Francis E. Wilde.

March 1907.

Clarendon Press Series

THE

CONSTITUTIONAL HISTORY

OF ENGLAND

IN ITS ORIGIN AND DEVELOPMENT

BY

WILLIAM STUBBS, D.D., Hon. LL.D.

Bishop of Oxford
and Honorary Student of Christ Church

VOL. I

SIXTH EDITION

OXFORD

AT THE CLARENDON PRESS

M DCCCC III

HENRY FROWDE, M.A.

PUBLISHER TO THE UNIVERSITY OF OXFORD

LONDON, EDINBURGH

NEW YORK

THE History of Institutions cannot be mastered,—can scarcely be approached,—without an effort. It affords little of the romantic incident or of the picturesque grouping which constitute the charm of History in general, and holds out small temptation to the mind that requires to be tempted to the study of Truth. But it has a deep value and an abiding interest to those who have courage to work upon it. It presents, in every branch, a regularly developed series of causes and consequences, and abounds in examples of that continuity of life, the realisation of which is necessary to give the reader a personal hold on the past and a right judgment of the present. For the roots of the present lie deep in the past, and nothing in the past is dead to the man who would learn how the present comes to be what it is. It is true, Constitutional History has a point of view, an insight, and a language of its own; it reads the exploits and characters of men by a different light from that shed by the false glare of arms, and interprets positions and facts in words that are voiceless to those who have only listened to the trumpet of fame. The world's heroes are no heroes to it, and it has an equitable consideration to give to many whom the verdict of ignorant posterity and the condemning sentence of events have consigned to obscurity or reproach. Without some knowledge of Constitutional History it is absolutely impossible to do justice to the characters and positions of the actors in the great drama; absolutely impossible to understand the origin of parties, the development of principles, the growth of nations in spite of parties and in defiance of principles. It alone can teach why it is that in politics good men do not always think alike, that the worst cause has often been illustrated with the most heroic virtue, and that the world owes some of its greatest debts to men from whose very memory it recoils.

In this department of study there is no portion more valuable than the Constitutional History of England.

I would fain hope that the labour spent on it in this book may at least not repel the student, and that the result may not wholly disappoint those friends in England, Germany and America, by whose advice it was begun, and whose sympathy and encouragement have mainly sustained me in the undertaking. To them I would dedicate a work which must stand or fall by their judgment. And I would put on record my grateful feeling for the unsparing good-will with which my work in other departments has been hitherto welcomed. A more special debt I would gladly acknowledge to the two Scholars (the Dean of Christ Church and the Rev. G. W. Kitchin) who have helped me with counsel and criticism whilst passing the book through the Press; to whom I am specially drawn by their association with my early Oxford ambitions, and whose patient kindness an acquaintance of now nearly thirty years has not exhausted.

KETTEL HALL,
Christmas Day, 1873.

CONTENTS.

CHAPTER I.

INTRODUCTION.

CHAPTER II.

CAESAR AND TACITUS.

CHAPTER III.

THE SAXONS AND ANGLES AT HOME.

CHAPTER IV.

THE MIGRATION.

CHAPTER V.

THE ANGLO-SAXON SYSTEM.

CHAPTER VI.

THE WITENAGEMOT AND THE KING.

CHAPTER VII.

DEVELOPMENT IN ANGLO-SAXON HISTORY.

CHAPTER VIII.

THE ANGLO-SAXON CHURCH.

CHAPTER IX.

THE NORMAN CONQUEST.

CHAPTER X.

POLITICAL SURVEY OF THE NORMAN PERIOD.

CHAPTER XI.

ADMINISTRATION DURING THE NORMAN PERIOD.

CHAPTER XII.

HENRY II AND HIS SONS.

CHAPTER XIII.

ADMINISTRATIVE AND REPRESENTATIVE INSTITUTIONS.

CHAPTER I.

INTRODUCTION.

1. THE growth of the English Constitution, which is the subject of this book, is the resultant of three forces, whose reciprocal influences are constant, subtle, and intricate. These are the national character, the external history, and the institutions of the people. The direct analysis of the combination forms no portion of our task, for it is not until a nation has arrived at a consciousness of its own identity that it can be said to have any constitutional existence, and long before that moment the three forces have become involved inextricably; the national character has been formed by the course of the national history quite as certainly as the national history has been developed by the working of the national character; and the institutions in which the newly conscious nation is clothed may be either the work of the constructive genius of the growing race, or simply the result of the discipline of its external history. It would then be very rash and unsafe to attempt to assign positively to any one of the three forces the causation of any particular movement or the origin of any particular measure, to the exclusion of the other two; or to argue back from result to cause without allowing for the operation of other co-ordinate and reciprocally acting factors.

But it does not follow that cautious speculation on matters

B

Preliminary
questions.

of interest, which are in themselves prior to the starting-point, would be thrown away; and some such questions must necessarily be discussed in order to complete the examination of the subject in its integrity by a comparison of its development with the corresponding stages and contemporary phenomena of the life of other nations. Of these questions the most important, and perhaps the only necessary ones, for all minor matters may be comprehended under them, are those of nationality and geographical position;—who were our forefathers, whence did they come, what did they bring with them, what did they find on their arrival, how far did the process of migration and settlement affect their own development, and in what measure was it indebted to the character and previous history of the land they colonised?

Germanic
origin of the
English.

Such a form of stating the questions suggests at least the character of the answer. The English are not aboriginal, that is, they are not identical with the race that occupied their home at the dawn of history. They are a people of German descent in the main constituents of blood, character, and language, but most especially, in connexion with our subject, in the possession of the elements of primitive German civilisation and the common germs of German institutions. This descent is not a matter of inference. It is a recorded fact of history, which these characteristics bear out to the fullest degree of certainty. The consensus of historians, placing the conquest and colonisation of Britain by nations of German origin between the middle of the fifth and the end of the sixth century, is confirmed by the evidence of a continuous series of monuments. These show the unbroken possession of the land thus occupied, and the growth of the language and institutions thus introduced, either in purity and unmolested integrity, or, where it has been modified by antagonism and by the admixture of alien forms, ultimately vindicating itself by eliminating the new and more strongly developing the genius of the old.

Influence of
the Ger-
manic races
in Europe
generally.

2. The four great states of Western Christendom—England, France, Spain, and Germany—owe the leading principles which are worked out in their constitutional history to the same

source. In the regions which had been thoroughly incorporated
with the Roman empire, every vestige of primitive indigenous
cultivation had been crushed out of existence. Roman civilisation in its turn fell before the Germanic races : in Britain it had
perished slowly in the midst of a perishing people, who were
able neither to maintain it nor to substitute for it anything of
their own. In Gaul and Spain it died a somewhat nobler death,
and left more lasting influences. In the greater part of Germany it had never made good its ground. In all four the constructive elements of new life are barbarian or Germanic,
though its development is varied by the degrees in which
the original stream of influence has been turned aside in its
course, or affected in purity and consistency by the infusion
of other elements and by the nature of the soil through which
it flows.

The system which has for the last twelve centuries formed
the history of France, and in a great measure the character of
the French people, of which the present condition of that kingdom is the logical result, was originally little more than a
simple adaptation of the old German polity to the government
of a conquered race. The long sway of the Romans in Gaul
had re-created, on their own principles of administration, the
nation which the Franks conquered. The Franks, gradually
uniting in religion, blood, and language with the Gauls, retained
and developed the idea of feudal subordination in the organisation of government unmodified by any tendencies towards
popular freedom. In France accordingly feudal government
runs its logical career. The royal power, that central force
which partly has originated, and partly owes its existence to the
conquest, is first limited in its action by the very agencies that
are necessary to its continuance ; then it is reduced to a shadow.
The shadow is still the centre round which the complex system,
in spite of itself, revolves : it is recognised by that system as its
solitary safeguard against disruption, and its witness of national
identity; it survives for ages, notwithstanding the attenuation
of its vitality, by its incapacity for mischief. In course of time
the system itself loses its original energy, and the central force

(margin note) Constitu-
tional His-
tory of
France.

gradually gathers into itself all the members of the nationality in detail, thus concentrating all the powers which in earlier struggles they had won from it, and incorporating in itself those very forces which the feudatories had imposed as limitations on

Changes in the consti- tution of France.

the sovereign power. So its character of nominal suzerainty is exchanged for that of absolute sovereignty. The only checks on the royal power had been the feudatories; the crown has outlived them, absorbed and assimilated their functions; but the increase of power is turned not to the strengthening of the central force, but to the personal interest of its possessor. Actual despotism becomes systematic tyranny, and its logical result is the explosion which is called revolution. The consti- tutional history of France is thus the summation of the series of feudal development in a logical sequence, which is indeed un- paralleled in the history of any great state, but which is thoroughly in harmony with the national character, forming it

The working out of feu- dalism.

and formed by it. We see in it the German system, modified by its work of foreign conquest and deprived of its home safe- guards, on a field exceptionally favourable, prepared and levelled by Roman agency under a civil system which was capable of speedy amalgamation, and into whose language most of the feudal forms readily translated themselves.

Kindred in- fluences of the Goths and other races in Spain.

3. In Spain too the permanency of the Germanic or of the kindred Visigothic influences is a fact of the first historical importance. Here, upon the substratum of an indigenous race conquered, crushed, re-created, remodelled into a Roman pro- vince more Roman than Rome itself, is superinduced the conquering race, first to ravage, then to govern, then to legis- late, then to unite in religion, and lastly to lead on to deliver- ance from Moorish tyranny. The rapidity with which Spanish history unfolds itself enables us to detect throughout its course the identity of the ruling, constructive nationality. The Visigothic element is kept to itself at first by its heresy; before the new- ness of its conversion has given it time to unite with the con- quered nation, it is forced into the position of a deliverer. The Moorish conquest compels union, sympathy, amalgamation, but still leaves the apparatus of government in the hands of the

Visigothic kings and nobles; the common law, the institutions, the names, are Germanic. Although the history of Spain, a crusade of seven centuries, forces into existence forms of civil life and expedients of administration which are peculiar to itself, they are distinctly coloured by the pertinacious freedom of the primitive customs; the constitutional life of Castille is, in close parallel or in marked contrast, never out of direct relation with that of Germany and England, as that of Aragon is in direct relation with French and Scottish history. To a German race of sovereigns Spain finally owed the subversion of her national system and ancient freedom.

4. In Germany itself, of course, the development of the primitive polity is everywhere traceable. Here there is no alien race, for Germany is never conquered but by Germans; there is much migration, but there is much also that is untouched by migration : where one tribe has conquered or colonised the territory of another, there feudal tenure of land and jurisdiction prevails : where the ancient race remains in its old seats, there the alod subsists and the free polity with which the alod is inseparably associated. The imperial system has originated other changes; there are Swabians in Saxony, Saxons in Thuringia : feudal customs in each case follow the tenure, but where the feod is not, there remains the alod, and even the village community and the mark. In the higher ranges of civil order, a mixed imperial and feudal organisation, which like the Spanish has no exact parallel, retains a varying, now substantial, now shadowy existence. The imperial tradition has substituted a fictitious for a true bond of union among the four nations of the German land. To the general reader the constitutional struggle is merely one of nationality against imperialism ; of the papal north against the imperial south; but under that surface of turmoil the lower depths of national life and constitutional organism heave constantly. Bavaria, Saxony, Franconia, Swabia have their national policy, and preserve their ancient modifications of the still more ancient customs. The weakness of the imperial centre, the absence of central legislature and judicature, allows the continued existence

General character of German Constitutional History.

of the most primitive forms; the want of cohesion prevents at once their development and their extinction. So to deeper study the wonderful fertility and variety of the local institutions of Germany presents a field of work bewildering and even wearying in its abundance: and great as might be the reward of penetrating it, the student strays off to a field more easily amenable to philosophic treatment. The constitutional history of Germany is the hardest, as that of France is the easiest, subject of historical study. As a study of principles, in continuous and uniform development, it lacks both unity and homogeneousness.

English Constitutional History a development of Germanic principles in comparative purity.

5. England, although less homogeneous in blood and character, is more so in uniform and progressive growth. The very diversity of the elements which are united within the isle of Britain serves to illustrate the strength and vitality of that one which for thirteen hundred years has maintained its position either unrivalled or in victorious supremacy. If its history is not the perfectly pure development of Germanic principles, it is the nearest existing approach to such a development [1]. England gained its sense of unity centuries before Germany: it developed its genius for government under influences more purely indigenous: spared from the curse of the imperial system and the Mezentian union with Italy, and escaping thus the practical abeyance of legislation and judicature, it developed its own common law free from the absolutist tendencies of Roman jurisprudence; and it grew equably, harmoniously, not merely by virtue of local effort and personal privilege.

The smaller states of Europe.

In the four great nationalities the Germanic influence is the dominant principle: in England, Germany and France directly; whilst in Spain all formative power is traceable to the kindred Gothic rule. The smaller states share more or less in the same general characteristics; Portugal with Spain; Scandinavia with Germany and England, with whose institutions it had originally everything in common, and whose development in great things

[1] Ranke, History of England (Oxf. tr.), i. p. 11; Bethmann-Hollweg, Civilprocess, iv. 10; Konrad Maurer, Kritische Ueberschau, i. 47; Gneist, Self-Government, i. 3.

and in small it seems to have followed with few variations, translating their constitutional systems into language of its own.   In Italy the confusion of nationalities is most complete, Italy. and there Roman institutions, owing perhaps to the rapid succession of conquerors and the shortlivedness of their organisations as contrasted with the permanency of the papal-imperial system, subsisted with the least change.   Yet there also, the Northern States through the German, and the Southern through the Norman connexion, both moreover having gone through the crucible of Lombard oppression, retain marks of Teutonic influence.   The institutions, national and free in one aspect, feudal and absolutist in another, testify, if not to the permanence, at least to the abiding impressions of the association.   The republican history of the North and the feudal system of the South, the municipalities of Lombardy and the parliaments of Naples, are much more German than Roman.

6. Nor do the great nationalities return a different answer Effect of the German and when interrogated by more convincing tests than that of ex- Gothic conternal history.   If language be appealed to, and language is language, quests on by itself the nearest approach to a perfect test of national extraction, the verdict is in close accordance.   The impact of barbarian conquest split up the unity of the Latin tongue as it did that of the Latin empire ; it destroyed its uniformity and broke up its constructional forms.   But in the breaking it created at least three great languages—the French, the Spanish, and the Italian ; each possessing new powers of development which the Latin had lost, and adapting itself to a new literature, fertile in beauty and vivacity, far surpassing the effete inanities that it superseded.   The breath of the life of the new literatures and on new literature. was Germanic, varied according to the measure of Germanic influence in other things.   The poetry of the new nations is that of the leading race : in South France and Spain Visigothic, in North France Norman, even in Italy it owes all its sweetness and light to the freedom which has breathed from beyond the Alps.   In these lands the barbarian tongue has yielded to that of the conquered ; in Spain and France because the disproportion of the numbers of the two races was very great ; both

Franks and Visigoths had become Romanised to a certain extent before the conquest; and the struggle with the native peoples assumed in neither case the character of extermination. In Italy the succession of masters was too rapid to allow a change of language to come into question among the greater and more abiding part of the people. Of the Germans of Germany and the English of early times it is scarcely necessary to speak, for, whatever may have been the later modifications, the influence of the Latin of the fifth century on the language of either must have been infinitesimal. No European tongue is more thoroughly homogeneous in vocabulary and in structure than that known as the Anglo-Saxon : it is as pure as those of Scandinavia, where no Roman influences ever penetrated, and no earlier race than the German left intelligible traces. Early and medieval German are also alike unadulterated. The analogy between language and institutions is in these cases direct : in Spain and France the outer garb is Roman, the spirit and life is Germanic : one influence preponderates in the language, the other in the polity; and the amalgamation is complete when the Gaul has learned to call himself a Frenchman, when the Goth, the Suevian, the Alan and the Vandal, are united under the name of Spaniard.

Analogy of language and polity.

Evidence of religion.

7. The most abiding influence of Rome is that of religion; the Roman church continues to exist when the old imperial administration has perished. Spain, Gaul and Italy, even Western Britain and Western Germany, retain the Christianity which Roman missions have planted. Yet in this very department the importance of the new spring of life is specially conspicuous. Spain alone of the four nations owes nothing to German Christianity. Her religious history is exactly analogous to that of her language : after a century's struggle the Visigoth and the Suevian become Catholic. In France and Western Germany, which had been Christianised mainly under the imperial influences, and had developed an independent theology during the Roman period, the influx of the Franks and their subsequent conversion produced a complex result. The Christianity which had stood out against Visigothic indifference or intolerance, withered under Frank patronage. The secular

Germanic influence on the Church.

tendencies of the imperial religious administration expanded under the Merovingian imitators, and, had it not been for the reformation begun by Boniface and worked out under the auspices of the Karolings, the Gallican church might have sunk to the level of the Italian or the Byzantine. But the same Austrasian influences which revivified the composite nationality, breathed new life into the fainting church, drawing from England and the converted North new models of study and devotion. The labours of English missionaries in German Saxony helped to consolidate and complete in both church and state the Germanic empire of the Karolings. The Austrasian domination was more purely Germanic than the Neustrian which it superseded. Charles the Great, as the reformer of the church and founder of the modern civilisation of France, was a German king who worked chiefly by German instruments.

8. In the domain of Law the comparison is equally clear. The number of possible factors is small: the primitive codes of the conquerors, the Roman law under which the conquered were living, and the feudal customs which were evolved from the relations of the two races. For there remain no original vestiges of the indigenous laws of Spain and Gaul, and it is only from Irish and Welsh remains of comparatively late date that we find that the Celtic tribes had any laws at all. *Influence of German customs on the common law of the nations.*

The common law of Spain is throughout the medieval period Germanic in its base: although the written law of the Visigoths is founded on the Theodosian code and the so-called Roman natives lived by Roman law, the *fueros* which contain the customary jurisprudence are distinctly akin to the customs of England and Germany; the wergild and the system of compurgation, the primitive elements of election and representation, are clearly traceable[1]. It is not until the fourteenth century that the civil law of Justinian supersedes the ancient customs, and then with its invariable results. *Spain.*

Medieval France is divided between the feudal customs of the *France.*

---

[1] Dunham, History of Spain and Portugal, iv. 109–118 : from Edinb. Review, No. 61 (an article attributed to Sir F. Palgrave). Palgrave, Commonwealth, pp. 128–131, &c. Lea, Superstition and Force, p. 65.

Law in
France.

North and the personal law of the South, which last was chiefly based on the Theodosian and earlier Roman jurisprudence. The former territory is more Frank in population, nearer to the German home, and bears more distinct marks of Karolingian legislation; the latter, before the Frank conquest, has borne the successive waves of Visigothic and Burgundian invasion, and has strengthened through them, or imparted to them, its own legal system as developed under the Romans. But feudal custom far more than Roman law is the characteristic jurisprudence of French history : and of the great expositions of feudal custom, the *Grand Coutumier* of Normandy and the *Coutumes de Beauvaisis* are from Northern France : the *Consuetudines Feudorum* were compiled by Lombard lawyers from the acts of the Franconian and Swabian emperors; the *Vetus Auctor de Beneficiis* wrote in Eastern Germany; and the Assizes of Jerusalem are based on the work of a Flemish or Lotharingian lawgiver[1]. The essence of feudal law is custom, and custom escapes the jealousies and antipathies that assail law imposed by a legislative centre : it grows and extends its area by imitation rather than by authority : and the scientific lawyer can borrow a custom of feudal jurisprudence where he cannot venture to lay down a principle of Roman law. Hence the uncertainty of detail contrasted with the uniformity of principle in feudal law.

Law in
Germany.

Germany, except in the few Capitularies of the Frank sovereigns, has no central or common written law; even the Capitularies are many of them only local in their operation : she does not, except by way of custom, adopt the Roman civil law; her feudal law is, like the feudal law elsewhere, based on the Frank custumals. Her common law, whether sought in the jurisprudence of the Alemanni, the Franks and the Saxons, or enunciated in the Sachsenspiegel and the Schwabenspiegel, is primitive, just as all her lower range of institutions may be said to be ; it subsists but it does not develop.

English
common law
based on
early Germanic
usages.

England has inherited no portion of the Roman legislation except in the form of scientific or professional axioms, introduced at a late period, and through the ecclesiastical or scholastic or

[1] Beugnot, Assises de Jerusalem, vol. i. pref. pp. xxxiii. sq.

international university studies. Her common law is, to a far greater extent than is commonly recognised, based on usages anterior to the influx of feudality, that is, on strictly primitive custom ; and what she has that is feudal may be traced through its Frank stage of development to the common Germanic sources [1].

9. The result of this comparison is to suggest the probability that the polity developed by the German races on British soil is the purest product of their primitive instinct. With the exception of the Gothic Bible of Ulfilas, the Anglo-Saxon remains are the earliest specimens of Germanic language as well as literature, and the development of modern English from the Anglo-Saxon is a fact of science as well as of history. The institutions of the Saxons of Germany long after the conquest of Britain were the most perfect exponent of the system which Tacitus saw and described in the Germania ; and the polity of their kinsmen in England, though it may be not older in its monuments than the Lex Salica, is more entirely free from Roman influences. In England the common germs were developed and ripened with the smallest intermixture of foreign elements. Not only were all the successive invasions of Britain, which from the eighth to the eleventh century diversify the history of the island, conducted by nations of common extraction, but, with the exception of ecclesiastical influence, no foreign interference that was not German in origin was admitted at all. Language, law, custom and religion preserve their original conformation and colouring. The German element is the paternal element in our system, natural and political. Analogy, however, is not proof, but illustration : the chain of proof is to be found in the progressive persistent development of English constitutional history from the primeval polity of the common fatherland.

General result.

The German element is the paternal element in the English polity.

[1] Brunner, in Holtzendorff's Encyclopädie, pp. 226, 227.

CHAPTER II.

CAESAR AND TACITUS.

Caesar's notices of the Germans.

10. THE earliest glimpses of the social and political life of our forefathers are derived from Caesar, who has in one passage of the Commentaries compressed into a few lines all that he could ascertain about the Germans in general; and in another describes, with very slight variations, the Suevi, whom he believed to be the greatest and most warlike of the kindred tribes. After contrasting the religion of the Germans with that of the Gauls, and praising the industry, chastity and hardiness of their lives, which he describes as divided between hunting and the studying of arms [1], he proceeds to remark that they do not devote themselves to husbandry, but live chiefly on milk, cheese and flesh. No one has a fixed quantity of land or boundaries that may be called his own, but the magistrates and chiefs assign annually, and for a single year's occupancy, to the several communities, larger or smaller, whom the tie of common religious rites or consanguinity has brought together, a portion of land, the extent and situation of which they fix according to circumstances. The next year they compel them to move elsewhere. Of this institution many accounts are given; one reason is that the people may not be induced by habitual em-

Annual change of land.

[1] Caesar, de Bello Gallico, vi. 21.

ployment in husbandry to exchange for it the pursuit of arms; Reasons for this. another that they may not devote themselves to the accumulation of estates; that the more powerful may not expel the meaner from their possessions; that they may not be led to build houses with too great care to avoid heat or cold; that they may prevent the growth of avarice and through it the creation of factions and dissensions; and that the general body of the people may be kept contented, which can be the case only so long as every man sees himself in material wealth on a level with the most powerful of his countrymen [1].

Of the several political communities, nations or states as they Isolation of the tribal may be called, the greatest glory is the extent of unpeopled territories. land which surrounds their territory, and which they have devastated. They regard it as a peculiar proof of prowess that their old neighbours have fled from their settlements for fear of them, and that no new comer has ventured to approach them. There is policy moreover in the plan; it is a guarantee of public security; sudden invasion is an impossibility.

When one of the states engages in war, offensive or defensive, Want of common or special officers are chosen to command, with power of life and central organisation. death; in time of peace there is no common or central magistracy, but the chiefs of the several divisions, 'principes regionum atque pagorum,' administer justice among their people, and do their best to diminish litigation [2]. Predatory expeditions undertaken beyond the borders of the particular state do not involve any infamy; on the contrary, they are openly regarded as expedient for the training of the young, and for the encouragement of active enterprise. One of the chiefs Warlike expeditions. offers himself in the public assembly as the leader of such an

[1] Caesar, de Bello Gallico, vi. 22 : 'Agriculturae non student; majorque pars eorum victus in lacte, caseo, carne consistit; neque quisquam agri modum certum aut fines habet proprios; sed magistratus ac principes in annos singulis gentibus cognationibusque hominum qui una coierunt, quantum et quo loco visum est agri attribuunt atque anno post alio transire cogunt.'

[2] Caesar, de Bello Gallico, vi. 23 : 'Cum bellum civitas aut illatum defendit aut infert, magistratus qui ei bello praesint, ut vitae necisque habeant potestatem, deliguntur. In pace nullus est communis magistratus, sed principes regionum atque pagorum inter suos jus dicunt controversiasque minuunt.'

expedition and calls on volunteers to join him; as soon as the
announcement is made, those warriors who approve the cause
and the man rise up and promise their aid, amidst the applause
of the assembled people.   If any of those who are pledged
betray their engagement, they are regarded as deserters and
traitors, and no trust is ever after reposed in them.

Comparison
of Germans
and Gauls.

The rights of hospitality are held sacred; it is strictly forbidden that any should injure the strangers who for any reason
whatever may visit them; they are considered as sacred; every
house is open to them, and every one will share his fare with
them[1].   There had been a time when the Gauls were superior
in prowess to the Germans, and even threw their colonies across
the Rhine, but matters were now altered; the Germans had
retained their simplicity, poverty and hardihood, the Gauls had
grown so used to defeat that they had ceased to claim equality
in valour[2].

The Suevi;
their tribal
divisions
and military
system.

The description of the Suevi is in one or two points more
circumstantial; their normal condition seems to be war, aggression for the purpose of conquest: they have a hundred
territorial divisions, or pagi, each of which furnishes to the
host a thousand champions; the rest stay at home and provide
food for themselves and for the warriors[3].   After a year's
service the warriors return home and till the land; their
places are supplied by the husbandmen of the previous year;
so agriculture and warlike discipline are perfectly maintained.

No several
estates of
land.

But private and separate estates of land do not exist, and the
term of occupation is restricted to the year.   Like the kindred
tribes, the Suevi find employment in hunting, live on animal
food, and possess great strength and power of endurance[4].   They

---

[1] Caesar, de Bello Gallico, vi. 23.   [2] Ibid. vi. 24.
[3] Just as in Alfred's war with the Danes in A.D. 894 he divided his
force into two bodies, so that one half was constantly at home, the other
half in the field. Chron. Sax. A.D. 894. Cf. Horace, Od. iii. 24. vv.
11–16.
[4] Caesar, de Bello Gallico, iv. 1: 'Hi centum pagos habere dicuntur,
ex quibus quotannis singula milia armatorum, bellandi causa, ex finibus
educunt; reliqui qui domi manserunt se atque illos alunt. Hi rursus
invicem anno post in armis sunt, illi domi remanent. Sic neque agricultura,
nec ratio atque usus belli intermittitur. Sed privati ac separati agri apud
eos nihil est, neque longius anno remanere uno in loco incolendi causa licet.'

also are proud of having no neighbours; on one side devastated
territory for six hundred miles testifies to their victorious might
and forms a barrier against invasion, on another side lies a
tributary nation which they have reduced to insignificance in
point of power[1].

This sketch, drawn by one of the greatest statesmen of the
world, has a value of its own; and, as a first attempt to cha-
racterise the race from which we spring, it has a special interest. But the details are scarcely distinct enough in themselves to furnish a trustworthy basis of theory, and even when
interpreted by later notices they contain much that is obscure.
Caesar wrote from the information of Gallic tribes who natur- Colouring
ally exaggerated the qualities of their triumphant rivals; and picture.
he himself dwells chiefly on the points in which the Germans
differed from the Gauls. To this must be attributed the stress
laid on the equality of the common lot, on the discouragement
of party struggles and personal litigation, and on the temperance and voluntary poverty which must have especially struck
him in contrast with the neighbour nation which was now
rapidly becoming mercenary, and, in the decay of liberty, de-
voting itself to the acquisition of wealth.

11. The general impression derived from the outline is, that He saw the
the tribes whom Caesar knew by report were in a state of state of
transition.
transition from the nomadic life to that of settled cultivation.
The nations had their defined territory surrounded by a belt of
unpeopled or subject land. But within the national area, the
customs of pastoral life still prevailed; the smaller communities moved annually in search of fresh pasturage; they cultivated only enough land to supply the year's provision of corn,
changing their occupancy every year, and having accordingly
no permanent homesteads or substantial dwelling-houses[2]. The
tie which united these smaller pastoral communities was simply
that of kindred; not that the social organisation depended on
nothing else, for the maintenance of the common peace and

[1] Caesar, de Bello Gallico, iv. 3; cf. vi. 23.
[2] See Bethmann-Hollweg, Civilprocess, iv. 79. Kemble, Saxons, i. 40,
rejects the testimony of Caesar on this point; see, on the whole question,
Waitz, Deutsche Verfassungs-Geschichte (Kiel, 1880), i. 97–107.

the administration of justice were provided by the tribal magistracy, but that the ideas of settled homes and the obligations of permanent neighbourhood were realised only in the form of relationship. Except for war the tribal communities had no general organisation; in war they followed leaders chosen and empowered for the particular occasion. The predatory expeditions which under the approval of the state were carried on by voluntary leaders, were not managed through the machinery of the state, or by warriors who were permanently attached to their captains; they volunteered and were bound by honour to their leaders only for the particular expedition[1]. In national wars, like those in which the Suevi lived, the whole population took part in active service and in reserve in alternate years; and their armies were arranged according to the contingents which represented the tribal sub-divisions. The only judicial organisation was that of the sub-divisions; their magistrates allotted the land annually, and administered justice: but, though there was no central magistracy, there was a national council which determined on wars and peace, and gave public sanction to volunteer enterprises.

Small amount of national organisation.

It is obvious that such a state of things must be transitional: that the determination of the territorial bounds of the nation is not permanently consistent with internal nomadic migrations, but can only allow them so long as the area is vastly too wide for its inhabitants. Nor is it conceivable that war should be the sole occupation of any tribe so far advanced in civilisation as the general description implies. The account of the Suevi can be true only of the populations bordering on Gaul or on the empire, which were kept on the defensive by the news of the approach of the Romans, or were still affected by the great migratory wave which had begun its course half a century before. Of the tribes of interior Germany we learn nothing directly, and can only infer from the looser details that their political and social organisation was very slight, consisting

Indistinctness of Caesar's outline.

[1] See Waitz, Deutsche Verfassungs-Geschichte, i. 382–384; Bethmann-Hollweg, Civilprocess, iv. 93; Konrad Maurer, Kritische Ueberschau, ii. 418.

mainly in the tie of kindred and local connexion under numerous chiefs who, whether chosen by the communities or inheriting power from their fathers, were independent one of another,
united only by tribal name, and of equal rank in the tribal
council. We must look to Tacitus for the filling in of details
as well as for the clearer, broader, and more definite elaboration
of the outline [1].

12. Tacitus wrote about a century and a half after Caesar. The Ger-
During this period the Romans had been constantly in collision mania of
Tacitus.
with the Germans, and the knowledge they now possessed of
them must have been direct, abundant, and explicit. The
Germania is an inestimable treasury of facts and generalisations, but it is not without many serious difficulties, arising
partly from the different stages of civilisation and political
organisation which the several tribes must be supposed to have
reached. In attempting to compress into a general sketch the
main features of so large a family of tribes, the historian is
scarcely able to avoid some inconsistencies. No one now be-
lieves him to have intended the Germania for a satire on Rome,
as was once suspected; yet it is possible that his eye was caught
in some instances rather by the points in which the German
institutions were contrasted with the Roman [2], than by those
which expressed their essential character. But of the general
faithfulness of the outline we have no doubt: the little inconsistencies of detail serve to preserve additional facts; and the
generality of statement enables us to obtain the idea of the
common Germanic system, which is approximately true of it
at every stage of its early development, although there may
never have been a time at which the whole description in its
exact details was true of any portion of it.

Germany as described by Tacitus was a vast congeries of Physical and
religious
tribes, indigenous and homogeneous throughout; speaking the unity of the
German
same language, worshipping the same gods; marked by common races.

[1] On the relation between Caesar and Tacitus in this point see Zeuss,
Die Deutschen und die Nachbarstämme, pp. 52 sq.; Bethmann-Hollweg,
Civilprocess, iv. 71, 72.
[2] Waitz, Deutsche Verfassungs-Geschichte, i. 21. See also Guizot,
Civilisation in France (ed. Hazlitt), i. 418.

physical characteristics and by common institutions, but having no collective name in their own tongue and no collective organisation [1]. They were singularly free from the commixture of blood with foreign races [2]; their primitive traditions and mythology were altogether their own. They had, as in Caesar's time, their own breeds of cattle, and their only wealth was the possession of herds [3]. Money and merchandise were of little account with them. They had no cities, nor even streets in their villages; their buildings were rudely put together from rough undressed materials [4]. Their chastity and regard for marriage, the plainness and simplicity of their dress, their general temperance and sobriety, are still strongly marked. In most of these points there is no difference between the accounts of the two great historians; but in the time of Tacitus the love of hunting has declined, and the warriors spend the seasons of peace in lazy enjoyment [5]; they have begun to use wine and that not in moderation, and they have become inveterate and business-like gamblers [6]. Agriculture of a simple description, and for the growth of wheat only, would seem to have increased; and the freemen and slaves alike have settled homes. Local organisation, too, is either much more largely developed, or forms a more prominent part of the general description.

Common features of German life.

It would be rash to affirm that these latter particulars prove a definite progress in civilisation since the days of Caesar; but in some respects such an advance was a necessity. The increase of population and the extension of settlements involve the dimi-

Advance on the state of things described by Caesar.

---

[1] Tac. Germania, cc. 1–3. On the origin of the name Germania see Waitz, D. V. G. i. 25 sq.; he rejects all German derivations, and concludes that it is originally Gallic, the name given (as Tacitus indicates) by the Gauls first to the Tungri and afterwards to all the kindred tribes. The meaning may be either 'good shouters' (Grimm, Geschichte der Deutschen Sprache, p. 787), or, according to other writers, 'East-men' or 'neighbours.'

[2] Tac. Germ. c. 4: 'Ipse eorum opinionibus accedo qui Germaniae populos nullis aliis aliarum nationum conubiis infectos propriam et sinceram et tantum sui similem gentem extitisse arbitror.'

[3] Tac. Germ. c. 5; Caesar, de Bello Gallico, vi. 26; Grimm, Geschichte der Deutschen Sprache, pp. 28–42.

[4] Tac. Germ. c. 16.   [5] Ibid. cc. 15, 22.

[6] Tac. Germ. c. 24.

nution of the number of animals of chase, and may account for the disuse of hunting and the absolute necessity of enlarged agriculture. The continuous struggle with the Romans may account alike for the creation of a more purely military spirit among the warriors, and for the misuse of their scarce and ungrateful seasons of leisure. But further than this it is scarcely safe to go; and it is unadvisable to undervalue the quantum of civilisation which had been attained in the time of Caesar, in order to point more graphically the bearing of Tacitus's encomium[1]. With all the drawbacks he mentions, there can be no doubt that the general tone of society and morality, so far as he knew it, was far higher in Germany than at Rome, 'plusque ibi boni mores valent quam alibi bonae leges[2].' It is, however, on points of social and political organisation that our greatest debt to Tacitus is owing.

13. Although the pursuit of agriculture is now general, the wealth of the Germans consists chiefly if not solely in their herds of cattle: for these the vast tracts of forest and unenclosed land afford abundant pasturage, and for the purpose of pasturage no particular appropriation of the soil is needed. The wide forests and untilled plains are common property. But there is not yet apparently any separate ownership even of the cultivated land. True, we read no longer of the annual migrations of families or small communities from one portion of the territory of the tribe to another. The village settlements are permanent, and the dwellings substantial and extensive. But the arable land is occupied by the community as a body, and allotments, changed annually, are assigned to the several freemen according to their estimation or social importance[3]. The extent of waste

Common property in land.

Character of the village settlements.

---

[1] Niebuhr thought that the Germans of Tacitus's time were not more uncivilised than the Westphalian and Lower Saxon peasants of his own time. Waitz, Deutsche Verfassungs-Geschichte, i. 33; Bethmann-Hollweg, Civilprocess, iv. 71, 72.

[2] Tac. Germ. c. 19: 'Nemo enim illic vitia ridet, nec corrumpere et corrumpi saeculum vocatur.'

[3] Tac. Germ. c. 26: 'Agri pro numero cultorum ab universis in vices (*al.* vicis) occupantur, quos mox inter se secundum dignationem partiuntur.' If the reading 'in vices' be retained and the annual change of allotment be understood, this passage must be translated, 'The fields are alternately occupied by the whole body of cultivators according to their number, and

land prevents any difficulty in the supply of divisible area. The arable area is changed every year, and there is abundance over [1]; for they do not attempt to utilise by labour the whole productive power or extent of the land, in planted orchards, divided meadows, or watered gardens; the only tribute levied on the soil is the crop of corn[2].

Several property in land.

Still, property in land can scarcely be said to be altogether unknown[3]. The villagers choose places for their homesteads as the supply of water, wood, or pasture tempts them. Their buildings are not crowded upon one another[4]: in collective villages or in solitary farmsteads each man has his own house and a space of ground surrounding it. Even if this arrangement, as Tacitus states, is the result of their dislike of neighbours or of their fear of fires, it is unnecessary to limit it by such considerations: the homestead of the rich and poor freemen alike must have included granaries, cow-houses, and stackyards[5]. And in this no one but the owner could have any

The homestead.

these they afterwards divide among themselves according to their individual estimation.' But Dr. Waitz, with good MS. authority, prefers to read *vicis*, and to understand the statement as referring to initial occupation;—'The lands are occupied by the collective townships according to the number of cultivators, and these they afterwards divide among themselves (the cultivators) according to their estimation.' The passage is confessedly one of great difficulty. See for an account of the very numerous interpretations, Waitz, D.V.G. i. 140–148. See also G. L. von Maurer, Einleitg. pp. 5, 6.

[1] Tac. Germ. c. 26: 'Arva per annos mutant et superest ager.' See Kemble, Saxons, i. 40, and p. 14 above.

[2] Tac. Germ. c. 26.

[3] Private possession of land is regarded as introduced after the Völkerwanderung (Bethmann-Hollweg, Civilprocess, iv. 15), and, in regions not affected by that change, as a development consequent on the improvements of agriculture, and strictly regulated by jealous custom. Bethmann-Hollweg, Civilprocess, iv. 16; G. L. von Maurer, Einleitg. pp. 93 sq.; Palgrave, Commonwealth, pp. 71, 93, &c.

[4] Tac. Germ. c. 16: 'Nullas Germanorum populis urbes habitari satis notum est; ne pati quidem inter se junctas sedes. Colunt discreti ac diversi, ut fons, ut campus, ut nemus placuit. Vicos locant non in nostrum morem conexis et cohaerentibus aedificiis; suam quisque domum spatio circumdat, sive adversus casus ignis remedium, sive inscitia aedificandi.' The houses in the villages are separated from one another; other houses are built apart wherever the settler chooses: the difference between the village-life and the separate farm-life already appearing. Waitz, D. V. G. i. 114–116.

[5] See Waitz, D. V. G. i. 118. Tacitus (Germ. c. 16) mentions subterranean storehouses.

right. It is possible that it contained land enough to furnish hay for the winter, for Tacitus mentions no annual re-apportionment of meadow-ground, although it is more probable that that was allotted on the same principle as the arable. But on any hypothesis the freeman had complete and several property in his homestead; he had a definite share in the arable field, annually assigned by the community itself, varying in situation and quality, but permanent in every other particular; and he had an undefined but proportionate right to the use of the common woods and pastures[1].

In this very general statement it may be thought possible to trace a distinct advance on the land system described by Caesar; the nomad stage has ceased[2], the communities have settled seats and each man his own home. It is however uncertain whether the tribes which Caesar describes as nomad are the same as those which Tacitus describes as settled; it has been contended that Caesar misled Tacitus and that Tacitus misunderstood Caesar. But the mere interpretation of the relation between the two authors does not affect the material truth of Tacitus's picture. The member of the community had a fixed share of a changing area of cultivated land, a proportionate share in the common pasturage, and a house and homestead of his own[3].

Relation of Caesar's statement to that of Tacitus.

14. But was this absolute equality in the character of the hold on land a sign of social equality in other relations of life? Although there is apparently no difference in the political status of all the fully qualified freemen, there are unmistakeable grades of class and rank. There are distinctions of wealth, although wealth consists of cattle only. There are distinctions of blood, some are noble and some are not; and of status, there are *nobiles, ingenui, liberti,* and *servi*[4]. There is further a distinct array of official personages, *principes, duces, sacerdotes, reges*[5].

Differences of ranks.

---

[1] Waitz, D. V. G. i. 119–125; G. L. von Maurer, Einleitg. pp. 139–152.
[2] Waitz, D. V. G. i. 36.
[3] The whole property, homestead, arable and pasture together, bore the name of *Hube,* hoba, in Germany; and was the higid, terra familiae, mansus, cassate or hide of the Anglo-Saxons. See G. L. von Maurer, Einleitg. pp. 126–134.
[4] Tac. Germ. cc. 7, 24, 25, 44; Grimm, Rechtsalterthümer, pp. 227, 308.
[5] Tac. Germ. cc. 7, 10, 11, 14, &c.

Of these differences, that based upon wealth does not require discussion, except so far as it implies a pre-eminence which would be marked by a larger allotment of arable land, and the possession of a larger homestead. Tacitus, in the obscure passage in which he describes the apportionment of the land, mentions, as one of the principles of partition, the *dignatio*[1], by which possibly he means the estimation of the individual recipient. The annual re-allotment involves an equality of subdivisions, but does not preclude the possibility of two or more subdivisions being assigned to the same person. The wealth in cattle involves of necessity a proportionate enjoyment of pasture and meadow, and the employment of servile cultivators implies an inequality in the shares of the arable which they cultivate for their respective masters. And the privilege which of necessity is granted to the rich man, can scarcely be withheld from the nobleman or magistrate who may demand it, if he possesses servants enough to cultivate a larger share than that of the simple freeman. But the inequalities in the use or possession of the land involve no inequalities in social and political rights[2].

Possible inequality of allotments.

The distinction between the *nobiles* and the *ingenui* must be taken in its ordinary sense: the nobility can be only that of descent, either from ancient kings, or from the gods, or from the great benefactors and military leaders of the race[3]. It is on the ground of nobility that the kings are chosen in the tribes that have adopted a monarchical government[4]; pre-eminent nobility, like great age, entitles a man to respectful hearing in the tribal councils, and to special rank in the *comitatus* of the magistrate to whom he attaches himself[5]; but it confers no political privilege, it involves no special claim to the office of

Character and rights of nobility.

---

[1] Above, p. 19, n. 3. Tac. Germ. c. 26; *dignitatem* is Grimm's reading; *dignationem* the common one, which is kept by Müllenhoff, may mean the deserved favour of the dividers; see below, p. 26, n. 2.

[2] Waitz, D. V. G. i. 198, 199. Kemble (Saxons, i. 135) seems to confound the *nobilis* with the *princeps*. See too Grimm, R. A. p. 280.

[3] Bethmann-Hollweg, Civilprocess, iv. 85. Cf. Tac. Germ. c. 13, 'magna patrum merita;' Waitz, D. V. G. i. 169–172; Grimm, R. A. pp. 265 sq.

[4] Tac. Germ. c. 7: 'Reges ex nobilitate, duces ex virtute sumunt.'

[5] Ibid. cc. 11, 13.

magistrate or leader in war[1], or to the right of having a comitatus or following such as belongs to the magistrate. The *ingenuus* or simple freeman is in every point except descent the equal of the noble. But it may be questioned whether freedom or nobility of birth implies in itself the possession of political rights. The young men are, until they are admitted to the use of arms, members of the family only, not of the state[2]. When they come to years of discretion, and the voice of the nation permits it, they are formally invested with a shield and spear either by the magistrate, or by father or kinsman, in the assembled Council. This investiture, or emancipation as it may be deemed, may entitle them to an honourable place in the host, but scarcely to a voice in the Council until they have obtained by inheritance or allotment their share in the common land[3].

On this point however Tacitus is silent. Nor can we discover from his words whether the *liberti* or freedmen, whom he mentions as constituting an important element in the tribes that are governed by kings[4], possessed more than merely personal freedom. It is most improbable on all analogies that they possessed any political rights.

The freedmen.

The unfree or servile class is divided by Tacitus into two[5]: one answering to the *coloni* of Roman civilisation, and the

The servile classes,

---

[1] Yet most of the *principes* mentioned in Tacitus are of noble birth: hence it is argued that nobility gave a presumptive if not exclusive claim to office. See Bethmann-Hollweg, Civilprocess, iv. 90. Waitz, D. V. G. i. 236, maintains that there is no such connexion, and it cannot be proved.

[2] Tac. Germ. c. 13: 'Ante hoc domus pars videntur, mox reipublicae.'

[3] Waitz, D. V. G. i. 347, 348; Sohm, Fränkische Reichs- und Gerichtsverfassung, pp. 545-558.

[4] Tac. Germ. c. 25: 'Liberti non multum supra servos sunt, raro aliquod momentum in domo, nunquam in civitate exceptis dumtaxat iis gentibus quae regnantur. Ibi enim et super ingenuos et super nobiles ascendunt.' Cf. Waitz, D. V. G. i. 153.

[5] Tac. Germ. cc. 24, 25: 'Ceteris servis non in nostrum morem descriptis per familiam ministeriis utuntur: suam quisque sedem, suos penates regit. Frumenti modum dominus aut pecoris aut vestis ut colono injungit, et servus hactenus paret; cetera domus officia uxor ac liberi exequuntur. Verberare servum ac vinculis et opere coercere rarum; occidere solent, non disciplina et severitate, sed impetu et ira, ut inimicum, nisi quod impune est.' See Grimm, R. A. pp. 300, 301; G. L. von Maurer, Hofverfassg. i. 5 sq.

other to slaves. Of the former each man has a house and home of his own. He pays to his lord a quantity of corn, of cattle, or of clothing; he must therefore hold land on which to grow the corn and feed the cattle, and this land is of course a portion of his lord's. Possibly the more dignified and richer freemen cultivate all their lands by these means; but if the analogy

The cultivating class.

with the Roman *coloni* holds good[1], the *servus* is personally free except in relation to his lord and his land, neither of which he can forsake. His condition is not a hard one; he is very rarely beaten or forced to labour; but if his lord kill him, as sometimes may be done in passion, it is done with impunity; no satisfaction can, it would seem, be recovered by his family. The origin of this servile class may be found in the subjugation, by the tribe, of the former occupiers of the land; a process which, in the nomadic and warlike phase of public life that had now passed away, must have been by no means uncommon, and which may have even created a subject population, cultivating the land of the tribe in immediate dependence on the state or king. There is no reason to suppose that the depressed population were other than German in origin, although of course unconnected by any tribal tie with their masters. Even the sons of the poorer freemen may be supposed to have taken service as cultivators under the richer men or on the public lands.

The slaves.

The second class of *servi* contained those who had lost their freedom by gambling; possibly also prisoners of war: of penal servitude there is no distinct trace. This cannot have been a large body: the gamblers were generally sold, the possession of such victims being no credit to the owner[2].

The official magistracy.

The *principes*, or official magistracy, have of course pre-eminence in dignity and privilege. They are elected in the

---

[1] Savigny has collected and arranged all the materials for the history of the *colonus* in a paper translated in the Philological Museum, ii. 117: he carefully points out that, notwithstanding a close analogy, there is no historical connexion whatever between the Roman *coloni* and the German serfs; pp. 144, 145. See also Waitz, D. V. G. i. 153 sq.; G. L. von Maurer, Hofverfassg. i. 27–37, 385–387.

[2] Tac. Germ. c. 24: 'Servos conditionis hujus per commercia tradunt, ut se quoque pudore victoriae exsolvant.'

national assemblies, and receive a provision in the shape of
voluntary offerings or distinct votes of corn and cattle, made by
the state itself [1]. Such votes imply the existence of some state
domain or public land, the cultivation of which must have
been performed by *servi* or *coloni;* and the natural tendency
of such an arrangement would be to annex some portion of the
territory as an official estate to the dignity of the *princeps.*
It is clear that it had not reached this stage in the age of
Tacitus [2]. Outside of his official authority, the chief or only
privilege of the *princeps* was the right of entertaining a *comitatus* [3].

This was a body of warlike companions, who attached themselves in the closest manner to the chieftain of their choice.
They were in many cases the sons of the nobles who were ambitious of renown or of a perfect education in arms. The *princeps* provided for them war-horses, arms, and such rough equipment as they wanted. These and plentiful entertainment were
accepted instead of wages [4]. In the time of war the *comites*
fought for their chief [5], at once his defenders and the rivals of
his prowess. For the *princeps* it was a disgrace to be surpassed, for the *comites* it was a disgrace not to equal the

The comitatus.

Tie of the comites to the princeps.

---

[1] 'Eliguntur in iisdem conciliis;' Tac. Germ. c. 12. 'Mos est civitatibus
ultro ac viritim conferre principibus quod pro honore acceptum etiam
necessitatibus subvenit;' ibid. c. 15. This is the origin of the *naturalia*
of the Frankish, and perhaps of the feorm-fultum of the Anglo-Saxon
kings. Kemble, Saxons, ii. 31.

[2] Waitz, D. V. G. i. 273.

[3] Whether the right of *comitatus* was attached to the office of king and
princeps is a matter of dispute; Bethmann-Hollweg, Civilprocess, iv. 93.
Waitz (D. V. G. i. 244–255) regards it as exclusively so. Konrad Maurer,
arguing that in an early stage of society the companions and free servants
of the *princeps* would be the same, inclines to regard the *comites* of the
princeps as corresponding with the servants of private persons; Krit.
Ueberschau, ii. 396–403. However this may be, it is enough for our purpose to remark that it was only the *princeps* who could give a public
status and character to his *comites.*

[4] 'Exigunt enim principis sui liberalitate illum bellatorem equum,
illam cruentam victricemque frameam. Nam epulae et quanquam incompti, largi tamen, apparatus pro stipendio cedunt.' Tac. Germ. c. 14.
The war-horse and spear were the gift of the *princeps* and the origin of
the later heriot.

[5] 'Principes pro victoria pugnant, comites pro principe.' Tac. Germ.
c. 14.

exploits of their leader, and perpetual infamy to retire from the
field on which he had fallen. They were bound by the closest
obligation to defend and protect him, and to ascribe to his
glory their own brave deeds [1]. In the body thus composed,
there were grades of rank determined by the judgment of the

The *comita-*
tus.

princeps [2]: and a high place in the *comitatus* was an object of
ambition to the noble youth just as much as the possession of
a numerous and spirited body of retainers was to his patron,
who found that his dignity, strength, glory, and security depended in no small degree on the character of his followers.
The *princeps* who entertained such a company was renowned
both abroad and at home; he was chosen to represent his
nation as ambassador; he was honoured with special gifts; and
sometimes the terror of his name would put an end to war

Their em-
ployments.

before blood had been shed. War was the chief if not the sole
employment of the *comites:* when there was peace at home,
the youth sought opportunities of distinguishing and enriching
themselves in distant warfare. In the times of forced and un-
welcome rest they were thoroughly idle; they cared neither
for farming nor for hunting, but spent the time in feasting and
sleep [3]. The *comitatus* is one of the strangest but most lasting
features of early civilisation, partly private and partly public
in its character, and furnishing a sort of supplement to an
otherwise imperfect organisation. The strong and close bond
of union thus described by Tacitus can scarcely be the same
institution as the voluntary and occasional adhesion to a military leader, which Caesar mentions in connexion with the

---

[1] Tac. Germ. c. 14: 'Cum ventum in aciem, turpe principi virtute
vinci, turpe comitatui virtutem principis non adaequare. Jam vero in-
fame in omnem vitam ac probrosum superstitem principi suo ex acie
recessisse. Illum defendere, tueri, sua quoque fortia facta gloriae ejus
assignare praecipuum sacramentum est.' Waitz understands this to imply
an actual oath; D. V. G. i. 373, 374.

[2] Tac. Germ. cc. 13, 14. The difficult passage 'Insignis nobilitas aut
magna patrum merita principis dignationem etiam adolescentulis assignant'
is commented on at great length by Waitz, D. V. G. i. 282–290; and Sohm,
Fr. R. G. V. pp. 555–558; both of whom give a transitive sense to *digna-*
tionem. Kemble translates 'principis dignationem assignant,' 'give the
rank of princes;' Saxons, i. 166.

[3] Tac. Germ. c. 15: a passage which does not refer exclusively to the
comites.

aggressive expeditions of his own time [1]; but the one may
have grown out of the other. Glory and booty seem to have
been the chief end of the expeditions organised by both, and
the tie of personal honour and attachment the common bond;
but in Caesar's account the leadership is not restricted to the
official magistrate, and the engagement of the follower is for a
single campaign only. That the relation to the *princeps* implies personal dependence is clear: no one need blush, says
Tacitus, to be seen among the *comites* [2]; but the fact that it
was necessary, from the Roman point of view, to say so, involves of necessity some idea of diminution of status. It may
be questioned whether any one in this relation would be regarded as fully competent to take part in the deliberations of
the tribe, but it is scarcely reasonable to suppose, as has been
sometimes maintained, that a position of so much honour, and
so much coveted, could only be obtained by the sacrifice of
freedom [3]. But the importance of the *comitatus* lies mainly in
the later history, and in its bearing on kindred but distinct
developments.

The princeps and comites.

Of the priests of the German races we learn little more
from Tacitus than that they formed a distinct class of men who
presided at the sacrifices, took the auspices for public under-
takings, proclaimed and enforced silence in the assembly, and in
the name of the god of war discharged the office of judge and
executioner in the host [4].

The priests.

It is, however, in relation to the administration of government that the notices of the Germania have their greatest
value.

15. There was not in the time of Tacitus, any more than in
that of Caesar, any general centre of administration, or any

The tribal constitution.

---

[1] Caesar, de Bello Gallico, vi. 23 ; above, § 11.   The idea of Sybel and
others that Caesar describes an earlier form of the institution is rejected
by Waitz, D. V. G. i. 382–384 ; K. Maurer, Krit. Ueberschau, ii. 418.

[2] Tac. Germ. c. 13 : 'Nec rubor inter comites aspici.'

[3] This seems to be Kemble's view ; Saxons, i. 173 ; 'it is clear that the
idea of freedom is entirely lost,' being replaced by that of honour.   It is
entirely rejected by Waitz, D. V. G. i. 374, and K. Maurer, Krit. Ueberschau, 394.

[4] Tac. Germ. cc. 7, 10, 11 ; Waitz, D. V. G. i. 275–279.

federal bond among the several tribes. The great kindred races had common religious rites and sanctuaries, but this bond of connexion seems to have involved no common political, military, or administrative organisation [1]. Each nation had a constitution of its own. In some there was a king with kindred nobility and of course a personal *comitatus*, the patron of freedmen and serfs [2]. But the king was by no means vested with irresponsible or unlimited powers [3]. He was elected from the body of the nobles, for strictly hereditary succession was confined to private property: he had not the sole command in war; that was engrossed by the *duces*, who also owed their position to election, determined by the renown they had already earned, and sustained by the willing obedience of their companions in arms [4]. He might take a leading part in council, but others qualified by age, nobility, honour, and eloquence had a not inferior claim to be heard [5]. He received a portion of the fines imposed in the courts of justice, but he did not appoint the judges [6]. His position was dignified and important, as impersonating the unity of the tribe and implying a dominion more extensive than that held by the other non-monarchical communities; but unless he were personally endowed with the gifts or reputation of a military leader, it could be one only of

Limited character of royalty.

[1] Tac. Germ. c. 39 : ' Vetustissimos se nobilissimosque Suevorum Semnones memorant. Fides antiquitatis religione firmatur. Stato tempore in sylvam auguriis patrum et prisca formidine sacram omnes ejusdem sanguinis populi legationibus coeunt, caesoque publice homine celebrant barbari ritus horrenda primordia.'

[2] Tac. Germ. cc. 7, 25. The essence of German kingship was not in the command of the host, or in the leadership of a *comitatus*, or in the union of several tribes under one sceptre, or in an authority more efficient than that of the *princeps*; but in its hereditary character, or in the choice, by the people, of a ruler from a distinct family; Waitz, D. V. G. i. 309-318; K. Maurer, Krit. Ueberschau, ii. 419-423. This hereditary character is absolutely inconsistent with the supposition that royalty originated in the *comitatus*: and is in distinct contrast with the elective principle applied in the case of the *principes*.

[3] Tac. Germ. c. 7 : ' Nec regibus infinita aut libera potestas.'

[4] ' Duces ex virtute sumunt . . . . et duces exemplo potius quam imperio, si prompti, si conspicui, si ante aciem agant, admiratione praesunt ;' Tac. Germ. c. 7. Waitz however maintains that the king was the regular general for the monarchic tribes; D. V. G. i. 333 sq.

[5] Tac. Germ. c. 11 ; see below, p. 30, n. 2.

[6] ' Pars mulctae regi vel civitati, pars ipsi qui vindicatur vel propinquis ejus exsolvitur ;' Tac. Germ. c. 12.

simple honour. There was no such relation between him and
the *principes*[1] as there was between the *principes* and their
comites : the *principes* fought not for him, but for victory, and
the only treason, except that which consisted in the betrayal of
the voluntary tie, was that which was committed against the
nation[2].

We may understand that a tribe which had adopted monarchy
must gradually have modified these conditions ; that a king
strong enough to maintain his position at all, must have
gathered the chiefs of the land into a *comitatus* of his own. But
there is no sign as yet that this was done : nor is there any
indication that the king exercised, except in the case of
auguries[3], any such sacerdotal influence as in ancient times
might be supposed to console a sovereign whose power bore no
proportion to his dignity. But it is not easy to argue with
certainty from the words of Tacitus, that those tribes, in which
the power and pre-eminence of the *principes* were of so great
importance, were really subject to kings at all.

For a very large proportion of the tribes dispensed altogether
with royalty : the state or *civitas*[4] was a sufficient centre, and
the tie of nationality a sufficient bond of cohesion. In these
still, as in Caesar's time, the *principes* chosen in the national
councils acted independently of one another in peace, and in war
obeyed the leader whose valour marked him out for election.
Under this system the state received the portion of the mulcts
which in the monarchies fell to the king[5] : there is no evidence

The central administration was in the civitas whether monarchic or not.

[1] Nor were the *nobiles* the king's *comitatus :* but the question belongs
to a later stage. Waitz, D. V. G. i. 392 sq.

[2] 'Proditores et transfugas arboribus suspendunt,' &c. ; Tac. Germ.
c. 12.

[3] Tac. Germ. c. 10 : 'Pressos (sc. equos) sacro curru sacerdos ac rex vel
princeps civitatis comitantur, hinnitusque ac fremitus observant.'

[4] Tacitus uses the word *civitas* to express the tribe in its constitutional aspect, in the Germania, cc. 8, 10, 12, 13, 14, 15, 19, 25, 30, 41 ; and Annales,
i. 37. *Gens* is also used in the same sense, but not so *pagus*, which always
means a subdivision ; as in Caesar, de Bello Gallico, i. 12, 'Omnis civitas
Helvetia in quattuor pagos divisa est.' Waitz, D. V. G. i. 203. Sohm
(Fr. R. G. V. pp. 1–8) carefully works out the position that, whereas the
unity of the German race was one of blood and religion only, the tribal or
state unity exhibited in the councils was political, and that of the pagi or
hundreds simply a judicial organisation.

[5] Tac. Germ. c. 12.

The *principes* of the non-monarchic tribes.

that the election of the *principes* was influenced by the hereditary principle[1], or that their status involved any of the honours of royalty.   In the monarchical tribes it is probable that the king may have gradually appropriated the powers and honours of the *principes*, but in the non-monarchical ones there is nothing to show that the *principes* were more than the elective magistrates of free and kindred communities.

The central assembly of the *civitas*, a gathering of the host.

16. Under both systems the central power was wielded by the national assemblies.   These were held at fixed times, generally at the new or full moon[2].   There was no distinction of place or seat[3]: all were free, all appeared in arms.   Silence was proclaimed by the priests, who had for the time the power of enforcing it.   Then the debate was opened by some one who had a personal claim to be heard, the king, or a *princeps*, or one whose age, nobility, military glory, or eloquence entitled him to rise.   He took the tone of persuasion, never that of command. Opposition was expressed by loud shouts; assent by the shaking of spears; enthusiastic applause by the clash of spear and shield.

Delibera-tions of the council of the *civitas*.

Of matters of deliberation the more important were transacted in the full assembly, at which all the freemen were entitled to be present.   But the business was canvassed and arranged by the *principes* before it was presented for national determina-tion; and matters of less import and ordinary routine were dispatched in the limited gatherings of the magistrates[4].   Of the greater questions were those of war and peace, although these,

---

[1] See above, p. 23, n. 1.

[2] Tac. Germ. c. 11 : 'Coeunt, nisi quid fortuitum et subitum incidit, certis diebus, cum aut inchoatur luna aut impletur. . . . Illud ex libertate vitium quod non simul nec ut jussi conveniunt, sed et alter et tertius dies cunctatione coeuntium absumitur.   Ut turba placuit considunt armati. Silentium per sacerdotes, quibus tum et coercendi jus est, imperatur.   Mox rex vel princeps, prout aetas cuique, prout nobilitas, prout decus bellorum, prout facundia est, audiuntur, auctoritate suadendi magis quam jubendi potestate.   Si displicuit sententia, fremitu aspernantur; sin placuit fra-meas concutiunt.   Honoratissimum assensus genus est armis laudare.'

[3] Possibly they arranged themselves, as in the host, in kindreds. Waitz, D. V. G. i. 349.

[4] Tac. Germ. c. 11 : 'De minoribus rebus principes consultant, de ma-joribus omnes, ita tamen ut ea quoque quorum penes plebem arbitrium est apud principes pertractentur (*v. l.* praetractentur).'

together with proposals of alliance and elections of magistrates, were frequently discussed in the convivial meetings which formed part of the regular session of the council[1]. The magistrates for the administration of justice in the *pagi* and *vici* were elected in the general council. It also acted, in its sovereign capacity, as a high court of justice, heard complaints and issued capital sentences[2].

The local courts of justice were held by the elected *principes* in the larger divisions or *pagi*, and in the villages or *vici*. But their office was rather that of president of the court than of judge. The *princeps* had, in the *pagus* at least, a hundred assessors or companions to whom he was indebted not only for advice but for authority also[3]: doubtless they both declared the law and weighed the evidence. Capital punishments were not rare; hanging was the reward of treason and desertion: the coward and the abandoned person were drowned or smothered under hurdles: other offences were expiated by fines, of which one portion went to the king or the state, the rest to the injured person or his relations. The system of compensation extended even to the reconciliation of hereditary quarrels: homicide itself might be atoned for by a fine of cattle: the whole house

Judicial assemblies of the pagus.

Fines in compensation for offences.

[1] 'De reconciliandis invicem inimicitiis et jungendis affinitatibus et adsciscendis principibus, de pace denique ac bello, plerumque in conviviis consultant;' Tac. Germ. c. 22. Whether the custom of drinking the fines for non-attendance, which was a time-honoured practice in the German mark-courts (G. L. von Maurer, Markenverfassg. p. 275), and still prevails in England in rural clubs, can be traced to this usage, need not be discussed. It certainly seems that the manorial courts still support their existence by dinner after business: and so in the time of Athelstan the 'bytt-fylling,' 'impletio vasorum,' was an important part of the proceedings of the local gatherings. The vexed question of *scot ales* and *church ales* and the functions of the ale-taster connect themselves with the primitive practice: and so also the guilds. See Ll. Hen. I. c. 81 ; and Chap. xi., below.

[2] Tac. Germ. c. 12 : 'Licet apud concilium accusare quoque et discrimen capitis intendere. Distinctio poenarum ex delicto. Proditores et transfugas arboribus suspendunt ; ignavos et imbelles et corpore infames caeno ac palude injecta insuper crate mergunt. Diversitas supplicii illuc respicit, tanquam scelera ostendi oporteat dum puniuntur, flagitia abscondi. Sed et levioribus delictis pro modo poena, equorum pecorumque numero convicti mulctantur. Pars mulctae regi vel civitati, pars ipsi qui vindicatur vel propinquis ejus exsolvitur.' See Sohm, Fr. R. G. V. p. 5.

[3] 'Eliguntur in iisdem conciliis et principes, qui jura per pagos vicosque reddunt. Centeni singulis ex plebe comites consilium simul et auctoritas adsunt ;' Tac. Germ. c. 12.

of the slain man joined in accepting it as an indemnity, and the
breach of the public peace was healed by a fixed share[1].

Organisa-
tion in time
of war.

17. In war the compulsory maintenance of discipline was
tempered greatly by the spirit of the *comitatus.* The leader of
the host was the chosen champion; not necessarily the king or
the local magistrate, but the *dux* whose prowess had earned the
confidence of the nation, and who as *princeps* was followed by
the largest train of companions[2]. From each *pagus* a hundred
champions were sent to the host[3], just as the hundred assessors
were furnished to the court of justice. Well-trained infantry
were thus supplied; they took the van in battle and were supported by or mingled with the cavalry. The chief burden fell on
the *duces*[4], who had to set an example rather than to enforce
command, and on the *principes* with their mounted *comites.*
The maintenance of discipline in the field as in the council was
left in great measure to the priests[5]; they took the auguries
and gave the signal for onset, they alone had power to visit
with legal punishment, to bind or to beat. Otherwise the
cohesion and order of battle was kept up by the voluntary
regularity of the armed freemen, who arranged themselves, when
not otherwise tied, in families and affinities[6]. Three principles
at least seem to be at work in this system; the national force
consisting of the *dux* and chosen centuries of infantry; the
professional warriors with their trains of disciples, the *principes*
fighting for victory, and the *comites* for their *princeps ;* and the

[1] The passages that illustrate this are of great importance on the whole
subject of German criminal law; the *bôt*, the *wergild*, the *wite ;* the
bannus, the *faidus*, and the *fredus ;* the character of the peace, the idea
of the right of private war, the so-called *fehde-recht*, and the position of
the king as guardian of the peace, and of the kindred as sharers in the feud.
Tac. Germ. cc. 12, 21, 22.   Waitz, D. V. G. i. 418–453; K. Maurer, Krit.
Ueberschau, iii. 26–36; Sohm, Fr. R. V. G. pp. 107, 108.

[2] ' Ipsa plerumque fama bella profligant ;' Tac. Germ. c. 13.

[3] Ibid. c. 6 : ' In universum aestimanti plus penes peditem roboris ;
eoque mixti proeliantur, apta et congruente ad equestrem pugnam veloci-
tate peditum quos ex omni juventute delectos ante aciem locant.   Definitur
et numerus: centeni ex singulis pagis sunt; idque ipsum inter suos
vocantur, et quod primo numerus fuit jam nomen et honor est.'

[4] ' Si prompti, si conspicui, si ante aciem agant ;' Ibid. c. 7.

[5] Ibid. c. 7.

[6] ' Non casus nec fortuita conglobatio turmam aut cuneum facit, sed
familiae et propinquitates ;' Ibid. c. 7.

mass of the freemen arranged in families fighting for their
homesteads and hearths.   It is to the influence of the last
association, according to Tacitus, that the host owes its strongest
impulse and the confidence of earnest valour, whether the immediate excitement be the rivalry of jealous neighbours or the
urgency of common interests. The host is thus the whole nation
in arms.

18. And the nation in its territorial aspect is not altogether
unlike the host in permanent encampment.   The *pagus* and
vicus are the divisions rather of the people than of the land,
and may be reasonably supposed to have been marked out with
reference to the numerical arrangement of the host, and in that
strict adherence to definite numbers which appears so constantly in new or loosely settled communities, whether civilised
or not.   The hundred warriors and the hundred judges of the
pagus, may on this supposition represent the hundred free
families to which the *pagus* was originally allotted, that primitive
institution of the hundred which appears in every branch of
the Germanic race in its earliest historical form; not yet a
definite geographical division, but a social and political one[1].
The *vici* may be subdivisions in equal proportions, both of the
personalities and of the territorial allotment of the hundred :
and their subdivision by re-allotment may have been equally
symmetrical.   But it would be wrong to state this as more
than a theory.

Personal basis of these arrangements.

19. With very few exceptions, by way of inference, this
description is a mere abstract and paraphrase of the language
of the Germania.   The general features of it are clear if not
minute.   It will probably always be a favourite exercise for
learned ingenuity to attempt to trace distinct reference to the

[1] Waitz, D. V. G. i. 218, understands the hundred companions of the
princeps in judgment to be the fully qualified members of the community;
no special stress is to be laid on the number, as Tacitus himself warns us.
They formed then a full hundred-court, and not a mere council of assessors,
as Tacitus supposed. Bethmann-Hollweg takes the same view (Civilprocess, iv. 102).   The older view, regarding them as a committee of the
freemen, is on the whole less likely.   The principle that in these courts all
the suitors are judges is very ancient.   See also Waitz, D. V. G. i. 358 ;
Sohm, Fr. R. V. G. pp. 6, 7.

Prospective and retrospective value of the Germania.

later institutions of the race: and it is quite lawful to work back, through obvious generalisations and comparisons with the early phenomena of society in other nations, to the primitive civilisation of the Aryan or the Indo-Germanic family. It would be foreign to our present purpose to attempt the latter task: and the former can only be partially undertaken in a work, the object of which is historical rather than philosophical. But the words of Tacitus require interpretation, and the unity of his sketch demands, for intelligent comprehension, some reference to the early principles of social development.

No principle works in isolation.

Among the first truths which the historical student, or indeed any scientific scholar, learns to recognise, this is perhaps the most important, that no theory or principle works in isolation. The most logical conclusions from the truest principle are practically false, unless in drawing them allowance is made for the counter-working of other principles equally true in theory, and equally dependent for practical truth on co-ordination with the first. No natural law is by itself sufficient to account for all the phenomena which on the most restricted view range themselves within its sphere. And with respect to primitive society, this is especially noteworthy. The patriarchal theory, as it is called, will certainly not account for any great proportion of the phenomena of the social system under any of

Traces of primitive society.

its phases: yet there are in the Germania some traces of the idea on which it is based; the union for some purposes of sacerdotal with royal functions[1], and the vast and permanent importance of the family tie[2]. Of the four chief forms of political life, which in their earlier stages are compatible with the existence of a people in the pastoral, the hunting, and the predatory stages of its development, the most complex, that of the city, is expressly excluded by the words of Tacitus; the Germans had no cities[3], no fortified places of resort or refuge;

[1] Tac. Germ. c. 10; above, p. 29, n. 3.
[2] In relation to the host, Tac. Germ. c. 7; to feuds, c. 21; to inheritance, c. 20; the relations witness the punishment of the unfaithful wife, c. 19; marriages with alien nations are unusual, c. 4. Waitz, D. V. G. i. 53-96.
[3] Tac. Germ. c. 16. They regarded them as 'munimenta servitii;' Tac. Hist. iv. 64.

and, when at a later period they adopt a city life, its constitution is based on that of the ancient villages rather than on any imported idea of the classical municipality[1]. The lordship,—that quasi-manorial system, in which the lord of the land lives among his free tenants and cultivates his proper demesne by serfs or hired labourers, possessing the original title to the whole, waste as well as cultivated, with jurisdiction over and right to service from all who dwell within the boundaries,—is only in very few particulars reconcileable with the sketch of Tacitus. The village system in which, the tie of community of land not necessarily existing, the freer and simpler institution of a common machinery for the preservation of peace, the administration of justice, and the fulfilment of public duties as part of a wider organisation, is the direct and primary bond, does fall in more easily with the general tenour of the description. The *vici* or villages exist and have justice administered by the *principes*. But further references, irrespective of the question of the land, are scanty and open to much discussion. The idea of the Mark System, as it is called, according to which the body of kindred freemen, scattered over a considerable area and cultivating their lands in common, use a domestic constitution based entirely or primarily on the community of tenure and cultivation, is an especially inviting one, and furnishes a basis on which a large proportion of the institutions of later constitutional life may theoretically be imposed. And there are nations in which such a system has ever been the rule, although they are not those whose progress has made a part of the world's history[2], whilst the very fact of their permanent insignificance may be regarded as a positive refutation of the claim of their system to include all the germs of greater and more active free institutions. But this system, in its bare simplicity, is scarcely consistent with

Marginal notes: Germs of later institutions contained in the Germania. The manor. The village. The Mark.

[1] See this worked out by G. L. von Maurer, Städteverfassg. i. 134 sq.: he rejects the idea of Roman municipality, of the manorial system, of the *Schöffenthum*, or of the guild, as the origin of city life among the Germans, and traces it to the *Mark*.

[2] See, especially in reference to India, Sir H. S. Maine's Lectures on Village Communities, London, 1871; and on the *Mir*, or Russian Village Community, Mackenzie Wallace, Russia, c. viii. pp. 179 sq.

the general sketch of the Germania, and totally insufficient as a key to the whole. The German communities, although they hold their land in common, are scarcely described as those of an agricultural people: while the mark system is wholly and entirely an agricultural one, and must, if it had existed in its integrity in Tacitus's time, have impressed its leading features more distinctly upon his memory. Nor can a mixture of the systems of the lordship, the village and the mark, claim a greater probability; we have no one of the three in its completeness and cannot be warranted in supposing the co-existence of all.

The sketch of Tacitus contains the several principles of later society.

It is only by viewing the description of the Roman historian as referring to a stage and state of society in which the causes are at work which at different periods and in different regions develop all the three, that any approach can be safely made towards bringing it into relation with the facts of historical sociology. We have not the mark system, but we have the principle of common tenure and cultivation, on which, in India, the native village communities still maintain a primitive practice much older probably than the Germania, and of which very distinct vestiges exist still in our own country, in Switzerland, and in Germany[1]. We have not the village system in its integrity, but we have the villages themselves, their relation to the *pagi*, and through them to the *civitas*, and the fact that they were centres or subdivisions for the administration of justice. We have not the manor, but we have the nobleman, we have the warlike magistrate with his attendant *comites*, whose services he must find some way of rewarding, and whose energies he must even in peace find some way of employing. The rich man too has his great house and court, and his family of slaves or dependents, who may be only less than free in that they cultivate the land that belongs to

---

[1] See below, pp. 53–58. It appears rash to make the mark system, pure and simple, the basis of Germanic society. No doubt in some cases not only villages, but hundreds, and still larger territories possessed common lands, but it does not follow that in these all constitutional relations were based upon it; and the preponderance of learned opinion is at present decidedly against the theory.

another. We dare not say that we have a perfect alodial system, although the land, so far as it may be held in severalty, is held alodially: we cannot say that we have feudality, for the tie between the lord and his dependent is distinctly not one of which land is either the exponent or the material basis.

But we have germs and traces of all. The military *princeps* has but to conquer and colonise a new territory, and reward his followers on a plan that will keep them faithful as well as free, and feudalism springs into existence. The members of the village society have but to commute their fluctuating shares in the annual redistribution of land for a fixed allotment with definite duties incumbent upon them as independent owners, and we have the alodial system of village life; let the warriors of the tribe sink their predatory ardour in the fulfilment of immediate duties, cultivate their land and live on the produce of it, and they will probably fall back into the simplicity of the primitive mark life, out of which they emerged, and into which their descendants, in many cases, when civilised and humanised by the arts of peace, chose, in the prospect of freedom and social independence, to return.

A slight development would turn these principles into systems.

If the free village organisation seems to recommend itself as the most adequate explanation of the facts recorded, it must be remembered that its plausibility depends on its obscurity and indefiniteness. It may contain or it may exclude the principle of common tenure and cultivation; it may include or exclude the estates of the rich men and their slaves, the halls of the *principes* and their companions. We can affirm little more than that the *vicus* was a community of common cultivators; a centre or a subdivision of the *pagus* for the purposes of police or judicature. On the analogy of the *pagus* we may infer that it furnished in its elders a body of assessors to assist the *princeps* on the bench of justice, and in its young men a contingent towards the chosen centuries of the host. All beyond this is theory, or derived from interpretation by later facts.

General indistinctness of the result.

The looseness and unjointed character of the upper organisation is by itself sufficient to prevent us from accepting a symmetrical theory. If the villages and the *pagi* are arranged on

The three
principles
of kindred,
community,
and personal
influence.
one principle, the supreme authority seems to be exercised at least on three. The king in the monarchic states does little more than represent the unity of race; he has a primacy of honour but not of power; he reigns but does not govern. The national council under the elective *principes* is sovereign in peace, but in war its powers are vested in the *dux;* and yet the authority of the *dux* over his *comites* does not rest on the election of the nation, but on the personal tie by which they are bound to him. Just so in each subordinate portion of the fabric, the three principles of the kindred, the community, and the personal influence, complement and complicate each other's action. The lower organisations are more coherent than the upper, because it is more possible for them to exist unmixed, or in personal union: the kindred may be the community, and the personal and official influence of the wise man or champion may be united in the chief of the family settlement. But even here the cohesive force may be exaggerated.

It is no part of our task to attempt here the higher point of view and the broader generalisations of the philosophic analyst. It is a tempting scheme which invites us to distinguish clearly the organic functions of the race, the state and the canton,—the *sanguis*, the *populus* or *civitas* and the *pagus*,—the *stamm*, the *volk* and the *hundertschaft*[1]; to recognise the common religious rites as the sole bond of union in the first, the assembly of the host as the sole expression of political unity in the second, and the judicial assembly of the hundred as the proper function of

the third of these associations. And it is perhaps a needless caution that withholds its assent from a theory which only fails to produce conviction because it is too sharply defined and too

---

[1] Sohm (Fr. R. G. V. pp. 1–8) combats the idea that the constitution of the race (*Stamm*), that of the civitas (*Volk*), and that of the pagus (*Hundertschaft*), are based on the same principle, so that one is the reproduction of the other on a different field. He contends that, in the Germania, they exhibit the people in three different phases: the religious, the political, and the judicial. 'The old German constitution is characterised by the organic connexion in which the different sides of the national life stand to the different stages of the national organism.' Grimm (R. A. p. 745), and Waitz (D. V. G. i. 339) are inclined to regard the several constitutions as conversant, in the main, with the same matters.

symmetrical. In the main such a theory is true, although it cannot be applied confidently or universally in minute particulars. Every tribe and every group has its own history; the migrating *populus* may retain only its religious unity, and the growing *pagus* may become a *civitas*. So the functions of the host and of justice may be united in one assembly, or by a reverse process the village may acquire powers of military and judicial administration. Some such changes and developments will show themselves as we proceed.

The conclusion that such a survey suggests, especially with a view to later history, is this: A great family of tribes whose institutions are all in common, and their bonds of political cohesion so untrustworthy, are singularly capable of entering into new combinations; singularly liable to be united and dissolved in short-lived confederations, and to reappear under new names, so long as they are without a great leader. Yet in that very community of institutions and languages, in the firmness of the common basis, and the strength of the lower organisation, if a leader can be found to impress on them the need of unity, and to consolidate the higher machinery of political action into a national constitution, instead of small aggregations and tumultuary associations, they possess a basis and a spring of life, from and by which they may rise into a great homogeneous people, symmetrically organised and united, progressive and thoroughly patriotic.

General conclusions.

CHAPTER III.

THE SAXONS AND ANGLES AT HOME.

20. Appearance of the Franks and Saxons.—21. The Angles and Jutes.
—22. Saxons in Germany as described by Bede, Nithard, Rudolf, and
Hucbald; and noticed in the Capitularies.—23. Notices of the Angles in
Germany.—24. The mark system and common husbandry.—25. Early
system illustrated by the Salian law.—26. Further illustrations.

Reappear-
ance of the
German
tribes under
new names.

20. FOR nearly two hundred years after the age of Tacitus
very little is known of the internal history of the German tribes,
and nothing new of their political institutions. From the
facility with which the latter, when they reappear, may be made
to harmonise with the account of the great historian, it is
almost necessarily inferred that they had continued without
change; nor is there any occasion to presume a development in
the direction of civilisation. The Germans of Caesar's time
were very far from being savages, but those of the fourth century
were still a very long way from the conditions of modern society.
How very long the institutions of a half-civilised nation may
remain stationary we have both in the East and in the West
very abundant evidence.

During these centuries, at various periods, the Roman empire
was alarmed and shaken by the appearance on her borders of
nations great in mass and strength, as their predecessors had
been, but bearing new names. In the reign of Caracalla Rome
first heard of the Goths and Alemanni[1]; a little more than
half a century later the Franks appear; and about the same time

[1] Ael. Spartianus, Caracalla, c. 10; Zeuss, Die Deutschen und die Nachbarstämme, pp. 304, 401.

the Saxons, who had been named and placed geographically by Ptolemy, make their first mark in history. They are found employed in naval and piratical expeditions on the coasts of Gaul in A. D. 287 [1].

Whatever degree of antiquity we may be inclined to ascribe to the names of these nations, and there is no need to put a precise limit to it, it can scarcely be supposed that they sprang from insignificance and obscurity to strength and power in a moment. It is far more probable that under the names of Frank and Saxon in the fourth century had been sunk the many better-known earlier names of tribes who occupied the same seats; as the Sigambri, the Salii and the Ubii were all now known as Franks [2], so the Cherusci, the Marsi, the Dulgibini, and the Chauci [3] may have been comprehended under the name of Saxons. The nations of the Germania had no common name recognised by themselves, and were content, when, ages after, they had realised their unity of tongue and descent, to speak of their language simply as the Lingua Theotisca, the language of the people [4] (theod). The general name by which the Romans knew them was one which they had received from their Gallic neighbours. Much of the minute and obscure nomenclature of the early geographers had probably a similar origin. The freemen of the *gentes* and *cognationes* might not care much about the collective name with which perhaps a casual combination under some great warrior had temporarily endowed them. So long as they retained amongst themselves their family or gentile names, it mattered little whether the foreigners called them Ingaevones [5] or Cherusci, Germans or Saxons. It is possible

Indetermi-nateness of the collective names.

---

[1] Eutropius, ix. 13; Zeuss, p. 381; Grimm, Gesch. der D. Spr. p. 625.

[2] Grimm, Gesch. der Deutschen Spr. pp. 520 sq.; Zeuss, pp. 326, 329.

[3] Grimm, Gesch. der Deutschen Spr. pp. 614, 624.

[4] Whence the name ' Deutsch.' Zeuss derives it rather from the root of ' deuten,' to explain, so that *theotisc* should mean 'significant.' But the root of *theod* and *deuten* is the same. See Max Müller, Lectures on the Science of Language, ii. 230; Grimm, Gesch. der Deutschen Spr. p. 790; Waitz, D. V. G. i. 30. All decide against the connexion with the Teutones. The word, as applied to language, occurs first A. D. 786.

[5] Grimm's identification of the Ingaevones with the Saxons, of the Iscaevones with the Franks, and of the Herminones with the Thuringians is convenient: Pref. to his edition of the Germania, p. iv; Gesch. der Deutschen Spr. pp. 825, 829, 830, 832; Waitz, D.V. G. i. 11, 12; Max Müller, Lectures

that the sudden prominence of new names sometimes signified the acquisition of dominion by a rising tribe; that the later career of the Franks may be but the fulfilment of a destiny that had begun to work centuries earlier; it is not impossible that a confederation of free and neighbour tribes may have become known to the world by a collective name which they were scarcely conscious of bearing[1]: nor is it unlikely that in some cases the collective name itself testifies to a series of rapid subjugations and annexations. But, however this may be, the bearing of the common name was in itself a long step towards political unity: the Saxon communities might have no yearning towards it themselves, but when they found that their neighbours treated them as one, they would find it gradually necessary to act as one. It is needless for us to attempt now to generalise on the widely varying causes that led to this constitution of the later nationalities. Some had originated in the necessity of defence against Rome, some in the tempting prospect of rich booty; the later ones perhaps in the turmoil which accompanied the great upheaval in Central Asia that first threw the Goths upon the empire. It is safer to ascribe them in general to some such external cause than to suppose them to have proceeded from, or even to have evinced, a tendency towards political union. The very causes which made combination easy would seem to preclude the possibility of any conscious active tendency towards it. Whilst the nations on the Lower Rhine were all becoming Franks, those between the Rhine and the Elbe were becoming Saxons; the name implied as yet no common organisation, at the most only an occasional combination for attack or defence.

Importance of the new collective names.

They are not to be referred to actual confederation.

The Saxons.

The Angles.

21. In close neighbourhood with the Saxons, in the middle of the fourth century, were the Angli, a tribe whose origin is

---

on the Science of Language, ii. 502, 503. There is, I believe, no etymological objection to connecting the *Ing* of the Ingaevones with the *Ang* of the Angles and the *Eng* of England.

[1] Waitz, D. V. G. i. 368, rejects the idea of anything like federal constitutions in these early times. But a long alliance may, for foreign nations, easily bear the appearance of a confederation. See also Grimm, Gesch. der Deutschen Spr. p. 518.

more uncertain and the application of whose name is still more
a matter of question. If the name belongs, in the pages of the *Movements of the Angli in Germany.*
several geographers, to the same nation, it was situated in the
time of Tacitus east of the Elbe ; in the time of Ptolemy it
was found on the middle Elbe between the Thuringians to the
south and the Varini to the north; and at a later period it
was forced, perhaps by the growth of the Thuringian power,
into the neck of the Cimbric peninsula. It may however be
reasonably doubted whether this hypothesis is sound, and it is
by no means clear whether, if it be so, the Angli were not
connected more closely with the Thuringians than with the
Saxons[1].

To the north of the Angli, after they had reached their *The Jutes.*
Schleswig home, were the Jutes, of whose early history we
know nothing, except their claim to be regarded as kinsmen of
the Goths, and the close similarity between their descendants
and the neighbour Frisians[2]. All these tribes spoke dialects of *Language of the three tribes.*
the language now known as the old low German, in contrast
with the Suevic or Swabian tribes, whose tongue was the basis
of the high German, and with the Frank, whose language, now
almost entirely lost, seems to have occupied a middle position
between the two[3]. That of the Goths was outside, but still
akin to all the three varieties.

It was by these tribes, the Saxons, the Angles, and the Jutes, *These tribes colonised Southern Britain.*
that Southern Britain was conquered and colonised in the fifth
and sixth centuries, according to the most ancient testimony.
Bede's assertion[4], although not confirmed by much independent
authority, is not opposed by any conflicting evidence; and such

---

[1] Grimm, Gesch. der Deutschen Spr. pp. 641, 642.
[2] Ibid. pp. 735, 736.
[3] Grimm, Gesch. der Deutschen Spr. pp. 535–547. The Malberg glosses
on the Lex Salica seem to be the chief if not the only relics of the primitive
Frank tongue. Dr. Kern (Haag, 1869) traces, in these, points of affinity
to the ancient Low German of the Netherlands, and K. J. Clement,
Forschungen über das Recht der Salischen Franken (ed. Zoepfl, 1876),
argues in favour of a Frisian relationship. This, if proved, would much
increase the importance of all parallels drawn between Frank and Anglo-
Saxon law. But the question is very far from decision.
[4] Hist. Eccl. i. 15.

arguments as can be gathered from language and institutions are in thorough harmony with it.

The three Tribes.

Of the three, the Angli almost if not altogether pass away into the migration : the Jutes and the Saxons, although migrating in great numbers, had yet an important part to play in their own homes and in other regions besides Britain ; the former at a later period in the train and under the name of the Danes ; the latter in German history from the eighth century to the present day[1]. The development of the Saxons, however, was more rapid, and is much more fully illustrated by history in England than in Germany ; and the traces of Anglian institutions in their ancient home are of the most insignificant character.

Historical notices of the old Saxons.

22. There are several notices extant of the social and political condition of the continental Saxons at the time when they first came into collision with the Frank empire, and when their conversion was first attempted. These seem to show that they had remained until then altogether free from Roman influences, and from any foreign intermixture of blood or institutions. They had preserved the ancient features of German life in their purest forms. Of these witnesses Bede is the most ancient.

Bede's statement.

He wrote, whilst they were still unconquered, from the report of the English missionaries. They are not only unconquered, but unconsolidated. ' These same old Saxons,' he writes, ' have not a king but a great number of satraps set over their nation, who in any case of imminent war cast lots equally ; and on whomsoever the lot falls, him they all follow as leader during the war ; him they obey for the time ; but, when the war is over, all the satraps again resume their equal power[2].' Except

---

[1] The name of Ambrones, given by Nennius as equivalent to ' Ald-Saxones,' and applied to the Northumbrians of the seventh century (M. H. B. p. 76), is found in Livy and Plutarch in connexion with the Teutones. Zeuss (Die Deutschen, &c. pp. 147, 151) collects the passages where the name occurs, and conjectures that it was a traditional name of the people known later as Saxons.

[2] Hist. Eccl. v. 10 : ' Non enim habent regem iidem Antiqui Saxones, sed satrapas plurimos suae genti praepositos, qui ingruente belli articulo mittunt aequaliter sortes, et quemcunque sors ostenderit, hunc tempore belli ducem omnes sequuntur, huic obtemperant ; peracto autem bello rursum aequalis potentiae omnes fiunt satrapae.' The word *ducem* is

the method of selection by lot, instead of election by merit, Bede's agreement with Tacitus.
this description is in close harmony with that of Tacitus. The
military leader is chosen for the time only : his success does not
make him a permanent ruler or king : the union of the *gentes*
or nations is temporary and occasional only ; when the emergency is over each tribal ruler is independent as before. In
connexion with the same story, the venerable historian describes
one of these satraps as acting with summary jurisdiction on the
inhabitants of a *vicus* which was under the mediate government
of a *villicus*[1]. King Alfred when he translated Bede had no The town-ship among the Old-Saxons.
difficulty in recognising in the satrap the *ealdorman*, in the
villicus the *tungerefa*, in the vicus the *tunscipe* of his own
land; possibly the same names were used in both the continental and the insular Saxonies[2].

The next historical witness is Nithard. The grandson of the Statement of Nithard.
great Charles, writing about A.D. 843, describes the nation
that his grandfather had converted as one of most ancient
nobility and most brilliant military skill. The whole race is
divided into three ranks, edhilingi or *nobiles*, frilingi or *in-
genuiles*, lazzi or *serviles*[3]. It was by promises made to the Three classes of men among the Saxons.
frilingi and the lazzi that the Emperor Lothar gained their aid
against his brothers : he undertook to restore to them the old
law under which they had lived before their conversion. Thus
encouraged they rose against their lords, and having expelled
them nearly all from their country, lived under their ancient
law, each man as he pleased. In the division of noble, free
and unfree, which is preserved also in a Capitulary[4] of A.D.

translated by Alfred ' to heretogan ' and ' to ladtheowe ;' Smith's Bede,
p. 624.

[1] ' Qui venientes in provinciam, intraverunt hospitium cujusdam villici,
petieruntque ab eo ut transmitterentur ad satrapam ;' Hist. Eccl. v. 10.

[2] ' Ða hi ða on eald Seaxan comon. Ða eodon hi on sumes tungerefan
gestærn, and hine bædon that he hi onsende to ðam ealdormen;' Smith's
Bede, p. 624.

[3] Nithard, Hist. iv. 2 : ' Saxones .... qui ab initio tam nobiles quam
et ad bella promptissimi multis indiciis saepe claruerunt. Quae gens omnis
in tribus ordinibus divisa consistit ; sunt enim inter illos qui edhilingi, sunt
qui frilingi, sunt qui lazzi illorum lingua dicuntur ; Latina vero lingua hoc
sunt, nobiles, ingenuiles atque serviles.'

[4] Capitulare Saxonicum, art. 3 : ' Item placuit omnibus Saxonibus ut
ubicunque Franci secundum legem solidos quindecim solvere debent, ibi

797, as the *nobilis,* the *ingenuus* and the *litus,* we have a clear
maintenance of Tacitus's distinction of the nobilis, the ingenuus, and the servus or colonus—the eorl, the ceorl and the
læt of the Kentish laws two centuries earlier in date.

Later
notices of
an earlier
state of
things.

Bede and Nithard both state the facts existing in their own
day; but we have two very valuable evidences of a much
earlier condition of things from writers of later date. Rudolf,
the author of the Translatio Sancti Alexandri, writing about
A.D. 863, describes the Saxons of the early Frank empire as a

Statement
of Rudolf.

nation 'most unquiet and hostile to the settlements of neighbours, but at home peaceable and benevolently mindful of the
interests of their own people. Of the distinctions of race and
nobility they are most tenaciously careful: they scarcely ever
(and here the writer quotes the Germania) allow themselves to
be infected by any marriages with other or inferior races, and
try to keep their nationality apart, sincere and unlike any
other.' Hence the universal prevalence of one physical type.
'The race consists of four ranks of men, the noble, the free,
the freedmen, and the servi. And it is by law established that
no order shall in contracting marriages remove the landmarks
of its own lot; but noble must marry noble, freeman freewoman, freedman freedwoman, serf handmaid. If any take a
wife of different or higher rank than his own, he has to expiate
the act with his life[1].' 'They used also most excellent laws for
the punishment of evildoers, and had taken pains to cultivate
many institutions beneficial and accordant with natural law,
which might have helped them in the way to true bliss, if they

nobiliores Saxones solidos duodecim, ingenui quinque, liti quatuor com-
ponant.' In art. 5: 'Si quis de nobilioribus ad placitum mannitus venire
contempserit, solidos quatuor componat, ingenui duos, liti unum.' Pertz,
Legg. i. 75, 76; v. 87, 90; Boret, i. 71, 72; Baluze, i. 199, 200. See Richthofen, Zur Lex Saxonum, p. 346.

[1] 'Quatuor igitur differentiis gens illa Saxonum consistit, nobilium
scilicet et liberorum, libertorum atque servorum. Et id legibus firmatum
ut nulla pars in copulandis conjugiis propriae sortis terminos fransferat,
sed nobilis nobilem ducat uxorem et liber liberam, libertus conjungatur
libertae et servus ancillae. Si vero quispiam horum sibi non con-
gruentem et genere praestantiorem duxerit uxorem, cum vitae suae damno
componat;' Rudolf, Transl. S. Alex.; Pertz, Scriptt. ii. 674. See Waitz,
D. V. G. i. 194, 195; Richthofen, Zur Lex Saxonum, pp. 223–229; Pertz,
Legg. v. 42.

had not been ignorant of their Creator and aliens from the truth of His worship.' Whatever this statement loses by the close imitation of the words of Tacitus, it more than gains by the clear identification of the Saxons as peculiarly answering to his account of the Germans generally.

Hucbald, the biographer of S. Lebuin, writing, in the middle of the tenth century, of the Saxons of the eighth, draws the following remarkable picture. 'In the nation of the Saxons in the most ancient times there existed neither a knowledge of the most High and Heavenly King, so that due reverence should be paid to His worship, nor any dignity of honour of any earthly king by whose providence, impartiality, and industry the nation might be ruled, corrected and defended. The race was, as it still is, divided into three orders; there are there those who are called in their tongue Edlingi; there are Frilingi; and there are what are called Lassi; words that are in Latin *nobiles, ingenui,* and *serviles.* Over each of their local divisions or *pagi,* at their own pleasure and on a plan which in their eyes was a prudent one, a single *princeps* or chieftain presided. Once every year, at a fixed season, out of each of these local divisions, and out of each of the three orders severally, twelve men were elected, who having assembled together in Mid-Saxony, near the Weser, at a place called Marklo, held a common council, deliberating, enacting, and publishing measures of common interest according to the tenour of a law adopted by themselves. And, moreover, whether there were an alarm of war or a prospect of steady peace, they consulted together as to what must be done to meet the case[1].' The Saxons then in the tenth century could look back on a time when they were under this primitive constitution. The orders

Marginal notes: Hucbald's description of the Old-Saxons. Their ranks, government, and annual councils.

---

[1] 'Sunt denique ibi qui illorum lingua Edlingi, sunt qui Frilingi, sunt qui Lassi dicuntur, quod in Latina sonat lingua nobiles, ingenui, atque serviles. Pro suo vero libitu, consilio quoque ut sibi videbatur prudenti, singulis pagis principes praeerant singuli. Statuto quoque tempore anni semel ex singulis pagis, atque ex iisdem ordinibus tripartitis singillatim, viri duodecim electi et in unum collecti, in media Saxonia seeus flumen Wiseram et locum Marklo nuncupatum, exercebant generale concilium;' V. S. Lebuini, Pertz, Scriptt. ii. 361; Surius, AA. SS. iv. fo. 90. The opening words are of course from Nithard: above, p. 45, note 3. See Grimm, Gesch. der Deutschen Spr. p. 628.

of men were what they had been in the days of Tacitus, although the servile class had got a new name and a far superior condition, which gave them some share even of political power.

Development of the principle of representation.

Still the *principes* ruled each his own *pagus*, and the national council was held once a year. That council alone expressed the national unity; there was no king; each chieftain ruled by the custom of the nation. The assembly was a representative council of the most perfect kind; and, stated simply, must have been as much in advance of the constitutional system of other countries in the tenth century as it had been in the eighth: for the double principle of representation, local and by orders, involves the double character of the gathering: in one aspect it is an assembly of estates, in another the concentration of local machinery: and in either it is a singular anticipation of polities which have their known and historical development centuries later. It may indeed be reasonably doubted whether such a complete and symmetrical system can have existed; it would be as startling a phenomenon if it existed only in the brain of the Frank monk, as it would be in proper history[1]. Nor have we any distinct information about it from any other source.

Illustrations from the Capitularies.

The Capitularies of Charles the Great, the Lex Saxonum, and other monuments of later Saxon jurisprudence down to the Sachsenspiegel, preserve a few traces of primitive law, and furnish now and then contrasts and analogies that illustrate the institutions of England. It would be premature in this place to enlarge upon these. The particulars in which they coincide with the traditions of the historians already quoted are sufficient to show the main points that are now of importance, the primitive character of the polity, the careful exclusiveness of the pure Saxon race, the existence of the general assemblies,

---

[1] Waitz, D. V. G. i. 157, 366, allows that the passage is suspicious, but declines to follow Schaumann in rejecting it altogether. See also vol. iii. p. 114. Richthofen, Zur Lex Saxonum, pp. 277, 278, regards it as problematical, especially with reference to the *liti*, but allows that a uniform rule respecting them did not prevail in the German tribes. In the edition of the Lex Saxonum, Pertz, Legg. v. 46, it is treated as fabulous.

and the threefold division of classes, with the exceptional position Illustrations from the Ca-pitularies.
of the lowest of the three. The Capitulatio de partibus Saxoniae,
issued immediately after the conquest, and during the process
of conversion, is strictly devoted to ecclesiastical regulations.
Amongst its clauses are two which direct the contribution of the
litus towards the maintenance of the clergy on the same principle
as that of the *nobilis* and *ingenuus* [1]; the *litus* is fined for neglect
of baptism, for transgression of the law of marriage, and for the
observance of heathen rites, and in a fixed proportion; he pays
half the mulct of the *ingenuus*, a fourth of that of the noble [2].
Another clause forbids the Saxons to hold any public assemblies
unless authorised by a royal *Missus*; and in this may be traced
a possible reference to the free national gatherings mentioned
by Hucbald; for the count, as the king's deputy, is still allowed
to hold pleas and do justice in his own government [3]. The
Saxon Capitulary of A.D. 797, which places the noble Saxon in
the point of pecuniary mulcts on a level with the Frank and
regulates the exercise of supreme jurisdiction, again recognises
the position of the *liti*. When the noble pays four solidi, the
ingenuus pays two, and the litus one [4]. The same conclusions From the Lex Saxo-num.
may be drawn from the Lex Saxonum, which furnishes besides
some interesting coincidences with the earliest English code in
regard to payment for personal injuries. The wergild of the
nobleman is 1440 shillings, that of the litus 120; the composition for the murder of a slave is 36. The lord of the *litus*
answers only for actions done at his command; in other cases
the *litus* must prove his innocence like a freeman: a *litus* of
the king may buy a wife wherever he pleases [5]. In each case

---

[1] 'Capitulatio de partibus Saxoniae,' Pertz, Legg. i. 50; v. 34 sq.; Boret,
i. 69; Baluze, i. 181; artt. 15, 17, 20, 21: 'Inter 120 homines, nobiles et
ingenuos, similiter et litos, servum et ancillam eidem ecclesiae tribuant;'
cap. 15; Pertz, Legg. v. 40, 41. Richthofen, p. 216, assigns A.D. 777 as the
date of this act: Pertz fixes A.D. 785; Waitz, A.D. 782; Boret, A.D. 775–790.

[2] Capp. 19, 20, 21; Pertz, Legg. v. 41, 42.

[3] Cap. 34 is this:—'Interdiximus ut omnes Saxones generaliter conventus publicos nec faciant nisi forte missus noster de verbo nostro eos
congregare fecerit. Sed unusquisque comes in suo ministerio placita et
justitias faciat; et hoc a sacerdotibus consideretur ne aliter faciat.' Pertz,
Legg. v. 46; Boret, i. 70. Cf. Richthofen, Zur Lex Saxonum, p. 171.

[4] Above, p. 45, note 4.

[5] Lex Saxonum, Pertz, Legg. v. 54, 56, 75. The wergild is 120 shillings,

Position of
the litus.

The laws of
the Anglii
and Werini.

the *litus* appears to be distinctly recognised as a member of the nation; he is valued for the wergild, summoned to the placitum, taxed for the church, allowed the right of compurgation and choice in marriage. It is probable from other evidence and on analogy that his services furnished part of the military resources of his country[1]. Instead of being a mere dependent with no political rights, the remnant of a conquered alien people[2], he is free in relation to every one but his lord, and simply unfree as cultivating land of which he is not the owner. The slave, *servus* or knecht, is in a very different plight. In this it may well be we have a proof of the freedom of the ancient life, notwithstanding the preponderance of the nobiles: liberty is more penetrating and more extensive than elsewhere, and the condition of the *liti* has no small importance in its bearing on the history of the colonisation of Britain.

23. Of the history of the Angli unconnected with that of England we have no details; but a code of laws is extant, dating perhaps from the ninth century, and entitled 'Lex Angliorum et Werinorum, hoc est Thuringorum[3].' It seems

cap. 16. See also cc. 17, 18, 36, 50. 'Lito regis liceat uxorem emere ubicunque voluerit, sed non liceat ullam feminam vendere;' cap. 65, p. 83. Richthofen, Zur Lex Saxonum, pp. 331 sq., fixes the date of this code between A.D. 777 and A.D. 797; perhaps in A.D. 785.

[1] See Waitz, D. V. G. iii. 115. He regards the high position of the adalings and the superior condition of the lazzi as Saxon peculiarities. They were an essential part of the Saxon people, iv. 299. A case in which they went to the host is given iv. 508; see also iv. 454. Richthofen, however, ap. Pertz, Legg. v. 55, 56, insists somewhat strongly on the servile condition of the litus, and maintains that his lord had true *dominium* over him.

[2] It is argued that the Saxon lazzi were not pure Germans, from the words of Nithard: 'Sclavi propter affinitatem Saxonibus qui se Stellinga nominaverant;' Hist. iv. 2. Robertson, Scotland under her Early Kings, ii. 235. But both frilingi and lazzi were named Stellinga, and affinity does not imply actual consanguinity. They were more probably the remains of a conquered Thuringian population. See Waitz, D. V. G. i. 157. The name (lazzus = slow or lazy), according to Grimm, R. A. pp. 305, 309, signifies condition not nationality. Kern, however, connects the *litus* with the Lettic or Lithuanian race, and regards it as equivalent to slave: Glossen, &c. p. 8.

[3] Edited by Merkel in 1851; Canciani, vol. iii.; Lindenbrog, pp. 482–486, and finally by the Richthofens in 1875; Pertz, Legg. v. pp. 103 sq.; see also Waitz, D. V. G. iii. 143; Richthofen, Zur Lex Saxonum, pp. 407–418. The theory that the laws belonged to two small communities, Englehem and Werinefeld, in Southern Thuringia (Richthofen, p. 411), is

to have belonged to two small communities in Thuringia, derived from the more ancient nationalities whose name they bore, and therefore removed by a considerable distance in both space and time from their English kinsmen. This document preserves several details which have been regarded as subordinate links in the chain between England and the Germania. Such are the proportions of the wergild and the money-fines; and the classification of the free people as adalings and liberi. Of the *ingenuus* and *litus* as opposed to one another there is no trace: the wergild of the adaling is thrice that of the free man; the corresponding payment for the slave is one-twentieth of that of the adaling; the slave is atoned for with thirty solidi, the freedman with eighty, the freeman with two hundred, and the adaling with six hundred [1]. The *litus* apparently does not exist. But although these points have a certain interest in themselves, they form part of a subject-matter which is common to all the Germanic races, and rest on an authority the exact value of which is too uncertain to make it worth while to examine them in detail. If we possessed a complete Mercian or Northumbrian code, and were quite certain of the connexion of the Anglii of these laws with the Angli of the migration, the case might be different.

The laws of the Frisians, a nation which both ancient and modern writers have regarded as closely associated with the immigrants from Germany, might be expected to furnish analogies that would illustrate alike the jurisprudence of the Angles, the Saxons and the Jutes. Whatever be their age or authority, they agree with the Saxon laws in giving prominence to the litus. His wergild is here half that of the freeman, a quarter of that of the nobleman, double the man-worth of the slave [2]. He has his definite place in every article of the tariff

The laws of the Frisians

accepted by Brunner, Schwurgericht, p. 19. See also Grimm, Gesch. der Deutschen Spr. pp. 604–606. The laws are referred by Richthofen to the end of the ninth century, at the earliest. It is noteworthy that they are cited in the Forest Constitutions of the Pseudo-Canute; Thorpe, Ancient Laws, p. 184.

[1] Capp. i, ii, iv–viii, xxxi; cf. Thorpe's Lappenberg, i. 93, 94.

[2] Lex Frisionum (A.D. 734–802), tit. 15, ed. Lindenbrog, p. 497; ed. Richthofen, Pertz, Legg. iv. p. 669.

of compositions and compurgations. The Frisian *litus* may redeem himself from his modified servitude with his own money; the freeman may place himself in the position of a *litus* by submitting to a nobleman, a freeman, or even a *litus*[1]. The freewoman who has married a *litus* unwittingly may renounce him when she has discovered the disparagement[2]. It is needless to multiply instances of minor coincidences.

Caution in the use of analogies.

Still less is it necessary to appeal to the evidence of later Danish institutions for the illustration of the polity of the Jutes[3]. It is true that the common law of a nation is even more certainly than its language a determining evidence of its extraction. But so great is the mass of material, and so much of it is common to this whole family of nations, that it is at once unnecessary to work it into detail, and unwise to dwell upon such detail as proof of more distinct closer affinities. The common law of the race is abundant and comparatively clear; but minute inferences from minute coincidences are sometimes deceptive: it would be unsafe to infer from such resemblances anything more than original consanguinity[4].

Importance of these early notices.

24. These scanty particulars have their value, first, as furnishing points and analogies illustrative of the tribal character of the Saxons and their neighbours, which throw light on some important features of their migration and early colonisation of Britain; and in the second place, as marking the peculiarities of their institutions which caught the eye of the historian and legislator by their contrast with those of the other nations of Germany. Only those details are noticed which serve to divide them from the nations whose system has now a less pure and primitive character. Hence we are warranted in concluding that in other points their social and political condition was not far removed from that of their neighbours, and are prepared to

---

[1] Lex Frisionum, tit. 11; Lind. p. 495; Pertz, iv. 666.
[2] Ibid. tit. 6; Lind. p. 494; Pertz, iv. 663.
[3] Lappenberg, i. 96, regards as possibly Jutish the Kentish division into *lathes*, and the custom of fixing the age of majority at fifteen.
[4] These remarks of course do not refer to the importance of Scandinavian analogies with Anglo-Saxon history, which is very great, but simply to the relics of Jute tradition as brought to prove special connexion.

look amongst the German tribes of the fifth and sixth centuries
generally for traces which may illustrate the polity of the particular race.

Such traces will be found chiefly in the department of land
tenure and local government, on the earlier phases of which
much has been said already. The laborious investigations of
recent scholars have successfully reconstituted the scheme of
land tenure as it existed among the Germanic races, by careful
generalisations from charters, records of usages, and the analogies of Scandinavian law and practice, which at a later date
reproduces, with very little that is adventitious, the early conditions of self-organising society. This scheme has been already
mentioned more than once under the name of the mark system[1].
Its essential character depends on the tenure and cultivation of
the land by the members of the community in partnership. The
general name of the *mark* is given to the territory which is
held by the community, the absolute ownership of which resides
in the community itself, or in the tribe or nation of which the
community forms a part. The mark has been formed by a
primitive settlement of a family or kindred in one of the great
plains or forests of the ancient world[2]; and it is accordingly,
like any other clearing, surrounded by a thick border of wood
or waste, which supplies the place or increases the strength of
a more effective natural boundary. In the centre of the clearing the primitive village is placed: each of the mark-men has
there his homestead, his house, court-yard, and farm-buildings[3].
This possession, the exponent as we may call it of his character
as a fully qualified freeman, entitles him to a share in the land
of the community[4]. He has a right to the enjoyment of the
woods, the pastures, the meadow, and the arable land of the
mark; but the right is of the nature of usufruct or possession

Common features of German life in the fifth and sixth centuries.

The Mark System.

---

[1] The great authority on this is G. L. von Maurer, who has collected
and arranged an enormous quantity of material on the subject in his
Einleitung, and in his works on the Markenverfassung, Dorfverfassung,
Hofverfassung, and Städteverfassung.

[2] The idea of a forest clearing is not necessary to the mark; K. Maurer,
Krit. Ueberschau, i. 65–72.

[3] G. L. von Maurer, Einleitg. p. 21.

[4] Dorfverfassg. i. 61–65; Markenverfassg. pp. 59–62.

only[1], his only title to absolute ownership being merged in the general title of the tribe which he of course shares. The woods and pastures being undivided, each mark-man has the right of using them, and can turn into them a number of swine and cattle: under primitive conditions this share is one of absolute equality[2]; when that has ceased to be the rule, it is regulated by strict proportion. The use of the meadow-land is also definitely apportioned. It lies open from hay harvest to the following spring, and during this time is treated as a portion of the common pasture, out of the area of which it is in fact annually selected. When the grass begins to grow the cattle are driven out, and the meadow is fenced round and divided into as many equal shares as there are mark-families in the village: each man has his own haytime and houses his own crop: that done, the fences are thrown down, and the meadow becomes again common pasture: another field in another part of the mark being chosen for the next year. For the arable land the same regulative measures are taken, although the task is somewhat more complex: for the supply of arable cannot be supposed to have been inexhaustible, nor would the mark-men be likely to spend their strength in bringing into tillage a larger area than they could permanently keep in cultivation. Hence the arable surface must be regarded as constant, subject to the alternation of crops. In the infancy of agriculture the alternation would be simply that of corn and fallow, and for this two divisions or common fields would suffice. But as tillage developed, as the land was fitter for winter or spring sowing, or as the use of other seed besides wheat was introduced, the community would have three, four, five, or even six such areas on which the proper rotation of crops and fallow might be observed[3]. In each of these areas the mark-man had his equal or proportionate share; and this share of the arable completed his occupation or possession.

This system of husbandry prevailed at different times over

Apportionment of land under the Mark System.

---

[1] Einleitg. pp. 6, 93, 97.

[2] Markenverfassg. pp. 142 sq.

[3] G. L. von Maurer, Einleitg. pp. 73–75, 77 sq.

the whole of Germany, and is in complete harmony with the idea of a nationality constituted on a basis of personal rather than territorial relations. As the king is the king of the nation, not of the land, the land is rather the sign or voucher for the freedom of its possessor than the basis of his rights. He possesses his land as being a full-free member of the community; henceforth the possession of it is the attestation, type, and embodiment of his freedom and political rights.

For every such mark becomes a political unit: every free mark-man has his place in the assembly of the mark, which regulates all the internal business of the partnership and of the relations that arise from it. The choice of the meadow, the rotation of the crops, the allotment of the shares from year to year, are determined in this council[1]; and without its consent no man may settle in the territory[2], build himself a house, or purchase the share of another. It is unnecessary to suppose that there was a period when the village marks administered justice amongst themselves; for within historical times they appear only as members of larger communities : but even these communities may have been originally constituted on the same principle, and have possessed common woods and pasture grounds in which the village marks had their definite shares. But the initiatory stage of legal proceedings may well have been gone through, complaints heard and presentments drawn up, in the village council. On such a hypothesis also it may have elected its own annual president[3], although again within historic times such magistrate seems to have been imposed by the king or governing council of the nation.

If a member of the mark, or a new settler with permission of the mark-men, chose to build his house apart from the village, in a remote portion of the common land or in a new clearing, he

---

[1] G. L. von Maurer, Einleitg. pp. 144–150.

[2] Ibid. pp. 141 sq. ; Lex Salica, tit. 45 ; ed. Merkel, p. 25 : ' Si quis super alterum in villa migrare voluerit, et unus vel aliqui de ipsis qui in villa subsistunt eum suscipere voluerit, si vel unus extiterit qui contradicat, migrandi ibidem licentiam non habebit. . . . Si vero quis migraverit et ei infra duodecim menses nullus testatus fuerit, securus sicut et alii vicini manent, ille maneat.'

[3] Ibid. p. 140.

might do so; and in such case he would have a permanent allotment of arable and meadow lying close to his farm, and not subject to the annual reapportionment. His partnership in the use of the common land would thus be limited to the use of wood and pasture, in which his rights would be determined on the common principle of proportion, by which also the extent of the original area which he was allowed to appropriate was limited [1].

Changes in the Mark System.

As the population increased and agriculture itself improved, the mark system must have been superseded everywhere. The foundation of new villages on the common lands, standing in a filial relation to the original settlement, and looking to it as the source of their political rights, must have soon exhausted the available territory. The partnership in tenure of the arable would necessarily become obsolete when the love of agriculture and the practice of careful husbandry demanded for the cultivator a tenant-right in his allotment: it could continue only so long as all men farmed equally well: as soon as the husbandman succeeded in keeping his annual plot better than his neighbour, he might fairly insist that a longer possession was therefore due to him, and that he might commute the annual for a perpetual allotment. So the arable fell into the condition of separate ownership together with the homestead; the rights to wood and pasture remaining in common, though liable also, when the process of inclosure has begun, to similar appro-

Inequality of estates of land.

priation. And the right of separate ownership being established, inequality of estate, which must have prevailed to some extent from the first, would become the rule instead of the exception. But, whilst the political importance of the system would thus pass away, the plan of common husbandry and common rights of wood and pasture, the local gatherings of the freemen and their by-laws or internal regulations, would remain and become available for administrative purposes guided on other principles. The old feeling of freedom and of the inseparable connexion between land ownership and the possession of public rights would continue; possibly also the habit of looking up to the

[1] G. L. von Maurer, Einleitg. p. 9.

owners of the primitive homesteads as the natural leaders, the Permanent results of the Mark usages. representatives of the half-mythical forefathers of the village.

The system, necessarily shortlived in its integrity, thus leaves deep and abiding impressions wherever it has once prevailed; and those, if we are to trust to the nomenclature which belongs to it, in regions of political life where we should hardly look for them. The homestead of the original settler, his house, farm-buildings and enclosure, 'the toft and croft,' with the share of arable and appurtenant common rights, bore among the northern nations the name of Odal, or Edhel; the primitive mother village was an Athelby or Athelham; the owner was an Athelbonde[1]: the same word Adel or Athel, signified also nobility of descent, and an adaling was a nobleman. Primitive nobility and pri- The Alod and the Adaling. mitive landownership thus bore the same name[2]. It may be questioned whether any etymological connexion exists between the words *odal* and *alod*, but their signification as applied to land is the same: the alod is the hereditary estate derived from primitive occupation; for which the owner owes no service except the personal obligation to appear in the host and in the court of law or council. The freeman who does not bear the The free-man. name of adaling, is the descendant of the later settler who has been admitted to full rights in the community; or he may be descended from the original settlers but has not inherited the homestead. Beneath these comes the free class of labourers The culti-vator of other men's land. who cultivate the land which others own. The three classes are kept distinct by the difference of the wergild: the killing of the adaling is atoned for by a fine twice or three times as large as that which can be demanded for the freeman; and his oath in compurgation is of twice or thrice the weight. Sometimes The distinct-tion of the wergild. this difference of valuation may be referred to the difference of the size of the estate which each holds; and the value of the oath bears an exact proportion to the acreage of the alod. But this rule belongs probably to later times. It is enough for the present to observe that the mark system preserves in itself the

---

[1] G. L. von Maurer, Einleitg. pp. 14–17.
[2] See Grimm, R. A. p. 265; Waitz, D. V. G. i. 164–166; K. Maurer, Krit. Ueberschau, i. 97; Vigfússon, Icelandic Dict. s. v. Aðal, Oðal.

two radical principles of German antiquity, the kindred and the community of land ; and their primitive appurtenances, the wergild and compurgation, in which the kindred share the rights and responsibilities of the individual freeman ; the right and obligation are based on the tie of kindred, regulated by the land tenure, and subject to the general administration of the peace.

The higher organisation as exemplified in the Salian law.

25. Ascending from the simplest form of local organisation to the juridical and political administration of the tribe, we have in the ' Pactus Legis Salicae,' or summary of the customs of Frank law in the fifth century, a store of facts which may illustrate a general theory although they cannot form the basis of one [1]. In some points the Salian law is contrasted with the customs of the interior nations of Germany, the Saxons for instance : such are those especially that have reference to royalty, which was unknown to the one nation long after it had become a regular institution of the other : where therefore the authority of the king is mentioned in it, we must, in applying the analogy to the Saxons, substitute for it the rule of the elective *princeps,* or of the assembly, or the local community, as the case may require.

Traces of the Mark.

The mark system has left its traces in the Salian law. The system of common cultivation may have passed away, but no settler is allowed to take up his dwelling in the vill without the express permission of the community, or authority from the king in whom the central rights of the community are vested [2]. The social organisation of the vill may be identical perhaps with that of the mark ; it is capable of holding assemblies, discussing grievances, and making by-laws, but it is not a court of justice ; its president is the officer who collects the royal dues, and is nominated by the king [3].

The ordinary court of justice is the mallus or court of the

---

[1] Lex Salica, ed. Merkel, 1851 ; Lindenbrog, Leges Barbarorum, pp. 309 sq.; Canciani, ii. 17 sq.; Baluze, Capitularia RR. Ff. i. 201 sq.; Waitz, Das Alte Recht, Kiel, 1846.

[2] Tit. xiv, xlv ; see above, p. 55, n. 2 ; Waitz, Das Alte Recht, pp. 124, 210, 228, 253 ; G. L. von Maurer, Einleitg. p. 141 sq.

[3] Waitz, D. V. G. ii. 314, 353, 354.

hundred, of which the centenarius or thunginus [1] is the pre- The court of justice, the mallus, or hundred-court.
sident, summoner and leader, elected by the national council.
With him sits the sacebaro, to represent and secure the king's
rights [2], especially the royal share of the compositions for the
breach of the peace. The court consists of all the fully qualified
landowners, who furnish the centenarius with a body of judicial
advisers qualified to draw up the formal decisions for the acceptance of the court. These are seven in number, selected
from time to time, and called, during their period of service,
the sitting rachimburgs [3], in opposition to the rest of the body
of 'boni homines,' who are the standing members. From the
decisions of the mallus there is no appeal, except to the king
himself; no court intervening between that of the hundred and
the supreme council of the nation [4]. The Graf, or administrative The Graf.
ruler of the province which is composed of the aggregations of
the hundreds, is a servant of the king, fiscal and judicial, and as
such executes the sentences of the mallus, but has no special
court of his own [5].

The Salian law recognises fully the importance of the kindred No tribunal of the kin.
in relation to the descent of property, the wergild and compurgation; but affords no trace of any political or juridical
organisation founded upon it, and contains no reference to any
primitive nobility [6], the only difference in the wergild of the No blood nobility.
freemen being the threefold rate arising from employment in
the host or in the king's service [7]. The position of the *letus* is
nearer to that of the slave here than in the Saxon institutions,

---

[1] Savigny, R. R. i. 273; Waitz, Das Alte Recht, p. 294; D. V. G. i.
265; Sohm, Fr. R. G. V. p. 73.

[2] Sohm, Fr. R. G. V. pp. 84–94.

[3] Waitz, D. V. G. i. 359, 494. According to Savigny the name belongs to
all fully qualified freemen among the Franks, and answers to Arimannus
among the Lombards; Röm. Recht. im Mittelalter, i. 191, 214 sq. Sohm
however restricts it to the seven acting officers (Fr. R. G. V. p. 386).
But see Waitz, D. V. G. ii. 36, 465, 485. On the derivation of the word
see Savigny, i. 222 (Rek = rich, great; and burg = borh, surety); Grimm,
R. A. pp. 293, 774 (ragin = consilium); Waitz, Das Alte Recht, p. 291.

[4] Waitz, D. V. G. ii. 493–495.

[5] Nor even a share in the jurisdiction of the mallus; Savigny, R. R. i.
256, 265; Sohm, Fr. R. G. Verf. i. 83, 93.

[6] Cf. Savigny, R. R. i. 223; Waitz, Das Alte Recht, p 103; D. V. G.
ii. 289–291.

[7] Cap. 41, ed. Merkel, p. 22; Waitz, Das Alte Recht, p. 104.

which however are in close conformity with the Frank law in the
prohibition of mixed marriages [1]. Separate ownership of land,
in the greatest completeness and in the most unequal proportions, has become the rule [2]: the more ancient system is to be
detected only by the vestiges of its nomenclature; the 'terra
salica' answering to the Alod or Adalsgut [3].

Inequality of estates.

The king is the ruler of the nation; he appoints the grafs
and the magistrates of the vills; he has a *comitatus* of personal
followers who supply the place of hereditary nobility and permanent guard. He is the guardian of the peace of the nation,
and supreme judge of appeal. The supreme political council is
the nation in arms: but of any central gathering of the people
for justice there is no mention; we can only infer that, if there
were any, it must have necessarily coincided with the assembly
of the host. The succession to the royalty is hereditary in one
family, but the person who succeeds is chosen by the nation [4].

The king.

The national council.

So simple was the governmental system of the Franks in the
fifth century: that of the Saxons was simpler still, for they were
without the complication of royalty. The name of the hundred,
the institution round which the Frank system circles, and the
origin of which has, as we shall see, its own complexities, does
not occur amongst the continental Saxons [5]: and although it
does not follow that it was unknown to them, its non-appearance
is a presumptive evidence of superior simplicity of organisation.
We shall trace, as we proceed in the history of the English,
vestiges of the systems, or of parts of the systems, thus briefly
characterised: perhaps we have shown already by implication
how very much any complete scheme or general picture must
be based on inferences and analogies, such as by their very

Difference of Salian and Saxon customs.

Danger of forming too complete theories.

---

[1] Waitz, Das Alte Recht, p. 106.

[2] Ibid., p. 117; D. V. G. ii. 217. This seems to be the consequence of the conquest of a Roman province.

[3] Waitz, D. V. G. ii. 220: the land attached to the 'sala' or house. The term does not occur in the oldest Text. Cf. Grimm, R. A. p. 493.

[4] Waitz, Das Alte Recht, pp. 203-214; D. V. G. ii. 148-164, 353, &c.

[5] Waitz, D. V. G. i. 213-215. The traces of the system alleged by Waitz are questioned by Richthofen. K. Maurer, Krit. Ueberschau, i. 76. It is also unknown among the Frisians. Waitz mentions however a 'Camminge hunderi' in Westphalia.

nature raise a suspicion of pretentious speculation and warrant us in contenting ourselves with a modest and tentative dogmatism.

26. And this consideration restrains us from even attempting to apply to the Saxons the minute and regular machinery of local divisions and jurisdictions which we find in the Scandinavian laws, and of which the colonisation of Iceland is the best and the favourite specimen. The existence of numerical divisions of the utmost minuteness is not inconsistent with great antiquity; but it is a sign not so much of antiquity as of the absence of more natural determinants. The nomad race has scarcely any possible principle of arrangement other than number: it is indispensable also to the machinery of the host; and in consequence the occupation of a conquered country, or the colonisation of one newly discovered, is regulated in this way. The usage is then no sign of either age or race. Yet it is useful to observe the analogy, especially when, as in Iceland, a perfect instance can be adduced. *Analogies in Scandinavian history.*

Iceland is divided into four fiordungs or quarters, as Yorkshire may have been divided by the Danes into three ridings. Each fiordung was divided into three *things*, and each thing into three godords or lordships: the northernmost fiordung however contained four things, so that there were thirty-nine godords in all. The godord was originally a personal not a territorial division[1]. In the court of the *thing* were thirty-six judges, twelve from each godord, named by the lord, who did not himself sit there. The general assembly of the island was called the Althing. The *lögretta*, the judicial and legislative committee of the *althing*, was composed of the thirty-nine gothar, or godordsmen proper, and nine supplementary ones chosen by those of the three southern fiordungs; each of the forty-eight had two nominated assessors, so that the whole number was 144; with these sat the bishop and the law-men; forty-eight being a quorum[2]. Here is a late but distinct product of the *Constitution of Iceland.* *The court of the Thing.* *The lögretta.*

[1] The godord (gothorth) was the lordship which looked to the Hof or temple as the centre of its religious and legal organisation under the Gothi or priest-lord.

[2] See Gragas, i. pp. 1–4; Palgrave, Commonwealth, p. 115; Bluntschli

Germanic centralising system marked by singular regard to numerical symmetry.

Constitution of Dithmarschen.

Another instance may be found, also at a late period, in the immediate neighbourhood of Saxony proper. The little territory of Dithmarschen was colonised by two kindreds from Friesland and two from Saxony: the Frisians formed two marks, the Norderstrand and the Süderstrand; the Saxons two others, Norderhamm and Süderhamm; and the four were in A.D. 804 made into a Gau, in which the archbishop of Bremen had the royal rights of Heerbann and Blutbann: a fifth mark or döfft was afterwards added. The rights of the archbishop being guarded by an advocatus or vogt, sometimes by one to each mark, the state was governed by its own landrath: each mark had twelve elected consules: the forty-eight constituted the landrath. When in the sixteenth century the vogts disappeared, the territory became, what it had been originally, a systematic organism for self-government[1]. This furnishes no bad commentary on the testimony of Hucbald[2].

in Krit. Ueberschau, i. 120–127; Vigfússon, Icelandic Dictionary, s. v. Althing, Gothi, Lögretta; K. Maurer's Beiträge zur Rechtsgeschichte des Germanischen Nordens, p. 176, and 'Island' (Munich, 1874), pp. 50–64.

[1] G. L. von Maurer, Einleitg. pp. 289–292.

[2] Above, p. 47.

CHAPTER IV.

THE MIGRATION.

27. THE fifth century saw the foundation of the Frank dominion in Gaul, and the first establishment of the German races in Britain. The former was effected in a single long reign, by the energy of one great ruling tribe, which had already modified its traditional usages, and now, by the adoption of the language and religion of the conquered, prepared the way for a permanent amalgamation with them. In this process, whilst the dominant tribe was to impose a new mould upon the material which Roman dominion had reduced to a plastic mass, it was in its turn to take forms which but for the pertinacious idiosyncrasy of the Gallic genius, and the Roman training to which it had been subjected, it would never have taken. Frank feudalism would scarcely have grown up as it did but for the pre-existence of the type of Gallic society which Caesar had remarked, and the care taken by the Roman governors to adapt the Gallic character to their own ends. It was a rapid if not an easy process : the Salian Frank entered into the place of the Roman and the Goth ; the Visigoth retired southwards ; the Ripuarian, the Alemannian, and the Burgundian accepted either feudal dependence or political extinction.

It was very different with Britain. The Saxons, Angles, and Jutes, although speaking the same language, worshipping the

Different circumstances of Frank and Saxon conquest.

same gods and using the same laws, had no political unity like
the Franks of Clovis; they were not moved by one impulse or
invited by one opportunity. The conquest of Britain was the
result of a series of separate expeditions, long continued and
perhaps, in point of time, continuous, but unconnected, and independent of one another. It was conducted by single chieftains, who had nothing whatever in common with the nations
they attacked, and who were about neither to amalgamate with
them nor to tolerate their continued existence. They were
men, too, on whom the charm of the Roman name had no
power, and whose institutions were, more than those of the
rest of the barbarians, free from Roman influences; for three
centuries after the conquest the Saxons in Germany were still
a pure nationality, unconquered by the Franks, untainted by
Roman manners, and still heathen.

These separate expeditions had doubtless changed their character in course of time. Beginning as mere piratical visitations
of the coast—such as were those of the Danes and Norsemen at
a later period—they had before the end of the third century
called forth the defensive powers of Rome, and tasked the
energies of the count of the Saxon shore[1]. It is not until the
middle of the fifth century that they assume the dimensions of
conquest, colonisation, migration; and when they have attained
that character, the progress and success of the several attempts
are not uniform; each little state reaches greatness by its own
route, and the history of its growth makes a mark upon its
constitution.

28. If the Saxons and Angles are contrasted with the Franks,
still more are the Britons with the Gauls. Rome had laid a
very strong hand on Gaul, and Gaul had repaid in a remarkable
degree the cultivation of her masters. At the time of the
downfall of the empire Gaul was far more Roman than Italy

Conquest of Britain.

Diverse character of the ex-peditions.

Difference between Gaul and Britain.

---

[1] The shore infested by the Saxon pirates, not the shore colonised by
Saxons, as sometimes understood. See Freeman, Norm. Conq. i. 11, and
the references given there; cf. Selden, Mare Clausum, lib. ii. c. 7. The
other view was held by Lappenberg (ed. Thorpe), i. 46, 47. Kemble
seems also to favour it, Saxons, i. 10, 11; Palgrave, Commonwealth,
p. 384.

itself ; she possessed more flourishing cities, a more active and
enlightened church, and a language and literature completely
Latin, although of course far beneath the standard of the classical ages.   Britain had been occupied by the Romans, but had Roman
not become Roman ; their formative and cultivating power had in Britain.
affected the land rather than the owners of it.   Here, too, had
been splendid cities, Christian churches, noble public works and
private mansions ; but whatever amount of real union may
have existed between the two populations ended when the
legions were withdrawn.   The Britons forgot the Latin tongue ; Its extinc-
their clergy lost all sympathy with the growth of religious tion.
thought : the arts of war had been disused, and the arts of
peace never thoroughly learned.   The old tribal divisions, which
had never been really extinguished by Roman rule, rose from
their hiding-places ; and Britain was as fertile in tyrants after
the Roman conquest as it was before it.   But Roman rule had Weakness
disarmed and enervated the people : constant foreign invasion Britons.
found them constantly unprepared, and without hope or energy
for resistance.   They could not utilise the public works or defend the cities of their masters.   So Britain was easy to be conquered in proportion as it was Romanised.   A succession of
calamities had diminished the population, already greatly reduced by the withdrawal of the dependents of the Romans into
Gaul ; and, when once the invitation or the concessions of the
British chiefs had given the invaders a standing-ground in the
island, the occupation of the eastern half at least was accomplished in a short time[1].   The middle of the fifth century is the Date of the
approved date for this settlement.   Kent seems to have been conquest.
won by a single victory : the kingdom of Sussex was the result
of the capture of Anderida ; the history of Wessex is the long
story of encroachments on the native people, who retired very
gradually, but became stronger in resistance as they approached
the mountains and the western sea, until a balance of forces
compelled an armed peace[2].   Mercia, the country of the

---

[1] Bede, H. E. i. 13-15 ; Gildas, xiv, xxii ; Hallam, Middle Ages,
chap. viii. note iv ; Kemble, Saxons, ii. 287 sq.
[2] See on the growth of Wessex, Freeman, Norm. Conq. i. 24, 25.

Diversity of growth of the kingdoms.

Southern and Middle Angles, was an aggregation of many smaller settlements, each apparently the result of detached Anglian expeditions. Of the formation of the Northumbrian and East Anglian kingdoms we have scarcely any of those legendary data, which, whether historical or not, serve to give an individuality to the others; but such traditions as have been preserved lead to the belief that in both cases the kingdom was created by the union of smaller separate conquests[1].

Want of union among the Britons.

The dislocated state of Britain seems, next to its desertion by the Romans, to have made way for the conquerors. The same weak obstinacy which had failed to combine against invasion, refused to accept the new dominion; and the Saxons, merciless by habit, were provoked by the sullen and treacherous attitude of their victims. The Britons fled from their homes: whom the sword spared famine and pestilence devoured: the few that remained either refused or failed altogether to civilise the conquerors[2].

Their refusal to combine with the conquerors.

For a century and a half after their arrival the Saxons remained heathen; for a century after their conversion they were repelled from communion with the Celts: the Britons retarded rather than promoted the religious change which the Spaniards forced on their Arian conquerors, and which Clovis voluntarily adopted to unite him with his Gallic subjects. This period, instead of being one of amalgamation, was one of divarication. There was room enough for both Britons and Saxons: the Roman cities might have been homes for the one, and the woods and broad pastures have furnished the others with their favourite prospects.

General desolation.

But the cities went to ruin; Christianity became extinct, and all culture with it. There were still Roman roads leading to the walls and towers of empty cities: the Roman divisions of the land were conspicuous: the intrenched and fortified camps, the great villas of the princely families, churches and burial-places; but they were become before the days of Bede mere haunted ruins, something like the mysterious

[1] See especially Henry of Huntingdon, M. H. B. p. 712, A. E.; Thorpe's Lappenberg, i. 116, 117; Freeman, Norm. Conq. i. 25, 26.
[2] Bede, H. E. i. 13–15; Gildas, xiv, xxii.

fabrics which in Central America tell of the rule of a mighty race whose name is forgotten [1].

It is not to be supposed that this desolation was uniform : in some of the cities there were probably elements of continuous life : London, the mart of the merchants, York, the capital of the North, and some others, have a continuous political exist- ence, although they wisely do not venture, like some of the towns of Southern France, to claim an unbroken succession from the Roman municipality. The new race found the convenience of ready-built houses and accumulated stores of material ; and wherever the cities were spared, a portion at least of the city population must have continued also. In the country, too, especially towards the West and the debateable border, great numbers of Britons may have survived in servile or half-servile condition : some few of the greater men may have made, and probably did make, terms for themselves, especially in the dis- tricts appropriated by the smaller detachments of adventurers; and the public lands of the new kingdoms must have required native cultivators. But all these probabilities only bring out more strongly the improbability of any general commixture or amalgamation of the races. Centuries after the conquest the Briton by extraction was distinguished by his wergild from the man of the ruling race. It is impossible that such a commix- ture could have taken place without leaving its traces on the language or the religion. The English of Alfred's time is, ex- cept where the common terms of ecclesiastical language come in, purely Germanic : British Christianity stood out against Saxon for a century after the death of Augustine ; and the vestiges of Romano-British law which have filtered through local custom into the common law of England, as distinct from those which were imported in the middle ages through the scientific study of law or the insensible infection of cosmopolitan civilisation, are in- finitesimal.

Local elements of life.

Remains of the Britons.

No general mixture of races,

or of insti- tutions:

29. The theory that some appreciable proportion of the population of Roman Britain was already Germanic, that the

---

[1] Kemble, Saxons, ii. 297.

Earlier
Germanic
settle-
ments.

Belgae[1] or Coritani or Catieuchlani[2] of the island might have
welcomed the Saxons and Angles as distant cousins, has had
learned supporters, but has no basis either in fact or in probability.
The Belgae of Caesar's days were Gauls, and their British kinsmen could scarcely have retained, five centuries later, any recollection of a language which their fathers, if they had ever known
it, had so long forgotten. It is neither impossible nor improbable that on the northern and eastern coasts shipwrecks and
piratic expeditions may have founded colonies of Germans much

Not im-
portant to
history.

earlier than the beginning of history. But to base any historical theory on such contingencies is about as wise as to
accept the notion that the German Saxons were a colony from
English Britain[3], or that the conquerors of Britain did not come
from Germany, but were a hypothetical colony from a hypothetical
settlement on the Littus Saxonicum of Gaul[4].

The parallels
of Welsh and
English laws
not to be
relied on.

30. Nor again can any weight be attached to the results of
the careful investigation of able scholars into Welsh social antiquities, as affecting the present question[5]. If the agreement
between the local machinery of the Welsh laws and the Anglo-
Saxon usages were much closer than it has ever been shown to
be ; if the most ancient remains of Welsh law could be shown
not to be much younger in date than the best established customs of Angle and Saxon jurisprudence ; the fact would still
remain that the historical civilisation is English and not Celtic.
The cantred of Howel dha may answer to the hundred of Edgar,
but the hundred of Edgar is distinctly the hundred of the
Franks, the Alemannians, and the Bavarians. If the price of
life and the value of the compurgatory oath among the Welsh

---

[1] Palgrave, Commonwealth, pp. 26 sq.   [2] Kemble, Saxons, i. 9.

[3] The old and curious inversion of the true story which appears in
Rudolf, Transl. S. Alexandri, Pertz, ii. 674.

[4] The view propounded by Dr. A. F. H. Schaumann, Göttingen, 1845 ;
see K. Maurer, Krit. Ueberschau, i. 51. The theory of Roman military
colonies of German race settled in Britain at a much earlier period is not
improbable, but rests on very scanty evidence : for Saxon settlements of
the kind there can be of course no evidence. But the root of the false
hypothesis lies in each case in the misunderstanding of the name Littus
Saxonicum. See above, p. 64.

[5] Much useless labour is spent by Sir F. Palgrave on this subject in the
' Rise and Progress of the English Commonwealth,' to a certain extent
impairing the value of that great work.

were exactly what they were among the Saxons, it would not be one degree less certain than it is that the wergild of the Saxons is the wergild of the Goth, the Frank, and the Lombard. The Welsh may in late times have adopted the institution from the English, or in all the nations the common features may be the signs of a common stage of civilisation; but the kinship is between the English and the German forms. The Welsh laws may be adduced for illustration and analogy, but not for historical argument. However, we have no remains of such laws that are not much later than the days of Alfred.

31. If it were possible to form a clear idea of the amount of civilisation which the invaders already possessed, or of the organisation which they were to substitute for that which thus vanished before them, we should be better able to determine the effect which was produced on them by the process of conquest. But as it is, only two great generalisations seem to be possible. In the first place, conquest under the circumstances compelled colonisation and migration. The wives and families were necessary to the comfort and continued existence of the settlements. It was not only that the attitude of the Britons forbade intermarriages; the Saxons, as all testimony has shown, declined the connubium of foreign races[1]: they could not give to the strange woman the sacred prerogative of the German woman, let her cast their lots or rear their children. The tie of the *cognatio* and the *gens* was as strong as it had been of old: the new settlements were called by Gentile names, and these names involved the retention of the rights and duties of the *mœgth*, the kindred. The invaders came in families, and kindreds, and in the full organisation of their tribes: the three ranks of men, the noble, the freeman, and the læt[2]. There seems to be no

Effect of the conquest on the new-comers.

Necessity of migration.

---

[1] See above, p. 46.
[2] Whether the Kentish læts were of German origin has been questioned. Lappenberg (ed. Thorpe), ii. 324, thinks that they were 'unfree of kindred race.' K. Maurer, Krit. Ueberschau, i. 421, thinks them a relic of ancient British population who come between the free wealh and the slave. Robertson, Scotland under her Early Kings, ii. 233, regards the *læt* of Kent as answering to the *wealh* of Wessex, and therefore British. The wergild of the Kentish læt was 40, 60, or 80 shillings according to rank, that of the ceorl being 200; Ll. Ethelb. § 26. On the general condition of the class, see G. L. von Maurer, Hofverfg. i. 12–18, Grimm, R. A.

reason for questioning that the eorl, ceorl, and læt of the earliest English laws, those of Ethelbert, answer exactly to the edhiling, the friling, and the lazzus of the old Saxons. Even the slaves were not left behind. The cattle of their native land were, it would appear, imported too: the store they set by their peculiar breeds is proved by the researches into the grave-places of the nations.

The coloni-
sation was
the work of
a regularly
constituted
body, or
nation.
It could scarcely be otherwise, unless we are to suppose an innate propension in the adventurers for reproducing one and the same system without historical connexion under the most different circumstances. The mere settlement of predatory bands without their homes and families must have resulted in their adoption of the institutions of the natives, those natives being their superiors in civilisation. They could not have re-produced pure German life and language from mixed materials, nor could they have retained their tribal organisation so long and so closely as they did, if it had been shattered at starting. It was far otherwise: the tribal identity was a reality bound down to no territorial area. The ownership of land was the out-ward expression rather than the basis of political freedom; and even that ownership was, under the primitive system, variable in its subject-matter, and in itself a usufruct rather than a pos-session. The tribe was as complete when it had removed to Kent as when it stayed in Jutland: the magistrate was the ruler of the tribe, not of the soil: the divisions were those of the folk and the host, not of the land; the laws were the usages of the nation, not of the territory. And, when they had found their new homes, the Angles at least left a desert behind them; for in the days of Bede the *Angulus*, the land between the con-tinental Saxons and Jutes, whence the Angles came, still lay without inhabitant[1], testifying to the truth of the tradition that they had gone forth old and young, noble, gentle and simple,

pp. 305–309; and on their position as a part of the Saxon nationality, on which their importance as illustrating the migration depends, see above, pp. 49–52.

[1] Bede, H. E. i. 15: 'De illa patria quae Angulus dicitur et ab eo tempore usque hodie manere desertus inter provincias Jutarum et Sax-onum perhibetur.'

free and slave, their flocks and herds with them. We may fairly argue that the amount of social and political organisation which the Saxons brought with them to Britain was not less than the sum of common civilisation possessed by them and their German kinsfolk in the eighth century, and that whatever differences existed in the eighth century were due to causes which had worked in one or both of the nations since the fifth. On their arrival in Britain, then, the Saxons had their threefold division of ranks : they had the association of the *vicus* or township, and that of the *pagus*, whether or no it bore the name of hundred ; some remains of the mark system of land-ownership and cultivation ; the principle of election to public functions ; and the tie of the kindred still preserving its legal rights and duties. It is unnecessary to suppose that a migrating family exactly reproduced its old condition : it is more probable that it would seek larger scope for extension and more abundant areas of cultivation : the adventurer of the conquest might seek to found a new family of nobles : every element of society would expect advancement and expansion. But all allowance being made for this, the framework of the older custom must have been the framework of the new. No creative genius can be expected among the rude leaders of the tribes of North Germany. The new life started at the point at which the old had been broken off. Hence we can scarcely suppose that the mark system was developed, lived its life, and faded away on English soil[1] ; or that it is necessary to begin the story of English civilisation by comparing the state of Britain in the fifth century with that of Germany in the first. Even if old ties were, more than we need suppose likely, broken in the process of migration, the names, functions, and rights of the magistrates, the principles of customary law and local organisation, survived and took new root and grew.

32. But in the second place, the process of migration and conquest must have produced such changes as are traceable at the beginning of our national history. It must have produced

Amount of civilisation brought by the colonists.

Expansion of older institutions.

Royalty one of the results of the migration.

---

[1] The importance of this seems to have been overlooked by Kemble in his invaluable work on the Saxons in England.

royalty, and the important political appurtenances of royalty[1].
The Saxons had no kings at home, but they create kingdoms in
Britain.   The testimony of tradition helps to confirm what is
a sufficiently safe inference.   According to the Chronicle the
Brito-Welsh in A.D. 443 invited to Britain the Ethelings of the
Angles: in A.D. 449, under two *heretogas,* Hengist and Horsa,
the strangers came : in A.D. 455 Hengist and Aesc his son came

Institution of royalty :

to the kingdom[2].   In A.D. 495 'came two *ealdormen* to Britain[3],
Cerdic and Cynric ; ' in A.D. 519 they became kings of the West
Saxons.   In Northumbria and East Anglia, when the 'proceres' had in long rivalry occupied provinces and fought battles,
they set up out of the most noble a king over them[4].   In each
case the erection of the throne was probably the result of some
great victory, or of the permanent securing of a definite territory ; but the institution was not a transference of British
royalty : the new kings are kings of the nations which they had

*its heredi-
tary charac-
ter.*

led to conquest, not of those they had conquered[5].   In each
case the son is named with his father as sharing in the first
assumption of the title, a recognition of the hereditary character[6]
which is almost the only mark distinguishing the German kingship from the elective chieftainship.   The royal houses thus
founded assume a divine pedigree; all trace their origin to

[1] See Allen, Inquiry into the Rise and Growth of the Royal Prerogative
(Lond. 1849), pp. 164, 165. Bethmann-Hollweg, Civilprocess, iv. 97,
gives several instances in which the separation of a tribe, by migration,
from the nation to which it belongs, is followed by the institution of
royalty. See also Freeman, Norm. Conq. i. 74, 75.

[2] Chr. S. Mon. Hist. Brit. pp. 298, 299.   [3] Ib. p. 300.

[4] e.g. 'Regnum Nordhanhumbrorum incipit xiii° anno regni Kinrici.
Cum enim proceres Anglorum multis et magnis praeliis patriam illam sibi
subjugassent, Idam quendam juvenem nobilissimum sibi regem constituerunt ; ' H. Hunt. p. 712.

[5] The origin of royalty is regarded by Kemble as ' rooted in the German
mind and institutions,' Saxons, i. 137 ; so also Bethmann-Hollweg, Civilprocess, iv. 84. Allen regards it as repugnant to the genius of the Germans and as a phantom borrowed from imperial Rome (Hist. Prerog.
p. 14). The common theory that it was the work of the comitatus of a
successful adventurer seems to rest on a misapprehension of the nature
of the comitatus.

[6] Bethmann-Hollweg, Civilprocess, iv. 94, 96, holding that nobility gave
a title to the office of princeps, questions whether the hereditary succession
was peculiar to royalty, and finds the differentia of monarchy in the headship of the collective people, as above.

Woden; and when they become extinct the independence of their nation comes to an end.   As the extension of the Frank dominion by the victories of Clovis resulted in an enormous enhancement of the royal authority of the Merovings, so the conquest of Britain by the English may be said to have necessitated the creation of the royal authority in their new home.   It would seem that the change of government followed almost necessarily on the creation of the new nationality; and the example of Frank conquest may have led the Saxons to adopt the monarchic form.   The nation is no longer one of a cluster of kindred nations, or itself a cluster of tribes united only in religion and language; it has to assert an identity that requires a distinct representation, a unity of which it has become more conscious than it was before.   It can no longer safely endure divided command, it must have a king who can deal with kings. Unquestionably individual prowess and ambition determined the change, but these deeper causes must have led the people to acquiesce in it.   For a hereditary king, however limited his authority may be by constitutional usage, is a stronger power than an elective magistrate: his personal interests are the interests of his people, which is in a certain sense his family : he toils for his children, but in toiling for them he works also for the people whom they will have to govern; he has no temptation to make for himself or them a standing-ground apart from his people.   He is trusted also with greater power : he becomes the regular leader of the host, or, if disabled by age, its guide and counsellor : he undertakes the maintenance of the national peace, and executes justice on the breakers of it; his power is co-ordinate with that of the national council, not subordinate to it, or a mere part of it.   Altogether his position is stronger and more dignified than that of the princeps.   He enters at the same time into a share of the common stock of the historic dignities of kings.   More can scarcely be affirmed until we come to ages in which we have clearer data.

Its character as representing national unity.

Advantages of hereditary royalty.

Superiority of the king to the ancient princeps, a reason for adopting royalty.

CHAPTER V.

THE ANGLO-SAXON SYSTEM.

The Anglo-Saxon system.

33. WE are scarcely justified in applying the name of system to any theoretical arrangement, by which the several notices of constitutional matters, scattered through the Anglo-Saxon histories, laws, and charters during a period of six centuries, can be harmonised. To do so would be to disregard both the development which certainly took place in the national character and organisation, and the several disturbing causes which gave to that development some part at least of its character. On the other hand, as we have scarcely any materials for determining the steps of such advance, and as at the close of the period we find only such organic differences between the common polity of the earliest and that of the latest ages as can easily be accounted for, we are at once compelled to fall back upon such a general theory, and are to a certain extent justified in the speculation. The disturbing causes, though startling, are not permanently potent; and they proceed from agencies closely analogous to those already at work in the normal action of society; the Danish conquest, and even the Norman, hastens and precipitates events that are already working to completion. But the developments themselves are rather political and dynastic than

constitutional or administrative [1]; they are the greatest in the upper ranges of the fabric, and leave the lower, in which we trace the greatest tenacity of primitive institutions, and on which the permanent continuity of the modern with the ancient English life depends for evidence, comparatively untouched. It is possible then to gather into two or three general groupings most of these features and their known developments.

34. In attempting to draw such a sketch of the system and to trace its connexion with that of the Germania, we have the great advantage of being able to use a distinct and intelligible terminology. Hitherto we have been indebted for all our information to Latin authors whose nomenclature could not be safely regarded as more than analogous to that of the ancient Germans, and we consequently run a certain risk in arguing from their expressions as if they had an ascertained and invariable definite force. It would be at first sight somewhat rash to argue from the use of such words as *princeps, dux, pagus, vicus, concilium, civitas, nobilis,* and *servus,* either that they always involve the same idea, or that that use is altogether unaffected by their common application to Roman ideas. Is the word *princeps* a definite translation of some German word? is it a mere general expression, like our 'prince' or 'chieftain,' that may cover a number of merely analogous relations, or has it an implicit relation to some Roman function, having been applied to the German in consequence of some fancied resemblance? It is most fortunate for us, as we have to rely on Caesar and Tacitus, that the former was obliged by circumstances to form a clear notion of the differences of the barbarian systems with which he was brought in contact; whilst Tacitus wrote from singularly good information, and is unrivalled as a writer for clearness of perception and distinctness of expression. The confidence which we derive from their consistent and precise use of words is borne out fully when we come to the investigation of later authorities. In the Ecclesiastical History of Bede we find the very same words used and in the same senses. Bede, writing in a foreign language, would be even more likely than Caesar and

(margin note: Correspondence of the Latin and English terminology.)

[1] See further on, Chapter VII.

Tacitus to use the same words to express the same things ; and, having a great acquaintance with classical Latin, would probably use also the most approved words. The *princeps, dux, nobilis, vicus* of Bede are the *princeps, dux, nobilis, vicus* of Tacitus. A hundred and fifty years after the death of Bede his History was translated into English, most probably under the eye of Alfred; and in this translation again the same English words are used regularly and almost uniformly as giving the sense of the same Latin. As the functions of the offices thus denoted are the same in the History of Bede and in the laws of Alfred, we have a link between the primitive and the medieval systems which no criticism is strong enough or sharp enough to sever.

Link between Tacitus and Alfred.

35. The exact process by which the transference of the German institutions to Britain was effected is not recorded : nor is it necessary to suppose that it was uniform in the several states and settlements. In some cases it may have been accomplished by unconnected bands of squatters, who took possession of an uninhabited tract, and, reproducing there the local system of their native land, continued practically independent until the whole surrounding districts were organised by a central state-power. In other cases, the successful leader of a large colony or a victorious host, having conquered and exterminated the natives, must have proceeded to divide their land according to a fixed scheme. The principle of this allotment he would find in the organisation of his host. That host was the people in arms, divided into hundreds of warriors, sustained and united by the principle of kindred. When the war was over the host became again the people: the hundreds of warriors[1] would require a territory in the new land to compensate them for what they had left in the old, and this when allotted to them they would sub-divide according to the divisions of the kindreds: and in such case the Anglo-Saxon village might reproduce the name, the local arrangements, the very personal relations of the German home. The isolated settlements would be then incorporated

Uncertainty of the exact process of colonisation.

The regular arrangements result from completed conquest.

[1] The non-existence of the territorial hundred among the continental Saxons, even if proved, does not affect the organisation of the host in hundreds. See above, p. 60.

and receive a share of political rights and duties. A regular Convenience of a general allotment. and authoritative division would prevent tribal quarrels for the possession of the best districts, and would maintain the national strength, the military organisation which, on the hypothesis of a haphazard and independent appropriation, must have broken up and perished long before the necessity of defence was past. This principle of allotment would do no violence to the pride or ambition of a German host[1]; in the time of Caesar, it was thus that the chieftains of the tribes provided for the annual resettlements of the pagi; and long after the Saxon migration, it was the rule with the Norsemen[2]. As in the fifth century the Vandals divided pro-consular Africa[3], as in the ninth Halfdane divided Northumbria and his fellow kings their conquests in Mercia and East Anglia[4], so in the fifth and sixth centuries the kingdoms of Wessex and Kent must have been portioned out. It does not follow that the division was in exact proportion and Allotment not necessarily uniform. symmetry; that every kindred contained the same number of households, or that every *pagus* or 'hundred' contained the same number of townships: or that the early independent settlements were reduced to an equality of area with the newer and more regularly constituted ones. The number of acres assigned to each family may well have been determined by exact rules, but the district assigned to the township as a whole may have been marked out by natural boundaries. The *centenae* or hundreds of the host, which in Tacitus's time had become an indefinite number, may have been still compelled to maintain a corporate completeness, and yet have occupied in peace areas of very

[1] It is unnecessary to refer to the system of tripartite division adopted by the Burgundians and other conquerors of the Roman empire on the continent, for there are no traces of such a plan in England. See on them Savigny, Röm. Recht im Mittelalter, i. 296, 300, 310, 331; Hallam, Middle Ages, i. 146; Allen, Prerogative, pp. 193–195.

[2] Godred Crovan offered to divide the Isle of Man by lot among his followers; Chron. Manniae (ed. Munch), p. 4; Kemble, Saxons, i. 90.

[3] Gibbon, viii. 227, 228; G. L. von Maurer, Einleitg. p. 72. 'Exercitui Zeugitanam vel proconsularem funiculo hereditatis divisit;' Victor Vitensis, Hist. pers. Vand. i. 4. So the tradition of Normandy, 'illam terram suis fidelibus funiculo divisit;' Dudo, p. 85; Thorpe's Lappenberg, iii. 18. The term *funiculus hereditatis* is borrowed from the Vulgate, Deut. xxx. 9; Ps. civ. 11.

[4] Chr. Sax. A.D. 876, 877, 880.

different character and dimensions. A perfect and symmetrical division of the whole land would be possible only on the theory that the colonising people were numerous enough to occupy it.

Importance of the public lands in this point.

That they were not is proved by the existence of the public lands, on the exact character of which some important questions of Anglo-Saxon history turn. Ultimately no doubt a territorial arrangement of hundreds and townships did cover the land exhaustively; but that result was attained only when the personal basis of the hundred was entirely lost sight of, and the term had a geographical, or rather an administrative, application only. Then the judicial organisation of one hundred extended to the borders of the next, the public lands were included within the same administrative district, and the name of hundred ceased to have any numerical signification. So the inequality of the existing divisions may partly be accounted for[1].

Existence of unequal estates.

The existence of the classes of nobles, freemen, and læts, among the conquerors, would seem further to imply the existence of larger and smaller private estates[2]. The extent of the land unappropriated to the simple freemen must have left it open for the new king to reward his chief followers with extensive grants, even if they did not from the first claim a larger share in the

The lætic and native cultivators.

allotment. On these domains and on the public land, the læts would find their home and occupation: the remnants of the native race would find more lenient treatment than they could expect at the hands of the common freemen, and might return

New estates cut out of the public land.

as cultivators to the land which had been their own. But although such estates are found existing as soon as documentary history begins, their origin cannot be safely referred to this cause only; for even if absolute equality were the rule in the original division, the extinction of families and the transfer of small estates might easily throw an accumulation of land into the hands of a single owner; and on the other hand the public land afforded a supply from which new properties might be carved continually, without any regard to size. In all respects except those resulting from ownership these estates might be,

[1] See further, § 45; p. 103, below.
[2] Cf. Gneist, Verwaltungsrecht, i. 4.

and seem to have been, regulated by the same machinery as the townships of simple freemen ; but the relations of the cultivator of another man's land to his lord belong to another portion of our investigation.

The general conclusion at which we arrive is that there must have been, over a large portion of each colony, a regular allotment of land to the bodies of colonists united in their native land by the tie of blood or of neighbourhood, and for the moment represented by the divisions of the host [1]; that these allotments varied according to the numbers of the kindred, the portion assigned to a single family or house being a hide of land [2]; that besides these the nobles or other great men received grants of estates, or perhaps attached themselves to the political centre on the condition of retaining estates which they had already appropriated; and that the surplus land remained the common property of the nation. This surplus land during a long period after the first invasion would go on increasing as the Britons were driven farther westward : after the conversion it furnished the stock from which the monasteries were endowed, and by grants to them and to individuals it was much diminished, until finally it became mere demesne of the king.

General theory of allotment.

36. The question of the primary allotment leads directly to that of the primitive tenure. The possession of land was, even whilst the idea of nationality was mainly a personal one, the

Question of primitive tenure.

---

[1] Kemble, Saxons, i. 69–71, 125.

[2] On the vexed question of the extent of the hide it is not necessary here to dilate ; Kemble, Saxons, i. 88 sq., attempts to fix it at thirty-three acres or thereabouts, or 120 acres of a size one-fourth of the present acre. But although his argument obviates many difficulties, it opens the way for many more. Grimm, R. A. p. 535, gives several passages in which the German *hoba* is made to contain thirty or forty acres. The mansus, mansa, manens, cassatum, terra aratri, of the charters are all interpreted to mean the same thing, although they may have had local differences. See Robertson, Historical Essays, pp. 88–102 : G. L. von Maurer, Einleitg. p. 120. The later hide was no doubt 120 or 100 acres. It is possible that some of the greatest inconsistencies in the use of these words may arise from their being used to express the whole share of one man in all the fields of his village. A hide of thirty acres in a system of common cultivation would represent such an allotment in each of the cultivated areas, i. e. if there were four common fields, it would be 120 acres. But this will not explain all. On the Domesday hide and on the question generally, see Round, Feudal England, pp. 36–44.

badge, if not the basis, of all political and constitutional right. On it depended, when the personal idea yielded to the territorial, the rights and obligations, the rank, value and credibility of the member of the body politic; it became the basis as well as the tangible expression of his status. According to the tenure by which it was held very much of the internal and external history of the nation changes its aspect. It is wrong to suppose that an early stage of society is favourable to simplicity in determining the character of tenure and the relations dependent upon it. Simple as the origin of property may have been, we have no historical data concerning it, and, when the subject does come within the ken of history, it is anything but simple and uniform. In the early Germanic system it is difficult, as we have seen, to prove the existence, except by way of inference, of any determinate property of land in severalty: the original gift comes from the community of which the receiver is a member, the gift is of itself mainly of the character of usufruct, the hold is ideal rather than actual; except in his own homestead the freeman can but set his foot on the soil and say, 'this is mine this year, next year it will be another's, and that which is another's now will be mine then.' It is only by way of further inference that we discover that there must have been larger and smaller properties; the larger held by those who had to support a larger household, the magistrate with his *comitatus*, or the noble with his great train of kinsmen. Without conjecturing how the change took place, we may safely assume that, although traces still remain of common land tenure at the opening of Anglo-Saxon History, absolute ownership of land in severalty was established and becoming the rule. We may then regard the land as referable to two great divisions: that which was held by individuals in full ownership, and that of which the ownership was in the state; the intermediate case of lands held by local communities in common, and used in common by the owners of land as appurtenances to their several estate, may be for the moment put out of sight. The land held in full ownership might be either an inherited[1] or otherwise acquired portion of

*Import-
ance of the
character
of tenure.*

*Absolute
ownership
the rule in
Anglo-
Saxon times.*

*Private and
public land.*

---

[1] For this the word *ethel* is used by Kemble, Grimm, Maurer and other

original allotment, or an estate of such full ownership created
by legal process out of the public land. Both these have been
regarded as coming under the continental denomination 'alod[1];'
but the former looks for its evidence in the pedigree of its   Bookland.
owner or in the witness of the community, while the latter can
produce the charter or book by which it is created, and is
called 'bocland[2].' As the primitive allotments gradually lost
their historical character, and the primitive modes of transfer
became obsolete, the use of written records took their place,
although much must still have been held by customary title[3].

writers on land; but whenever the word occurs in history it is equivalent
to 'patria,' and has no special reference to landed estate. See Bede,
H. E. iii. 1, 8, 9, 28, &c. &c.; and the Anglo-Saxon Gospels.

[1] The word *alod* does not occur in Anglo-Saxon documents before the
eleventh century, when it appears in the Latin of Canute's laws in the
Colbertine MS. as the equivalent of *bócland* or *hereditas.* Schmid, Gesetze,
&c. p. 261.

[2] Probably far too much importance, as regards Constitutional History,
has been attached to the terms *bookland* and *folkland.* The explanations
given at different periods are collected by Schmid, Gesetze, &c. p. 538.
Spelman thought that bookland implied a written title, whilst folkland
was based on the witness of the people, and this interpretation is now
accepted by legal antiquaries. Verelius interpreted bookland as feudal;
Phillips thought bookland feudal, and folkland alodial; and was followed
by Grimm and Gaupp. Even Palgrave connected folkland with the odal,
and bookland with lænland. On the other hand, Somner, Lambard, Lye,
and other antiquaries, considered bookland to be freehold held under
charter, folkland to be held at the will of the lord. The contention that
folkland was public or national property was propounded by Allen, On the
Prerogative, pp. 125–153; and accepted by Kemble, Saxons, i. 289; K.
Maurer, Krit. Ueberschau, i. 69, 107; Hallam, Middle Ages, ii. 406–410;
Gneist, Verwaltungsrecht, i. 4. The Anglo-Saxon law of Land is further
illustrated by Mr. H. C. Lodge in 'Essays on Anglo-Saxon Law,' Boston,
1876, pp. 55 sq. Mr. Lodge, in the Essay above referred to, divides Anglo-
Saxon land into estates created by book, 'bookland,' and estates that were
not so created. The latter class he divides into three, (1) the '*family
land*' or '*yrfeland*;' held by the individual, created by customary law; an
estate of inheritance, subject to certain rights of the family and therefore
inalienable or only alienable with their consent, and liable to no burdens
but the trinoda necessitas: therefore equivalent to the original *ethel*;
(2) common lands, those of the village communities, whether free or under
a lord; and (3) the public or folkland, administered by the king and witan.
The folkland as held by individuals was 'in its nature an unbooked
læn, not heritable, not devisable, alienable in that the holder could grant
all the right and title possessed by him; capable of underletting, and
finally the special and primary taxpaying estate of the community;' p. 98.
Under *bookland* he includes all estates that were held by written title,
whether they were held in fee simple or for life or otherwise.

[3] It is to this hold by folk-right or customary title that the much contested term folkland is now understood to belong. Bócland is the term

Public land.

All the land that is not so accounted for is public land, comprising the whole area that was not at the original allotment assigned to individuals or communities, and that was not subsequently divided into estates of bookland. This constituted the standing treasury of the country: no alienation of any part of it could be made without the consent of the national council. The charters that deal with it are construed to imply that individuals might hold portions of it subject to rents and other services to the state, from which the owners of alods or

The 'trinoda necessitas.'

bookland were exempt. The three obligations of the *fyrd* or military service, the repair of bridges, and the maintenance of fortifications [1] were incumbent on all freemen, and therefore on all holders of land whether alodial or not. Out of this stock were created estates for life or lives; they were alienable only to the extent of the right possessed by the holder; he might by testamentary disposition express a wish for the disposal of them, but a distinct act of the king and witan was necessary to give operation to such provision; the ownership continued to reside in the state, and the proceeds to furnish a portion of

Public land distinct from royal estate.

the revenue. This disposition of the public land, if indeed the interpretation of the charters is correct, was peculiar to

---

used in Alfred's Bede as equivalent to possessio or possessiuncula. *Bóclanda æhte* is *possessiones praediorum*, H. E. iii. 24. In the Latin of Alfred's laws (art. 41), it is *terra hereditaria*; in Athelstan, vi. 1, it is *terra testamentalis*; in Edgar, ii. 2, it is *feudum*; in Ethelred, I. i. 14, *libera terra*; in Canute, i. 11, *hereditas* or *alodium*, though the passage is a mere re-enactment of Edgar, ii. 2 (feudum); in Canute, ii. 77, *terra hereditaria*; in other places the vernacular is retained.

[1] The trinoda necessitas first appears in genuine Anglo-Saxon charters about the beginning of the eighth century. It occurs however earlier in disputed ones, e. g. A.D. 616, Cod. Dipl. dcccclxxxiii. It is mentioned in the act of the council of Clovesho of A.D. 742, Councils, &c. iii. 341; and in a charter of Ethelbald, issued at Godmundesleah in A.D. 749, ibid. p. 386. It occurs two or three times in charters of Offa, more frequently in those of Kenulf, and becomes very general after the time of Egbert. The corresponding obligations in the Frank empire are attendance on the host, repairing of roads, fortifications, and bridges, and watch; Waitz, D. V. G. iv. 30, 31. This is called by Charles the Bald 'antiquam et aliarum gentium consuetudinem;' and although first traceable on the continent in the reign of Charles the Great, is probably much older in custom; but the arguments which refer it to Roman origin want both congruity and continuity. The nearest approach to it is in a law of A.D. 423, in the code of Justinian, xi. 74. § 4: 'igitur ad instructiones reparationesque itinerum pontiumque nullum genus hominum nulliusque dignitatis ac venerationis meritis cessare oportet.' Mr. Coote, in his 'Neglected Fact,' has argued with great

England[1]; in the other Germanic kingdoms there seems to have been no difference between the royal demesne and the other lands of the nation. Here the king himself could not appropriate a part of the public land without the consent of the witenagemot[2].

All estates in land could be let, lent or leased out by its holders; and, under the name of *lænland*[3], held by free cultivators: the greater owners could so let their distant estates to hereditary dependents, such as læts and freedmen, whilst their home farm was cultivated by hired labourers or by slaves. The multiplicity of ranks in the cultivating classes, which was thus engendered, according to the legal status of the individual, his relation to the landlord, the extent or character of his holding, and the nature of his service, produced the somewhat bewildering nomenclature that meets us in Domesday-book; and these have an importance of their own in social history.

Diversity of tenant cultivators.

37. There is no department of Anglo-Saxon law which presents greater difficulties, or has been more variously viewed, than that of status. In one aspect all men are free except the slave pure and simple who is his master's chattel. In another all are unfree except the fully qualified freeman, the owner of land for which he owes no dependence on another[4]; all who stand in

Question of freedom.

learning and ingenuity for the Roman origin: he refers further to Code, viii. 12, §§ 7, 12, 18. Cf. Pearson, Middle Ages, i. 266; Robertson, Scotland under her Early Kings, ii. 337.

[1] The Lombards had public or state lands, the disposal of which was at the pleasure of the king. The Vandals gave their king a separate allotment of very great extent. Among the Franks and other conquering races all the land not in private hands was royal property. Waitz, D. V. G. iv. 239, 240; Sohm, Fr. R. G. V. i. 31–34.

[2] The change of learned opinion as to the meaning of *folkland* involves certain alterations in the terminology; but it does not seem to militate against the idea of the public land as here stated; and some such explanation seems absolutely necessary for the interpretation of the charters.

[3] Kemble, Saxons, i. 310–326; K. Maurer, Krit. Ueberschau, i. 104–107. Mr. Lodge (p. 95) gives a careful account of *læns* and *lænland*. See Robertson, Historical Essays, pp. 102–112.

[4] Savigny, R. R. i. 235. This is Kemble's view (Saxons, i. 122 sq.), but seems to be exaggerated by him beyond reasonable dimensions. He treats the wife and son as unfree in relation to the father, as being in his *mund*. K. Maurer however lays it down as a principle that 'only the free can stand in *mund*: the unfree can stand only in possession' (gewere = seizin). Bethmann-Hollweg explains the *mund* as covering the relations of lord and unfree as well as husband and wife, father and child; Civil-process, iv. 11. Waitz thinks it best to describe the dependent class

the relations of personal dependence, however entered and however terminable, are regarded as unfree. The former view appears the more simple and true.

Slavery a primitive institution.

Classes of slaves.

It cannot be denied that slavery in the strictest sense was an early, if not a primitive, institution of the race. Tacitus knew that the slave had no remedy against the violence of his master ; even his life could be taken with impunity. And in the earliest English laws such slaves are found ; the *theow*[1] or slave simple, whether *wealh*—that is, of British extraction captured or purchased—or of the common German stock descended from the slaves of the first colonists; the *esne*[2] or slave who works for hire ; the *wite-theow*[3] who is reduced to slavery because he cannot pay his debts; the man who has sold himself or his children to avoid starvation[4]; the slave who works in his master's house and the slave who works on the farm : all are regarded as a part of the stock of their owner and are valued according to their importance to him : their offences against a third person he must answer for, as for the mischief done by his cattle : the price of their life is a mere *man-wyrth*, they have no *wergild*, no credibility, no legal rights ; wrongs done to them are regarded as done to their master. In some respects the practice of the law is better than the theory : the slave is entitled to his two loaves a day[5], and his holydays are secured to him[6]; he can purchase his freedom with

The slave is his owner's chattel.

(Hörige, læts, &c.) as neither free nor unfree ; D. V. G. i. 155, 156. See K. Maurer, Krit. Ueberschau, i. 405 sq.; Sohm, Fr. R. G. V. i. 359.

[1] *Theow*, from the same root as *dienen*, to serve; Grimm, R. A. p. 303; Schmid, Gesetze, &c. p. 669.

[2] *Esne* (Gothic *asneis*), an unfree hireling; Grimm, R. A. p. 304. Kemble, Saxons, i. 215, considers the *'esne* as superior in position to the *theow*. See, however, Schmid, Gesetze, &c. p. 568, who regards vir, juvenis, as the original meaning.

[3] *Wite-theow*, possibly the man who is reduced to slavery as not able to pay the fines by which the breach of the peace is redeemed ; so that he is in a state of penal servitude. See Schmid, Gesetze, &c. p. 679; K. Maurer, Krit. Ueberschau, i. 409.

[4] There is in Kemble, C. D. dccccxxv, a manumission of several men who had ' bowed their heads for meat in the evil days.' Theodore's Penitential (Councils, &c. iii. 202) allows this voluntary servitude.

[5] ' Seven hundred and twenty loaves, besides morning meals and noon meals.' Dialogue of Salomon and Saturn, ap. Kemble, Saxons, i. 38.

[6] By Ini's law a slave working on Sunday at his master's command became free (Ini, § 3). See also Canute, Sec. 45 ; Ethelred, vii. 2, § 2 ; Alfred,

savings[1] which in some unexplained way the law has allowed him to keep, and the spiritual law can enforce a penance on the master for ill-treating him. But his status descends to his children; all his posterity, unless the chain is broken by emancipation, are born slaves[2]. *Slavery hereditary.*

If the status of the free be held to include all who have legal rights, the class may be divided, first, into those who have land of their own, and those who have not. Of the former the law can take immediate cognisance, they have a tangible stake in the community through which the law can enforce its obligations. Of the latter it can take cognisance only mediately, through some person whom the law can touch, and they are therefore compelled to put themselves in dependence on some one with whom it can deal as answerable for their forthcoming. The relation of dependence on a lord may however be entered into by a free landowner for the sake of honour or protection[3]. The dependent class thus includes a great variety of relations; the *comitatus* or personal following of the king or ealdorman; all freemen hired as household servants or field labourers; the rent-paying tenants of other men's lands; and the hereditary dependents who have personal rights, the læts and the freedmen: the landless, the homeless, the kinless, must all seek a lord whose protection is to be secured by voluntary service, who is responsible for their appearance in the law courts, and who in some cases exercises over them an authority which is scarcely less than legal jurisdiction[4]. *The fully free: landed or landless.* *The landless man must have a lord.* *Classes of dependent freemen.*

§ 43; Theodore, Penit. ii. 13, § 3. 'Non licet homini a servo tollere pecuniam quam ipse labore suo adquesierit;' Councils, &c. iii. 202.

[1] Kemble, C. D. mcccli: a slave buys his own liberty of the abbot of Bath; others buy their own children. See also dcccxxxiv, &c.

[2] On Anglo-Saxon slavery see Kemble, Saxons, i. 185–225; Sharon Turner, Hist. Ang.-Sax. ii. 96–102; and on German and Anglo-Saxon slavery in general, an essay by Dr. Ignaz Jastrow, Breslau, 1878.

[3] This practice is traceable throughout Anglo-Saxon history from the hlafæta, the bread-eater of the hlaford or bread-giver (Ethelb. § 24), to the liber homo of Domesday, 'terram tenens et quo vellet abire valens,' who 'summisit se in manu Walterii pro defensione sua;' i. 36. But the practice of commendation in England was generally the result of the police organisation, not of the land system. See Chapter VII below; Gneist, Self-government, i. 42; Verwaltungsrecht, i. 11, 12.

[4] Konrad Maurer, Krit. Ueberschau, i. 415 sq. The law of Athelstan,

Classes of
landed
freemen.

The fully qualified freeman who has an estate of land may be
of various degrees of wealth and dignity, from the ceorl, with a
single hide, to the thegn with five hides, a place in the king's
hall, a bell-house and burh-geat seat; to the still more powerful
man who has 'thriven to eorl-right,' or who has his forty hides[1];
to the ealdorman and the etheling. He may be a simple husbandman or the lord of a soken and patron of hundreds of servants
and followers. The cross division according to blood and
wergild affects both classes of the free: the noble may be forced
to have a lord, the ceorl having land may dispense with one.

Gradation
of classes.

The eorlcundman is worth his high wergild even if he be landless: the ceorl may attain to thegn-right and yet his children to
the third generation will not be gesithcund[2]. But there is no
impassable barrier between the classes: the ceorl may become
thegn-worthy, and the thegn eorl-worthy[3]. And there are gra-
dations in every class; four ranks of the eorlcund, the three of the

ii. § 2, is as follows: 'Et diximus de illis, qui dominos non habent, de
quibus rectum difficile conquiritur aut nullum; praecipiatur cognationi
eorum ut eos ad rectum adducat et dominum eis inveniat in conventu
publico.' Maurer points to the Edictum Pistense of Charles the Bald as
a parallel (A.D. 864), § 6: 'Quidam leves homines de istis comitatibus qui
devastati sunt a Nortmannis, in quibus res et mancipia et domos habuerunt, quia nunc mancipia et domos non habent, quasi licenter malum
faciunt; et quia non habent domos ad quas secundum legem manniri et
banniri possint, dicunt quod de mannitione vel bannitione legibus com-
probari et legaliter judicari non possunt.' The count is therefore to send
a missus into the district and 'si necesse fuerit ipse in forbannum mit-
tatur qui ad justitiam reddendam venire noluerit.' Athelstan's law continues, 'et si hoc efficere nolit vel non possit, ad terminum sit ille for-
bannitus deinceps:' the parallel seems more than accidental, although
the remedial measures are different. In Iceland every one who is not
himself settled as a peasant proprietor must choose himself a domicile
(grið); as by the law of Canute every freeman must be in hundred and
in tithing; Canute, ii. 20. Maurer, p. 427. The Capitulum of A.D. 847,
'Volumus etiam ut unusquisque liber homo in nostro regno seniorem
qualem voluerit in nobis et in nostris fidelibus accipiat,' merely gives the
liberty of choosing a lord, does not enforce it as a duty; Waitz, D. V. G.
iv. 234. The Capitula Lombardorum afford a better parallel: 'Et quia
sunt nonnulli qui sine proprietatibus in regno nostro degentes judicia
comitum effugiunt, atque non habentes res aut substantiam quibus con-
stringi possint, ideo circumquaque malitias exercere non cessant, de illis
nobis placuit ut ipsi cum quibus videntur manere aut eos praesentent aut
pro eorum malefactis rationem reddant;' Waitz, D. V. G. iv. 363.

[1] Ranks; Schmid, Gesetze, &c. p. 389; Thorpe, Ancient Laws, p. 81.
[2] Wergilds; Schmid, Gesetze, p. 399; Thorpe, p. 79.
[3] Ranks; Schmid, Gesetze, p. 389; Thorpe, p. 81.

læts; three even of the household slaves[1]. The great distinction however is that of wealth, the landless ceorl is little better off than the slave, except that he may choose his own master.

38. The primary element which the law regards is the land-owning freeman; the first relation in which he stands is that of the family[2]. The political importance of the tie of kindred is prehistoric: the early Germans were associated in families for the service of the host and for the occupation and cultivation of land, but the family had no jurisdiction over its own members, nor any representation in the state. So also in England, it is probable that all the primitive villages in whose name the patronymic syllable *ing* occurs were originally colonised by communities united either really by blood or by the belief in a common descent[3]: but the legal relations were for most purposes merged already in those of the township or the mark, and the political weight of the kindred was accidental only. Yet significant traces of the old importance of the bond remain: as in the Germania, the kindred have a share in the fines paid for the wrongs of their kinsman[4], so in England the mægth share in the wergild paid for their slain brother, and contribute to the payment for one whom their brother has slain[5]; they have certain claims on his hereditary bookland

Importance of the family relation in England as in Germany.

Duties of the kin.

---

[1] The Law of Ethelbert, § 75, mentions four classes of the eorlcund; § 26, three classes of læts; §§ 11 and 16, three classes of theows.

[2] K. Maurer, Kritische Ueberschau, i. 52–62. The view of Kemble (Saxons, i. 234 sq.) seems to exaggerate the political importance of the *mægburh*, at least if it refers to Anglo-Saxon institutions however early. See also Robertson, Scotland under her Early Kings, ii. 309–340: where likewise far too much latitude of conjecture is taken. As for the importance of the principle in the development of the German state-system generally, the views of Sybel are combated by Waitz, Das Alte Recht, pp. 126, 127; Deutsche Verfassungs-Geschichte, i. 53–60 sq., and rejected by K. Maurer, Kritische Ueberschau, i. 61. On the Anglo-Saxon family Law generally see an Essay by Mr. Ernest Young, in Essays on Anglo-Saxon Law, pp. 121–182. It is true that in the nomad state the family bond is the only trustworthy one, but the Germans had passed that stage when they entered history. Still there are sufficient vestiges of the prior importance of the principle to make the inquiry valuable.

[3] On this and on its connexion with the Mark system see Kemble, Saxons, i. 58 sq. and Appendix A.

[4] Tac. Germ. c. 21.

[5] For the share of the kindred in the receipt see Schmid, Gesetze, p. 394; for their share in the payment, Alfred, §§ 27, 28; Edmund, ii. 7, &c.

which limit his power of alienating it[1]; they are the legal compurgators for one another[2] in accusation or defence, they are bound to protect their kinsman in his minority[3], to seek a lord and find a home for him if he is lordless or homeless[4]. All these however are legal rather than constitutional obligations.

The township.

39. The unit of the constitutional machinery or local administration, the simplest form of social organisation, is the township, the *villata* or *vicus*[5]. It may represent the original allotment of the smallest subdivision of the free community, or the settlement of the kindred colonising on their own account, or the estate of the great proprietor who has a tribe of dependents.

Free and dependent townships.

Its headman is the *tun-gerefa*, who in the dependent townships is of course nominated by the lord[6], but in the independent ones may have been originally a chosen officer, although when

---

[1] Alfred, § 41 ; Ll. Hen. I, tit. 70, § 21 ; tit. 88, § 14 ; Schmid, pp. 95, 472, 484 ; Thorpe, pp. 39, 251, 260.

[2] Laws of the Northumbrian Priests, § 51 ; Henry I, tit. 64, § 4.

[3] Hlothere and Eadric, § 6.   [4] Athelstan, ii. §§ 2, 8.

[5] *Tûn*, viculus, vicus, Bede, H. E. iii. 17 ; *tûn-scipe*, vicus, v. 10 ; *tûn-gerefa*, villicus, iv. 24, v. 10 ; *tûn-scipe*, Edgar, iv. 8 ; *tûnes-man*, ibid. iv. 8, 13. The *tûn* is originally the enclosure or hedge, whether of the single farm or of the enclosed village, as the *burh* is the fortified house of the powerful man. The corresponding word in Norse is *gardr*, our *garth* or *yard*. The equivalent German termination is *heim*, our *ham* ; the Danish form is *by* (Norse *bû* = German *bau*). Some inferences might be drawn from these differences as to the contrasts of early colonisation. See Grimm, R. A. p. 534. The notion of the *dorf* or *thorpe* seems to stand a little further from the primitive settlement.

[6] Athelstan, iii. § 7 : 'Si tunc sit aliquis qui tot homines habeat, quod non sufficiat omnes custodire, praeponat sibi singulis villis praepositum unum,' &c. On the origin of the word gerefa, see Max Müller's Lectures on Language, ii. 281. It has been regarded generally as the same word with the German graf, and derived from *grau*, grey = senior, but many other explanations have found favour ; Grimm connected it with *râvo*, tignum, tectum, and interpreted it as comes, socius, the inmate of the same house ; Spelman connected it with *reafan*, to plunder, and thus accounted for the Latin word *exactor* used to translate it ; Kemble with rófan or réfan, to call aloud, making it originally mean the *bannitor* or proclaimer of the court ; Richthofen derives it from the Greek γράφω ; and other derivations are also imagined. Max Müller would not 'be at all surprised if the Anglo-Saxon gerefa turned out to be etymologically unconnected with the German *graf*' (Lectures, ii. 284), and this is so far probable, that whereas the fundamental, universal and permanent idea of the gerefa is stewardship (gerefa = dispensator ; Alf. Gloss. Schmid, p. 597), the graf is not, so far as appears, a steward at all, but primarily and universally a magistrate. If then they are the same word, the English application seems to be most primitive, and there is at least one link missing between it and the graf.

the central power has become stronger he may be, as in the
Frank *villa*, the nominee of the king, or his officer.   The internal organisation in both cases must have been much the
same, for the dependent communities had probably in most
instances been originally free, and reduced to dependence by
a powerful neighbour; or were composed of his tenants who
entered into the rights and duties of men whose estates their
lord had purchased or accumulated by inheritance.

This corporate unity is subjected to changes both by way of
development and under legislative action.   In its earlier stage
it may have been the community of free and kindred cultivators,
or what is called the *mark*[1].   It cannot be safely affirmed that
the German settlers in Britain brought with them the entire
system of the mark organisation, or that that system was ever
in Anglo-Saxon times the basis of local administration.   The
comparative rarity of the word, whether in laws and charters or
in local names, forbids the idea of such completeness, universality, or fundamental constitutional significance[2].   But such

Relation of the mark to the town- ship.

---

[1] Kemble has the credit of being the first to recognise the applicability
to English history of the results of German investigations into the mark
system : but with his usual tendency to exaggeration.   Since he wrote,
the whole subject has been worked out by Dr. G. L. von Maurer in
several treatises : the most important results of which for the history of
early society agree with the view of Dr. Waitz in the Deutsche Verfassungs-Geschichte.   Sir Henry Maine, on Village Communities, and
Dr. Nasse, on The Land-Community of the Middle Ages, have some
important remarks on the English side of the subject : which is also
illustrated in a curious Essay by William Maurer, published at Man-
chester in 1855.   The whole question has been elaborately discussed by
Mr. Seebohm in 'The English Village Community,' 1883 ; where the relics
of primitive tenure are interpreted on a different theory from that of the
text, and much greater influence assigned to the permanent elements of
Roman administration and British population.   The results are extremely
interesting but, so far as they are proved, do not interfere materially with
our conclusions as to the *constitutional* bearing of the subject.   Dr. Gneist,
Self-government, i. 2, goes too far in regarding the expenditure of
learned investigation on this part of the subject as unfruitful, but he is
undoubtedly right in refusing to recognise the Mark as the basis of our
polity.   See too Schmid, Gesetze, p. 630 ; Gneist, Verwaltungsrecht, i.
61.

[2] Kemble ascribes the rarity of the term to the fact that ' the system
founded upon what it represents yielded in England earlier than in Germany to extraneous influences ;' Saxons, i. 36. The word occurs in charters
—e. g. Cod. Dipl. dcxxxiii—in the full signification ; but more generally as
a simple boundary.   The 'mercemot,' mentioned in Cod. Dipl. dlxviii,

Traces of
the mark,

an institution there are distinct traces. We nowhere see the qualification of the freeman for political right depending on a partnership in tenure and cultivation of common land. It may have been the case very early, but it is more probable that the settlers had passed beyond this stage before they migrated. Yet in the nomenclature of the villages the same significant syllable that points to the idea of *cognatio* points equally to the

in the
commons,

mark: and what is indisputable, the existence of the common system of cultivation, and of common lands belonging in usufruct to the members of the township, proves the abiding influence of the mark principle[1]. Community of land and joint action in cultivation might exist without forming the basis of the political unity of the community: it cannot be shown to have precluded the possession of private estate among the sharers of it, and in its later form it appears merely as an appendage to such private possession. Common lands of manors and townships exist at the present day, and, within a century, common cultivation also existed in many parts of England. It is to this system that the origin of some part of the machinery of local courts of the manor and township which still exist may be

and in the
court baron
of the
manor.

traced[2]. The right of the markmen to determine whether a new settler should be admitted to the township exists in the form of admitting a tenant at the court baron and customary court of every manor[3]; the right of the markmen to determine the by-laws[4], the local arrangement for the common husbandry,

is referred by Kemble to the place where the markmoot was held; Saxons. i. 55. Schmid, Gesetze, p. 631, gives some other passages where the word *mark* occurs, but it is not found in the full sense in the laws.

[1] Ini, § 42 : 'If ceorls have a common meadow, or other partible land to fence, and some have fenced their part, some have not, and [strange cattle come in and] eat up the common corn or grass, let those go who own the gap and compensate to the others.' The common wood, 'commune silfa quam nos Saxonice in gemennisse dicimus,' is mentioned in a charter of Ethelwulf, Cod. Dipl. ii. 1 ; the common land, 'gemanan lande,' ib. iv. 326.

[2] Kemble, Saxons, i. 54 ; Maine, Village Communities, pp. 138–140; and W. Maurer's Essay.

[3] See Kemble, Saxons, i. 54. That the markmoot was a court of justice, as Kemble conjectures, seems altogether improbable. See Mr. Adams's Essay on Anglo-Saxon Courts of Law, in Essays on Anglo-Saxon Law, p. 23.

[4] Kitchin, Court Leet and Court Baron (ed. 1587), fo. 79; Nelson, Lex Maneriorum, pp. 54–58.

or the fencing of the hay-fields [1], or the proportion of cattle [2] to
be turned into the common pasture, exists still in the manorial
courts and in the meetings of the townships: the very customs
of relief and surrender which are often regarded as distinctly
feudal, are remnants of the polity of the time when every transfer
of property required the witness of the community, to whose
membership the new tenant was thereby admitted. Still between all this and the enjoyment of political rights there is no
immediate connexion. It is as an owner of land, or as a fully
qualified ' lawful man,' not as a member of the mark community, that the freeman has rights and duties, and there is no
evidence that in England the only way of owning land was the
membership of the mark.

The historical township has outgrown the mark.

The historical township is the body of alodial owners who
have advanced beyond the stage of land-community, retaining
many vestiges of that organisation; or the body of tenants of
a lord who regulates them or allows them to regulate themselves
on principles derived from the same.

40. In a further stage the township appears in its ecclesiastical form as the parish [3] or portion of a parish, the district
assigned to a church or priest; to whom its ecclesiastical dues
and generally also its tithes are paid. The boundaries of the
parish and the township or townships with which it coincides,
are generally the same; in small parishes the idea and even
name of township is frequently, at the present day, sunk in
that of the parish; and all the business that is not manorial is
dispatched in vestry meetings, which are however primarily
meetings of the township for church purposes.

The township as a district of a priest; the parish.

41. In some parts of England, especially if not solely those
which constituted the West Saxon kingdom, the name of tithing
replaces that of township as the unit of local administration.
This term occurs as early as the time of Edgar [4], and must be

The Tithing.

---

[1] Nasse, Land Community, ed. Ouvry, pp. 17, 18 sq.; G. L. von Maurer,
Dorfverfassg. i. 358.
[2] Nelson, Lex Maneriorum, pp. 59, 67.
[3] Pearson, Early and Middle Ages, i. 251; Toulmin Smith, The Parish.
On the formation of parishes see below, Chapter VIII. The 'Church of
town' is mentioned by Bede, H. E. v. 12.
[4] In the Judicia civitatis Lundoniae, Ath. vi. 2, 8, § 1, it is not a local

understood as then signifying a local or personal subdivision of the hundred, although it now appears generally as a subdivision

of a parish. Naturally the word would mean the tenth part of the larger division; and if an instance were forthcoming of the historical introduction of the hundred, or the colonisation of border territory, it would probably be found that the hundred

and tithing were measured in proper proportion. But as that cannot be done, it is safer to allow to the tithing the same laxity of interpretation that Tacitus allowed to the hundred. It is however quite possible that the term was a relic of the same system that the hundred itself represents [1], that, as the hundred

was the sphere of the hundred court, so the tithing was the sphere of the tithingman, and that the arrangement, being found applicable to both police and fiscal purposes, was used for personal as well as a territorial division. Thus when Ethelwulf released one out of every ten hides of folkland from the payment of geld, or when he ordered that every ten hides of his land should maintain one poor man, the arrangement might result in the formation of local tithings; or might even presuppose their existence. The convenience of rating a number of hides together produced the Lincolnshire hundreds and the Richmondshire 'tenmentales,' and as a fiscal arrangement the West Saxon tithing may have had the same origin before the time of Canute;

but a personal association of ten. See Chapter XI. § 131 below. Edgar i. 2, 4, mentions the tithingman as taking part in the action of the hundred in the matter of theft. The only other place where the tithing occurs is in the Secular law of Canute, § 20. It is curious that *teothung* should be ordinarily used for an association of ten, as the only whole of which the tithe is ten must be the hundred; and if, as generally believed, the Anglo-Saxon hundred was the long one of six score, the tithing ought to have contained twelve; and Fleta speaks of the frankpledges as *dozein.* Palgrave, Commonwealth, pp. cxxi–cxxvi.

[1] The *decanus* and *decania,* or *decuria,* occur in the organisation of the host, in the laws of the Visigoths and Bavarians; and in connexion with the police system in the Lombard laws also. The *decanus* in Frank law is the lowest officer in the host, or in police administration; but nowhere is there any trace of a division of land connected with the number. The Frank host recognised the *contubernium* of ten men, but there is no certainty that this was connected with the *decanus.* Waitz, D. V. G. i. 488–491. Cf. Gneist, Self-government, i. 9; Palgrave, Commonwealth, p. 199.

[2] Tithings at present exist in Somerset, Wilts, Berks, Devon, Dorset, Hants, Surrey, and Sussex; there are isolated instances in Warwickshire,

whose enactment, 'We will that every freeman be brought into hundred and tithing,' seems virtually, at least, to secure to every man his proper domicile, and to the public service his proper contribution. If however the tithing ever existed as a territorial subdivision outside the West Saxon kingdom, it must at an early date have sunk both the name and the functions in that of the villata or township[1]. The local tithing may then possibly mark a stage in the process by which the personal organisation of the free people passed into the territorial system. But the name has been very commonly applied both by historical writers and in legal custom to denote an institution only incidentally connected with territorial arrangements, the association of ten men in common responsibility legally embodied in the *frithborh* or frankpledge.

This institution[2], of which there is no definite trace before   The frith-borh or

Gloucestershire, and Worcestershire; and the township occurs here and there in the former list. In the other counties the subdivision of the parish bears the name of township, except in Kent, Cornwall, Hertford, and Suffolk, where only parishes and hamlets are ordinarily reckoned. The Cornish tithings seem to be coincident with the manors, and thus may be merely the areas of the court-leet view of frankpledge. Palgrave, p. cxxi, gives instances of both personal frankpledges and local tithings in the reign of Henry III; the former in Kent and Warwickshire, the latter in Devon. In the Pipe Roll of 1 Rich. I. the personal tithing in Bedfordshire, Gloucestershire, Berkshire, Sussex and Surrey, and the local tithing in Cornwall, Somerset and Hants, alike discharge the function of the frankpledge; see pp. 36, 114, 153, 168, 169, &c. These illustrations might determine the question of the origin of the tithing generally, were it not that the term occurs before the frankpledge tithing was instituted. Finally, it is not impossible that there may have been a connexion between the ecclesiastical tithe and the domiciliary tithing; for the ciricsceat, or church-scot, was paid by every man to the parish church of the place where he had his hearth at Midwinter; Ini, § 61. As his hundred was the district where he paid suit to the hundred court, his tithing was the district where he paid his tenth to the church. But this is only a speculation.

[1] Pearson, Middle Ages, i. 250, says, ' Ten families constituted a tithing, the self-governing unit of the state, which is now represented among us by the parish, the ten tithings were a hundred.' Robertson, Hist. Essays, p. lxv, also uses the word as *generally* equivalent to township. It is however very rash to adopt any such generalisation. Gneist, Verwaltungsrecht, i. 51, 59, alleges that the word is not found in Domesday (Schmid, p. 648), and rejects the territorial application of it. Palgrave also suggests that the local tithings in the West may have been remains of the British divisions of Cantreds and Trefs. Mr. Pearson says that the hundreds of Devon generally contain about ten parishes, and infers thence the original identity of the parish with the tithing.

[2] On this subject a great literature exists, which may be seen summed

frank-
pledge.

Principle of
pledges.

the Norman Conquest, is based on a principle akin to that of the law which directs every landless man to have a lord who shall answer for his appearance in the courts of law. That measure, which was enacted by Athelstan[1], was enlarged by a law of Edgar[2], who required that every man should have a surety who should be bound to produce him in case of litigation, and answer for him if he were not forthcoming. A law of Canute[3] re-enacts this direction, in close juxtaposition with another police order ; namely, that every man, who wishes to be entitled to any free rights, shall be in a hundred and in a tithing. The laws of Edward the Confessor, a compilation of supposed Anglo-Saxon customs issued in the twelfth century, contain a clause on which the later practice of frankpledge is founded, but which seems to originate in the confusion of the

The accept-
ed law of
the frank-
pledge.

two clauses of the law of Canute. By this article, which describes itself as a comparatively recent enactment[4], all men are bound to combine themselves in associations of ten, to which the name of *frithborh* is given in the South, and that of *tenmannetale* in the North of England[5]. Each association has a headman, a ' capital pledge,' *borhs-ealdor* or *frithborge-head*, to manage the

Law of
frank-
pledge.

business of the ten. Thus constituted, they are standing sureties for one another : if one break the law, the other nine shall hold him to right ; if they cannot produce him, the capital pledge with two of his fellows, and the head men and two others out of each of the three nearest *frithborhs*, are to purge their association of

---

up in Waitz, D. V. G. i. 454–496 ; Schmid, Gesetze, pp. 646–648 ; K Maurer, Krit. Ueberschau, i. 87–96 ; Gneist, Verwaltgsr. i. 166 ; Self government, i. 26 sq.; Hallam, M. A. ii. 289. Palgrave (Commonwealth p. 196 sq. and notes), who anticipates most of the later arguments, refer the institution to Canute.

[1] Athelstan, ii. 2. If a reeve dare not warrant any of his lord's men the suspected man must find twelve pledges among his kindred, who shall stand in security for him ; ibid. iii. 7, § 2. This looks like a frank-pledge, but probably is a variety of the compurgatory obligation of the kin.

[2] Edgar, iii. 6 ; iv. 3.

[3] Canute, ii. 20 ; Gneist, Self-government, i. 26.

[4] Edw. Conf. §§ 19, 26 ; Schmid, pp. 502, 507 ; Thorpe, pp. 194, 196.

[5] Edw. Conf. § 19. Tenmentale, however, in Richmondshire, was in Henry II's reign an extent of 14 carucates which paid 4*s.* 7*d.* as an annual tax ; see Gale, Regist. Hon. de Richmond, p. 22.

complicity in the flight of the criminal, or to make good the mischief he has done. The association of the ten is called also the tithing[1], and the 'capital pledge' the *tithing*-man. Whether before the Conquest this union or confusion of the two distinct ideas had taken the form of a law, there is nothing to show: and the word frankpledge is used in the so-called laws of the Conqueror simply for the surety[2]; but it is probable from the view of his legislation in the case of murder, by which the responsibility of producing the criminal was laid on the hundred[3], that a kindred measure of universal application may have then been introduced, and that thus the mutual responsibility of the frankpledge was imported into the English law. The 'view of frankpledge,' the business of seeing that these associations were kept in perfect order and number and of enforcing the same by fine, was one of the agenda of the local courts, and became ultimately, with the other remunerative parts of petty criminal jurisdiction, a manorial right exercised in the courts leet, where it still exists[4]. It was made one way of maintaining the practice of local representation: the capital pledge and a portion of his tithing taking the duty of appearing for their township or berewic in the popular courts[5]; and thus again the ideas of the township and the tithing come into connexion. It is in this point that the frankpledge has its chief historical importance. It has been very much exaggerated; some writers having even gone so far as to make it a common institution of the whole German race, and possibly the basis of political combination: by others

(marginal notes:) Possibly of the date of the Conquest.

Continued existence in court leet.

Exaggeration of the importance of the frankpledge.

---

[1] Madox, Hist. Exch. p. 392 ; Palgrave, Commonwealth, pp. 196 sq.
[2] William, i. 25, 52.   [3] Ibid. iii. 3.
[4] Palgrave (Commonwealth, pp. 202, cxxiii) asserts that the view of frankpledge did not exist in the 'shires which constituted the ancient kingdom of Northumbria,' and gives reference to records to prove that it was not general in Mercia in the reign of Henry III. However this may have been, it is certainly found in Yorkshire at the present day. The exceptions may be perhaps accounted for on the ground of the inhabitants of exempt districts being under the pledge of the lord of the soil at the time of the institution. But the question is obscure. Cf. Gneist, Verwaltungsrecht, i. 178.
[5] Customs of Kent, Statutes of the Realm, i. 223. The borghesaldor and four men appeared for each 'commune' of tenants in Gavelkind, in the court of the justices in Eyre; each borough however was represented by twelve men.

again, it has been regarded as a form of guild[1]; and as a substitute for, or development of, the principle of the accountability
of the kindred for wergild[2]. These views, and others equally
speculative, may be safely discarded: there is no trace of any
similar institution on the Continent, or even in England, earlier
than the middle of the twelfth century, although, as has been
said, the enactment of the law would be not strange to the
legislation of the Conqueror. If it were not that the term
tithing occurs in the laws long before we have any evidence of
the existence of the frankpledge, the latter institution might be
regarded as the origin of the name, if not of the local subdivision which in particular districts takes the place of the more
usual *township*.

The town-
ship as the
manor.

42. To return however to the township. Besides its character
as representing the principle of the mark, and forming the basis
of the parish, the township has a share in the creation of the
later territorial jurisdiction of the manor: and those early
townships which were founded on the land of a lord are in

Original and
created
jurisdiction
of the
manor.

many respects much the same as manors[3]. The lord exercised
in both the functions depending on the free possession of the
land, which in the free community belonged to all the townsmen, and likewise a jurisdiction in civil and criminal suits
which, with all the profits,—for in early time the pecuniary
interests of justice formed no small part of the advantages of

[1] The *gegildan* who are mentioned in the laws on which this theory is
built, are the associates or companions of strangers, and kinless people
and furnish no evidence of any institution of the kind for collective responsibility. Waitz, D. V. G. i. 461–466. The guilds themselves had a
quite different object. See the next note and Chapter XI below.

[2] The importance of the subject of frankpledge is much exaggerated,
owing to the extraordinary variety of views that have been entertained
upon it. It is obvious that associations of ten men may be embodied
(1) as in a guild for mutual help and obtaining of redress; (2) in police
organisation, to join in the pursuit of a thief who has robbed and may
be concealed within their neighbourhood: this is supposed to be the
character of the decima or decenna when mentioned in connexion with the
hundred; (3) as a compulsory organisation of collective responsibility as
in the frankpledge.

[3] Ordericus Vitalis (lib. iv. c. 7) regarded the township and the manor
as identical: 'villas quas a manendo manerios vulgo vocamus.' Palgrave
seems to hold that nearly all townships in Anglo-Saxon times were under
the rule of a lord; Commonwealth, p. 65.

judicial power,—was conferred on him by the original gift, and removed from the cognisance of the hundred. In consequence of this system, the exact development of which belongs to a later stage of our inquiry, some part of the business properly belonging to the township is dispatched in the manorial courts, varied of course by local custom and the terms of particular grants.

43. In all these forms and relations the townsmen retain their right of meeting and exercising some sorts of judicial work, although, until the criminal jurisdiction in court leet comes to the lords of manors by special grant, their participation in such matters is of the character simply of police-agency. Their assemblies are rather *gemots* or meetings than proper courts; for any contentious proceedings amongst men so closely connected and so few in number must have been carried immediately to the hundred court. But they may be safely understood to have had the power of making their own by-laws : the word *by-law* itself is said to mean the laws enacted by the township, the 'by' of the Northern shires [1] : the *gemot* also elected its own officers, possibly the *gerefa* and the *bydel* [2] ; it arranged the representation of its interests in the courts of the hundred and the shire, where the *gerefa* and four best men appeared for the township ; it carried into effect the requisitions of the higher courts in the way of taxes and other exactions, the pursuit of criminals and the search for stolen goods [3] ; on the institution of the frankpledge it prepared the tithing lists for the view of the sheriff. In the dependent townships some of these functions devolved on the lord's steward, or nominated gerefa, as the delegate of the master on whom the original gift had conferred the power of enforcing these sections of jurisdiction : but the actual process must have been much the same as in the freer

The assembly of the township.

The by-laws.

Election of officers,

Similar process in dependent townships.

---

[1] Palgrave, Commonwealth, p. 80 : he quotes Jornandes for the use of the word 'bellagines' in the same sense ; de Rebus Geticis, c. 2.

[2] The usual custom after the Conquest and still. Palgrave, Commonwealth, p. 82. The tithingman is of course an elective officer. The idea that he was a sort of village magistrate is without basis ; although in a simple community of peasants the office of a constable, for such seems to have been the position of the tithingman, was held in more honour than it is now. See Hallam, M. A. ii. 282.

[3] Hlothere and Eadric, § 5 ; Edgar, iv. §§ 8, 13 ; Ethelred, iii. § 15.

communities, if we may judge by the common law of the later manors where the suitors are judges in court baron still [1].

Township organisation at the present day.

As the national customs which belong to the lowest range of machinery are subject to the fewest organic changes, these courts have continued to exist until the present day. In the vestry-meeting the freemen of the township, the ratepayers, still assemble for purposes of local interest, not involved in the manorial jurisdiction; elect the parish officers, properly the township officers,—for there is no primary connexion between the maintenance of roads and collection of taxes and the parish as an ecclesiastical unity,—the churchwardens, the waywardens, the assessors, and the overseers of the poor. In the courts of the manor are transacted the other remaining portions of the old township jurisdiction; the enforcing of pains and penalties on the breakers of by-laws; the election of the capital-pledges of frankpledges, of *plebiscitarii*[2] or by-law men, aletasters, constables, and other officers of a character of which nine-tenths of Englishmen know nothing. The court-baron and customary court continues, in its admission of tenants and witnessing of surrenders, the ancient business of the markmoot; the court leet exercises the remaining share of the higher jurisdiction involved in the grant or exemption of the original gift. The vestry is the representative of the *gemot*, with which it was once identical; but as the jurisdiction of the courts of the manor was defined by charter, or by the customary law existing at the moment of their creation, all matters arising outside that jurisdiction come under the management of the vestry. Nor can the importance of this point be exaggerated, when we look further on and see in these local gatherings the chief element in the origination of the borough system of later date. The com-

[1] As in Domesday, i. 193 : 'Hanc terram tenuerunt VI. sochemanni et dare et vendere terram suam potuerunt. Unus eorum homo regis Edwardi fuit et inwardum invenit vicecomiti. Tres istorum sochemannorum accommodavit Picotus Rogerio comiti, propter placita sua tenenda, sed postea occupaverunt eos homines comitis et retinuerunt cum terris suis sine liberatore, et rex inde servitium non habuit nec habet, sicut ipse vicecomes dicit.' An important passage, showing further how manors were enlarged by usurpation.

[2] Manorial Register of Aldborough, Yorkshire : the officers elected in the ninth of Charles I were four by-lawmen or *plebiscitarii*, two constables, two aletasters, and one 'communis impercator' or pinder.

paratively restricted character of the powers of the local courts Importance
was probably the cause why liberty of election was suffered to
exist in them during ages in which in the higher ranges of the
polity it was entirely lost. A curious instance of the early
confusion of the ideas of the township and the parish may be
found in the defensive war of A.D. 1138[1], when the parish priests
with their parishioners assembled and joined the army of the
barons. In the hundred-courts the parson still joined in the
representation of the township[2]. The host was the nation in
arms; here it is the church in arms also.

Importance of these vestiges of early institutions.

44. The 'burh' of the Anglo-Saxon period was simply a more *The burh.*
strictly organised form of the township. It was probably in a
more defensible position; had a ditch and mound instead of the
quickset hedge or 'tun' from which the township took its name;
and, as the 'tun' originally was the fenced homestead of the
cultivator, the 'burh' was the fortified house and court-yard
of the mighty man—the king, the magistrate, or the noble.
Although there is no evidence which connects the *burhs* of the *Growth of*
Anglo-Saxons with the remains of Roman civilisation[3], and *the burhs.*
although like the rest of the Germans they abhorred walled
towns as the defences of slavery and the graves of freedom[4],
they must necessarily have used, during the process of conquest,
fortified camps which, after peace was obtained, served as civil
centres for the districts in which they were placed. Other
towns grew up round the country houses of the kings and
ealdormen, round the great monasteries in which the bishops
had their seats[5], and in such situations as were pointed out by

---

[1] R. Hexham, ed. Twysden, c. 321.   [2] Hen. I, vii. §§ 7, 8.
[3] Pearson, Early and Middle Ages, i. 264, follows Mr. T. Wright
(Archaeologia, xxxii) in an ingenious argument for the continuity of
Roman municipal institutions in Anglo-Saxon Britain: illustrating the
subject by reference to the *trinoda necessitas*, extra-mural burial, and
some other particulars; all, however, capable of other and far more probable explanation.
[4] Tacitus, Hist. iv. 64.
[5] We have the *cyninges burh*, Edm. ii. 2, &c.; the *cyninges tun*, Alfred,
i. 2; the *eorles tun*, Ethelbert, § 13; *cyninges ealdor botl* (villa regalis),
Bede, H. E. ii. 9; *ceastre* (i. e. Carlisle), ibid. iv. 29; the *mynster stowe*
and *folc-stowe*, urbana et rustica loca, Bede, H. E. iii. 5. The five Danish
burhs, Lincoln, Nottingham, Derby, Leicester, and Stamford, had not only
special privileges of their own, but a common organisation, apparently of

They retain the forms of the free township.

nature as suited for trade and commerce. Where such communities were developed out of the village townships, or founded on the folkland, their institutions and organisation would continue free until the time at which the king began to be regarded as the owner of the public land, and the lord of every man who had no other lord. In these the idea of the free township was retained : municipal authority depended on no different organisation ; the presiding magistrate was the *gerefa* ; in mercantile places such as London or Bath, the *port-gerefa* ; in others the *wic-gerefa* or the *tun-gerefa* simply [1] : his assessors were the owners of the homesteads which had been allotted to the original settlers, or of the estates which had been formed by the union of such allotments. The common lands of the burh testified to its origin in a state of society in which the mark system was not yet forgotten [2].

The jurisdiction of the burh.

Very little indeed can be stated with certainty about the *burh* constitution of early times. We know from Bede that Lincoln had a *gerefa* [3] in the seventh century, and from Domesday that in the eleventh it was governed by twelve lawmen, who inherited their jurisdiction, their sac and soc, with their tenements [4] ; but Lincoln had gone through several centuries of Danish rule in the meantime. The city of Chester on the other hand belonged, in the reign of Edward the Confessor, to the Earl of Mercia, subject to the rights of the king and bishop, and had a governing body of twelve judges, chosen from the tenants of the three [5]. It would appear from the use in these instances

the nature of confederation ; but the history is very obscure. Cf. Laws of Ethelred, iii. 1 ; Chron. Sax. A.D. 1013, 1015 ; Palgrave, Commonwealth, p. 49.

[1] London and Winchester had a *wic-gerefa* ; London, Bath, Bodmin, and Canterbury had a *port-gerefa* ; the *burh-gerefa* does not occur ; Schmid, Gesetze, p. 598.

[2] On the common lands of the Scottish burghs, see Maine, Village Communities, p. 95. Each of the four wards of York has its own common pasture, on which only freemen have rights ; the same rule may be found in most ancient towns, Oxford, Colchester, &c.

[3] Hist. Eccl. ii. 6.

[4] ' In ipsa civitate erant xii lageman, id est habentes sacam et socam ... Modo sunt ibi totidem habentes sacam et socam ;' Lincoln Dom. i. 336. Stamford also had twelve lagemanni with sac and soc in their own houses and over their men ; ibid. : and there were lagemanni also in Cambridge. The burh-thegns in London may have been the same sort of dignitaries. Kemble, C. D. iv. 214, 221.

[5] ' Civitas de Cestre ... Tunc erant xii judices civitatis ; et hi erant de

of the number of twelve for the governing magistracy, that the The government of the burh resembles that of the hundred. constitution of the larger towns resembled that of the hundred rather than that of the township[1]; and, in fact, each such town generally contained several parish churches with a township organisation belonging to each. Its jurisdiction was a section cut out of the jurisdiction of the hundred court, or created by a grant of immunity. Hence, in the law of Edgar directing the election of witnesses in each community to legalise transfers of cattle and goods, the number fixed for the larger burhs is thirty-three, that for the hundreds and smaller burhs twelve only[2]. The burh-gemot is to be held three times a year, when that of the hundred is held monthly, and that of the shire half-yearly[3]. Probably the townships which made up the *burh* had their weekly meetings also, and the weekly market day would serve as a general gathering for the whole. But it is far easier to trace in existing monuments vestiges of early differing systems than to construct out of them any consistent idea of a uniform constitution. All the definite knowledge that we have of the subject belongs to a later date. Of the influence of guilds, as a subsidiary part of town organisation, there are some traces which at a later period assume great historical importance; but there is nothing to justify the notion that they were the basis on which the corporate constitution of the burh was founded[4].

The city of London, when it springs into historical light, is a Examples of great towns. collection of communities based on the lordship, the township, the parish, and the guild; and there is no reason to doubt that similar coincident causes helped the growth of such towns as York[5] and Exeter. Their size and power, and perhaps also the

---

hominibus regis et episcopi et comitis. Horum si quis de hundret remane-bat die quo sedebat sine excusatione manifesta x solidis emendabat inter regem et comitem;' Dom. i. 262.

[1] Palgrave, Commonwealth, p. 102; Somner's Canterbury, p. 32. It is however necessary to remember that a hundred might take its name from a borough, and the hundred court be held in the borough, without extinguishing the proper township court, or borough-moot.

[2] Edgar, iv. §§ 4, 5.   [3] Ibid. iii. § 5.

[4] See below in Chapter XI.

[5] 'In Eboraco civitate tempore regis Edwardi praeter scyram Archie-piscopi fuerunt sex scyrae. Una ex his wasta in castellis;' Dom. i. 298. The wards of Canterbury were called hundreds, or rather their courts were called hundred-courts; Somner, p. 52; App. vi. p. 4.

extent of the suburban common lands, entitled many of them to the name as well as the constitution of the hundred; Canterbury, Feversham, Norwich, Thetford, Cambridge[1], and many others, appear in Domesday as hundreds. But the basis of the system was that of the township or cluster of townships which had coalesced or grown up into the city organisation. The duty of 'burh-bot,' which formed part of the *trinoda necessitas*, threw the burden of repairing the fortifications on the land-owning townsmen and householders of the particular *burh*, or in some cases on the county; every *burh* was to be put in good repair within a fortnight of the Rogation days[2]; just as in Germany the duty of keeping the town hedge and ditch in order was a part of the general business of the village communities[3].

With the exception of the *burhs*, the townships were generally very small communities, and the heads of families would not be so numerous as to require a select body of magistrates. The *tun-gerefa*, answering to the schulz or schultheiss of the German *dorf*[4], and the tithingman, are the only officers of whom we read at all; the duties of the former were, like those of all the *gerefan*, connected with the fiscal as well as with the police administration; in the dependent townships he was the officer responsible for the production, and even for the credibility of his lord's men[5]; he may also have commanded them in the fyrd. In the free townships, he and the four best men were the legal representatives of the community in the court of the hundred and the shire[6]. The tithingman is only known as the executive officer of the police system of the hundred[7].

---

[1] Cambridge 'defendit se pro uno hundret;' Dom. i. 190.

[2] Athelstan, ii. § 15. See the customs of repairing the walls of Oxford, where the walls were maintained by the 'mansiones murales,' which were therefore free from all taxes save the trinoda necessitas; Domesday, i. 154; and those of Chester, where the repairs were executed by the county, one man serving for each hide of land; ibid. i. 262.

[3] G. L. von Maurer, Dorfverfassg. i. 356–361.

[4] Ibid. ii. 22–30; Waitz, D. V. G. ii. 350–353; Grimm, R. A. p. 755.

[5] Athelstan, iii. § 7.

[6] Hen. I, vii. § 8.

[7] I can find no authority whatever for regarding the tithingman as the head of the free township or tithing, and the tun-gerefa that of the dependent one. The apparent analogy of shireman, hundredman, and tithingman, with sheriff, hundred-reeve and town-reeve, is of course inviting, but

45. The union of a number of townships for the purpose of The hundred and wapentake. judicial administration, peace, and defence, formed what is known as the *hundred* or *wapentake*; a district answering to the *pagus* of Tacitus, the *hærred* of Scandinavia, the *huntari* or *gau*[1] of Germany. The terms wapentake and hundred are both, in Anglo-Saxon records, of somewhat late occurrence, and the exact steps by which they acquired their geographical application are among the vexed questions of English archæology. Perhaps the simplest theory is that, on English soil, both names belong primarily to the popular court of justice, and secondarily to the district which looked to that court as its judicial centre. This would enable us to dispense with any general speculation as to the symmetrical division of lands or the systematic concretion of minor communities.

The wapentake is found only in the Anglian districts, York- The wapentake. shire, Lincolnshire, Nottinghamshire, Derbyshire, Northampton-shire, Rutland, and Leicestershire. To the north of these districts the shires[2] are divided into wards, and to the south into hundreds. Hence the wapentake may be a relic of Scan- Danish origin. dinavian occupation. It finds a kindred form in the Norse *vapnatak*, which is however not applied to the district but to the form of ratifying the decisions of the local court by the clash of arms; a reminiscence of the primitive custom of the Germania: from this mode of acceptance it was transferred to the decisions themselves[3]. In the Icelandic *althing* the vap- The wapentake. natak was the word used for the closing of the court when the members 'resumed the weapons which had been laid aside during the session.' It is just possible that the uplifted shield which the tunginus set up at the opening of the mallus, or the custom of investing the young warrior with his arms, may

there is nothing in the earlier or later functions of the tithingman that gives him the character of a magistrate. He is the mere servant or executor of the law.

[1] Grimm, R. A. p. 532; Kemble (Saxons, i. 72) uses the word 'gá' for the aggregation of 'marks,' but the word is found only in one document of very questionable value, cf. pp. 81, 82; Gale, Script. XV, 748. See Gneist, Verwaltungsrecht, i. 47.

[2] The wapentake of Sadberge in Durham is one instance north of Tees. Script. Dunelm., App. xi; Boldon Buke, p. xxxvii.

[3] Grimm, R. A. p. 770; Schmid, p. 672; Vigfússon, Icel. Dict., p. 685.

have had some connexion with the name of wapentake. The Norman lawyers explained it in reference to the formal recognition of the local magistrate by touching his arms [1]; but this is more than questionable. In some way or other however it has reference to the armed gathering of the freemen, and so to the assembly rather than to the district which it represents. If we could argue from the fact that, in Lincolnshire, the hundreds appear as subdivisions of the wapentake, we might infer that the latter was in its origin the meeting of a cluster of associated hundreds for the purpose of armament, or contribution of armed men, under some such arrangement as provided that every three hundreds should furnish a ship, and every eight hides a helm and breastplate. But the data are too scanty to warrant more than a conjecture [2].

The hundred.

The hundred, which, like the wapentake, first appears in the laws of Edgar [3] as the name of an English institution, has its origin far back in the remotest German antiquity, but the use of it as a geographical expression is discoverable only in com-

The territorial hundred.

paratively late evidences. The *pagus* of the Germania sent its hundred warriors to the host, and appeared by its hundred judges in the court of the *princeps*. The Lex Salica contains abundant evidence that in the fifth century the administration of the hundred by the *tunginus* in the *mallus* was the chief, if not the only, machinery of the Frank judicial system [4]; and the word in one form or other enters into the constitution of all the German nations. It may be regarded then as a certain

Its relation to the hundreds of the Germania.

vestige of primitive organisation. But the exact relation of the territorial hundred to the hundred of the Germania is a point which is capable of, and has received, much discussion. It has been regarded as denoting simply a division of a hundred hides of land; as the district which furnished a hundred warriors to the host; as representing the original settlement of the hundred warriors; or as composed of a hundred hides,

[1] Edw. Conf. § 30. Cf. Grimm, R. A. 851, 852, 956; Sohm, p. 371.
[2] See below, p. 118.
[3] Edgar, i. Constitutio de hundredis. The wapentake is first mentioned in Edgar's Secular Law, § 6.
[4] Above, p. 59.

each of which furnished a single warrior[1]. The question is
not peculiar to English history, and the same result may
have followed from very different causes, as probably as from
the same causes, here and on the continent. It is very probable, as already stated, that the colonists of Britain arranged
themselves in hundreds of warriors; it is not probable that
they carved out the country into equal districts[2]. It may be
regarded as certain that they brought with them the judicial
institution which the Franks knew as the mallus or court of
the hundred. But if the judicial system were fully developed
when it was introduced, there is no reason to suppose that in
England it went anew through the whole process of development. It was enough that a hundred court should be erected
in every convenient district. The district which centered in
the hundred court would soon take the name of hundred, just
as the district which met at the wapentake court took the
name of wapentake. This may seem only one more unwar-

English hundreds.

[1] The several views are enumerated by Konrad Maurer; Philipps,
Turner, and Palgrave despair of any explanation; Lingard combats the
ideas of earlier inquirers without suggesting one of his own; Spelman
refers the hundred to the collective responsibility of an association like
the frankpledge; Leo takes a similar view. Verelius regarded it as
an aggregate of a hundred households; and Grimm (R. A. p. 533) accepts
the same notion. Ihre, with some diffidence, suggests that the hundred
was merely the district which furnished the hundred warriors; Schmid
and Lappenberg accept this. Eichhorn maintained that the hundred was
originally the personal union of the hundred warriors; and, on their
settlement, was used to denote the territorial area which they occupied. Vel-
schow and Waitz hold that a warrior was due from every hide of land, and
accordingly the hundred was at once an area of a hundred hides and a district responsible for a hundred warriors. Maurer himself follows the view
of Eichhorn, which is also Kemble's; Krit. Ueberschau, i. 77, 78. See too
Gneist, Verwaltungsrecht, i. 49, 50, 58, 59; Hallam, Mid. Ages, ii. 281.

[2] Neither the hundreds in England nor the shires appear ever to have
had common lands, like the *härraths-almanningar* and *lands-almanningar*
in Sweden, where the *bys-almanningar* answer to the common lands of
the township; K. Maurer, Krit. Ueberschau, i. 69. But too much stress
must not be laid on this statement. The several townships in the forest
of Knaresborough each had an allotment at the enclosure, and this seems
a fair instance of common lands of a hundred, although the particular hundred is regarded as a manor. Kemble regards the public buildings of the
county as representing the common land of the shire (i. 76). Whatever
was the case with the hundreds, before the shire system had become
general the idea of the common mark had given way to that of folkland.
If Sussex had folkland when it became part of Wessex, that folkland became part of the folkland of Wessex, did not remain as common land of
the shire to Sussex.

The hundred is the *pagus.* ranted speculation; but it need not interfere with the one warranted and reasonable conclusion that, under the name of geographical hundreds, we have the variously sized pagi or districts in which the original clusters of families or hundred warriors settled, or into which the new kings subdivided their realms; the extent and boundaries of these must have been determined by other causes, as the courses of the rivers, the ranges of hills, the distribution of estates to the chieftains, and the remnants of British independence.

Variety in size and distribution of hundreds, But although the numerical element may be thus eliminated, an equal difficulty remains; the variety in size and distribution which marks the existing hundreds. There are at the present day in England proper about 729 of these subdivisions, known as hundreds, wapentakes and wards; most of these are noted by name in Domesday book; all may be presumably as old as that record, and consequently very much older. Of these, 88 are included in the eight counties which constituted the old division known as the Mercian law, 241 in the fifteen counties of the Dane law, 30 in the districts not included in this arrangement, and not less than 370 in the nine counties of the West Saxon law. The seacoast counties are minutely subdivided; the closeness of organisation diminishes as we proceed inland or go northwards; the hundreds become thinner and larger and the name itself disappears, superseded by the wapentake and the ward.

Relation to the West Saxon administration. Now the West Saxon shires appear in history under their permanent names and with a shire organisation much earlier than those of Mercia and Northumbria; whilst Kent, Essex and East Anglia had throughout an organisation derived from their old status as kingdoms. It is in Wessex, further, that the hundredal division is, as we have seen, supplemented by that of the tithings. It may then be argued that the whole hundredal system radiates from the West Saxon kingdom, and that the variations mark the gradual extension of that power as it won its way to supremacy under Egbert and Ethelwulf, or recovered territory from the Danes under Alfred and Edward, Athelstan, Edmund, Edred and Edgar. If this be

VIEW OF THE SUBDIVISION OF ENGLAND INTO SHIRES, WAPENTAKES, AND HUNDREDS.

Shires.	Kingdoms.	Laws.	I. Sub-divisions.	II. Subdivisions into Wapentakes and Hundreds.[8]	Number in Domesday.	Number at present.	III. Subdivisions into Townships and Tithings.	Acreage.
Northumberland	Northumbria		Wards			6	Townships	1,290,312
Durham	Northumbria		Wards			4	Townships	647,502
Westmoreland	Northumbria and Strath-		Wards			4	Townships	500,956
Cumberland	clyde		Wards			5	Townships	970,161
Yorkshire	Northumbria		3 Ridings	1 Wapentake	15 W. 13 H.	31	Townships	3,882,851
Norfolk	East Anglia			Wapentakes	33	33	Townships	1,356,173
Suffolk	East Anglia			Hundreds	28	23	Townships	949,825
Essex	Essex			Hundreds	20	20	Townships	1,055,133
Nottinghamshire	Mercia			Wapentakes	7	6	Townships	526,176
Lincolnshire	Mercia	15 Shires of the Dane Law	3 Parts[1]	Wapentakes and Hundreds	30 W. 80 H.	27	Townships	1,767,962
Leicestershire	Mercia			Wapentakes and Hundreds	4	8	Townships	511,719
Derbyshire	Mercia			Wapentakes and Hundreds	6	6	Townships	656,243
Rutland	Mercia			Hundreds[2]	2 W. 3 H.	5	Townships	94,889
Northamptonshire	Mercia and East Anglia			Hundreds	28	19	Townships	639,912
Cambridgeshire	Mercia and East Anglia			Hundreds[3]	17	17	Townships	524,926
Huntingdonshire	Mercia			Hundreds	4	8	Townships	229,515
Buckinghamshire	Mercia			Hundreds	18	8	Townships	467,009
Bedfordshire	Mercia			Hundreds	12	9	Townships	295,509
Hertfordshire	Mercia and Essex			Hundreds	9	9	Townships	391,141
Middlesex	Mercia and Essex			Hundreds	6	6	Townships	181,317
Lancashire	Mercia and Northumbria			Hundreds	7	7	Townships	1,207,926
Cheshire	Mercia			Hundreds[4]	12	5	Townships	705,493
Staffordshire	Mercia	8 Shires of the Mercian Law		Hundreds	5	12	Townships	734,434
Shropshire	Mercia		Sipesocns	Hundreds	13	5	Townships and Tithings	841,167
Worcestershire	Mercia			Hundreds	12	4	Townships and Tithings	472,453
Warwickshire	Mercia			Hundreds	12	14	Townships	566,458
Oxfordshire	Mercia			Hundreds			Townships	470,095
Herefordshire	Mercia			Hundreds	19	11	Townships and Tithings	533,898
Gloucestershire	Mercia			Hundreds	39	30	Tithings	804,977
Somersetshire	Wessex			Hundreds	58	50	Tithings	1,049,815
Berkshire	Wessex			Hundreds	21	20	Tithings	450,132
Wiltshire	Wessex	9 Shires of the West Saxon Law		Hundreds	40	34	Tithings	859,303
Dorsetshire	Wessex			Hundreds	38	40	Tithings	627,265
Devonshire	Wessex			Hundreds	33	33	Tithings	1,655,161
Hampshire	Wessex			Hundreds	44	40	Tithings	1,032,105
Surrey	Wessex			Hundreds	13	14	Tithings	483,178
Sussex	Sussex		6 Rapes	Hundreds	58	71	Tithings	934,006
Kent	Kent		5 Lathes[5]	Hundreds	68	68	Tithings	1,004,984
Cornwall	West Saxon and Cornish			Hundreds	7	9	Vills	869,878

1 Lindsey is divided into three Ridings.   2 One Wapentake.   3 Including Ely.   4 Including two Hundreds in Flintshire.
5 Six and two half Lathes in Domesday.   6 Including Islandshire and Northamshire.   7 Including Sokes.

Alfred as
organiser.

allowed, the claim of Alfred, as founder not of the hundred-law, but of the hundredal divisions, may rest on something firmer than legend. As the national power extended northwards the recovered territory was consolidated into shires and hundreds, the latter becoming larger as the distance from the court increased, and as the larger and more ancient subdivisions adhered to their old associations. Other considerations lead to, or at least admit, a similar inference. The smallness and symmetry of the West Saxon and maritime hundreds suggests a closer organisation for defence. If, as seems unlikely, it should be held that the earlier the settlement the larger would be the allotments,—a doctrine which would not be necessarily true anywhere, and which need not be applied to England at all,—it might fairly be answered that the existing arrangement was the result of a redistribution at a later time, testifying to the greater activity and coherence of administrative order which led Wessex to her final supremacy.

The hypothesis of a redistribution under the West Saxon dynasty would meet almost every objection. The fact that a ship was due from every three hundreds will certainly help to account for the great number of the maritime hundreds, and the date of that enactment, which was in force under Edgar, may possibly be suggested as marking the final arrangements of these districts[1]. It has been already referred to as possibly bearing on the development of the wapentake.

Edgar's law
of the hun-
dred.

The fact that the hundred appears first in the laws of Edgar[2], and with an adaptation to a particular police in-

[1] See below, p. 118. Kemble's theory was that the increase of the size of the hundreds towards the interior of the country is owing to the fact that the original free families settled in close companionship on the coast, whilst in the interior they were placed at comparatively wide distances in the midst of a servile population; the hundred representing only the free settlers. But although the Saxon population was much thinner towards the West and the number of servi greater, the argument does not hold good; Gloucestershire and Wiltshire are as minutely subdivided as Devonshire and Dorsetshire.

[2] Edgar, i; Schmid, p. 183; Thorpe, p. 109; 'Hoc est judicium qualiter hundredum teneri debeat. c. 1. Imprimis ut conveniant semper ad iiii ebdomadas et faciat omnis homo rectum alii.... c. 5. Amplius diximus si hundredum minet vestigium in aliud hundredum, ut notificetur homini ipsius hundredi (A. S. hundredesmen) .... c. 7. In hundredo sicut in

stitution, the pursuit and capture of thieves, has sometimes
been held to mark the definite application of the name to the
territorial area, which may have been called wapentake, ward,
or even shire, at an earlier period. But the particular measure
then adopted implies the previous existence of the district
name [1]. In this case, we may refer to a parallel institution of The police
the Frank kings, Childebert and Clothair, three centuries and a hundred of
the Franks.
half before the days of Edgar; to which the introduction of
the name as that of a local division in the Frank kingdom has
been ascribed, although the hundred system is known from the
Salian law to have been in full working ages earlier [2].

The tradition preserved by William of Malmesbury, that The tra-
Alfred devised the arrangement into hundreds and tithings, Alfred.
although, as it stands, irreconcileable with facts, may, as has
been said already, embody a portion of a historical truth [3].
Alfred may have re-arranged the areas of the hundred-court
jurisdiction; or he may have adopted the hundred as a basis

---

omni placito (swa on other gemote) volumus ut rectum et jus publicum
judicetur in omni causa, et adterminetur quando hoc impleatur,' &c. The
other gemote must be the shiremoot and boroughmoot. See also Edgar, iii.
5; Schmid, p. 191. Brompton (Twysden, pp. 847, 848) places it amongst
Athelstan's laws, and so it was regarded by Palgrave, Commonwealth,
p. cxxi; it is however certainly later than Edmund, and can scarcely be
thrown later than Edgar. See Schmid, Gesetze, p. xlviii.

[1] Robertson, Scotland under her Early Kings, ii. 335, refers to this act
as the introduction of the territorial hundred: and regards the law of
Childebert and Clothair as instituting the same on the continent.

[2] Baluze, Capit. i. 14; Select Charters, p. 69. The words of Clothair,
A.D. 595, 'Decretum est ut qui ad vigilias, hoc est ad wactas, constituti
nocturnas diversos fures non caperent, eo quod per diversa intercedente
conludio scelera sua praetermissa custodias exercerent, centenas fierent'
—are scarcely strong enough to prove the usage an innovation; though
it may well have been an application of old machinery to a new purpose.
And Sohm, who has thoroughly examined the subject, decides that the
centenae now instituted were merely a police force arranged numerically
for the watching of the already existing territorial hundreds. Reichs- und
Gerichtsverfassg. i. 182–190.

[3] Will. Malmesb. G. R. ii. § 122: 'Et quia occasione barbarorum etiam
indigenae in rapinas anhelaverant, adeo ut nulli tutus commeatus esset
sine armorum praesidio, centurias quas dicunt hundrez, et decimas quas
thethingas vocant, instituit, ut omnis Anglus legaliter duntaxat vivens
haberet et centuriam et decimam. Quod si quis alicujus delicti insimu-
laretur, statim ex centuria et decima exhiberet qui eum vadarentur; qui
vero hujusmodi vadem non reperiret severitatem legum horreret. Si quis
autem reus vel ante vadiationem vel post transfugeret, omnes ex centuria
et decima regis mulctam incurrerent.'

of rating, as Edgar did for police; or he may have anticipated the measures of his descendant. If in the several recoveries of territory from the Danes, or conquests on the British border, a re-division or re-measurement of lands was requisite, either to satisfy old claims or to provide for the security of the frontier, it is probable that the measure of a hundred hides of land would be adopted, as in the reign of Ethelred it was for the purpose of taxation [1]. But the inequality of the hundreds, as we everywhere find it [2], precludes any hypothesis of a primitive symmetrical division on any such principle; and we may rest satisfied on the whole with recognising in the name the vestige of the primitive settlement, and, in the district itself, an earlier or a later subdivision of the kingdom to which it belonged ; possibly a greater mark, possibly a smaller shire.

Improbability of a symmetrical division.

The wapentake, so far as its history is illustrated by records, answers in all respects of administration directly to the hundred, and, except possibly the conjecture that it represents an association of smaller hundreds, no attempt has been made to refer it to a principle of symmetrical division. Nor is it easy to determine the origin of the variety of systems into which the hundred jurisdiction is worked. In Kent, for instance, the hundreds are arranged in Lathes or Lests ; and in Sussex in Rapes. The Lathe and the Rape may represent the undershires of the Heptarchic kingdom ; but the Lathe, which is an ancient, possibly a Jutish expression, is the organised judicial division of which the hundreds are mere geographical subdivisions, while the Rape, which was probably introduced by the Normans, is on the contrary a mere geographical ex-

The wapentake.

Various arrangements of the hundreds.

[1] Chron. Sax. A.D. 1008.
[2] Pearson, Hist. Maps, p. 51, discusses the statement of the Leiger book of Peterborough, that the hundred contained a hundred hides : he shows that the Domesday hidage in each of the counties of Bedford, Huntingdon, Northampton and Wilts, taken in the aggregate, nearly contains as many hundred hides as they do territorial hundreds, but without any agreement between the single hundred and the hundred hides. The document given by Ellis, Intr. to Domesday, i. 184, giving the hidage of Northamptonshire, shows variations in the several hundreds from 100 to 40 hides. Eyton (Shropshire, xii. 184) thinks that ‘ districts which were originally half-hundreds or quarter-hundreds came to be called hundreds ; ’ and this is certainly true in some cases.

pression, the judicial organisation remaining in the hundred[1]. In Cornwall, in the twelfth century, the subdivisions were not called hundreds but shires[2]; one of which, Triconscire, now the hundred of Trigg, is mentioned in Alfred's will[3]. York-shire was divided into Trithings or Ridings, subdivided gene-rally into wapentakes. Lincolnshire was divided into three parts, Lindsey, Kesteven, and Holland; Lindsey was sub-divided into three ridings, North, West and South; these ridings again were subdivided into wapentakes, and the wapen-takes into hundreds of twelve carucates each[4]. A similar arrangement prevailed in Rutland and probably in North-amptonshire, where also the wapentake is found[5]. The East riding of Yorkshire appears in Domesday as divided into hun-dreds, Holderness containing three, North, Middle and South; whilst in Richmondshire in the reign of Henry II, the ten-mentale, which contained fourteen carucates, and paid a geld of four shillings and sevenpence, must have been the result of a corresponding arrangement. Of the Yorkshire subdivisions two, Borgheshire and Craveshire, the latter of which is never called a wapentake, retain the name of shire; and it is given in later documents to Richmondshire, Kirbyshire, Riponshire, Hallamshire, Islandshire, Norhamshire, and probably other similar districts[6]. Nottinghamshire, Derbyshire, and Leicester-

(margin notes:) Ridings. Small shires of Yorkshire. Small shires.

---

[1] The names of the Lathes, Borowarlest, Wiwarlest, Limowarlest, Es-trelest, are clearly native and ancient; the Rapes assigned in Domesday to William of Braiose, William of Warenne, the Count of Eu, and the Earl Roger, seem more like a novelty. Lest or Lathe is the same word probably as Leet. Rape corresponds with the Norse and Icelandic Hrepp, which is now applied to 'a poor-law district,' and was perhaps introduced into Iceland in the eleventh century. See Vigfússon, Icel. Dict. s. v. Hrepp; Palgrave, Commonwealth, p. 101; Ellis, Intr. to Domesday, i. 178 sq.

[2] Simeon Dun. ed. Hinde, i. 221 : ' In Cornewalas sunt sex parvae scirae.'

[3] Cod. Dipl. ii. 114. Kemble explains Triconshire as Cornwall generally ; it is the Trigerscire hundred of the Pipe Roll of A.D. 1130, p. 159.

[4] Hearne, Liber Niger Scaccarii, pp. 399 sq.; Gale, Reg. Honoris de Richmond, p. 22.

[5] In Rutland, the wapentake of Alfnodestou contains two hundreds ; but half of it is in Turgastune wapentake, and half in Brochelestou, in Not-tinghamshire. Martinsley wapentake contains one hundred. Dom. i. 293 b.

[6] Robertson, Scotland under her Early Kings, ii. 433, is inclined to trace the trithing in Kent and Sussex ; Kent was divided into East and West, each arranged into three lathes, which in East Kent are double. Sussex was divided into East and West, each again divided into three

Variety of
arrangement.
shire are, in Domesday, arranged in wapentakes, but in one place the term 'hundred' is used in reference to a division of the last-named county. It may seem not impossible that the original name of the subdivision immediately above the township was scir or shire, a term of various application. The city of York was divided into seven shires [1], and the use of the word in northern Northumbria, the present Lowlands of Scotland, a territory which was peopled by Saxons and little disturbed by Danish aggression, points to the same conclusion [2]. It would be rash however even to attempt a generalisation on these obscure differences, much more so to attempt to force them into conformity with the local arrangements existing under the later Scandinavian institutions whose symmetry testifies to an artificial origin [3].

Chief officer
of the hundred.
The presiding officer of the hundred or wapentake bears various names: nor is it quite certain that we are right in ascribing the functions so denoted to a single magistrate. The *centenarius* or *thunginus* was under the Salian law the head of his hundred, elected by the national council; he exercised his jurisdiction in company with the king's sacebaro, and in Merovingian times in subordination to the graf, the royal repre-

rapes. In the trithing he sees the threefold division of the land allotted to the Norse odallers; thus Yorkshire and Lindsey, which were so divided, represented the lands measured out by Halfdane in A.D. 876 : the other portions of the Danish conquests being left to their Saxon proprietors, under the special rule of the king : the trithings were thus left as odalland, and the other parts as gafol-land or tributary. The view is very interesting, but very conjectural.

[1] Above, p. 101, note 5.

[2] See, for example, the Records of the Priory of May, Cartae, p. 3: 'Sira de Chellin,' 'Sira de Cherel ;' p. 5, 'Sire de Erdros.' The diocese of St. Aldhelm is called Selwoodshire by Ethelwerd, M. H. B. p. 507.

[3] The idea of Sachse (Grundlagen des Deutschen Staats- und Rechtslebens, §§ 11, 12) is that each kingdom was divided into four provinces, each province into three shires; each shire into three trithings, each trithing into four hundreds; each hundred into twelve tithings and each tithing into twelve free households; Gneist, Verwaltgsr. i. 55. Mr. Robertson's theory, which however is put forth only as a theory, makes a square league equal to a turbe or tithing; four tithings a small shire or barony; three such shires one hundred; three hundreds one quarter; two quarters one larger shire or fylki; and two such shires one province or thiufada; Essays, p. 131. Palgrave, Commonwealth, p. 97, arranges East Anglia in hundreds, distributed in four head leets or tribes, and each tribe divided into three subordinate leets.

sentative in the larger province of which the hundred was
a subdivision[1]. The officer answering to the centenarius in
England may be the hundreds-ealdor[2], to whom the laws of
Edgar direct the townsmen to refer in questions of witness, or
the hundred-man who with his tithing-men goes forth to execute justice on the thief[3]. The officer who, according to the
law of Edward the Elder, holds the monthly court, that is the
court which we know as the hundred-court, is called the
gerefa[4]. The headman of the wapentake is called in the laws
of Ethelred likewise the gerefa[5]. It is possible to trace here
the existence of two officers, answering to the graf and the
centenarius of the Merovingian period of Frank law; the representative of the king's interest in the gerefa, who becomes
after the Conquest the bailiff of the hundred; and the representative of the freemen in the hundredes-ealdor, who also survives the Conquest and is found in the thirteenth century,
as the elected ealdorman of the hundred, representing his hundred in the shire-moot[6]. There is not sufficient evidence to
allow us to claim for the hundred-man the presidency of the
hundred-court; that seems to belong to the *gerefa*[7]: and later
usage would incline us to regard him as the convener rather
than the chairman. The hundred-man of the Exeter Domesday is simply the collector of the fees, *fegadrus*[8]. But at the

Possible double go-vernment of the hundred.

Hundred-reeve and Hundred-man.

[1] Above, p. 59. Sohm, Fr. G. V. G. pp. 154, 162.
[2] Edgar, iv. §§ 8, 10.   [3] Ibid. i. §§ 2, 4, 5.
[4] The gerefa, mentioned in Edward, ii. 8, must also have been the reeve
of the hundred or wapentake. See Schmid, Gesetze, p. 589. Cf. Palgrave,
Commonwealth, p. 99. The mot-gerefa of Edward the Confessor's charter
to Abingdon, Kemble, C. D. iv. 200, is doubtless the same. In Domesday
he is the praefectus, or praepositus hundredi ; Ellis, Introd. i. 188.
[5] Ethelred, iii. § 3.
[6] Hen. I, viii. § 1. See Palgrave, Commonwealth, pp. 635, cccli : ' Et
hundreda baroniae (de Aquila) dant ad auxilium Vicecomitis £9 17s. 6d.
per quod barones et milites totius baroniae quieti sunt de secta ad comitatum, salvis Aldermannis Hundredorum qui faciunt sectam ad comitatum
pro hundredo ; ' Rot. Hund. ii. 204, 205. ' Bedellus qui vocatur Aldre-
man, qui dat pro balliva sua per annum quatuor marcas, et nihil habet de
certo de quo possit dictam firmam levare, nisi quod poterit extorquere de
populo sibi subdito, et injuste. Et aliquo tempore solebant hujusmodi
bedelli eligi per sectatores hundredi, et tunc parum vel nihil dederunt pro
balliva sua ; ' Ibid. ii. 214.
[7] See p. 116, note 1.
[8] Domesd. iii. ff. 65 sq.

time at which the name first occurs, the management and profits of the local courts had already passed into the hands of the great men to whom the name of land-rica is given, and who appear later as lords having sac and soc in whole hundreds and wapentakes. This change must have tended to depress the status of all elected officers, although it might not much affect the judicial process: the old names continue, but the reeve or grave of the hundred-court is the servant rather than the president, whilst the hundreds-ealdor has sunk to the position of a bedel. On analogy, however, we may fairly maintain that the original hundred-man or hundredes-ealdor was an elected officer, and the convener and constituting functionary of the court which he held.

Hundred-
moot.

46. This court, the hundred-gemot or wapentake court, was held every month[1], according to the laws of Edward and Edgar; but the term of thirty days for the completion in one gemot of the work begun in a previous one is at least as early as the reign of Egbert[2]. In this point we fail to find any very exact analogy among the continental courts of law. The meetings of the German mallus, ding, or placitum varied in different regions and eras. Under the Salian law according to one view the court was held weekly, according to another at intervals of forty days.

Times of
meeting.

By the Alemannian law the conventus was weekly in troubled times, fortnightly in the time of peace. The Bavarians however met ordinarily every month; if there were a need, every fortnight[3]. The meeting of the English hundred-moot was summoned seven days beforehand, and could not be held on a Sunday. It was termed *gemot*, *thing*, or *methel*, the last name, which occurs in the Kentish laws, being equivalent to the Frankish *mallus*[4].

Place of
meeting.

The place of meeting was notified by the summoner; it may have originally been the place from which the territorial hundred or wapentake took its name. This class of names is

---

[1] Edw. ii. § 8; Edgar, i. § 1; iii. § 5; Canute, E. 15; Henr. §§ 7, 51.
[2] See Kemble, Cod. Dipl. No. 218.
[3] See Waitz, D. V. G. i. 342–345; ii. 460, 461; Sohm, Fr. G. V. G. i. 396.
[4] Cf. Legg. Hen. I, c. 89, § 3; an extract from a Capitulary.

itself very curious. In the south of England the names of the Names of
Hundreds. hundreds are often derived from those of the central towns; but in the midland and northern districts they seem like echoes of a wilder and more primitive society. The Yorkshire wapentake of Skyrack recalls the Shire Oak as the place of meeting; so in Derbyshire we have Appletree, in Hertfordshire Edwinstree, in Herefordshire Webtree and Greytree; in Worcestershire Doddingtree, in Leicestershire Gartree. Osgodcross, Ewcross, Staincross, Buckross, mark centres of jurisdiction which received names after the acceptance of Christianity. Claro or Clarhow in Yorkshire was the moot-hill of its wapentake; similarly Leicestershire has Sparkinho, Norfolk Greenho and Grimshoe, and Lincolnshire Calnodshoe. Others preserve the name of some ancient lord or hero, as the Worcestershire Oswalds-law and the Lincolnshire Aslacoe; or the holy well, as the Yorkshire Hallikeld. The Suffolk Thingoe preserves a reminiscence of the court itself as the Thing. These may all have been originally the constant moot-places of the hundreds; but at a later period and in the larger wapentakes the court was held at different villages in rotation; a rule which must have greatly facilitated the breaking up of the hundredal jurisdiction into manorial courts leet.

The court was attended by the lords of lands within the hundred, or their stewards representing them, and by the parish priest, the reeve, and four best men of each township[1]. The Judges of the
hundred-
moot. judges of the court were the whole body of suitors, the freeholders answering to the 'rachimburgii' of the Franks; but as various inconveniences might arise from the uncertainty of the number, qualifications, or attendance of the whole, a representative body of twelve seems to have been instituted as a judicial committee of the court. These twelve may have been in some cases like the scabini or schöffen[2], a fixed body holding their

---

[1] Hen. I, vii. §§ 4, 7; li. § 2.

[2] Compare Savigny, i. 239, who argues that the official scabini were instituted by Charles the Great. Seven scabini were requisite for a full mallus; Ibid. i. 248. See also Sohm, Fr. G. V. G. i. 377, 380. No other freemen but the scabini and the vassi comitum were compelled to attend the extraordinary or specially summoned placita after the capitulary of A.D. 803; Sohm, p. 375. Dr. Sohm holds that the Merovingian kings

appointment for life; or like the lawmen of Lincoln, the hereditary owners of sac and soc in the territory; or chosen merely for the occasion, like the Salian rachimburgs. They may be discovered in the twelve thegns of the wapentake, who by the law of Ethelred declared the report of the district in the gemot[1]; or in the twelve chosen witnesses of Edgar's law, before whom all bargains and sales are to be transacted[2]; in the thirty-six 'barons' or twenty-four 'judices' chosen in the East Anglian county courts to determine the suits of Ramsey and Ely[3]; and in the twelve legal men of the hundred, who are directed in the Assize of Clarendon[4] to act as part of the Grand Jury before the judges in Eyre, and who play so important a part in the legal reforms of Henry II and his ministers.

The ealdorman in the hundred-moot.

Whether the ealdorman of the shire, the sheriff or the bishop, sat regularly in the hundred court at any period may be doubted[5]: the number of hundreds in each shire must have prevented a monthly attendance at each, and it is more likely that the one or two occasions on which the ealdorman is mentioned as present were cases of exceptional importance. The sheriff may not improbably have been represented by a deputy, 'gingra'[6] or junior; who would look after the king's rights.

Jurisdiction of the hundred.

The hundred court was entitled to declare folk right in every suit[7]; its jurisdiction was criminal as well as civil, and volun-

reduced the number of malli to two a year in each hundred, and that Charles increased them to three: but Waitz holds a different view.

[1] 'Let pleas be held in each wapentake, and let the twelve senior thegns go out and the reeve with them and swear on the halidome which shall be put in their hands that they will accuse no innocent man and conceal no guilty one;' Ethelred, iii. § 3. 'Et judicium stet ubi tayni consenserint; si dissideant, stet quod ipsi viii dicent;' Ibid. § 13. K. Maurer, Krit. Ueberschau, v. 389, refers this to the Danelaw only: and its whole purport is contested by Brunner, Schwurgericht, pp. 402, 403. See below, § 164.　　　　　　　　　　　　　　　　　[2] Edgar, iv. §§ 4, 5.

[3] Hist. Ramsey, Gale, p. 415: 'xxxvi barones de amicis utriusque partis pari numero electos, ipsi judices constituerunt.' Hist. Ely, Gale, p. 471: 'coram xxiv judicibus.' 'Tandem veniens Aegelwinus Alderman ad Granteburge habuit ibi grande placitum civium et hundretanorum coram xxiv judicibus;' Ibid. p. 478; cf. Legg. Henr. I, c. 29.

[4] Select Charters, p. 137. See also Hallam, M. A. ii. 386 sq.

[5] Gneist, Verwaltungsrecht, i. 78; Palgrave, Commonwealth, pp. 98, 99.

[6] Alfred, 38, § 2, speaks of the king's ealdorman's gingra or junior as holding pleas. They are mentioned also in three charters of Berhtwulf king of Mercia; Kemble, C. D. ii. pp. 14, 25, 34.　　　　　[7] Edgar, i. § 7.

tary as well as contentious. It tried criminals, settled disputes, and witnessed transfers of land. The testimony of the country and the record of the law were supplemented by the compurgatory oath and ordeal. It had also a common chest which divided the profits of jurisdiction with the king and the lord or land-rica[1]; and no suit might be carried to a higher court unless it had been refused justice in the hundred[2]. It had a special peace protected by a special fine; its suitors were under special protection of the law on their way to and from it; and those who neglected the special summons to it were fined[3].

As was the case with the township, the organisation of the hundred lent itself readily to the judicial, ecclesiastical and fiscal developments of later times. The criminal jurisdiction of the hundred is perpetuated in the manorial court leet. On the institution of the frankpledge, a hundred court was held twice a year to ascertain the observance of the law[4]. This became the business of the sheriff's tourn of later times, held twice a year, in the octave of Easter and Michaelmas, in different parts of the county. It was the great court leet, as the old hundred court was the court baron of the hundred, and the county court that of the shire[5]: the distinction of origin being maintained in the principle that in the courts baron, whether in the manor, the hundred or the shire, the suitors were the judges, whilst it was otherwise in the courts leet[6], and in the sheriff's tourn

The hundred court as sheriff's tourn.

---

[1] Edgar, i. § 3. The peace given in the hundred or wapentake was, when broken, amended by the payment of a fine of eight pounds. This fine bore the name of hundred, possibly as being the hundred-fine, possibly as being the sum of a hundred (120) ores (of 15*d.* each). This hundred is often mentioned both in the laws and in Domesday as a measure of account. In Lincolnshire the peace given by the king's hand is amended by the payment of 18 hundreds, of which a third goes to the earl, two thirds to the king; Domesd. i. 336. 'Forisfacturam hundredi Dani et Norwicenses vocabant viii libras;' Ll. Edw. Conf. c. 24.

[2] Athelstan, i. § 3; Edgar, iii. 2; Canute, ii. 17, 19.

[3] It would seem from the Legg. Henr. I, c. 29, that the *judices* were specially summoned and fined for non-attendance. For some illustrations see below, p. 128, note 4.

[4] Hen. I, viii. § 1.   [5] Blackstone, Comm. iii. 33, 34; iv. 273.

[6] Viner's Abridgment, vii. 8. Although the suitors are judges in the court baron, the steward is judge in the court customary of the copyholders, a result of the early depression of the free into dependent townships, as well as of the later organisation of manors.

among them, the steward being judge in the leet, the sheriff judge in the tourn[1]. The criminal jurisdiction of the hundred was early cut up by grants of sac and soc, and later on was lost or merged in the general jurisdiction of the crown exercised by the judges in assize, in which it appears only as helping to constitute the juries.

The hundred as an area for rating.

There can be no doubt that the organisation of the hundred had a fiscal importance, not merely as furnishing the profits of fines and the produce of demesne or folkland, but as forming a rateable division of the county. The fiscal system of the Anglo-Saxons is very obscure ; and it may be questioned whether any money taxation properly so called ever existed before the imposition of Danegeld by Ethelred the Unready. The tribute from the remaining folkland, and the rent of the royal demesne, which was scarcely a tax, sufficed for most of the expenses of the king's household. The obligations of the trinoda necessitas were discharged by personal service. The profits however of each hundred were no doubt accounted for by the sheriffs, and when general taxation became necessary it would be collected by the same machinery. When King Edgar confirmed the bishop of Worcester in the possession of his estates he made up the amount of land by new grants to the extent of three hundreds, which he directed to furnish one scypfylled or 'navipletio'[2] to the national fleet. In the year 1008 Ethelred ordered that a ship should be furnished by every three hundred hides[3], and we learn from Domesday that the hundred of Oswald's law, comprising the three hundreds of Edgar's charter, contained three hundred hides[4]. It may be inferred then that every three hundreds were liable to be called on to furnish one ship,

---

[1] Viner's Abridgment, vi. 586 ; vii. 3.

[2] Dugdale, Mon. Angl. i. 617, 618 : 'Scilicet ut ipse episcopus cum monachis suis de istis tribus centuriatibus ... constituant unam navipletionem quod Anglice dicitur scypfilled oththe Scypborne.' Kemble, C. D. vi. 240, for the last word reads ' scypsocne.' The town of Bedford paid towards ships as much as a third of a hundred; Domesd. i. 209. Warwick furnished four batsweins ; Ibid. i. 238.

[3] Chron. Sax. A.D. 1008.

[4] Domesd. i. 172 : 'Ecclesia S. Mariae ... habet unum hundret quod vocatur Oswaldeslaw, in quo jacent ccc hidae.'

whilst every ten hides were accountable for a boat, and every eight hides for a helm and breastplate [1].

47. In Anglo-Saxon as in later times, there existed, as is generally believed, side by side with the hundreds and wapentakes, large *franchises* or *liberties* in which the jurisdiction, or at least the execution and profit of jurisdiction, was vested in private hands [2]. The particular rights thus exercised were termed sac and soc, to which others, toll and team and the like, were frequently added [3]. In some grants of land exemption from the hundred is specially mentioned [4], in which case the grantee would hold the courts on his own estate. In other cases the jurisdiction of the hundred is itself granted, even when the ownership of the soil was not affected by the grant. In the latter

Franchises or liberties.

---

[1] Chron. Sax. A.D. 1008, with Earle's note, pp. 336, 337.

[2] To these exempt districts the name of *sithesocn* has been given, on somewhat scanty authority, indicating their origin in a grant by the king to one of his gesiths or companions, of an estate upon which he may enjoy all the rights and profits that had belonged to the king, nominating the officers and exercising the jurisdiction. The word ' sithesocn ' does not occur in any ancient document, unless in the form ' sipessocna,' which Dugdale and other scholars following him regarded as a misreading of ' sipesocna.' It is found in the laws of Henry I, vi. § 1, and two or three times in the Pipe Rolls. In the Pipe Roll of 16 Hen. II the hundreds of Warwickshire, which were ten or twelve in Domesday, appear as four sipesocnas. This instance certainly seems to favour the opinion of Archdeacon Hale, who argued from the use of the word ' scypsocne ' in Edgar's charter, quoted above, p. 118, n. 2, that it referred to the association of three hundreds to provide a ship's crew; Hale, Register of Worcester, p. xxxiii. This explanation illustrates the conjecture that the original wapentake was based on a like principle. Anyhow, the disputed word cannot be taken as an authentic term for the jurisdiction of a franchise. See Robertson, Scotland under her Early Kings, ii. 336, 457; Essays, p. lxvi; Dugdale's Warwickshire, p. 4; Thorpe, Anglo-Saxon Laws, p. 221; Lappenberg, ii. 331.

[3] See for examples, Kemble, C. D. iv. 138, 187, 233, 247.

[4] Edward the Confessor frees certain lands of Westminster from the shire and the hundred; Kemble, C. D. iv. 191, 213. There were seven hundreds in Worcestershire, ' ita quieti, sicut scira dicit, quod vicecomes nichil habet in eis;' Domesd. i. 172. Mr. Adams, Essays on Anglo-Saxon Law, p. 44, declares against the existence of private jurisdictions before the Conquest, and insists on the uniform hundredal jurisdiction as the only real jurisdiction in such reputed cases. The importance of the point is legal rather than historical. No doubt the hundred law (' secundum hundret' Will. I, Thorpe, p. 213) was administered in all these courts, but there is no difficulty in supposing a bishop, or even a private magnate being put in the place of the king's official representative in such courts and so constituting a hereditary private jurisdiction. Mr. Adams also urges that the word soken, *socn,* before the Conquest does not mean jurisdiction, but the profit of jurisdiction (p. 43), the exaction of the fines of jurisdiction.

case the status of the free tenant within the hundred would not
be at first changed by the gift. Far the largest proportion of
these jurisdictions belonged to the churches and coincided with
the ownership of the soil, which the clergy leased out to their
sokemen on fairly liberal terms: Edward the Confessor gave the
hundred of Hornemere to Abingdon [1], and that of Goddelie to
Chertsey [2]. The extent to which these exemptions must have
weakened the hundred organisation may be inferred from the
statement that the thegn holding five hides often if not always
had a right of magistracy, a burh-geat-setl [3]. But although separated from the body of the hundred in this way, the liberties were
not exempt from the jurisdiction or organisation of the shire, and
may be regarded as private hundreds standing to the others in
a relation analogous to that which existed between the free township and the manor of the lord : and they are often regarded simply
as larger manors. In all these the machinery of the hundred or
wapentake was strictly preserved, and the law was administered
on the same principle. The sokemen elected their officers and
made report, the steward of the lord acting as president in their
courts and leading them in a separate body to the host. This
is especially provided by Edgar in the charter already referred
to : the tenants of the see of Worcester are to fulfil their military
duties not with the king's servants or the exactors of the hundred, but under the bishop as their archiductor [4].

The courts of the great franchises, where they still exist, will be
found to furnish the best instances of the ancient constitution of
the hundred court : for they were less touched than the hundred
courts themselves by general legislation, and have preserved
their constitution in greater integrity. In the courts of the
Forest of Knaresborough each of the townships or berewics

*The hundred
court in
private
hands.*

*Modern
illustrations.*

---

[1] Kemble, C. D. iv. 200. In Domesday, i. 280, the Countess Godeva
is said to have had sac and soc in the whole wapentake of Newark.

[2] Kemble, C. D. iv. 206, 207. The jurisdiction of eight hundreds and
a half was granted by the same king to S. Edmund's ; Ibid. iv. 243, 253 ;
vi. 203. The gifts of hundreds to Ely and Peterborough by Edgar, ibid.
iii. 61, 93, are of questionable authenticity.

[3] Ranks, § 2.

[4] Mon. Angl. i. 617. So in Domesday, i. 87, the men of Taunton attend
the courts of the bishop of Winchester : ' profectio in exercitum cum hominibus episcopi.'

which form the manor of the forest is represented by the constable and four men [1]; from these the jurors of the leet are
chosen; and by them the praepositus or grave, and the bedel.
In the manor of Wakefield the representation is by the constable
and two men, just as in 1181 in the half hundred of Chingford
in Essex the tenants of St. Paul's were represented by the reeve
and two men [2]. There is no ground for connecting the hundred
with the tithing of frankpledge, other than the right of the former
to view the frankpledges in a half-yearly court. In the ecclesiastical system the hundred bore the same relation to the deanery
rural as the township bore to the parish: but the deaneries
do not always coincide geographically with the hundreds.

48. Between the hundred, or wapentake, and what is now
the shire, it is possible that other intermediate divisions may at
an early period have come in; answering to the trithings and
ridings of Yorkshire and Lincolnshire, the rapes of Sussex and
the lathes of Kent. If this were the case they may have had
courts of their own as is the case with the lathe, and officers of
their own such as the trithing-reeve and the leide-reeve who
occur in two manuscripts of the so-called laws of Henry I [3]. The
trithings of Lincolnshire and Yorkshire had their moots in the
age of the Conqueror, although little is known of them [4]. There
is however no evidence of any such general arrangement. The
association of two, three or more hundreds is occasionally mentioned as used for the purpose of witness [5], a custom which may
be interpreted as the relic of some more symmetrical arrangement, but is more probably a mere expedient for extending the
application of the compurgatory system. The reduction of the
numbers of Domesday hundreds to the existing number, in
several of the Midland counties, may be accounted for on such
a principle of association or combination. All the intermediate
districts which bear the name of shire, and have been already
referred to, are of too late formation to illustrate this supposition.

Interme-diate divi-sions: com-binations of hundreds.

[1] Hargrove, Hist. of Knaresborough (ed. 1798), pp. 44, 45.
[2] Hale, Domesday of St. Paul's, p. 144.
[3] Schmid, Gesetze, p. 663.
[4] See Ellis's Introduction to Domesday (folio ed.), p. lvii.
[5] Ethelred, i. 1, § 3; Canute, ii. 30, § 3; Hist. Ely, pp. 473, 475, 479.

The lathe system in Kent answers closely to that of the hundred elsewhere, and all the existing machinery of the ridings, save the name and boundaries, is comparatively modern [1].

The shire.

The name scir or shire, which marks the division immediately superior to the hundred, merely means a subdivision or share of a larger whole, and was early used in connexion with an official name to designate the territorial sphere appointed to the particular magistracy denoted by that name. So the diocese was the bishop's scire [2], and the stewardship of the unjust steward is called in the Anglo-Saxon translation of the Gospel his groefscire [3]. We have seen that the original territorial hundreds may have been smaller shires [4]. The historical shires or counties owe their origin to different causes [5]. Kent and Sussex are two of the Heptarchic kingdoms, of which their lathes and rapes are perhaps the original shires. Kent however appears as 'Cantescyre' as early as the reign of Athelstan [6]. Essex, Middlesex and Surrey are also ancient kingdoms. Norfolk and Suffolk are the two divisions of East Anglia, representing possibly the two ' fylkis ' or folks into which the Norsemen divided their province [7], or possibly the two dioceses assigned to Elmham and Dunwich before the invasions of the Danes. Of the Northumbrian kingdom, Yorkshire is the only one of the

Creation of modern shires.

[1] The territorial arrangements of the Domesday hundreds are now so much changed that it is dangerous to generalise from them, but some instances may be given. Buckinghamshire in Domesday contained eighteen hundreds ; these are now combined into five hundreds of three each, and three old hundreds which also have a collective name, the Chiltern hundreds. The twelve Domesday hundreds of Warwickshire were reduced to four before the reign of Henry II by some similar process. (Rot. Hund. ii. 225.) The arrangement in threes may be as old as the navipletio referred to above (p. 118). Of the twelve hundreds of Worcestershire, only five were geldable at the time of the Inquest. Lancashire and Leicestershire, which Mr. Robertson (Essays, p. 120) refers to as retaining the ancient division into six hundreds (above, p. 112, note 3), have been somewhat re-arranged since the Domesday Survey, but the fact may go in support of the same theory.

[2] Bede, H. E. iii. 7, &c. &c. (Alfred).

[3] Lindisfarne Gospels, iii. 130 ; St. Luke xvi. 2.

[4] Above, pp. 110, 111.

[5] On this see Palgrave, Commonwealth, pp. 116, 117; Gneist, Verwaltungsrecht, i. 56, 57.

[6] Athelstan, ii : ' omnes Cantescyrae thaini ;' possibly only a late translation of an Anglo-Saxon document; Thorpe, p. 91.

[7] Robertson, Hist. Essays, p. 120.

existing subdivisions which dates as a shire before the Conquest.
Mercia, during its existence as a kingdom, was arranged in five Shires of Mercia;
regions none of which bore the name of shires: Lindsey, the
district of the Lindisfari and diocese of Sidnacester; Hwiccia
the diocese of Worcester and its appendant Magasætania; Mercia
proper with its bishop of Lichfield and its royal city at Tam-
worth; Middle Anglia and South Anglia, dependent ecclesiastically on Leicester and later on Dorchester. These represent
the early settlements out of which the Mercian kingdom was
created by Penda and his immediate predecessors, and which
were arranged as dioceses by Theodore before their several
nationality had been forgotten; nor were they rearranged as
shires and named after their chief towns before the reconquest
of Mercia from the Danes under Edward the Elder. In Wessex of Wessex;
however the division is more ancient; Ini speaks of the Scirman;
the names Hamptonscire, Defnascire, and Bearrocscire[1] appear
in the Anglo-Saxon Chronicle as early as the reign of Ethelwulf,
side by side with the Dorsætas, the Wilsætas, and the Sumer-
sætas. As the earliest possible date of the Chronicle is the age
of Alfred, it is not impossible that the arrangement may be due
to that king[2]: but it is probably much earlier, and determined
by the divisions of the early settlements of the West Saxons, or
their successive conquests. The terminology was not however
general in the time of Bede, who knew only the larger provinces
of Mercia as regiones, mægths or settlements of kindred tribes,
and those of Wessex as dioceses. The arrangement of the whole
kingdom in shires is of course a work which could not be completed until it was permanently united under Edgar; and the
existing sub-divisions of Southern England are all traceable
back to his day at the latest. The Northern counties have of North-umbria.
undergone some changes since the Conquest, although the new
lines have been drawn on older landmarks: Durham is the
county palatine of the Conqueror's minister, formed out of the
patrimony of St. Cuthbert; Lancashire was formed in the

[1] Chron. Sax. A.D 851, 860.
[2] Gneist, Verwaltungsrecht, i. 56, considers A.D. 880 as the most probable date, and inclines to connect the division with the treaty arrangements of Alfred and Guthrum.

twelfth century by joining the Mercian lands between Ribble and Mersey with the northern hundreds, which in Domesday were reckoned to the West Riding of Yorkshire; Cumberland is the English share of the old Cumbrian or Strathclyde kingdom; Northumberland and Westmoreland are the remnants of Northumbria and the Cumbrian frontier, appropriated ecclesiastically to Durham or York, and temporally to Appleby and Newcastle.

The constitutional machinery of the shire thus represents either the national organisation of the several divisions created by West Saxon conquest; or that of the early settlements which united in the Mercian kingdom, as it advanced westwards; or the rearrangement by the West Saxon dynasty of the whole of England on the principles already at work in its own shires. A shire system had been at work in Wessex as early as the
Question as
to an earlier
name for the
shire.
reign of Ini[1]. Whether, before the name of shire was introduced into Mercia, the several mægths or regions bore any common designation, such as that of *gau*, must remain in entire obscurity. There is extant a list of thirty-four divisions of England, gathered out of Bede and perhaps other sources now lost, and recording the number of hides contained in each; the termination 'ga' which is found here, in some cases, may be the German 'gau'; but the age and value of the document are very uncertain, and the divisions as a rule do not correspond with the historical shires[2].

Each shire contained a number of hundreds, so various however that it seems almost impossible to suppose that in any case it was arranged on a numerical principle; although, as each three hundreds had to supply a ship, the number of hundreds in each of the later constituted shires might be expected to be a
multiple of three. The organisation of the shire was of much the same character as that of the hundred, but it was ruled by an ealdorman as well as by a gerefa, and in some other respects bore evidence of its previous existence as an independent unity.

[1] The scir-man is spoken of as the president of a court, Ini, § 8; the ealdorman may forfeit his *scir*, ibid. § 39; and the dependent is forbidden to withdraw from his lord into another *scir*, ibid. § 36.

[2] Gale, Rer. Angl. Scriptores, xv. 748; Kemble, Saxons, i. 81, 82; two of the ga's are Noxga-ga and Ohtga-ga.

Its gemot was not only the scir-gemot but the folc-gemot [1] also, the assembly of the people; its ealdorman commanded not merely the military force of the hundreds, but the lords of the franchises and the church vassals with their men. Its gerefa or sheriff collected the fiscal as well as the local imposts. Its ealdorman was one of the king's witan.

49. The ealdorman, the princeps of Tacitus, and princeps [2], or satrapa, or subregulus of Bede, the dux of the Latin chroniclers and the comes of the Normans, was originally elected in the general assembly of the nation, and down to the Norman Conquest, even when hereditary succession had become almost the rule, his nomination required the consent of the king and the witenagemot. There is no reason to suppose that he was ever elected by the body over which he was to rule [3], although some form of acceptance by the shire may not improbably have been gone through. The hereditary principle appears however in the early days of the kingdom as well as in those of Edward the Confessor; in the case of an under-kingdom being annexed to a greater, the royal dynasty seems to have continued to hand down its delegated authority from father to son. The under-kings of Hwiccia thus continued to act as ealdormen under Mercia for a century; and the ealdormanship of the Gyrwas [4] or fen-countrymen seems likewise to have been hereditary. The title of ealdorman is thus much older than the existing division of shires, nor was it ever the rule for every shire to have an ealdorman to itself as it had its sheriff. The ealdormanship of Mercia comprised a very large portion of the Mercian kingdom; Wessex in the reign of Ethelred was arranged under two ealdormen [5]. But each shire was under an ealdorman, who sat

[Marginal notes:] The ealdorman. Nominated by the king and witan. Hereditary succession. The ealdorman administered several shires.

[1] Alfred, 38, § 1; Athelstan, ii. § 12; v. 1, § 1; Ethelred, v. § 13; vi. § 22.
[2] Ealdorman stands for *princeps*, Bede, H. E. iii. 15; and, generally, for *optimas*, iii. 30; for *subregulus*, iv. 12; for *satrapa*, v. 10; for *dux*, iv. 13, 15. The first writer who uses 'comes' as equivalent to ealdorman is Asser, and the fact has been used as an argument against the genuineness of his book. It occurs however in some of the questionable charters of Ethelwulf apparently in the same sense; Kemble, C. D. ii. 50; v. 97.
[3] Gneist, Verwaltungsrecht, i. 76.
[4] Bede, H. E. iii. 20; iv. 19; Hugo Candidus (Sparke, p. 2); Felix, Vita S. Guthlac.; Mabillon, Acta Sanctorum, iii. 260.
[5] On this point Mr. Robertson's essay on the 'King's kin' (Essays, pp.

with the sheriff and bishop in the folkmoot, and received a third
part of the profits of the jurisdiction[1], a proportion which represents no doubt the composition for the breach of the peace
which according to Tacitus was paid to the civitas, and which
bore the name of *fredus* in the Frank law. He also commanded
the military force of the whole division. From the latter
character he derived the name of heretoga[2], leader of the host
(*here*), or dux, which is occasionally given him in charters and
which marks the military function as the chief distinction of the
ealdorman.

The sheriff.   The sheriff or scir-gerefa, the scir-man of the laws of Ini[3],
was the king's steward and judicial president of the shire, the
administrator of the royal demesne and executor of the law.
His sphere of jurisdiction was distinctly a single shire, although
after the Conquest for a long period the shires were administered
in pairs. It is probable on early analogy that the gerefa was
chosen in the folkmoot; but there is no proof that within his-

177–189) is highly instructive and suggestive. He argues that the great
ealdordom of Mercia subsisted until the banishment of Elfric the child in
985, and that of East Anglia until the death of Ethelwin in 992, after
which they were administered by high-reeves under the king until Canute
reconstituted them. Wessex he regards as divided into two great ealdor-
doms, that of the western and that of the central provinces; which, with
Kent under archbishop Sigeric, made a threefold division of the south of
England. These, with Essex and Northumbria, would make up seven
great territorial magistracies. But Sussex had an ealdorman as late as
982, and the arrangements are so short-lived that it is impossible to regard them as parts of a permanent methodical system. And the same may
be said even of Canute's fourfold division.

    [1] The third penny of the county appears from Domesday (i. 1, 26, 203,
246, 252, 280, 298, 336) to have been paid to the earl in the time of Edward
the Confessor; but see Round, Geoff. de Mandeville, pp. 288 sq. Compare
the share of the count in the Capitulary of A.D. 783; one third to the
count, two thirds to the palace; Waitz, D. V. G. ii. 628; iv. 145.
    [2] Elfhere, ealdorman of Mercia under Edgar, is called heretoga, Cod.
Dipl. ii. 383; iii. 5, 49, 159, 259 sq. His son Elfric is called ealdorman.
See Kemble, Saxons, ii. 126; Freeman, Norm. Conq. i. 581.
    [3] Scirman, Ini, § 8; Ethelwin is scirman in Kent under Canute, Kemble,
C. D. iv. 9; see also iv. 304; Leofric, scires-man, iv. 267; and Wulfsi
priest, the shire-man, vi. 127. Pontius Pilate is scirman of Judaea, St.
Luke iii. 1. The word used in the laws is generally gerefa simply; scir-
gerefa however is found in charters, Kemble, C. D. iv. 10, where Ethelwin,
the scirman in Kent, is called scir-gerefa; also iv. 54, 201, &c. &c. The
Latin word is generally praepositus or praefectus. Ethelwerd (M. H. B.
p. 509) calls the sheriff of Dorset *exactor* in A.D. 787. See above, p. 88.

torical times this was the case [1], although the constitutionalists
of the thirteenth century attempted to assert it as a right, and
it was for a few years conceded by the crown. As a rule he
was, as a royal officer, nominated by the king; the ealdorman,
as a national one, by the king and witan. The sheriff as well
as the ealdorman was entitled to a share of the profits of administration, and possibly had in some cases an endowment
in land [2].

The system of double administration by a national leader and
a royal steward, although common to the early Germanic constitutions, the Frank, the Gothic and the Lombard, is in its
later form almost peculiar to England. In the later Frank
kingdom the graf, who now stood in the place of the national as
well as the royal officers of early days, exercised the functions
of both in immediate dependence on the king [3]; and in medieval
Germany, where the title of duke or herzog presents some
analogy with that of the ealdorman, he is rather a national
prince than an imperial officer: for every attempt made by the
central authority to assert its power through counts or counts-
palatine, ended in the foundation of new hereditary principalities, either coordinate with or subordinate to the dukes, but
in both cases equally neglectful of any duties to the emperor.
In England, on the contrary, the sheriffdom as a rule never
became hereditary, and after the Norman Conquest, under the
changed title or translation of vice-comes [4], it was used by the

Double go-
vernment by
ealdorman
and sheriff.

---

[1] The statement of the chapter ' de heretochiis ' in the so-called laws of
Edward the Confessor is a fabrication of the thirteenth century at the
earliest; Schmid, Gesetze, p. 510. See Gneist, Verwaltungsr. i. 78.

[2] The allowances made to the sheriff of Wilts, in kind, are enumerated
in Domesd. vol. i. 69; and he also had rights in reveland, which possibly
were attached to his office. Reveland is mentioned also in Herefordshire,
Domesd. i. 179, 181; Ellis, Introd. to Domesd. i. 168, 231; Allen, Prerog.
p. 214. The sheriff of Shropshire had the third penny of the town of
Shrewsbury, ibid. i. 252. In Surrey were three manors from which the
sheriff had £7, ' de eo quod impendit eis adjutorium cum opus habent ;'
Domesd. i. 30. See above, p. 113, note 6. The folkland held by the
ealdorman Alfred (Kemble, C. D. No. 316) may have been an official
endowment. See Sohm, Fr. G. V. G. p. 32.

[3] Waitz, D. V. G. ii. 363; Sohm, Fr. R. G. V. i. 156-181, 463-472.

[4] Vicecomes occurs as the Latin word for sheriff in Canute's letter to the
bishops, given by Florence of Worcester: but this is clearly a translation
of Norman date.

kings as a means of ousting or preventing the creation of any
feudal rule such as that of the counts and dukes of the continent. The history of the sheriffdom is thus one of the most
important departments of Constitutional History.

The shire-
moot.

50. The sheriff held the shiremoot, according to Edgar's law,
twice in the year [1]. Although the ealdorman and bishop sat in it
to declare the law secular and spiritual, the sheriff was the constituting officer [2]. The suitors were the same as those of the
hundred court : all lords of lands [3], all public officers, and from

Attendance
of the reeve
and four
men.

every township the reeve and four men [4]. The latter point, left
questionable in the laws, is proved by the later practice. In the
county courts of the reign of Henry III, the reeve and four
men took part in matters of election, of arming and of assessment; and in the reign of Edward I the Kentish *borhs-ealdor*
and his four fellows represented each township in the court of
the itinerant justices, itself a form of the county court. Every
one on his way to and from the gemot was under the special
protection of the law.

Jurisdiction
of the shire-
moot.

The shiremoot, like the hundredmoot, was competent to declare folkright in every suit, but its relation to the lower court
was not, properly speaking, an appellate jurisdiction. Its
function was to secure to the suitor the right which he had

---

[1] 'Et requiratur hundretum sicut antea fuit institutum, habeatur in
anno burgmotus ter, et scyremotus bis, et intersit praesul comitatus et
aldremannus, et utrique doceant Dei rectum et saeculi ;' Edgar, iii. § 5.

[2] Hallam, M. A. ii. 283; Kemble, Saxons, ii. 158, 159.

[3] Called in this aspect scir-thegns, Kemble, C. D. vi. 198; iv. 170;
Saxons, ii. 234, 235. Kemble contends, and with good reason, that these
scir-thegns are not necessarily king's thegns. It may be added that there
is no reason to regard them as all possessed of five hides of land, very
many of the thegns of Domesday having far less. See too Gneist, Verwaltgsr. i. 37.

[4] Compare the following passages from Domesday : in Archenefield, i.
179, ' Si vicecomes evocat eos ad sciremot, meliores ex eis, vi aut vii, vadunt
cum eo. Qui vocatus non vadit dat ii solidos aut unum bovem regi, et qui
de hundret remanet, tantundem persolvit.' In the city of Hereford, ' qui
equum habebat ter in anno pergebat cum vicecomite ad placita et ad hundret ;' Ibid. In Derby hundred (inter Ribble et Merse), ' Si de hundredo
remanebat aut non ibat ad placitum ubi praepositus jubebat, per v solidos
emendabat ;' Ibid. i. 269. At Dover, ' Si fuerint praemoniti ut conveniant ad sciram, ibunt usque ad Pinnedennam, non longius ;' p. 1.
The participation of ceorls in the shiremoot is mentioned in a charter of
Canute, Cod. Dipl. iv. 11, and illustrated by the direction of writs to all
thegns of the shire twelf-hynd or twy-hynd.

failed to obtain in the hundred. He could not apply to the
shire until he had thrice demanded his right in the hundred court.
If the respondent failed to appear when the shiremoot had
fixed for him a fourth day for appearing, the applicant was
allowed to enforce his claim. In the same way it was forbidden
to apply to the king until shire and hundred had been tried in
vain[1]. It is possible that by a direct writ from the king the
shiremoot might be used as a court of primary instance, but of
this we have no distinct evidence.

Here again the suitors were the judges; but the twelve senior
thegns appear in the county court as well as in the hundred[2],
and, on the institution of the grand-jury, present the report of
the hundred. Thus limited, the authority of the sheriff was
rather that of a chairman or moderator than that of a judge.
The duty of seeing the law executed devolved upon him, and in
fiscal as well as judicial matters he exercised a good deal of
somewhat irresponsible power.

The twelve thegns.

Besides the judicial power of the shiremoot, and its function
of giving validity to private acts by way of witness[3], some
shadow of legislative authority seems to have remained to it in
the time of Athelstan, when the bishops of Kent and all the
thegns, eorl and ceorl[4], of Cantescyre, declared to him in their

Vestiges of legislative action in the shire-moot.

---

[1] See Athelstan, i. § 3 ; Edgar, iii. § 2 ; Canute, ii. § 17, &c. The words
of the law of Canute are these: 'Nemo regem requirat de justitia facienda
dum ei rectum offertur in hundreto suo, et requiratur hundretum super
witam sicut justum est;' 'Nemo namium capiat in comitatu vel extra
comitatum priusquam ter in hundreto suo rectum sibi perquisierit. Si
tertia vice rectum non habeat, eat quarta vice ad conventum totius
comitatus, quod Anglice dicitur scyremotus, et ipse comitatus ponat ei
quartum terminum. Qui si fallat tunc licentiam accipiat ut abhinc et
inde suum audeat requirere.'

[2] Compare the direction of Lewis the Pious in A.D. 819, that every
graf should attend the general placita with twelve scabini, or, if there
were not so many, the number should be made up from the best men of
the county. See Savigny, i. 248 ; Waitz, D. V. G. iv. 329 sq. The appearance of the senior thegns in the shiremoot is mentioned in Cod. Dipl. iv.
137: 'Ealla tha yldestan thegnas on Wigeraceastrescire Denisce and
Englisce;' No. 804.

[3] Wills are frequently attested by it, e. g. Kemble, C. D. vi. 198. Other
acts done before the shire will be found in Cod. Dipl. iv. 117, 137, 138,
234; iii. 292.

[4] Comites et villani, Athelstan, iii. 148 ; Kemble, Saxons, ii. 233, 234 ;
Hallam, M. A. ii. 376 ; Palgrave, Commonwealth, p. 637.

gemot at Faversham their acceptance of the measures taken for the maintenance of the peace in the recent witenagemot of Greatley. In this we may trace a recognition of the importance of the popular reception of a law [1], which appears even in the narrative preamble of the Salian law itself, which induced Charles the Great to ask the consent of the mallus to the capitularies which he had drawn up [2], and which occurs in England among the measures taken for the publication and preservation of Magna Carta.

Evidence of the ancient nationality of the shire.

The institution of the shiremoot in England is not paralleled by any similar arrangement in the primitive Frank kingdom, in which the hundred court or mallus admits of no further recourse for justice, except, by special favour, to the judgment of the king [3]. This point further illustrates the theory that in the shiremoot, as a folkmoot, we have a monument of the original independence of the population which it represents. If the shire be the ancient under-kingdom, or the district whose administrative system is created in imitation of that of the under-kingdom, the shiremoot is the folkmoot in a double sense, not merely the popular court of the district, but the chief council of the ancient nation who possessed that district in independence, the witenagemot of the pre-heptarchic kingdom. Such a theory would imply the much greater preponderance of popular liberties in the earlier system, for the shiremoot is a representative assembly, which the historical witenagemot is not. And this is indeed natural, for the smaller the size of the districts and the more nearly equal the condition of the landowners or sharers in the common land, the more easy it would be to assemble the nation, and so much the less danger of the supreme authority falling into the hands of the king and the magistrates without reference to the national voice. But this can only be matter of conjecture.

Rating of the shire.

Under the late shire-system, before as after the Conquest, the

[1] Kemble, Saxons, ii. 238.
[2] Waitz, D. V. G. iii. 506–510; Sohm, Fr. G. V. G. pp. 281, 293: see below, vol. ii. § 224.
[3] See Waitz, D. V. G. ii. 494. It was however usual among the Bavarians and, at a later period, general.

shire was a unit for purposes of rating. Each shire was bound to furnish ships in proportion to its number of hundreds[1], and, from the produce of what had been the folkland contained in it, to pay a composition for the feorm-fultum, or sustentation, of the king[2]. The military contingents of the shire were also made a matter of composition, the number of fighting men furnished for the fyrd being often much smaller than the number of hides which furnished them[3]. Whether these compositions were, as in the case of the churches, a matter of privilege, can scarcely be determined in the almost entire deficiency of secular charters before the Norman Conquest. It is however probable from Domesday that long before that event the shires had been allowed to acquit themselves of several of these duties by paying fixed sums or furnishing fixed contingents, answering in some measure to the firms, ferms or farms, for which the sheriffs were liable.

Composition for military service.

In ecclesiastical matters the shire had the same indefinite status which belonged to the hundred: the archdeaconries, as geographical divisions, do not occur earlier than the twelfth century. At that time the archdeacons, who had been ministers of the bishop in all parts of the diocese alike, received each his own district, which in most cases coincided with the county.

The shire ecclesiastically.

The system adopted by Edgar and Ethelred of combining the government of a whole cluster of shires in the hands of a single ealdorman, is so nearly contemporary with the general institution of a shire-system for all England, that it can scarcely be determined whether it is an exceptional departure from, or a

Combination of several shires under an ealdorman.

---

[1] Chron. Sax. A.D. 1008; with Earle's note, pp. 336, 337; see above, p. 118. Hence Archbishop Elfric leaves a ship to the people of Kent, and another to Wiltshire; Kemble, C. D. iii. 352.

[2] The county of Oxford paid firm of three nights, or £150. That of Warwick paid £65 and 36 sextaries of honey; Domesday, i. 154, 238. Northamptonshire paid firm of three nights; Ibid. i. 219. Many other instances are adduced by Ellis, Introd. to Domesd. i. 261, 262.

[3] In Berkshire one man went for each five hides, each hide paying four shillings for his maintenance. The whole city of Exeter furnished only the service of five hides. Oxford sent twenty burgesses to represent all the rest; Leicester sent twelve, and, if the king was going to sea, furnished four horses to convey arms to the fleet; Domesday, i. 56, 100, 154, 230. Warwick sent ten; Ibid. i. 238: Wilton one man for five hides; Ibid. i. 64. Cf. Rot. Pip. 31 Hen. I. pp. 123, 125.

The great
earldoms do
not involve
a new or-
ganisation of
the shire-
moot.

stage in, the development of the new rule. Until the shire-
system was made uniform, it is quite possible that the witenagemots of the heptarchic kingdoms may have continued to
exist[1]. But after that organisation was completed, though one
ealdorman might govern and lead to battle the forces of several
shires, he had no general court or gemot of his jurisdiction :
the ealdorman of the Western provinces would take his seat in
the folkmoot of Devonshire and Cornwall, but would not have
a united council for the two. Nor is there any reason to suppose that, after Canute had divided the whole realm into four
earldoms, any such provincial witenagemots followed the institution. The royal writs are directed to the bishop and earl
and sheriff of each shire, although both bishop and earl presided over many such shires. Whether any subordinate officer
took in the shire the place of these powerful earls and ealdormen, or whether, if it were so, he also bore the title of ealdorman, can scarcely be determined from our existing materials.
On the one hand there is no distinct mention of such official :
on the other hand the use of the word ealdorman was becoming
very different from what it had been ; it was superseded in the
higher ranks of organisation by the title of earl, and in the
lower was acquiring, or returning to, the primary and loose
meaning of a head-man, in which it could be applied to almost
any local officer. But however this may have been, there was
no intermediate organisation between the shire with its folkmoot and the central one of the kingdom with its witenagemot.

[1] The charters of Ethelred, ealdorman of Mercia under Alfred, are
generally attested by Mercian bishops only, and therefore very probably
issued in Mercian witenagemots; Cod. Dipl. ii. 107, 112; v. 126, 134,
140. In the last case Ethelred states that he has summoned to Gloucester
'ælle Mercna weotan . . . bisceopas and aldermen and alle his duguthe,'
and that with King Alfred's witness and leave. See also Cod. Dipl. v.
143, 154. There are also charters of Edgar drawn up whilst he was king
of the Mercians only, and attested by the Mercian witan; Cod. Dipl. ii.
348, 358. The charters of the kings of the West Saxon dynasty are of
course often attested by the West Saxon witan only. See Gneist, Verwaltgsr. i. 48. An East Anglian witenagemot of A.D. 1004 is spoken of in
the Chronicle, which may or may not have been a folkmoot; for East
Anglia, like Kent, was only one administrative division. See Freeman,
Norm. Conq. i. 102.

CHAPTER VI.

THE WITENAGEMOT AND THE KING.

51. The witenagemot.—52. Its composition.—53. Its powers in legislation.—54. In grants of land.—55. In judicature.—56. In taxing and
general politics.—57. In election of magistrates.—58. In election and
deposition of kings.—59. The king.—60. Coronation and unction.—61.
His promises to his people.—62. The oath of the people.—63. The comitatus.—64. Nobility by birth.—65. Nobility by service.—66. The ealdormanship.—67. Use of the wergild.—68. The Bretwalda.

51. The civitas or populus of Tacitus, the union of several *The supreme assembly of the kingdom.*
pagi, is in Anglo-Saxon history the *rice*, or kingdom; and its
council, the concilium principum, is the witenagemot or assembly of the wise. This is the supreme council of the nation,
whether the nation be Kent or Mercia as in the earlier, or the
whole gens Anglorum et Saxonum as in the later history. The
character of the national council testifies to its history as a
later development than the lower courts, and as a consequence
of the institution of royalty. The folkmoot, or popular assembly of the shire, is a representative body to a certain extent: it
is attended by the representatives of the hundreds and townships, and has a representative body of witnesses to give validity
to the acts that are executed in it. If each shire represented a
complete kingdom, the shiremoot would give a complete repre-
sentative system existing in each kingdom. But as the small *The witena-gemot not a folkmoot.*
kingdoms coalesced or were united by conquest, it does not
seem to have been thought necessary to extend the system ; the
council of the aggregated state is not a folkmoot but a witenagemot. In those early kingdoms again, which were identical

Question as
to the co-
existence of
the folkmoot
and witena-
gemot.
with the later shires, Kent for instance, it might be expected
that we should find two central councils, the folkmoot or council
of the people of Kent, and the witenagemot or council of the
chiefs, answering to the greater and narrower assemblies of the
plebs and of the *principes* in the Germania. It is by no means
improbable that such was the case ; but as our knowledge on
the subject is derived from the charters attested by these assemblies, or issued with their consent, and as the consent of the
witan only was necessary for the transfers of land, we have not
the documentary evidence that would suffice for proof. We
have many charters issued in witenagemots under the kings of
Kent ; but the only document issued by a folkmoot of Kent
belongs to a date when it had long been without a king[1].
The customs, however, of the folkmoot are so common and so
ancient, that they afford a strong presumption of their universality ; so that Kent and Sussex, and perhaps Essex and East
Anglia, may be fairly supposed to have had the two regular
assemblies in primitive simplicity as long as they continued independent[2]. With regard to Wessex and Mercia, which were
aggregations of smaller states, no such hypothesis will hold
good. There is no probability that a Mercian king would introduce a new constitution into the organisation of his kingdom.
It was enough that the Hwiccians, or Hecanians, or Maga-
sætanians had their folkmoot, without the Mercians having one
too ; and it was enough for the king, as ruler of Mercia, to
have his witenagemot without continuing to hold similar gatherings as overlord of Hwiccia and the associated districts. The
folkmoot was left to the shire, the witenagemot was gathered
round the king.

Question as
to the ga-
thering of
the folk-
moots in
arms.
Yet even in the seven kingdoms, even in the united kingdom,
when there was a general summons to the host, some concentration of the armed folkmoots must have taken place. For

---

[1] Athelstan, iii. : ' Karissime, Episcopi tui de Kancia et omnes Cantescyrae thaini, comites et villani.' See Kemble's comment, Saxons, ii. 234,
235 ; Hallam, M. A. ii. 377.
[2] See Gneist, Verwaltungsrecht, i. 43, who seems to take a contrary
view, and regards the witenagemot and folkmoot of the small kingdoms as
identical. Both views are of course conjectural.

the promulgation of the laws also, at least in the period before
Alfred, the national assembly must have comprised a much
wider class than the witan[1]. On great occasions too, corona- General
tions and the like, during the history of the later West Saxon gatherings of the nation at
dynasty[2], or on the sudden emergency of a Danish invasion, or the witena-
for the reception of Canute's promulgation of Edgar's laws[3], gemot,
we must understand the witenagemot to have been attended by
a concourse of people whose voices could be raised in applause
or in resistance to the proposals of the chiefs[4]. But that such not organ-
gatherings shared in any way the constitutional powers of the ised or repre-
witan, that they were organised in any way corresponding to the sentative.
machinery of the folkmoot, that they had any representative
character in the modern sense, as having full powers to act on
behalf of constituents, that they shared the judicial work, or
except by applause and hooting influenced in any way the decision of the chiefs, there is no evidence whatever. They
might, by an easy and welcome fiction, be considered as representing the nation, although they were really the mere retainers of the nobles or the inhabitants of the neighbouring
villages.

[1] See the prologues to the laws of Wihtræd and Ini.

[2] For example, in A.D. 1051, when Godwin was exiled: 'Rex in suo
concilio et omnis exercitus unanimi consensu . . . decreverunt;' Flor. Wig.
A.D. 1051.

[3] Freeman, Norm. Conq. i. 103, and Appendix Q, thinks that 'every
freeman retained in theory the right of appearing in the Assembly of the
kingdom;' and adds, 'expressions are found which are quite enough to
show that the mass of the people were theoretically looked on as present
in the national Assembly, and as consenting to its decrees.' Most of the
passages quoted in favour of this opinion refer to the occasions on which
a king was elected, or laws promulgated. Kemble, Saxons, ii. 239,
furnishes similar quotations from charters: Cod. Dipl. lxxiii, 'cum praesentia populationis;' ccclxiv, 'tota populi generalitate;' mciii, 'tota
plebis generalitate.' He sums up thus: 'Whether expressions of this
kind were intended to denote the actual presence of the people on the
spot; or whether *populus* is used in a strict and technical sense, that sense
which is confined to those who enjoy the full franchise, those who form
part of the πολίτευμα, or finally, whether the assembly of the witan making
laws is considered to represent in our modern form an assembly of the
whole people, it is clear that the power of self-government is recognised in
the latter;' Ibid. 240.

[4] Such was the case in the shiremoot: Cod. Dipl. mcxxix, where all the
people who stood around cried out, 'Si hyt swa, Amen, Amen;' Kemble,
Saxons, ii. 238.

The ecclesiastical the only unity.

So long as the heptarchic kingdoms lasted, each having its own witenagemot, there was no attempt at general organisation even for cases of the greatest emergency, except the ecclesiastical. The provincial or family tie was as strong as ever, and although the gens Anglorum had learned to recognise itself under one collective name as early as the time of Augustine, it was only on the ancient lines that any power of organisation was developed until the church was strong enough to form a

Occasional meetings of kings in the heptarchic period.

national union. The kings met occasionally for alliance or for arbitration; for some great purpose, such as the choice of a primate [1]; but the nation met only in the ecclesiastical councils, which were held with some frequency, from the days of Theodore to those of Athelstan, quite apart from and independently of the witenagemots of the several states. As occasionally the kings, and frequently the ealdormen, of different kingdoms attended these assemblies, and as they were, like other courts, useful for the witnessing of acts which required powerful attestation and general promulgation, the nation learned from them

Ascendency of one great king or dynasty.

the benefit of common action. Another powerful help in the same direction must have been the ascendency, during the whole of that period, of some one great prince, who by war or alliances exercised an overwhelming influence over the rest. Such a position was occupied after the middle of the seventh century by the kings of Northumbria, during the eighth by those of Mercia, and, after the rise of the West Saxon power, by Egbert and his successors. But the existence of this hegemony, whether or no its possessor bore the title of Bretwalda, was not accompanied by unity of organisation or even by any act of confederation.

Frank assemblies.

In the Frank kingdom, if we may accept the testimony of

---

[1] Bede, H. E. iii. 29: 'Reges Angliae nobilissimi, Oswiu provinciae Nordanhymbrorum et Ecgberct Cantuariorum, habito inter se consilio,' &c. Many instances of deliberation between the kings preparatory to the reception of Christianity may be found in Bede. A clear example of more general deliberation is furnished by Bishop Waldhere, in his letter to Brihtwald (Councils, &c. iii. 274): 'Ante paucos autem dies hoc placitum communi consensione condixerunt, ut in idus Kalendarum Octobrium, in loco qui dicitur Breguntford omnes advenissent reges ambarum partium, episcopi et abbates judicesque reliquos, et inibi adunato consilio omnium dissimultatum causae determinarentur.'

Adalhard to the existence of the rule, some shadow of the double council of the Germania seems to have been preserved[1]. Charles the Great held two great annual assemblies of his people, one in May at the Campus Madius, which Pippin had substituted for the Campus Martius of the Merovingians; and another in the autumn. The spring meeting was attended by the majores, optimates, and seniores, and held at the same time with the great military levy, the assembly of the people in arms. The autumnal one comprised the royal counsellors only, and answered nearly to the witenagemot[2]. But although these assemblies afford a superficial parallel with the system sketched by Tacitus, the functions of the principes and the plebs were interchanged: in the first, the optimates were assembled 'propter consilium ordinandum;' the minores were allowed to be present 'ad consilium suscipiendum,' sometimes also 'pariter tractandum,' but not as of old to give authority to the determinations of the lords. It was in the autumn council, to which only the seniores and chief counsellors were admitted, that the policy of the ensuing year was settled.

The spring and autumn gathering.

Without denying that occasionally an Anglo-Saxon king might call together his witan, and hold his military review at the same time, it may be generally concluded that, if such had

Question as to the similar practice in England.

---

[1] 'Consuetudo autem tunc temporis erat ut non saepius sed bis in anno placita duo tenerentur. Unum quando ordinabatur status totius regni ad anni vertentis spacium, quod ordinatum nullus eventus rerum, nisi summa necessitas quae similiter toto regno incumbebat, mutabatur. In quo placito generalitas universorum majorum tam clericorum quam laicorum conveniebat; seniores propter consilium ordinandum, minores propter idem consilium suscipiendum et interdum pariter tractandum, et non ex potestate, sed ex proprio mentis intellectu vel sententia, confirmandum. Caeterum autem propter dona generaliter danda aliud placitum cum senioribus tantum et praecipuis consiliariis habebatur; in quo jam futuri anni status tractari incipiebatur, si forte talia aliqua se praemonstrabant, pro quibus necesse erat praemeditando ordinare, si quid mox transacto anno priore incumberet pro quo anticipando aliquid statuere aut providere necessitas esset;' Adalhard (ap. Hincmar), cc. 29, 30. On the interpretation, see Waitz, D. V. G. iii. 463 sq.; Kemble, Saxons, ii. 187–191. The Capitulary of Pippin (Baluze, i. 119), § 4, orders, 'ut bis in anno *synodus* fiat,' on March 1 and Oct. 1, in the king's presence: the ecclesiastical assembly was thus in strict analogy with the general one.

[2] There are difficulties in harmonising Adalhard's account with historical data; but the principle enunciated in it is the only important question as illustrating early practice. See Waitz, D. V. G. iii. 465.

been the rule, some evidence would have been forthcoming. Of anything like the Campus Madius there is no trace: but very many of the dated charters of the period were issued in the autumn[1]; and it is by no means improbable that the reception of annual presents[2] after harvest, which was a regular part of the agenda of the Frank court, may have caused a similar meeting in the early kingdoms. As we approach the Conquest, it seems more probable that the great courts were held as they were by William the Conqueror, at Easter, Whitsuntide, and Christmas[3] and that the deliberations of the witan took place in them Such courts would account for large gatherings of the people who, although without organisation, might be regarded as representing the nation at large[4].

Three great annual courts.

Members of the witenagemot.

52. The members of the assembly were the wise men, the *sapientes, witan*; the king, sometimes accompanied by his wife and sons; the bishops of the kingdom, the ealdormen of the shires or provinces, and a number of the king's friends and dependents. These last generally describe themselves as *ministri* king's thegns, and numbered amongst themselves no doubt the chief officers of the household, and the most eminent of the persons who, in the relation of gesith or *comes* to the king, held portions of folkland or of royal demesne, and were bound to him by the oath of fealty. These ministri answer roughly to

[1] See Cod. Dipl. lxxix, Nov. 24: xcvii, Sept. 29: cxl, Sept. 22: cxc Aug. 6: cxcvi, Aug. 1: cci, Nov. 25: ccxvi, Sept. 20: ccxviii, Sept. 30 ccxxvii, Aug. 28:—the later charters are seldom dated, and the dating of such documents generally weakens rather than confirms their claims to genuineness. The ecclesiastical councils were mostly held in autumn that of Hertford on Sept. 24, 673: in this an annual council on the 1st of August at Clovesho was ordered. The council of Hatfield was Sept. 17 680: that of Berghamsted on the 6th of Rugern or August (Schmid Gesetze, p. 15): that of Brentford, Oct. 16, 705: that of Clovesho, July 716: another at Clovesho, Sept. 747: one at Pincahala, Sept. 2, 787: one at Aclech, Sept. 29, 788: the great council of Clovesho, Oct. 6–12, 803 and that of Chelsea, July 27, 816. (See Councils, &c. iii.)

[2] Annual presents were offered also at the spring gathering; but the autumn must have been the most natural time. Instances of both are given by Waitz, D. V. G. iii. 479.

[3] 'Easter and Christmas were usual times for the meetings of the witan;' Kemble, Saxons, ii. 191. Documents are dated at Easter, Cod Dipl. cxciv, cclxx, cclxxi, &c.: at Christmas, cciii, ccxxxii (Egbert), ccxlvii ccxlviii, ccxlix: at Whitsuntide, ccxvii, &c.

[4] Kemble, Saxons, ii. 237–240.

the antrustions and vassi of the Frank court ; but the term is a very general one, and perhaps embraced others than the sworn dependents of the king[1].   Occasionally a *praefectus* or *gerefa* appears in the early charters ; he is probably the heah-gerefa or high-steward of the household[2] ; the ealdormen appear under the variable title of princeps or dux, applied indiscriminately : now and then the names of the bishops are followed by that of an abbot, who may have been the king's chaplain or the prede- cessor of the later chancellor, as the heah-gerefa might be of the justiciar.   Under the later kings, a considerable number of abbots attest the charters, a fact which may be ascribed either to the increased power of the monasteries, or to the advance in secular importance of the ecclesiastical body generally, after the reign of Athelstan.

Classes of members.

The number of the witan was thus never very large.   The Mercian charters of the reign of Offa furnish us with an enumeration of all the members who could be ranged under the heads already mentioned, and may be taken as acts of the most completely organised assemblies, the Kentish and West Saxon charters being as a rule very scantily attested.   These documents are witnessed by the five Mercian bishops, five, six, or seven ealdormen, principes or duces, and a number of ministri about equal to that of each of the other classes[3].   The list of bishops is certainly exhaustive, for Mercia contained only five dioceses : the list of ealdormen is probably as complete, for the names recur in all the charters of Offa ; and the whole number of persons who bore the title during his reign is not much more than a dozen.   The list of ministri is more variable, but they are still a very limited body, and, on the analogy of the bishops and ealdormen, must have been exhaustively enumerated ; nor is it

Number of the witan in early times.

---

[1] Kemble, Saxons, ii. 195–197, thinks that the ministri of the charters may many of them have been sheriffs, which is quite possible ; but he goes too far when he argues from Athelstan, vi. 10, that all the sheriffs were present even at a particular witenagemot.

[2] The Northumbrian highreeves probably answered to the sheriffs of the other kingdoms ; Robertson, Essays, p. 177.

[3] See Cod. Dipl. cxxi, cxxii, cxxxi, (five bishops, seven abbots and six ealdormen); cxxxvii, (five bishops, one abbot, seven principes and two duces); cxxxviii, (four bishops and four ealdormen) ; cxl, clii, cliii, &c. &c.

to be supposed that the king would venture to outnumber by
his own nominees the national officers, lay and clerical, who
formed the older and more authoritative portion of the council.

Number
under the
later kings.

The witenagemots of Athelstan and Edgar are of course much
more numerous, but only in proportion to the increased size of
the realm. The whole tale of the bishops and ealdormen are
easily identified, but the number of ministri is variable, and the
abbots form occasionally a formidable addition. In a witenagemot, held at Luton in November A.D. 931 [1], were the two
archbishops, two Welsh princes, seventeen bishops, fifteen
ealdormen, five abbots, and fifty-nine ministri. In another,
that of Winchester of A.D. 934 [2], were present the two archbishops, four Welsh kings, seventeen bishops, four abbots,
twelve ealdormen, and fifty-two ministri. These are perhaps the
fullest extant lists. Of Edgar's witenagemots, the one of A.D.
966 contained the King's mother, two archbishops, seven bishops,
five ealdormen, and fifteen ministri [3]; and this is a fair specimen
of the usual proportion. It is clear that as the feudal principle

Increase in
the number
of ministri.

grew stronger the number of king's thegns must have largely increased, and, as their power became preponderant in the assembly,
the royal authority became supreme in the country at large ; the
office of ealdorman also began at this period to be held chiefly
by persons connected with the king's kin. A further inference
may be drawn from the attestations of the charters. They are
most of them those of the bishops and ealdormen, whose local
duties would keep them generally distant from the court. The
charters are therefore not the acts of a standing council of the
king, or of casual gatherings of his nobles, but evidences of
assemblies regularly constituted, and probably, for the paucity of
exact dates prevents us from being certain, held at fixed times
and places.

Proceedings
of the
witena-
gemot.

53. The part taken by the witan in the transaction of business
was full and authoritative. Bede gives an account of the
Northumbrian council which received Christianity, and represents

---

[1] Cod. Dipl. cccliii.
[2] Ibid. ccclxiv. See also mcvii. Kemble says that the largest number
given is 106. Saxons, ii. 200 ; Gneist, Self-government, i. 49.
[3] Cod. Dipl. dxviii.

the king as consulting his princes and counsellors one by one: each
declares his mind ; and the king decides accordingly [1].   Eddius
describes the assemblies in which Wilfrid was banished and
recalled ; accusation, defence and sentence fall into their regular
order ; the bishops and ealdormen speak, and the king or ruling
ealdorman pronounces the determination, 'haec est voluntas
regis et principum ejus [2].'   With these exceptions we have not
at any period much material evidence to show the order of
deliberation ; most of the early councils in which speeches and
votings are recorded being ecclesiastical.   The clergy were no   Independ-
doubt very influential, and the great ealdormen, if we may   ence of the
                                                                clergy and
judge by their action under Edred and Edwy, were not less inde-   ealdormen.
pendent.   Under Edward the Confessor, Godwin and Leofric
are able to sway the policy of the sovereign, or to neutralise
each other's influence.   It may be presumed that in the early
stages and under the weaker sovereigns, the determination was
elicited by *bonâ fide* voting.   And, under the stronger and later
kings, it was decided by the sovereign himself, as he chose to
follow or to thwart the policy of his leading adviser.   But we
have little more than conjecture and analogy to guide us.   It is
rarely that even the Frank kings are described as acting under
the constraint of their people [3]: the days of Ethelred the Unready, and even of Edward the Confessor, can scarcely be
appealed to as giving the normal condition of the relations of
king and council ; nor is it until the reign of Henry II that we
find any historical data as to deliberations in which the king
does not get his own way.

   The formula however by which the co-operation of the witena-   Counsel and
gemot was expressed is definite and distinct [4].   The laws of Ini   consent of
                                                                    the witan.
are enacted 'with the counsel and teaching of the bishops, with
all the ealdormen and the most distinguished witan of the

---

[1] Bede, H. E. ii. 13.   [2] Eddius, c. lix. (ed. Gale, p. 86.)
   [3] As for example, when the host compelled King Clothair to go to war,
pulling down his tent and loading him with abuse ; Greg. Turon. iv. 14 ;
Waitz, D. V. G. ii. 146.
   [4] The legislative authority of the witan is the subject of Kemble's
second canon, Saxons, ii. 205.   'The witan deliberated upon the making
of new laws which were to be added to the existing folkright, and which
were then promulgated by their own and the king's authority.'

Counsel and
consent. nation, and with a large gathering of God's servants [1];' those of
Wihtræd are decreed 'by the great men with the suffrages of
all, as an addition to the lawful customs of the Kentish people[2].'
Alfred issues his code [3] with the counsel and consent of his
witan; Athelstan writes to the reeves with the counsel of the
bishops [4]; at Exeter the witan decree with the counsel of the
king, and the king with theirs [5]. Edmund before he legislates
has deliberated [6] with the counsel of his witan, both ecclesiastical
and secular. Edgar ordains with the counsel of his witan in
praise of God, and in honour of himself and for the behoof of all
the people [7]. Ethelred and his witan issue ordinances at Woodstock [8]; Canute at Winchester with the counsel of his witan [9].

Examples
of this
usage in the
German
laws.   Such in fact was the traditional theory of all the German
races. The Burgundian laws are stated to be issued by Gunde-
bald 'ex tractatu nostro et communi omnium voluntate,' and
are signed by thirty-one *comites* [10]. The Salian laws had been
settled by the Franks and their proceres before they were repro-
mulgated by Clovis and Charles [11]; those of the Lombards were
issued by Rotharis, 'cum primatibus meis judicibus [12];' those of
the Alemannians are reissued by King Clothair with his princes,
thirty-three bishops, thirty-four duces, and sixty-two comites,
'vel cetero populo [13].' The Bavarian laws are re-enacted, reformed, and augmented, 'apud regem et principes suos et apud
cunctum populum [14].'

In the
Frank laws.   The Capitularies of the Merovingian kings of Neustria, who to
a certain extent aped Roman forms and ruled mainly over a
conquered population of Romanised Gauls, are more distinctly
imperative; but Childebert of Austrasia declares, before he

---

[1] Schmid, Gesetze, p. 21.   [2] Ibid. p. 15.   [3] Ibid. p. 69.
[4] Ibid. pp. 126, 127.   [5] Ibid. pp. 150, 153.
[6] Ibid. pp. 172, 173, 177.   [7] Ibid. pp. 184–187.
[8] Ibid. pp. 198, 199.   [9] Ibid. pp. 250, 251.
[10] Pertz, Legg. iii. 529; Lindenbrog, p. 267; Canciani, iv. 13, 14.
[11] Lindenbrog, pp. 313, 314; Canciani, ii. 10, 13, 15, 121.
[12] Canciani, i. 63.
[13] Pertz, Legg. iii. 45; Lindenbrog, p. 363; Canciani, ii. 323.
[14] Pertz, Legg. iii. 269; Lindenbrog, p. 399; Canciani, ii. 296; Baluze,
i. 18. In all these cases the Codes are republications of national laws,
for the attestation of which the witness of the wise would be absolutely
necessary.

issues his 'decretio,' that he has treated of the matter with his *optimates*[1]. And when the Austrasian influence becomes supreme, the form reverts at once to the ancient type. Carloman ordains ' per consilium sacerdotum et optimatum [2];' Pippin ' cum consensu episcoporum sive sacerdotum vel servorum Dei consilio; seu comitibus et optimatibus Francorum [3];' Charles the Great augments the Lombard laws as emperor, king of Italy, and conqueror [4], but his Capitularies are the result of synodical deliberation often expressed and generally implied. The succeeding Karolingians acknowledge almost always the counsel and consent of their optimates, in a way remarkably contrasted with the legislation of the third race, and with the principles of the imperial system which they imagined themselves to represent. Instead of ' quod principi placuit legis habet vigorem,' Charles the Bald, in the famous Edictum Pistense, enunciates the doctrine that ' lex consensu populi fit et constitutione regis [5],' the consent of the people being sought not merely in the assembly of the chiefs but, as we have seen, in the acceptance by the *mallus*.

The laws in the enactment of which the witenagemot joins are not merely secular ones : the ecclesiastical legislation of Ini, Alfred, Ethelred and Canute is, equally with the temporal, transacted with the counsel of the witan. The great influence exercised by the bishops and other ecclesiastics in the assembly may account for the fact that no jealousy of this legislation appears during this long period. Even the more distinctly ecclesiastical assemblies which, like the councils of Clovesho [6] and Chelsea [7], issued canons and spiritual dooms of their own,

Ecclesiastical laws of the witenagemots.

---

[1] Pertz, Legg. i. 9; Baluze, i. 11 (A.D. 595).

[2] Pertz, Legg. i. 16; Baluze, i. 103; Karloman, c. i. § 1.

[3] Pertz, Legg. i. 20; Baluze, i. 133.

[4] Pertz, Legg. i. 82; Baluze, i. 247.

[5] Pertz, Legg. i. 490; Baluze, ii. 120; Edict. Pistense, § 6. Cf. Hincmar, Opp. ii. 204 : 'Habent enim reges et rei publicae ministri leges, quibus in quacunque provincia degentes regere debent; habent capitula Christianorum regum ac progenitorum suorum quae generali consensu fidelium suorum tenere legaliter promulgaverunt.' See Sohm, Fr. G. V. G. p. 135.

[6] Council of Clovesho, A.D. 747 : ' Anno autem regni Aedilbaldi regis Merciorum, qui tunc aderat cum suis principibus ac ducibus, xxxii°;' Councils, &c. iii. 362.

[7] 'Qui (sc. Coenwulf, K. Mercia) tunc temporis praesens adfuit cum

Ecclesiasti-
cal councils.

admitted the great counsellors of the kingdom to their sittings, and allowed their acts to be confirmed by lay subscription. That in both cases the spiritual witan prepared the enactments, in the initial as well as in the final form, there can be no question; but it would be unsafe to argue with reference to the spiritual dooms of the general witenagemots, that this participation of the lay witan was admitted simply to give public or legal ratification to the resolutions of the clergy. It is more probable that in this, as in the action of the folkmoots, the distinction between spiritual and temporal authorisation, as also between moral or religious and legal obligation, was very lightly drawn. The Legatine Councils of A.D. 787[1], which in their very nature were entirely ecclesiastical, were attended by kings and ealdormen as well as by bishops and abbots, and must therefore be numbered amongst true legislative witenagemots. Amongst the ecclesiastical articles which come most naturally within the scope of secular confirmation, are the enforcement of Sunday and festival holydays, the payment of tithe, the establishment of the sanctity of oaths, of marriage and of holy orders, all of them frequent matters of early legislation[2].

Consent of
the witan
to royal
grants of
land.

54. A second class of subjects submitted to these councils, of which we have abundant documentary evidence, concerns the transfer of lands[3], and especially the grants made by charters involving questions of the public burdens. It is not necessary to suppose that every transfer of land required the assent of a court of law, although it might be necessary that it should be conducted under a certain form and before witnesses; that form being symbolical, before as well as after the use of

suis principibus, ducibus et optimatibus, dum undique sacri ordines praesules, cum abbatibus, presbiteriis, diaconibus pariter tractantes;' 'praesidente vero Wlfredo archiepiscopo;' Councils, &c. iii. 579.

[1] Councils, &c. iii. 447–461.

[2] With such limitations we may accept Kemble's seventh canon, Saxons, ii. 222: 'The king and the witan had also power to regulate ecclesiastical matters, appoint fasts and festivals, and decide upon the levy and expenditure of ecclesiastical revenue.' Cf. Gneist, Self-government, i. 44.

[3] Kemble's tenth canon, Saxons, ii. 225: 'The witan possessed the power of recommending, assenting to, and guaranteeing grants of land, and of permitting the conversion of folkland into bookland, and vice versâ.' See also i. 305.

charters for the purpose.   Still, in cases where a large grant of Consent of the witan.
private estate was made by a powerful person, to the possible
detriment of his heirs, the confirmation of the gift might be
sought in the witness of the witenagemot and even by a ratification under their hand and that of the king.   And this was
no doubt the reason why so many monastic charters of confirmation passed under the eye of this assembly.   But where
a grant was made by which the land given was released from
special obligations and made alodial or heritable for ever, the
consent of the nation, the owner, as must be supposed, of
the land so released, was imperatively necessary.   In such
cases the king who makes the grant states that it is done
with the advice and consent of the principes[1].   The sub- Examples.
scribing witnesses are of course the principes whose counsel
and consent are rehearsed in the body of the grant, and who
were the witenagemot in session.   It is with such a form that
Ethelwulf added twenty hides of land to his own inheritance in
A.D. 847[2]; and in the great majority of royal grants the circumstances were the same.   Occasionally a king made a grant
out of his private estate with like formality; the necessity for
counsel and consent in such cases arising probably from the
immunities which formed part of the grant[3].   Where the
witness of a select body of freemen was necessary even for

[1] This is the case in a very large proportion of charters ; e. g. that of
Ceolwulf of Mercia to Archbishop Wulfred in A.D. 823 : 'Actum est . . .
cum consensu et consultu episcoporum meorum ac principum quorum
nomina adnotata tenentur, &c. ;' Cod. Dipl. ccxvii. Egbert's grant to
Shaftesbury : 'Ego Ecgbertus gratia Dei Occidentalium Saxonum rex,
cum consensu et communi consilio episcoporum et principum meorum ac
totius plebis meae seniorum, hanc testimonii cartulam conscribere jussi ;'
Ibid. ccxxxii.

[2] 'Ego Ethelwulf Deo auxiliante Occidentalium Saxonum rex cum consensu ac licentia episcoporum et principum meorum aliquantulam ruris
partem viginti manentium mihi in hereditatem propriam describere jussi ;'
Kemble, C. D. cclx. Edgar also (ibid. mccxlv) takes an estate of five
hides and frees it, with the attestation but without the expressed counsel
and consent of the witan. A similar act of Offa is mentioned : 'Quas
scilicet terras olim rex Offa sibi viventi conscribere fecit, suisque heredibus
post eum, et post eorum cursum vitae, ecclesiae quae sita est apud Beod-
ford consignari praecepit ;' Ibid. mxix.

[3] E. g. Ethelwulf in A.D. 841 : 'Dabo et concedo Beornmodo Hrobensis
ecclesiae episcopo aliquam partem terrae juris mei . . . cum consilio et
licentia episcoporum et principum meorum ;' Kemble, C. D. no. cclii.

the sale of cattle, it cannot be regarded as improbable that in the case of land also security would be sought by publicity quite as much as by careful performance of the legal routine. That the great majority of the charters are gifts to churches may show that, notwithstanding the pious liberality of the period, such endowments required special guarantees; in most other transfers, where no special or prominent public right was concerned, the transaction would be completed by a 'livery of seisin' in the presence of the neighbours. In the greater gifts the witenagemot occupies an analogous position to that held by the townsmen when they admit the new-comer to his share in the common land. The gift of a king to one of his courtiers[1] would require the same security and publicity as a grant to a church; both would be very liable to be resumed. That the participation of the witan in royal grants had any connection with the supposed right of the comites to limit the liberality of their princeps is a theory that cannot bear investigation for a moment[2]. The members of the witenagemot whose consent is generally rehearsed, the ealdormen and bishops, did not, as ealdormen and bishops, stand in the relation of comites to the king; it is far more in concert with history to understand these acts as based on the ancient right of the community to regulate all changes of ownership which affected their own body. This principle of course applies primarily and necessarily to conversions of public land into private estate.

Publicity and security thus acquired.

Judicial power of the witenagemot.

55. The witenagemot was, further, a court of justice, although only in the last resort, or in cases in which the parties concerned were amenable to no other than the royal jurisdiction[3]. They decided suits and tried criminals. Of the contentious jurisdiction there are sufficient proofs in the charters[4]; the king himself

[1] E. g. Cod. Dipl. mccxlvi, ccliii.

[2] Kemble, C. D. i. pref. pp. cii–civ sq.

[3] Kemble's twelfth canon, Saxons, ii. 229: 'The witan acted as a supreme court of justice both in civil and in criminal causes.' The eleventh (ibid. ii. 228); 'The witan possessed the power of adjudging the lands of offenders and intestates to be forfeit to the king.'

[4] Examples will be found in Cod. Dipl. ccxx, ccxlv, mcclviii; many of the earlier and more interesting suits were decided by arbitration in the

was liable to be compelled by a judicial decision to restore the Trials by the witan. property of those whom he had unjustly despoiled [1]. The chroniclers furnish less abundant, but not less satisfactory, proof of the exercise of a criminal judicature also. The witenagemot of Northumbria condemned Wilfrid to imprisonment and exile in the seventh century [2]; Elfric, Ethelweard, Swegen, and Alfgar were outlawed by like assemblies in the eleventh; and there are many instances in which the lands forfeited by criminals were assigned by the witan to the king [3]. Even in Norman times the Anglo-Saxon chronicler does not find a better name for the court of the justiciar that hanged forty-four thieves at Hundehoge in A.D. 1124 than 'gewitenemot [4].' The criminal jurisdiction was much the same under Edward the Confessor as it had been in the days of Tacitus. The king and witenagemot may be said to have possessed a supreme jurisdiction 'over all persons and over all causes,' although from the nature of the case it may not have been frequently exercised. The sentence of outlawry issued so often in the struggle between the houses of Leofric and Godwin may stand as the best illustration [5].

ecclesiastical councils, which were to a certain extent international and cannot be regarded as simple witenagemots; e. g. Cod. Dipl. clxxxvi, ccxix.

[1] In 840 Berhtulf king of Mercia had taken an estate from the church of Worcester and given it to his own men : ' Tunc perrexit ille episcopus Heaberht cum suis secum senioribus, in Pascha, ad Tomeworthie, et suas libertates et cartulas ante-nominatorum terrarum secum habentes, et ibi ante regem ejusque proceres fuerunt allecta, et ibi Merciorum optimates dejudicaverunt illi ut male ac injuste dispoliati essent in suo proprio;' Kemble, C. D. no. ccxlv. See below, vol. ii. § 220; Sohm, Fr. G. V. G. i. 27; Roth, Beneficialwesen, p. 222.

[2] Eddius, V. Wilfr. cc. 33, 45.

[3] Chron. Sax. A.D. 1020, 1051, 1035. Cod. Dipl. mcccxii : 'Synodale concilium ad Cyrneceastre universi optimates mei simul in unum convenerunt et eundem Elfricum majestatis reum de hac patria profugum expulerunt et universa ab illo possessa mihi jure possidenda omnes unanimo consensu decreverunt.' So Leofsin was condemned by the sapientes for the murder of Aefic the high reeve ; Cod. Dipl. dccxix ; Chr. Sax. A.D. 1002.

[4] Chron. Sax. A.D. 1124.

[5] The cases of grant of forfeited land quoted by Kemble, Saxons, ii. 53, 228, are Cod. Dipl. mcxii, mcccxcv, ccclxxiv, mcccxii. Mr. Lodge, Essays on Anglo-Saxon Law, pp. 65, 66, has mustered twenty-one examples of such forfeitures. The king receives in the same way the lands of a person dying intestate ; Ibid. mxxxv.

Taxation
by king and
witan.

56. The imposition of extraordinary taxation was directed by the king with the counsel of the witan[1]; this is more especially conspicuous in the case of the taxes levied for war against the Danes, or to buy off their hostility. In A.D. 991 tribute was given to the Danes by decree of the witan, amongst whom the Archbishop Sigeric and the ealdormen Ethelweard and Elfric are specially mentioned[2]; three years later the unhappy king 'procerum suorum consilio,' levied sixteen thousand pounds for the same purpose; the measure was repeated under the same advice in A.D. 1002, 1007, and 1011[3]. These are indeed the only cases of extraordinary imposts of which there is any record: the maintenance of the royal state being fully provided for by the proceeds of the royal farms and public lands, and all local requirements being met by the alodial obligations discharged by personal service.

General
political
delibera-
tion.

The participation of the witan in the determination of war and peace[4], in the direction of the fleet and army[5], as well as in the furnishing of funds, is abundantly proved by the chronicles of the same reign. The highest subject on which their general powers of deliberation could be exercised is exemplified in the acceptance of Christianity by the Northumbrian witan, as related by Bede[6]. It may be safely affirmed that no business of any importance could be transacted by the king in which they had not, in theory at least, a consultative voice[7].

---

[1] Kemble's eighth canon, Saxons, ii. 223 : 'The king and the witan had power to levy taxes for the public service.'
[2] Chron. Sax. A.D. 991.   [3] Chron. Sax. ; Flor. Wig.
[4] Kemble's third canon, Saxons, ii. 213 : 'The witan had the power of making alliances and treaties of peace, and of settling their terms.' See the peace of Alfred and Guthrum : 'Haec sunt instituta pacis quae Alfredus rex et Godrun rex et omnes Angliae sapientes et omnis populus qui sunt in East-Anglia constituerunt;' Schmid, p. 106 : and the terms made by Ethelred with Anlaf : 'Tha geræde se cyng and his witan thæt him man to sende and him gafol behete and metsunge ;' Chron. Sax. A.D. 994.
[5] Kemble's ninth canon, Saxons, ii. 224 : 'The king and his witan had power to raise land and sea forces, when occasion demanded.' See Chron. Sax. A.D. 999, 1047, 1048. They also arranged for the command of the fleet; Ibid. A.D. 1052.
[6] Hist. Eccl. ii. 13.
[7] This is Kemble's first canon, and it is large enough to cover all the rest. Saxons, ii. 204 : 'First, and in general, they possessed a consul-

57. As one of the chief powers of the councils of the Ger- Election of ealdormen.
mania was the election of the *principes,* and as the consent
of the witenagemot to the deposition of the ealdormen was
apparently requisite [1], it is probable that in theory the election
of those officers belonged to the king and witan conjointly [2].
But the constant tendency, in all the important offices, to the
principle of hereditary succession, must have been a limit to the
exercise of the right; and it would not be safe to regard the
expressed consent of the witan as an absolute condition of appointment. In the election of bishops the same uncertainty of Of bishops.
both theory and practice exists. In the earliest days the kings
of Northumbria and Kent deliberated on the election to Canterbury, as a matter of international interest [3]: and in A.D.
1051 Edward the Confessor summarily set aside the choice
of the monks [4]. Dunstan was appointed 'ex respectu Divino
et sapientum consilio [5].' Edward the Confessor appointed
Archbishop Robert in a witenagemot at London, and nominated Spearhafoc in London at the same time [6]. Yet nothing
can be more certain than that in many cases the clergy and
even the people of the dioceses were consulted. Alcuin writes
to the priests of York, urging them to make a right election [7]:
the chapter of St. Paul's could exhibit a bull of Pope Agatho

tative voice and a right to consider every public act which could be
authorised by the king.'
  [1] See the Chronicle, A.D. 1055; Freeman, Norm. Conq. i. 126.
  [2] Kemble's sixth canon, Saxons, ii. 221 : 'The king and the witan had
power to appoint prelates to vacant sees.' The same right with respect to
the ealdormen is discussed; Ibid. ii. 148, 149.
  [3] Bede, H. E. iii. 29 : 'Cum electione et consensu sanctae ecclesiae
gentis Anglorum.'
  [4] V. Edw. Conf. (ed. Luard), p. 400 : 'Rodbertus vero . . . . regis
munere archiepiscopus, totius ecclesiae filiis hanc injuriam pro nisu suo
reclamantibus.' It was done in a gemot at London; Chron. Sax. A.D.
1050.
  [5] See the contemporary life of Dunstan, in Memorials of St. Dunstan,
pp. 36, 38; Flor. Wigorn. A.D. 959. Oskytel was made archbishop in
A.D. 971, by favour of the king and his witan; Chron. Sax. A.D. 971.
Elfric was chosen by Ethelred and all his witan in 995 ; Ibid.
  [6] Chron. Sax. A.D. 1050.
  [7] Alcuin writes in A.D. 796 to a powerful man in Northumbria, urging
him to defend the freedom of the election to York, and to the clergy of
York praying them to avoid simony; Alc. Epp. 40, 48 ; Councils, &c. iii.
499, 500.

Election of
bishops.

conferring on them the exclusive right[1]. A bishop of Lichfield in the ninth century declares himself elected by the whole church of the province[2]; and Helmstan, of Winchester, in A.D. 839, mentions the pope, the king, the church of Winchester, and all the bishops, optimates, and nation of the West Saxons, as joining in his appointment[3]. It is probable then that under the heptarchic kings the action of the churches was comparatively free in this respect, and that the restriction was a result of the growth of royal power; but that, like all other ecclesiastical business, the appointment of bishops was a matter of arrangement between the parties concerned: the election by the clergy was the rule in quiet times, and for the less important sees; the nomination by the king in the witenagemot was frequent in the case of the archiepiscopal and greater sees; the consent of the national assembly to the admission of a new member to their body being in all cases implied, on behalf of the most important element in it, by the act of consecration performed by the comprovincial bishops[4].

Election of
kings.

58. Of all elections, the most important was no doubt that of the kings; and this belonged both in form and substance to the witan[5], although exercised by them in general assemblies of the whole nation. The king was in theory always elected, and the fact of election was stated in the coronation service throughout the middle ages, in accordance with most ancient precedent. It is not less true, that the succession was by constitutional practice restricted to one family, and that the rule of hereditary succession was never, except in great emergencies and in the most trying times, set aside. The principle may be generally stated thus,—the choice was limited to the best qua-

[1] Councils, &c. iii. 161.

[2] 'Quoniam me indignum famulum tuum tota ecclesia provinciae nostrae sibi in episcopatus officium elegerunt;' Councils, &c. iii. 613.

[3] 'A sancta et apostolicae sedis dignitate, et ab congregatione civitatis Wentanae, necnon Aethel . . . . regis et episcoporum optimatorumque ejus et totius genti Occidentalium Saxonum unanimiter ad episcopalis officii gradum electus;' Councils, &c. iii. 622.

[4] Gneist regards the bishops as royal nominees far too exclusively; Self-government, i. 44; Verwaltungsrecht, i. 73.

[5] Kemble's fourth canon, Saxons, ii. 214: 'The witan had the power of electing the king;' Freeman, Norm. Conq. i. 593–597.

lified person standing in close relationship to the last sovereign :
for it is seldom, except in case of revolution or conspiracy, that
any one but a son, brother, or near kinsman is chosen ; and in
the case of a king dying in mature years, his eldest son would
be, and was in practice held to be, in every respect the safest
successor[1]. It may be sufficient however here to lay down the Formal elec-
rule, that both the formal election preparatory to the act of king.
coronation, and the actual selection when the necessity for a
free choice occurred, belonged to the witan : they included
among them both the principes or national magistrates, to
whom, on the most ancient precedents of heathen times, the
power appertained ; the bishops, whose recognition by the act
of anointing and coronation was religiously viewed as conveying the Divine sanction, and as requisite for the enforcement The three-
of the moral duty of the subject ; and the ministri or personal tion.
retainers of the crown, whose adhesion, expressed in their
particular oath of fealty, was in the highest degree necessary
for the safety and peace of the new reign[2]. The recognition
by the assembled people was a complementary security, but
implied no more real right of admission or rejection than
belonged to the persons actually present : for the crowd that
surrounded the coronation chair was no organised or authorised
representation of the nation[3].

But although the principle of electing the best qualified

---

[1] Hallam, M. A. ii. 273. The instances in which express mention is
made of the act of election, are collected by Kemble, Saxons, ii. 215–219,
and Freeman, Norm. Conq. i. 591. They are, Alfred (Asser, M. H. B.
477, Sim. Dun. A.D. 871) ; Edward the Elder (Ethelwerd, c. 4, M. H. B.
519) ; Athelstan (Chron. Sax. A.D. 924) ; Edred, 'electione optimatum
subrogatus' (Cod. Dipl. ccccxi) ; Edgar 'eligitur' (Flor. Wig. A.D. 957) ;
Edward (Flor. Wig. A.D. 975) ; Ethelred (Chron. Sax. A.D. 979) ; Edmund
(Chron. Sax. A.D. 1016) ; Canute (Chron. Sax. A.D. 1017) ; Harold I (Flor.
Wig. A.D. 1035: 'consentientibus quam plurimis majoribus natu,' A.D.
1037, 'rex eligitur') ; Edward the Confessor (Chron. Sax. A.D. 1042) ;
Harold II (Flor. Wig. A.D. 1066).

[2] In the case of Alfred it is said, 'a ducibus et a praesulibus totius
gentis eligitur et non solum ab ipsis verum etiam ab omni populo
adoratur ;' Sim. Dun. ad 871. Edred 'frater ejus (i. e. Edmundi)
uterinus, electione optimatum subrogatus, pontificali auctoritate eodem
anno catholice est rex et rector ad regna quadripertiti regiminis consecratus ;' Cod. Dipl. ccccxi.

[3] Freeman, Norm. Conq. i. 591.

member of the royal house may be accepted as giving the basis of a rule, the cases in which son succeeded father directly are, from various causes, very few during the whole period. In Wessex there is not one example of the kind between the years 685 and 839[1]. In Mercia the history tells nearly the same tale[2]. In Northumbria the confusion is increased by numerous cases of conspiracy, murder and deposition[3]. In the West Saxon dynasty, after it had won the supremacy under Egbert, the hereditary principle is maintained[4], but the short-

---

[1] To confine the reckoning to Christian times: In WESSEX; after the death of Cynewalh in 672, his wife Sexburga is said to have reigned a year, but the kingdom was really broken up by the ealdormen. The line of succession continues; Cenfus a distant kinsman succeeds Sexburga, and Escwin son of Cenfus succeeds him. Kentwin the next king, Ceadwalla his successor, Ini, Ethelheard, whose successor Cuthred is called his brother, Sim. Dun. A.D. 739; Sigebert, Cynewulf, Brihtric, and Egbert, are in no case so nearly related as to be described by a more distinct term than kinsmen; and the pedigrees show that they were not near kinsmen.

[2] In Mercia, after Penda, his sons Wulfhere and Ethelred reigned in succession. Ethelred was followed by his nephew Cenred son of Wulfhere; Cenred by Ceolred son of Ethelred. Ethelbald the next king was a distant kinsman, great-nephew of Penda; Beornred who followed was a usurper. Offa recovered the throne for the royal house, but himself was only sprung from a brother of Penda. His son Egfrith succeeded him; on Egfrith's death Coenwulf, a distant collateral, came in; his brother Ceolwulf succeeded after the murder of the child Kenelm; and the rest of the Mercian kings are not within the pedigree.

[3] See note, p. 153.

[4] In the West-Saxon family after the reign of Egbert the chief exceptions to hereditary succession are found in the fact that the four sons of Ethelwulf followed in order of birth, the brother being preferred to the son of the last king; Alfred at least succeeded, although he certainly had two nephews, sons of an elder brother. But in this case it may be observed, (1) that the kingdoms held by Ethelwulf were not yet consolidated: Ethelstan had reigned as king of Kent with Ethelwulf until A.D. 850; Ethelbald had been king of Wessex from A.D. 856; Ethelbert had been king of Kent as early as A.D. 853 (Cod. Dipl. cclxix); and during the reign of Ethelred, Alfred had been *secundarius*, that is, had probably an inchoate royalty of a stronger character than that of heir presumptive; so that the family arrangement which provided for the descent of the inherited estate (see Alfred's Will) may have been followed in the succession to the kingdom also; (2) the sons of the elder brother must have been minors at the time of Alfred's succession. That Edward the Elder should succeed his father to the exclusion of his cousins, was quite natural. The three sons of Edward the Elder succeeded one another in the same way; Athelstan however seems to have had no children: and as Edmund was only eighteen when he began to reign in 940, his children must have been infants when he died in 946. It is not necessary here to examine into the nature of Alfred's anointing at Rome, which Asser describes as royal unction, but which has been explained of confirmation. See

ness of the reigns and the youthfulness of the kings at their
accession seldom admits of the direct transmission of the crown
from father to son.   Hence the elective principle had a sphere
and exercised an influence much greater than might appear from
the direct assertion of the chroniclers.

The right of deposing a worthless king seems to be a corollary   Deposition
from the right of election[1]; but it is not in reality so simple   of the king.
a matter either in history or in theory; for the right of an
elected, accepted, crowned and anointed king is fenced round
with sanctions that cannot be broken by the mere resolution of
his electors.   The cases in which the power was exercised by
the witenagemot must be dealt with singly.   Most if not all of
these belong to the heptarchic period.   In the eighth century   In North-
there were fifteen kings of Northumbria all duly elected, of   umbria.
whom at least thirteen ended their reigns by extraordinary
means[2]: of these, two, Ceolwulf and Eadbert, are recorded to

Pauli, Life of Alfred (ed. Thorpe), pp. 54, 84; Kemble, C. D. cccxiv;
Liber de Hyda, p. 327.
   [1] Kemble's fifth canon, Saxons, ii. 219: 'The witan had the power to
depose the king, if his government was not conducted for the benefit of his
people.'
   [2] The order of their reigns is as follows :—
     1. Aldfrith, died in A.D. 705 ; Bede, H. E. v. 18.
     2. Eadwulf, ' de regno quod duos menses tenuit, conjuratione facta
        adversus eum expulsus est;' Edd. V. Wilfr. c. 57.
     3. Osred, son of Aldfrith, ' cognatorum insidiis caesus ;' W. Malmesb.
        G. R. § 53.   'Immatura et terribili morte praeventus;' Ep.
        Bonif. 59.
     4. Coenred, 'infirmatus ;' Henry of Hunting- ⎫ ' Foedo exitu auras pol-
        don, M. H. B. 734.   ⎬ luere ;' W. Malmesb.
     5. Osric, killed ; Chron. Sax. A.D. 731.   ⎭ G. R. § 53.
     6. Ceolwulf, brother of Coenred, ' captus, attonsus et remissus est in
        regnum ;' Cont. Bedae, A.D. 731 : ' sua voluntate attonsus reg-
        num Eadbercto reliquit;' Ibid. A.D. 737.
     7. Eadbert, 'filius patrui Ceolwulfi'—'accepta Sancti Petri tonsura,
        filio suo Oswulfo regnum reliquit;' Ibid. A.D. 758.
     8. Oswulf, ' a suis ministris facinorose occisus ;' Ibid. A.D. 759 :
        ' occisus est nequiter a sua familia ;' Sim. Dun. A.D. 758.
     9. Ethelwald, ' a sua plebe electus;' Cont. Bed. 759 : 'regnum
        amisit in Winchenheale ;' Sim. Dun. A.D. 765.
    10. Alcred, ' prosapia Idae regis exortus ;' Ibid.   ' Consilio et con-
        sensu suorum omnium, regiae familiae ac principum destitutus
        societate, exilio imperii mutavit majestatem ;' Ibid. A.D. 774.
    11. Ethelred, son of Ethelwald, ' tanto honore coronatus ;' Ibid.
        ' Expulso de regali solio et in exilium fugato ;' Ibid. A.D. 779.
    12. Elfwald, son of Oswulf, ' conjuratione facta ab ejus patricio, Sicgan
        nomine, miserabili occisus est morte ;' Ibid. 788.

have resigned quietly and entered the ranks of the clergy; one,
Osric, is simply said to have been killed; three, Osred, Oswulf,
and Elfwald, were slain by conspiracy of their own officers or
retainers; two, Eadwulf and another Osred, were expelled by
similar bodies without being murdered; Osbald was set up and
set aside by a faction; of the end of Coenred we are told nothing,
but that it was calamitous; Alcred was deprived of his kingdom
by the counsel and consent of his own people, that is no doubt
by regular act of the witenagemot; his predecessor, Ethelwald,
lost his kingdom at Wincenheale, the meeting-place of the
Northumbrian councils,—most probably therefore by a similar
act; Ethelred was displaced in A.D. 779, and restored in A.D.
790, only to be murdered six years later by equally competent
authority; Eardulf was expelled from his throne and country in
A.D. 808, and sought restoration through the intercession of the
pope and emperor.　In Wessex the tale is somewhat different:
during the same period Ini, following the example of his predecessor Ceadwalla, resigned his crown and went to Rome; Ethelheard and Cuthred, who followed him, reigned as long as they
lived; Sigebert, the next king, was[1], after a year's reign, deposed by Kynewulf and the West Saxon witan, one province
being left him for his maintenance; Kynewulf was murdered,
and Brihtric was poisoned by his wife.

In such a record it is scarcely wise to look for constitutional

---

13. Osred, son of Alcred: 'dolo suorum principum circumventus et
　　captus ac regno privatus attonsus est—coactus exilium petit;'
　　Ibid. 790.　'De exilio sacramentis et fide quorundam principum
　　clam .... venit .... captus .... occisus;' Ibid. 792.

11. Ethelred restored; killed by his subjects in A.D. 796; Sim. Dun. :—
　　Letter of Alcuin to Offa; Councils, iii. 499.

14. Osbald: 'patricius a quibusdam ipsius gentis principibus in reg-
　　num est constitutus et post xxvii dies omni regiae familiae ac
　　principum est societate destitutus, fugatusque et de regno ex-
　　pulsus;' Sim. Dun. A.D. 796.

15. Eardulf: 'De exilio vocatus regni infulis est sublimatus;' Sim.
　　Dun. 796.　'Regno et patria pulsus;' Einhard, A.D. 808.　'Per
　　legatos Romani pontificis et domini imperatoris in regnum suum
　　reducitur;' Ibid.; Councils, iii. 561.

[1] Chron. Sax. A.D. 755: 'This year Cynewulf and the West Saxon
witan deprived Sigebert of his kingdom, except Hampshire, for his unjust
doings.'

precedents [1]. The depositions, however, of Alcred and Sigebert stand out as two regular and formal acts; the authority by which they were sanctioned being fully though briefly stated, the deposition not being followed by murder, and, in one case, provision being made for the support of the royal dignity. It is probable that these instances might be multiplied, if we had fuller details as to the conspiracies by which the Northumbrian kings were unseated. The depositions of Alcred and Sigebert may have been the result of a conspiracy, and those of the others may have been determined in a witenagemot, all under the inspiration of a competitor for the throne : but in these cases, on any theory, the deposition was decreed in the national council. Whether such depositions were completed by any act of degradation or renunciation of allegiance, we are not told : at a later period, when coronation and the national recognition by homage and fealty were regular parts of the inauguration of a king, something more than a mere sentence of the supreme court would have been necessary, if all such ceremonies had not been summarily dispensed with by murder. In the cases of Ceolwulf and Eadbert, the voluntary tonsure was regarded as a renunciation of the rights conferred by coronation. In the cases in which the expulsion or deposition is said to be the result of conspiracy or desertion of the 'familia' of the luckless prince, we have an indication of some process on the part of the comitatus, the ministri, or king's thegns, analogous to the renunciation of allegiance in feudal times. But our authorities are scanty and brief, and, even if such conjectures are true, it would be unsafe to regard these cases as instances under a general rule. The time was one of unexampled civil anarchy, and there is no instance in which, without the pressure of a competitor, who had perhaps an equal title to the throne by hereditary or personal qualifications, a king was simply set aside for

Marginal notes: Cases of Alcred and Sigebert. Complication of the question. Scarcity of constitutional precedents.

[1] The deposition of Beornred, king of Mercia, in A.D. 758, related in the *Vitae duorum Offarum*, by Matthew Paris (ed. Wats, pp. 10, 11), is scarcely historical, but may be quite true : 'Pro eo quod populum non equis legibus sed per tyrannidem gubernaret, convenerunt in unum omnes tam nobiles quam ignobiles, et Offa duce . . . . ipsum a regno expulerunt ;' M. Paris, ed. Luard, i. 342, 343.

misgovernment. The immorality and other misdeeds of the Northumbrian kings would have been amply sufficient to justify more regular proceedings than a succession of conspiracies among their near kinsmen.

Later cases
exceptional.

Among the descendants of Egbert three cases occur; the western half of the West Saxons discard Ethelwulf after his return from Rome, in favour of Ethelbald[1] : the Mercians reject Edwy and elect Edgar[2]; and the whole kingdom renounces Ethelred the Unready[3]. In the first two instances, however, it is a revolt or civil war rather than a legal deposition, and it results in a division of an ill-consolidated kingdom between two competitors. Ethelred also is renounced in favour of his conqueror, rather than formally deposed, and the action of the witan is more clearly concerned with his restoration than with his expulsion.

---

[1] Asser, V. Alfredi, Mon. Hist. Brit. pp. 470, 471 : 'Interea tamen Ethelwulfo rege ultra mare tantillo tempore immorante . . . . Ethelbald rex, Ethelwulfi regis filius et Ealhstan Scireburnensis ecclesiae episcopus, Eanwulf quoque Summurtunensis pagae comes, conjurasse referuntur, ne unquam Ethelwulf rex a Roma revertens iterum in regno reciperetur, ... redeunte eo a Roma, ... ineffabili patris clementia et omnium adstipulatione nobilium, adunatum antea regnum inter patrem et filium dividitur.'

[2] V. Dunstani (Memorials of S. Dunstan), pp. 35, 36 : 'Factum est autem ut rex praefatus in praetereuntibus annis penitus a brumali populo relinqueretur contemptus . . . . Hunc ita omnium conspiratione relictum elegere sibi Deo dictante Eadgarum fratrem ejusdem Eadwigi germanum in regem . . . . Sicque universo populo testante publica res regum ex diffinitione sagacium sejuncta est ut famosum flumen Tamesae regnum disterminaret amborum.'

[3] 'Quibus omnibus ad velle peractis, ad suam classem reversus ab omni Anglorum populo rex, si jure queat rex vocari qui fere cuncta tyrannice faciebat, et appellabatur (sc. Sweyn) et habebatur ;' Flor. Wig. A.D. 1013. 'Quo mortuo filium ejus Canutum sibi regem constituit classica manus Danorum. At majores natu totius Angliae ad regem Ethelredum par. consensu nuntios festinanter misere dicentes, se nullum plus amare vel amaturos esse quam suum naturalem dominum, si ipse vel rectius gubernare vel mitius eos tractare vellet quam prius tractarat. Quibus auditis Eadwardum filium suum cum legatis suis ad eos dirigens, majores minoresque gentis suae amicabiliter salutavit, promittens se mitem devotumque dominum futurum, in omnibus eorum voluntati consensurum, consilii. acquieturum et quidquid sibi vel suis ab illis probrose et dedecorose dictum vel contrarie factum fuerat, placido animo condonaturum, si omnes unanimiter et sine perfidia illum recipere vellent in regnum. Ad haec cuncti benigne responderunt. Dein amicitia plenaria ex utraque parte verbis et pacto confirmatur. Ad haec principes se non amplius Danicum regem admissuros in Angliam unanimiter responderunt ;' Ibid. A.D. 1014.

In all these points, the actual exercise by the witenagemot of their allowed and recognised right must have depended very much on the circumstances of the case, and on the character of the sovereign with whom they had to deal. It is in legislation alone that we can affirm that their right to advise and consent was invariably recognised; their participation in grants of land is not much less frequently particularised, but is often mentioned in a way that shows it to have been formal and perfunctory, and after the end of the tenth century often ceases to be expressed at all. The election to the office of ealdorman was regulated more by the king's favour and by hereditary claims than by a substantive selection, except in a few extraordinary cases; that to the episcopal sees was limited both by canonical custom and by the piety or determination of the king; in either case, the election might easily obtain constitutional confirmation, for both the friends of the monks and the retainers of the king were numerous in the gemot.

Rights really exerted by the witan.

Thus the English king, although fettered both in theory and in practice by important restrictions, was scarcely more like the king of German antiquity than like the king of feudal times. He was hedged in by constitutional forms, but they were very easy to break through, and were broken through with impunity wherever and whenever it was not found easier to manipulate them to the end in view. The reason why the West Saxon kings of united England had so few difficulties with either clergy or lay counsellors may have been that, their power of increasing the number of their dependents in the witenagemot by nomination being admitted, they could at any time command a majority in favour of their own policy. Under such circumstances, the witenagemot was verging towards a condition in which it would become simply the council of the king, instead of the council of the nation; the only limit on the power of nomination being on the one hand the importance of canonical sanction, and on the other the difficulty of setting aside hereditary claims among the ealdormen and the ministri. The feudal principle advances until it stands face to face with the determination of the tax-payer.

The limited character of the kingship. 59. The king [1] then, who crowns the fabric of the state, is neither a mere ornamental appendage nor a ruler after the imperial model. He is not the supreme landowner, for he cannot without consent of the witan add a portion of the public land to his own demesne. He requires their consent for legislation or taxation, for the exercise of jurisdiction, for the determination of war and peace. He is elected by them, and liable to be deposed by them. He cannot settle the succession to the throne without their sanction. He is not the fountain of justice, which has always been administered in the local courts; he is the defender of the public peace, not the autocratic maintainer of the rights of subjects who derive all their rights from him. But, notwithstanding, he is the representative of the unity and dignity, and of the historical career of the race; the unquestioned leader of the host; the supreme judge of ultimate resort. The national officers are his officers; the sheriffs are his stewards; the bishops, ealdormen, and witan are his bishops, ealdormen, and witan. The public peace is his peace; the sanction which makes him inviolable and secure, is not the simple toleration of his people, but the character impressed on him by unction and coronation, and acknowledged by himself in the promises he has made to govern well and maintain religion, peace, and justice.

Privileges of royalty. Royalty has besides many distinctive and most important privileges or prerogatives; rights which only in a very modified way exist among the subjects, and which are practically limited only in a slight degree by the action of the council. In the first place, it is hereditary; that is, the successor or competitor pos-

[1] On the origin of the word *king*, see Max Müller's Lectures on the Science of Language, ii. 282, 284; Freeman, Norm. Conq. i. 583, 584; Grimm, R. A. p. 230; Schmid, Gesetze, p. 551. Max Müller decides that 'the old Norse konr and konungr, the old high German chuninc, and the Anglo-Saxon cyning, were common Aryan words, not formed out of German materials, and therefore not to be explained as regular German derivatives. . . . . It corresponds with the Sanskrit ganaka . . . . It simply meant father of a family.' Therefore it is not cyn-ing, the child of the race. But the Anglo-Saxons probably connected the *cyning* with the *cyn* more closely than scientific etymology would permit; witness such words as cyne-hlaford, in which however we are told that cyne means *nobilis*, not *genus*; Schmid, Gesetze, p. 551. Sir F. Palgrave's idea of deriving the word from the Celtic *cen*, 'head,' and the notion connecting it with 'can' and 'cunning,' are alike absurd.

sible to the reigning sovereign cannot be any merely ambitious ealdorman or factious neighbour; royalty, though elective, belongs to one house, one family, always kept within comparatively narrow proportions by the hazardousness of their employments, by private jealousy, and not unfrequently by stern cruelty. The king is safe from competition, except by his own immediate kinsmen, and if he live long enough to have a grown-up son, he may count surely on not being deposed. This mark seems to be universal : the Visigoths are the only tribe of Germanic connexion which we know to have maintained royalty unfettered by hereditary right, and that only in their decline, and after the extinction of the house of Alaric [1]. In all other cases, save that of simple alodial inheritance, public offices were filled and political position bestowed by nomination or election for life only. As hereditary sovereign, the king had every inducement to labour for the consolidation of the state, the government of which he should leave to his son, and not for the mere accumulation of wealth or territory for heirs who would sink into a private station when he was gone.

The king had, in the next place, a large property in land and revenue. His property in land may fall under three heads : first, his private estate, which he could dispose of by his will, and which might be either alodial property, bookland [2], or possibly public land of which he had taken leases of lives ; secondly, the proper demesne of the crown, comprising palaces and their appendant farms, the *cyninges botl* and the *cyninges tun*, and even cities and burghs founded upon old royal estates : these belonged to the king as king, and could not be alienated or burdened without the consent of the witenagemot [3]. And he

---

[1] The fifth council of Toledo anathematises aspirants to the throne whom ' nec electio omnium probat nec Gothicae gentis nobilitas ad hunc honoris apicem trahit ; ' Labbe, Conc. v. 1739.

[2] Such as are disposed of in the wills of Alfred and Edred ; Liber de Hyda, pp. 62, 153.

[3] The ' dominicatus regis ad regnum pertinens ; ' Exon. Domesd. p. 75. See a grant of Ethelred II to Abingdon (Cod. Dipl. mcccxii), in which he carefully distinguishes between his *propria hereditas,* which he could alienate, and the *terrae regales et ad regios filios pertinentes,* the alienation of which the witan had refused to sanction ; Kemble, Saxons, ii. 30. On the king's authority over the folkland see Sohm, Fr. G. V. G. i. 31–33.

had, thirdly, rights over the public land of the kingdom, rather of the nature of claim than of possession; the right of feorm-fultum for himself, and that of making provision for his followers with the consent of the witan. After the reign of Ethelred, this third class of property seems to have been merged in the crown demesne.

Revenue of the crown.

Under the head of revenue may be placed the fines and other proceeds of the courts of law which the king shared as guardian of the peace [1]; the proceeds of forfeited lands and goods secured to him by the sentence of the witan [2]; the right of maintenance or procurations for himself and his retinue in public progresses [3]; the produce of wreck and treasure trove [4], mines and saltworks [5], the tolls and other dues of markets, ports and transport generally [6]; and the heriots and other semifeudal payments resulting from the relation between the sovereign and his special dependents [7]. The existence of many of these sources of income is known only from grants of land in which they are retained or remitted. It is probable that the character of many of them varied much from time to time; but there is no subject on which we have less information than the administration of public revenue in the Anglo-Saxon times: a curious point of contrast with the age that follows, that of Domesday and the Pipe Rolls. With these sources of profit may be noted such minor rights as the protection of strangers, and the power of erecting bridges and castles [8].

The king's wergild.

The higher price set on the king's life [9], the wergild payable to his kin on his violent death, testifies to the importance attached to his person. By the Mercian law it was 7,200 shillings, by that of the North people 15,000 thrymsas, or

The king's cynebot.

nearly half as much again. A fine of equal amount, the *cynebot*, was at the same time due to his people. The existence of these regulations may be interpreted as showing that

[1] Kemble, Saxons, i. 157; ii. 54, 55.　　　[2] See above, p. 147.
[3] Kemble, Saxons, i. 152; ii. 58–61.　　　[4] Ibid. ii. 55, 64.
[5] Ibid. ii. 69.　　　　　　　　　　　　　[6] Ibid. ii. 75.
[7] Ibid. ii. 98 sq.　　　　　　　　　　　　[8] Ibid. ii. 88, 91.
[9] Ibid. i. 153; ii. 32; Schmid, Gesetze, p. 552; Allen, Prerogative, pp. 36, 40; Gneist, Verwaltungsrecht, i. 21.

the idea of treason against the king was as yet unknown, no other punishment being prescribed for the regicide, and the value of the king's life being made to differ in degree only from that of the subject [1]. How far this is true in theory we may consider further on; as to the fact, it may be stated that in the earliest laws no wergild is assigned to the king, and hence it may be inferred that none would be accepted; in the cases in which it is assigned, the sum is so large that it would necessitate the enslaving of the murderer and his kin, if not such a failure of payment as death alone could expiate. The fines for transgressing the king's protection, breaking into his 'burh,' and injuring his dependents, were correspondingly high, but not so much so as to imply a difference in kind from like offences against private men.

The raised seat or throne, the crown or royal helmet, the sceptre, the standard, tufa or lance [2], all the ordinary insignia of historical royalty, seem to have been used by one or other of the Anglo-Saxon kings. The ceremony of anointing and coronation has however an especial interest in their case. *Honorary privileges.*

60. The royal consecration in its most perfect form included both coronation and unction. The wearing of a crown was a most ancient sign of royalty, into the origin of which it is useless now to inquire; but the solemn rite of crowning was borrowed from the Old Testament by the Byzantine Caesars; the second Theodosius was the first emperor crowned with religious ceremonies in Christian times [3]. The introduction of the rite of anointing is less certainly ascertained. It did not always accompany coronation, and, although usual with the later emperors, is not recorded in the case of the earlier ones, whilst in *Consecration, including crowning and unction.*

[1] Allen, Prerogative, p. 40: 'It appears ... from these legal and historical details that in early times he had no other security for his life than what the law afforded to the meanest of his subjects.'

[2] Sceptra, Sim. Dun. A.D. 755; tufa, Bede, H. E. ii. 16.

[3] Maskell, Monumenta Ritualia, iii. p. iv; Robertson, Essays, pp. 203-215. The word 'consecration' would as a rule imply unction, and, *a fortiori*, coronation. But the unction of Alfred at Rome was rather a prophetic and presumptive inauguration than a formal act, and can scarcely have included coronation. Alfred at any rate did not receive the title of king with it, and it is most reasonably referred to his confirmation. The point is however an interesting one; see Will. Malmesb. (ed. Stubbs), ii. pref. pp. xli, sq.

Origin of
coronation
and unction.

the middle ages the kings of England, France, Jerusalem and
Sicily, are said to have been the only sovereigns below the imperial rank who were entitled to it. There is no evidence that
Theodosius was anointed, but his successor Justin certainly
was; and in general, where unction is stated to have taken
place, coronation may be understood to have accompanied it.
It is not easy to determine, when crowned and anointed kings
are spoken of rhetorically, whether anything more is meant
than a figurative statement that their power is ordained of
God: and consequently the fact that Gildas speaks thus of the
British kings can scarcely be pleaded as actual evidence of the
performance of the rite[1]. S. Columba however 'ordained,'
that is crowned and consecrated, King Aidan of Dalriada[2].
The unction of Clovis by S. Remigius, so far as it is true at all,
is better understood of his baptism than of his coronation[3];
and between Clovis and Pippin there is no authenticated case
of any Frank king being anointed[4], although it was customary
among the Visigothic kings of Spain[5]. From the ancient Pontifical ascribed to Egbert archbishop of York, in the eighth
century, we learn that the English kings were both crowned
with a helmet and anointed[6]. Whether the custom was bor-

---

[1] Gildas, Hist. cxix. (M. H. B. 12): 'Ungebantur reges et non per
Deum; sed qui ceteris crudeliores extarent; et paulo post ab unctoribus
non pro veri examinatione trucidabantur, aliis electis trucioribus.'

[2] 'Sanctus verbo obsecutus Domini ad Iovam transnavigavit insulam
ibidemque Aidanum iisdem adventantem diebus in regem, sicut erat
jussus, ordinavit;' Adamnan, V. S. Columbae; ed. Reeves, n. 198. Councils,
&c. ii. 108.

[3] Waitz, D. V. G. ii. 130, 131; iii. 219. Maskell regards the whole as
a fabrication; Mon. Rit. iii. p. vi. Waitz refers the unction to the
baptism. Clovis wore a diadem, after receiving the consular insignia from
Constantinople; D. V. G. ii. 133. Cf. Hallam, M. A. i. 107, 108.

[4] Waitz, D. V. G. iii. 61.

[5] Robertson, Essays, p. 204; Waitz, D. V. G. iii. 63.

[6] Pont. Egb. (dated between 733 and 766), Surtees Soc., pp. 100–105.
See also Kemble, Saxons, i. 155. Bede does not, so far as I remember,
mention any coronation or unction. The ancient Northumbrian annals,
used by Simeon of Durham, say of Ethelred of Northumbria, A.D. 774,
'tanto honore coronatus;' of Eadbert, A.D. 758, 'regnum sibi a Deo colla-
tum;' of Eardulf, A.D. 796, 'regni infulis est sublimatus, et in Eboraca, in
ecclesia Sancti Petri, ad altare beati apostoli Pauli, ubi illa gens primum
perceperat gratiam baptismi, consecratus est.' Of the other kingdoms we
have no contemporary Chronicles; but the consecration of Egfrith the heir
of Offa is mentioned in the Chronicle under the year 785, and there is a

rowed from the Britons or taken direct from the Old Testament may be made a matter of question. The ceremony was understood as bestowing the divine ratification on the election that had preceded it, and as typifying rather than conveying the spiritual gifts for which prayer was made[1]. That it was regarded as conferring any spiritual character or any special ecclesiastical prerogative there is nothing to show : rather from the facility with which crowned kings could be set aside and new ones put in their place without any objection on the part of the bishops, the exact contrary may be inferred. That 'the powers that be are ordained of God' was a truth recognised as a motive to obedience, without any suspicion of the doctrine, so falsely imputed to churchmen of all ages, of the indefeasible sanctity of royalty[2]. The same conclusion may be drawn from the compact made by the king with his people and the oaths taken by both. If coronation and unction had implied an indefeasible right to obedience, the oath of allegiance on the one side, and the promise of good government on the other, would have been superfluous. Yet both were given.

Import of the ceremony.

61. The undertaking of the king to govern righteously is not improbably a ceremony of much older date than either of the symbolical rites. But the earliest instance of an oath to that effect is that of the Frank king Caribert of Paris, father of the Kentish Queen Bertha, who is recorded to have sworn

Royal oath on accession.

charter of Ceolwulf of Mercia in which he mentions his consecration as having been performed by Archbishop Wulfred on the 15 Kal. Oct. 822. (Cod. Dipl. ccxvi.) The coronation of Edmund, king of the East Angles, does not rest on any good authority; but the practice had probably become general before the time of Alfred. Florence of Worcester mentions the consecration of Athelstan at Kingston, A.D. 924; that of Edred at the same place in A.D. 946 ; that of Edwy, also at Kingston, in A.D. 955 ; but none of these are specified in the Chronicle. The Chronicles (not contemporary) which give an account of Egbert's consecration at Winchester are of no authority whatever. Ethelwerd states that Edward the Elder was crowned at Whitsuntide in the year after Alfred's death : he also mentions the coronation of Edgar.

[1] The term 'christus Domini,' the Lord's anointed, applied to kings in the canons of the legatine synod of A.D. 787, must be regarded as a presumptive evidence of the existence of the practice commonly at that date ; Councils, &c. iii. 453.

[2] The statements of Allen, Prerogative, p. 22, on this point are very shallow and unfair. To attribute the ideas of the seventeenth century to the ages of S. Gregory, Anselm, and Becket, seems an excess of absurdity.

that he would not inflict new laws and customs upon his people, but would thenceforward maintain them in the state in which they had lived under his father's rule, and that he would impose on them no new ordinance, to their damage; there is some doubt however to whom the promise was made [1]. In the Pontifical of archbishop Egbert the declaration is made in the form of a decree [2]: 'It is the duty of a king newly ordained and inthroned to enjoin on the Christian people subject to him these three precepts; first, that the Church of God and all the Christian people preserve true peace at all times; secondly, that he forbid rapacity and all iniquities to all degrees; thirdly, that in all judgments he enjoin equity and mercy, that therefore the clement and merciful God may grant us His mercy.' In almost exactly the same form is the oath taken by Ethelred the Unready at the bidding of Dunstan [3]: 'In the name of the Holy Trinity, three things do I promise to this Christian people

Oath at consecration.

[1] Greg. Turon. ix. 30: 'Post mortem vero Chlothacharii regis, Chariberto regi populus hic sacramentum dedit; similiter etiam et ille cum juramento promisit, ut leges consuetudinesque novas populo non infligeret, sed in illo quo quondam sub patris dominatione statu vixerant in ipso hic eos deinceps retineret, neque ullam novam ordinationem se inflicturum super eos quod pertineret ad spolium, spopondit.' See Waitz, D. V. G. ii. 158, 161.

[2] Pont. Egb. p. 105; Select Charters, pp. 61, 62. I quote the Pontifical of Egbert under that name as usually given to it; but it is by no means clearly ascertained whether the service it contains is to be regarded as an edition by Egbert of a service for an Anglo-Saxon coronation, or as a common form already in use. It certainly appears to contain the germ of the ceremony which was expanded in later times according to local circumstances; as in the service for the Emperor Henry, Canciani, i. 281. On the later question, as to whether the kings of France borrowed their service from England, see Selden, Titles of Honour, pp. 177, 189; and Maskell, Mon. Rit. iii. 14, 15. In the service of Charles V of France (MS. Cotton. Tiberius B. 8) the archbishop prays for the king, 'ut regale solium videlicet Saxonum, Merciorum, Nordanchimbrorum sceptra non deserat.' Maskell further quotes a service for the coronation of the king of the Franks in which the prayer runs, 'et totius Albionis ecclesiam deinceps cum plebibus sibi annexis ita enutriat,' &c.; and the form given by Canciani may be compared in both particulars. The conclusion seems pretty certain that English MSS. had been used for the original drawing up of the service in both instances. See also Freeman, Norm. Conq. iii. 622-625. The earliest coronation service that we have, to which a certain date can be given, is that of Ethelred II, printed in Taylor's 'Glory of Regality.'

[3] Kemble, Saxons, ii. 36, from Reliquiae Antiquae, ii. 194; Maskell, Mon. Rit. iii. 5; Memorials of S. Dunstan, p. 355.

my subjects: first, that God's Church and all the Christian people of my realm hold true peace; secondly, that I forbid all rapine and injustice to men of all conditions; thirdly, that I promise and enjoin justice and mercy in all judgments, that the just and merciful God of his everlasting mercy may forgive us all.' The promise made by the same Ethelred on his restoration to the throne in A.D. 1014 is an illustrative commentary on this, for it shows the alteration in the relations of the king and his people which had taken place since the more ancient oath was drawn up; 'he promised that he would be to them a *Royal oath.* mild and devoted lord, would consent in all things to their will: whatever had been said of reproach or shame, or done frowardly to him or his, he would placably condone; if all with one mind and without perfidy would receive him to the kingdom[1].' The promise to do the will of his people although they receive him as their lord is a step towards the form of the medieval coronation oath, 'to maintain just laws and protect and strengthen, as far as lies in you, such laws as the people shall choose, according to your strength[2].'

62. The duties and obligations of the people towards the *Oath of the* king may very probably have taken the form of an oath of *people to* allegiance in primitive times, although no such form has been *the king.* preserved. The Frank kings on their accession made a progress through their kingdoms, showed themselves to the nation, and received an oath from all[3]. The oath does not however appear in our own records until the ancient idea of kingship had been somewhat modified. It is the first found in the laws of Edmund, and it there bears the same mark as the legislation of Alfred respecting treason[4]. 'All shall swear, in the name of the Lord, fealty to King Edmund as a man ought to be faithful to

---

[1] See above, p. 156, n. 3; Flor. Wigorn. A.D. 1014.

[2] See vol. ii. § 249.

[3] Greg. Turon. vii. 7: 'Priores quoque de regno Chilperici ... ad filium ejus ... se collegerunt, quem Chlotharium vocitaverunt, exigentes sacramenta per civitates quae ad Chilpericum prius aspexerant, ut scilicet fideles esse debeant Guntchramno regi ac nepoti suo Chlothario.' Also ix. 30, quoted above; other instances are given by Waitz, D. V. G. ii. 158. See also Roth, Beneficialwesen, p. 280.

[4] See Chapter VII.

his lord, without any controversy or quarrel, in open and in secret, in loving what he shall love, and in not willing what he shall not will[1].' This however is no unconditional promise; for the oath taken by the man to his lord, on which the above is framed, specially adds ' on condition that he keep me as I am willing to deserve, and fulfil all that was agreed on when I became his man and chose his will as mine[2].' But it is not the less clear that the obligation, though mutual and conditional still, is not the mere right and duty of both to maintain the peace of the people, but a stage in the development of those mutual relations by which the subject became personally dependent on the sovereign as lord rather than as king.

Conditional oath.

The royal comitatus, gesiths or companions.

63. The greatest constitutional prerogative of the king, his right to nominate and maintain a *comitatus*[3] to which he could give territory and political power, is marked by similar developments. Like the Frank king, the Anglo-Saxon king seems to have entered on the full possession of what had been the right of the elective principes: but the very principle of the comitatus, when it reappears in our historians, had undergone a change from what it was in the time of Tacitus; and it seems to have had in England a peculiar development and a bearing of special importance on the constitution. In Tacitus the comites are the personal following of the princeps; they live in his house, are maintained by his gifts, fight for him in the field. If there is little difference between companions and servants, it

---

[1] Edmund, iii. § 1; Schmid, p. 180: 'Imprimis ut omnes jurent in nomine Domini, pro quo sanctum illud sanctum est, fidelitatem Edmundo regi, sicut homo debet esse fidelis domino suo, sine omni controversia et seditione, in manifesto, in occulto, in amando quod amabit, nolendo quod nolet; et antequam juramentum hoc dabitur, ut nemo concelet hoc in fratre vel proximo suo plusquam in extraneo.' The importance of ' amare quod amet et nolle quod nolit' appears in the earlier law of Edward; Edward, ii. § 1; Schmid, p. 115.

[2] Oaths; Schmid, Gesetze, p. 405: 'In illo Deo pro quo sanctum hoc sanctificatum est, volo esse domino meo N. fidelis et credibilis, et amare quae amet, et absoniare quae absoniet, per Dei rectum et seculi competentiam, et nunquam ex velle et posse, verbo vel opere, quicquam facere quod ei magis displiceat; ut me teneat sicut deservire volo, et totum mihi compleat quod in nostra praelocutione fuit, quando suus deveni et ejus elegi voluntatem.'

[3] See above, pp. 25–27; Kemble, Saxons, i. 162; K. Maurer, Wesen des ältesten Adels, &c. pp. 137 sq.; Krit. Ueberschau, ii. 388 sq.

is because civilisation has not yet introduced voluntary helplessness. The difference between the comites of the princeps
and the household of the private man [1] depends fundamentally
only on the public and political position of the master. Now,
the king, the perpetual princeps and representative of the race,
conveys to his personal following public dignity and importance. His gesiths and thegns are among the great and wise
men of the land. The right of having such dependents is not
restricted to him, but the gesith of the ealdorman or bishop is
simply a retainer [2], a pupil or a ward [3] : the free household
servants of the ceorl are in a certain sense his gesiths also.
But the gesiths of the king are his guard and private council;
they may be endowed by him from the folkland and admitted
by him to the witenagemot. They supply him with an armed
force, not only one on which he can rely, but the only one
directly amenable to his orders; for to summon the fyrd he
must have the consent of the witan. The Danish huscarls of
Canute are a late reproduction of what the familia of the Northumbrian kings must have been in the eighth century [4]. The
gesiths are attached to the king by oath as well as by gratitude
for substantial favours [5]; they may have exempt jurisdictions

The royal
gesiths.

---

[1] Gneist, Self-government, i. 6 ; K. Maurer, Krit. Ueberschau, ii. 396;
G. L. von Maurer, Hofverfassg. i. 138–142. The equivalents of gesith
(*comes*) are hlafæta, the loaf-eater, who eats the bread of the hlaford;
folgarius, the follower ; geneat, the companion (genoss).

[2] Others besides kings and ealdormen might have gesiths or gesith-
cundmen in dependence on them; see Ini, § 50. The under-kings of
the Hwiccii retained the right of endowing their comites ; see Cod. Dipl.
xxxvi, cxvii, cxxv. So too Queen Ethelswitha of Mercia; Ibid. ccxcviii,
ccxcix.

[3] The household of Wilfrid is described by Eddius, c. 21 : ' Principes
quoque saeculares, viri nobiles, filios suos ad erudiendum sibi dederunt, ut
aut Deo servirent si eligerent, aut adultos si maluissent regi armatos
commendaret.' No wonder king Egfrith was jealous of his ' innumerum
sodalium exercitum, regalibus vestibus et armis ornatum ; ' Ibid. c. 24.

[4] K. Maurer, Krit. Ueberschau, ii. 400. The *huskarlar* are of three
classes : (1) Servants; (2) Gestir, who do the king's business abroad and
meet at his table only on holydays, guests ; (3) Hiredhmenn, the inmates
of the court.

[5] Cod. Dipl. clxxix : Cenulf grants land to Suithun ' eo videlicet jure si
ipse nobis et optimatibus nostris fidelis manserit minister et inconvulsus
amicus.' Ibid. ccccxxxvii: Edwy describes Elfhere as 'cuidam comiti non
solum mihi per omnia fideli subjectione obtemperanti, verum etiam in
omnibus meum velle subjicienti.' Ibid. cccclxii : ' vassallo.'

from which the national officers are partially excluded, and dependents of their own whom they may make available for the king's service. The king is not therefore left alone in forlorn majesty like the later Merovingian monarchs; he is his own mayor of the palace, the leader of his own comitatus, and that comitatus supplies him with strength both in the council and in the field. But the chief importance of the gesiths lies in their relation to the territorial nobility, at its origin.

Questions as to the existence of a nobility of blood.

64. It has been sometimes held that the only nobility of blood[1] recognised in England before the Norman Conquest was that of the king's kin[2]. The statement may be regarded as deficient in authority, and as the result of a too hasty generalisation from the fact that only the sons and brothers of the kings bear the name of ætheling. On the other hand must be alleged the existence of a noble (edhiling) class among the continental Saxons who had no kings at all: and the improbability that the kindred nations should undertake so large expeditions for conquest and colonisation with but one noble family in each, or that every noble family that came to England should succeed in obtaining a kingdom[3]. The common use of the word *nobilis* in Bede and Eddius shows that the statement is far too sweeping, and the laws of Ethelbert prove the existence of a class bearing the name of eorl of which no other interpretation can be given[4]. That these, *eorlas* and *æthel*, were the descendants of the primitive nobles of the first settlement, who, on the institution of royalty, sank one step in dignity from the ancient state of rude independence in which they had

The eorl and æthel.

[1] On the subject of nobility see K. Maurer, Ueber das Wesen des ältesten Adels der Deutschen Stämme, München, 1846, and Krit. Ueberschau, iii. 424–440.
[2] Thorpe's Lappenberg, ii. 312, 313. The Franks had no true ancient nobility, such as the rest of the German tribes had; Waitz, D. V. G. ii. 289–291. See above, p. 59.
[3] K. Maurer, Krit. Ueberschau, ii. 424. See Bede, H. E. iii. 14: 'nobilibus simul atque ignobilibus,' translated ' æthelum and unæthelum.' Similar expressions are countless. For the 'eorl' see Ethelbert's laws, §§ 13. 14, 75, &c. &c.; Schmid, Gesetze, pp. 566–568. The word eorl is said to be the same as the Norse jarl, and another form of ealdor (?); whilst the ceorl answers to the Norse karl ; the orginal meaning of the two being old man and young man. See Max Müller, Lectures on Language, ii. 280.　　　　[4] K. Maurer, Wesen des ältesten Adels, &c. p. 187.

elected their own chiefs and ruled their own dependents, may be very reasonably conjectured: and when the heptarchic kingdoms gathered in the petty royalties of the earlier date, and were themselves in turn gathered in under the West Saxon supremacy, the numbers of the families which claimed blood-nobility must have largely increased, whilst the accumulation of power in the king's hand must have at the same time widened the interval between nobility and royalty. The rise of royal dignity and the diminishing importance of the ancient nobles may likewise have tended to restrict the title of ætheling to the royal house. And this would certainly follow as soon as the nobility of blood began to be merged in the much more numerous nobility of official and territorial growth. The ancient name of *eorl* likewise changed it application and, under the influence perhaps of Danish association, was given like that of *jarl* to the official ealdorman. Henceforth the *thegn* takes the place of the *æthel*, and the class of *thegns* probably embraces all the remaining families of noble blood. The change may have been very gradual; the *north people's law* of the tenth or early eleventh century still distinguishes the eorl and ætheling with a wergild nearly double that of the ealdorman and seven times that of the thegn[1]: but the north people's law was penetrated with Danish influence, and the eorl probably represents the jarl rather than the ealdorman, the great earl of the fourth part of England as it was divided by Canute[2]. The eorl-riht to which the successful thegn might aspire, and which he perhaps acquired by the possession of forty hides, may possibly be otherwise explained than by the supposition of a class of eorls as distinct from ealdormen, of which the histories preserve no individual names[3].

Changes of names and titles.

---

[1] The wergild of the king is 15,000 thrymsas, and his cynebot the same; the wergild of the archbishop and ætheling or eorl is 15,000; that of the bishop and ealdorman, 8000; that of the hold and high reeve, 4000; that of the thegn, 2000; that of the ceorl, 267; Schmid, Gesetze, pp. 396, 397.

[2] Robertson, Scotland under her Early Kings, ii. 281, refers the ealdorman and thegn to Saxon Northumbria, the earl and hold to the Scandinavian lords. This is most probable, but it is unnecessary to suppose the document earlier than the time of Canute.

[3] See below, p. 174, n. 4.

Peculiar
growth of
nobility by
service.

65. The development of the comitatus into a territorial nobility seems to be a feature peculiar to English History. Something of the kind might have occurred in the other Germanic races if they had not been united and assimilated under the Frank empire, and worked out their feudalism under the influence of the Frank system. The Lombard gasind and the Bavarian sindman were originally the same thing as the Anglo-Saxon gesith [1]; but they sank into the general mass of vassalage as it

Frank
vassalage.

grew up in the ninth and tenth centuries. Frank vassalage, although it superseded and swamped the comitatus, grew out of circumstances entirely unconnected with it [2]. Frank vassalage was based on the practice of commendation and the beneficiary system. The beneficiary system bound the receiver of land to the king who gave it; and the act of commendation placed the freeman and his land under the protection of the lord to whom he adhered; the result was to bring all the land-

---

[1] Waitz, D. V. G. ii. 182; iv. 190; Grimm, R. A. p. 318; G. L. von Maurer, Hofverfassg. i. 167–170.

[2] Waitz, D. V. G. ii. 262: 'It is usual to derive the later vassalage from the ancient comitatus, but there are no grounds whatever for doing so. The former, wherever we find it, appears in wider extension, in relation to private persons as well as to the king; in relation to them it gives no honours or rights such as the members of the comitatus enjoyed; nor does it create that close personal connexion in which the comites stand to their lord.' See also vol. iv. 210 sq. The dependent might be connected with the king (1) by service, (2) by comitatus, (3) by commendation, (4) by reception of land as a benefice. Frank feudalism grew out of the two latter, the English nobility of service from the two first. It is not contended that either the principles at work in English society or the results at which they arrived before the Norman Conquest were very different from the corresponding influences and results on the continent; but they had a distinct history which was different in every stage, especially in the point that, as in so many other things, the personal relation in England takes the place of the territorial, as it was in France; and the feudalism that followed the Conquest was Frank and territorial, that which preceded it grew from personal and legal, not from territorial influences. On the growth of Frank feudalism, see Waitz, as quoted above; on the growth of dependence among the English, see the following chapter. Here the important point is this, that, whereas the later Anglo-Saxon nobility grew out of gesith-ship and thegn-ship, on the continent the feudal nobility grew out of vassalage, the beneficiary system and immunity. There are however two points in question, (1) the creation of the Anglo-Saxon nobility of service, and (2) the creation of the general system of dependence of which the king was the centre and head: of these only the first is here noticed. In the Frank empire the beneficiary system is unconnected with the comitatus, in the English they are in the closest connexion. See below, § 93.

holders of the country gradually into personal dependence on
the king. Each of these practices had its parallel in England. Anglo-Saxon
Here, however, the bestowal of the gift rather presupposed analogies.
than created the close relation between the king and the receiver of the gift, and in most cases it was made to a gesith in
consideration of past services, implying no new connexion. The
choice of a lord by the landless man for his surety and protector, and even the extension of the practice to the free landowner who required such protection, was less liable in England
than on the continent to be confounded with feudal dependence, and in fact created no indissoluble relation. Hence the
important difference. The comitatus with its antrustions is on
the continent absorbed in the landed vassalage. The comitatus
of gesiths and thegns forms the basis of a new and only partially
vassalised nobility.

But in the process the character of the gesith and thegn is Change in
largely modified. He who had at first been a regular inmate the character of the
of the king's house begins to have an estate of land assigned gesith.
him. He may be a noble, the son of a landed noble, like
Benedict Biscop, who received a provision of land from King
Egfrith which he resigned when he became a monk [1]. To the
public land the sons of the nobles, and the warriors who had
earned their rest, looked for at least a life estate [2]; and according to Bede the pretended church endowments, the pseudo-
monasteries, of his day had so far encroached on the available
stock as to be a public evil. It is unreasonable to suppose
that the relation to his lord diminished at all the personal
status of the gesith [3]. In the time of Tacitus, the noble Ger-

---

[1] 'Cum esset minister Osuiu regis et possessionem terrae suo gradui
competentem illo donante perciperet, . . . fastidivit possessionem caducam
ut adquirere posset aeternam ; despexit militiam cum corruptibili donativo
terrestrem, ut vero Regi militaret, regnum in superna civitate mereretur
habere perpetuum ;' Bede, Hist. Abbatum, c. 1.

[2] 'Quod enim turpe est dicere, tot sub nomine monasteriorum loca hi qui
monachicae vitae prorsus sunt expertes in suam ditionem acceperunt . . . ut
omnino desit locus ubi filii nobilium aut emeritorum militum possessionem
accipere possint ; ideoque vacantes . . . hanc ob rem vel patriam suam pro
qua militare debuerant trans mare abeuntes reliquant, vel,' &c. &c. ; Bede,
Letter to Egbert, c. 7.

[3] Kemble regards the status of the comes as unfree, 'the unfree chattel
of a prince,' Saxons, i. 175 ; see above, p. 27. n. 3.

man did not blush to be seen amongst the comites. Beowulf the son of the noble Ecgtheow became the gesith of King Hygelac, and, when he rose to be a chieftain, had lands, treasures, and gesiths of his own[1]. Of gifts of land to the gesiths we have abundant instances in the charters, and, in almost every instance in which the *comes* is mentioned by Bede, it is as possessor of an estate. In this respect almost at the dawn of History the character of the association is varied: the ancient *comes* lived with his lord, and was repaid for his services by gifts and banquets; the English *gesith*, although bound by oaths to his lord still, lives on his own domain. There are still of course gesiths without land[2], who may live in the palace; but the ancient rule has become the exception.

The thegn.   Closely connected with the *gesith* is the *thegn*[3]; so closely that it is scarcely possible to see the difference except in the nature of the employment. The *thegn* seems to be primarily the warrior *gesith*; in this idea Alfred uses the word as translating the *miles* of Bede[4]. He is probably the *gesith* who has a particular military duty in his master's service. But he also

---

[1] Kemble, Saxons, i. 168; Beowulf, ed. Thorpe, v. 391.

[2] Ini, §§ 45, 50, 51, 63; K. Maurer, Wesen d. ält. Adels, &c. pp. 138, 139. Maurer understands the gesith of Ini's law, where contrasted with the thegn, as the landless gesith; p. 141. He also maintains that the original difference was that the gesith was bound only to military service, whilst the thegn had a special office in the court over and above the military one; the second stage is reached when the thegn has special service in the field; and a third when the military service is united to the possession of five hides; pp. 160–163.

[3] Thegn, 'thegen, vir fortis, miles, minister;' Kemble, Saxons, i. 131, who however, at p. 169, regards the word as meaning originally a servant. Waitz compares the gesith with the Frank antrustion, and the thegn with the vassus; D. V. G., i. 363. K. Maurer identifies the geneat with the gesith (Wesen des ältesten Adels, &c. p. 146), and points out that the original meaning of thegn is not a servant, but a warlike man. Its origin is not the same as that of the German *dienen*, to serve; the cognate word with which is *theow*, a slave. See too K. Maurer, Kritische Ueberschau, ii. 389.

[4] Bede, H. E. iii. 14: 'Divertitque ipse cum uno tantum milite (thegn) sibi fidelissimo nomine Tondheri, celandus in domo comitis (gesithes) Hunvaldi, quem etiam ipsum sibi amicissimum autumabat . . . ab eodem comite (gesith) proditum eum Osuiu, cum praefato ipsius milite (thegn) per praefectum (gerefan) suum . . . interfecit.' Hist. Eccl. iv. 22: 'Ad dominum ipsorum, comitem (gesith) videlicet Aedilredi regis, adductus; a quo interrogatus quis esset, timuit se militem (cyninges thegn) fuisse confiteri,' &c.

appears as a landowner. The ceorl who has acquired five hides of land, and a special appointment in the king's hall, with other judicial rights, becomes thegn-worthy; his oath and protection and wergild are those of a thegn[1]. The thegn therefore is now the possessor of five hides of land, and as such bound to service in war, not necessarily by his relation to the king, but simply as a landowner. And from this point, the time of Athelstan, the gesith is lost sight of except very occasionally; the more important members of the class having become thegns[2], and the lesser sort sinking into the rank of mere servants to the king. The class of thegns now widens; on the one hand the name is given to all who possess the proper quantity of land whether or no they stand in the old relation to the king[3]; on the other the remains of the older nobility place themselves in the king's service. The name of thegn covers the whole class which after the Conquest appears under the name of knights, with the same qualification in land and nearly the same obligations[4]. It also carried so much of nobility as is implied in hereditary privilege. The thegn-born are contrasted with the ceorl-born; and are perhaps much the same as the gesithcund. Such thegn-born

The land-owning thegn.

The gesith disappears.

Nobility of the thegn.

---

[1] As the Danish wars compelled the king to call out the whole population to arms and not to rely on his own comitatus, or on his gesiths and king's thegns, the distinction of the king's thegn from other land-owners disappeared (K. Maurer, Krit. Ueberschau, ii. 409, 410), and the gesith with it.

[2] This is self-evident in the case of the laws. As to charters the following is the general conclusion: down to the time of Egbert grants are made to comites and ministri in nearly equal numbers; Ethelwulf's grants are all to ministri; so are those of his successors down to Edmund, who grants twice to his comites Ethelstan and Eadric, both of whom are ealdormen; and from this time comes frequently has that signification; the terms miles (Cod. Dipl. ccccxxvi, mclvi, mclviii), homo (ccclxxxvi, ccccxii), and vassallus (ccccxxxi, mlxxx), occur occasionally during the tenth century. It would appear from this that the use of the word *gesith* in Alfred's translation of Bede may have been an intentional archaism.

[3] This is the great point maintained by K. Maurer, Wesen d. ält. Adels, p. 158; who asserts that in the later Anglo-Saxons times, the king's service without the five hides did not confer the rank of thegn, whilst the five hides without the king's special service did. The whole view is combated by Schmid, Gesetze, pp. 664–668. See Gneist, Self-government, i. 13, 16, 17. See also Lodge, Essays, &c. pp. 116–118.

[4] Select Charters, p. 87; above, p. 172. The word *cniht* occurs in the charters occasionally, e. g. Cod. Dipl. dlvii, dcxii, dclxxxv, dcxciv, mcccii, mcccxxxvi, apparently in the sense of minister or thegn to a noble person. See Schmid, Gesetze, p. 548.

and gesithcund men may themselves be called thegns even where they hold no land, but they do not acquire the privilege of their blood until they have reached the third generation from the founder of the family dignity [1].

Ranks of thegns.

Under the name of thegn are included however various grades of dignity [2]. The class of king's thegns is distinguished from that of the medial thegns, and from a residuum that falls in rank below the latter [3]. The heriot of an earl by the law of Canute is eight horses, four saddled and four unsaddled, eight lances, four coats of mail and four swords, and two hundred mancuses; that of the king's thegn is half as much armour and fifty mancuses; that of the medial thegn a single horse with equipment and two pounds; that of the simple thegn, who has soken, four pounds. The heriot then of the king's thegn comes midway between that of an eorl and that of the medial thegn.

Differences of rank among thegns.

His estate of land would seem then to fall between the forty hides of the one and the five hides of the other [4]. Over a king's

---

[1] There are doubts about the reading of the passage on which this depends, Wergilds, §§ 9–12. See K. Maurer, Wesen d. ält. Adels, &c. pp. 139, 140; who understands that although every possessor of five hides was a thegn, it was only in three generations that he became gesithcund or ennobled in blood; if a ceorl was a gesith or military follower without the five hides, he was not a thegn and could have only a ceorl's wergild.

[2] Of the official thegns of the king's household, the hors-thegn, disc-thegn and the rest, it is not necessary to speak here ; they are officers, not classes or ranks of society.

[3] Canute, Sec. § 71. Maurer (p. 171) refers this graduation merely to the extent of the possessions held by each class; citing Domesday, Nottinghamshire, p. 280; Yorkshire, p. 298; where the thegn who has more than six manors pays a relief of eight pounds to the king; he who has six or less pays three marks to the sheriff. The custom of Berkshire was different; there the whole armour was given to the king, with one horse saddled and another unsaddled. Gneist (Self-government, i. 17) connects the extension of the heriot to alodial owners with the acquisition of the position of thegn by every owner of five hides.

[4] The statement that forty hides conveyed the rank or status of an eorl is a matter of inference, from two or three somewhat precarious data. (1) The statement of the 'Ranks' that a thegn might thrive to *eorlriht*; a statement which in the ancient Latin translation appears as 'si tainus provehebatur ad consulatum,' which means simply the attaining of the office of ealdorman. The analogy of the other passages of the Ranks favours the former and simpler explanation. (2) In the Liber Eliensis (ed. Gale, 513), lib. ii. c. 40, a compilation of the twelfth century, occurs a story of Gudmund, brother of Abbot Wulfric, who lived in the days of Edgar. Gudmund was engaged to marry the daughter of a powerful man ; 'sed quoniam ille quadraginta

hegn none but the king himself could exercise jurisdiction[1], whilst there were thegns who were in actual dependence on others bearing the same title[2]: and Canute in one of his charters addresses his thegns as 'twelfhynde and twyhynde,' as if some at least of the order were in wergild indistinguishable from the ceorls[3]. Some thegns had soken or jurisdiction over their own lands, and others not[4]. We may well believe that the combinations and permutations of nobility by blood, office, and service would create considerable differences among men bearing the common title. The alodial eorl who for security Different sorts of thegns. has commended himself to the king and bears an honorary office at court, the official ealdorman who owes his place to royal favour earned in the humbler status of a dependent, the mere courtier who occupies the place of the ancient gesith, the ceorl who has thriven to thegn-right, the landowner of five hides or more, and the smaller landowner who has his own place in the shiremoot, all stand on different steps of dignity. The very name, like that of the gesith, has different senses in different ages and kingdoms; but the original idea of military service runs through all the meanings of thegn, as that of personal association is traceable in all the applications of gesith. The king's thegn was both the landowner and the military gesith. In the latter character he was bound by a very stringent oath

hidarum terræ dominium minime obtineret, licet nobilis esset, inter proceres tunc numerari non potuit, illum puella repudiavit.' In another passage of the same book (lib. i. c. 5. p. 466) forty hides are mentioned as the patrimonium of an ealdorman. (3) The heriot of the eorl was eight times that of the thegn; the wergild of the eorl 15,000 thrymsas, that of the thegn 2000; Schmid, p. 397. I confess that I see no other explanation of the passage and of the similar one in the Ranks, than that the possession of forty hides entitled a man to the wergild and credibility of an earl; it could scarcely confer a claim on the ealdormanship in its character of magistracy, although the passage in Hist. Eliens. i. 5 might lead to such a conclusion; Robertson, Essays, p. 169. But there may have been a rule, such as that of Clothair II (Baluze, i. 16), that no one should be an ealdorman who did not hold forty hides of land in the territory he was to rule; or the forty hides may have been the appanage or official estate of the earl.

[1] Ethelred, iii. § 11.

[2] Ranks, § 3.

[3] Cod. Dipl. dcccxxxi. K. Maurer doubts the pertinency of this passage. Such persons were probably the scir-thegns to a large extent, simply landowners, such as the numerous taini of the Western shires, noticed in Domesday-book. See Schmid, Gesetze, p. 667.

[4] Canute, ii. § 71. 3.

of fidelity; and he received from his lord the equipment which was returned as a heriot on his death. He was a member of his personal council, and as such attested the acts of the witena-gemot. Sometimes the assent and counsel of the comites is expressed in a charter [1], and occasionally a comes attests a grant, but more frequently the king's retainers style themselves ministri or thegns, and when the term *comes* ultimately emerges, it is as the translation of eorl or ealdorman, in the century immediately preceding the Conquest [2].

The title of ætheling.

When the more ancient blood nobility which had existed in the time of Ethelbert of Kent, and survived as late as that of Alfred, had finally merged in the nobility of service, when the eorl and æthel were lost in the thegn, it is no wonder that the title of ætheling was restricted to the king's kin. Then too the position of the ceorl seems to have sunk, although not so low as it did after the Conquest : the mere possession of land, however free, was no longer the sole qualification for political power.

The ealdor-man.

66. Whilst the title of thegn speaks distinctly of the origin of the rank in military service, that of ealdorman evinces equally clearly its connexion with military command and executive government ; for although it is sometimes loosely or generically applied as an equivalent to lord, senior, or noble, it is, when given to a particular person, or appearing in a public document, always referable to the chief magistrate of a shire or cluster of shires. It thus answers to the *comes* or *graf* of the continent, and by Asser and the other historians who have used his work, the word *comes* is employed as its Latin equivalent. Alfred, however, uses *ealdorman* to translate the *princeps* of Bede.

The *dux*.

The use of *dux* for *ealdorman* is not rare in the Latin chronicles, and the term is occasionally found in charters as early as the eighth century interchangeably with *princeps* [3]. Whether in such cases the dux should be understood to have the military command of the shire, whilst the ealdorman possessed the civil, and the gerefa was simply the guardian of

---

[1] But only in suspicious documents, such as the grant of Ethelwulf; Cod. Dipl. ml.

[2] See above, p. 125, n. 2.   [3] Cod. Dipl. lxvii, &c.

the king's interest; whether the dux ruled over a wider territory than the simple ealdorman; or whether the terms are not really equivalents, can only be conjecturally decided.

The history of the ealdormanship is thus in close connexion with that of the shire[1]. The smaller principalities of Mercia, retaining, under the rule of Penda and his sons, somewhat of their earlier individuality, have their ealdormen in the descendants of their royal house. Oshere, Osric, and their race[2] rule the Hwiccii for a century and a half as hereditary lords; the ealdorman of the Gyrwas is in the seventh century sufficiently noble to marry the daughter of the king of East Anglia[3]: and the ealdorman of the Gaini in the ninth took a wife of the royal house of Mercia, and gave his daughter as wife to King Alfred[4]. In the cases in which such an origin is clear, the relation of the ealdorman to the king has probably been created by commendation rather than by conquest; and consequently the hereditary descent of the office is only occasionally interfered with by royal nomination, as was the rule in Saxon Northumbria[5].

Ealdormen as under-kings.

As the heptarchic kingdoms successively came under West Saxon domination, their ruling houses being extinct, ealdormen were placed over them. The Mercian kingdom, or so much of it as was not in Danish hands, was administered by the son-in-law of Alfred as ealdorman, and an attempt was made to render the dignity hereditary in the person of his daughter[6]. Each of the West Saxon shires already had its ealdorman[7]; and as soon as the subjugation of the Danes made it possible to introduce a uniform shire-administration, the same organisation was adopted

Ealdormen as viceroys.

Ealdormen of shires or provinces.

---

[1] Above, p. 125.
[2] See the charters in the Cod. Dipl. lv, lxxxiii, cii, cxvii, cxxv. Cf. Palgrave, Commonwealth, p. cclxxxviii.
[3] Bede, H. E. iv. 19.
[4] Asser, M. H. B. p. 475. Her mother was of the royal house of Mercia.
[5] See the succession in Hoveden, i. 57 sq.
[6] Flor. Wig. A.D. 920.
[7] Ethelwulf is ealdorman of Berks in A.D. 860, Asser, M. H. B. p. 473; Athelhelm of Wilts in A.D. 887, ibid. p. 491; Eanwulf of Somerset, A.D. 867, Ethelw. M. H. B. p. 513; Osric of Hants in A.D. 860, Asser, p. 473; Odda of Devon, A.D. 878, Ethelw. p. 515; Ceolmund of Kent in A.D. 897, Chron. Sax.; Huda of Surrey in A.D. 853, Asser, p. 470; Osric is ealdorman of Dorset in A.D. 845, Chron. Sax. See Palgrave, Commonwealth, Appendix.

throughout the kingdom. But either the arrangement was carried into effect by the collection of several shires under one ealdorman, or a superior ealdormanship was established over a number of subordinate ones[1] : for in the time of Edgar and earlier, these great jurisdictions existed, as we have seen already[2], and led the way for the summary division of the country by Canute into four earldoms, which continued with

Title of earl.
some slight variations until the Norman Conquest. The title of earl had begun to supplant that of ealdorman in the reign of Ethelred : and the Danish jarl, from whom its use in this sense was borrowed, seems to have been more certainly connected by the tie of comitatus with his king than the Anglo-Saxon ealdorman need be supposed to have been[3]. Hence in the laws of Canute the heriot of the earl appears side by side with that of the thegn, and he himself is included in the servitial nobility. The original idea of the ealdormanship is, however, magistracy or jurisdiction, as implied in the attribute of age, and is not necessarily connected with either nobility of blood or with that of service, or even with the possession of a separate estate of land greater than that of the ordinary freeman.

The wergild as a distinction of rank.
67. Although the various origins of the various ranks of dignity are thus involved, the distinction between man and man was sharply drawn for all the most important purposes of judicature by the institution of the wergild. Every man's life had its value, and according to that valuation the value of his oath in the courts of justice varied, and offences against his protection and person were atoned for. The oath of the twelfhynd man was worth six times that of the twyhynd man, and twice that of

[1] I cannot find that, after the consolidation of the kingdom, the Mercian shires ever had their own ealdormen like the West Saxon, except Lindsey, the ealdorman of which district was killed at Assandun. They were under the great ealdormen of Mercia ; yet Offa had governed by ealdormen, and something must be allowed for the scantiness of records. See above, p. 125, note 5.

[2] Above, p. 131 ; Robertson, Essays, pp. 177–189. The title of *patricius*, which appears from time to time in Anglo-Saxon records from the eighth century to the eleventh, is referred by Robertson to the senior ealdorman of the king's kin ; according to Sohm it is equivalent to *dux*.

[3] K. Maurer, Wesen d. ält. Adels, p. 180.

the sixhynd man. Each of the Germanic races had its own Wergilds.
tariff of wergilds, varying according to the circumstances of the
case[1]; as the freemen were mingled more or less with lætic or
native races, or affected by the influences of royalty and nobility[2].
The most significant feature of the Frank tariff was the threefold wergild assigned to all persons who were employed in the
king's service. In most of the English kingdoms the basis of
the calculation was the wergild of two hundred shillings, which
marked the ceorl, twyhynd or simple free man. The thegn was
worth twelve hundred shillings. The Briton or wealh was
worth half as much as the Saxon or Angle : if he possessed five
hides he was sixhynd, if he possessed but one he was worth a
hundred shillings[3]. The higher ranks, the king, archbishop,
bishop, ealdorman, and earl, were estimated in multiples of the
same sort: the king's high reeve was worth twice the thegn,
the bishop and ealdorman four times, the king and archbishop
six times; but the rules are neither general nor constant.

But although English society was divided by sharp lines and No caste
system.
broad intervals, it was not a system of caste either in the stricter
or in the looser sense. It had much elasticity in practice, and Possibility
of rising in
rank.
the boundaries between the ranks were passable. The ceorl
who had thriven so well as to have five hides of land rose to the
rank of a thegn ; his wergild became twelve hundred shillings ;
the value of his oath and the penalty of trespass against him increased in proportion; his descendants in the third generation

---

[1] See them collected by Robertson, Scotland under her Early Kings, ii.
275-308.

[2] On this subject, which is in itself of great importance, but cannot be
worked out here, see K. Maurer, Wesen des ältesten Adels, pp. 130-132,
where the different usages of Kent, Wessex, and Mercia are compared.

[3] The sixhynd-man is a difficulty. K. Maurer holds the twyhynd-man
to be the landless ceorl, the freeman on another's land; and therefore the
sixhynd-man would be the ceorl who had land of his own, but less than
five hides, which was the qualification of the twelfhynd-man; p. 134.
Robertson, Scotland, &c. ii. 280, 297, thought that the British owner of
five hides (Ini, § 24) was the only sixhynd-man, and, as such proprietors
became extinct or merged early in the mass of the people, the rarity of
the term may be thus accounted for; but in his Essays (p. xlviii) he
includes the Northumbrian dreng, and also the landless gesithcund-man
of Wessex. If we suppose however that the Frank system had any
analogies in England, the sixhynd-man might be the ceorl in the king's
service.

became gesithcund. Nor was the character of the thriving defined : it might, so far as the terms of the custom went, be either purchase, or inheritance, or the tenure of important office, or the receipt of royal bounty. The successful merchant might also thrive to thegn-right. The thegn himself might rise to the rank, the estimation, and status of an eorl.

Intricacy of the system.

68. With such an intricate system was royalty surrounded : a system rendered the more intricate by poverty of nomenclature, variety of provincial custom, and multiplicity of ranks, tenures, and offices. Most of these characteristics belong both to the heptarchic and to the aggregated kingdom. Under the former system the organisation ends here; for no higher machinery either of race or territorial nationality can be shown to have existed until the hegemony of the West Saxon kings began the work of consolidation. At several periods the most powerful monarch of the seven did, as we have seen, exercise a supremacy more than honorary, although not strictly of the nature of government. Bede mentions seven kings who had a primacy (imperium or ducatus)—Ella of Sussex, Ceawlin of Wessex, Ethelbert of Kent, Redwald of East Anglia, Edwin, Oswald, and Oswy, of Northumbria. One of these, Oswald, is called by Adamnan, who wrote before Bede, 'totius Britanniae imperator ordinatus a Deo.' The Anglo-Saxon Chronicle, A.D. 827, gives to these seven the title of Bretwalda[1]; and makes

[1] See Bede, H. E. ii. 5 ; Chr. S. A.D. 827. On the Bretwalda see Hallam, M. A. ii. 270, 352, and Archaeologia, xxxii. 245 ; Kemble, Saxons, ii. 8–22; Freeman, Norm. Conq. i. 542–556. The word occurs in a bilingual charter of Athelstan, Cod. Dipl. mcx, as Brytænwalda, translating the title 'rex et rector totius hujus Britanniae insulae.' Kemble, however, derived it from the Anglo-Saxon breotan, to ' distribute,' and explained it ' widely ruling.' Rapin, who seems to have been the first historian who attached much importance to it, regarded it as denoting the headship of a federal union of kings ; Sharon Turner also mentions it ; Lingard goes so far as to assume that it was a regular title borne by several kings in succession, and arranges the early history under them as Bretwalda I, Bretwalda II, &c. Palgrave went on to connect it with the imperial status of the kings, as sharers in the remains of the Roman Caesarship, and supposed the Bretwaldas to be the successors of the British pseudo-emperors Maximus and Carausius. Mr. Freeman of course throws over the latter part of Palgrave's theory, but regards the title as significative of a real and substantial hegemony, though in no way derived from Roman or British dominion. The supremacy of Egbert was acknowledged by all the English princes

Egbert of Wessex the eighth. On this evidence the theory of a What was the Bretwalda?
formal hegemony or Bretwaldaship has been maintained by
historians; but the denomination is not contemporaneous or of
common use. It is most probable that the superiority was one
of power and influence only; but it may have been recognised
by occasional acts of commendation by which the weaker sovereign placed himself under the protection of the stronger,
entering on an alliance for defence and offence in which the
determination of the defence and offence belonged to the
superior. The commendation was ratified by oath and was one
of the chief steps towards organised feudalism. In itself however it was not feudal any more than the comitatus: the origin
of the tie in both these cases being personal and not territorial,
whilst in the feudal system the origin of the obligation is in the
land, and not in the persons connected by it. Such a theory,
however, will not account for all cases in which the title of
Bretwalda is given: some may have been due to conquest and
occupation of short duration, such as the alternate superiority
of Mercia and Northumbria in the seventh century: some to the
mere threat of war, or to the flattery of courtiers, or to the renown of the great king whose very name, as in Tacitus's time,
settled the fate of battles.

During this period the unity of the church was the only Ecclesiastical unity.
working unity, the law of religion the only universally recognised common jurisprudence. The archbishop of Canterbury
stood constantly, as the Bretwalda never stood, at the head of
an organised and symmetrical system, all the officers of which
were bound by their profession of obedience to him. The archbishop of York governed Northumbria with a much firmer and
more permanent hold than the kings, and in secular as well as
ecclesiastical matters occupied a position stronger and safer.
The bishops of the several kingdoms could meet for common

in Britain, and his successors took titles of imperator, basileus, &c., which
express the same supremacy, and, although in themselves quaint and
pedantic imitations of foreign usage, imply a distinct assertion of the
independence of the English crown of all earthly superiority. The Appendix B. to Mr. Freeman's first volume contains all the information on
the subject, which is only very incidentally connected with constitutional
history.

council and issue canons that were of equal validity all over the land. And this fact was recognised by Offa and Egbert, the two kings who made the greatest strides towards a union of the kingdoms. But the origin, growth, and constitutional development of the English church requires separate and independent treatment.

CHAPTER VII.

DEVELOPMENT IN ANGLO-SAXON HISTORY.

69. ALTHOUGH the framework of Anglo-Saxon society was permanent, and its simple organisation easily adapted itself to the circumstances that fill the five centuries of its history, it was capable of development and liable to much internal modification, according to the variations of the balance of its parts and the character of its regulative or motive force. The exact chronological sequence of these variations it is difficult to determine, but as to the fact of the development there can be no question. A comparison of the state of affairs represented in Domesday book with the picture that can be drawn from Bede sufficiently proves it. The ages had been ages of struggle and of growth, although the struggle was often fruitless and the growth ended in weariness and vexation. But the transition is more distinctly apparent if we look back further than Bede, and rely on the analogies of the other Germanic nationalities in drawing our initial outline. And this we are justified in doing by the completeness and homogeneousness of the constitution when it first appears to us, and by the general character of the early laws. But the subject is not without its difficulties: the

Development ment in Anglo-Saxon history.

Difficulties
of treat-
ment.

first and last terms of the development are as remote from each
other in character as in date. There is a very great difference
between the extreme and confusing minuteness of Domesday and
the simplicity and elasticity of the ideal German system of the
sixth century: whilst on the other hand the scantiness of our
knowledge of the latter is compensated by its clearness, and the
abundant information of the former is deprived of much of its
value by the uncertainty of its terminology. For it is un-
questionable that great part of the Anglo-Saxon customary
law, of which Domesday is the treasury, was unintelligible to the
Norman lawyers of the next century, on whose interpretation of
it the legal historian is wont to rely. The process of change
too was very gradual: it is not marked by distinct steps of
legal enactment; the charters afford only incidental illustrations,
and the historians were, for the most part, too far removed in
time from the events they described to have a distinct idea of
it, even if it had been possible for the annalist to realise the
working of causes in so slow and so constant action. But all the
great changes in the early history of institutions are of this
character, and can be realised only by the comparison of
sufficiently distant epochs. There are no constitutional revo-
lutions, no violent reversals of legislation; custom is far more
potent than law, and custom is modified infinitesimally every
day. An alteration of law is often the mere registration of a
custom, when men have recognised its altered character. The
names of offices and assemblies are permanent, whilst their
character has imperceptibly undergone essential change.

General
character
of the
develop-
ment.

The general tendency of the process may be described as a
movement from the personal to the territorial organisation [1];
from a state of things in which personal freedom and political
right were the leading ideas, to one in which personal freedom
and political right had become so much bound up with the relations created by the possession of land, as to be actually subservient to it: the Angel-cynn of Alfred becomes the Engla-
lande of Canute. The main steps also are apparent. In the
primitive German constitution the free man of pure blood is the

[1] Palgrave, Commonwealth, p. 62.

fully qualified political unit[1]; the king is the king of the race; the host is the people in arms; the peace is the national peace; the courts are the people in council; the land is the property of the race, and the free man has a right to his share. In the next stage the possession of land has become the badge of freedom; the freeman is fully free because he possesses land, he does not possess the land because he is free; the host is the body of landowners in arms; the courts are the courts of the landowners. But the personal basis is not lost sight of: the landless man may still select his lord; the hide is the provision of the family; the peace implies the maintenance of rights and duties between man and man; the full-free is the equal of the noble in all political respects. In a further stage the land becomes the sacramental tie of all public relations; the poor man depends on the rich, not as his chosen patron but as the owner of the land that he cultivates, the lord of the court to which he does suit and service, the leader whom he is bound to follow to the host: the administration of law depends on the peace of the land rather than on that of the people; the great landowner has his own peace and administers his own justice. The king still calls himself the king of the nation, but he has added to his old title new and cumbersome obligations towards all classes of his subjects, as lord and patron, supreme landowner, the representative of all original, and the fountain of all derived, political right.

The first of these stages was passed when the conquest of

Progress from personal to territorial system.

---

[1] Sohm, Fr. R. G. Verfg. i. 333 sq., maintains that in the Frank dominion it was not the possession of land but personal freedom that entitled or obliged a man to attend in the courts of law, in the host and other assemblies; and that it was only in trials in which land was concerned that the witnesses were required to have a land qualification (ibid. p. 355). In this as in many other points, this writer combats the received view. 'The full freedom of the German law is, in host and in court, given by personal freedom' (ibid. p. 359). Waitz on the other hand holds that 'the hide was the basis of freedom in the full sense of the word;' D. Verfassgs.-Gesch. i. 127; and 'only he who possessed land was fully qualified in the community;' ibid. iv. 450. Where there is so much divergence in the application of terms, it is somewhat dangerous to speak positively about stages of development; and in this, as in many other points, the statements of the text must be understood as referring chiefly if not solely to English history.

Britain was completed[1]; and only showed what it had been in the vestiges of the mark system, and in the permanence of the personal nomenclature. The village was the kindred settlement, the hide of land the allotment of the head of the family, the tribal divisions—the hundred, the mægth, the theod,—all personal[2]. The tracing of the process of change under the second and third stages is the problem of Anglo-Saxon Constitutional History. The series is not fully worked out. The Anglo-Saxon king never ceases to be the king of the nation, but he has become its lord and patron rather than its father; and that in a state of society in which all lordship is bound up with land-ownership : he is the lord of the national land, and needs only one step to become the lord of the people by that title. This step was however taken by the Norman lawyers and not by the English king; and it was only because the transition seemed to them so easy, that they left the ancient local organisation unimpaired, out of which a system was to grow that would ultimately reduce the landownership to its proper dimensions and functions. If the system had in England ripened into feudalism, that feudalism would in all probability have been permanent. Happily the change that produced feudalism for a time, introduced with it the necessity of repulsion. The English, who might never have struggled against native lords, were roused by

The great
question of
Anglo-Saxon
History.

[1] It may be thought that in granting so much, we are placing the landless Englishman on a lower level than the landless Frank; see the last note. But it is to be remembered that in Gaul and the other Romanised provinces, the fully free Frank was surrounded by a vast servile population, whilst in England the servile class formed a minority comparatively insignificant. The contrast is between full freedom and servitude in the former case; and in the latter between greater and smaller duties and liabilities. But it is quite probable that the rights of attending court and host were burdens rather than privileges to the Anglo-Saxons; and the rule that the landless man must have a lord was a measure rather compelling him to his duty, than depriving him of right. Until that rule was laid down, it is probable that the fully free Englishman, whether he owned land or not, was capable of taking part in the judicial business. Large numbers of landless men must have constantly attended the courts; and mere residence as well as possession of estate must have determined in what court they should attend.

[2] The mægth of Alfred is the provincia of Bede; the theod lande of Alfred is the regio, the theod being the gens; Bede, H. E. ii. 9, iii. 20, v. 12, &c.

the fact that their lords were strangers as well as oppressors, and the Norman kings realised the certainty that if they would retain the land they must make common cause with the people.

Five historical events mark the periods within which these changes were working: the accretion of the small settlements in heptarchic kingdoms; the union of the heptarchic kingdoms under the house of Cerdic; the first struggle with the Danes; the pacification of England under Edgar; and the introduction of new forms and principles of government by Canute.

Historical landmarks.

70. The development of constitutional life depends largely on the historical career of the nation, on the consolidation of its governmental machinery in equality and uniformity over all its area, on the expansion or limitation of the regulative power for the time being: in other words, on the general and external history marked by these eras; on the extension of the kingdom and on the condition of the royal power. England at the period of the Conversion, when for the first time we are able really to grasp an idea of its condition, was composed of a large number of small states or provinces bound in seven or eight kingdoms[1]. The form of government was in each monarchical, and that of the same limited character. By the middle of the tenth century it has become one kingdom, and the royal power is much more extensive in character. During a great part of the intervening period the consolidation of the kingdom and the power of the king have undergone many variations. The tendency towards union has been developed first under one tribal supremacy and then under another, and the royal power, whose growth is of necessity greatly affected by the extension of its territory, and the presence or absence of rival royalties, has fluctuated also. The two of course rise and fall together. But as a rule, at the end of any fixed period, both manifest a decided advance.

Growth of the kingdom.

It can scarcely be said that the tendency towards territorial

---

[1] I use the word heptarchy for the sake of brevity and convenience, and of course without vouching either for its accuracy of form or for its exact applicability to the state of things preceding the West Saxon hegemony. During far the greater portion of its duration there were actually seven kingdoms of Germanic origin in the island, and I see nothing in the term that implies any unity of organisation.

Causes of
union of
the seven
kingdoms.

union proceeded from any consciousness of national unity or from any instinct of self-government. Nor can it be attributed solely to the religious unity, which rather helped than originated such a tendency. This tendency resulted not so much from the strivings of the peoples as from the ambition of the kings. The task which was accomplished by the West Saxon dynasty had been tried before by the rulers of Kent, Northumbria, and Mercia, and the attempt in their hands failed. Nor would it have been more successful under the genius of Athelstan and Edgar, but for the Danish invasions, the extinction of the old royal houses, and the removal, to a certain extent, of the old tribal landmarks.

Mainten-
ance of
ancient
boundaries,
and royal
families.

The ancient German spirit showed its tenacity in this. The land had been settled by tribes of kinsmen, under rulers who as kings acquired the headship of the kin as well as the command of the host. Whilst the kin of the kings subsisted, and the original landmarks were preserved, neither religion nor common law, nor even common subjection sufficed to weld the incoherent mass. And it may have been the consciousness of this which hindered the victorious kings from suppressing royalty altogether in the kingdoms they subdued : the vassal kings either became insignificant, sinking into *eorls* and hereditary *ealdormen*, or gradually died out. But, until after the Danish wars, provincial royalty remained, and the cohesion of the mass was maintained only by the necessities of common defence. When Ethelbert of Kent acquired the rule of Essex, when Ethelred of Mercia annexed Hwiccia, when Egbert conquered Mercia, the form of a separate kingdom was preserved ; and the royal house still reigned under the authority of the conquerors until it became extinct. Such a system gave of course occasion for frequent rebellions and rearrangements of territory; when a weak king succeeded a strong one in the sovereign kingdom, or a strong chief succeeded a weak one in the dependent realm. But the continuance of such a system has the effect of gradually eliminating all the weaker elements.

The process of natural selection was in constant working; it is best exemplified in the gradual formation of the seven kingdoms and in their final union under Wessex: the heptarchic king was as much stronger than the tribal king, as the king of united England was stronger than the heptarchic king.

The kings of the smaller divisions disappear first, either alto-gether, or to emerge for a moment when the greater kingdom itself loses its royal house or falls into decrepitude. In the early days of Mercia, kings of Hwiccia, Hecana, Middle Anglia, and Lindsey, still subsisted [1]. Kent in the eighth century broke up into the kingdoms of the East and West Kentings, probably on the lines of the earlier kingdoms which are said to have been united by Ethelbert [2]. In Wessex, besides the kings of Sussex [3] which has a claim to be numbered among the seven great states, were kings of Surrey [4] also. In 626 Cynegils and Cwichelm were kings of the West Saxons, but five other kings of the same nation fell before Edwin. On the death of Cynewalh in A. D. 672, Wessex was divided among the ealdormen (just as the

Gradual disappearance of the smaller sovereignties.

[1] The Hwiccian kings were connected with those of Sussex and Northumbria, and were under the protection of the Mercian kings until they sank into the rank of ealdormen. Bede gives to Osric, one of these princes, the title of king, and the see of Worcester no doubt owes its existence to the fact that their national existence apart from Mercia was still recognised. Hecana or Herefordshire was the kingdom of Merewald, one of Penda's sons (Flor. Wig. M. H. B. p. 638), and has Hereford for its see. Middle Anglia was the kingdom of Peada, another of his sons, and retained its separate organisation long enough to have a see of its own,—Leicester, settled like the other three by Theodore. The pedigree of the kings of Lindsey is preserved by Florence (M. H. B. p. 631), and although none of them are known in history, the territory was in dispute between Mercia and Northumbria in 678, so that they could not have been long extinct; its nationality also was recognised by the foundation of a see, at Sidnacester.

[2] The existence of the see of Rochester is adduced in proof of the existence of a separate tribal kingdom in Kent, and the same inference is drawn from the fact that double settlements, as in Norfolk and Suffolk (of two fylkis), were common among the German tribes. See Freeman, Norm. Conq. i. 342; Robertson, Essays, p. 120; Kemble, Saxons, i. 148. But the historical mention of the East and West Kentings is later; and where two kings are found reigning together they seem to be of the same family.

[3] Mr. Robertson infers a twofold arrangement in Sussex from the fact that two ealdormen were slain there by Cædwalla (Essays, p. 120), but Sussex as an independent kingdom must have always been united. After its subjection to Wessex it seems to have had two or three kings at a time. (Palgrave, Commonwealth, p. cclxxiv.) They are no longer heard of under Egbert.

[4] Frithewold, subregulus or ealdorman of Surrey, was the founder of Chertsey Abbey; Malmesb. G. P. lib. ii. The name seems sufficient to prove it an independent settlement.

Small pro-
vincial
kingdoms.

Lombard kingdom broke up on the death of Clephis), and was reunited thirteen years later by Cædwalla[1] : Hampshire was separated from the body of Wessex in A.D. 755[2], as a provision for the deposed Sigebert. The Isle of Wight had a king of its own[3]. In East Anglia several traditionary kingdoms are commemorated by poetical traditions[4]. Northumbria was in constant division between Bernicia and Deira : and besides the Anglian and Saxon kingdoms, there were in Cornwall, Wales, Cumbria, and on the borders of Yorkshire[5], small states of British origin whose rulers were styled kings. These kings were not merely titular; the kings of Hwiccia, in the endowment of their *comites*, exercised one at least of the most important powers of royalty, and continued to subsist as *subreguli* or ealdormen, ruling their province hereditarily under the sovereignty of Mercia. But they died out, and by their extinction their territory was consolidated permanently with the superior state. And so it probably was in the other cases.

Extinction
of the
greater
kingdoms.

Again, when Wessex and Mercia have worked their way to the rival hegemonies, Sussex and Essex do not cease to be numbered among the kingdoms until their royal houses are extinct. When Wessex has conquered Mercia and brought Northumbria on its knees, there are still kings in both Northumbria and Mercia : the royal house of Kent dies out, but the title of king of Kent is bestowed on an *ætheling*, first of the Mercian, then of the West Saxon house[6]. Until the

---

[1] Bede, H. E. iv. 12 ; above, p. 152.   [2] Chron. Sax. A.D. 755.
[3] Bede, H. E. iv. 16.   [4] Thorpe's Lappenberg, i. 116.
[5] Elmet had a king according to Nennius ; M. H. B. p. 76.
[6] The succession of the later kings of Kent is extremely obscure, and the chronology as generally received is certainly wrong. It would seem that it had become dynastically connected with Wessex in the latter part of the eighth century. Ealhmund, father of the great Egbert, was king in Kent in the time of Offa ; Chron. Sax. A.D. 784 or 786 : after Offa's death the kingdom was seized by Eadbert Præn, a kinsman of Egbert ; he was overcome by Kenulf of Mercia, who made his brother Cuthred king; after Cuthred's death it was ruled by Kenulf himself ; and on his death was seized by Baldred, who in his turn was conquered by Egbert. Ethelwulf son of Egbert ruled Kent during his father's life ; when he succeeded to Wessex, Ethelstan and Ethelbert reigned successively in Kent : and on Ethelbert's succession to Wessex, Kent was consolidated with the rest of Southern England.

Danish conquest the dependent royalties seem to have been spared; and even afterwards organic union can scarcely be said to exist. Alfred governs Mercia by his son-in-law as ealdorman, just as Ethelwulf had done by his son-in-law as king[1]: but he himself is king of the West-Saxons; Edward the Elder is king of the Angul-Saxones[2], sometimes 'of the Angles;' Athelstan is 'rex Anglorum,' king of the English, and 'curagulus' of the whole of Britain[3]. The Danish kingdom still maintains an uncertain existence in Northumbria; Mercia under Edgar sets itself against Wessex under Edwy. At last Edgar having outlived the Northumbrian royalty and made up his mind to consolidate Dane, Angle and Saxon, to unite what could be united and to tolerate what would not, receives the crown as king of all England[4] and transmits it to his son.

Consolidation under Wessex.

[1] Egbert conquered Mercia and deposed King Wiglaf in A.D. 828: he restored him in 830; in 839 Berhtwulf succeeded him and reigned till 851. Burhred his successor was Ethelwulf's son-in-law, and reigned until 874. Ceolwulf his successor was a puppet of the Danes. As soon as Alfred had made good his hold on Western Mercia he gave it to Ethelred as ealdorman, and married him to his daughter Ethelfleda; Ethelred died in 912, and Ethelfleda in 920. Her daughter Elfwina, after attempting to hold the government, was set aside by Edward the elder, by whom Mercia was for the first time organically united with Wessex.

[2] See Hallam, M. A. ii. 271. Edward is rex 'Angul-Saxonum,' or 'Anglorum et Saxonum,' in charters, Cod. Dipl. cccxxxiii, cccxxxv, mlxxvii, mlxxviii, mlxxx, mlxxxiv, mxc, mxcvi; 'Rex Anglorum' simply in cccxxxvii; and king of the West Saxons in mlxxxv.

[3] A list of the titles assumed by the succeeding kings is given by Mr. Freeman, Norm. Conq. i. 548–551. Athelstan's title of Curagulus or Coregulus is explained as derived from cura, caretaker (ibid. p. 552) = mundbora, and as coregulus or corregulus in its natural sense seems to be opposed to monarcha, it is probable that the derivation is right; the *cura* representing the *mund* under which all the other princes had placed themselves.

[4] On this subject see Mr. Robertson's remarkable essay, Hist. Essays, pp. 203–216; and Freeman, Norm. Conq. i. 626. The last Danish king of Northumbria was killed in 954. In 959, Edgar succeeded to the kingdom of the West Saxons, Mercians and Northumbrians. Edgar's coronation at Bath took place in 973 immediately after Archbishop Oswald's return from Rome, which may be supposed to have been connected with it. Mr. Robertson concludes that Edgar 'would appear to have postponed his coronation until every solemnity could be fulfilled that was considered necessary for the unction and coronation of the elect of all three provinces of England, the first sovereign who in the presence of both archbishops— of the "sacerdotes et principes" of the whole of England—was crowned and anointed as the sole representative of the threefold sovereignty of the West Saxons, Mercians and Northumbrians.' The ancient theories about this coronation may be seen in the Memorials of S. Dunstan, pp. 112, 214,

Influence of
the Danish
struggle.

If the extinction of the smaller royalties opened the way for permanent consolidation, the long struggle with the Danes prevented that tendency from being counteracted. The attempts of Ethelwulf to keep central England through the agency of Mercian and East Anglian subject kings signally failed. It was only Wessex, although with a far larger seaboard, that successfully resisted conquest. Mercia and Northumbria, though conquered with great slaughter, and divided by the victorious Norsemen, exchanged masters with some equanimity, and the Danes within a very few years were amalgamated in blood and religion with their neighbours. The Danish king of East Anglia accepted the protection of the West Saxon monarch, and Mercia was brought back to allegiance. Alfred, by patient laborious resistance as well as by brilliant victories, asserted for Wessex the dominion, as his grandfather had the hegemony, of the other kingdoms; and his son and grandsons perfected his work [1].

Amalgamation of the
Danes with
the English.

The king
increases in
strength
as the
kingdom
increases
in area.

It could not fail to result from this long process that the character of royalty itself was strengthened. Continual war gave to the king who was capable of conducting it an unintermitted hold and exercise of military command: the kings of the united territory had no longer to deal alone with the *witan* of their original kingdom, but stood before their subjects as

423. In connexion with this process of consolidation occurs the council of Wihtbordesstane (Wilbarstone) in Northamptonshire, held between the years 966 and 975, in which measures were taken for bringing the Danelaw into harmony with the rest of the kingdom, and the laws were confirmed in what is called the *Supplementum Legum Eadgari;* Schmid, p. 193.

[1] The story that Egbert after his coronation at Winchester directed that the whole state should bear the name of England is mythical. It originates in the Monastic Annals of Winchester, MS. Cotton, Dom. A. xiii; extracts from which are printed in the Monasticon Anglicanum, i. 205. 'Edixit illa die rex Egbertus ut insula in posterum vocaretur Anglia, et qui Juti vel Saxones dicebantur omnes communi nomine Angli vocarentur.' On the names England and English, see Freeman, Norm. Conq. i. App. A. The era of Egbert's acquisition of the *ducatus,* by which he dates some of his charters to Winchester (Cod. Dipl. mxxxv, mxxxvi, mxxxviii), must be A.D. 816; and, if the ducatus be really a Bretwaldaship, may be marked by his conquest of West Wales or Cornwall, which is placed by the Chronicles in A.D. 813, but belongs properly to A.D. 815. At this period however Kenulf of Mercia was still in a more commanding position than Egbert.

supreme rulers over neighbouring states; the council of their *witan* was composed no longer of men as noble and almost as independent as themselves, *ealdormen* strong in the affection of their tribes and enabled by union to maintain a hold over the kings, but of members of the royal house itself, to whom the kings had deputed the government of kingdoms and who strengthened rather than limited their personal authority[1]. So, as the kingdom became united, the royal power increased, and this power extending with the extension of the territory, royalty became territorial also. The consolidated realm enters into continental politics and borrows somewhat of the imperial form and spirit; and this brings on some important changes.

71. The earliest legislation exhibits the king as already in a position in which personal preeminence is secured and fortified by legal provisions. In the laws of Ethelbert the king's *mund-byrd* is fixed at fifty shillings, that of the *eorl* at twelve, and that of the *ceorl* at six; and wrongs done to members of his household are punished in proportion[2]. These laws mention no wergild for the king, but it seems probable that if there were one it also would be calculated on a like scale. A century later the laws of Wihtræd direct that the king is to be prayed for without command, that is, that intercession for him shall be part of the ordinary service of the church; his word without oath is incontrovertible, and even his *thegn* may clear himself by his own oath. The king's *mundbyrd* is still fifty shillings[3]. The laws of Ini king of Wessex, who was contemporary with Wihtræd, show that in that conquering and advancing kingdom the tendency was more strongly developed. If a man fight in the king's house both his life and property lie at the king's mercy; the king's *geneat* may 'swear for sixty hides;' his *burh-bryce* is a hundred and twenty shillings[4]. But in the reign of Alfred the king's *borh-bryce* or *mundbyrd* was five pounds, his *burh-bryce* a hundred and twenty shillings, whilst that of the *ceorl* was only five[5]. The value of the protection given by the

Marginal notes: Earliest status of the Anglo-Saxon king. Increase in his personal importance.

---

[1] See Mr. Robertson's essay on the king's kin ; Hist. Essays, pp. 177–189.
[2] Ethelbert, §§ 8, 15, &c.   [3] Wihtræd, §§ 1, 2, 16, 20.
[4] Ini, §§ 6, 19, 45.
[5] Alfred, §§ 3, 40. The first mention of treason in the Saxon law on

higher classes rises in proportion to that given by the king,
whilst that of the simple freeman remains as before, or is
actually depressed. It is by the same code that the relation
between the king and his subjects is defined as that between
lord and dependent; 'if any one plot against the king's life, of
himself or by harbouring of exiles, or of his men, let him be
liable in his life and in all that he has. If he desire to prove
himself true, let him do so according to the king's wergild. So
also we ordain for all degrees whether *eorl* or *ceorl*. He who
plots against his lord's life let him be liable in his life to him
and in all that he has, or let him prove himself true according
to his lord's *wer*[1].' The law of Edward the elder contains an
exhortation to the *witan* for the maintenance of the public
peace, in which it is proposed that they should 'be in that
fellowship in which the king was, and love that which he loved,
and shun that which he shunned, both on sea and land[2]:' a
clear reference to the relation between the lord and his dependent as expressed in the oath of fealty. The same king, in
A.D. 921, received the submission of the East Anglian Danes
on the same condition: 'they would observe peace towards all
to whom the king should grant his peace, both by sea and
land[3]:' and the people of Northamptonshire and Cambridgeshire especially chose him 'to *hlaforde* and to *mundbora*,' so
placing themselves under his personal protection. The principle

the continent occurs in the Capit. de partibus Saxoniae, c. 11: 'Si quis
domino regi infidelis apparuerit capitali sententia punietur;' Pertz, Legg.
v. 39: cf. Lex Sax. ib. p. 62.

[1] Alfred, § 4. In the introduction to his laws, § 49. 7, he also excepts
treason from the list of offences for which a *bot* may be taken: 'In prima
culpa pecunialem emendationem capere quam ibi decreverunt, praeter
proditionem domini, in qua nullam pietatem ausi sunt intueri, quia Deus
omnipotens nullam adjudicavit contemptoribus Suis.' This is referred to
as a judgment of ancient synods.

[2] Edward, ii. 1, § 1; above, p. 166.

[3] Thurferth the eorl and the holds and all the army that owed obedience
to Northampton sought him 'to hlaforde and to mundboran;' all who
were left in the Huntingdon country sought 'his frith and his mund-
byrde;' the East Anglians swore to be one with him, that they would all
that he would, and would keep peace with all with whom the king should
keep peace either on sea or on land; and the army that owed obedience
to Cambridge chose him 'to hlaforde and to mundbora;' Chron. Sax.
A.D. 921.

is enunciated with greater clearness in the law of his son The king becomes the lord of his people.
Edmund, in which the oath of fealty is generally imposed; all
are to swear to be faithful to him as a man ought to be faithful
to his lord, loving what he loves, shunning what he shuns[1].
This series of enactments must be regarded as fixing the date of
the change of relation, and may perhaps be interpreted as explaining it. The rapid consolidation of the Danish with the
Angle and Saxon population involved the necessity of the
uniform tie between them and the king: the Danes became
the king's men and entered into the public peace; the native
English could not be left in a less close connexion with their
king: the commendation of the one involved the tightening of
the cords that united the latter to their native ruler. Something of the same kind must have taken place as each of the
heptarchic kingdoms fell under West Saxon rule, but the principle is most strongly brought out in connexion with the Danish
submission.

From this time accordingly the personal dignity of royalty Imperial titles adopted.
becomes more strongly marked. Edmund and his successors
take high sounding titles borrowed from the imperial court;
to the real dignity of king of the English they add the shadowy
claim to the empire of Britain which rested on the commendation of Welsh and Scottish princes[2]. The tradition that
Edgar was rowed by eight kings upon the Dee is the expression
of this idea which it was left for far distant generations to
realise[3].

Under Ethelred still higher claims are urged: again and
again the witan resolve as a religious duty to adhere to one

---

[1] Edmund, iii. § 1; above, p. 166.

[2] Athelstan is 'rex Anglorum, et curagulus totius Britanniae,' or 'primi-
cerius totius Albionis,' or 'rex et rector totius Britanniae.' Edred is
'imperator,' 'cyning and casere totius Britanniae,' 'basileus Anglorum
hujusque insulae barbarorum;' Edwy is 'Angulsaxonum basileus' &c., or
'Angulsaexna et Northanhumbrorum imperator, paganorum gubernator,
Breotonumque propugnator;' Edgar is 'totius Albionis imperator Augustus;' and so on. See Freeman, Norm. Conq. i. 548 sq.

[3] In A.D. 922 the kings of the North Welsh took Edward for their lord;
in 924 he was chosen for father and lord by the king and nation of the
Scots, by the Northumbrians, Dane and English, and by the Strathclyde
Britons and their king. On the real force of these commendations see
Freeman, Norm. Conq. i. 565; and Robertson, Scotland, &c. ii. 384 sq.

Religious
duty of
obedience.

cyne-hlaford[1]: and the king himself is declared to be Christ's vicegerent among Christian people, with the special duty of defending God's church and people, and with the consequent claim on their obedience; 'he who holds an outlaw of God in his power over the term that the king may have appointed, acts, at peril of himself and all his property, against Christ's vicegerent who preserves and holds sway over Christendom and kingdom as long as God grants it[2].' The unity of the kingdom, endangered by Sweyn and Canute, is now fenced about with sanctions which imply religious duty. Both state and church are in peril; Ethelred is regarded as the representative of both. A few years later Canute had made good his claim to be looked on as a Christian and national king. The first article of his laws, passed with the counsel of his witan, to the praise of God, and his own honour and behoof, is this: 'that above all other things, they should ever love and worship one God, and unanimously observe one Christianity, and love King Canute with strict fidelity[3].'

The increase
of royal
assumption
not to be
attributed
to clerical
adulation.

It is wrong to regard the influence of the clergy as one of the chief causes of the increase in the personal dignity of the kings. The rite of coronation substituted for the rude ceremony, whatever it may have been, which marked the inauguration of a heathen king, contained a distinct charge as to the nature of royal duties[4], but no words of adulation nor even any statement of the personal sacro-sanctity of the recipient. The enactments of the councils are directed, where they refer to royalty at all, rather to the enforcement of reforms than to the encouragement of despotic claims[5]. The letters of the early Anglo-Saxon

---

[1] Ethelred, v. § 5; viii. §§ 2, 44.   [2] Ibid. viii. § 42.

[3] Canute, i. § 1.

[4] Above, p. 163; where I have protested distinctly against the view of Allen, Prerogative, pp. 18–24; and see Memorials of S. Dunstan, p. 355.

[5] The canon (12) of the legatine council in A.D. 787 (Councils, &c. iii. 453) attempts to prohibit the murder of kings, so frightfully common at the time, by enforcing regular election and forbidding conspiracy; 'nec christus domini esse valet et rex totius regni, et heres patriae, qui ex legitimo non fuerit connubio generatus,' &c., but the preceding canon (11) is an exhortation to kings; the bishops and others are warned, ' fiducialiter et veraciter absque ullo timore vel adulatione loqui verbum Dei regibus,' the kings are exhorted to obey their bishops, to honour the church, to

bishops are full of complaints of royal misbehaviour: the sins
of the kings of the eighth century seem almost to cancel the
memory of the benefits received from the nursing-fathers of
the seventh [1]. Far from maintaining either in theory or in
practice the divine right of the anointed, the prelates seem
to have joined in, or at least acquiesced in, the rapid series of
displacements in Northumbria [2]. Alcuin mourns over the fate
of the national rulers, but grants that by their crimes they
deserved all that fell on them. They are, like Saul, the
anointed of the Lord [3], but they have no indefeasible status.
In the preaching of peace and good-will, the maintenance of
obedience to constituted powers is indeed insisted on, but the
duty of obeying the powers that be is construed simply and
equitably [4]. It is only when, in the presence of the heathen
foe, Christendom and kingdom seem for a moment to rest on
the support of a single weak hand, that the duty of obedience
to the king is made to outweigh the consideration of his de-
merits. And yet Dunstan had prophesied of Ethelred that the
sword should not depart from his house until his kingdom
should be transferred to a strange nation whose worship and
tongue his people knew not [5].

Importance of the religious side of the question.

Nor is it necessary to regard the growth of royal power, as
distinct from personal pomp, among the Anglo-Saxons, as having
been to any great extent affected by the precedents and model of
the Frank empire [6]. Athough the theory of kingship was in

Royal assumption not the result of imitation of Frankish practice.

have prudent counsellors fearing the Lord and honest in conversation,
that the people, instructed and comforted by the good examples of kings
and princes, may profit to the praise and glory of Almighty God.

[1] See especially the letter of Boniface to Ethelbald, Councils, &c. iii. 350.
[2] Above, p. 153.
[3] See Councils, &c. iii. 476. Writing to Ethelred of Northumbria he
says, 'vidistis quomodo perierint antecessores vestri reges et principes
propter injustitias et rapinas et immunditias .... timete illorum per-
ditionem ...;' p. 491. 'Qui sanctas legit scripturas ... inveniet pro
hujusmodi peccatis reges regna et populos patriam perdidisse;' p. 493.
[4] 'The words of the old writer followed by Simeon, "deinde Domini
suffragio potitus," clearly show the opinion of the age that the God of
battles gave his verdict in victory, and that war was only an appeal to the
judgment of God on a large scale;' Robertson, Essays, p. 208. The
principle thus expressed might be extended still further; there were no
kings *de jure* except the kings *de facto*.
[5] Flor. Wig. ad ann. 1016.   [6] Allen, Prerogative, p. 20.

Gaul perhaps scarcely less exalted than at Constantinople, the practice was very different, for the Merovingian puppets were set up and thrown down at pleasure. But during the eighth century the influence of England on the continent was greater than that of the continent on England. The great missionaries of Germany looked to their native land as the guide and pattern of the country of their adoption. It is only with the Karolingian dynasty that the imitation of foreign custom in England could begin; but, even if the fact were far more clearly ascertained than it is, the circumstances that made it possible, the creation of national unity and the need of united defence, were much more important than a mere tendency to superficial imitation. The causes at work in Gaul and Britain were distinct and the results, in this point at least, widely different.

The king becomes the source of justice.

Growth of the idea.

72. As the personal dignity of the king increased and the character of his relation to his people was modified, his official powers were developed, and his function as fountain of justice became more distinctly recognised. The germ of this attribute lay in the idea of royalty itself. The peace, as it was called [1], the primitive alliance for mutual good behaviour, for the performance and enforcement of rights and duties, the voluntary restraint of free society in its earliest form, was from the beginning of monarchy under the protection of the king. Of the three classes of offences that came under the view of the law [2], the minor infraction of right was atoned for by a compensation

The king's share in the fines for breach of the peace.

[1] Wilda, Strafrecht, pp. 255 sq., 264 sq.; Waitz, D. V. G. i. 421: 'The peace is the relation in which all stand whilst and in so far as all continue in the union and in the right on which the community rests. He who acts against this commits a breach of the peace. The breach of the peace is unright; the transgression against right is a breach of the peace.' He who sins against one, sins against all; and no man may redress his own wrongs until he has appealed to the guardians of the peace for justice. Hence the peace is the great check on the practice of private war, blood feuds, and the so-called *lex talionis*. I think the German writers take too high a view of the power of the Anglo-Saxon king as guardian of the peace. See Schmid, Gesetze, p. 584; Gneist, Verwaltungsrecht, i. 26. On the whole subject of Anglo-Saxon criminal procedure see Mr. Laughlin's Essay in the Essays on Anglo-Saxon Law, pp. 262 sq.

[2] K. Maurer, Krit. Ueberschau, iii. 26 sq.; Bethmann-Hollweg, Civil-process, iv. 25 sq.; Schmid, Gesetze, p. 584; Palgrave, Commonwealth, p. 204; Waitz, D. V. G. i. 422; ii. 40.

to the injured, the *bot* with which his individual good-will was redeemed, and by a payment of equal amount to the king by which the offender bought back his admission into the public peace[1]. The greater breaches of the peace arising either from refusal to pay the fines, or from the commission of offences for which fines were inadequate, were punished by outlawry; the offender was a public enemy, set outside the law and the peace; his adversary might execute his own vengeance, and even common hospitality towards him was a breach of the law, until the king restored him to his place as a member of society[2]. The third class of offences, which seemed beyond the scope of outlawry, and demanded strict, public, and direct rather than casual and private punishment, were yet like the former capable of composition, the acceptance of which to a certain extent depended on the king as representing the people[3]. In all this the king is not only the executor of the peace, but a sharer in its authority and claims. But this position is far from that of the fountain of justice and source of jurisdiction. The king's guarantee was not the sole safeguard of the peace: the hundred had its peace as well as the king[4]: the king too had a distinct peace which like that of the church was not that of the country at large, a special guarantee for those who were under special protection[5].

His power of accepting money compensation.

The king is guardian of the peace.

The *grith*[6], a term which comes into use in the Danish

[1] K. Maurer, Krit. Ueberschau, iii. 45; Ll. Hloth. and Eadr. §§ 11, 12, 13; Ini, §§ 3, 6, 7, 10; Schmid, Gesetze, p. 679.

[2] Athelstan, ii. § 20, 3. Edgar, i. § 3: 'et sit utlaga, id est exul vel exlex, nisi rex ei patriam concedat.' Ethelred, viii. § 2.

[3] Alfred, § 7, 'sit in arbitrio regis sic vita sic mors, sicut ei condonare voluerit.' Also Ini, § 6; Edmund, ii. § 6; Ethelred, iv. § 4; but compare Alfred, Introd. § 49. 7; as given above, p. 194.

[4] Edmund, iii. § 2; Edgar, i. §§ 2, 3; iii. 7; Ethelred, iii. 3; Canute, ii. §§ 15, 20.

[5] Schmid, Gesetze, p. 584.

[6] Grith [gridh] is properly the *domicile*, Vigfússon (Icelandic Dict. s. v.), and consequently, asylum; then truce or peace limited to place or time; Schmid, Gesetze, pp. 584, 604. So Church-grith is sometimes used for sanctuary; but it really means as much as Church-frith, the peace and security which the law guarantees to those under the Church's protection. Schmid arranges the special peaces or several griths under three heads: (1) Place; churches, private houses, the king's palace and precincts; (2) Time; fasts and festivals, coronation days, days of public gemots and

The people
pass into the
king's peace
or protec-
tion.
struggle, is a limited or localised peace, under the special
guarantee of the individual, and differs little from the protection
implied in the *mund* or personal guardianship which appears
much earlier[1]; although it may be regarded as another mark
of territorial development. When the king becomes the lord,
patron and *mundborh* of his whole people, they pass from the
ancient national peace of which he is the guardian into the closer
personal or territorial relation of which he is the source. The
peace is now the king's peace[2]; although the *grith* and the
mund still retain their limited and local application, they entitle
their possessor to no higher rights, they do but involve the
transgressor in more special penalties; the *frith* is enforced by
the national officers, the *grith* by the king's personal servants;
the one is official, the other personal; the one the business of
the country, the other that of the court[3]. The special peace is
further extended to places where the national peace is not fully

courts, special gatherings at drinking-parties, sales, markets, guilds, &c.,
and the times when the fyrd is summoned; (3) Persons; clergy, widows,
and nuns; Gesetze, p. 585; Gneist, Verwaltgsr. i. 38, 39. The curious
enactment of Ethelred, iii. § 1, distinguishing the grith of the king, that
of the ealdorman, that given in the burh-moot, the wapentake and the
alehouse, with different fines for breach, is very noteworthy.

[1] Gneist, Verwaltungsrecht, i. 26. The original meaning of *mund* is said
to be *hand*, Schmid, Gesetze, p. 634; but it also has the meaning of *word*,
sermo; and of *patria potestas*; Waitz, D. V. G. i. 55.

[2] Edward, ii. 1, § 1 : ' Inquisivit itaque qui ad emendationem velit redire,
et in societate permanere quâ ipse sit.' Edmund, ii. § 7 : ' Pax regis.'
See Gneist, Verwaltungsrecht, i. 26; Self-government, i. 29; K. Maurer,
Krit. Ueberschau, iii. 46.

[3] The king's hand-grith, in the law of Edward and Guthrum, § 1, must
mean the king's *mund*; the special peace given by the king's hand; see
too Ethelred, vi. § 14; and the 'pax quam manu sua dederit,' Canute, i.
§ 2. 2.   To this belongs also the chapter on the *Pax regis* in the laws of
Edward the Confessor, in which the peace of the coronation-days, that is,
a week at Easter, Whitsuntide and Christmas; the peace of the four great
highways, Watling-street, Ikenild-street, Ermin-street, and Foss-way, and
the peace of the navigable rivers, are protected with special fines that
distinguish them from the common-law peace of the country, which also is
the king's peace. Besides these there is a fourth peace called the king's
hands-sealde grith, and one given by the king's writ, which answer more
closely to the idea of the *mund* as personal protection; and with this are
connected the original pleas of the crown (see below, p. 205). Other
offences against the peace, and the protection of other roads and rivers,
belong to the view of the local courts, the shire and the sheriff, although not less closely related to the king's peace and jurisdiction. Cf.
Glanvill, de Legg. i. 1 ; Ll. Edw. Conf. § 12; Palgrave, Commonwealth,
pp. 284, 285.

provided for : the great highways, on which questions of local
jurisdiction might arise to the delay of justice, are under the
king's peace.   But the process by which the national peace   The peace
became the king's peace is almost imperceptible : and it is very   the king's peace.
gradually that we arrive at the time at which all peace and law
are supposed to die with the old king, and rise again at the
proclamation of the new [1].   In Anglo-Saxon times the transition
is mainly important as touching the organisation of jurisdiction.
The national officers now execute their functions as the king's
officers, and executors of his peace; the shire and hundred
courts, although they still call the peace their own, act in his
name; the idea gains ground and becomes a form of law.
Offences against the law become offences against the king, and   Contempt of
the crime of disobedience a crime of contempt to be expiated   the king's law is spe-
by a special sort of fine, the *oferhyrnesse* [2], to the outraged   cially pun-
majesty of the lawgiver and judge.   The first mention of the   ishable.
oferhyrnesse occurs in the laws of Edward the elder [3].   It is
probable that the reforms which Alfred, according to his
biographer, introduced into the administration of justice had a
similar tendency; and these two reigns may be accepted as the

[1] ' The Sovereign was the fountain of justice ; therefore the stream ceased
to flow when the well-spring was covered by the tomb.   The judicial bench
vacant; all tribunals closed.   Such was the ancient doctrine—a doctrine
still recognised in Anglo-Norman England ;' Palgrave, Normandy and
England, iii. 193.   Speaking of the special protections above referred to,
the same writer says : ' Sometime after the Conquest all these special
protections were replaced by a general proclamation of the king's peace
which was made when the community assented to the accession of the
new monarch, and this first proclamation was considered to be in force
during the remainder of his life, so as to bring any disturber of the public
tranquillity within its penalties.   So much importance was attached to the
ceremonial that even in the reign of John, offences committed during the
interregnum, or period elapsing between the day of the death of the last
monarch and the recognition of his successor, were unpunishable in those
tribunals whose authority was derived from the Crown ;' Commonwealth,
p. 285.

[2] Ofer-hyrnesse (subauditio, male audire) answers to the later over-
seunnesse (over-looking, contempt) ; it is marked by special penalty in the
cases of buying outside markets, refusal of justice, accepting another man's
dependent without his leave, refusing Peter's pence, sounding the king's
coin, neglect of summons to gemot or pursuit of thieves, and disobedience
to the king's officers.   See Schmid, Gesetze, p. 638.

[3] ' Si quis extra portum barganniet, oferhyrnesse regis culpa est ;' Edward, i. § 1.

period at which the change of idea seems to have become permanent [1].

Growth of the idea of royal jurisdiction.

73. But, although it may be convenient to accept this approximation to a date, the influence of the idea may be traced much further back. The administration of the peace is inseparable from the exercise of jurisdiction; those who are in the national peace are subject only to the national courts; those who are in the church's *grith*, are also in the church's *socn*; those who are in the king's *mund*, are under his cognisance; those who are amenable to any jurisdiction, owe suit and service to the courts of the jurisdiction; when all are in the *mund* or *grith* or *frith* of the king, he is the supreme judge of all persons and over all causes, limited however by the counsel and consent of his *witan*.

Royal jurisdiction over the tenants of folkland.

In regard to the holders of *folkland*, the special royal jurisdiction must have been much older than the time of Alfred; as these tenants were liable to special burdens payable directly to the state, and as the profits of jurisdiction, which were counted among these burdens, were inseparable from jurisdiction itself, it is probable that the jurisdiction of these lands was administered by royal officers, not necessarily separate from the business of the hundred courts, but as a part of their work, having special reference to the king's interests [2]. They would be from the first

[1] The concluding chapter of Asser's Life of Alfred (M. H. B. p. 497) gives some important data, not only as to the participation of the king in judicature, but as to the composition of the local courts in his day. The nobiles and ignobiles, the eorls and ceorls, were constantly disagreeing in the gemots ' in concionibus comitum et praepositorum;' a proof that ealdorman and gerefa, eorl and ceorl, had their places in these courts. None of the suitors were willing to allow that what the ealdormen and gerefan determined was true; a proof that although the officers might declare the law the ultimate determination rested in each case with the suitors. This caused a great number of causes to be brought before the king: he summoned the faulty judges before him and carefully examined into each case; or examined them through his messengers: insisting when he found them guilty that they should either resign the offices which he had committed to them, or devote themselves to the study of equity. We learn from this that the appointments to the sheriffdoms and ealdormanships were made by him, not by election of the people; and, as ignorance was the excuse of their sin, equity the object of their enforced study, that it is clearly in the declaration of law not in the determination of suits that they were faulty. The same general conclusion results from the reading of his laws.

[2] In the Salian Mallus (above, p. 59), the thunginus acted on behalf

in the peace of the king rather than in that of the hundred. When, however, folklands were turned into booklands in favour of either churches or individuals, and all their obligations save the *trinoda necessitas* transferred with them, the profits of jurisdiction and jurisdiction itself followed too.   Such jurisdiction as had been exercised on behalf of the king, in or out of the popular courts, was now vested in the recipient of the grant.   This may have been a very early innovation.   The terms *sac* and *soc* [1], which imply it, are not found until late in the period, but occur almost universally in Norman grants of confirmation, as describing definite immunities which may have been only implied, though necessarily implied, in the original grant, and customarily recognised under these names [2].   The idea of jurisdiction accompanying the possession of the soil must be allowed to be thus ancient, although it may be questioned whether, except in the large territorial lordships, it was actually exercised, or whether

Private jurisdictions.

Sac and soc.

Grants of sac and soc removed the lands from the jurisdiction of the hundred court.

of the nation, the sacebaro looked after the interests of the king.   In the later county court, some such division of duties and interests must have existed between the sheriff and the coroner; and in the Anglo-Saxon time, there may have been a hundred-reeve as well as a hundreds-ealdor (above, p. 113).   Yet in the county court the sheriff was nominated by the crown, the coroner chosen by the people; and earlier, the ealdorman was appointed by the king and witan, the sheriff apparently by the king alone.   And it is extremely difficult to distinguish between the duties of the sheriff executing the peace as the officer of the nation, and collecting the revenue as steward of the king.

[1] Sac, or sacu, seems to mean litigation, and sôcn to mean jurisdiction; the former from the thing (sacu) in dispute; the latter from the seeking of redress; but the form is an alliterative jingle, which will not bear close analysis.   Kemble refers sacu to the preliminary and initiative process, and sôcn to the right of investigation; Cod. Dipl. i. p. xlv.   Ellis makes *sac* the jurisdiction, and *soc* the territory within which it was exercised; Introd. i. 273.   See also Schmid, Gesetze, p. 654.

[2] Kemble (C. D. i. p. xliv) remarks, that except in one questionable grant of Edgar, sac and soc are never mentioned in charters before the reign of Edward the Confessor; and concludes that ' they were so inherent in the land as not to require particularisation; but that under the Normans, when every right and privilege must be struggled for, and the consequences of the Norman love of litigation were bitterly felt, it became a matter of necessity to have them not only tacitly recognised but solemnly recorded.'   The idea that the manor originates in the gradual acquisition by one family of a hereditary right to the headship of the township and the accumulation in that capacity of lands and jurisdiction, does not seem to have anything to recommend it.   In fact, within historic times the headman of the township does not occupy a position of jurisdiction, simply one of police agency.

the proprietor would not as a rule satisfy himself with the profits of jurisdiction, and transact the business of it through the ordinary courts. It is probable that, except in a very few special cases, the *sac* and *soc* thus granted were before the Conquest exemptions from the hundred courts only, and not from those of the shire [1]; and that thus they are the basis of the manorial court-leet, as the mark-system is that of the court baron. There is no evidence of the existence of a domestic tribunal by which the lord tried the offences or settled the disputes of his servants, serfs, or free tenantry; he satisfied himself with arbitrating in the latter case, and producing the criminal in the public courts [2]. But when grants of *sac* and *soc* became common, these questions would swell the business of his private courts, and his jurisdiction would apply as much to those who were under his personal, as to those who were in his territorial protection. By such grants then, indirectly as well as directly, large sections of jurisdiction which had been royal or national, fell into private hands, and as the tendency was for all land ultimately to become bookland, the national courts became more and more the courts of the landowners. The ancient process was retained, but exercised by men who derived their title from the new source of justice. Their jurisdiction was further modified by enactment: as the *thegn* had *socn* over his own men, the king had *socn* over his *thegns*; none but the king could exercise or have the profits of jurisdiction over a king's *thegn* [3]; none but the king could have the fines arising from the offences of the owner of bookland [4]. And, although this might practically be

Growth of private courts.

Jurisdiction of the thegns.

---

[1] In Cod. Dipl. dcccxxviii and dcccviii, Edward frees certain estates of Westminster, 'mid sace and mid socne, scotfreo and gavelfreo, *on hundrede and on scire*,' but the exemption is unusual, and even in these passages may not be a full exemption from jurisdiction. However, when in Domesday the sheriff of Worcestershire reports that there are seven hundreds out of the twelve in which he has no authority, it is clear that such jurisdictions must have been already in being.

[2] K. Maurer, Krit. Ueberschau, ii. 56.

[3] Ethelred, iii. § 11: 'Et nemo habeat socnam super taynum regis, nisi solus rex.' Gneist insists that this refers only to thegns who were members of the witenagemot; Verwaltungsrecht, i. 25, 37, 38.

[4] Ethelred, i. §§ 1, 14: 'Et habeat rex forisfacturas omnium eorum qui liberas terras (bôcland) habent, nec componat aliquis pro ulla tyhtla, si non intersit testimonium praepositi regis.' See also Canute, ii. §§ 13, 77.

observed by recognising the popular courts as royal courts for the smaller owners of bookland, the king had a '*thening-manna*' court, in which his greater vassals settled their disputes [1]. But the time came when the great local landowner was vested with the right of representing the king as judge and *land-rica* in his whole district, and so exercised jurisdiction over minor land-owners. This change, the bearing of which on the history of the hundred courts, which also were placed in private hands, is very uncertain, seems to have begun to operate in the reign of Canute [2]. It is at that date that the *land-rica* becomes pro-minent in the laws; the further development of the practice, as shown in large and almost exhaustive grants of immunity, must be referred to the weak reign and feudal proclivities of Edward the Confessor. Wherever it prevailed it must have brought the local jurisdictions into close conformity with the feudalism of the continent, and may thus serve to explain some of the anomalies of the system of tenure as it existed in the times reported in Domesday.

Hereditary jurisdic-tions.

These immunities, tying the judicature, as it may be said, to the land, and forming one of the most potent causes of the territorial tendency, so far ousted the jurisdiction of the national courts, whether held in the name of the king or of the people, that it might be almost said that the theoretical character of the sovereign rises as the scope for his action is limited. This, how-ever, was to some extent counteracted by the special retention of royal rights in laws and charters. Accordingly, in the later laws, the king specifies the pleas of criminal justice, which he

Weakening of the real power of the king.

Pleas of the crown re-served in grants of jurisdiction.

---

[1] Kemble, Cod. Dipl. mcclviii ; Saxons, ii. 46, 47. In this instance the bishop of Rochester sues the widow of Elfric in the king's 'theningmanna gemot' for certain title deeds alleged to have been stolen : the court ad-judged them to the bishop. Afterwards her relations brought the matter before the ealdorman and the folk, who compelled the bishop to restore them. It is a very curious case, and certainly serves to illustrate the principle that the shire could compel recourse to itself in the first instance even where such high interests were concerned. See K. Maurer, Krit. Ueberschau, ii. 57.

[2] Laws of the Northumbrian Priests, §§ 49, 54, 58, 59 : cf. Ethelred, iii. § 3 ; K. Maurer, Krit. Ueberschau, ii. 50. Mr. Adams urges with a great deal of force the importance of the reign of the Confessor as an epoch in this alteration.

Pleas of the crown. retains for his own administration and profit; such a list is given in the laws of Canute; breach of the king's protection, house-breaking, assault, neglect of the fyrd, and outlawry[1]. These were the original pleas of the crown, and for them special fines were received by the king's officers in the local courts. By a converse process, such small parts of criminal process as still belonged to these courts, arising from the offences of smaller freemen, together with the voluntary and contentious jurisdiction for which the courts of the landowners were not competent, came to be exercised in the king's name. He interfered in suits which had not passed through the earlier stage of the hundred and the shire[2], and asserted himself as supreme judge in all causes, not in appeals only. All jurisdiction was thus exercised either by the king through his officers, or by landowners who had their title from him. The royal officers acted in the hundred courts with freemen of all classes that still owed suit to them; and the shire courts were composed of all lords of land, *scir-thegns*, and others, including a representation of the humblest landowners.

Difficulties of Anglo-Saxon tenure. 74. The subject of tenure in Anglo-Saxon times is beset with many apparently insuperable difficulties[3]. We have not materials for deciding whether a uniform rule was observed in the several kingdoms or in the legal divisions which continued to represent them down to the Norman Conquest and later: whether the Danish Conquest may not have created differences in Mercia, Northumbria, and East Anglia; or whether the variety of nomenclature found in Domesday Book implies a difference of character in the relations described, or merely the variations of local and customary terminology. It was the result of an investigation transacted by different officers, many of whom were Normans and scarcely understood the meaning

---

[1] Canute, ii. § 12; K. Maurer, Krit. Ueberschau, ii. 55. The charter of Alfred, in which these rights are granted away to the abbey of Shaftesbury (Cod. Dipl. cccx), seems to be very doubtful.

[2] Kemble, Saxons, ii. 46 ; Cod. Dipl. dcxciii, dcclv. In the reign of Ethelred the king sends his insegel or writ to the shiremoot of Berkshire, bidding them arbitrate between Leofwine and Wynflæd; C. D. dcxciii.

[3] Hallam, M. A. ii. 293; Palgrave, Commonwealth, pp. 576 sq.

of the witnesses whose evidence they were taking. There is, The Anglo-
Saxon
system of
vassalage however, no question of any general subversion of the primitive rule before the Norman Conquest. No legislation turned the grew out of
the law not
out of the
land. free owner into the feudal tenant: whatever changes in that direction took place were the result of individual acts, or of very gradual changes of custom arising indirectly from the fact that other relations were assuming a territorial character. Domesday Book attests the existence in the time of Edward the Practice of
commenda-
tion as it
appears in
Domesday. Confessor of a large class of freemen who, by commendation, had placed themselves in the relation of dependence on a superior lord [1]; whether any power of transferring their service still remained, or whether the protection which the commended free-man received from his lord extended so far as to give a feudal character to his tenure of land, cannot be certainly determined; but the very use of the term seems to imply that vassalage had not in these cases attained its full growth: the origin of the relation was in the act of the dependent. On the other hand, the occupation of the land of the greater owners by the tenants, or dependents to whom it was granted by the lord, prevailed according to principles little changed from primitive times and incapable of much development. It would seem, however, wiser to look for the chief cause of change in the alteration of other relations. This tendency with reference to judicature we have just examined. When every man who was not, by his own free Growth of
the idea of
lordship as
connected
with land. possession of land, a fully qualified member of the common-wealth, had of necessity to find himself a lord, and the king had asserted for himself the position of lord and patron of the whole nation; when every free man had to provide himself with a permanent security for his own appearance in the courts of justice, of which the king was the source, and for the mainten-ance of the peace, of which the king was the protector; when every thegn aspired to *sac* and *soc*, and the king alone had *socn* over his thegns and the owners of bookland; the relation of the

---

[1] Ellis, Introd. to Domesday, i. 64–66. The term is most frequent in Essex and East Anglia; but descriptions that imply the general use of the practice are abundant; such as 'ire cum terra ubi voluerit,' 'quaerere dominum ubi voluerit;' Hallam, M. A. ii. 276, note z.

Growth of
the idea of
lordship as
connected
with land.

small landowner to the greater or to the king, and the relation
of the landless man to his lord, created a perfectly graduated
system of jurisdiction, every step of which rested on the possession of land by one or both of the persons by whose relations
it was created. The man who had land judged the man who
had not, and the constant assimilation going on between the
poor landowner and the mere cultivator of his lord's land, had
the result of throwing both alike under the courts of the greater
proprietors. As soon as a man found himself obliged to suit and
service in the court of his stronger neighbour, it needed but a
single step to turn the practice into theory, and to regard him
as holding his land in consideration of that suit and service [1].
Still more so, when by special grant other royal rights, such
as the collection of Danegeld and the enforcement of military
service, are made over to the great lords [2]; the occupation,
though it still bears the name of alodial, returns to the character
of usufruct out of which it sprang, when the national ownership,
after first vesting itself in the king as national representative,
has been broken up into particulars, every one of which is
capable of being alienated in detail.

Military
service
originally
a personal
obligation.

75. In the obligation of military service may be found a
second strong impulse towards a national feudalism. The host
was originally the people in arms; the whole free population,
whether landowners or dependents, their sons, servants, and
tenants. Military service was a personal obligation: military
organisation depended largely on tribal and family relations:

---

[1] Hence the alodiaries of Domesday are represented as holding their
lands of a superior: not because they had received them of him, but because they did suit and service at his court, and followed his banner.
Hence, too, Edward the Confessor was able to give to the abbey of S.
Augustine's his own alodiaries; the king being lord of all who had no
other lord. They remained alodiaries by title and inheritance, and probably escaped some of the burdens of territorial dependence.

[2] Gneist, who treats this subject from a different point of view, inclines
to refer the sinking of the ceorl into dependence generally to three
causes: (1) The burden of military service, which led him to commend
himself to a lord who would then be answerable for the military service;
(2) to the convenience which the poor alodial owners found in seeking justice from a strong neighbour rather than from a distant court; and (3) in
the need of military defence during the Danish wars, which drove men
into the protection of fortified houses; Verwaltungsrecht, i. 52, 53.

in the process of conquest, land was the reward of service ; the
service was the obligation of freedom, of which the land was
the outward and visible sign. But very early, as soon perhaps
as the idea of separate property in land was developed, the
military service became, not indeed a burden upon the land,
but a personal duty that practically depended on the tenure of
land ; it may be that every hide had to maintain its warrior ; it
is certain that every owner of land was obliged to the *fyrd* or
expeditio; the owner of bookland as liable to the *trinoda necessitas* alone, and all others by the common obligation. It
would perhaps be hazardous to apply too closely to England
the distinctions that existed under the Frank and Imperial
systems. The holder of alodial land was subject on the continent to the fine for neglecting the Heerbann[1]; the holder
of a beneficium to forfeiture[2]. The same practice might apply
in England to lands analogously held, although, from the
peculiarly defensive character of English warfare after the
consolidation of the kingdom, it might very early be disused.
The law of Ini, that the landowning gesithcundman in case
of neglecting the fyrd, should forfeit his land as well as pay
120 shillings as fyrdwite[3], may be explained either of the
gesith holding an estate of public land, or of the landowner
standing in the relation of gesith to the king : it seems
natural however to refer the fine to the betrayal of his
character of free man, his forfeiture to his desertion of
his duty as gesith. The later legislation, which directs forfeiture in case of the king's presence with the host, whilst
a fine of 120 shillings was sufficient atonement if he were not
present, would seem to be the natural result of the change

It becomes connected with land.

Penalty for neglect of the host.

---

[1] 'Quicumque liber homo in hostem bannitus fuerit et venire contempserit plenum heribannum id est solidos 60 persolvat;' Cap. Bonon. 811, c.
1; Baluze, i. 337; Waitz, D. V. G. iv. 486.
[2] 'Quicumque ex his qui beneficium principis habent parem suum contra
hostes in exercitu pergentem dimiserit, et cum eo ire vel stare noluerit,
honorem suum et beneficium perdat;' Cap. Bonon. 811, c. 5; Baluze, i.
338; Waitz, D. V. G. iv. 492.
[3] Ini, § 51 : 'Si homo sithcundus terrarius expeditionem supersedeat,
emendet cxx solidis et perdat terram suam; non habens terram lx solidis;
cirliscus xxx solidis pro fyrdwita.'

which placed the whole population in dependence on him as lord [1].

The military obligation of the thegn.

It is by no means improbable that the final binding of land-ownership with military attendance on the king in the form of the thegn's service [2], is connected with the same legislation of Alfred and Edward, which we have already examined in reference to treason and the maintenance of the peace. To their date approximately belong the definitions of the thegn as possessing five hides of his own land, church and kitchen, bell-house and burh-geat-setl, and special service in the king's hall: the thegn of Alfred is the miles of Bede; the history of the year A.D. 894 shows an amount of military organisation on Alfred's part, of which there is no earlier evidence, an army of reserve and a definite term of service. 'The king had divided his forces (fierd) into two, so that one half was constantly at home, half out in the field; besides those men whose duty it was to defend the burhs [3].' The military policy too of Charles the Great may by this time have affected England. The improvement of organisation involves a more distinct definition of military duties; and it is certain that the increased importance and costliness of equipment must have confined effective service to the rich [4]. But although the thegn was bound to military

---

[1] Ethelred, v. § 28; vi. § 35. 'Quando rex in hostem pergit, si quis edictu ejus vocatus remanserit, si ita liber homo est ut habeat socam suam et sacam et cum terra sua possit ire quo voluerit, de omni terra sua est in misericordia Regis. Cujuscunque vero alterius domini liber homo si de hoste remanserit, et dominus ejus pro eo alium hominem duxerit, xl solidis domino suo qui vocatus fuit emendabit. Quod si ex toto nullus pro eo abierit ipse quidem domino suo xl sol., dominus autem ejus totidem sol. regi emendabit;' Domesday, i. 172, Worcestershire. In Canute, ii. § 65, neglect of the fyrd involves a fine of 120 shillings, but in § 77, whoever flies from his lord or his companion, in sea or land expedition, is to lose all that he has, and even his bookland is forfeited to the king. His lord enters on the land that he has given him, and his life is forfeit; but this is not the neglect of the fyrd, but the *herisliz* of the continental law, which was punishable by death; Cap. Bonon. 811, c. 4; Baluze, i. 338.

[2] Gneist, Self-government, i. 11: The thegn's service was clearly, (1) personal; (2) at his own cost of equipment; (3) he paid his own expenses during the campaign.

[3] Chron. Sax. A.D. 894.

[4] Gneist, Self-government, i. 10. The stages may be thus marked: (1)

service, we have not sufficient warrant for accepting the theory that his service bore to the extent of his land the exact proportion that is laid down in feudal times[1]. The hide might furnish its man; the thegn might be answerable for five men, or for one warrior five times as well equipped as the ordinary free man: in the reign of Ethelred, eight hides furnished a helm and a coat of mail[2]; in Berkshire in the time of Edward the Confessor, the custom was that every five hides sent one warrior (miles)[3], and each furnished him with four shillings for the provision of two months: if he failed to attend he suffered forfeiture. But we have few more indications of local, and none of general practice, and it is probable that the complete following out of the idea of proportion was reserved for Henry II, unless his military reforms are to be understood, as so many of his other measures are, as the revival and strengthening of anti-feudal and prae-feudal custom. Still even these traces are sufficient to show the tendency to bind up special possession with special service, and consequently to substitute some other liability for that of military service in cases where that special qualification did not exist. Whether the simple freeman served as the follower of the lord to whom he had commended himself or to whose court he did service, or as the king's dependent under the banner of the sheriff or other lord to whom the king had deputed the leading, he found himself a member of a host bound together with territorial relations[4].

(margin note: No exact parallel with feudal legislation on military matters.*)*

the universal obligation; (2) the obligation of the hundred to furnish a hundred warriors; (3) the increased cost of armour restricting effective service. In the seventh century, on the continent, full equipment was worth 33 solidi, that is the price of as many oxen, or of a hide of land: in England, the service was on foot. (4) Although the fully armed warrior might be the king's thegn, all owners of five hides were liable to the same service, and the whole population was still summoned to defensive war, like that against the Danes; Ibid. i. 11–13, 14. Robertson, Hist. Essays, pp. vii–xix, has some very valuable remarks on the whole subject.

[1] Gneist, Self-government, i. 13.
[2] Chron. Sax. A.D. 1008.
[3] Above, p. 131.
[4] Gneist (Self-government, i. 15; Verwaltgsr. i. 15) rightly maintains that the military service was still a personal duty, not a burden on the land; but the personal duty was at every turn conditioned by the possession of the land.

Commuta-
tion of
military
service.

If he were too poor to provide his arms, or preferred safe servitude to dangerous employment in warfare, there was no lack of warlike neighbours who, in consideration of his acceptance of their superiority, would undertake the duty that lay upon his land: he was easily tempted to become a socager, paying rent or gavel, instead of a free but over-worked and short-lived man-at-arms.

Public land
becomes royal
property.

But a further conclusion may be drawn on other grounds. From the time of Alfred the charters contain less and less frequently the clause expressing the counsel and consent of the witan to the grant. It never altogether disappears; but the witan gradually sink into the position of witnesses, and their consent, probably perfunctory enough at any time, becomes a mere attestation. It would seem to follow from this that the public land was becoming virtually king's land, from the moment that the West Saxon monarch became sole ruler of the English; a date agreeing nearly with those which we have fixed for the turning point of the system. If then the king was henceforth special lord of the national land, that land itself becomes scarcely distinguishable from the royal demesne; and every estate cut out of it, whether turned into bookland or not, would seem to place the holder in a personal relation to the

The duty of
national
defence.

king which was fulfilled by military service. Every man who was in the king's peace was liable to be summoned to the host at the king's call, but the king's vassals especially; the former for national defence, the latter for all service[1]: but all the

---

[1] See Gneist, Self-government, i. 13, 18. In the Karoling period this general armament already bore the name of the *landwehr*. 'Ad defensionem patriae omnes sine ulla excusatione veniant;' Edict. Pistense, A.D. 864, c. 27. 'Et volumus ut cujuscumque nostrum homo, in cujuscunque regno sit, cum seniore suo in hostem vel aliis suis utilitatibus pergat, nisi talis regni invasio, quam lantweri dicunt, quod absit, acciderit, ut omnis populus illius regni ad eam repellendam communiter pergat;' Conv. Marsn. A.D. 847. *adn. Karoli.* § 5. The continuance of the fyrd as a general armament of the people during Anglo-Saxon times was no doubt the result of the defensive character of the warfare with the Danes; otherwise it might have sunk, as on the continent, to the mere *wacta* or police of the country (see above, p. 82); a character which it possessed in England also, and which was called out by the legislation of Edward I. It is important to note this double character of the third obligation of the trinoda necessitas; watch and ward; one against male-

English wars of the tenth and eleventh centuries were wars of defence, and hence the fyrd system was maintained in its integrity, although the special duty of the thegns, as afterwards that of the knights, subsisted side by side with it. Still, as in the most primitive times, the host contained the free people fighting in their local organisation, and the specially qualified, specially bound, servants and companions of the leaders[1]. The cultivators of Kent might not be bound by the special service[2], might pay gavel, or rent, instead of fighting, be drengs instead of thegns or knights, but they had no right to hold back from the defence of the country. *(margin: Composition of the army.)*

76. In the region of legislation, beside the general tone and tendency which have been illustrated under the heads of justice and land-tenure, the growth of the royal power and the accompanying increase of territorial influences could appear only in the form of enactment, or in the growth or elimination of the principle of personal law. In the former point no change is perceptible. Ethelred and Canute invariably express the counsel and consent of the wise men of the nation to their promulgation of the laws, just as Ini and Alfred had done. The king never legislates by his own ordinance. The codes are in fact not so much the introductions of new principles as the declarations of the customs or common law of the race, dating from far beyond the existence of written record, preserved in the memories of the wise, and kept alive for the most part in constant general experience. It may be that, when the knowledge of law has become professional, or when under new influences indigenous customs are becoming obsolete, they are written down in books; but as a rule it may be said that a publication of laws is the result of some political change or *(margin: Form of legislation unchanged.)*

---

factors, the other against armed hosts. In the German trinoda necessitas the *wacta* is more important, because in more constant requisition, than the *lantweri*; in England the fyrd is in more constant requisition, until after the Conquest, than the watch; but the two ideas are never really divorced.

[1] Above, p. 32.

[2] See Robertson, Essays, pp. l–liv. Elton, Tenures of Kent, pp. 45–48. The drengs who held lands under the archbishop were turned into knights by Lanfranc; Epp. Cantuar. p. 225; Domesday, i. 4.

New legis-
lation the
result of
some
national
crisis.

series of changes ; so that the very act of legislation implies some crisis in the history of the legislator. The most ancient Germanic code, the Pactus Legis Salicae, seems to mark the period at which the several Frank tribes admitted the sovereignty of the Salian king. The laws of Ethelbert of Kent were the immediate result of the conversion[1] ; those of Wihtræd and Ini, of the changes which a century of church organisation made necessary in that kingdom and in Wessex. The codes of Alfred and Edgar are the legislation which the consolidation of the several earlier kingdoms under the West Saxon house demanded, the former for Wessex, Kent and Mercia[2], the latter for the whole of England. Not the least important parts of the laws of Alfred and Edward are clothed in the form of treaty with the East Anglian Danes; and the Supplementum of Edgar, issued in the witenagemot of Wihtbordesstane, shares the same character[3]. The laws of Canute are the enunciation, with the confirmation of the conqueror, now the elected king, of the legislation which he had promised to preserve to the people who accepted him. Most of the shorter laws are of the nature of amendments, but serve occasionally to illustrate the growth of a common and uniform jurisprudence which testifies to the increase in strength of the power that could enforce it. Thus the very fact of the issue of a code illustrates the progress of legislative power in assimilating old customs or enacting provisions of general authority. The share of the provincial folkmoots in authorising legislation, though not in originating it, appears as late as the reign of Athelstan ; the king in a witenagemot at Greatley enacts certain laws; these are accepted by the men of Kent, bishop, thegns, eorls and ceorls, in a gemot at Faversham, and finally confirmed by the wise men

---

[1] Bede, H. E. ii. 5 : 'Inter cetera bona quae genti suae consulendo conferebat, etiam decreta illi judiciorum juxta exempla Romanorum cum consilio sapientium constituit.'

[2] 'Nolui multa de meis in scriptura ponere quia dubitamus quid posteris inde placeret; sed quae repperi diebus Inae regis cognati mei, vel Offae Mercenorum regis, vel Æthelbrihtes qui primus in Anglorum gente baptizatus est rex, quae mihi justiora visa sunt, haec collegi et cetera dimisi ; ' Alfred, Introd. 49, § 9.

[3] Edgar, iv. 14; Schmid, p. 198.

of Exeter at Thundersfield. The three readings recall the
primitive redaction of the Salian law and its reception in three
malli[1].

The increase of territorial influences might naturally be ex- Question of
pected to put an end to the system of personal law wherever it law.
existed, except in the border territories of Wales and Scotland.
But in spite of the differences of local custom, it may be questioned whether in England the system of personal law ever
prevailed to an extent worth recording. It is true that the Tables of
table of wergilds differs in the different kingdoms [2]; but the wergilds.
differences are very superficial, nor is there anything that shows
certainly that the wergild of the slain stranger was estimated by
the law of his own nation and not by that of the province in
which he was slain. But if there ever was a period at which Division of
the former was the rule, it must have disappeared as soon as according
the united kingdom was ranged under the threefold division of to law.
West Saxon, Mercian and Danish law, an arrangement which
appears to be entirely territorial [3]. The practice of presentment
of Englishry in the case of murder, which was once attributed
to Canute [4], is now generally regarded as one of the innovations
of the Norman Conquest. The laws of Edgar however contain
an enactment which seems to give to the Danes some privilege
of personal law, if not also of actual legislation. In the Supplementum enacted at the Council of Wihtbordesstane, the king
and witan enact an ordinance for the whole population of the
kingdom, English, Danish and British; but with a sort of
saving clause, ' I will that secular rights stand among the Danes Right of
with as good laws as they best may choose. But with the the Danes.

---

[1] See above, p. 130; Athelstan, iii. iv; Lex Salica, ed. Merkel, p. 94;
Sohm, Fr. G. V. G. p. 52.

[2] Schmid, Gesetze, pp. 394–400.

[3] See Freeman, Norm. Conq. i. 433.

[4] Ll. Edw. Conf. § 16. Dialogus de Scaccario, I. cap. x (Select Charters,
p. 193). If an unknown man was found slain, he was presumed to be a
Norman, and the hundred fined accordingly, unless they could prove that
he was English. ' Non procedit nec solvatur pro murdro Anglicus sed
Francigena ; ex quo vero deest qui interfectum hominem comprobet An-
glicum esse, Francigena reputatur ;' Ll. Henr. I. § 92. 6. A similar measure may possibly have been taken by Canute.

English let that stand which I and my witan have added to the dooms of my forefathers for the behoof of all my people. Only let this ordinance be common to all [1].' This is a distinct recognition of the right of the Danes of the Danelaga not only to retain their own customs, but to modify them on occasion : the few customs which they specially retained are enumerated by Canute, and seem to be only nominally at variance with those of their neighbours, whilst of their exercise of the right of

Personal law not important in England.

separate legislation there seems to be no evidence. And what is true of the Danes, is equally true of the Mercians and Northumbrians; the variations of custom are verbal rather than real ; and where, as in the case of the wergilds, they are real, they are territorial rather than personal. The deeper differences of Briton and Saxon laws on the Western border, or of early Danish and English custom in East Anglia were settled by special treaty, such as those of Alfred and Edward with the two Guthrums, and the ordinance of the Dunsætas. The subject of personal law then illustrates the Anglo-Saxon development only incidentally ; there was no such difference amongst the customs of the English races as existed between Frank, Visigoth and Roman, or even between Frank, Alemannian and Lombard.

Effect of Danish invasion.

77. Of the influence of the Danes and Norsemen on the constitutional life of England, whether in their character as conquerors generally, or in special relation to the districts which they ravaged, divided and colonised, little that is affirmative can be certainly stated. For nothing is known of their native institutions at the time of their first inroads ; and the differences between the customs of the Danelaga and those of the rest of England, which follow the Norse occupation, are small in themselves and might almost with equal certainty be

Limits of Danish occupation.

ascribed to the distinction between Angle and Saxon. The extent of the Danish occupation southward is marked by the treaty of Alfred and Guthrum, 'upon the Thames, along the Lea to its source, then right to Bedford and then upon the Ouse to Watling Street [2].' To the north they were advanced as

[1] Edgar, iv. § 2. 1.
[2] Alf. and Guthr. § 1.

far as the Tyne ; and their Western boundary was the mountain
district of Yorkshire, Westmoreland and Cumberland [1].   Over
all this region the traces of their colonisation abound in the
villages whose names end in ' by,' the Scandinavian equivalent
of the English ' tun,' or ' ham ' : the division into wapentakes
may be accepted as Scandinavian more probably than Anglian,
and the larger arrangement of the trithings or ridings of Yorkshire and Lincolnshire is doubtless of the same origin.   But it   The infusion
of Danish
is not probable that they introduced any substantial changes   usages was
not great,
into the customs of the common law, for several reasons.   In   owing to
their own
the first place, their organisation for the purpose of colonisation   condition ;
was apparently only temporary.   It was nearly two centuries
before they effected a permanent settlement, during which period
they ravaged the coasts in the summer, and in the winter either
returned home or remained in camp.   Their expeditions were
headed by independent chieftains allied, as the old Saxons had
been, for the purpose of war, and after the war was over returning to equality and isolation.   They were accordingly far
more likely to amalgamate with the Anglian population which
submitted to them [2] than to create a great and new nation upon
lines of their own.   The evidence of a popular migration, as
distinguished from mere settlement, is wanting, and although
the local extermination of the natives must have occasionally
made the institution of a new organisation necessary [3], it would
appear that such instances were not numerous enough to alter
the general complexion of society.   In the second place, the   and possibly
to their af-
Angles whom they conquered were, of all the English tribes,   finity with
the Angles.
the most closely connected with them in their primitive homes.
The civilisation which the Danes now possessed was probably
about equal to that which the Angles had had three centuries
before ; they were still heathens, and of their legal system we
know no more than that they used the universal customs of

---

[1] See Mr. Robertson's Essay on the Dane-law, in Scotland under her
Early Kings, ii. 430–444.   Freeman, Norm. Conq. i. 644–647.
[2] Freeman, Norm. Conq. i. 148.
[3] Such perhaps was the original confederation of the Five Boroughs;
above, p. 100.

The Danes coalesce with the English.

compurgation, wergild, and other pecuniary compositions for the breach of the peace[1]. Their heathenism they renounced with scarcely a struggle, and the rest of their jurisprudence needed only to be translated into English: the lahslit of the Danes is the wite of the Anglo-Saxons; and in many cases, as we have already seen, new names, rather than new customs, date from the Danish occupation: the earl, the hold, the grith, the trithing, the wapentake perhaps, supersede the old names, but with no perceptible difference of meaning. For the word *law* itself (lah) we are, it is said, indebted to the Danes. Just as in France the Normans adopted the religion and institutions of the conquered, so in England the Danes sank almost immediately into the mass of the Angles.

Bracing influence of the Danish infusion.

It cannot be doubted that the influx of a body of new settlers whose ideas of freedom had not been trained or shackled with three centuries of civilisation, must have introduced a strong impulse in favour of the older institutions which were already on the wane. The alodial tenure of the North must have been reinstated in Yorkshire and East Anglia in its full strength[2], even if the subject Angle sank one degree in the scale of liberty. The institutions of the Danish settlements of the Five Boroughs[3] stand out as late as the Conquest, in the possession of a local constitution which, as well as their confederation, seems to date from their foundation in the ninth century. But speculation on

[1] See the laws of Alfred and Guthrum, and Edward and Guthrum.

[2] Robertson, Scotland, &c. ii. 269: 'It will be found that at the date of the Norman Conquest, contrary to the usually received idea, a greater amount of freedom was enjoyed in the Danelage than in England proper, or in other words Wessex and English Mercia. Throughout the latter district, except in the case of the Gavellers of East Kent, military tenure seems to have prevailed with hardly any exception . . . In the Danelage, on the contrary, omitting Yorkshire from the calculation, between a third and a fourth of the entire population were classified either as liberi homines, or as socmen . . . Free socage, the very tenure of which is sometimes supposed to have been peculiarly a relic of Anglo-Saxon liberty, appears to have been absolutely unknown except among the Anglo-Danes.' Whether these conclusions are to be accepted may be questionable, but the argument illustrates remarkably the expression in the text.

[3] The 'North People's Law,' Schmid, Gesetze, p. 396, seems to imply that the Danes estimated their own wergilds at twice the value of the Angles, just as in early days the Saxons had valued themselves at twice as much as the wealh. See above, p. 169, n. 1.

such points is scarcely necessary. The amalgamation of the Dane and Angle population began from the moment of the conversion. The peace of Alfred and Guthrum established the social equality of the races: the prowess and policy of Edward and of Ethelfleda reunited the Southern Danes under the West Saxon dynasty, and the royal houses of Northumbria and Wessex intermarried. The attraction of the larger and more coherent mass, itself consolidated by the necessity of defence, and the quarrels of the Danish chieftains amongst themselves, led the way to their incorporation. The spasmodic efforts of the Northumbrian Danes were checked by Edmund and Edred; and Edgar, who saw that the time was come to join Dane and Mercian on equality in all respects with the West Saxon, consolidated the Northumbrian kingdom with his own. The Danish Odo, Oskytel, and Oswald were archbishops in less than a century after Halfdane had divided Northumbria; and in the struggles of Ethelred, Sweyn and Canute, the national differences can scarcely be traced. The facility with which the Danes of the eleventh century conquered the provinces which their kinsmen had occupied in the ninth can scarcely be referred to this cause with more probability than to the fact that Mercia and East Anglia during the Anglian period had never united with Wessex. The ill-consolidated realm of Edred broke up between Edwy and Edgar, just as that of Ethelred broke up between Edmund and Canute, and that of Canute between Harold and Hardicanute.

It may be concluded then, that whilst very considerable political modifications and even territorial changes followed the Danish conquest of the ninth century, whilst a rougher, stronger, and perhaps freer element was introduced into the society, into the language, and even into the blood of the Angles, the institutional history is not largely affected by it. During the conquest the Danes were the *host*, or *here*; when it was over they subsided into the conditions of settled society as they found it; their magistrates, their coins, their local customs, like their dwelling places, retained for a while their old names; but under those names they were substantially identical with the

Marginal notes:

Speedy union of Danes and English.

Ecclesiastics of Danish extraction.

The want of cohesion not a result of Danish infusion only.

General conclusion as to the first Danish struggle.

magistrates, coins and customs of the Angles, and in the course of time sank all differences in a common nomenclature.

Nor again can much of the constitutional change which followed the second Danish domination, that founded by Sweyn and Canute, be attributed to the infusion of new customs from the North[1]. Its chief effects were political, and its constitutional consequences may be referred to political far more than to ethnical causes. The laws of Canute are but a reproduction of those of Edgar and Ethelred: 'I will that all people clerk and lay hold fast Edgar's law which all men have chosen and sworn to at Oxford[2].' Not a single custom can be assigned to his rule with any certainty that it cannot be found earlier; and the infusion of Danish blood and language is less important in the

[1] If the authenticity of the Constitutiones Forestae, ascribed to Canute, were proved, they might be useful as marking the introduction of forest law into England; but they are either spurious, or so much interpolated as to be without value. They are accepted indeed by Kemble and Lappenberg, and with some hesitation by Schmid also (Gesetze, p. lvi); but K. Maurer rejects them as a fabrication of much later date (Krit. Ueberschau, ii. 410). Liebermann places them between 1130 and 1215, probably about 1180; see his edition, Halle, 1894. Besides these laws the institution of the huskarls is the only peculiarity of the Danish régime: on them see Freeman, Norm. Conq. i. 733; Langebek, Scr. Rer. Danic. iii. 146. Although they recall very distinctly the features of the primitive comitatus (above, p. 167, n. 4), they do not concern Constitutional History further, and add in no important degree to the elements already existing in English society. It is just possible that the *ornest* or trial by battle, which occurs once in an Anglo-Saxon charter of A.D. 1062 (K. C. D. 813), may have been introduced by the Danes; but its first legal appearance is in the edict of the Conqueror on the subject; Schmid, p. 352. The heriot is often regarded as an institution of Canute; but there are many examples of the custom in the charters much earlier, which show that he simply declared the law of an ancient, probably primitive, usage; Kemble, Saxons, ii. 99. The heriots of Theodred, Bishop of Elmham (Cod. Dipl. dcccclvii), Ethelwald the ealdorman (mclxxiii), Elfgar (mccxxiii), Beorhtric (ccccxcii), and many others are known; and they seem to imply an assessment similar to Canute's own. And in this view of the case, where the payment had become a settled amount due from persons of a particular rank, it 'became possible for women to be charged with it.' In other words, the heriot was become a burden on the land rather than on the person.

[2] Charter of Canute, Select Charters, pp. 75, 76; from the York Gospel Book; see Chr. Sax., A.D. 1018, 'The Danes and the English agreed at Oxford to live under Edgar's law.' The Code of Canute issued at Winchester (Ll. Canuti, Schmid, p. 251) is somewhat later, dating after his conquest of Norway and probably after his visit to Rome in 1027.

eleventh century than in the ninth. The changes which are traceable, and which have been adverted to in the general sketch just given of the growth of the royal power, are to be ascribed to the fact that Canute was a great conqueror and the ruler of other far wider if less civilised territories than England. His changes in the forms of charters and writs, if they were really anything more than clerical variations, simply show that he did with a strong hand what Ethelred had done with a weak one. Even the great mark of his policy, the division of England into four great earldoms or duchies, may be paralleled with the state of things under Edgar and his sons.

It is however possible to refer the last measure to an idea of reproducing something like the imperial system which Canute saw in Germany. He ruled, nominally at least, a larger European dominion than any English sovereign has ever done ; and perhaps also a more homogeneous one. No potentate of the time came near him except the king of Germany, the emperor, with whom he was allied as an equal. The king of the Norwegians, the Danes, and a great part of the Swedes [1], was in a position which might have suggested the foundation of a Scandinavian empire with Britain annexed. Canute's division of his dominions on his death-bed showed that he saw this to be impossible ; Norway, for a century and a half after his strong hand was removed, was broken up amongst an anarchical crew of piratic and bloodthirsty princes, nor could Denmark be regarded as likely to continue united with England. The English nation was too much divided and demoralised to retain hold on Scandinavia, even if the condition of the latter had allowed it. Hence Canute determined that during his life, as after his death, the nations should be governed on their own principles, and as the Saxons, the Bavarians, the Swabians and the Franconians obeyed Conrad the Salic, so the Danes, the Norwegians, the Swedes and the English should obey him. But still further, the four nations of the English, Northumbrians, East Angles, Mercians and West Saxons, might, each under their own national

Imperial character of Canute.

Canute's empire not permanent or consolidated.

---

[1] See his letter to the bishops, in Florence of Worcester, A.D. 1031.

leader, obey a sovereign who was strong enough to enforce peace amongst them. The great earldoms of Canute's reign were perhaps a nearer approach to a feudal division of England than anything which followed the Norman Conquest. That of Mercia was a vast territory in which the earl, an old Mercian noble, united the great territories of the national æthel with the official authority and domain of the ealdorman, and exercised the whole administration of justice, limited only by the king's reeves and the bishops. And the extent to which this creation of the four earldoms affected the history of the next half century cannot be exaggerated. The certain tendency of such an arrangement to become hereditary, and the certain tendency of the hereditary occupation of great fiefs ultimately to overwhelm the royal power, are well exemplified. The process by which, as we have seen, the king concentrates in himself the representation of the nation, as judge, patron, and landlord, reaches its climax only to break up, save where the king's hand is strong enough to hold fast what he has inherited, and the people are
coherent enough to sustain him. The history of the reign of Edward the Confessor is little more than the variation of the balance of power between the families of Godwin and Leofric ; the power of the witenagemot is wielded by the great earls in turn ; each has his allies among the Welsh, Irish and Scottish princes, each his friends and refuge on the continent : at their alternate dictation the king receives and dismisses his wife, names and sets aside his bishops. The disruption of the realm
is imminent. The work of Godwin is crowned by the exaltation of Harold, who saw the evils of the existing state and attempted at the sacrifice of his own family interests to unite the house of Leofric in the support of a national sovereignty. But the policy of Leofric, followed out by the lukewarm patriotism of Edwin and Morcar, opened the way to the Norman Conquest by disabling the right arm of Harold. The Norman Conquest restored national unity at a tremendous temporary sacrifice, just as the Danish Conquest in other ways, and by a reverse process, had helped to create it.

In all this however there is nothing that would lead to the

conclusion of any formal infusion of Scandinavian polity[1]. The measure, so far as it is new, is rather Frank or German, and in advance rather than in the rear of the indigenous development.

78. A glance at the Karolingian legislation of the ninth century suggests the important question whether the legal measures adopted by Alfred and his descendants were to any extent influenced by continental precedents. The intercourse between the two courts had been close and constant, the social condition of the two nations was far more uniform than a superficial view of their history would lead us to believe, and in the laws of their respective legislative periods there are coincidences which can scarcely be regarded as accidental. During the reign of the Great Charles the Frank court was the home of English exiles, as well as of English scholars[2]. Egbert spent as a banished man in France three years, one of which was marked by Charles's assumption of the imperial dignity[3]. It is quite possible that there he conceived the desire of establishing a supremacy over the English kingdoms as well as the idea of binding to himself and his dynasty the mother church of the land in alliance for mutual patronage[4]. The character and some part of the history of Ethelwulf are in strict parallel with those of Lewis the Pious, whose correspondent he was in

(margin notes: Question of the infusion of Frank elements in the later Anglo-Saxon system. Intercourse of the West Saxon kings with the Karolings.*)*

---

[1] Hallam, M. A. ii. 272, comes to the same conclusion. The views of Northern antiquaries, who refer every point of similarity between Scandinavia and England to Norse and Danish influences in Britain, seem to be maintained in ignorance of the body of English History which existed earlier than the Norse invasions, the civilising and Christianising influence of England on Scandinavia, and the common stock of institutions that both nationalities possessed. The temperate and critical treatment of Konrad Maurer is strongly in contrast with this. But even the introduction of the huskarls and the forest law are to a certain extent outside our present subject: the former was no permanent institution, and the latter rests on too weak evidence to be accepted. I have therefore preferred to mention what is important about them under other heads.

[2] See the letters of Offa, Alcuin and Charles, in the Councils and Ecclesiastical Documents, iii. 487, 498, 561–565.

[3] Chron. Sax. A.D. 836. Brihtric died in A.D. 802 ; Egbert's stay in France is sometimes computed at thirteen years (Lappenberg, ed. Thorpe, ii. 1), but on either computation it must have covered the date of Charles's coronation.

[4] See Chapter VIII.

his early years and whose granddaughter he married on his return from his Roman pilgrimage. Alfred drew from the empire some at least of the scholars whose assistance in the restoration of learning repaid to a great extent the debt due to England for the services of Alcuin. Charles the Simple and Otto the Great were married to two of the sisters of Athelstan; and, whilst Otto was consolidating the Saxon empire on the continent, his nephew Edgar was gathering subject kings at his court and taking to himself the titles of emperor and Augustus. As Otto collected the great duchies of Germany into the hands of his sons and sons-in-law, Edgar placed the great ealdormanships of England in the hands of his own kinsmen. In ecclesiastical legislation at the same time England was largely copying from the manuals of Frank statesmanship. The Anglo-Saxon Canons and Penitentials of the tenth century are in great part translations and expansions of the Frank books of discipline which had a hundred years earlier been based on the works of Theodore and Egbert. It would be very rash to affirm that while the bishops, who composed so large a part of the witenagemot, sought foreign models for their canons, they did not seek foreign models for the secular laws. Dunstan had learned monastic discipline where he might also have furnished himself with the knowledge needed for the great office of first adviser to the king. But the brilliant period of imperial legislation was over before the time of Alfred; in the disorganisation of the latter period of the Karolings much of the framework of their system had ceased to exist except in the law books; and the parallels between Frank and English law must not be pressed without allowing for the similarity of the circumstances which prompted them and for the fundamental stock of common principles and customs which underlay them. The law which provided that the landless man must have a lord appears in the Capitularies of Charles the Bald half a century before it appears in the dooms of Athelstan[1]. The judicial investigations made by Alfred through his 'fideles' may remind us of the jurisdic-

Connexion with the Karolings.

Contemporary policy of the Saxon emperors.

Intercourse of churches.

Periods of Frank and English legislation do not coincide.

Coincidences of law and usage.

---

[1] Above, p. 86.

tion of the Frank ' missi ' [1]: in England, as in the empire, the
head of the shire receives a third part of the profits of the law
courts [2], and the great thegn is allowed to swear by the agency
of a representative [3].   Yet all these may be merely the results
of similar circumstances.   In other points, where the coincidences are more striking, difference of circumstances may be
fatal to an affirmative theory.   It cannot be safely said that Uncer-
Edgar's regulations for the hundred were borrowed from the tainty of connexion.
law of Childebert and Clothair, or that Ethelred's rating of the
eight hides to furnish a helm and coat of mail was an imitation of the Frank practice [4], or that the payment of Danegeld
in A.D. 991 was consciously adopted on the precedent created
by Charles the Bald in A.D. 861, 866 and 877 in Gaul and
Lotharingia [5].   Jurists will probably always differ as to the
relation between the scabini of Lewis the Pious and the as-
sistant thegns of the shiremoot [6]; whether the twelve senior Parallels
thegns who swear to accuse none falsely are a jury of inquest not proofs.
like the inquisitors of Lewis, or a compurgatory body to determine on the application of the ordeal.   The oath imposed by
Canute on every one above the age of twelve, that he will

---

[1] Asser, M.H.B. 497 : 'Nam omnia pene totius suae regionis judicia, quae
in absentia sua fiebant, sagaciter investigabat qualiter fierent, justa aut
etiam injusta; aut vero si aliquam in illis judiciis iniquitatem intelligere
posset, leniter advocatos illos ipsos judices aut per se ipsum aut per alios
suos fideles quoslibet interrogabat.'
[2] Above, p. 126.
[3] Ranks, § 3 : 'Iste poterat deinceps jurare pro domino suo.' Waitz,
D. V. G. iv. 228.   'Honorem enim talem nostris vassallis dominicis con-
cedimus, ut ipsi non sicut reliqui manu propria sacramentum jurent, sed
melior homo illorum et credibilior illud agere non differat;' Cap. Vern.
A.D. 884, c. 11.   'Exceptis nostris vassis dominicis pro quibus illorum
homines meliores juramentum persolvent;' Ibid. c. 4; Baluze, ii. 195, 197.
But this existed a century before in the Lex Saxonum, where the noble is
allowed to swear 'in manu liti sui vel sua armata;' c. 8.
[4] Robertson, Essays, p. x.
[5] See the Capitularies of A.D. 861 (Pertz, Legg. i. 477 ; Baluze, ii. 103)
and 877 : 'Haec constituta est exactio Nortmannis qui erant in Sequana
tribuenda ut a regione ejus recederent.' The tax in A.D. 877 is twelve
denarii from the mansus indominicatus ; from the mansus ingenuilis four
from the rent, four from the tenant; from the mansus servilis two from
the rent and two from the tenant. Pertz, Legg. i. 536; Baluze, ii. 175,
176; Waitz, D. V. G. iv. 102 ; Robertson, Essays, pp. 116, 117; Ann. S.
Bertin, A.D. 866.
[6] See above, p. 116.

not be a thief nor cognisant of theft [1], runs back through the common form of Edmund's oath of allegiance [2], and finds parallels in the earliest legislation of Charles the Great [3]. In more than one passage the collection of early English usages, known as the Leges Henrici Primi, recalls the exact language of the Capitularies and of still earlier laws [4]. But, although we may be inclined to reject the theory that refers all such importations of Frank law to the Norman lawyers, and to claim for the institutions, which like trial by jury came to full growth on English soil, a native or at least a common Germanic origin, it is wiser and safer to allow the coincidences to speak for themselves; and to avoid a positive theory that the first independent investigator may find means of demolishing. It is enough that, although in different lines and in widely contrasted political circumstances, royalty was both in England and on the continent working itself into forms in which the old Germanic idea of the king is scarcely recognisable, whilst the influence of long-established organisations, of settled homes, and hereditary jurisdictions, was producing a territorial system of government unknown to the race in its early stages. A strong current of similar events will produce coincidences in the history of nations whose whole institutions are distinct; much more

Similar tendencies in Frank and English history.

---

[1] 'Volumus ut omnis homo post duodecimum aetatis suae annum juret quod fur esse nolit nec furi consentaneus;' Canute, ii. § 21. Compare with this the later regulations of Henry II and Richard I; Select Charters, pp. 137, 256.

[2] Select Charters, p. 66: 'Ut nemo concelet hoc in fratre vel proximo suo plus quam in extraneo.'

[3] Waitz, D. V. G. iv. 368. 'Judex unusquisque per civitatem faciat jurare ad Dei judicia homines credentes juxta quantos praeviderit, seu foris per curtes vel vicoras mansuros, ut cui ex ipsis cognitum fuerit, id est homicidia, furta, adulteria et de inlicitas conjunctiones, ut nemo eas concelet;' Capit. Langobard. A.D. 782, c. 8; Pertz, Legg. i. 43. Cf. Capit. Silvac. A.D. 853; Baluze, ii. 44, 45; Pertz, Legg. i. 424.

[4] See Schmid, Gesetze, pp. 437, 438, 471, 472, 484, 485; Thorpe, Ancient Laws, pp. 507, 509, 510, &c. The regulations of Athelstan (ii. § 14), Edgar (iii. § 8) and Ethelred (iv. § 6) respecting coin, may be compared with those of Lewis the Pious (Pertz, Legg. i. 245; Baluze, i. 432), and Charles the Bald (Baluze, ii. 120, 121). Cf. both with the Roman Law (Just. Cod. ii. § 24), from which they were doubtless derived. The law against holding gemots on Sundays and festivals (Ethelred, v. 13; Canute, i. 15) also resembles that of Charles the Great (Pertz, v. 41; Baluze, i. 183) and Charles the Bald (Baluze, ii. 140, 141).

will like circumstances force similarly constituted nations into like expedients; nay, great legislators will think together even if the events that suggest the thought be of the most dissimilar character. No amount of analogy between two systems can by itself prove the actual derivation of the one from the other.

79. Although the progress of the Anglo-Saxon system, from the condition in which its whole organisation depends on personal relations to that in which everything depends on territorial ones, is marked at each step by some change in the royal power, it is better described in this formula than as a progress from democracy to monarchy, or from a democratic to an aristocratic monarchy, or from alodialism to feudalism. The growth of the royal power was theoretical rather than practical; what it gained on one side, it lost on another. The king became the source of justice, the lord and patron of his people, the owner of the public lands; but he had almost immediately to part with the substantial exercise of the powers so appropriated. By the grants of land, constantly increasing in number, the royal demesne was continually diminished, and the diminution of royal demesne made the taxation of the people the only available means of meeting public emergencies. The immunities which, by grant or by prescription, were vested in the holders of bookland, actually withdrew the profits and powers of jurisdiction from the source from which they themselves emanated. The patronage or lordship which was to unite the king more closely than ever before with the people, was intercepted by a number of mesne lordships and superiorities, which kept them in reality further asunder.

Formula of development.

Diminution of the king's real powers.

Edgar had perfected, so far as we can see, the theory of royalty. He had collected, we are told, a fleet of not less than 3600 ships, which every summer he reviewed and exercised in circumnavigating Britain, thus providing for present defence and for the maintenance of permanent discipline. The winter and spring he devoted to judicial circuits, in which he traversed all the provinces of the English, and accurately inquired how the magistrates observed the laws of the nation and his own decrees, that the poor might not suffer injury or oppression at

Royalty reached its highest point in Edgar.

the hands of the mighty [1]. Possibly the tradition is brighter
than the reality, for the evil times that followed may well have
suggested an exaggeration of past blessings. But the spirit of
Edgar's legislation is good. The preamble of his secular laws
declares that every man shall be worthy of folkright, poor
as well as rich; and the penalties for unrighteous judgment,
with the promise of redress by the king in the last resort,
immediately follow [2]. With his death the evil days began at
once. The strong men whom he had curbed to his service,
took advantage of the youth and weakness of his sons; and
internal divisions rendered the kingdom of Ethelred an easy
prey to the Danes. The real benefit of the changes of the preceding century fell into the hands of the great ealdormen, and
through them to the thegns. The local jurisdictions grew:
the feeling of national union which had been springing up, was
thrown back: the tribal divisions had become territorial, but

they were divisions still. The great lords rounded off their
estates and consolidated their jurisdictions: each had his own
national and ecclesiastical policy. The Mercian Elfhere banished
the monks and replaced them with married clerks; the East
Anglian Ethelwin, God's friend, and the East Saxon Brihtnoth,
drove out the clerks and replaced the monks [3]. Where ecclesiastical order was settled by the local rulers notwithstanding
the strong hand of Dunstan, it was scarcely to be expected that
temporal liberties could be sustained by Ethelred. Another
Danish inroad seemed needed to restore the state of things that
Edgar had created.

80. One good result attended this apparent retrogression.
There had been centralisation without concentration: all rights
and duties were ranging themselves round the person of the

---

[1] Florence of Worcester, A.D. 975. Edgar's judicial circuits were copied
by Canute; Hist. Ramsey (ap. Gale), p. 441: and they may have been
copied from the practice of Alfred; Asser, M. H. B. 497.

[2] Edgar, iii. § 1: 'Volo ut omnis homo sit dignus juris publici, pauper
et dives, quicunque sit, et eis justa judicia judicentur; et sit in emendationibus remissio venialis apud Deum et apud saeculum tolerabilis.' The
latter clause is re-echoed in the charters of Henry I and John; and may
be traced further back in the legislation of Alfred; Ll. Introd. § 49. 7.

[3] Flor. Wig. A.D. 975.

king, and there was a danger that the old local organisations might become obsolete. Edgar had found it necessary to renew the law of the hundreds and to forbid recourse to the king's audience until the local means of obtaining justice had been exhausted [1]. His fleets and armies may not improbably have been organised on a plan of centralisation. Such a tendency was almost a necessity where the royal authority was becoming recognised as imperial, or as limited only by a witenagemot of royal nominees in which no representation or concentration of local machinery had a place. The fact then that the great lords, by the extension of their own rights and the practical assertion of independence, took to themselves the advantages of the change and maintained their jurisdictions apart, gave a longer tenure of life to the provincial divisions. The national unity was weakened by the sense of provincial unity, and individual liberty was strengthened against the time when the national unity should be, not the centralisation of powers, but the concentration of all organisation ; a period long distant and to be reached through strange vicissitudes. In the maintenance of provincial courts and armies was inherent the maintenance of ancient liberty.

The events that followed his death had the result of maintaining local divisions and popular institutions.

For, notwithstanding the series of developments which have been traced so far, the forms of primitive organisation still generally survived. The warriors of the shire, whether free men of full political right, or the church vassals, or the contingents of the great thegns, fought as men of the shire under the ealdorman or his officer. The local force of Devonshire and Somersetshire was beaten by the Danes at Penho ; the East Anglians and the men of Cambridgeshire fought apart at Ringmere ; the men of Dorset, Wilts and Devon at Sherstone [2]. Even the political attitude of the province was determined by the ealdorman and the thegns. The Northumbrian earl Uhtred and the West Saxon earl Ethelmar made their separate agreements with Sweyn, and in doing so declared their independence

Maintenance of provincial administration in military matters.

Political independence of the earls.

---

[1] Edgar, iii. § 2 : 'Nemo requirat regem pro aliqua causa nisi domi negetur ei omne dignum recti vel rectum impetrare non possit.' See above, p. 129.

[2] Flor. Wig. A.D. 1001, 1010, 1016.

Permanence of old customs.

of Ethelred [1]. But still more certainly in the local courts the old spirit of freedom found room. The forms were the same whether the king's gerefa or the lord's steward called the suitors together: the hundred retained its peace, the township its customs: the very disruption of society preserved these things for the better days.

Old customs contain the seed of new liberties.

In the preservation of the old forms,—the compurgation by the kindred of the accused, the responsibility for the wergild, the representation of the township in the court of the hundred, and that of the hundred in the court of the shire; the choice of witnesses; the delegation to chosen committees of the common judicial rights of the suitors of the folkmoot; the need of witness for the transfer of chattels, and the evidence of the hundred or shire to the title to lands; the report of the hundred and shire as to criminals, and the duty of enforcing their production and punishment, and the countless diversity of customs in which the several committees went to work to fulfil the general injunctions of the law,—in these remained the seeds of future liberties; themselves perhaps the mere shakings of the olive tree, the scattered grains that royal and noble gleaners had scorned to gather, but destined for a new life after many days of burial. They were the humble discipline by which a down-trodden people were schooled to act together in small things, until the time came when they could act together for great ones.

Growth of national character.

81. The growth of national character under these changes is a matter of further interest. Although the national experience was not enough to produce a strong and thorough feeling of union, it had been equable and general. No part of England was far behind any other in civilisation. The several kingdoms had been Christianised in rapid succession, and the process of amalgamation, by which the Danes became incorporated with the English, had been so speedy as little to affect the comparative civilisation of the districts they occupied after it had once fairly begun. Northumbria had indeed never recovered the learning and cultivation of her early days, but Kent and

Uniform condition of England.

[1] Flor. Wig. A.D. 1013.

Wessex had retrograded nearly as much during the dark century that preceded Alfred. The depression of national life under Ethelred was much the same everywhere. The free man learned that he had little beyond his own arm and the circle of his friends to trust to. The cohesion of the nation was greatest in the lowest ranges. Family, township, hundred, shire held together when ealdorman was struggling with ealdorman and the king was left in isolated dignity. Kent, Devonshire, Northumbria, had a corporate life which England had not, or which she could not bring to action in the greatest emergencies. The witenagemot represented the wisdom, but concentrated neither the power nor the will, of the nation.

Greatest cohesion in the lowest ranges of organisation.

The individual Englishman must have been formed under circumstances that called forth much self-reliance and little hearty patriotism. His sympathies must have run into very narrow and provincial channels. His own home and parish were much more to him than the house of Cerdic or the safety of the nation. As a Christian, too, he had more real, more appreciable social duties than as an Englishman. He could accept Sweyn or Canute, if he would be his good lord and not change the laws or customs that regulated his daily life. There was a strong sense of social freedom without much care about political power. It was inherent in the blood. Caesar had seen it in the ancient German, and the empire of Charles and Otto strove in vain to remodel it in the medieval aggregation of the German-speaking nationalities; Bavarian, Saxon, Franconian, Swabian, were even less inclined to recognise their unity than were the nations which now called themselves English.

Effect of national history on character.

The form however which this tendency took in the Anglo-Saxon of the eleventh century, is distinct from the corresponding phases of French and German character. The Frenchman can indeed scarcely be said as yet to have developed any national character; or rather the heavy hand of Frank supremacy had not so far relaxed its pressure as to allow the elastic nature of the Gallic element to assert itself; and the historical Frank of the age is still for the most part German. The territory itself

Contrast with French.

scarcely ventures to take a collective name, and resembles the
Gallia of Caesar more than that of Honorius. But the new
life that is growing up is city life, and the liberties at which it
grasps are collective rather than individual privileges. The
rural populations of France are, as they were in the latter days
of Roman rule, and as they continued to be more or less until
the Revolution, a people from whom social freedom had so long
departed that it was scarcely regretted, scarcely coveted ; to
whom Christianity had brought little more than the idea of
liberty in another life to be waited for and laboured for in the
patient endurance of the present. The true life was in the
towns, where, in the interests of commerce, or under the favour
of some native lord temporal or spiritual, or under the patronage of a king who would fain purchase help on all sides against
the overwhelming pressure of his too powerful friends, in the
guild and the commune, men were making their puny efforts
after free action. But this life had scarcely reached the surface : the acts of kings and councils fill the pages of history.
Law was either slowly evolving itself in the shape of feudal
custom, or resting on the changeless rock of Roman jurisprudence : the one unconscious of its development and calling forth
no active participation in the people, the other subject to no
development at all. Even the language had scarcely declared
itself, except in the fragments of courtly minstrelsy.

The contrast between the Englishman and the native German
is not so strong. The disruptive tendency in the English
state is little connected with primitive national divisions. There
is little evidence to show that the people in general felt their
nationality as West Saxons or Mercians, however much they
might realise their connexion as Yorkshiremen or men of Kent.
The Saxon and Bavarian of the continent had each their national policy : their national consciousness was so strong that,
like that of the Irish, it constantly impressed itself even upon
alien rulers. The Saxon emperor made his nearest kinsman
duke of Bavaria only to discover that he had made his son or
brother a Bavarian instead of making the Bavarians loyal. The
Swabian emperor sent a Swabian duke to Saxony in the idea

The grow-
ing life in
France is
civic rather
than rural.

But it is
as yet
scarcely
conscious.

Contrast
with the
German.

Absence of
a feeling of
nationality
among the
English.

Strength of
political
provincial

that the Saxons would cling rather to the emperor than to an feeling
alien governor; but the Swabian duke became forthwith a among the Germans.
Saxon, and the loyalty that was called forth was devoted entirely to the adopted ruler.   And these nations had their
political and ecclesiastical aims; the Saxons preferred the pope
to any emperor but a Saxon one; the Bavarians were ready
to give up the empire altogether if they might have a king
of their own.   In both there was a singular development of And of
personal loyalty with a distinctly national aim in the politics personal loyalty.
of the empire.   But in the Anglo-Saxon history there is an
equally singular lack of personal loyalty, and a very languid
appreciation of national action.   Such loyalty as really appears
is loyalty to the king, not to the provincial rulers whom they
saw more closely and knew better.   The poetic lamentations
of the chronicler over the dead kings may perhaps express the
feeling of the churchmen and the courtiers, but have nothing
to answer to them in the case of the provincial rulers.   The
great earls had not, it would seem, an hereditary hold upon
their people; and although they had political aims of their
own, these were not such as the people could sympathise with.
The popularity of Harold the son of Godwin is only an apparent exception: it was won indeed by his personal gifts and
his ubiquitous activity, but carried with it no feeling of loyalty.
Much even of that higher sentiment which was bestowed on his Languid
kingly career was retrospective; they valued him most when consciousness of
he was lost.   Throughout, the connexion between patriotism loyalty and patriotism
and loyalty, such patriotism and loyalty as exist, seems to want among the
that basis of personal affection which is so natural and necessary English.
to it.   It is not on national glories, but on national miseries
that the Chronicler expatiates; and the misery brings out,
perhaps more than is necessary, the querulous and helpless tone
of national feeling; a tone which no doubt is called forth by
the oppressions of the Norman régime, but which might, under
the same circumstances, in the mouths of other men, have been
exchanged for one of very different character: the song of the
people emulous of ancient glories, girding itself up for a strong
and united effort after liberty.   There is no breath of this in

the English remains of the eleventh century, and the history of the ill-contrived and worse executed attempts to shake off the yoke of the Conqueror proves that there was little life of the kind. Yet there was life; although it lay deep now, it would be strong enough when it reached the surface: nor had the Conqueror any wish to break the bruised reed.

Little interest felt in England as to the ecclesiastical quarrels of the continent. The lack of political aims which might give a stimulus to provincial patriotism, was not compensated by ecclesiastical partisanship, although the struggle between the seculars and regulars does fill a page in English history to the loss it may be feared of more important matter. But the great disputes between the imperial and papal pretensions that moved the continent, found no echo here, and called forth no sympathy. The English, like the continental Saxons, were proud of their faithfulness to Rome; but it was a far distant Rome that interfered very little with them, and that in the minds of their kings and prelates had the aspect of a spiritual city, very different from anything that was really to be found there. The clergy had but a faint notion of the difference between pope and antipope; even in doctrine they had scarcely advanced with the age, and there were points on which they were falling as far behind Roman orthodoxy as the British bishops had been in the Paschal controversy. When an English archbishop visited Rome he spent his time in pilgrimages to holy places: the pope received him with a splendid hospitality which showed him only what it was desireable that he should see; and he came back rich in relics, but as poor as ever in political experience. The secular world was still farther away from him: Canute, who had certain cosmopolitan and imperial instincts, knew better than to involve England in foreign complications. For a century and a half scarcely one Englishman has left his name on record in the work of any foreign historian.

The reasons of this isolation are apparent. The Englishman had enough to do at home in constant resistance to a persevering foe. But the isolation is not, as might be expected, combined with intenser patriotism. The fire of sympathy burns in a very narrow circle: there is little to call forth or diversify the latent energies.

But this is only one aspect of the Englishman. He may be phlegmatic, narrow, languid in political development, but he is neither uncivilised nor uncultivated. The isolation which has been fatal to political growth, has encouraged and concentrated other energies. Since the time of Alfred a national literature has been growing up, of which the very fragments that have survived the revolution of conquest and many centuries of literary neglect, are greater than the native contemporaneous literature of any other people in Europe. No other nation possesses a body of history such as the Anglo-Saxon Bede and the Chronicles. The theological literature, although slight in comparison with that of the Latin-speaking nations, testifies, by the fact that it is in the tongue of the people, to a far more thorough religious sympathy between the teachers and the taught than can be with any degree of probability attributed to the continental churches. In medicine, natural science, grammar, geography, the English of the eleventh century had manuals in their own tongue. They had arts too of their own; goldsmith's work, embroidery, illumination of manuscripts, flourished as well as the craft of the weaver and the armourer. The domestic civilisation of England, with all its drawbacks, was far beyond that of France. The Norman knights despised, undervalued and destroyed much that they could not comprehend. England was behind Europe in some of the arts which they had in common, but she had much that was her own, and developed what she had in common by her own genius. She might be behind in architecture, although that remains to be proved, for much that we know as the work of Northern architects was imitated from Roman models; an imitation which, although it later developed into systems far freer and nobler than anything that had existed before, was still only advancing from its rudest stage in France and Germany. England was slow in following the architecture as she was in following the politics of the continent. It is seldom remembered in comparing Norman and Anglo-Saxon in point of civilisation, how very little the Norman brought in comparison with what he destroyed, and how very little he brought that

Development of national life in other forms.

National literature.

National art and domestic life.

was his own. His law was Frank or Lombard, his general
cultivation that of Lanfranc and Anselm, far more Italian than
native: in civilisation—taken in the truer sense of the word,—
in the organisation of the social life, in the means of obtaining
speedy and equal justice, in the whole domain of national jurisprudence, he was far behind those whom he despised with the
insolence of a barbarian: he had forgotten his own language,
he had no literature, his art was foreign and purchased. But
he was a splendid soldier, he had seen the great world east and
west, he knew the balance of power between popes and emperors; and he was a conqueror: he held the rod of discipline
which was to school England to the knowledge of her own
strength and power of freedom: he was to drag her into the
general network of the spiritual and temporal politics of the
world, rousing her thereby to a consciousness of unsuspected,
undeveloped powers: he was to give a new direction to her
energies, to widen and unite and consolidate her sympathies:
to train her to loyalty and patriotism; and in the process to
impart so much, and to cast away so much, that when the time
of awakening came, the conqueror and the conquered, the race
of the oppressor and the race of the oppressed, were to find
themselves one people [1].

[1] 'After the closing scenes of the great drama commenced at Hastings,
it ceased to exist as a national character; and the beaten, ruined and demoralised Anglo-Saxon found himself launched in a new career of honour,
and rising into all the might and majesty of an Englishman. Let us re-
flect that the defeats upon the Thames and Avon were probably necessary
preliminaries to victories upon the Sutlej;' Kemble, Cod. Dipl. iv. pref.
vi. Carlyle, Fred. II., i. 415, taking a different view of the Anglo-Saxon
temperament, says, 'without them (i. e. the Normans and Plantagenets)
what had it ever been? a gluttonous race of Jutes and Angles, capable of
no grand combinations; lumbering about in pot-bellied equanimity; not
dreaming of heroic toil, and silence, and endurance, such as leads to the
high places of this universe and the golden mountain tops where dwell the
spirits of the dawn.' . . . 'Nothing but collision, intolerable interpressure
(as of men not perpendicular), and consequent battle often supervening,
could have been appointed those undrilled Anglo-Saxons; their pot-bellied
equanimity itself continuing liable to perpetual interruption, as in the
heptarchy times.' This recalls the words of earls Ralph and Roger, 'Angli
sua solummodo rura colunt, conviviis et potationibus non praeliis intendunt;' Ord. Vit. lib. iv. c. 13.

CHAPTER VIII.

THE ANGLO-SAXON CHURCH.

82. Growth of the church organisation in England.—83. Freedom from
the leaven of Roman imperialism.—84. Monasticism.—85. Divisions of
dioceses and origin of parishes.—86. Tithes and endowments.—87. Ecclesiastical councils.—88. Relation of the church to the states.—89. Revival
under Alfred.—90. The eleventh century.

82. THE conversion of the heptarchic kingdoms during the The nation
awakes to
seventh century not only revealed to Europe and Christendom the consciousness
the existence of a new nation, but may be said to have ren- of its unity
at the con-
dered the new nation conscious of its unity in a way in which, version.
under the influence of heathenism, community of language and
custom had failed to do so. The injunctions of Pope Gregory S. Gregory's
scheme for
to the first mission would seem to show that he knew the organising
the church.
whole cluster of tribes under the name of English [1], and regarding them as one nationality provided a simple scheme of ecclesiastical organisation for them; there were to be two provinces each
containing twelve episcopal sees, governed by two metropolitans,
one at London, the other at York. But the comparative failure
of the Kentish mission after the death of Ethelbert, and the fact
that each of the seven kingdoms owed its evangelisation to a
different source, must have rendered the success of S. Gregory's
scheme problematical from the very first. Kent remained per- Distinct
sources of
manently Christian under the successors of Augustine; but mission in
the several
Wessex was converted by Birinus, a missionary from Northern kingdoms.
Italy, East Anglia by a Burgundian, Northumbria and Mercia

[1] Bede, H. E. i. 27, 29.

by Irishmen, Essex and Sussex by the labours of Cedd and Wilfrid. It might have seemed by the middle of the century that the heptarchic divisions were to be reproduced in the ecclesiastical ones. The questions of discipline arising between the Roman and the Irish converts lent an additional element of division. Each kingdom might have had a church of its own, distinct in ritual and traditions from all the rest. This danger was averted by the kings Oswy and Egbert when they joined in sending to Rome a candidate for the see of Canterbury[1]; and Oswy himself, by renouncing the Irish custom of Easter at the synod of Streoneshalch, set the seven churches at peace on that most fruitful matter of discord[2]. The policy of Oswy was thoroughly carried out by Archbishop Theodore of Tarsus. Theodore's scheme of organisation opened the prospect of a more complete unity than that of S. Gregory: there was to be one metropolitan at Canterbury under whom the whole of England was to be carved out into new dioceses. Oswy died before it could be seen whether he and Theodore could work together, and the merit of the scheme actually carried into effect is due to the latter.

This great prelate, himself a philosopher and divine of Eastern training, who had accepted the Roman tonsure and credentials for his message of peace, began his career by consolidating as well as he could the several elements of life that had survived the great pestilence of A.D. 664. The Augustinian succession had almost, if not entirely, died out[3]. Wilfrid and Chad, although they had ceased to differ on points of discipline, represented in their history, their sympathy and their claims, the two opposing schools. Theodore's first care was to settle the personal disputes between them, and through them to make permanent peace between the two sources of mission. He next, in A.D. 673, at the council of Hertford, combined the whole episcopate in a single synod, and provided, by instituting an

Causes of division in the early English church.

Policy of Oswy and Theodore.

Theodore's scheme of organisation.

---

[1] Bede, H. E. iii. 29.
[2] Ibid. iii. 25.
[3] It is questionable whether Boniface of East Anglia survived at the arrival of Theodore; but if so he must have died shortly after: and Damian of Rochester is described as having been long dead; Ibid. iv. 2.

annual council of Clovesho[1], for their permanent cooperation. In A.D. 678 he divided Northumbria, and in the following year Mercia also, into new dioceses: Wessex alone of the larger kingdoms resisted; but a few years after Theodore's death it was subdivided and the whole nation then ranged under sixteen sees, subject to the metropolitan primacy of Canterbury. The arrangement was broken up shortly after, so far as to allow to the see of York its title of archbishop and the obedience of three suffragans; but until the Norman Conquest the Northern primate occupied a very subordinate position to his brother at Canterbury. The institution of the archbishopric of Lichfield by Offa, in A.D. 787, threatened once more to break up the ecclesiastical system. The third metropolitanate however was very short-lived[2]. The final subdivision of Wessex by Edward the elder completed the scheme of Theodore and the territorial organisation of the dioceses, which has continued with some minor changes and additions to the present day. *Creation of dioceses.*

Besides devising this constitution, Theodore did his best to secure and promote cultivation and civilisation in other ways, especially by educating the clergy and tightening the reins of moral and religious discipline. In this he was assisted by the kings, without whose cooperation it could not have been attempted, and who showed an amount of policy, judgment and foresight, in these matters, which could scarcely be looked for in the rulers of a half-Christianised people, themselves as much marked by internecine family bloodshed as by religious devotion. In a single century England became known to Christendom as a fountain of light, as a land of learned men, of devout and unwearied missions, of strong, rich and pious kings. *Other features of Theodore's policy.*

83. The whole material fabric had to be built up from the foundation. Roman Christianity had passed away from Eastern Britain leaving few and indistinct traces. The greater part of the Britons either had never been converted or during the attacks of the Saxons had fallen back into heathenism[3]. British *Attitude of British Christianity towards the English church.*

---

[1] Bede, H. E. iv. 5.

[2] Councils, &c. iii. 444, 445, 542–545. It lasted from A.D. 787 to A.D. 803. The only archbishop of Lichfield was named Higbert.

[3] Bede, H. E. iv. 13, 16, describes Sussex and the Isle of Wight as

Christianity had taken refuge in the Welsh mountains, and made no attempt either to convert the conquerors or to maintain a spiritual hold on the conquered. There was no reason why the English should not have become Christian when and as the Franks did, but from the condition and temper of the native population, on whom the continuance of the conquerors in idolatry and persecuting cruelty brought ultimate extermination. The positive paganism of the Anglo-Saxons was, as far as concerns its mythology and ritual, in the most attenuated condition. Scarcely was Christianity presented to them by the seventh-century missions when they embraced it with singular fidelity and singleness of heart. It could not have failed to prevail earlier but for the attitude of the Britons, who, demoralised by desertion and cut off from all the supports and advantages of communion with foreign churches, had sunk into a despairing lethargy which took for its main principle obstinate and indiscriminating isolation.

Result on the Britons themselves.

Anglo-Saxon Christianity was thus saved from the danger of inheriting the traditions and the burdens of the earlier system. The wave of conquest obliterated in all the South and East of Britain every vestige of Romano-British Christianity. The seats of the bishops had become desolated ruins : the diocesan divisions, if they had ever existed, had been effaced with the civil landmarks on whose lines they may have been drawn[1]. And thus the wonderful vitality of imperialist traditions which did so much to leaven the character and history of the churches

The English church saved from the traditions of the Romano-British system.

entirely heathen in the time of Wilfrid ; that is, either the Christian Britons had been exterminated or they had become heathenised. From the words of Eddius, c. 40, referring to the same transaction, it would seem that the pagans were Saxons, 'gentis nostrae quaedam provincia gentilis usque ad illud tempus perseverans.' In the North of England the British clergy had fled long before, deserting their property, which Wilfrid accordingly claimed for the Northumbrian church ; Eddius, c. 17. Except on the borders of Wessex and Mercia no traces of British church organisation are discoverable from Bede.

[1] Haddan, Councils, i. 142, regards the attestation of the British bishops at Arles in A.D. 314, as proving the existence of diocesan episcopacy in the British church, as opposed to the Irish and Scottish system 'of government by abbots, with bishops as subordinate officers discharging episcopal functions but without jurisdiction.' Wales also had diocesan bishops, and their *parochiae* are mentioned by Gildas ; Ibid. p. 143.

of France and the Rhineland, finding their way to light, in some cases, after devastation and desolation scarcely less than that which befell Britain, took no hold here.   Escaping this, the English church was saved from the infection of court-life and corruption which forms nearly the whole history of the early Franco-Gallican church.   Nor was it called on to act as the protector of a down-trodden people, and undergo the risks that attend political and party religion ; it escaped the position forced upon the bishops of France as secular officers, defensors, and civil magistrates.   And this fact is marked by the choice of the sees of the bishops.   They were in many cases selected in full agreement with the German instinct of avoiding cities; and planted in villages or country monasteries which served as a nucleus for the later towns[1].   Hence, with some few exceptions, the bishops were not local potentates in the way that the French and German prelates were[2].   They were members of the council of the realm to which they belonged and sat also in the local folkmoot with the prestige of wisdom and sanctity, with higher wergild and oath incontrovertible ; but they did not become the counts or dukes of their dioceses, or entangle themselves with the secular intricacies of the divided and bewildered nation whose spiritual guides they were.   Thus Archbishop Egbert sat at York undisturbed in his primacy during the reigns of five princes bound in close relationship with himself, all of whom owed their elevation and deposition to revolt.   In Kent the archbishops ruled from A.D. 740 to A.D. 789, during a period of so much subdivision and anarchy in the kingdom that not even the names of the rival kings or the dates of their reigns have been preserved.   In scarcely any case was a bishop removed from his see for

It escapes the danger of becoming political.

Important position of the prelates apart from secular commotions.

---

[1] In the cases of York, London, Canterbury, Rochester, Leicester, Winchester, and possibly Sidnacester and Worcester, the mother church was placed in the chief town of the kingdom.   In the cases of Lichfield, Lindisfarne, Hereford, Sherborne, Selsey, Elmham, Dunwich, Hexham, villages were chosen or created for the purpose ; and of the new sees of Edward the Elder, Wells, Ramsbury, and Crediton were villages.

[2] The archbishops seem always to have had a more distinctly secular position than the diocesan bishops, a consequence no doubt of their exercising jurisdiction in several kingdoms.   They also coined money bearing their own name and likeness.   The coins of the archbishops of Canterbury run back to the middle of the eighth century, and those of York are only a little later ; Councils, &c. iii. 403.

political causes[1], until Offa attempted to disturb the balance and reform the provincial arrangement of the dioceses. The bishops were occasionally able to act as peacemakers, they were probably always the friends and advisers of their kings, but they were distinctly spiritual men and unfettered by secularity, at least until the consolidation of the West Saxon hegemony.

84. The universality of monasticism is the less pleasant side of this picture; and yet it may be questioned whether anything but monasticism could have kept the church and clergy free from the political combinations and dangers of the early time. The original missionaries were nearly all monks; the mission stations, the bishops' houses, and the homes of the country clergy, were all monasteries; not, it is true, in the strict sense of the Benedictine rule, but sufficiently near to claim all the rights, privileges and immunities which were accorded to it. There were great evils in this arrangement; the privileges and immunities were so great as to invite false brethren. Many houses in which no rule or system of religion was observed, took the name of monasteries to escape public burdens, and brought discredit and reproach upon those that truly bore the name[2]. Even the regularly endowed communities grew too rich, and in the time of Bede engrossed too large a share of the public land[3]:

---

[1] There are very few cases of deposition of bishops in the Anglo-Saxon church history at all. Archbishop Theodore deposed Winfrith of Mercia for disobedience, and Trumbert of Hexham also; Bede, H. E. iv. 6, 28; Wilfrid of York was banished and restored more than once; Acca of Hexham had to fly from his see in A.D. 732, probably in consequence of the disorders of Northumbria; Wulfstan of York was set aside and imprisoned for treason in A.D. 952, but afterwards restored; Brihthelm, the bishop appointed by Edwy to Canterbury, was set aside by Edgar. Of resignation there are very many instances.

[2] Council of Clovesho, A.D. 747, c. 5: 'Monasteria, si tamen ea fas est ita nominare, quae utique quamvis temporibus istis, propter vim tyrannicae quandam avaritiae, ad religionis Christianae statum nullatenus immutari possint; id est a saecularibus, non divinae scilicet legis ordinatione, sed humanae adinventionis praesumptione, utcunque tenentur;' Councils, &c. iii. 364. Bede also speaks of innumerable places 'in monasteriorum ascripta vocabulum sed nihil prorsus monasticae conversationis habentia;' Ep. ad Ecgbert.; Councils, iii. 319.

[3] 'Tot sub nomine monasteriorum loca hi qui monachicae vitae prorsus sunt expertes in suam ditionem acceperunt. . . . ut omnino desit locus ubi filii nobilium aut emeritorum militum possessionem accipere possint;' Ibid. p. 320.

in their wealth they lost sight of the strict obligations of a religious life, so that, before the middle of the eighth century, a stringent reform was demanded, and the secular were synodically divided from the monastic clerks[1]. But with all these draw-backs, the monastic system did its work well, and that a most important work for the time. It colonised the country by means of missions, furnished the supply of teachers in districts too poor and too thinly peopled to provide for their own clergy; and in a manner levelled and equalised the country for parochial adminis-tration. The monastic spirit has, further, had in all ages a singular corporate consciousness; and, besides the influence of common councils and canonical customs, the fact that the clergy felt their vows and spiritual relations to be a much more real tie and basis of consolidation than mere nationality, must have led to the elimination of provincial feeling amongst them. A Mercian priest was free of all the churches. A Mercian or West Saxon prelate might rule at Canterbury; the bishop of East Anglia might be a Kentish man, and a South Saxon rule at Rochester[2].

Real ser-vices of the monastic system.

Whilst then the church formed a basis of national union, the clergy escaped the danger of sinking into an hereditary caste, as was the case largely both in the Irish churches and on the con-tinent. Some marked traces of this tendency however are found in England, in the age immediately preceding the Conquest[3];

No clerical caste.

---

[1] Council of Clovesho, A.D. 747, cc. 4, 5, 19, 28. Still more strongly is it insisted on in the decrees of the legatine councils of A.D. 787: 'Ut episcopi diligenti cura provideant quo omnes canonici sui canonice vivant et monachi seu monachae regulariter conversentur;' Councils, iii. 450. This is the first time the title of *canon* occurs in an English docu-ment; and the term never became common until the eve of the Norman Conquest.

[2] Instances of the international character of the priesthood, and espe-cially of monachism, are abundant. Deusdedit, the sixth archbishop of Canterbury, was a West Saxon; Tatwin, the ninth, was a Mercian (Bede, H. E. v. 20, 23); and after the time of Alfred the archbishops were generally West Saxons. Pecthelm, the deacon of Aldhelm, was made bishop of Whithern; Boniface, a Kentishman, was bishop of East Anglia; Damian, a South Saxon, was bishop of Rochester; Ibid. v. 13, iii. 20. In the North of England, and during the later Anglo-Saxon period, the instances are less frequent; freedom of election, or local influence, would generally determine in favour of a native candidate.

[3] On the descent of ecclesiastical property through an hereditary line of priests, see Raine's preface to the Memorials of Hexham. The institution of the Culdees, which was maintained by this custom, had probably spread

and that the escape was a narrow one is shown by the number
of early charters, which distinctly prove the descent of the half-
secular monastic estates through a series of generations, in which
either clerical celibacy was unknown, or the successive heads of
the monasteries must have delayed ordination until they became
fathers and mothers of families large enough to continue the
succession. These occur throughout the history of the early
Anglo-Saxon church, and must not be regarded as a mark of
monastic decadence, though distinctly an abuse [1]. The royal and
noble monasteries were clearly regarded as family benefices, for
which the only requisite was the assumption of orders or the
taking of vows; they served as places of retirement for worn-
out statesmen and for public functionaries—kings, queens, and
ealdormen, whose forced seclusion gave to their retreats somewhat of the character of reformatories [2].

85. The development of the local machinery of the church
was in a reverse order to that of the state; the bishoprics
being first formed, then the parishes; and at a much later
period, the archdeaconries and deaneries. The original bishoprics of the conversion were the heptarchic kingdoms; and the

into the Northumbrian church. 'The particular Keledean laxity appears
to have been that, precisely like their Irish and Welsh congeners, they
lapsed into something like impropriators (to use the modern term), married,
and transmitting their church endowments, as if they had been their own,
to their children, but retaining, at any rate in most cases, their clerical
office;' Haddan, Councils, ii. 178.

[1] See, for example, the charters referring to monasteries at Fladbury,
Sture and Withington, in the Cod. Dipl. xxxiii, cxlvi, ccxv; lxxx, cxxvii;
lxxxii, cxxiv. In one case the principle is laid down thus: Abbot Headda
left his monastery at Onnanford to the see of Worcester, under condition
'quod mei heredes in mea genealogia in ecclesiastico gradu de virili sexu
percipiant, quamdiu in mea prosapia tam sapiens et praesciens inveniri
potest qui rite et monastice ecclesiasticam normam regere queat, et nunquam potestati laicorum subdetur;' Ibid. clxix. Benedict Biscop thought
differently; he declared that he would rather his monastery should become an eternal solitude than that his brother should be elected abbot,
not having entered the way of truth; Bede, Hist. Abbat. c. 9. It was
forbidden also by Theodore, Penit. ii. 6: 'Ipse non potest aliquem ordinare de suis propinquis.'

[2] Abundant instances, in which the retirement can scarcely be regarded
as voluntary, may be found in Simeon of Durham's annals of the eighth
century. An adulteress may retire to a monastery; Theod. Penit. ii. 12.
The thief has a choice between a monastery and slavery: 'Aut intret in
monasterium Deo servire aut humanum subeat servitium;' Ibid. i. 3.
'Eat in monasterium et poeniteat usque ad mortem;' Ibid. i. 7.

see was in some instances the capital. The kingdom of Kent
formed the dioceses of Canterbury and her suffragan Rochester;
Essex was the diocese of London; Wessex that of Dorchester
or Winchester; Northumbria that of York; East Anglia that
of Dunwich : the site of the original Mercian see is not fixed,
but within a few years of the conversion it was placed by S.
Chad at Lichfield. In all cases, for a short time, the diocese The diocese
coincided with the kingdom, and needed no other limitation; at first
coincided
the court was the chief mission-station, and sent out monks or with the
kingdom.
priests to convert the outlying settlements. There were as yet Simplicity
very few churches; crosses were set up in the villages and on of organisation.
the estates of Christian nobles, at the foot of which the missionaries preached, said mass, and baptized[1]. The only officer of
the bishop was his deacon, who acted as his secretary and companion in travel, and occasionally as interpreter. The bishop's
house, however, contained a number of clerks, priests, monks
and nuns, and was both a home of retreat to the weary missionary and a school for the young. These inmates lived by a
sort of rule, which was regarded as monastic, and the house and
church were the *monasterium* or minster. Gifts of land were at Early endowments.
this very early stage bestowed both on the bishop's minster and
on others, which, although under his governance spiritually,
were less exclusively his own, having their abbots and abbesses
with full powers of economical administration. These houses
were frequently of royal foundation, ruled by persons of noble
blood ; some of them contained both male and female votaries,
and might be ruled by persons of either sex[2].

---

[1] 'Quia sic mos est Saxonicae gentis, quod in nonnullis nobilium bono-
rumque hominum praediis, non ecclesiam sed sanctae crucis signum Domino dicatum cum magno honore almum, in alto erectum, ad commodam
diurnae orationis sedulitatem solent habere;' V. S. Willibaldi, Mab.
AA. SS. saec. iii. pt. 2, p. 334. This is late in the eighth century. Bede
describes the building of churches throughout Northumbria under Oswald,
H. E. iii. 3: 'Construebantur ergo ecclesiae per loca, confluebant ad audiendum verbum populi gaudentes, donabantur regio munere possessiones.'
[2] These mixed monasteries are animadverted on but not forbidden by
Theodore, Penit. ii. 6 : 'Non licet viris feminas habere monachas neque
feminis viros, tamen non destruamus illud quod consuetudo est in hac
terra.' The custom was perhaps derived from Ireland. S. Hilda's monastery at Whitby is the most famous instance. The practice seems to have
subsisted until the ninth century.

Scanty
materials
for Theo-
dore's work.

Subdivision
of dioceses
on the still
earlier pro-
vincial lines.

When archbishop Theodore undertook to organise the church, he found little more than this to work on. He found dioceses identical with kingdoms; no settled clergy, and no definite territorial subdivisions. His first measure was, as we have seen, to break up the dioceses; and in doing so, he followed the lines of the still existing territorial or tribal arrangements which had preceded the creation of the seven kingdoms. East Anglia was first divided between the northern and southern divisions of the folk; the former with its see at Elmham, the latter clinging to Dunwich. Northumbria followed: York, the capital of Deira, had already put in its claim, according to the direction of S. Gregory, and had its own bishop. Bernicia remained to Lindisfarne and Hexham; and the Picts had a missionary bishop at Whithern: the Lindisfari, of modern Lincolnshire, who at the moment of the division were under the Northumbrian king, received a bishop with his see at Sidnacester. Next, Mercia was divided; the recovered province of Lindsey was recognised as a new diocese; the kingdom of the Hwiccas, which still existed as an under-kingdom, furnished another with its see at Worcester; North and South Hecana had their bishop at Hereford, and the Middle Angles theirs at Leicester. The work was not without its difficulties. The old bishops in particular resisted any infringement on their power. Winfrith of Lichfield had to be deposed before Mercia was divided: the struggle for the retention of his Northumbrian dioceses was the work of the life of Wilfrid. In Wessex the opposition was so strong as to thwart Theodore himself, and it was not until after his death, when Brihtwald was archbishop of Canterbury and Ini king of the West Saxons, that the unwieldy diocese was broken up; Sussex, which now was permanently subject as a kingdom, was made the diocese of the mission see at Selsey; the kingdom of Wessex proper was divided by the forest of Selwood into two convenient divisions, of which the western half had its see at Sherborne, Winchester remaining the see of the eastern half, with a sort of primacy of its own, as the mother church[1].

[1] The dates of the foundation of these sees are as follows: Canterbury, A.D. 597; London and Rochester, A.D. 604; York, A.D. 625, restored in

The subdivision of the dioceses was followed by a great de- Great development of monasti-cism. velopment of monasticism ; the monastery continued to be the typical church settlement, and the monastic history casts almost all other into the shade. Still we may learn from Bede that the country churches were also multiplied, and local provision of some sort was made for the village clergy[1]. What measures Organisation of parishes. Theodore, who is the traditional creator of the parochial system[2], took in this direction can only be conjectured : it is unnecessary to suppose that he founded it, for it needed no foundation. As the kingdom and shire were the natural sphere of the bishop, so was the township of the single priest ; and the parish was but the township or cluster of townships to which that priest minis-tered[3]. The fact that the two systems, the parish and the township, have existed for more than a thousand years side by side, identical in area and administered by the same persons, and yet separate in character and machinery, is a sufficient proof that no legislative act could have been needed in the first place ; nor was there any lay council of the whole nation which could have sanctioned such a general measure. Considering, moreover, the thorough harmony of church and state in these ages, any legislation would probably have altogether sunk one of the two systems in the other. The parish, then, is the ancient *vicus* or tun-scipe regarded ecclesiastically. As many

A.D. 664 and 678, and endowed with the pall in A.D. 735 ; Dunwich, in A.D. 630 ; the see of Wessex, at Dorchester, A.D. 634 (afterwards at Win-chester) ; Lindisfarne, A.D. 635 ; that of Mercia, A.D. 656, settled at Lich-field in A.D. 669. In A.D. 673 Theodore instituted the see of Elmham ; in A.D. 676, Hereford ; in A.D. 678, Sidnacester and Hexham ; in A.D. 680, Worcester and Leicester ; in A.D. 681, Whithern. In A.D. 705 Sherborne was founded ; and in A.D. 709, Selsey.

[1] Bede urges on Egbert the importance of this : ' necessarium satis est ut plures tibi sacri operis adjutores adsciscas, presbyteros videlicet ordinando atque instituendo doctores qui in singulis viculis praedicando Dei verbo, et consecrandis mysteriis caelestibus ac maxime peragendis sacri baptismatis officiis, ubi opportunitas ingruerit, insistant ; ' Ep. ad Ecgb. c. 3.

[2] Elmham, ed. Hardwick, pp. 285, 286 : ' Excitabat fidelium devotionem et voluntatem, in quarumlibet provinciarum civitatibus necnon villis, ecclesias fabricandi, parochias distinguendi, assensu eisdem regios pro-curando, ut qui sufficientes essent et ad Dei honorem pro voto haberent super proprium fundum ecclesias construere earundem perpetuo patronatu gauderent.' This is mere tradition or invention.

[3] Above, p. 91.

The parish
is the town-
ship in its
ecclesias-
tical cha-
racter.

townships were too small to require or to support a separate church and priest, many parishes contain several townships; but the fact of a township lying partly in one parish and partly in another, without being very uncommon, is rare enough to be exceptional, and may generally be accounted for by more recent local history [1].

Mainten-
ance of the
clergy.

Origin of
Tithes.

86. The maintenance of the clergy thus settled was provided chiefly by the offerings of the people : for the obligation of tithe in its modern sense was not yet recognised. It is true that the duty of bestowing on God's service a tenth part of the goods was a portion of the common law of Christianity, and as such was impressed by the priest on his parishioners [2]. But it was not possible or desirable to enforce it by spiritual penalties : nor was the actual expenditure determined except by custom, or by the will of the bishop, who usually divided it between the church, the clergy, and the poor. It was thus precarious and uncertain, and the bestowal of a little estate on the church of the township was probably the most usual way of eking out what the voluntary gifts supplied [3].

Legislation
on the
subject of
Tithes.

The recognition of the legal obligation of tithe dates from the eighth century, both on the continent and in England. In A.D.

[1] Many alterations in the boundaries of parishes, townships, hundreds, and counties, have of course taken place in thirteen centuries of English history, but the whole of the 'irregularities of boundary' of parishes and counties are contained in three pages of the Population Report of 1831, vol. ii. pp. 1064–1066.

[2] Tithes are mentioned by Theodore in the genuine Penitential, in a way that proves the duty of making the payment, but not the right of the clergy to the sole use of them : ' Presbiter (or presbitero) decimas dare non cogitur;' Lib. ii. 2. ' Tributum ecclesiae sit, sicut consuetudo provinciae, id est ne tantum pauperes inde in decimis aut in aliquibus rebus vim patientur. Decimas non est legitimum dare nisi pauperibus et peregrinis, sive laici suas ad ecclesias;' Lib. ii. 14. Bede praises Bishop Eadberct of Lindisfarne, as ' maxime eleemosynarum operatione insignis, ita ut juxta legem omnibus annis decimam non solum quadrupedum verum etiam frugum omnium atque pomorum, necnon et vestimentorum partem pauperibus daret;' Hist. Eccl. iv. 29. In the laws of Edward the Confessor the obligation is alleged to have been introduced by Augustine, that is, at the Conversion.

[3] See Cap. de partibus Saxoniae ; Pertz, Legg. v. p. 40 ; Baluze, i. 183, Art. 15, which shows that this was the rule approved by Charles : ' ad unamquamque ecclesiam curtem et duos mansos terrae pagenses ad ecclesiam recurrentes condonent, et inter centum viginti homines nobiles et ingenuos, similiter et litos, servum et ancillam eidem ecclesiae tribuant.'

779 Charles the Great ordained that every one should pay tithe, and that the proceeds should be disposed of by the bishop[1]: and in A.D. 787 it was made imperative by the legatine councils held in England, which, being attended and confirmed by the kings and ealdormen, had the authority of witenagemots[2]. From that time it was enforced by not unfrequent legislation. The famous donation of Ethelwulf had nothing to do with tithe[3]; but almost all the laws issued after the death of Alfred contain some mention of it. The legislation of Edgar is somewhat minute on the subject; directing the tithe of young to be paid at Whitsuntide, and that of the fruits of the earth at the autumnal equinox, thus testifying to the general devotion of the tithe of increase[4]. The legal determination of the church to which the tithe was to be paid was not yet settled. The same king directs that it shall be paid to the ' eald mynster,' or mother church to which the district belongs[5]; the thegn who had on his bookland a church with a buryingplace was bound to give a third of his own tithe to that church; if there were no buryingplace, his gift to the priest might be what he pleased[6]: the cathedral church being it would seem the normal recipient, and the bishop the distributor. But the actual determination was really left very much to the owner of the land from which the tithe arose; and although in the free townships it must have become the rule to give it to the parish priests, the lords of franchises found

Law of Tithe.

---

[1] Cap. A.D. 779, Art. 7: ' De decimis, ut unusquisque suam decimam donet atque per jussionem pontificis dispensentur.' Pertz, Legg. i. p. 36; Baluze, i. 142.

[2] 'Praecipimus ut omnes studeant de omnibus quae possident decimas dare, quia speciale Domini Dei est;' Can. 17; Councils, &c. iii. 456. On these councils see Lord Selborne, Ancient Facts and Fictions, 159 sq.; where the author argues that the injunctions of the councils were not strictly canons, and certainly were not legislative enactments by kings or witenagemots. Whether the injunctions were or were not canons, it is difficult to see how they could have had more direct legislative authority than was given them by the acceptance, attestation and promise of observance given by the kings, in councils, with *senatores, principes, duces,* and *populus,* who received them in words apparently taken from the apostolic legislation; Acts, 16. 4.

[3] Except as showing the sanctity of the tenth portion. See Councils, &c. iii. 636 sq.; Kemble, Saxons, ii. 481–490. See p. 258 below.

[4] Edgar, ii. § 3.

[5] Edgar, ii. §§ 1, 2.

[6] Ibid. § 2.

it a convenient way of making friends and procuring intercessions to bestow it on monasteries. This custom became very frequent after the Norman Conquest, and it was not until the council held at Westminster in A.D. 1200 that the principle was summarily stated that the parochial clergy have the first claim on the tithe even of newly cultivated lands[1]. Even after that time, by the connivance of bishops and popes, the appropriation system worked widely and banefully. Besides the tithe, the clergy received, under the name of cyric-sceat or church-scot, a sort of commutation for firstfruits paid by every householder. The church-scot was paid at Martinmas, 'according to the hearth that a man is at at midwinter,' that is, in the township where he keeps Christmas. There was also sawl-sceat, soul-scot or mortuary-dues, with other occasional spontaneous offerings[2].

Bede's desire for progress and reform.

Rapidly and regularly as the organisation and endowment of the church proceeded under Theodore and his successors, it was not such as to satisfy the pious longings or to silence the severe judgment of Bede. He saw that in the northern province much greater subdivision was necessary[3], and he viewed with fear and anger the corruptions of the monastic life, which the rich and

Mischievous effects of Mercian supremacy.

vicious were perverting in a strange degree. But the bright days of the early church were already over, and notwithstanding the efforts of Cuthbert of Canterbury in his councils, and of Egbert of York in court, school, and study, the evil days of

Archbishopric of Lichfield.

Mercian supremacy told heavily on the church. These reached their climax when Offa in A.D. 787 proposed and effected the division of the province of Canterbury, established a new archbishopric at Lichfield to which the sees now included in the Mercian kingdom should pay obedience, and obtained by a liberal tribute to Rome the papal authorisation of his plan[4].

---

[1] Can. Westm. 9 ; Johnson's Canons, ii. 89.

[2] Ini, §§ 4, 61. See on the whole subject, Kemble, Saxons, vol. ii. ; Schmid, Gesetze, 545 sq.

[3] See especially the letter to Archbishop Egbert, c. 5 ; Councils, &c. iii. 319 ; and compare the appeals of Boniface to Ethelbald, King of Mercia, ibid. 350–356.

[4] The annual tribute of 365 mancuses was, according to Pope Leo III,

This payment,—for there is a want of evidence as to the institu- Rome-scot.
tion by Ini of a similar tribute for the maintenance of the English
school at Rome,—is probably the origin of the Rom-feoh, or
Peter's pence, a tax of a penny on every hearth, which was collected and sent to Rome from the beginning of the tenth century,
and was a subject of frequent legislation[1]. But the archiepiscopate of Lichfield scarcely survived its founder. After Offa's
death archbishop Ethelheard, who had submitted as long as he
lived, took advantage of the devotion or weakness of Kenulf to
obtain a reversal of the measure; Leo III was prevailed on to
annul the act of Hadrian I, and in a great council at Clovesho in
803 the primitive dignity of Canterbury was finally and fully
recognised.

87. The ecclesiastical councils of the heptarchic period were Ecclesias-
tical coun-
cils.
either national, such as those of Hertford and Hatfield under
Theodore[2], or provincial, as was generally the case after the vindication of the metropolitical claims of York under Egbert. Of
ecclesiastical assemblies of the single kingdoms there are perhaps
occasional traces, but they are scarcely distinguishable from the
separate witenagemots. All these councils in many respects
resemble the witenagemots. The presence of the kings and Presence of
kings and
ealdormen.
ealdormen seems to have been by no means unusual[3]: and,
although actual participation by the latter in ecclesiastical legislation may not have been permitted, their confirmation and
attestation of the results was not undervalued. The bishops, Members
of these
councils:
however, were the chief permanent element: abbots are not un-
frequently mentioned as attending, though not in large numbers: bishops and
abbots.
and in one case, that of the Council of Clovesho of A.D. 803,
each bishop appears at the head of a body of diocesan clergy,

---

bestowed by Offa in the legatine council of A.D. 787; Councils, &c. iii. 445.
A similar benefaction of Ethelwulf (W. Malmesb.; Councils, iii. 646) is
also recorded.

[1] Edw. and Guthr. 6, § 1; Ethelred, v. 11. It was paid on the feast of
S. Peter and S. Paul, June 29.

[2] Bede, H. E. iv. 5, 17, 18.

[3] At the legatine council of A.D. 787 Offa was present 'cum senatoribus
terrae;' Councils, &c. iii. 460. At the council of Chelsea in A.D. 816
Kenulf was present 'cum suis principibus, ducibus et optimatibus;' Ibid.
p. 579. See above, p. 143.

many of whom are abbots[1]. These are not necessarily to be regarded as the heads of strictly Benedictine houses, but as the rulers of churches which had lost much of the cenobitic character, and answer rather to the holders of large family preferment or other benefices, like the mass-thegns of the laws.

Places of assembly. It was part of Theodore's plan that these assemblies should be held every August at Clovesho[2], a now forgotten place in the Mercian kingdom, probably near London. But the rule, although frequently observed as to place, does not seem to have prevailed as to time or frequency. Yet on the whole the councils are more numerous than could be expected in the unsettled state of the kingdoms. Most of them are held on the confines of the states, where the subjects of each king could at nightfall retire into their own country. Such places were Brentford and Chelsea, and most likely Clovesho also. As during this period there could be no witenagemots of the whole nation, any council at any of these places, or at which all or a majority of the bishops were present, must be regarded as either an ecclesiastical council pure and simple, or as a mixed gathering under the eye of some king who at the moment was supreme in church and state.

Subjects of discussion. The subjects of discussion were various, but the strictly ecclesiastical councils contented themselves with ecclesiastical legislation. They passed canons in which any interference with secular law or custom is wisely avoided, and they never imitate the Theocratic system of the Spanish councils with which in some respects they have much in common. They seem also to have exercised a friendly jurisdiction in suits for property between different churches or between kings and ealdormen of the different nations who had disputed with the churches or with each other. Herein they acted rather as arbitrators than as judges, and probably expected review or confirmation by the folkmoot or witenagemot. Their legislation shows no sign of needing any further confirmation, but, from the frequency of ecclesiastical regulations in the general codes of the

Harmony of lay and church councils.

[1] Councils, &c. iii. 546, 547.
[2] Bede, H. E. iv. 5.

kings and witan, it is certain that no jealousy as yet existed between the two systems; the bishops were members of both bodies, and did not hesitate to accept the confirmation of the national council to strengthen the pressure or increase the publicity of their own enactments.

The judicial power and coercive jurisdiction of the great spiritual officers are matters of further question. The bishops sat in the popular courts as they sat in the witenagemot, and in both with much the same power as the lay witan. They had also temporal jurisdiction within the limits of their own franchises, in which the legal process by compurgation and ordeal was in no wise distinguishable from that of the hundred moot. They had further, as a result of that penitential discipline which, partly perhaps through the oriental training of Theodore, and partly through the labours of the Irish missionaries, obtained an early and general acceptance in the Anglo-Saxon church, a powerful coercive machinery quite apart from the common law or customs of the nation at large, for the enforcement of which they must have been indebted to the pious assistance or neutrality of the laity. But between these two regions of judicature there lay a class of suits, concerning the disputes and offences of the clergy and the morals of the laity, with which it would seem the bishops were especially charged. Unfortunately our evidence on this head is very small. The Penitential of Theodore contains provision that the bishop shall determine the causes of the poor up to fifty shillings, the king if the sum in question be greater. At the other end of the period, in Domesday book, we find among the Customs of Kent, that in cases of adultery, the king is to have the man, the archbishop the woman [1]. There is no reason to suppose that in such cases any peculiar court was provided. They would be tried in the hundred-moot and shire-moot, and the bishop would claim his share in the penalties as well as declare the law and the

Marginal notes: Power of the bishops in the popular courts; in their own franchises; in penitential discipline; over the clergy; in questions of morals; and others. Much of their jurisdiction exercised in the popular courts.

[1] The law of Wihtræd orders the excommunication of such offenders, § 3. The penalty of the adultery of the gesithcundman goes to his lord, ' according to ancient usage;' Ibid. § 5. Alfred directs the excommunication of the fugitive perjurer; Ll. Alfr. § 1, and Canute also joins outlawry and excommunication in his denunciation of evil doers.

sentence of the judges[1]: just as the king's officers would in cases where royal rights and interests were concerned. And the criminal offences of the clergy would be tried in the same way; the special rules for compurgation in their case being observed under the eye of the bishop, who stood to them in the relation of lord and patron[2]. In contentious suits it is difficult to draw the line between judicial decision and arbitration; the bishop with his clerks would however be fully competent to arbitrate, and were probably frequently called upon to do so. None of these generalisations however cover the cases in which the spiritual offences of the clergy, disobedience, heresy, drunkenness, and the like, called for authoritative treatment: they would not come before the popular courts, for they were not breaches of secular law; and they were not crimes for which the penitential

Probable existence of separate ecclesiastical courts.

jurisdiction alone was sufficient. For such, then, it is probable that the bishops had domestic tribunals not differing in kind from the ecclesiastical courts of the later ages[3] and of matured canon law: in which, according to the common practice of the post-Nicene church, the archdeacon[4] as the bishop's officer executed the sentence of his superior[5]; whilst for the enforce-

---

[1] See Ll. Hen. I, vii. § 3. This he would have to do in other causes in which no specially religious principle was involved, as for example in cases where the property of churches had been stolen, or their peace infringed. It is observable that the very first of our written laws, Ethelb. § 1, places the property of the churches under the special protection of the law.

[2] If a priest kill a man his property is confiscated, and the bishop is ordered to 'secularise' him, after which he is to be given up (to the relations of the slain?) unless his lord will compound for his wer; Alfred, § 21. This looks as if the clergy had some personal immunities which could not be infringed until they were formally degraded. The bishop is indeed the 'mæg and mundbora' of clergy and strangers; Edw. and Guthr. § 12. According to the Ll. Henrici, c. 68, the wergild of the man in holy orders was determined by his birth, but there was a graduated fine *pro infractura ordinis* in addition.

[3] The doom of the bishop is referred to in the case of a criminal priest, in the law of Wihtræd, § 6; Edw. and Guthr. § 4. If any one before a bishop belie his testimony, he pays a fine of 120s.; Ini, § 13.

[4] The first person who is called archdeacon is Wulfred, who became archbishop of Canterbury in A.D. 805, and who is so named in a charter of his predecessor. Bede knew only the deacon as the bishop's officer: throughout the period his office is simply ministerial.

[5] The archdeacon is only once mentioned in the laws, 'If a priest disobey the order of the archdeacon he has to pay 12 ores;' Northumbrian Priests' law, § 6. The deans mentioned in the so-called laws of Edward

ment of these decisions the servants of the bishop were competent and sufficient. In such circumstances it is probable Spiritual enough that the secular and ecclesiastical powers would act in sentences enforced by concert: and, even if the national force were not called in to the secular arm. the assistance of the clergy, it can scarcely be doubted that it offered no hindrance to the execution of the spiritual sentence. The outlaw of God and the outlaw of the king, the excommunicated man and the convicted criminal, are alike set outside of the protection of the peace.

The relation of the church to the state was thus close, Peculiar relation of although there was not the least confusion as to the organisa- church and state. tion of functions, or uncertainty as to the limits of the powers of each[1]. It was a state of things that could exist only in a race that was entirely homogeneous and becoming conscious of political unity. The history, however, of the church of the united or West-Saxon dominion, on which the fury of the Danes fell, and which rose from ruin in closer union than before with the national polity, has many features in marked contrast with the earlier and simpler life of the heptarchic churches.

88. The rapid growth of the power of Egbert was the result The West-Saxon not merely of his own valour and policy but of the weakness of period. the enemies with whom he had to contend: the same exhaustion and incapacity for resistance which laid the nation open to the Danes. Mercia in the early years of Kenulf[2], who Growth of West-Saxon ruled contemporaneously with Egbert for nearly twenty years, power. sustained some of the glory that she gained under Offa; but

the Confessor, § 27, are also officers of the bishop. The territorial deaneries, however, as well as the territorial archdeaconries, are later than the Conquest. The Anglo-Saxon deans mentioned in the Chronicle and in the lives of the saints are generally either monastic officers exercising discipline within the house, like the later deans of colleges, or possibly the executors of the spiritual authority of exempt monasteries, in the way in which the archdeacons executed the sentence of the bishops.

[1] Religion, morality, and law, seem to be regarded throughout the period as much the same thing. The principle stated by Tacitus that among the ancient Germans, 'plus ibi boni mores valent quam alibi bonae leges,' is thus amplified by Alfred: 'Ex hoc uno judicio perpendi potest, ut unicuique justum judicetur; *nec opus est aliquo libro judiciali* praeter hoc fatigari, quam ne quis alii judicet quod sibi judicari nollet si judicium haberetur super eum.' The *unum judicium* is of course 'Quod vobis non vultis fieri non faciatis aliis;' Alfr. Ll. Intr. § 49. 6.

[2] Kenulf reigned from A.D. 796 to 821 or 822.

the end of his reign was inglorious, and a rapid and disputed
succession of kings after his death deprived the kingdom of any
hope of continued independence.   Kent was now only nominally
a kingdom, becoming a mere appendage to Mercia and Wessex
in turn, with a spasmodic effort between times to revive the
ancient status.   The history of East Anglia is exactly parallel,
sometimes under Mercia, sometimes broken up under several
ealdormen.   Northumbria continues the tale of revolution and
anarchy which marked her history in the preceding century.

The royal power, and with it the tribal nationality, was in suspension or solution.   One result of this was the supremacy of
Wessex; another was prostration before the Danes; the third
was the throwing of much power and secular work on the clergy
especially the bishops, who represented the most permanent

element of society; and the fourth, the consequence of the
others, the general decline of civilisation and learning.   It was
natural that in those kingdoms in which the church was
strong, the extinction or other defeasance of the old royal
houses should increase the importance of the bishops.   The
Kentish church under archbishop Wulfred had sustained a
long and fatal dispute with Mercia, in which appeals to the
pope and emperor were discussed as a possible solution.   Not
only had Canterbury succeeded in effecting the humiliation of
the rival archiepiscopate, but on the death of Cuthred, the
brother and dependent of Kenulf, Wulfred is found in open
opposition to Kenulf[1]; for seven years he contested with him
and his heiress the possession of the royal monasteries in
Thanet, and was at last victorious.   Baldred, the king who
attempted to assert the independence of Kent during the
Mercian troubles[2], seems to have been in alliance with Wulfred,
and we may conjecture that the sturdy prelate submitted with

---

[1] Kemble, C. D. ccxx; Councils, &c. iii. 596.   In a council at London
Kenulf threatened to send Wulfred into exile 'et nunquam nec verbis
domini papae nec Caesaris seu alterius alicujus gradu huc in patriam
iterum recipisse.'

[2] Baldred was king from A.D. 823 to 825, when he was dethroned by
Egbert.   He had attempted to secure the good will of the archbishop by
the gift of Malling to Christ Church (Kemble, C. D. ccxl.) at the very
moment of his downfall.

reluctance to the rule of Egbert although he also was of Kentish descent. Archbishop Ceolnoth however, who succeeded Wulfred, was wise enough to throw himself into the arms of Egbert, even if he did not, as is possible, owe his promotion to him[1]; and in A.D. 838 at Kingston a permanent alliance was concluded between the church of Canterbury and the house of Cerdic. Ceolnoth undertook to maintain 'firm and unshaken friendship from henceforth for ever,' and received in return a promise of perpetual peace and protection[2]. A like agreement was made at the same time with the church of Winchester: and both were repeatedly confirmed by Ethelwulf[3].

Alliance of the West-Saxon kings with the church of Canterbury.

A similar state of things existed in the North of England. Eanbald the archbishop of York, after a long struggle with the king Eardulf, had seen him dethroned and a fugitive; he was restored by the intervention of the pope and emperor, but on the immediate result the veil of ninth century darkness settles down. We know the consequences only from the Danish conquest of the North. One or two letters of the succeeding archbishops show that the light of learning was not quite extinct, although it was becoming obscured by the superstitious and impious fabrications which were made possible by its decline. Whilst continental scholars were still applying to England for manuscripts[4], the English bishops were puzzled with strange forms of heresy at home. Nial the deacon was said to have risen from the dead after seven weeks; letters were spoken of[5], written by the hand of God in letters of gold, and the whole court of Ethelwulf was perplexed with the vision of a priest, portending grievous calamities on account of the profanation of Sunday[6].

Decline of religion in the North.

---

[1] Robertson, Hist. Essays, 196, 200, conjectures that Ceolnoth was a West Saxon in whose favour the Kentish Feologeld, who had been elected to succeed Wulfred, was set aside. See Councils, &c. iii. 609.

[2] Council of Kingston ; Councils, iii. 617.

[3] Ibid. p. 619.

[4] See the letters of Lupus of Ferrières to Ethelwulf, and Wigmund archbishop of York ; Councils, iii. 634, 635, 648, 649.

[5] Letter of Egred, bishop of Lindisfarne to Wulfsige, archbishop of York ; Councils, iii. 615. Alcuin had had to protest against the wearing of relics by way of charms ; Epp. ed. Dümmler, pp. 719, 721.

[6] Prudentius Trecens. ap. Pertz, Scr. i. 433 ; Councils, &c. iii. 621.

Decline of monachism.

The bishops act as warriors.

The Donation of Ethelwulf.

The same period is traditionally fixed for the extinction of primitive monachism throughout the nation[1]. It is now for the first time that we find the bishops in arms; two West-Saxon prelates fell in the battle of Charmouth in A.D. 835[2]; and bishop Ealhstan of Sherborne acted as Egbert's general in Kent A.D. 825, and was one of the commanders who defeated the Danes on the Parret in A.D. 845[3]. The same prelate thirteen years later took a leading part in the supplanting of Ethelwulf by his son Ethelbald[4]. Ethelwulf was a poor substitute for his father: his pilgrimage to Rome, contemplated in his first year[5] and performed nearly at the end of his reign, his magnificent gifts to the pope[6], and his marriage with the daughter of Charles the Bald[7], are, with the exception of his famous *Donation*, the best-known parts of his history. That celebrated act, the devotion of a tenth part of his private estate to ecclesiastical purposes, the relief of a tenth part of the folk-land from all payments except the trinoda necessitas, and the direction that every ten hides of his land should provide for one poor man or stranger, testifies to his piety and liberality[8]. Possibly the further subdivision of the West-Saxon dioceses was begun under him: we find Ethelred the bishop of Wiltshire appointed to the see of Canterbury by his sons[9]. This is

[1] See the Anglo-Saxon Chronicle, A.D. 870.

[2] Chr. Sax. A.D. 833.

[3] Ibid. A.D. 823, 845.

[4] Asser, V. Alfr. M. H. B. 470.

[5] Prud. Trec., Pertz, Scr. i. 433; Councils, iii. 621.

[6] Anastasius, Vit. Bened. III. ap. Mansi, xv. 100, 110. It was on this occasion, it is said, that he obtained from the pope a decree that English penitents should no more be forced to work in chains; T. Rudborne, in Ang. Sac. i. 202. See Lappenberg, ii. 26.

[7] Ann. Bertin. Pertz, Scr. i. 450; Baluze, ii. 209–212.

[8] Councils, iii. 636–648; Kemble, Saxons, ii. 481–490.

[9] Chr. Sax. A.D. 780. There seems to be no reasonable doubt that this was finally effected by Edward the Elder, who mentions in more than one charter that he had divided the old diocese of Winchester into two parts; Cod. Dipl. mxc. &c.; and we know from the lists of bishops drawn up in the tenth century, that a further division almost immediately followed by which the West-Saxon sees became five in number. Of the three new sees, one, that of Ramsbury, had no cathedral, and was moved about in Wiltshire and Berkshire, resting sometimes at Sunning, but finally joined to Sherborne just before the Conquest. It may have existed in the same way before the time of Alfred, and been a sort of suffragan see to Win-

the age of Swithun also. But, notwithstanding occasional flashes of light, the darkness in church and state deepens. Alfred has to record that when he came to the throne there were none south of the Thames who could understand their rituals in English, or translate a letter from the Latin; very few south of the Humber, and not many beyond [1]. The monasteries still stood with their libraries, but the books were unintelligible to their owners. Then the Danes had come and destroyed all.

Increased darkness of the period.

It is perhaps not unreasonable to connect the revival of learning and ecclesiastical order under Alfred and his son with the bracing up of the national vigour that resulted from the Danish struggle, and so with the growth of royal power which was traced in the last chapter. At all events they coincide in time. It was Plegmund, the associate of Alfred in his labours in the service of English literature [2], who consecrated the seven bishops at Canterbury in Edward's reign. This completed the diocesan arrangement which divided Wessex into dioceses corresponding almost exactly with the shires of which the kingdom was composed, by the foundation of sees in Somerset, Wilts, and Devon [3]. The final annexation of Cornwall is marked by the foundation of a new see under Athelstan [4]. The prelates, too, begin to be statesmen. Odo of Ramsbury goes as ambassador to France to secure the succession of Lewis the Fourth [5]: as archbishop of Canterbury he acts as prime minister to Edmund and Edred; a position which he leaves to Dunstan and a long series of successors. But whilst they acquire this new secular position, the bishops lose somewhat of their old

Revival of learning and religion under Alfred, coinciding with the restoration of national vigour in the Danish wars.

chester. The idea of having a bishop to each shire of Wessex seems to have been in the mind of the creator of the new sees; Somersetshire had Wells, Dorsetshire Sherborne, Sussex Selsey, Devonshire Crediton, Cornwall Bodmin or S. German's, Hampshire Winchester; whilst Wilts and Berks joined at the bishop of Ramsbury. None of the other kingdoms had such a complete organisation of either bishops or ealdormen.

[1] Preface to the translation of S. Gregory's Pastoral Care, ed. Sweet, p. 1.

[2] Ibid. p. 6.

[3] W. Malmesb. G. R. ii. § 129; Reg. Sacr. Angl. p. 13.

[4] Between A.D. 924 and 931. See Pedler's Ancient Bishopric of Cornwall.

[5] Hist. Richer. ii. c. 4; ed. Pertz, p. 53.

security. Brihthelm, the immediate predecessor of Dunstan, is

The bishops
are found
acting as
statesmen.
summarily set aside by Edgar for incapacity [1]. Notwithstanding the restoration of monastic order, canonical custom is set at naught for party or political purposes; one bishop holds two or even three sees: translations become more common, and the great prelates constantly find themselves in positions in which they have to choose between their duties as bishops, as ministers of the king, and as patriots. Archbishop Sigeric acts as chief magistrate temporally and spiritually in Kent [2], and earns the discredit of having been the first to propose the Danegeld [3].

Stigand a
representa-
tive of the
secular
prelate.
Under the later kings the successor of Augustine appears far more as a secular than as a spiritual potentate; and the last of the native primates, Stigand, has an unhappy pre-eminence, as holding the richest see of England in plurality, as the partisan of a schismatic pope, and as the chief minister of a distinctly patriotic but not thoroughly spiritual party organisation.

Effects of
the Danish
conquest on
the North-
umbrian
church.
But the Danish conquest of the north and middle of England had other effects than the rousing of the spirit of the people and kings. It cut off the Northumbrian church from the see of Canterbury almost as completely as it had been cut off before the days of Oswy. The archbishop of York became the head of a distinct nationality, preserving his seat—with one exception, the seven years exile of Wulfhere [4]—during the numerous vicissitudes of the Danish kingdom. Under Athelstan the northern primate appears at the English court [5], but not quite as a subject. Wulfstan, after Athelstan's death, took sides with the Ostman Anlaf, and had to fly before Edmund [6]. In A.D. 947 at Tanshelf he brought the Northumbrian witan to plight their troth to Edred [7], but the next year he revolted with his people, and in A.D. 952 was imprisoned [8]. Two years

---

[1] Memorials of S. Dunstan, p. 38.
[2] Ethelred, ii. § 1; Robertson, Hist. Essays, p. 178.
[3] Chron. Sax. A.D. 991.
[4] Sim. Dun. Hist. Arch. ed. Twysden, p. 79.
[5] Rodward archbishop of York appears as witness to three charters of Athelstan, which are questionable, Cod. Dipl. cccxlvi, cccxlix, mcl; and to one which is less suspicious, dated in A.D. 929, Ibid. cccxlviii.
[6] Chron. Sax. A.D. 943.   [7] Ibid. A.D. 947.
[8] Ibid. A.D. 952.

after, he made his peace with the king and was restored. His Settlement of the North. immediate successor Oskytel ruled peaceably under Edgar; but the importance of the position of the archbishop is shown by the fact that from the year A.D. 963 to the Conquest, the see of Worcester was generally either held by him in plurality, or bestowed on one of his near kinsmen, at once a reward of faithfulness and a pledge of obedience[1]. The wisdom of the arrangement is shown by the adhesion of Northumbria generally to the English king. Whilst the mother church of York underwent these changes, the northern suffragan sees of Hexham and Whithern became extinct; and the church of Lindisfarne only survived in exile and pilgrimage with S. Cuthbert's bones, not settling finally at Durham until A.D. 995.

The ecclesiastical machinery of Mercia and East Anglia Extinction and abeyance of Mercian and East-Anglian sees. suffered scarcely less. The see of Dunwich perished altogether: and in that of Elmham the succession of the bishops is uncertain for nearly a century after the martyrdom of S. Edmund[2]. The bishop of Leicester fled southwards, and placed his chair at Dorchester in Oxfordshire, close to the West-Saxon border. The succession in Lindsey vanishes[3]; and the see of Lichfield itself only occasionally emerges, although there is reason to suppose that there was no long vacancy. Even in London the episcopate seems to have had a narrow escape from extinction. As much as was possible of the old system was restored under

[1] S. Oswald and his two immediate successors held Worcester and York together from A.D. 963 to A.D. 1016, when Leofsi seems to have been appointed, probably in consequence of political events. On his death Brihtege, nephew of archbishop Wulfstan, held Worcester until A.D. 1038. It was then disputed between archbishop Elfric and the bishop of Crediton. Ealdred, who ultimately obtained it, was obliged to resign on his promotion to York in A.D. 1061; and S. Wulfstan followed, A.D. 1062–1096. Bishop Sampson, his successor, was brother to archbishop Thomas I of York, and father to Thomas II. The disputes about the property of the two sees were continued until the reign of Henry II. The later archbishops possessed the church of S. Oswald at Gloucester, which was given them by William Rufus.

[2] The year 870 is the epoch at which the Mercian churches seem to collapse; they emerge in the time of Edward the Elder, but the succession of bishops is very uncertain until the middle of the century; Reg. Sac. Angl. pp. 12–14.

[3] It re-appears in A.D. 953, but is joined with Dorchester about fifty years later.

Edgar, but the modifications in the arrangement of the dioceses were permanent. We do not know enough of the local history of the period to ascertain how far the Mercian church underwent the same secularising process as the West-Saxon and Northumbrian.

The glories of the tenth century in church and state.

89. The process of restoration begun by Alfred was carried still further by the great kings who succeeded him on the lines which he had drawn. The vernacular literature which he had founded flourished continuously: the tenth century not only is the great age of the chroniclers, but abounds in legal and disciplinary enactments in the native tongue. Every attempt to secure the consolidation of the national and royal power in the state is accompanied by a similar effort for the re-establish-

Influence of Dunstan.

ment of the church in strength and purity. The memory of Dunstan has suffered rather than gained by the praises of his monastic admirers, but it cannot be doubted that his monastic reforms were among the least of the measures that he had at heart, and that the exaggerated views entertained of them in

Renewal of foreign intercourse.

the middle ages threw his greater deeds into the shade [1]. He was the prime minister, perhaps the inspirer, of the consolidating policy of Edgar ; he restored, through the monastic and educational revival, the intercourse between the Church of England and those of France and Flanders [2], and established a more intimate communication with the Apostolic See; in so doing he did what could be done to restore piety and learning. Under his influence the Mercian bishoprics again lift up their heads : the archbishops henceforth go to Rome for their palls : the Frank writers begin to record the lives of English saints. Abbot of Fleury wrote the life of S. Edmund ; Adelard of Blandinium wrote a eulogy on Dunstan himself. But the contrast between this restored life and communion and the state of things that had existed earlier is strongly marked. Now, England, instead of setting the example to France, borrows from her

---

[1] See Robertson's Essay on Dunstan, Hist. Essays, pp. 189–262 ; Hook's life of him in volume i. of the Lives of the Archbishops of Canterbury ; and the preface to the Memorials of S. Dunstan in the Rolls Series.

[2] He spent his exile in the monastery of Blandinium at Ghent ; Flor. Wig. A.D. 956.

neighbour.   John the Old Saxon and Grimbald had come from England borrows from the continent. the northern provinces of the empire; the restored Benedictine monachism is brought by S. Oswald from Fleury[1].   The English scribes copy the disciplinary works of Theodulf of Orleans and Halitgar of Cambray[2], just as a century and a half before the Franks had copied the penitentials of Theodore and Egbert. The royal marriages[3] promote intercourse with the German churches also.   The countess Elfthritha of Flanders, Alfred's daughter, endowed the church of S. Peter at Ghent with lands in Kent.   Bishop Kinewold of Worcester in A.D. 929 visited all the monasteries of Germany with offerings from Athelstan, and concluded a league for mutual intercession with the monks of S. Gall[4].

Some marks of this intercourse are left on the constitutional Decline of conciliar activity. history of the church.   Although the pontifical claims of Odo and Dunstan play so great a part in the popular histories, their secular position somewhat derogated from their ecclesiastical one.   It can hardly be supposed that purely conciliar action ceased; it is however quite possible that the assimilation of the national witenagemots to the older ecclesiastical councils was a consequence of the union of the seven kingdoms; and this renders it difficult to distinguish between lay and spiritual assemblies.   There are few if any records of councils distinctly ecclesiastical held during the tenth century in England; and every royal code contains large ecclesiastical regulations.   The Compilations of canons. abundant bodies of canons which exist are clad either in the form of constitutions, such as those of Odo and Edgar[5], or in the form of private compilations such as that of Elfric[6].   It would almost seem as if the union between church and state

---

[1] Hist. Rams. (Gale), p. 391.

[2] One of the penitentials ascribed to Egbert (Wilkins, Conc. i. 113–143, Thorpe, Anglo-Saxon Laws, pp. 343–392) is a translation from Halitgar. The laws of Theodulf are also translated, in Wilkins, i. 265 sq.

[3] See above, p. 224.

[4] Goldastus, Rer. Alamann. Scr. ii. 152, 153 ; Memorials of S. Dunstan, p. lxxv.

[5] See Wilkins, Concilia, i. pp. 212, 225.

[6] Ibid. p. 250 ; Johnson's Canons, i. 388–407 ; Thorpe, Ancient Laws, pp. 441 sq.

had become so intimate as to supersede one of the most important functions of the former; for the break in the list of councils cannot be attributed to the loss of records; abundance of charters in both Latin and English attest the activity of the church and of the monasteries, and abundant penitential literature shows that the want of canonical legislation was felt. It is perhaps most probable that business of both sorts was transacted in the same assemblies, as was done in the councils of the twelfth and thirteenth centuries, when the difficulties of collecting the clerical witan more than once or twice a year were still considerable. The fact that the persons who composed the two were the same, or nearly so, contributes to the uncertainty, and possibly occasioned the confusion of which this obscurity is the result.

The eleventh century.

90. The ecclesiastical history of the eleventh century is of an equally varied character. On the one hand there is a great development of English literature. Elfric nobly carries on what Alfred had begun. More than ever the chroniclers and sermon-writers put forth their strength. The society which is unable to withstand the arms of Canute almost immediately humanises

Intercourse with the colleges of Lorraine.

and elevates him. The court of Edward the Confessor, although too much divided and leavened with unpatriotic counsels, is an advance in cultivation on that of his father; Frankish elegance falls into ready association with English wealth[1]; and England, although she has very much to lose by this foreign admixture, has much also to gain. The school which Harold founded at Waltham[2], the whole revival of the canonical life as a more honest and more practicable system than the monastic, was one result of the increased intercourse with the empire and especially with Lorraine. The introduction of foreign ecclesiastics into English bishoprics was another. Robert of Jumieges sat at

---

[1] Guibert of Nogent says of bishop Helinandus, the Confessor's French chaplain, ‘quia Francicam elegantiam norat, Anglicus ille ad Francorum regem Henricum eum saepius destinabat .... quoniam Anglia infinitis eo tempore florebat opibus, multos pecuniarum montes aggesserat;’ Opp. ed. D'Achery, p. 496.

[2] See the Tractatus de S. Cruce, pref. pp. v–xii; Freeman, Norm. Conq. ii. 440 sq.; Epistolae Cantuarienses, pref.

London and Canterbury successively; bishops Herman of Rams- Foreign ecclesias-
bury and Walter of Hereford were Lorrainers; Wells was held tics in Eng-lish sees.
by Duduc a Saxon, and after him by Giso a Brabanter; William
of London and Ulf of Dorchester were Normans[1]. For so large
an infusion of foreign influence the church was not ready:
English isolation has always resisted it, and the fact of the unpopularity of the new-comers, the absolute necessity that fell on
them of throwing themselves for support on other agencies than
the result of their work and the love of the people, must have
counteracted any possible benefit that could have been derived
from freer intercourse with the churches of the continent.
Amongst the prelates of this era there are very few except S. Wulfstan and Ealdred.
Wulfstan who are spoken of with honour. Archbishop Ealdred
of York, the traveller, pilgrim and ambassador, stands high on the
list of Anglo-Saxon statesmen, but it is not until after the Conquest that he shows much of the spirit of the patriot. The
practice of holding bishoprics in plurality reaches its climax in
him. He held, or at least administered, at one time Worcester,
Hereford and Sherborne: it is fair to say that he was a good
bishop when such were very scarce, and that he kept foreigners
out. The abuse may perhaps be excused on the same grounds
as the nomination of the foreign prelates—the default of native
candidates.

In the extreme difficulty of discriminating between the eccle- Analogy of church and
siastical and civil relations of men and things, to enter now into state.
the special development of church institutions in the tenth and
eleventh century would be to traverse again the ground already
gone over. The devolution of judicial powers on the lords of Assimila-tion of lay
bookland, the king's thegns, and others having grants of sac and and spiritual systems.
soc, affected the territorial power of the bishops and monasteries
just as it affected that of the lay landowners: it is in fact from
the charters of immunity to the churches that we are able to
draw the scanty conclusions which can be drawn as to the status
of the lay lords. The obligation of 'borh,' by which every man

---

[1] Freeman (Norm. Conq. ii. 80, 81) regards the Lotharingian prelates
as German in speech, and therefore possibly welcome to Godwin and his
party.

was obliged to have a security for his keeping the peace, was enforced on ecclesiastics also. An unpublished list of the 'festormen' of archbishop Elfric exists on a fly-leaf of the York Gospel Book; every priest had to find himself twelve such bondsmen[1];

Arch-
deacons.

Elfric has sixty or more. The office of archdeacon, which appears first at the end of the eighth century, has now risen into a place of jurisdiction, although the creation of territorial arch-

Suffragan
bishops.

deaconries has not yet been required. The bishops, instead of resigning when age and infirmity incapacitate them, employ deputies to perform their spiritual functions, as the prince-bishops did in the later middle ages. The distinctive character of the Anglo-Saxon church, like that of the state, is being changed to the general pattern of the continental churches. The same cries of simony and immorality against the clergy which are heard in France and Germany are prevalent here, and the means taken to silence them are as weak in England as abroad. The revival of life and energy under Dunstan and Elfric has worn itself out before the days of the Confessor.

Need of
restoration
in church
and state.

The exhaustion of the church coincided with that of the state, of which Edward is a fair type, and which the zeal of Siward, of Godwin, and even of Harold could not counteract. The time was come for Lanfranc and Anselm as well as for William of Normandy and Henry of Anjou.

Importance
of church
history in
constitu-
tional his-
tory.

It is scarcely necessary to point out the special importance of this portion of history in its bearing on our constitutional growth. The Church of England is not only the agency by which Christianity is brought to a heathen people, a herald of spiritual blessings and glorious hopes in another life; it is not merely the tamer of cruel natures, the civiliser of the rude, the cultivator of the waste places, the educator, the guide and the protector, whose guardianship is the only safeguard of the woman, the child, and the slave against the tyranny of their lord and master. The church is this in many other countries besides Britain; but here it is much more. The unity of the church in England was the pattern of the unity of the state: the cohesion of the church was for ages the substitute for the cohesion which the divided

---

[1] Laws of the Northumbrian Priests, § 2.

nation was unable otherwise to realise. Strong in its own con- Bearing of the English church history in the life of the nation.
formation, it was more than a match for the despotic rule of
such kings as Offa, and was the guardian of liberties as well as
the defence of the oppressed.   It was to an extraordinary degree
a national church: national in its comprehensiveness as well as
in its exclusiveness.   Englishmen were in their lay aspect Mercians or West Saxons ; only in their ecclesiastical relations
could they feel themselves fellow-countrymen and fellow-subjects.
And for a great part of the period under our view, the interference of foreign churches was scarcely if at all felt.   There
was no Roman legation from the days of Theodore to those of
Offa, and there are only scanty vestiges of such interference for
the next three centuries : the joint intercession of Leo III and
Charles the Great effected the restoration of king Eardulf in
Northumbria ; an envoy of Eugenius II, bearing an English
name, attests the acts of the council of Clovesho in 824 ; the
action of pope Formosus appears, in a legendary way, in the
final division of the West Saxon dioceses.   But there are few
other traces of Roman influence.   Dunstan boldly refused to
obey a papal sentence [1].   Until the eve of the Conquest, therefore, the development of the system was free and spontaneous,
although its sphere was a small one.   The use of the native
tongue in prayers and sermons is continuous ; the observance of
native festivals also, and the reverence paid to native saints.   If
the stimulating force of foreign intercourse was wanting, the
intensity with which the church threw itself into the interest of
the nation more than made up what was lacking.   The ecclesiastical and the national spirit thus growing into one another
supplied something at least of that strong passive power which
the Norman despotism was unable to break.   The churches
were schools and nurseries of patriots ; depositories of old tra-

---

[1] See Adelard's Life of Dunstan, in Memorials of S. Dunstan, p. 67 :
'Quidam illustrium pro illicito matrimonio saepius ab eo redargutus, sed
non correctus, gladio tandem evangelico est a Christo divisus ; qui Romam
adiens dominum apostolicum pro se Dunstano scriptis satisfacere optinuit.
Hic Dunstanus . . . . moveri non potuit, sed ipso apostolico mente altior in
se solidus perstitit ; "Scias" inquiens legato, "nec capitis plexione me a
Domini mei auctoritate movendum."'

ditional glories and the refuge of the persecuted. The English clergy supplied the basis of the strength of Anselm when the Norman bishops sided with the king. They trained the English people for the time when the kings should court their support and purchase their adherence by the restoration of liberties that would otherwise have been forgotten. The unity of the church was in the early period the only working unity; and its liberty, in the evil days that followed, the only form in which the traditions of the ancient freedom lingered. It was again to be the tie between the conquered and the conquerors; to give to the oppressed a hold on the conscience of the despot; to win new liberties and revive the old; to unite Norman and Englishman in the resistance to tyrants, and educate the growing nation for its distant destiny as the teacher and herald of freedom to all the world.

CHAPTER IX.

THE NORMAN CONQUEST.

91. THE effect of the Norman Conquest on the character and constitution of the English was threefold. The Norman rule invigorated the whole national system; it stimulated the growth of freedom and the sense of unity, and it supplied, partly from its own stock of jurisprudence, and partly under the pressure of the circumstances in which the conquerors found themselves, a formative power which helped to develop and concentrate the wasted energies of the native race. In the first place it brought the nation at once and permanently within the circle of European interests, and the Crusades, which followed within a few years, and which were recruited largely from the Normans and the English, prevented a relapse into isolation. The adventurous and highly-strung energy of the ruling race communicated itself to the people whom it ruled; its restless activity and strong political instinct roused the dormant spirit and disciplined even while it oppressed it. For, in the second place, the powers which it called forth were largely exercised in counteracting its own influence. The Normans so far as they became English added nerve and force to the system with which

[marginal notes:] Complex results of the Conquest.

Its invigorating effect.

It calls forth strength in opposition.

they identified themselves; so far as they continued Norman they provoked and stimulated by opposition and oppression the latent energies of the English. The Norman kings fostered, and the Norman nobility forced out the new growth of life. In the third place, however, the importation of new systems of administration, and the development of new expedients, in every department of government, by men who had a genius not only for jurisprudence but for every branch of organisation, furnished a disciplinary and formative machinery in which the new and revived powers might be trained:—a system which through oppression prepared the way for order, and by routine educated men for the dominion of law: law and order which when completed should attest by the pertinacious retention and development of primitive institutions, that the discipline which had called them forth and trained men for them, was a discipline only, not the imposition of a new and adventitious polity. For the Norman polity had very little substantial organisation of its own; and what it brought with it to England was soon worn out or merged in that of the nation with which it united. Only the vigour and vitality which it had called forth was permanent.

The Normans in Normandy.

92. Of the constitutional history of the Normans of Normandy we have very little information [1]. A century and a half before the Conquest of England, Rollo had received the province from Charles the Simple: he and his people in becoming Christian had become to a certain extent Frank also. They retained much of the Scandinavian character, but of the Norse customs only those which fell into easy agreement with Frank law; and their native language they entirely forgot. Of Frank law in its

[1] See Palgrave, Normandy and England, i. 113. Palgrave enumerates three traditions or legal legends of Rollo: (1) The custom of the *clameur de haro,* by which whoever sustained or feared to sustain any damage of goods or chattels, life or limb, was entitled to raise the country by the cry Haro. (2) The legend of the Roumare, according to which he tried the obedience of his people by hanging his bracelets on a tree, where they remained unguarded for three years and unmolested. (3) The legend of Long-paon, according to which he hanged a husband and wife who had conspired to cheat him. The first two stories are common to England and other countries; the last is in conformity with Scandinavian jurisprudence; Ibid. i. 696–699.

early Norman form we have equally scanty evidence. What little is known is learned from later jurisprudence, and that by inference rather than historic evidence. Even the existence of the ordinary language of feudalism in Normandy[1] before the Conquest of England has been questioned, unreasonably indeed, but not without such probability as arises from lack of documentary materials of proof. The little that is clearly known seems to be that the Norman duke or count ruled his people as a personal sovereign, and with the advice of a council of great men[2]; that under him were a number of barons, who owed their position to the possession of land for which they were under feudal obligations to him, which they took every opportunity of discarding; who had the status of nobility derived from ancient Norse descent or from connexion with the ducal family, although that nobility neither possessed purity of blood, nor was accompanied by any feeling of honour or loyalty; and who therefore were kept faithful partly by a sense of interest and partly by the strong hand of their master. The Norman counts were at the time of the Conquest, in most cases, younger branches of the ducal house or closely connected with it by affinity. The counts of Brionne, Evreux, and Eu were descended from sons of Richard I; Count Odo of Aumâle was the Conqueror's brother-in-law; Count Robert of Mortain his half-brother. The three great patriarchs of the other Norman houses were Yvo of

Obscurity of their constitutional history.

The nobles.

---

[1] Sismondi's idea that Rollo introduced full-grown feudality into Normandy (Palgrave, Normandy and England, i. 693) is of course quite untenable. Palgrave remarks that 'it remains to be proved whether any system of Norman tenure had been matured into consistency by fiscal talent until after the seventh duke of Normandy won the Anglo-Saxon crown;' Ibid. i. 694. He regards however Richard Sanspeur, the third duke, as the founder of Norman feudalism; Ibid. ii. 534. Waitz agrees with Palgrave as to the comparatively late growth of it; Göttingische Gelehrte Anzeigen, Nachrichten, Feb. 14, 1866; pp. 95, 96.

[2] Freeman, Norm. Conq. iii. 289 sq. Palgrave, Normandy and England, ii. 257, regards William Longsword the son of Rollo as absolute. 'His was the law, his was the state, his was the church.' 'No baronage surrounded his curule chair, no clerk sat at his feet. He spake the law, he gave the law, he made the law, he executed the law;' Ibid. p. 258. 'At no period after the first development of the duchy until it has been united to the crown of France, can we discern any courts or conventions of prelates and nobles equivalent to the Great Councils, States General, or Parliaments of subsequent times;' Ibid. p. 259.

Belesme, ancestor of the Montgomery counts of Ponthieu and Alençon, and earls of Shrewsbury; Bernard the Dane, and Osmund de Centville. The Beaumonts, whose county of Meulan, or Mellent, was in the French Vexin, and who were the ancestors of the earls of Warwick and Leicester, were descended from a sister of Gunnoris, the wife of Duke Richard I; the houses of Montgomery, Warenne and Giffard, from other sisters of the same famous lady; and the house of Breteuil from her brother Herfast [1].

The cultivators.

Under this aristocracy lived the population of cultivators, Gallic in extraction, Frank in law and custom, and speaking the language which had been created by their early history. These people were in strict dependence on their Norman lords, although they now and then showed some remembrance of the comparative freedom they had enjoyed under the Frank empire, and retained the local organisation which neither Franks nor Normans were numerous enough to displace [2]; and commercial

The towns.

prosperity and a strong communal feeling subsisted in the great towns. Nothing but the personal character of the dukes had

Ducal policy.

saved the territory thus lightly held from dismemberment. The strong hand had gathered all the great fiefs into the hands of kinsmen whose fidelity was secured by the right of the duke to garrison their castles, and whose tyrannies were limited by the right of the duke to enforce his own peace. Their attempts at

Relation of the duke to the king of France.

independence were checked by ruthless bloodshed. The duke himself was by commendation a vassal of the king, not so much as king, for the gift to Rollo had left him free, but as duke of the French: Richard of Normandy had commended himself to Hugh the Great, whose descendants had since become kings [3].

[1] Palgrave, Normandy and England, ii. 535, 536; iii. 28, 29, 148. See also the pedigrees at the end of Du Chesne's Scriptores Hist. Normannorum.

[2] Palgrave, Normandy and England, iii. 41, 42: 'When we reach the era of written evidence all absolute servitude has become obsolete. The very charter which designates the *Terre-tenant* as a servus guarantees his personal freedom;' Ibid. p. 44.

[3] On the status of the Norman dukes, and the changes of the relation in which they stood to the Karolings, the German kings of the Saxon line, the dukes of the Franks and the kings, see Palgrave, Normandy and England, ii. 125, 227–234, 347, 533; Freeman, Norm. Conq. i. 167, 220, 221, 609; Waitz, Nachrichten (as above), pp. 69–96.

But the hold of the royal hand on Normandy was scarcely perceptible; and its constitutional connexion is with the polity of the Karolingian rather than with that of the third race of kings. What little legal system subsisted was derived from the Frank institutions as they were when Normandy was separated from the body of the Frank dominion.

93. Feudalism, the comprehensive idea which includes the whole governmental policy of the French kingdom, was, by its historic origin and growth, distinctly Frank[1]. The principle which underlies it may be universal; but the actual presentation of it with which the constitutional history of Europe is concerned may be traced step by step under Frank influence, from its first appearance on the conquered soil of Roman Gaul to its full development in the jurisprudence of the Middle Ages[2].

Frank growth of feudalism.

---

[1] The word *feudum*, fief or fee, is derived from the German word for cattle (Gothic *faihu*; Old High German *fihu*; Old Saxon *fehu*; Anglo-Saxon *feoh*); the secondary meaning being goods, especially money: hence property in general. The letter *d* is perhaps a mere insertion for sound's sake; but it has been interpreted as a part of a second root, *od*, also meaning property, in which case the first syllable has a third meaning, that of fee or reward, and the whole word means property given by way of reward for service. But this is improbable; and the connexion of the word with the Greek ἐμφύτευσις, which is suggested by the similarity of feudal and emphyteutic tenure of land, will not stand the test of criticism. The legal emphyteusis is 'a perpetual right in a piece of land that is the property of another.' This word occurs first in the Digest of Justinian, and the emphyteutic possessor seems generally to be a mere lessee: it appears in the Lombard Capitulary of A.D. 819. The word *feodum* is not found earlier than the close of the ninth century. But neither the etymology of the latter word nor the development of its several meanings can be regarded as certain. See Smith's Dictionary of Antiquities, s. v. *Emphyteusis*; Robertson, Scotland, ii. 454; Du Cange, &c.

[2] As feudalism in both tenure and government was, so far as it existed in England, brought full-grown from France, it is not necessary here to trace in detail its growth in its native country. But it is important to note the change in the opinion of scholars on the subject, which has resulted from the recent investigations of German writers. The view accepted in the last century on the authority of Montesquieu, and generally maintained by the French writers, is that the conquests of the Franks were made by independent nobles, who had a powerful comitatus, and that the lands so acquired were divided amongst the comites, each of whom was bound by a special oath of fidelity to his lord, and held his land by the obligation of military service. Eichhorn, accepting this theory, distinguished the divisions of territory made before Clovis, on the principle of free allotment, from those made by that king and his successors, on a feudal principle: the recipients of the latter grants were supposed to be the *leudes*, and amongst the leudes a narrower class of comites bore the

Condition
of feudalism
at the time
of the
Norman
Conquest.

In the form which it has reached at the Norman Conquest, it may be described as a complete organisation of society through the medium of land tenure, in which from the king down to the lowest landowner all are bound together by obligation of service and defence : the lord to protect his vassal, the vassal to do service to his lord ; the defence and service being based on and regulated by the nature and extent of the land held by the one of the other. In those states which have reached the territorial stage of development, the rights of defence and service are supplemented by the right of jurisdiction. The lord judges as well as defends his vassal; the vassal does suit as well as service to his lord. In states in which feudal government has reached its utmost growth, the political, financial, judicial, every branch of public administration is regulated by the same conditions. The central authority is a mere shadow of a name.

name of *antrustions*. The Merovingian kingdom was, on this hypothesis, a state built up on vassalage; the bond of unity being the connexion of classes in subordination to one another, not the common and immediate subjection to a sovereign government. This theory has been entirely refuted by Waitz, whose authority has been, in this work, regarded as conclusive as to the ancient German system. It was no irregular unorganised fabric, but a complete governmental system. Its conquests were the work of the nations moving in entire order ; the comitatus was not the bond of cohesion ; the leudes were not comites : all the people were bound to be faithful to the king; the gift of an estate by the king involved no defined obligation of service ; all the nation was alike bound to military service ; the only comites were the antrustions, and these were few in number ; the basis of the Merovingian polity was not the relation of lord and vassal, but that of the subject to the sovereign. The arguments of Roth (Geschichte des Beneficialwesens, and Feudalität und Unterthanverband) so far coincide with those of Waitz ; and the work of Sohm (Altdeutsche Reichs-und-Gerichtsverfassung) completes the overthrow of the old theory by reconstructing in a very remarkable manner the old German system in Salian and Merovingian times. It remains now to account for the growth of the feudal system. This is done by Waitz on the theory of a conjunction and interpenetration of the beneficial system and the vassal relation, both being fostered by the growth of immunities ; and this is the view adopted in the text. Roth, however, goes further, connecting the antrustionship with the vassal relation, and making the former a link between the primitive comitatus and later feudalism. The infeudation of benefices and transfer of magisterial jurisdictions to the landowners (the seigniorial system), he traces not to any general movement in society, but to the violent innovation of the early Karoling period, which itself resulted from the great secularisations of the eighth century. Waitz's theory is maintained as against Roth, in the points in which the two writers differ, in the last edition of his invaluable work. See also Richter, Annalen der Deutschen Geschichte, pp. 108–111.

This institution had grown up from two great sources—the Elements of feudalism. beneficium, and the practice of commendation,—and had been specially fostered on Gallic soil by the existence of a subject population which admitted of any amount of extension in the methods of dependence. The beneficiary system[1] originated The *beneficium*. partly in gifts of land made by the kings out of their own estates to their own kinsmen and servants, with a special undertaking to be faithful[2]; partly in the surrender by landowners of their estates to churches or powerful men, to be received back again and held by them as tenants for rent or service. By the latter arrangement the weaker man obtained the protection of the stronger, and he who felt himself insecure placed his title under the defence of the church. By the practice of commenda- Commendation. tion[3], on the other hand, the inferior put himself under the personal care of a lord, but without altering his title or divesting himself of his right to his estate; he became a vassal[4] and did homage. The placing of his hands between those of his lord was the typical act by which the connexion was formed. And the oath of fealty was taken at the same time. The union Twofold nature of vassalage. of the beneficiary tie with that of commendation completed the idea of feudal obligation; the two-fold hold on the land, that of the lord and that of the vassal, was supplemented by the two-fold engagement, that of the lord to defend, and that of the vassal to be faithful. A third ingredient was supplied by the

[1] Waitz, D. V. G. ii. 226–258.

[2] Not a promise of definite service but a pledge to continue faithful in the conduct in consideration of which the reward is given; Waitz, D. V. G. ii. 251. Such a condition of course preserved to the giver a hold on or interest in the land, through which he was able to enforce fidelity. See also Roth, Beneficialwesen, p. 385; who points out that even when the possessors of great benefices commended themselves to the kings, they did not in the days of Charles the Bald fall into the class of vassals: 'episcopi, abbates, comites et vassalli dominici . . . beneficia habentes Carolo se commendaverunt, et fidelitatem sacramento firmaverunt;' Ann. Bertin. A.D. 837. But this was a period of transition, and if they did not become vassals in name, they entered into a relation which differed very little from later vassalage.

[3] Waitz, D. V. G. ii. 258–262.

[4] Vassus in the Merovingian period was used, according to Roth, invariably for an unfree person; in the Karolingian period, for a freeman commended, or, as he states it, placed in the relation of comitatus, to a lord; Beneficialwesen, p. 367. Waitz, as has been repeatedly mentioned, rejects the idea of connecting the comitatus with commendation.

Grants of
immunity.

grants of immunity by which in the Frank empire, as in England, the possession of land was united with the right of judicature: the dwellers on a feudal property were placed under the tribunal of the lord, and the rights and profits which had belonged to the nation or to its chosen head were devolved upon

Benefices
hereditary.

the receiver of a fief [1]. The rapid spread of the system thus originated, and the assimilation of all other tenures to it, may be regarded as the work of the tenth century; but as early as A.D. 877 Charles the Bald recognised the hereditary character of all benefices [2]; and from that year the growth of strictly feudal jurisprudence may be held to date.

National
origin of
feudalism.

The system testifies to the country and causes of its birth. The beneficium is partly of Roman, partly of German origin: in the Roman system the usufruct, the occupation of land belonging to another person, involved no diminution of status [3]; in the Germanic system he who tilled land that was not his own was imperfectly free: the reduction of a large Roman population to dependence placed the two classes on a level, and conduced to the wide extension of the institution. Commendation on the other hand may have had a Gallic or Celtic origin [4], and an analogy only with the Roman clientship. The German comitatus, which seems to have ultimately merged its existence in one or other of these developments, is of course to be carefully distinguished in its origin from them. The tie of the benefice or of commendation could be formed between any two persons

Importance
of the Anglo-
Saxon form
of comitatus.

whatever; none but the king could have antrustions. But the comitatus of Anglo-Saxon history preserved, as we have seen, a

---

[1] Waitz, D. V. G. ii. 634-645; iv. 243-273.

[2] The practice has been growing up for a long period, and the clause of the Capitulary of Kiersi is rather a recognition of a presumptive right than an authoritative enunciation of a principle. See on it Roth, Beneficialwesen, p. 420; Waitz, D. V. G. iv. 193. The hereditary usage was not yet universal, nor did this recognition make it so; the emperor simply makes provision as to what is to be done by his son during his absence, in case of the death of a count or other holder of a benefice. It is, however, a clear proof of the generality of the usage. See Pertz, Legg. i. 539; Baluze, ii. 179.

[3] See Waitz, D. V. G. ii. 225, 234.

[4] Ibid. iv. 199. The arguments in favour of this theory rest on Breton usages.

more distinct existence [1], and this perhaps was one of the causes
that distinguished the later Anglo-Saxon system most definitely
from the feudalism of the Frank empire.

The process by which the machinery of government became
feudalised, although rapid, was gradual. The weakness of the
Karoling kings [2] and emperors gave room for the speedy development of disruptive tendencies in a territory so extensive
and so little consolidated. The duchies and counties of the
eighth and ninth centuries were still official magistracies, the
holders of which discharged the functions of imperial judges or
generals. Such officers were of course men whom the kings
could trust, in most cases Franks, courtiers or kinsmen, who at
an earlier date would have been *comites* or *antrustions,* and who
were provided for by feudal benefices. The official magistracy
had in itself the tendency to become hereditary, and, when the
benefice was recognised as heritable, the provincial governorship
became so too. But the provincial governor had many opportunities of improving his position, especially if he could throw
himself into the manners and aspirations of the people he ruled.
By marriage or inheritance he might accumulate in his family
not only the old alodial estates which, especially on German
soil, still continued to subsist, but the traditions and local
loyalties which were connected with the possession of them. So
in a few years the Frank magistrate could unite in his own
person the beneficiary endowment, the imperial deputation, and
the headship of the nation over which he presided. And then
it was only necessary for the central power to be a little weakened,
and the independence of duke or count was limited by his
homage and fealty alone, that is by obligations that depended
on conscience only for their fulfilment. It is in Germany that
the disruptive tendency most distinctly takes the political form;

Introduction of feudalism into the machinery of government.

Growth of feudal magistracies into provincial principalities.

[1] See above, p. 170.
[2] The tendency had begun to work during the Merovingian period.
It was a regulation of Clothair II, that the count (judex) must be a
native of the province over which he was placed; Edict. Cloth. II, c. 12;
Pertz, Legg. i. 15 ; Baluze, i. 16 ; Waitz, D. V. G. ii. 377. The intention
was that he should have a substantial stake in the well-being of the
province, such that compensation could be exacted from him in case of
misgovernment.

Disruptive
tendencies
of feudal
government.
Saxony and Bavaria assert their national independence under
Swabian and Saxon dukes who have identified the interests of
their subjects with their own. Abundant proof of this position
will be found in minuter history. The rise of the successive
families of Saxon dukes, and the whole history of Bavaria under
the Saxon emperors, furnish illustrations. The Saxon dukes of
Bavaria maintain the Bavarian policy in opposition to their
near kinsmen on the imperial throne. The growth of the
Swabian Welfs into perfect identification with the Saxons whom
they governed affords another striking instance. In a less
degree, but still to some extent, this was the case in France
also; but the Gallic populations had lost before the Karoling
period most of their national aspirations; nor did the Frank
governors identify themselves at any time with the people.
Hence the great difference in social results between French and
German feudalism. In France, where the ancient tribal divisions
had been long obsolete, and where the existence of the alod involved little or no feeling of loyalty, the process was simpler
than in Germany; the provincial rulers aimed at practical
rather than political sovereignty; the people were too weak to
have any aspirations at all: the disruption was due more to the
abeyance of central attraction than to any centrifugal force existing in the provinces. But the result was the same; feudal
government, a graduated system of jurisdiction based on land
tenure, in which every lord judged, taxed, and commanded the
class next below him; in which abject slavery formed the lowest,
and irresponsible tyranny the highest grade; in which private
war, private coinage, private prisons, took the place of the imperial institutions of government.

Opposition
between the
interest of
the Con-
queror and
that of his
barons.
94. This was the social system which William the Conqueror and his barons had been accustomed to see at work in
France. One part of it, the feudal tenure of land, was perhaps
the only description of tenure which they could understand;
the king was the original lord, and every title issued mediately
or immediately from him. The other part, the governmental
system of feudalism, was the point on which sooner or later the
duke and his barons were sure to differ; already the incom-

patibility of the system with the existence of the strong central power had been exemplified in Normandy ; the strength of the dukes had been tasked to maintain their hold on the castles and to enforce their own high justice : much more difficult would England be to retain in Norman hands if the new king allowed himself to be fettered by the French system. On the other hand the Norman barons would fain rise a step in the social scale answering to that by which their duke had become a king; and they aspired to the same independence which they had seen enjoyed by the counts of Southern and Eastern France. Nor was the aspiration on their part altogether unreasonable ; they had joined in the Conquest rather as sharers in the great adventure than as mere vassals of the duke whose birth they despised as much as they feared his strength [1]. William, however, was wise and wary as well as strong. Hence it was that, whilst by the insensible process of custom, or rather by the mere assumption that feudal tenure of land was the only lawful and reasonable one, the Frankish system of tenure was substituted for the Anglo-Saxon, the organisation of government on the same basis was not equally a matter of course. The Conqueror himself was too strong to suffer that organisation to become formidable in his reign, but neither the brutal force of

Feudal tenure of land received without feudal principles of government.

---

[1] On the descent of the great barons of Normandy see above, p. 271. Ordericus Vitalis names the chiefs who joined in the deliberation of Lillebonne preparatory to the expedition to England ; the Counts Richard of Evreux, Robert of Eu, Robert of Mortain, Ralph de Conches, son of the standard-bearer of Normandy, William Fitz Osbern the steward, William de Warenne and Hugh the butler ; Hugh de Grantmesnil and Roger de Mowbray, Roger de Beaumont and Roger de Montgomeri, Baldwin and Richard sons of Count Gilbert of Brionne ; lib. iii. c. 11. At the battle of Hastings, besides most of these, he mentions (iv. c. 14) Count Eustace of Boulogne, Aimer Viscount of Thouars, Hugh de Montfort the constable, and Walter Giffard. The curious, but questionable, list of the contributions to the fleet by the allied barons is briefly this :—William Fitz Osbern the steward furnished 60 ships ; Hugh, afterwards earl of Chester, 60 ; Hugh de Montfort the constable, 50 ships and 60 knights ; Remi, afterwards bishop of Lincoln, a ship with 20 knights ; Nicholas, abbot of S. Ouen, 20 ships and 100 knights ; Count Robert of Eu, 60 ships ; Fulk the lame, 40 ; Gerald the steward, 40 ; Count William of Evreux, 80 ; Roger of Montgomery, 60 ; Roger of Beaumont, 60 ; Bishop Odo, 100 ; Robert of Mortain, 120 ; Walter Giffard, 30 and 100 knights ; Lyttelton, Hist. of Henry II, vol. i. p. 523. These lists are useful as helps in tracing the gradual extinction of the Conquest families during the struggles of the Norman reigns.

William Rufus, nor the heavy and equal pressure of the government of Henry I, could extinguish the tendency towards it. It was only after it had under Stephen broken out into anarchy and plunged the whole nation in long misery, when the great houses founded by the barons of the Conquest had suffered forfeiture or extinction, when the Normans had become Englishmen under the legal and constitutional reforms of Henry II, that the royal authority in close alliance with the nation was enabled to put an end to the evil.

William tries to reign as an English king.

95. William the Conqueror claimed the crown of England as the chosen heir of Edward the Confessor[1]. It was a claim which the English did not admit, and of which the Normans saw the fallacy, but which he himself consistently maintained and did his best to justify. In that claim he saw not only the justification of the conquest in the eyes of the Church, but his great safeguard against the jealous and aggressive host by whose aid he had realised it. Accordingly, immediately after the battle of Hastings, he proceeded to seek the national recognition. He obtained it from the divided and dismayed witan with no great trouble, and was crowned by the archbishop of York, the most influential and patriotic amongst them, binding himself by the constitutional promises of justice and good laws. Standing before the altar at Westminster, 'in the presence of the clergy and people he promised with an oath that he would defend God's holy churches and their rulers, that he would moreover rule the whole people subject to him with righteousness and royal providence, would enact and hold fast right law, utterly forbid rapine and unrighteous judgments[2].'

His coronation engagement.

---

[1] Freeman, Norm. Conq. ii. 169; Ord. Vit. iii. 11; Chron. de Bello, p. 2; W. Pictav. ed. Maseres, pp. 105, 145. The Durham charters in which the king states that he is 'Rex Anglorum hereditario jure factus' are forgeries. See Greenwell, Feodary of Durham, pp. lxvii, lxxii, lxxxii. The king himself on his deathbed declared that he had won the crown by the grace of God, not by hereditary right; Ord. Vit. vii. 15. See Gneist, Verwaltungsr., i. 111.

[2] Flor. Wig. A.D. 1066; W. Pictav. ed. Maseres, p. 145. See Freeman, Norm. Conq. iii. 559. No doubt the coronation service used was that which had been employed in the case of Ethelred, and the words of Florence represent the coronation engagement : 'Sanctas Dei ecclesias ac rectores illarum defendere, necnon et cunctum populum subjectum juste et

The form of election and acceptance was regularly observed and the legal position of the new king completed before he went forth to finish the conquest.

Had it not been for this the Norman host might have fairly claimed a division of the land such as the Northmen had made in the ninth century[1]. But to the people who had recognised William it was but just that the chance should be given them of retaining what was their own. Accordingly, when the lands of all those who had fought for Harold were confiscated[2], those who were willing to acknowledge William were allowed to redeem theirs, either paying money at once or giving hostages for the payment[3]. That under this redemption lay the idea of a new title to the lands redeemed may be regarded as questionable. The feudal lawyer might take one view, and the plundered proprietor another. But if charters of confirmation or regrant were generally issued on the occasion to those who were willing to redeem, there can be no doubt that, as soon as the feudal law gained general acceptance, these would be regarded as conveying a feudal title. What to the English might be a

No general division of lands.

Redemption of lands.

regali providentia regere, rectam legem statuere et tenere, rapinas injustaque judicia penitus interdicere.' See above, p. 164.

[1] See above, p. 77.

[2] 'The evidence that we have leads us to believe that the whole of the lands of those men, dead or living, who had fought at Senlac, was at once dealt with as land forfeited to the king;' Freeman, Norm. Conq. iv. 24. The evidence consists of references to these confiscations in the Domesday survey. See too Dialogus de Scaccario, i. c. 10, where the traditionary view of the government officials is preserved: 'Post regni conquisitionem, post justam rebellium subversionem, cum rex ipse regisque proceres loca nova perlustrarent, facta est inquisitio diligens qui fuerint qui contra regem in bello dimicantes per fugam se salvaverint. His omnibus et item heredibus eorum qui in bello occubuerunt spes omnis terrarum et fundorum atque redituum quos ante possederant praeclusa est; magnum namque reputabant frui vitae beneficio sub inimicis.'

[3] Chron. Sax. A.D. 1066: 'And com to Westmynstre. and Ealdred arcebisceop hine to cynge gehalgode. and menn guldon him gyld. and gislas sealdon. and syththan heora land bohtan.' The Dialogus de Scaccario states that the landowners who had not fought at Hastings were allowed to hold their property or a portion of it at the will of their new lords, but without hope of hereditary succession; but when this power of the lords was misused the king allowed those who had made agreement with the lords to acquire a vested right, only they must content themselves with the new title, 'ceterum autem nomine successionis a temporibus subactae gentis nihil sibi vindicarent;' lib. i. c. 10. This is perhaps too definite a statement to be really historically true, but it contains the germ of a truth.

mere payment of *fyrdwite,* or composition for a recognised offence, might to the Normans seem equivalent to forfeiture and restoration.   But however this was, the process of confiscation and redistribution of lands under the new title began from the

Divisible stock of land increased after each struggle against the Conqueror.

moment of the coronation.   The next few years, occupied in the reduction of Western and Northern England, added largely to the stock of divisible estates.   The tyranny of Odo of Bayeux and William Fitz Osbern which provoked attempts at rebellion in A.D. 1067 ; the stand made by the house of Godwin in Devonshire in A.D. 1068; the attempts of Mercia and Northumbria to shake off the Normans in A.D. 1069 and 1070 ; the last struggle for independence in A.D. 1071 in which Edwin and Morcar finally fell ; the conspiracy of the Norman earls in A.D. 1075 in consequence of which Waltheof perished, all

Change of tenure followed with change of owner.

tended to the same result.   After each effort the royal hand was laid on more heavily : more and more land changed owners, and with the change of owners the title changed.   The complicated and unintelligible irregularities of the Anglo-Saxon tenures were exchanged for the simple and uniform feudal theory.   The fifteen hundred tenants-in-chief of Domesday take the place of the countless landowners of king Edward's time : and the loose unsystematic arrangements which had grown up in the confusion of title, tenure and jurisdiction, were replaced by systematic custom.   The change was effected without any legislative act, simply by the process of transfer under circumstances in which simplicity and uniformity were an absolute

Assimilation of all tenures to the feudal tenure.

necessity.   It was not the change from alodial to feudal so much as from confusion to order.   The actual amount of dispossession was no doubt greatest in the higher ranks; the smaller owners, to a large extent, remained in a mediatised position on their estates ; but even Domesday with all its fulness and accuracy cannot be supposed to enumerate all the changes of the twenty eventful years that followed the battle of Hastings.   It is enough for our purpose to ascertain that a universal assimilation of title followed the general changes of ownership.   The king of Domesday is the supreme landlord; all the land of the nation, the old folkland, has become the king's ; and all private land is held mediately or immediately of him ; all holders are bound to their lords by homage and fealty, either actually demanded or understood to be demandable in every case of transfer by inheritance or otherwise.

96. The result of this process is partly legal and partly con- Results. stitutional or political. The legal result is the introduction of an elaborate system of customs, tenures, rights, duties, profits and jurisdictions. The constitutional result is the creation of several intermediate links between the body of the nation and the king, in the place of or side by side with the duty of allegiance.

On the former of these points we have very insufficient data ; Legal changes for we are quite in the dark as to the development of feudal law consequent in Normandy before the invasion, and may be reasonably inclined change of to refer some at least of the peculiarities of English feudal law tenure. to the leaven of the system which it superseded [1]. Nor is it easy to reduce the organisation described in Domesday to strict conformity with feudal law as it appears later, especially with the general prevalence of military tenure. The growth of knighthood is a subject on which the greatest obscurity prevails; and the most probable explanation of its existence in England, the theory that it is a translation into Norman forms of the thegnage of the Anglo-Saxon law, can only be stated as probable. Between the picture drawn in Domesday and the state of affairs Develop- ment be- which the charter of Henry I was designed to remedy, there is tween 1086 a difference which the short interval of time will not account for, and 1100. and which testifies to the action of some skilful organising hand working with neither justice nor mercy, hardening and sharpening all lines and points to the perfecting of strong government.

It is unnecessary to recapitulate here all the points in which Resem- blance of the Anglo-Saxon institutions were already approaching the the thegn feudal model; it may be assumed that the actual obligation of and knight. military service was much the same in both systems, and that even the amount of land which was bound to furnish a mounted warrior was the same, however the conformity may have been produced. The heriot of the English earl or thegn was in close

[1] See more on this question in Chapter XI.

resemblance with the relief of the Norman count or knight. But however close the resemblance, something was now added that made the two identical. The change of the heriot to the relief implies a suspension of ownership, and carries with it the custom of livery of seisin. The heriot was the payment of a debt from the dead man to his lord; his son succeeded to his lands by alodial right. The relief was paid by the heir before he could obtain his father's lands; between the death of the father and livery of seisin to the son the right of the overlord had entered, the ownership was to a certain extent resumed, and the succession of the heir took somewhat of the character of a new grant. The right of wardship also became in the same way a re-entry by the lord on the profits of the estate of the minor, instead of being as before a protection, by the head of the kin, of the indefeasible rights of the heir, which it was the duty of the whole community to maintain.

It has, for want of direct and distinct historical statement, been held that the military tenure, the most prominent feature of historical feudalism, was itself introduced by the same gradual process which we have assumed in the case of the feudal usages in general. We have no light on the point from any original grant made by the Conqueror to a lay follower;

and in the absence of any general enactment we cannot assign the introduction of the system to any direct measure of law. Nor does the exaction of military service involve the immediate carving out of the land into knights' fees[1]. The obligation of national defence was incumbent as of old on all land-owners, and the customary service of one fully-armed man for each five hides was probably at the rate at which the newly-endowed follower of the king would be expected to discharge his duty. The wording of the Domesday survey does not imply that in this respect the new military service differed from the old: the land is marked out not into knights' fees but into hides, and the number of knights to be furnished by a particular feudatory would be ascertained by inquiring the number of hides that he

[1] See Pollock and Maitland, Hist. Eng. Law, i. 236–238; Round, Feudal England, pp. 225–261.

held, without apportioning the particular acres that were to support the particular knight. On the other hand, the early date at which the due service (debitum servitium) of feudal tenants appears as fixed, goes a long way to prove that it was settled in each case at the time of the royal grant.

It must not however be assumed that this process was other than gradual. Our earliest information is derived from the notices of ecclesiastical practice. Lanfranc, we are told, turned the drengs, the rent-paying tenants of his archiepiscopal estates, into knights for the defence of the country[1]: he enfeoffed a certain number of knights who performed the military service due from the archiepiscopal barony. This had been done before the Domesday survey[2], and almost necessarily implies that a like measure had been taken by the lay vassals. Lanfranc likewise maintained ten knights to answer for the military service due from the convent of Christ Church, which made over to him, in consideration of the relief, land worth two hundred pounds annually. The value of the knight's fee must already have been fixed at twenty pounds a year. In the reign of William Rufus the abbot of Ramsey obtained a charter which exempted his monastery from the service of ten knights due from it on festivals, substituting the obligation to furnish three knights to perform service on the north of the Thames[3]: a proof that the lands of that house had

Knights' fees gradually introduced.

Case in Kent.

Case of Ramsey.

---

[1] Elton's Tenures of Kent, pp. 68, 69. ' Sed et haec attestantur scripta vetustissima, quae lingua Anglorum *land-bokes*, id est, terrarum libros vocat. Quia vero non erant adhuc tempore regis Willelmi milites in Anglia, sed threnges, praecepit rex ut de eis milites fierent ad terram defendendam. Fecit autem Lanfrancus threngos suos milites ; monachi vero id non fecerunt sed de portione sua ducentas libratas terrae dederunt archiepiscopo, ut per milites suos terras eorum defenderet et omnia negotia eorum apud curiam Romanam suis expensis expediret, unde adhuc in tota terra monachorum nullus miles est, sed in terra archiepiscopi ;' Epp. Cantuar. p. 225. As late as 1201 the archbishop obtained a charter for the same purpose ; Houard, Anc. Loix, ii. 352. M. Paris, ii. 6, places the fixing of the service of bishops and monasteries in 1070. See Round, Feudal England, p. 299 ; and on the whole subject, pp. 225–261.

[2] Domesday, i. fol. 3.

[3] Ramsey Cartulary, fol. 54 b : in the 29th report of the Deputy Keeper of the Records, app. p. 45. The abbot in 1167 replies to the royal inquiry as to the number of knights enfeoffed in the monastic lands : ' Homines faciunt iiii. milites in communi ad servitium domini regis, ita quod tota terra abbatiae communicata est cum eis per hidas ad praedictum servitium faciendum ;' Liber Niger Scaccarii, ed. Hearne, i. 257. The lands were

not yet been divided into knights' fees. In the next reign we may infer from the favour granted by the king to the knights who defend their lands ' per loricas,' that is, by the hauberk, that their demesne lands shall be exempt from pecuniary taxation, that the process of definite military infeudation had largely advanced. But it was not even yet forced on the

Case of Milton.

clerical or monastic estates. When in 1167 the abbot of Milton in Dorset was questioned as to the number of knights' fees for which he had to account, he replied that all the services due from his monastery were discharged out of the demesne; but he added that in the reign of Henry I, during a vacancy in the abbacy, bishop Roger of Salisbury had enfeoffed two knights out of the abbey lands [1]; he had however subsequently reversed the act and had restored the lands whose tenure had been thus altered to their original condition of rent-paying estate or socage.

Old and new feoffment.

The very term ' the new feoffment,' which was applied to the knights' fees created between the death of Henry I and the year in which the account preserved in the Black Book of the Exchequer was taken, proves that the process was going on for nearly a hundred years [2], and that the form in which the

---

not yet cut into knights' fees. Similarly the bishop of Durham's service for his demesne land was that of ten knights, but it was not cut up into fees; Ibid. 309.

[1] Liber Niger Scaccarii, i. 75 : ' Contigit tamen aliquando, ecclesia nostra vacante, Rogerum episcopum Saresberiae illam ex mandato regis Henrici avi vestri in custodiam annis quinque suscepisse. Tunc praedictus episcopus de quodam tenemento quod tenuit R. de Monasteriis feodo censuali, scilicet de duabus hidis, unum fefavit militem. Postmodo vero bonae memoriae R. praedecessore meo constituto abbate, per justitiam regis Henrici et consilio praefati episcopi R. feoda praedicta ad antiquum statum revocata sunt; et quos episcopus constituit milites facti sunt censuarii.'

[2] An objection to this argument may be found in a clause of the so-called Charter of the Conqueror (Ll. Will. iii. § 8), in which the full-grown doctrine of military tenure is expressed thus : ' Omnes comites et barones et milites et servientes, et universi liberi homines totius regni nostri praedicti, habeant et teneant se semper bene in armis et in equis ut decet et oportet ; et sint semper prompti et bene parati ad servitium suum integrum nobis explendum et peragendum cum opus fuerit, secundum quod nobis debent de feodis et tenementis suis de jure facere; et sicut illis statuimus per commune consilium totius regni nostri praedicti, et illis dedimus et concessimus in feodo jure hereditario.' But this charter is a mere fabrication, and gives no authority whatever to the articles which are not found in the earlier and simpler form. See Hoveden, ii. pref. pp. xxxv, xxxvi. If this clause be genuine, or any part of it, it must be under-

knights' fees appear when called on by Henry II for scutage was most probably the result of a series of compositions by which the great vassals relieved their lands from a general burden by carving out particular estates the holders of which performed the services due from the whole; it was a matter of convenience and not of tyrannical pressure. The statement of Ordericus Vitalis that the Conqueror 'distributed lands to his knights in such fashion that the kingdom of England should have for ever 60,000 knights, and furnish them at the king's command according to the occasion,' must be regarded as one of the many numerical exaggerations of the early historians. The officers of the Exchequer in the twelfth century were quite unable to fix the number of existing knights' fees [1].

It cannot even be granted that a definite area of land was necessary to constitute a knight's fee; for, although at a later period and in local computations we may find four or five hides adopted as a basis of calculation, where the extent of the particular knight's fee is given exactly, it affords no ground for such a conclusion. In the Liber Niger we find knights' fees of two hides and a half [2], of two hides [3], of four [4], five [5], and six hides [6]. Geoffrey Ridel states that his father held 184 carucates and a virgate, for which the service of fifteen knights was due, but that no knights' fees had been carved out of it, the obligation lying equally on every carucate [7]. The archbishop of York had

stood to refer only to the cases in which the knights' fees had been actually apportioned.

[1] Ord. Vit. iv. 7. See below, c. xi. § 133.
[2] Lib. Nig. i. 64, 75.
[3] Ibid. i. 75.   [4] Ibid. i. 79.
[5] Ibid. i. 79, 104, 165.
[6] Ibid. i. 79; where one hide is reckoned as the sixth part of a knight's fee; and also as a fifth part: the difference being of course accounted for by the quality of the land, or by the tenour of the enfeoffment. These variations continue to subsist throughout the middle ages. In Lancashire a knight's fee contained twenty-four carucates; Testa de Nevill, p. 408. The Percy Feodary's book (Kirkby's Quest, ed. Skaife, pp. 442 sq.) gives a calculation of the acreage of the knight's fee varying from four carucates to twenty-eight. The recognised extent of the fee was 640 acres at five score to the hundred, or 540 at six score; the intermediate calculations for the carucate and oxgang varying according to the number of carucates in the fee. This is of the reign of Edward I.
[7] Lib. Nig. i. 210: 'Nullus militum de veteri illo fefamento feofatus

The knight's fee was of the annual value of £20.

far more knights than his tenure required [1]. It is impossible to avoid the conclusion that the extent of a knight's fee was determined by rent or valuation rather than acreage, and that the common quantity was really expressed in the twenty librates [2], and twenty pounds' worth of annual value which until the reign of Edward I was the qualification for knighthood [3]. It is most probable that no regular account of the knights' fees was ever taken until they became liable to taxation, either in the form of *auxilium militum* under Henry I, or in that of scutage under his grandson. The facts, however, which are here adduced, preclude the possibility of referring this portion of the feudal in-

Questionable relation of knighthood to knight-service.

novations to the direct legislation of the Conqueror. It may be regarded as a secondary question whether the knighthood here referred to was completed by the investiture with knightly arms and the honourable accolade. The ceremonial of knighthood was practised by the Normans, whereas the evidence that the English had retained the primitive practice of investing the youthful warrior is insufficient : yet it would be rash to infer that so early as this, if indeed it ever was the case, every possessor of a knight's fee received formal initiation before he assumed his spurs. But every such analogy would make the process of transition easier and prevent the necessity of any general legislative act of change.

Feudalism not involved in the oath exacted by William.

It has been maintained that a formal and definitive act, forming the initial point of the feudalisation of England, is to be found in a clause of the laws, as they are called, of the Conqueror ; which directs that every free man shall affirm by

---

fuit nominatim per feodum militis ; sed unaquaeque carrucata terrae ad faciendum milites xv. par est alii ad omnia servitia facienda et in exercitibus et in custodiis et ubique.'

[1] Lib. Nig. i. 303: 'Sciatis, domine, quod super dominium archiepiscopatus Eboracensis nullum feodum est militis, quoniam tot habemus fefatos milites per quos acquietavimus omne servitium quod vobis debemus, sicut et praecessores nostri fecerunt, et plures etiam habemus quam vobis debeamus. Antecessores enim nostri, non pro necessitate servitii quod deberent, sed quia cognatis et servientibus suis providere volebant, plures quam debebant regi feodaverunt.'

[2] See above, p. 285. In the return of Nigel de Luvetot in the Liber Niger, i. 258, the fractions of the knight's fee are calculated in solidates, or shillings' worths. See also pp. 293, 294.

[3] Select Charters, pp. 446, 447. Cf. Gneist, Verwalt. i. 11, 117.

covenant and oath that 'he will be faithful to King William within England and without, will join him in preserving his lands and honour with all fidelity, and defend him against his enemies[1].' But this injunction is little more than the demand of the oath of allegiance which had been taken to the Anglo-Saxon kings, and which is here required, not of every feudal dependent of the king, but of every freeman or freeholder whatsoever. In that famous Council of Salisbury of A.D. 1086, which was summoned immediately after the making of the Domesday survey, we learn from the Chronicle that there came to the king 'all his witan, and all the landowners of substance in England whose vassals soever they were, and they all submitted to him, and became his men and swore oaths of allegiance that they would be faithful to him against all others.' In this act has been seen the formal acceptance and date of the introduction of feudalism, but it has a very different meaning. The oath described is the oath of allegiance, combined with the act of homage, and obtained from all landowners whoever their feudal lord might be[2]. It is a measure of precaution taken against

The general oath of allegiance is not feudal.

The oath taken at Salisbury was really anti-feudal.

---

[1] Ll. Will. I, iii. § 2 ; below, note 2. See Hoveden, ii. pref. pp. xxv. sq., where I have attempted to prove the spuriousness of the document called the charter of William I in the Ancient Laws, ed. Thorpe, p. 211. The way in which the regulation of the Conqueror here referred to has been misunderstood and misused is curious. Lambarde in the Archaionomia, p. 170, printed the false charter, in which this genuine article is incorporated, as an appendix to the French version of the Conqueror's laws ; numbering the clauses 51 to 67 ; from Lambarde the whole thing was transferred by Wilkins into his collection of Anglo-Saxon laws. Blackstone, Commentaries, ii. 49, suggested that '*perhaps* the very law [which introduced feudal tenures] thus made at the Council of Salisbury, is that which is still extant and couched in these remarkable words,' i. e. the injunction in question ; and referred to Wilkins, p. 228. Ellis, in the introduction to Domesday, i. 16, quotes Blackstone, but adds a reference to Wilkins without verifying Blackstone's citation from his Collection of Laws, substituting for that work the *Concilia* in which the law does not occur. Many modern writers have followed him in referring the enactment of the article to the Council of Salisbury.

[2] It is as well to give here the text of both passages. That in the laws runs thus: 'Statuimus etiam ut omnis liber homo foedere et sacramento affirmet quod infra et extra Angliam Willelmo regi fideles esse volunt, terras et honorem illius omni fidelitate cum eo servare et ante eum contra inimicos defendere ;' Select Charters, p. 80. The homage done at Salisbury is described by Florence thus : 'Nec multo post mandavit ut archiepiscopi, abbates, comites et barones, et vicecomites cum suis militibus die Kalendarum Augustarum sibi occurrerent Saresberiae ; quo cum

the disintegrating power of feudalism, providing a direct tie between the sovereign and all freeholders which no inferior relation existing between them and the mesne lords would justify them in breaking. But this may be discussed further

It shows that the feudal theory was already accepted.

on. The real importance of the passage as bearing on the date of the introduction of feudal tenure is merely that it shows the system to have already become consolidated; all the landowners of the kingdom had already become, somehow or other, vassals, either of the king or of some tenant under him. The lesson may be learned from the fact of the Domesday survey.

The Conqueror's policy was to defeat the disruptive tendency of feudal institutions.

97. The introduction of such a system would necessarily have effects far wider than the mere modification of the law of tenure; it might be regarded as a means of consolidating and concentrating the whole machinery of government; legislation, taxation, judicature, and military defence were all capable of being organised on the feudal principle, and might have been so had the moral and political results been in harmony with the legal. But we have seen that its tendency when applied to governmental machinery is disruptive. The great feature of the Conqueror's policy is his defeat of that tendency. Guarding against it he obtained recognition as the king of the nation and, so far as he could understand them and the attitude of the nation allowed, he maintained the usages of the nation. He kept up the popular institutions of the hundred court and the shire court[1]. He confirmed the laws which had been in use in King Edward's days with the additions which he himself made for the benefit, as he especially tells us, of the English[2]. We are told,

venissent, milites eorum sibi fidelitatem contra omnes homines jurare coegit.' The Chronicle is a little more full : 'Thær him comon to his witan and ealle tha landsittende men the ahtes wæron ofer eall Engleland, wæron thæs mannes men the hi wæron, and ealle hi bugon to him and wæron his menn and him hold athas sworon thæt hi woldon ongean ealle othre men him holde beon.' Gneist, Verwalt. i. 116, rightly points out this oath as giving to the English polity a direction very different from that of the continental states.

[1] Statutes of William, § 8 : 'Requiratur hundredus et comitatus sicut antecessores nostri statuerunt.'

[2] Ibid. § 7 : 'Hoc quoque praecipio et volo ut omnes habeant et teneant legem Edwardi regis in terris et in omnibus rebus, adauctis iis quae constitui ad utilitatem populi Anglorum.' This is re-echoed by Henry I in

on what seems to be the highest legal authority of the next century, that he issued in his fourth year a commission of inquiry into the national customs, and obtained from sworn representatives of each county a declaration of the laws under which they wished to live [1]. The compilation that bears his name is very little more than a reissue of the code of Canute. And this proceeding helped greatly to reconcile the English people to his rule. Although the oppressions of his later years were far heavier than the measures taken to secure the immediate success of the Conquest, all the troubles of the kingdom after A.D. 1075, in his sons' reigns as well as in his own, proceeded from the insubordination of the Normans, not from the attempts of the English to dethrone the king. Very early they learned that, if their interest was not the king's, at least their enemies were his enemies ; hence they are invariably found on the royal side against the feudatories.

Maintenance of national customs.

William's laws a reissue of the earlier codes.

This accounts for the maintenance of the national force of defence, over and above the feudal army. The *fyrd* of the English, the general armament of the men of the counties and hundreds, was not abolished at the Conquest, but subsisted even through the reigns of William Rufus and Henry I, to be reformed and reconstituted under Henry II ; and in each reign it gave proof of its strength and faithfulness. The witenagemot itself retained the ancient form ; the bishops and abbots formed a chief part of it, instead of being, as in Normandy, so insignificant an element that their very participation in deliberation has been doubted. The king sat crowned three times in the

Maintenance of the national militia.

Of the witenagemot.

---

his Charter, § 13 : 'Lagam Edwardi regis vobis reddo cum illis emendationibus quibus pater meus eam emendavit consilio baronum suorum.'

[1] 'Willelmus rex quarto anno regni sui, consilio baronum suorum fecit summoneri per universos consulatus Angliae Anglos nobiles et sapientes et sua lege eruditos ut eorum et jura et consuetudines ab ipsis audiret. Electi igitur de singulis totius patriae comitatibus viri duodecim jurejurando confirmaverunt primo ut, quoad possent, recto tramite neque ad dextram neque ad sinistram partem devertentes legum suarum consuetudinem et sancita patefacerent, nil praetermittentes, nil addentes, nil praevaricando mutantes;' Hoveden, ii. 218. The authority on which the statement is made seems to be that of the justiciar Ranulf Glanvill. See Hoveden, ii. pref. p. xlvii. According to the tradition preserved in the same document the laws ultimately granted by William were those of Edgar ; Ibid. p. 235.

year in the old royal towns of Westminster, Winchester, and
Gloucester[1], hearing the complaints of his people, and executing
such justice as his knowledge of their law and language and
his own imperious will allowed.   In all this there is no violent
innovation, only such gradual essential changes as twenty eventful years of new actors and new principles must bring, however
insensibly the people, themselves passing away and being replaced by their children, may be educated to endurance.

No violent innovation.

Changes resulting from change of adminis- trators.

98. It would be wrong to impute to the Conqueror any intention of deceiving the nation by maintaining its official forms
whilst introducing new principles and a new race of administrators.   What he saw required change he changed with a high
hand.   But not the less surely did the change of administrators
involve a change of custom, both in the church and in the state.
The bishops, ealdormen, and sheriffs of English birth were replaced by Normans : not unreasonably perhaps, considering the
necessity of preserving the balance of the state.   With the
change of officials came a sort of amalgamation or duplication of
titles ; the ealdorman or earl became the comes or count ; the
sheriff became the vicecomes[2]; the office in each case receiving

New names bring in new princi- ples.

---

[1] Chron. Sax. A.D. 1087 ; W. Malmesb. G. R. iii. § 279.

[2] The correspondence of the offices of count and earl is obvious, and need
not be discussed further, since *comes* had even before the Conquest been
adopted as the Latin word for earl or ealdorman; see above, pp. 125,177,178.
The identification of the vicecomes with the sheriff requires a little more
illustration, for many writers have tried to explain the term as if it were
of native growth, and have been accordingly puzzled by the fact that the
vicecomes is the vicegerent, not of the earl, but of the king.   See Madox,
Dialogus de Scaccario, pp. 31, 32.   Hence also, when it was ascertained
that the vicecomes was imported full-grown from Normandy, it was thought
probable that the *comes* whom he represented there was the *comes Normannorum,* the Duke of Normandy.   But the term is really one of Frank
origin.   The vicecomes is the missus comitis of the Karolings, as distinguished from the vicarius or centenarius, who stands to him in a
subordinate relation.   The vicecomes is the judicial representative of the
Karolingian *comes* : and somewhat later, but still as early as the ninth
century, he appears as administrator of the county immediately under the
king.   The name appears first in Southern France under Lewis the Pious,
but never was domesticated in Germany; Sohm, Fr. R. G. Verfg. pp. 508–
525.   It had been maintained in Normandy by the Normans without any
question of verbal correctness, and was in the same loose way transferred
to England.   The duties of the Norman viscounts very much of course
resembled those of the sheriffs both fiscally and judicially, but we know
little of their action before the Conquest.

the name of that which corresponded most closely with it in Normandy itself. With the amalgamation of titles came an importation of new principles and possibly new functions; for the Norman count and viscount had not exactly the same customs as the earls and sheriffs. And this ran up into the highest grades of organisation; the king's court of counsellors was composed of his feudal tenants; the ownership and tenure of land now became the qualification for the witenagemot instead of wisdom; the earldoms became fiefs instead of magistracies, and even the bishops had to accept the status of barons. There was a very certain danger that the mere change of persons might bring in the whole machinery of hereditary magistracies, and that king and people might be edged out of the administration of justice, taxation, and other functions of supreme or local independence. Against this it was most important to guard; as the Conqueror learned from the events of the first year of his reign, when the severe rule of Odo and William Fitz-Osbern had provoked Herefordshire and Kent into hopeless resistance.

It was no part of William's policy to break up the unity of the royal authority by the creation of great hereditary territorial jurisdictions: but the absolute necessity of measures by which the disruptive tendency should be defeated forced itself upon him probably by degrees; and every opportunity that was furnished by the forfeitures of the first ten years of the reign was turned to progressive advantage. His first earls were merely successors of the earls of Edward the Confessor; William Fitz-Osbern held Herefordshire as it had been held by earl Ralph, the Confessor's nephew; Ralph Guader, Roger Montgomery, and Hugh of Avranches filled the places of Edwin and Morcar and the brothers of Harold. But the conspiracy of the earls in A.D. 1075 opened William's eyes to the danger of this proceeding, and from that time onward he governed the provinces through sheriffs immediately dependent on himself, avoiding the foreign plan of appointing hereditary counts, as well as the English custom of ruling by viceregal ealdormen. He was however very sparing in giving earldoms at all, and inclined to confine the title to those who were already counts

Hereditary jurisdictions, a thing to be avoided.

William gives very few earldoms.

in Normandy or in France. To this plan there were some marked exceptions, which may be accounted for either on the ground that the arrangements had been completed before the need of watchfulness was impressed on the king by the treachery of the Normans, or on that of the exigencies of national defence.

Existence of palatine earldoms.

In these cases he created, or suffered the continuance of, great jurisdictions of the kind that is denominated *palatine*; earldoms in which the earls were endowed with the superiority of whole counties, so that all the landowners held feudally of them; in which they received the whole profits of the courts and exercised all the regalia or royal rights, nominated the sheriffs, held their own councils and acted as independent princes except in the owing of homage and fealty to the king. Two of these great franchises, the earldom of Chester and the bishopric of Durham, retained much of their character to our own days[1]. A third, the palatinate of bishop Odo in Kent, if it were really a jurisdiction of the same sort, came to an end when Odo forfeited the confidence of his brother and nephew[2]. A fourth, the earldom of Shropshire, which is not commonly counted amongst the palatine jurisdictions, but which possessed under the Montgomery earls all the characteristics of such a dignity, was confiscated by Henry I after the treason of Robert of Belesme[3]. These had been all founded before the conspiracy of A.D. 1075;

[1] The earldom of Chester has, with the principality of Wales, belonged to the eldest son of the sovereign since 1301; the palatinate jurisdiction of Durham was transferred to the crown in 1836 by act of Parliament, 6 Will. IV. c. 19.

[2] The palatine jurisdiction of Odo rests on the authority of Ordericus Vitalis, who speaks as if he understood what he meant by the term; he mentions the gift of Kent three times, (1) in A.D. 1067, ' totam Cantiam fratri suo commendavit; ' at that time the archbishop Stigand was a prisoner, and Odo was acting as cojusticiar; (2) under the year 1087 he speaks of him as viceroy, ' in Anglia praeposuit Cantiae regno; ' and (3) in 1088, ' palatinus Cantiae comes erat, et plures sub se comites virosque potentes habebat.' This seems distinct enough, but it may be explained perhaps by supposing the writer to have confused Odo's position as justiciar with his territorial endowment in Kent. The overwhelming character of his power may be inferred from the action of the *Placitum apud Pinnendenam*, below, p. 301; in the record of which he is called comes Cantiae; Ang. Sac. i. 335; as he is by Osbern, his contemporary; Vita S. Dunstani, p. 144.

[3] Mr. Eyton, in his History of Shropshire, claims it as a palatine earldom for Roger Montgomery, vol. i. 22, 70, 242 sq. See too Nicolas's Historic

they were also, like the later lordships of the marches, a part Their
of the national defence; Chester and Shropshire kept the character.
Welsh marches in order; Kent was the frontier exposed to
attack from Picardy; and Durham, the patrimony of St.
Cuthbert, lay as a sacred boundary between England and
Scotland; Northumberland and Cumberland were still a
debateable ground between the two kingdoms. Chester was
held by its earls as freely by the sword as the king held
England by the crown; no lay vassal in the county held of
the king, all held of the earl. In Shropshire there were only
five lay tenants in capite besides Roger Montgomery; in Kent
Bishop Odo held an enormous proportion of the manors, but
the nature of his jurisdiction is not very clear, and its duration
is too short to make it of much importance. If William
founded any earldoms at all after A.D. 1075, which may be
doubted, he did it on a very different scale.

The hereditary sheriffdoms he did not guard against with Sheriffdoms
equal care. The Norman viscounties were hereditary[1], and hereditary.
there was some risk that the English ones would become so
too; and with the worst consequences, for the English counties
were much larger than the bailiwicks of the Norman viscounts,
and the authority of the sheriff, when he was relieved from
the supervision of the ealdorman, and was soon to lose the
society of the bishop, would have no check except the direct
control of the king. If William perceived this, it was too late
to prevent it entirely; some of the sheriffdoms became hereditary, and continued to be so long after the abuse had become
constitutionally dangerous[2].

The independence of the greater feudatories was still further Contiguous
limited by the principle, which the Conqueror seems to have accumu-
observed, of avoiding the accumulation in any one hand of a avoided.
great number of contiguous estates[3]. The rule is not without

Peerage, ed. Courthope, p. 434, where Selden is quoted as an authority
for the same statement; and the Report on the Dignity of a Peer, i. 407;
and see below, Chapter XI.
[1] See Stapleton, 'Rotuli Scaccarii Normanniae,' i. pp. lviii, lix, &c.
[2] See Chapter XI.
[3] See Thorpe's Lappenberg, iii. 201. The estates of Odo lay in seventeen

Distribution of great fiefs in distant counties.

some important exceptions, such as the gift of Richmondshire to Alan of Brittany, and may have been suggested by the diversity of occasions on which the fiefs were bestowed, but the result is one which William must have foreseen. An insubordinate baron whose strength lay in twelve different counties would have to rouse the suspicions and perhaps to defy the arms of twelve powerful sheriffs, before he could draw his forces to a head. In his manorial courts, scattered and unconnected, he could set up no central tribunal, nor even force a new custom upon his tenants, nor could he attempt oppression on any extensive scale. By such limitation the people were protected and the central power secured.

Legal theory of the origin of manors.

Yet the changes of ownership, even thus guarded, wrought other changes. It is not to be supposed that the Norman baron, when he had received his fief, proceeded to carve it out into demesne and tenants' land as if he were making a new settlement in an uninhabited country. He might indeed build his castle and enclose his chase with very little respect to the rights of his weaker neighbours, but he did not attempt any such radical change as the legal theory of the creation of manors seems to presume. The name 'manor' is of Norman origin, but the estate to which it was given existed, in its essential character, long before the Conquest; it received a new name as the shire also did, but neither the one nor the other was created by this change. The distinction between the *in-land* and *out-land* of the *hlaford* already existed. The local jurisdictions of the thegns who had grants of sac and soc, or who exercised judicial functions amongst their free neighbours, were identical with the manorial jurisdictions of the new owners. It may be

Growth of manorial customs.

counties, those of Robert of Mortain in twenty; Eustace of Boulogne had fiefs in twelve counties, and Hugh of Avranches in twenty-one, besides his palatine earldom. Gneist, Self-government, i. 66, 67, gives more details, chiefly from Kelham's 'Domesday Illustrated,' and Ellis's Introduction to Domesday:—There are forty-one great vassals, each of whom has estates in more than six counties : of these five have lands in seven, six in eight, two in nine, four in ten, four in eleven, three in twelve, one in thirteen, two in fourteen, one in twenty, and one in twenty-one; all these are laymen. The greatest number of manors is held by Robert of Mortain, 793; Odo has 439; Alan of Brittany 442.

conjectured with great probability that in many cases the weaker freemen, who had either willingly or under constraint attended the courts of their great neighbours, were now, under the general infusion of feudal principle, regarded as holding their lands of them as lords; it is not less probable that in a great number of grants the right to suit and service from small landowners passed from the king to the receiver of the fief as a matter of course; but it is certain that even before the Conquest such a proceeding was not uncommon; Edward the Confessor had transferred to St. Augustine's monastery a number of alodiaries in Kent [1], and every such measure in the case of a church must have had its parallel in similar grants to laymen. The manorial system brought in a number of new names; and perhaps a duplication of offices. The gerefa of the old thegn or of the ancient township was replaced, as president of the courts, by a Norman steward or seneschal; and the bydel of the old system by the bailiff of the new; but the gerefa and bydel still continued to exist in a subordinate capacity as the grave or reeve and the bedell; and, when the lord's steward takes his place in the county court, the reeve and four men of the township are there also. The common of the township may be treated as the lord's waste, but the townsmen do not lose their customary share. The changes that take place in the state have their resulting analogies in every village, but no new England is created; new forms displace but do not destroy the old, and old rights remain, although changed in title and forced into symmetry with a new legal and pseudo-historical theory. The changes may not seem at first sight very oppressive, but they opened the way for oppression; the forms they had introduced tended, under the spirit of Norman legality and feudal selfishness, to become hard realities, and in the profound miseries of Stephen's reign the people learned how completely the new theory left them at the mercy of their lords; nor were all the reforms of his successor more stringent or the struggles of the century that followed a whit more impassioned, than were

Manorial institutions.

Estimate of the amount of change.

The new forms oppressive in result.

---

[1] Kemble, C. D. iv. 239.   See above, p. 208.

necessary to protect the English yeoman from the men who lived upon his strength.

99. In attempting thus to estimate the real amount of change introduced by the feudalism of the Conquest, many points of further interest have been touched upon, to which it is necessary to recur only so far as to give them their proper place in a more general view of the reformed organisation. The Norman king is still the king of the nation. He has become the supreme landlord; all estates are held of him mediately or immediately, but he still demands the allegiance of all his subjects. The oath which he exacted at Salisbury in A.D. 1086, and which is embodied in the semi-legal form already quoted, was a modification of the oath taken to Edmund [1], and was intended to set the general obligation of obedience to the king in its proper relation to the new tie of homage and fealty by which the tenant was bound to his lord. All men continued to be primarily the king's men, and the public peace to be his peace. Their lords might demand their service to fulfil their own obligations, but the king could call them to the fyrd, summon them to his courts, and tax them without the intervention of their lords; and to the king they could look for protection against all foes. Accordingly the king could rely on the help of the bulk of the free people in all struggles with his feudatories, and the people, finding that their connexion with their lords would be no excuse for unfaithfulness to the king, had a further inducement to adhere to the more permanent institutions.

In the department of law the direct changes introduced by the Conquest were not great. Much that is regarded as peculiarly Norman was developed upon English soil, and, although originated and systematised by Norman lawyers, contained elements which would have worked in a very different way in Normandy. Even the vestiges of Karolingian practice which appear in the inquests of the Norman reigns are modified by English usage. The great inquest of all, the Domesday survey, may owe its principle to a foreign source; the oath of the reporters may be Norman, but the machinery that furnishes

Position of the Norman king.

Direct relations between king and people.

Amount of change in jurisprudence uncertain.

Inquests.

---

[1] Above, p. 166.

the jurors is native ; 'the king's barons inquire by the oath of the sheriff of the shire, and of all the barons and their Frenchmen, and of the whole hundred, the priest, the reeve, and six ceorls of every township [1].' The institution of the collective Frankpledge, which recent writers incline to treat as a Norman innovation, is so distinctly coloured by English custom that it has been generally regarded as purely indigenous. If it were indeed a precaution taken by the new rulers against the avoidance of justice by the absconding or harbouring of criminals, it fell with ease into the usages and even the legal terms which had been common for other similar purposes since the reign of Athelstan [2]. The trial by battle, which on clearer evidence seems to have been brought in by the Normans, is a relic of old Teutonic jurisprudence, the absence of which from the Anglo-Saxon courts is far more curious than its introduction from abroad [3].

Frankpledges.

Trial by battle.

The organisation of jurisdiction required and underwent no great change in these respects. The Norman lord who undertook the office of sheriff had, as we have seen, more unrestricted power than the sheriffs of old. He was the king's representative in all matters, judicial, military, and financial in his shire, and had many opportunities of tyrannising in each of those departments : but he introduced no new machinery. From him, or from the courts of which he was the presiding officer, appeal lay to the king alone ; but the king was often absent from England and did not understand the language of his subjects. In his absence the administration was entrusted to a justiciar, a regent or lieutenant of the kingdom ; and the convenience being once ascertained of having a minister who could in the whole kingdom represent the king, as the sheriff did in the

Jurisdiction of the sheriff unaltered.

The justiciar as the king's deputy.

[1] Domesday of Ely ; Domesd. iii. 497.
[2] See above, pp. 93, 94.
[3] Palgrave argues, from the fact that trial by battle is mentioned in a record of a Worcester shiremoot soon after the Conquest, that the custom may possibly have been of earlier introduction ; but it is never mentioned in the laws, and as exemption from it was one of the privileges conferred by charter on towns in the next century, there can be no doubt that it was an innovation, and one which was much disliked. See Palgrave, Commonwealth, p. 225 ; and above, p. 220, note 1.

shire, the justiciar became a permanent functionary. This however cannot be certainly affirmed of the reign of the Conqueror,
who, when present at Christmas, Easter, and Whitsuntide, held
great courts of justice as well as for other purposes of state;
and the legal importance of the office of justiciar belongs to a
later stage. The royal court, containing the tenants in chief of
the crown, both lay and clerical, and entering into all the functions of the witenagemot, was the supreme council of the nation,
with the advice and consent of which the king legislated, taxed,
and judged.

The Con-
queror legis-
lates with
the advice of
his council.

In the chief authentic monument of William's jurisprudence,
the act which removed ecclesiastical suits from the secular courts
and recognised the spiritual jurisdictions, he tells us that he acts
'with the common council and counsel of the archbishops,
bishops, abbots, and all the princes of the kingdom [1].' The
ancient summary of his laws contained in the Textus Roffensis
is entitled, 'What William King of the English with his princes
enacted after the conquest of England [2].' The same form is
preserved in the tradition of his confirming the ancient laws
reported to him by the representatives of the shires : ' King
William in the fourth year of his reign, by the council of his
barons, caused to be summoned through all the counties of
England the noble, the wise, and the learned in their law, that
he might hear from them their rights and customs [3].' The
Anglo-Saxon Chronicle enumerates the classes of men who
attended his great courts : 'There were with him all the great
men over all England, archbishops and bishops, abbots and earls,
thegns and knights [4].' We are not without a few good illustrations of the supreme jurisdiction exercised by the Conqueror
in the ancient courts of law.

A trial of
the Con-
queror's
reign.

The great suit between Lanfranc as archbishop of Canterbury
and Odo as earl of Kent, which is perhaps the best reported

---

[1] ' Communi concilio et consilio archiepiscoporum, episcoporum et abbatum et omnium principum regni mei;' Ancient Laws, p. 213; Select
Charters, p. 82.
[2] Select Charters, p. 80.
[3] Ll. Edw. Conf., Schmid, p. 491.
[4] Chron. Sax. A.D. 1087.

trial of the reign, was tried in the county court of Kent before
the king's representative, Gosfrid bishop of Coutances ; whose
presence and that of most of the great men of the kingdom seem
to have made it a witenagemot.   The archbishop pleaded the
cause of his church in a session of three days on Pennenden
Heath [1] ; the aged South-Saxon bishop, Ethelric, was brought
by the king's command to declare the ancient customs of the
laws, and with him several other Englishmen skilled in ancient
laws and customs.   All these good and wise men supported the
archbishop's claim, and the decision was agreed on and determined by the whole county.   The sentence was laid before the   Trial at
king, and confirmed by him.   Here we have probably a good   Pennenden.
instance of the principle universally adopted ; all the lower
machinery of the court was retained entire, but the presence of
the Norman justiciar and barons gave it an additional authority,
a more direct connexion with the king, and the appearance at
least of a joint tribunal.   Exactly the same principle was involved in the institution of regular eyres or circuits of the justices
by Henry I or Henry II.

The liberties of the church of Ely were ascertained in a   Law-suit
session of three neighbouring county courts, held under a precept   of Ely.
of bishop Odo as justiciar and attended by four abbots, four
sheriffs, and three delegates of royal appointment, besides a
large assembly of knights [2].

Another trial of great interest took place between Gundulf   Trial in
bishop of Rochester and Picot sheriff of Cambridgeshire.   The   Cambridge-
                                                                   shire.
suit was brought before the king ; he called together the county
court of Cambridgeshire, and directed that the right to the disputed land should be decided by their judgment.   Bishop Odo
presided.   The Cambridgeshire men, in fear of the sheriff, decided against Gundulf.   Odo thereupon directed that they should
choose twelve out of their number to swear to the truth of their
report.   The twelve swore falsely ; and, one of them having

---

[1] It is printed in Anglia Sacra, i. 334–336, from the Textus Roffensis, in
Wilkins, Concilia, i. 323, 324 ; and in Bigelow's Placita Anglo-Normannica,
pp. 5–9.   The litigation is referred to in Domesday, i. fol. 5.
[2] Lib. Eliens, ii. 116 ; Bigelow, Plac. Angl. p. 22.

confessed his perjury to Odo, he ordered the sheriff to send the jurors up to London, and with them twelve of the best men of the county. He also summoned a body of barons. This court of appeal reversed the decision of the shire. The twelve best men tried to deny their complicity with the perjurers, and Odo offered them the ordeal of iron. They failed under the test, and were fined by the rest of the county three hundred pounds, to be paid to the king[1].

Principle of amalgamation.

The principle of amalgamating the two laws and nationalities by superimposing the better consolidated Norman superstructure on the better consolidated English substructure, runs through the whole policy. The English system was strong in the cohesion of its lower organisms, the association of individuals in the township, in the hundred and in the shire; the Norman system was strong in its higher ranges, in the close relation to the crown of the tenants in chief whom the king had enriched. On the other hand, the English system was weak in the higher organisation, and the Normans in England had hardly any subordinate organisation at all. The strongest elements of both were brought together.

The same principle carried out in taxation.

100. The same idea of consolidating the royal power by amalgamating the institutions of the two races was probably followed also in the department of finance; although in this point neither party was likely to discern much immediate benefit to any one but the king. William, whose besetting vice was said by his contemporaries to be avarice, retained the revenues of his predecessors and added new imposts of his own. The ordinary revenue of the English king had been derived solely from the royal estates and the produce of what had been the folkland, with such commuted payments of feormfultum, or provision in kind, as represented either the reserved rents from ancient possessions of the crown, or the quasi-voluntary tribute paid by the nation to its chosen head. The Danegeld, that is, the extraordinary revenue arising from the cultivated land, —originally levied as tribute to the Danes, although it had been continued long after the occasion for it had ceased,—had been

The Danegeld.

---

[1] Angl. Sac. i. 339; Bigelow, p. 34; see below, Chap. XI.

abolished by Edward the Confessor[1]. The Conqueror not only
retained the royal estates, but imposed the Danegeld anew. In
A.D. 1084 he demanded from every hide of land not held by
himself in demesne, or by his barons, a sum of six shillings,
three times the old rate[2]. The measure may have been part of
the defensive policy which he adopted after discovering the
faithlessness of his brother Odo, and which connects itself with
the Domesday survey and the Salisbury council two years later;
but it became a permanent source of revenue. On the Norman *Feudal im-*
side the supreme landlord was entitled to all the profits of the *posts.*
feudal position, a description of income of which we have no
details proper to the reign of the Conqueror, but which becomes
prominent immediately after his death. It is needless to observe
that the actual burden of the feudal imposts, as well as the
older taxation, fell on the English; for the Norman lords had
no other way of raising their reliefs, aids, tallages, and the rest,
than from the labours of their native dependents. The exaction
may have been treated by them as a tyrannical one, but the hardship directly affected the English.

The income thus accumulated was no doubt very great. The *The Con-*
royal lands are known from Domesday to have produced in the *queror's*
reign of William the Conqueror nearly £20,000[3]; and the *income.*
Danegeld of A.D. 1084, if levied from two-thirds of the hidage
of the kingdom, would be nearly as much more. To this must
be added the profits of jurisdictions and the other occasional
items which we have no means of estimating. Giraldus Cambrensis[4] mentions £40,000 as the amount which in his days

---

[1] Edward imagined that he saw the devil sitting on the bags in the
treasury; Hoveden, i. 110. The author of the Dialogus de Scaccario says
that William turned the Danegeld from a regular into an occasional tax;
Lib. i. c. 11.

[2] Chron. Sax. A.D. 1083; Flor. Wig. A.D. 1084; Freeman, Norm. Conq.
iv. 685. The accounts of this geld for the five counties of Devon, Cornwall, Dorset, Wilts, and Somerset, are preserved in the Domesday of
Exeter: the sum paid by those counties collectively was somewhat under
£2000.

[3] Pearson, Early and Middle Ages, i. 385.

[4] De Inst. Princ. iii. c. 30: 'Angliae, regum Anglorum tempore et
etiam penultimi Edwardi Westmonasteriensis diebus, annui fiscales redditus, sicut in rotulo Wintoniae reperitur, ad sexaginta millia marcarum
summam implebant.'

The Conqueror's income.

was regarded as representing the income ascribed, on the evidence of Domesday, to Edward the Confessor. Ordericus Vitalis, a well-informed Norman monk of the next century, boldly states William's revenue at £1061 10s. 1½d. a day, besides the profits of the law courts[1]. If, as has been cleverly conjectured, this circumstantial statement refers properly to the weekly revenue, we arrive at a sum of between fifty and sixty thousand pounds a year. A comparison with the revenue of Henry I, which in his thirty-first year reached a gross amount of £66,000, may show that this is not improbable[2]. But the numerical statements of the early writers are very untrustworthy, and no approach can yet be made to a precise estimate. It is evident, however, that the same general principle was at work in the collection of revenue as in the courts of justice and in the furnishing of military defence. No class was left untaxed; all men had a distinct relation to the king over and above the relation to their lords; and the strongest points of the two national systems are brought into joint working.

Ecclesiastical policy of the Conqueror.

101. The ecclesiastical policy of the Conqueror presents marks of coincidence, and also of contrast, with his secular administration. There is the same change of administrators, but not the same fusion or modification of offices. The change of administrators is gradual in the church as in the state, and nearly as complete: the English church was drawn into the general tide of ecclesiastical politics and lost much of its insular character: it gained in symmetry and definiteness of action, and was started on a new career. But the immediate motives of

Relations to the pope.

William's measures are somewhat complex. His attack on England was planned and carried out with the approval of Pope

---

[1] Ord. Vit. iv. 7 : 'Ipsi vero regi, ut fertur, mille et sexaginta librae sterilensis monetae, solidique triginta et tres oboli, ex justis redditibus Angliae per singulos dies redduntur ; exceptis muneribus regiis et reatuum redemptionibus, aliisque multiplicibus negotiis quae regis aerarium quotidie adaugent.'

[2] Ben. Pet. ii. pref. xcix. The sum, roughly added up, reaches this amount ; but it includes debts and old accounts, and cannot be regarded as an approximation to the true revenue. The Roll moreover is imperfect. The treasure in Henry's hands at his death was at least £160,000, of which £100,000 fell to Stephen, Will. Malmesb. Hist. Nov. i. § 14 ; and £60,000 was in Normandy, Ord. Vit. xiii. 19.

Alexander II, and the hard measure dealt out to the English bishops personally was due quite as much to the desire of satisfying the pope, who had his own jealousies and grudges, as to William's belief that the influence of the great ecclesiastics was secretly working against him, or that the support of a strong Norman hierarchy was absolutely necessary for his safety. But William had no intention of following the papal guidance further than was convenient to himself; and in the great adviser whom he chose on his own responsibility he found a very able and conscientious helper. Lanfranc was a statesman as well as a theologian, a lawyer as well as a scholar, and in feeling quite as much an Englishman as a Norman: he was an Italian too, and therefore, perhaps, not a papalist[1]. Hence whilst attempting the reformation of abuses, which either the national easiness and self-complacency, or the evil influence of the Norman clergy had originated, he adopted no violent or rigorous scheme of discipline, provoked no national antipathies, sacrificed neither the state to the church nor the church to the state. His policy was uniformly in agreement with the king's, and his personal influence kept in harmonious working two systems, which contained elements that after his death were to produce a long and bitter quarrel.

Influence of Lanfranc.

William's own ideas of managing the church were probably developed in England itself. The Norman prelates, with whom as duke he had to do, were either sons of the ruling families[2] or personally insignificant. They had not the position of the English prelates with reference either to the people or to the duke. They were but a small element in his council, and in no close relation with the native population, whilst in England

William's church policy worked out in England.

---

[1] Several letters of Lanfranc and Gregory VII are extant, from which a certain amount of coolness may be inferred to have existed between them. Gregory complains and Lanfranc excuses himself. See Freeman, Norm. Conq. iv. 434–437.

[2] Ordericus names them, lib. iii. c. xi. Odo of Bayeux was the Conqueror's brother; the bishop of Lisieux was brother of the count of Eu, and the bishop of Avranches son of Count Ralph of Bayeux, both cousins of the king; the bishop of Seez belonged to the family of Belesme; Gosfrid of Coutances was a mighty man on both sides the Channel. The archbishop of Rouen and the bishop of Evreux were of less personal importance.

Position
of the
English
bishops.

they were the most numerous and coherent body in the witena-gemot; and, although many of Edward's bishops were foreigners, they had inherited the loyalty and traditional support of the districts over which they presided. The ready submission of the witan in A.D. 1066 saved the bishops for the moment: the Conqueror had no wish to make enemies, and they had no champion to take the place of Harold. But when in A.D. 1070 he had found that the influence of the episcopate was so strong that it must be put into safer hands, and when the legates of Alexander II demanded the humiliation of the ignorant supporters of the antipope Benedict, the deposition of the bishops consecrated by Stigand, and the enforcement of canonical order,

Deposition
of English
bishops.

he proceeded to displace most of the native bishops. Then Stigand, who occupied two sees, one of which he had taken in the lifetime of a Norman predecessor, and who had received the pall from a schismatic pope, was deposed and imprisoned. With him fell his brother, the bishop of Elmham, and the faultless bishop of Selsey whom he had consecrated, and who might be regarded as sharing his schismatic attitude[1]. The brother bishops of Durham, Ethelwin and Ethelric, had incurred the penalties of treason. York and Lichfield were vacant by death. Dorchester had been filled up by the Norman Remigius since the battle of Hastings; he too had been consecrated by Stigand, but the offence was not so fatal in a Norman as in an Englishman; he declares in his profession of obedience to Lanfranc that he was ignorant of Stigand's uncanonical status[2]. Hereford, Wells, Ramsbury, Exeter, and London were already in the hands of foreigners. It was by no act of extraordinary severity that the change was made; but at the end of A.D. 1070 only two sees retained native bishops, Worcester and Rochester[3]. The way was open for Lanfranc, and his appointment satisfied both king and pope. Henceforth the bishops and most of the

---

[1] Flor. Wig. A.D. 1070. Remigius, in his profession of obedience to Lanfranc, mentions the mission of legates from the pope with orders that all who had been ordained by Stigand should be deposed or suspended.

[2] MS. Cotton, Cleopatra, E. 1.

[3] Siward of Rochester is said by William of Malmesbury to have died a few days after the Conquest. But he lived several years longer, was present at a council at Winchester in 1072, and died probably in 1075.

abbots were Norman [1]; but they, like the king, realised their new position as Englishmen by adoption; entering immediately on all the claims of their predecessors and declaring that, so far as their power went, the churches they espoused should suffer no detriment. The Conqueror's bishops were generally good and able men, though not of the English type of character. They were not mere Norman barons, as was the case later on, but scholars and divines chosen under Lanfranc's influence. The abbots were less wisely selected, and had perhaps a more difficult part to play, for the monasteries were still full of English monks, and preserved, and probably concentrated, most of the national aspirations after deliverance which all came to naught.

The most important ecclesiastical measure of the reign, order- ing the separation of the church jurisdiction from the secular business of the courts of law, is unfortunately, like all other charters of the time, undated. Its contents however show the influence of the ideas which under the genius of Hildebrand were forming the character of the continental churches. From henceforth the bishops and archdeacons are no longer to hold ecclesiastical pleas in the hundred-court, but to have courts of their own; to try causes by canonical not by customary law, and to allow no spiritual questions to come before laymen as judges. In case of contumacy the offender may be excommunicated and the king and sheriff will enforce the punishment. In the same way laymen are forbidden to interfere in spiritual causes [2]. The reform

---

[1] The deposition of the abbots was also gradual. See the Chronicle (ed. Earle), pp. 271–275.

[2] Ancient Laws, ed. Thorpe, p. 213: 'Ut nullus episcopus vel archidiaconus de legibus episcopalibus amplius in hundret placita teneant, nec causam quae ad regimen animarum pertinet ad judicium secularium hominum adducant, sed quicunque secundum episcopales leges de quacunque causa vel culpa interpellatus fuerit, ad locum quem ad hoc episcopus elegerit vel nominaverit veniat, ibique de causa vel culpa sua respondeat, et, non secundum hundret sed secundum canones et episcopales leges, rectum Deo et episcopo suo faciat. Si vero aliquis per superbiam elatus ad justitiam episcopalem venire contempserit vel noluerit, vocetur semel, secundo et tertio; quod si nec sic ad emendationem venerit, excommunicetur et, si opus fuerit, ad hoc vindicandum fortitudo et justitia regis vel vicecomitis adhibeatur. Ille autem qui vocatus ad justitiam episcopi venire noluerit, pro unaquaque vocatione legem episcopalem emendabit. Hoc etiam defendo et mea auctoritate interdico, ne ullus vicecomes, aut praepositus seu minister regis, nec aliquis laicus homo de legibus quae ad episcopum pertinent se

is one which might very naturally recommend itself to a man like Lanfranc. The practice which it superseded was full of anomalies and disadvantages to both justice and religion. But the change involved far more than appeared at first. The growth of the canon law, in the succeeding century, from a quantity of detached local or occasional rules to a great body of universal authoritative jurisprudence, arranged and digested by scholars who were beginning to reap the advantages of a revived study of the Roman civil law, gave to the clergy generally a far more distinctive and definite civil status than they had ever possessed before, and drew into church courts a mass of business with which the church had previously had only an indirect connexion. The question of investitures, the marriage of the clergy, and the crying prevalence of simony, within a very few years of the Conqueror's death, forced on the minds of statesmen everywhere the necessity of some uniform system of law. The need of a system of law once felt, the recognition of the supremacy of the papal court as a tribunal of appeal followed of course : and with it the great extension of the legatine administration. The clergy thus found themselves in a position external, if they chose to regard it so, to the common law of the land; able to claim exemption from the temporal tribunals, and by appeals to Rome to paralyse the regular jurisdiction of the diocesans. Disorder followed disorder, and the anarchy of Stephen's reign, in which every secular abuse was paralleled or reflected in an ecclesiastical one, prepared the way for the Constitutions of Clarendon, and the struggle that followed with all its results down to the Reformation itself. The same facility of employing the newly developed jurisprudence of the canonists drew into the ecclesiastical courts the matrimonial and testamentary jurisdiction, and strengthened that most mischievous, because most abused, system

Consequence of the separation of the spiritual and secular courts.

Growth of the canon law.

intromittat, nec aliquis laicus homo alium hominem sine justitia episcopi ad judicium adducat ; judicium vero in nullo loco portetur, nisi in episcopali sede aut in illo loco quem ad hoc episcopus constituerit.' Notwithstanding this enactment the Custumal, known as the ' Leges Henrici primi ' (Schmid, p. 440), places the ' debita veræ Christianitatis jura ' first among the agenda of the full county court. The author, however, seems to be referring to those cases of offences against the church, in which the king had a share of the fines ; and he may be reproducing old materials.

of enforcing moral discipline by spiritual penalties, at the instance of men whose first object was the accumulation of money.

The reformation of the spiritual courts, and the exemption of their proceedings from the common usages of Anglo-Saxon law, had a bearing on the relations of the church to the state in these ways; but it must not be supposed that it was in itself a sign of any disposition in either William or Lanfranc to admit extreme claims on the part of the popes. The results that have been mentioned flowed from a state of things which was now in process of development, and which attained full growth far more rapidly than they could have expected, through circumstances which they could not foresee. Anything like a direct claim on the part of the papacy William repudiated at once. Not only did he distinctly refuse the demand of fealty made by the legate Hubert on behalf of Gregory VII [1], but he seems to have established an understanding with the English church which had the force of a concordat for future times. The arrangement is described by the faithful historian Eadmer as a novelty, but it was a novelty necessitated by the newness of the circumstances in which the king found himself. 'He would not suffer that any one in all his dominions should receive the pontiff of the city of Rome as apostolic pope, except at his command, or should on any condition receive his letters if they had not been first shown to himself.' This principle, which was abused by William Rufus, and which could only work well when

Attitude of William and Lanfranc towards the papacy.

William's rules of dealing with Rome.

---

[1] Freeman, Norm. Conq. iv. 432–434, has traced the history of Gregory's correspondence with the Conqueror. Some time about A.D. 1076, the pope sent a legate to William to ask for a more regular payment of Peter's pence and to demand fealty. The king's answer was this : after the greeting ' salutem cum amicitia,' ' Hubertus legatus tuus, religiose pater, ad me veniens ex tua parte me admonuit, quatenus tibi et successoribus tuis fidelitatem facerem, et de pecunia quam antecessores mei ad Romanam ecclesiam mittere solebant melius cogitarem. Unum admisi, alterum non admisi ; fidelitatem facere nolui nec volo ; quia nec ego promisi nec antecessores meos antecessoribus tuis id fecisse comperio. Pecunia tribus ferme annis, in Galliis me agente, negligenter collecta est ; nunc vero Divina misericordia me in regnum meum reverso, quod collectum est per praesentem legatum mittetur ; et quod reliquum est per legatos Lanfranci archiepiscopi fidelis nostri, cum opportunum fuerit, transmittetur. Orate pro nobis et pro statu regni nostri, quia antecessores vestros dileximus et vos prae omnibus sincere diligere et obedienter audire desideramus ; ' Selden, App. to Eadmer, p. 164 ; Lanfr. Epp. ed. Giles, No. x.

The Con-
queror's
rules of
dealing
with the
Church.
the chiefs in church and state were in thorough concert, expresses rather than overcomes the difficulty. But it is a difficulty which has never yet been overcome; and it is probable that the Conqueror's rule went as near to the solution as any state theory has ever done. A second rule was this, ' He did not suffer the primate of his kingdom, the archbishop of Canterbury, if he had called together under his presidency an assembly of bishops, to enact or prohibit anything but what was agreeable to his will and had been first ordained by him.' This was a most necessary limitation of the powers recognized as belonging to the spiritual courts, nor did it, in an age in which there was no discord of religious opinion, create any of the scandals which might arise under more modern conditions. The two rules together express the principle of the maxim so well known in later times, ' cujus regio, ejus religio ' in that early form in which it recommended itself to the great Charles. A third rule was this; ' he did not allow any of his bishops publicly to implead, excommunicate, or constrain by penalty of ecclesiastical rigour, any of his barons or servants, who was informed against either for adultery or for any capital crime, except by his own command.' Of this also it may be said that it might work well when regulated by himself and Lanfranc, but that otherwise it created rather than solved a difficulty [1]. A further usage, which was claimed by Henry I as a precedent, was the prohibition of the exercise of legatine power in England, or even of the legate's landing on the soil of the kingdom without royal licence [2].

Such precautions as these show little more than an incipient misgiving as to the relations of church and state: a misgiving

---

[1] Eadmer, Hist. Nov. i. (ed. Selden, p. 6). The rules of William Rufus are thus stated by Anselm, Epp. iii. 40: ' Exigebat enim a me rex ut voluntatibus suis, quae contra legem et voluntatem Dei erant, sub nomine rectitudinis assensum praeberem: nam sine jussione apostolicum nolebat recipi aut appellari in Anglia, nec ut epistolam ei mitterem, aut ab eo missam reciperem, vel decretis ejus obedirem. Concilium non permisit celebrari in regno suo ex quo rex factus jam per tredecim annos.'

[2] Eadmer, Hist. Nov. v. p. 118: ' Rex Henricus antiquis Angliae consuetudinibus praejudicium inferri non sustinens, illum ab ingressu Angliae detinebat.' See also Flor. Wig. A.D. 1116. In this case the objection to receive the legate arose from the bishops, abbots, and nobles who discussed the question ' communi consilio.' See also below, vol. iii. c. xix.

which might well suggest itself either to the king or to the
thoughtful mind of the adviser, who saw himself at the head of
a church which had been long at uneasy anchorage apart from
those ecclesiastical tumults into the midst of which it was soon
to be hurried. There is something Karolingian in their simplicity, and possibly they may have been suggested by the
germinating Gallicanism of the day. They are, however, of   Their im-
                                                              portance.
great prospective importance and form the basis of that ancient
customary law on which throughout the middle ages the English
church relied in her struggles with the papacy.

The removal of the episcopal sees from the villages or decayed   Removal of
                                                                  episcopal
towns to the cities[1] is another mark of the reign which is signi-   sees.
ficant of change in the ideas of clerical life, but is not of important consequence. The Norman prelate preferred Bath to Wells
and Chester to Lichfield: he felt that he was more at home in
the company of the courtier and warrior than in the monastery.
In the council of London, A.D. 1075, it was determined to remove the see of Sherborne to Old Sarum; that of Selsey to
Chichester; and that of Lichfield to Chester. The see of
Dorchester was removed to Lincoln in 1085; that of Elmham,
which had been transferred to Thetford about 1078, was moved
to Norwich in 1101. The see of Crediton had been transferred
to Exeter in 1050. Bishop John of Wells took up his station
at Bath in 1088[1]. But the change went little further than
this: the monastic rigour was tenacious and aggressive: Lanfranc was himself a monk, and allowed the monastic traditions
of the early English church even more than their due weight in
his reforms[2]. It is now that the secular clerks finally disappear
from those cathedrals which remained monastic until the Reformation. The archbishop seems to have been urged by Alexander   The cathe-
                                                                drals.
II to reorganise the cathedral of Canterbury on monastic principles; and the same pope forbade bishop Walkelin of Winchester to expel the monks from his church. In the reigns of   Canons
                                                                secular and
Edward the Confessor and William, the bishops of Wells, Exeter,   regular.
and York attempted to reduce their canons to rule by ordering

---

[1] See Wilkins, Concilia, i. 363.
[2] See Epistolae Cantuarienses, pref. pp. xx–xxvi.

them to have a common refectory and dormitory. They were unable to enforce the command. The institution of Augustinian, or Regular, canons, which resulted from the like projects of reform was not adopted in any English cathedral until the see of Carlisle was founded by Henry I, and thus continued the only Augustinian cathedral in England until the Reformation, although many of the Scottish cathedrals were made Augustinian

Question of monasticism in the cathedrals.

in the twelfth and thirteenth centuries. The abuses of the rich foundations by married canons, who would perpetuate a hereditary clerical caste, were glaring; and so strong was their interest in both Normandy and England that neither legal nor ecclesiastical discouragement could, for a century and a half, avail to extinguish the evil[1]. The cathedrals were at last divided between the two monastic and secular systems in nearly equal proportions. Canterbury, Winchester, Durham, Coventry, Norwich, Rochester, Worcester, Ely, and Bath were left to the monks; York, London, Exeter, Lichfield, Wells, Hereford, Lincoln, Salisbury, and Chichester were secured to the canons. But the reforming prelates showed no wish to

Growth of the chapters and convents.

throw in their lot with their churches. The bishop's share of the estates was separated from that of the monks, and the exemptions which had been obtained by the favoured noncathedral monasteries were grasped at by the conventual cathedrals in order to oust the jurisdiction of the bishop in the house and in the property of his chapter. Thus even when the sees were transferred to the cities, it was rather the cathedral body than its nominal head that increased in power and pomp. New churches rivalling in beauty and size those of the continent began to be built, and hospitable establishments to be doubled.

New orders of monks.

New orders were instituted in quick succession. The canonical reform failed, but the Augustinian canons grew up out of the failure: every attempt at monastic development took ultimately the form of a new rule, and in England all found a ready and too liberal welcome. In many instances this liberality was exercised at the expense of the parish churches, and an evil precedent was established which outlived in its effects very much

[1] Epp. Cantuar. pref. xxvi.

of the advantage gained from monastic piety and cultivation. But these results are yet far distant.

102. A general view of the reign of the Conqueror suggests the conclusion that, notwithstanding the strength of his personal character, and his maintenance of his right as king of the English and patron of the people both in church and in state;—notwithstanding the clearness of his political designs and the definiteness and solidity of his principles of action, there was very much in the state system which he initiated that still lay in solution. So much depended on the personal relations between himself and Lanfranc in church matters, that after their deaths the whole ecclesiastical fabric narrowly escaped destruction; and in temporal matters also, Lanfranc's influence excepted, the king had no constitutional adviser, no personal friend whose authority contained any element of independence. William is his own minister. His policy, so far as it is his own, owes its stability to his will. His witan are of his own creation,—feudatories powerful in enmity, no source of strength even when they are friends and allies,—with a policy of their own which he is determined to combat. His people fear him even when and where they trust him: he is under no real constraint, whether of law or conscience, to rule them well. His rule is despotic therefore, in spite of the old national and constitutional forms which he suffers to exist: it is the rule of a wise and wary, a strong and resolute, not a wanton and arbitrary despot; it avoids the evils of irresponsible tyranny, because he who exercises it has learned to command himself as well as other men. But a change of sovereign can turn the severe and wary rule into savage licence; and the people, who have grown up and have been educated under a loose, disorganised polity, see no difference between discipline and oppression. The constitutional effects of the Conquest are not worked out in William's reign, but in that of Henry I. The moral training of the nation does not as yet go beyond castigation: the lowest depth of humiliation has yet to be reached, but even that yields necessary lessons of its own. It is useless to ask what the result would have been if the first Norman king had been such a man as William

Transitional character of the Conqueror's reign.

General character of his government.

Rufus: but it was most fortunate for the English that in the hour of their great peril, when they had neither ruler, counsel, nor system, they fell under the rule of one who was a law to himself, who saw the coincidence of duty and policy, and preferred the forms of ancient royalty to the more ostentatious position of a feudal conqueror. He was a hard man, austere, exacting, oppressive: his heavy hand made the English themselves comprehend their own national unity through a community of suffering. Yet in the suffering they were able to discern that there might be still worse things to bear: one strong master was better than many weak ones, general oppression than actual anarchy. The king made and kept good peace. The Danegeld and the Forest-law were not too much to pay for the escape from private war and feudal disruption.

CHAPTER X.

103. THE political history of the Conqueror's reign consists Political
mainly in the three great struggles with the native English, history of
with the rebellious earls, and with the disobedient heir. The queror's
foreign wars and the constitutional measures which they in- reign.
volved were in close connexion with one or other of these
struggles.

Under the first head are comprised the several contests with
the English which either arose from the unextinguished spirit
of resistance to conquest, or were provoked by the severity of
the Norman ministers, or were stimulated by the hopes entertained by dynastic partisans that the crown might be recovered
for their respective leaders. In 1067, when William was in
Normandy, the Northumbrians slew Copsi, the intruded earl ;
the men of Herefordshire with the aid of the Welsh rose against
William Fitz-Osbern, and Kent, prompted by Eustace of Boulogne, revolted against Odo of Bayeux. In 1068 the family of
Godwin were in arms ; the widowed Gytha held out at Exeter,

and after the submission of Exeter the sons of Harold attempted to seize Bristol. The same year Edwin and Morcar raised the standard of resistance in Mercia, Edgar Atheling and Gospatric in Northumbria. The next year the sons of Harold again attacked Devonshire, and the Danish allies of Edgar Atheling drew down William's exemplary vengeance on the North. In 1070 and 1071 the embers of English independence burst into flame and were extinguished in the Fen country; Edwin lost his life and Morcar his liberty. The result of the disjointed struggles was to throw the whole country under the feet of the Conqueror in a prostration more abject than any to which his mere aggressive ambition could have reduced it. In detail and in sum William was victorious, partly through the still unbroken force of his own power as leader of the Norman host, and partly through the want of concert among his enemies. The family of Godwin, whose strength lay in the support of Welsh and Irish princes, had not a single principle in common with the remnant of the West-Saxon house, whose allies were in Scotland and Denmark. Eadric the Wild might raise Herefordshire, but he was too far away to help the men of Kent. The strong and united Norman force met them and crushed them separately. The terrible vengeance wreaked on the Northumbrian population effectually prevented any further attempt at a rising, and the English found in obedience to one strong ruler a source of unity, strength, and safety, such as they had not possessed since the days of Edgar. They suffered, without power to rebel, until all the old causes of division amongst them were forgotten.

Struggles of the English.

The second series of events begins with the conspiracy of the earls in A.D. 1075. This conspiracy opens a new page of history which possesses far more constitutional interest than that which preceded it. The speeches put by Ordericus Vitalis in the mouths of the conspirators give a clue to the understanding of the next century. Roger of Breteuil and Ralph Guader, the former being earl of Herefordshire, the latter of Norfolk or East-Anglia, were discontented with the ample provision that the king had made for them, and made a statement of their

Conspiracy of the earls.

grievances, which the historian elaborates into a speech [1]. Its objects
and pleas.
William they said was a bastard and had seized the English
crown unrighteously ; he had oppressed his nobles in Normandy,
despoiled the count of Mortain, poisoned the counts of Brittany
and of the Vexin ; he had refused to reward the followers who
had fought his battles, or had given them only barren and
desolate lands. The English, although they would gladly have
had revenge, are described as contentedly cultivating their
lands, and more intent on enjoyment than on battle. The mal-
contents propose to earl Waltheof that England should be restored to the state in which it was in King Edward's time ; one
of the three should be king, the other two should be dukes [2].
Waltheof declined the project, but fell a victim to the suspicious
hatred of William, who spared the lives of the real offenders.
The grounds of the discontent thus stated seem to include three Objects of
the conspi-
points—the title of the king, the condition of the English, and racy of the
earls.
the restrictions imposed upon the Norman vassals : and these
are the very points which give interest to the history of the
Norman period ; for a century, no king succeeds with undis-
puted title ; the Norman baronage is incessantly in arms in

---

[1] Ord. Vit. iv. 14 : 'Degener, utpote nothus, est qui rex nuncupatur, et
in propatulo divinitus monstratur quod Deo displicet, dum talis herus regno
praesidet. . . . Ipse Willelmum Warlengum Moritolii comitem pro uno verbo
exhereditavit, et de Neustria penitus effugavit ; Walterium Pontesii comitem
Edwardi regis nepotem, cum Biota uxore sua Falesiae hospitavit, et nefaria
potione simul ambos una nocte peremit. Conanum quoque strenuissimum
consulem veneno infecit. . . . Haec et alia multa erga cognatos et affines suos
scelera Willelmus peregit, qui super nos et compares nostros adhuc similia
perpetrare non desistit. Nobile regnum Angliae temere invasit, genuinos
heredes injuste trucidavit vel in exilium crudeliter pepulit. Suos quoque
adjutores, per quos super omne genus suum sublimatus est, non ut decuisset
honoravit, sed multis qui sanguinem suum in ejus satellitio fuderunt ingratus
exstitit, et pro frivolis occasionibus ad mortem usque velut hostes puniit.
Vulneratis victoribus steriles fundos et hostium depopulatione desolatos
donavit, et eisdem postmodum restauratos avaritia cogente abstulit seu
minoravit. . . . Ecce major pars exercitus trans pontum moratur, assiduisque
bellis acriter occupatus detinetur. Angli sua solummodo rura colunt,
conviviis et potationibus, non praeliis intendunt, summopere tamen pro
suorum exitio parentum ultionem videre concupiscunt.'

[2] Ibid. 'Acquiesce nobis et indesinenter inhaere, et tertiam partem
Angliae nobiscum sine dubio poteris habere. Volumus enim ut status regni
Albionis redintegretur omnimodis sicut olim fuit tempore Edwardi piissimi
regis. Unus ex nobis sit rex et duo sint duces et sic nobis tribus omnes
Anglorum subjicientur honores.'

order to extend their own power, taking advantage of every quarrel, and ranging themselves with the king or against him on no principle save the desire of strengthening their own position; and the English are found by the king and his ministers to be the only trustworthy element in society, notwithstanding their sufferings and the many attempts made to draw them from their allegiance. The reign of William Rufus exhibits the several elements of disturbance in open working, and throws into light the different interests which had been operating obscurely and confusedly under the sagacious pressure of his father's hand.

Importance of the question of title in its bearings on other points of constitutional interest.

104. The question of personal title, the right to the headship of the races ruled by the Conqueror, on which the third class of his difficulties turn, is not directly connected with constitutional history. But its bearing on the political development of England is most important, and in its many complexities it touches the main sources of constitutional growth. The duke of the Normans had acquired the realm of England, by the gift of God, as he himself said, and by the acceptance of the English witenagemot, but directly by the arms of the Norman race. The Normans had availed themselves of William's ambition, strength, and supposititious claims as Edward's heir, and had established their hold on England ; but William himself they had never loved, they despised his birth, and feared and detested the very strength which sustained them. His position as duke of the Normans had been won through rivers of blood, and by the violent extinction of every element of rivalry. England was the conquest of the race, or of a voluntary association under the head of the race. But William's hold on England could not be shaken without risking the loss of England to the race itself. And yet William had most grudgingly rewarded their aid and reluctantly acknowledged their claims. Should England and Normandy be separated, should the headship of the race continue in the progeny of the bastard, or should advantage be taken of every opportunity of raising either question, to secure more independent power to the feudatories and reduce their king-duke to the position of the king-duke of the

The great vassals take advantage of every question of royal title.

French? On whatever plea the struggle arose, the main object of the Norman nobles was the securing of feudal power,
and the unavoidable result of such a consummation would be
the entire enslaving of the English. Hence it was that none
of the great houses maintained a consistent policy; none of
them sincerely believed in the grounds put forth as pretexts of
quarrel; but they fought first on one side and then on the other,
and purchased promises from either side by alternate offers of
support. And the necessary result of this was their own destruction. In such a struggle royalty must win in the end,
and whichever of the competitors for it ultimately succeeds
will take care to make his position safe against such uncertain
friends and such certain foes.

The conspiracy of A.D. 1075 is the first epoch of the struggle; Rebellion
of Robert.
the last of the English earls perished in consequence, and the
first of the Norman earls suffered forfeiture. The long series
of humiliations which they brought upon themselves began.
They had asserted the right of the race and the deserts of the
confederacy. The rebellion of Robert followed in A.D. 1078; He is sup-
ported by
the younger
men.
he claimed the Norman duchy by his father's gift, and was
supported by four of the greatest barons of the new aristocracy,
Robert of Belesme, William of Breteuil, Roger of Bienfaite, and
Robert Mowbray, the heirs of William's oldest and most trusted
ministers[1]. That rebellion was quelled, and without much
bloodshed or confiscation, though the king did not feel himself
secure without imprisoning and dispossessing his brother Odo
of Bayeux: and the war that was kindled by it opened the way
for the aggression of the French king which William was en-
gaged in repelling at the time of his death. His confession on William's
retrospect
on his death-
bed.
his deathbed, if actually made as related by Ordericus, is one of
the most singular monuments of history. He looked back for
fifty-six years on Normandy, and recounted what he suffered at

---

[1] Robert of Belesme was son of Roger Montgomery, earl of Shrewsbury;
William of Breteuil, son of William Fitz-Osbern; Roger of Bienfaite, son
of Richard and grandson of Gilbert of Brionne, the Conqueror's guardian;
Robert Mowbray was nephew and heir of Bishop Gosfrid of Coutances:
all trusted ministers of William, three of whom had actually been justiciars,
or royal lieutenants. See Ord. Vit. v. 10.

the hand of his enemies and how he had repaid them. He looked forward also, and augured for the future; but he did not attempt to do violence to destiny. Robert must have Normandy; William he wished, but dared not command, should have England; Henry he was sure would have all in the end. His experience suggested much misgiving, but furnished no means of directing the future. He saw the struggle that must come as soon as his death opened the question[1]. He died on the 9th of September, 1087.

Robert's claim on England defeated.

The claim of Robert to the whole of his father's dominions was taken up by the restless barons at once: far the larger part adhered to him, especially his father's brothers Odo of Bayeux and Robert of Mortain; also Gosfrid of Coutances, Robert Mowbray and Roger Montgomery: indeed, all the princes of the Conquest except the earl of Chester and William of Warenne[2]. William overcame the opposition, but was not yet strong enough to punish it. The only great forfeiture was Odo's earldom of Kent. Seven years later, in 1095, an attempt was made to get rid altogether of the Conqueror's heirs, and to assert for Count Stephen of Aumâle, the grandson of duke Robert the Second[3], the headship of the race[4]. This also failed, and was followed by considerable but still cautious forfeitures; the great earl Robert Mowbray of Northumberland lost his liberty and estates; Roger de Lacy was deprived of his

Stephen of Aumâle set up against William Rufus.

Forfeitures.

---

[1] Ord. Vit. vii. 15, 16.

[2] Ordericus mentions, as taking part in the first rising on Robert's behalf, Bishop Odo, Eustace of Boulogne, Robert of Belesme, and his father Roger Montgomery (secretly), Hugh of Grantmesnil, and Bernard of Neufmarché; lib. viii. c. 2. Florence adds Gosfrid of Coutances, Robert of Mortain, and Robert Mowbray, the last of whom is placed by Ordericus on the side of William Rufus, and the bishop of Durham. On the king's side were Hugh of Chester, William of Warenne, and Robert Fitz-Hamon; but the mainstay of the party was Lanfranc.

[3] Odo of Aumâle, the father of count Stephen, was married to a sister of the Conqueror, who is said distinctly by Ordericus to have been daughter of duke Robert and Harlotta (lib. iv. c. 7). The Continuator of William of Jumieges (ed. Camden, p. 687) calls her the uterine sister of the Conqueror; it is impossible that the Normans should have accepted the idea of electing an entire stranger to the ducal house. See Stapleton, Rot. Scacc. Norm. vol. ii. p. xxxi.

[4] The heads of this revolt were, according to Florence, Robert Mowbray earl of Northumberland, and William of Eu. Orderic adds Roger de Lacy and earl Hugh of Shrewsbury. Ord. Vit. viii. 23.

hundred and sixteen manors, the earl of Shrewsbury paid an enormous fine, William of Eu was mutilated. A great gap was already made in the phalanx of the feudatories; the death of William stayed but did not avert the destruction of the rest.

105. But far more important in principle than the demo-lition of the single feudatories is the relation created and strengthened between the king and the native English. The Conqueror's last wish for the disposal of England was confided to Lanfranc, as the head of the witenagemot of the kingdom: and Lanfranc proceeded to secure the fulfilment of it in such a constitutional way as lay open to him, when the majority of the baronage were inclining to duke Robert. William was ready to make any promise to secure his crown. He swore to Lan-franc that if he were made king he would preserve justice and equity and mercy throughout the realm, would defend against all men the peace, liberty, and security of the churches, and would in all things and through all things comply with his precepts and counsels[1]. On this understanding Lanfranc crowned him and re-ceived the formal enunciation of the engagement in the coronation oaths. The outbreak of war immediately after forced from him another acknowledgment of his duty. He found Lanfranc his ablest adviser, Wulfstan his most energetic supporter; he called the English together, declared to them the treason of the Normans, and begged their aid. If they would assist him and be faithful in this need, he would grant them even a better law than they would choose for themselves; he forbade on the instant all unjust taxation, and surrendered his hold on their forests[2].

The people are thrown on the side of the crown.

Promise of William Rufus: at his coro-nation:

in the time of rebellion.

---

[1] 'Verens ne dilatio consecrationis suae inferret ei dispendium cupiti honoris, coepit, tam per se quam per omnes quos poterat, fide sacramentoque Lanfranco promittere justitiam, aequitatem et misericordiam se per totum regnum, si rex foret, in omni negotio servaturum; pacem, libertatem, secu-ritatem ecclesiarum contra omnes defensurum; necnon praeceptis atque consiliis ejus per omnia et in omnibus obtemperaturum.' Eadmer, Hist. Nov. i. p. 14.

[2] Of this second formal engagement to govern well we have four accounts. (1) Florence says: 'Congregato vero quantum ad praesens poterat Nor-mannorum, sed tamen maxime Anglorum, equestri et pedestri licet mediocri exercitu, statuens leges, promittens fautoribus omnia bona . . . tendere

Promises of
William
Rufus;

The English too willingly believed him, and, throwing themselves with energy into the struggle, brought it to a successful
issue. The king forgot his promises, and, when reminded of
them by Lanfranc, answered in wrath, 'Who is there who can
fulfil all that he promises?' Lanfranc's death removed his
best counsellor, and he began to act with unrestrained and

during his
illness.

wanton tyranny. A third time, in A.D. 1093, when he either
believed himself to be dying or wished to purchase a reprieve by
repentance, he made a formal declaration, pledging his faith and
making the bishops the sureties between himself and his God,
sending them to make the promises for him before the altar. A
written proclamation was made and sealed, all prisoners were to
be released, all debts pardoned, and all offences forgiven and forgotten. To all the people moreover were promised good and
holy laws, the inviolable observance of right, and a severe
examination into wrongs such as should frighten all men from

disposuit Roveceastram.' (2) Simeon of Durham: ' Hoc audito rex fecit
convocare Anglos et ostendit eis traditionem Normannorum et rogavit ut
sibi auxilio essent, eo tenore ut, si in hac necessitate sibi fideles existerent,
meliorem legem quam vellent eligere eis concederet, et omnem injustum
scottum interdixit et concessit omnibus silvas suas et venationem.   Sed
quicquid promisit parvo tempore custodivit. Angli tamen fideliter eum
juvabant.' (3) William of Malmesbury, G. R. iv. § 306: ' Videns Normannos pene omnes in una rabie conspiratos, Anglos probos et fortes viros
qui adhuc residui erant, invitatoriis scriptis accersiit; quibus super injuriis
suis querimoniam faciens, bonasque leges et tributorum levamen liberasque
venationes pollicens, fidelitati suae obligavit . . . Anglos suos appellat;
jubet ut compatriotas advocent ad obsidionem venire, nisi si qui velint sub
nomine *Nithing*, quod nequam sonat, remanere. Angli qui nihil miserius
putarent quam hujusce vocabuli dedecore aduri, catervatim ad regem
confluunt et invincibilem exercitum faciunt.' (4) Ordericus, viii. 2:
' Lanfrancum itaque archiepiscopum cum suffraganeis praesulibus, comites,
Anglosque naturales convocavit, et conatus adversariorum ac velle suum
expugnandi eos indicavit. At illi regem ut perturbatores pacis comprimeret
adhortati sunt, seseque promptissimos ad adjuvandum polliciti sunt.
Anglorum vero triginta millia tunc ad servitium regis sponte sua convenerunt, regemque ut perfidos proditores absque respectu puniret admonuerunt,
dicentes "Viriliter age ut regis filius et legitime ad regnum assumptus,
securus in hoc regno dominare omnibus. Nonne vides quot tecum sumus,
tibique gratanter paremus? Passim per totam Albionem impera omnesque
rebelles dejice regali justitia. Usque ad mortem pro te certabimus, nec
unquam tibi alium praeponemus. Stultum nimis et profanum noto regi
praeferre hostem extraneum. Detestabilis gens est quae principi suo infida
est. Phalanx morti sit vicina quae domini sui gaudet ruina. Solerter
Anglorum rimare historias, inveniesque semper fidos principibus suis
Angligenas."'

evil-doing [1]. The king recovered, but behaved worse than ever [2].

The acknowledgments of his duty were however not without their value. The charter, if it ever existed, was lost, and the benefits it promised were withheld. The quarrel with the Church followed, and the wretched king cast away even the outward observance of morality and religion. But he had testified to the nation his own duty and their right. He had revealed to them their moral and material strength at the same time. Fear of man and dread of God's present judgment forced him to the promise which was a confession of justice, and placed means in their hands which would set their rights on a firmer basis than the conscience of a tyrant. If the reign of William Rufus had no other importance, it taught a lesson of profoundly valuable consequence to his successor.

Value of these acknowledgments of duty.

106. It is not easy at first sight to determine exactly the particular measures by which, in spite of his professions of good government and the support which he purchased by them, William Rufus earned the detestation of all classes of his subjects. The historians describe him as a strong, fierce, and arrogant man, of abandoned habits, cruel, profane, and avaricious ; but their general declamatory tone hides rather than reveals the constitutional grievances, except where they touched the Church.

Special acts of tyranny of William Rufus.

---

[1] Florence says : ' Cum se putaret cito moriturum, ut ei sui barones suggesserunt, vitam suam corrigere, ecclesias non amplius vendere nec ad censum ponere, sed illas regia tueri potestate, irrectas leges destruere ac rectas statuere Deo promisit.' Eadmer, Hist. Nov. i. p. 16 : ' Adquiescit ipse, et corde compunctus cuncta quae viri sententia tulit se facturum necnon totam vitam suam in mansuetudine et justitia amplius servaturum pollicetur. Spondet in hoc fidem suam, et vades inter se et Deum facit episcopos suos, mittens qui hoc votum suum Deo super altare sua vice promittant. Scribitur edictum regioque sigillo firmatur, quatenus captivi quicunque sunt in omni dominatione sua relaxentur, omnia debita irrevocabiliter remittantur, omnes offensiones ante haec perpetratae indulta remissione perpetuae oblivioni tradantur. Promittuntur insuper omni populo bonae et sanctae leges, inviolabilis observatio juris, injuriarum gravis et quae terreat ceteros examinatio.'

[2] ' Willelmus in principio infirmius laboriosiusque imperaret, et ad conciliandos sibi animos subditorum modestior mitiorque appareret. At postquam, perdomitis hostibus et fratre mollius agente, roboratum est regnum ejus, exaltatum est illico cor ejus, apparuitque succedentibus prosperis qualis apud se latuisset dum premeretur adversis ; ' Will. Newb. i. 2.

We may however, by comparing the remedial measures of **Henry** I with what is known of the law and custom of the Conqueror's reign, form some idea of the nature of the tyranny of William Rufus. Ranulf Flambard, an able and unprincipled clerk, who had been long acquainted with England [1], and was restrained by no sympathies with either the Norman nobles, the native population, or the clergy, was after the death of Lanfranc taken by the king into his confidence. Whether or not it is fair to ascribe to Ranulf the suggestion of the tyrannical policy which marks the reign, it is to him without doubt that the systematic organisation of the exactions is to be attributed. He possessed, as the king's justiciar, the management of all the fiscal and judicial business of the kingdom, and seems to have exercised the functions of his office with indefatigable zeal. William, on the other hand, although an able soldier and not deficient in political craft, has left no traces of administrative power such as mark the rule of his father and brother.

Ranulf's policy seems to have been to tighten as much as possible the hold which the feudal law gave to the king on all feudatories temporal and spiritual, taking the fullest advantage of every opportunity, and delaying by unscrupulous chicanery the determination of every dispute. In ecclesiastical matters this plan was systematically pursued. The analogy of lay fiefs was applied to the churches with as much minuteness as was possible. The feudal relation had been recognised in the Conqueror's reign, the great question of investitures being set aside by the mutual good understanding of king and primate; but the obligation was liberally construed on both sides. Lanfranc did his duty as a great noble, and William contented himself with the constitutional claims to which the earlier system had regarded the archbishop as liable. No advantage was taken of the vacancies of sees or abbeys to draw the revenues of the Church into the royal treasury, or by prolonging the vacancy to increase the accumulations on which the king might lay his hand; on the contrary, we are distinctly informed that the revenues of the vacant churches were collected and preserved in

Administration of Ranulf Flambard.

In ecclesiastical matters.

Prolongation of vacancies.

[1] See Chap. XI, below.

safe custody for the new prelates, and that the elections were not unduly postponed[1]. The elections were themselves scarcely canonical, but all difficulties were avoided by Lanfranc, who suggested the best men to the king for that formal nomination which had taken the place of election.

Ranulf Flambard saw no other difference between an ecclesi- astical and a lay fief than the superior facilities which the first gave for extortion; the dead bishop left no heir who could importunately insist on receiving seisin of his inheritance; and it was in his master's power to determine how soon or at what price an heir should be created and admitted. The vacancies of the churches were prolonged indefinitely, in spite of canon and custom; their property was taken into the king's hands and administered by his officers just as the barony of a ward of the crown might be; and all proceeds were claimed for the king. Not only so; the lands were let out on farm[2], a large fine paid down at once, and a small rent promised for the future: the king secured the fine, the bishop might or might not recover the rent. Further, the longer the vacancy lasted the less chance there was of redress being enforced when it was at last filled up; the king could even grant away the lands of the Church as hereditary fiefs to his knights, and refuse to admit a new bishop until he had promised to ratify his gifts. Lastly, he might, on the analogy of the relief payable by the heir of a lay fief, demand of the new bishop such a payment on entry as gave to the whole transaction a simoniacal complexion[3]. All these claims were contrary to the terms on which the endowments of the Church

Churches treated as lay fees.

---

[1] W. Malmesb. iv. § 314: 'Tempore patris post decessum episcopi vel abbatis omnes reditus integre custodiebantur, substituendo pastori resig- nandi, eligebanturque personae religionis merito laudabiles.' See also Ord. Vit. viii. 8, who distinctly charges Ranulf Flambard with introducing the evil custom.

[2] 'Ad censum primitus abbatias, dehinc episcopatus, quorum patres e vita discesserant noviter, accepit a rege et inde singulis annis summam pecuniae non modicam persolvit illi;' Flor. Wig. A.D. 1100.

[3] Henry's promises in his charter prove the existence of all these exactions under his brother: 'Sanctam Dei ecclesiam imprimis liberam facio, ita quod nec vendam, nec ad firmam ponam, nec mortuo archiepiscopo sive episcopo sive abbate aliquid accipiam de dominico ecclesiae vel de hominibus ejus donec successor in eam ingrediatur.'

had been granted ; but they were in accord to a certain extent with the feudal spirit now introduced into the country, and the very fact that they were made shows how strongly that spirit had made itself felt. The Church was open to these claims because she furnished no opportunity for reliefs, wardships, marriage, escheat, or forfeiture[1].

Treatment of feudal vassals by William Rufus.

107. From the treatment of the churches conversely the treatment of the feudal landowners may be inferred : and the charter of Henry I confirms the inference ; although it is not quite so clear as in the former case that all the evil customs owed their origin to the reign of William Rufus. On the death of a vassal the heir was not admitted until he paid such relief as the king would accept[2]; the amount demanded was sometimes so great as to equal the value of the property ; the estate might therefore be altogether resumed, or it might be retained in the king's hands as long as he pleased : and this shameless exercise of power was aggravated by the practice of disregarding the testamentary disposition of the vassal, so as to leave his family pauperised[3]. The right of marriage, that is, of consenting to the marriage of the daughters of vassals, was interpreted to mean the right to exact a sum of money for consent[4] : if the marriage in question were that of an heiress or widow, the king disposed of it without any reference to the will of the bride or her relations. The right of wardship was asserted unrestrictedly.

Indefiniteness of the royal claims.

The amercements for offences were arbitrary : a vassal might be accused of crime and find himself liable to forfeiture, or to give such security as made him constantly amenable to forfeiture[5]. In all these points the royal claims were unrelentingly pressed.

---

[1] 'He desired to be the heir of every one, churchman or layman ;' Chron. Sax. A.D. 1100.

[2] Art. 2 of Henry's charter : 'Si quis .... mortuus fuerit, heres suus non redimet terram suam sicut faciebat tempore fratris mei ;' see Ord. Vit. viii. 8.

[3] See Henry's charter, art. 7 : 'Si quis baronum vel hominum meorum infirmabitur, sicut ipse dabit vel dare disponet pecuniam suam, ita datam esse concedo. Quod si ipse praeventus armis vel infirmitate, pecuniam suam non dederit vel dare disposuerit, uxor sua sive liberi aut parentes, et legitimi homines ejus, eam pro anima ejus dividant, sicut eis melius visum fuerit.'

[4] See art. 3 of Henry's charter.　　　　[5] See art. 8 of Henry's charter.

Not less heavy was the king's hand on the body of the people. Oppression of the people at large. On them in the first instance fell the burden of the imposts laid on their feudal masters. It was from them, by similar exactions of reliefs, wardship, marriage, and forfeitures, that the vassals raised money to redeem their own rights: every wrong that the king inflicted on his vassals they might inflict on theirs. But the king too had a direct hold on them; he demanded the old tribute, the hateful Danegeld: he had the power to insist on their military service, and did so: on one occasion Ranulf brought down a great force of the fyrd to Hastings, and there took from them the money that the shires had furnished them with, the ten shillings for maintenance, and sent them penniless home[1]. He took advantage of the simple machinery of justice to tax them further. Ranulf was not only the ' exactor ' of all the business of the kingdom, but the ' placitator' also. ' He drove and commanded all his gemots over all England[2].' His management broke up for a time the old arrangements of the hundred and shire-moots, making them mere engines of extortion, so that men rather acquiesced in wrong than sought redress at such a price. It is probable further that the assemblies which met on these occasions were turned to profit, being forced or persuaded to give sums towards the king's necessities. The subordinates of the court followed the example of their chief; no man was safe against them; the poor man was not protected by his poverty, nor the rich by his abundance[3]. The very recent Story of the new survey. Domesday taxation was, we are told, superseded by a new valuation; the old English hide was cut down to the acreage of the Norman carucate[4]: and thus estates were curtailed and taxation increased at the same time. Whether the charge is definitely

---

[1] 'Quibus ut mare transirent Heastingae congregatis, pecuniam quae data fuerat eis ad victum Rannulfus Passeflambardus praecepto regis abstulit, scilicet unicuique decem solidos, et eos domum repedare mandavit, pecuniam vero regi transmisit;' Flor. Wig. A.D. 1094.

[2] Chron. Sax. A.D. 1099. On the justiciarship in the hands of Ranulf, see further, Chap. XI, below.

[3] On the enormities of the king's followers, who made his progresses through the country resemble the march of a devastating army, see W. Malmesb. G. R. iv. §§ 314, 319; Eadmer, iv. p. 94; Ord. Vit. viii. 4.

[4] Ord. Vit. viii. 8; see below, Chap. XI, §§ 107, 120, 126.

true may be questioned, for the testimony on which it rests is not confirmed by distinct statements of the English annalists; but it is not improbable; and the burden was but one of many.

Forest op-pressions. The forest law or lawlessness now comes into marked prominence. William the Conqueror had afforested and desolated large territories for the chase. His son made the practice burdensome to baron and villein alike; a vexation to the one, destruction and extermination to the other. Unrestrained by religion, by principle, or by policy, with no family interests to limit his greed, extravagance, or hatred of his kind, a foul incarnation of selfishness in its most abhorrent form, the enemy of God and man, William Rufus gave to England and Christendom a pattern of

Death of William Rufus, Aug. 2, 1100. absolutism. It is only to be ascribed to the weakness and disunion of those whom he wronged that he burdened the throne and nation for twelve long years of misery.

Succession of Henry I. 108. The great question whether England should or should not be ruled by the head of the Norman race was decided by the promptness of Henry in his own favour. Robert continued indeed to represent to the mind of the feudatories the principle of the Conquest; by the treaty arranged at Caen in A.D. 1091 he was entitled, as far as William's power of disposition went, to the succession: he had received the homage of his brother and of the great barons of the kingdom, and he had few personal enemies. But he was far away from England at the critical moment; his right to the crown had been disregarded by his father in his settlement of his estates; he had grievously mismanaged the government of Normandy, and, if he had few enemies, he had still fewer friends who would imperil themselves for a prince who might be prompt only to avenge them. Henry was on the spot. The opportunity that a seeming accident supplied he had energy to seize and courage and counsel to improve. The very suddenness of William's death precluded the possibility of preparation on either side. This he turned to profit. The kingdom was taken by surprise, and, when the world knew that William was dead, it knew that Henry had succeeded him.

The accession of Henry was transacted with as much deference

to national precedent as was possible consistently with his pur- Formality of his elec-
pose. Among the few barons who were in attendance on tion.
William on the day of his death were the two Beaumonts, the
earl of Warwick and the count of Meulan, Robert Fitz-Hamon
and William of Breteuil [1]. The last of these made a bold claim
on behalf of Robert, but was overruled by the others [2]; the form
of election was hastily gone through by the barons on the spot ;
and the seizure of the royal hoard in the castle of Winchester
placed in the hands of Henry the means of securing his advantage [3]. His first act was to bestow the vacant see of Winchester
on William Giffard the chancellor, so providing himself with a
strong supporter in the episcopal body. He then hastened to Election and coro-
London, where a few prelates and other nobles were found, who nation of Henry I,
after some discussion determined to accept him as king. The Aug. 5, 1100.
seizure of the royal treasure on Thursday, August 2, was followed by the coronation on the Sunday, August 5. On that
day a comprehensive charter of liberties was published, and
Anselm was recalled. Shortly after Ranulf Flambard was im- His mar-riage, Nov.
prisoned, and before the end of the year the marriage of the 11, 1100.
king with the daughter of Malcolm and Margaret completed the
consolidation of the title by which he intended to reign.

The election was however no mere form. Even in the handful
of barons who were present there were divisions and questionings,
which were allayed, as we are told, by the arguments of the earl
of Warwick [4]. The oaths taken by Ethelred were also required His corona-tion oath.
of Henry : the form of his coronation has been preserved, and it
contains the threefold promise of peace, justice, and equity [5]. In

---

[1] Ordericus mentions Robert of Meulan and William of Breteuil; lib. x.
c. 14. William of Malmesbury mentions the exertions of Henry of
Warwick on Henry's behalf; G. R. v. § 393.

[2] Ord. Vit. x. 14.

[3] William 'was slain on a Thursday and buried the next morning; and
after he was buried, the witan who were then near at hand chose
his brother Henry as king, and he forthwith gave the bishopric of
Winchester to William Giffard, and then went to London;' Chron. Sax.
A.D. 1100.

[4] 'In regem electus est, aliquantis tamen ante controversiis inter proceres agitatis atque sopitis, annitente maxime comite Warwicensi Henrico;'
W. Malmesb. G. R. v. § 393.

[5] Taylor's Glory of Regality, pp. 245, 330 ; Maskell, Mon. Rit. iii. 5, 6.
The oath is as follows: 'In Christi Nomine promitto haec tria populo

His letter
to Anselm.

the letter written by the newly-crowned king to Anselm to recall him to England and to account for the rite of coronation being performed in his absence, Henry states that he has been chosen by the clergy and people of England, and repeats to the archbishop the engagement that his brother had made with Lanfranc : ‘Myself and the people of the whole realm of England I commit to your counsel and that of those who ought with

Charter of
Henry I.

you to counsel me [1].’ The undertaking to govern well was made not only with the archbishop as the first constitutional adviser of the crown, but with the whole nation : it was embodied in a charter addressed to all the faithful, and attested by the witan who were present, the paucity of whose names may perhaps indicate the small number of powerful men who had as yet adhered to him,—the bishops of London and Rochester, the elect of Winchester, the earls of Warwick and Northampton, and four barons [2]. The form of the charter forcibly declares the ground which he was taking : ‘Know ye that by the mercy of God and the common counsel of the barons of the whole realm of England I have been crowned king of the same realm [3].’ The abuses of the late reign are specified and forbidden for the

Privileges
of the
church,

future. The Church is made free from all the unjust exactions; and the kingdom from the evil customs : to the English people are restored the laws of King Edward with the Conqueror’s amendments ; the feudal innovations, inordinate and arbitrary

---

Christiano mihi subdito. In primis, me praecepturum et operam pro viribus impensurum ut ecclesia Dei et omnis populus Christianus veram pacem nostro arbitrio in omni tempore servet ; aliud ut rapacitates et omnes iniquitates omnibus gradibus interdicam ; tertium ut in omnibus judiciis aequitatem et misericordiam praecipiam, ut mihi et vobis indulgeat Suam misericordiam clemens et misericors Deus ;’ see above, p. 164.

[1] It is printed among Anselm’s letters; lib. iii. Ep. 41 : ‘Ego nutu Dei a clero et a populo Angliae electus, et, quamvis invitus propter absentiam tui, rex jam consecratus, requiro te sicut patrem cum omni populo Angliae, quatenus mihi filio tuo et eidem populo cujus tibi animarum cura commissa est quam citius poteris venias ad consulendum. Meipsum quidem ac totius regni Angliae populum tuo eorumque consilio qui tecum mihi consulere debent committo.’

[2] The four barons are Walter Giffard, Robert de Montfort, Roger Bigot, and Henry de Port. The letter to Anselm furnishes the additional names of Gerard bishop of Hereford, William Warelwast, Robert Fitz-Hamon, and Haimo dapifer.

[3] Ancient Laws, ed. Thorpe, p. 215 ; Select Charters, p. 96.

reliefs and amercements, the abuse of the rights of wardship and of the vassals,
marriage, the despotic interference with testamentary disposition,
all of which had been common in the last reign, are renounced;
and, as a special boon to tenants by knight-service, their demesne lands are freed from all demands except service in the
field. To the whole nation is promised peace and good coin- and of the nation.
age : the debts due to William Rufus, and the murder-fines
incurred before the day of coronation, are forgiven. But the
forests, as they were in the Conqueror's time, are retained by
the king with the common consent of his barons[1]. Perhaps
the most significant articles of the whole document are those by
which he provides that the benefit of the feudal concessions
shall not be engrossed by the tenants in chief: 'in like manner Henry I provides
shall the men of my barons relieve their lands at the hand of for the ex-
their lords by a just and lawful relief;' 'in like manner I enjoin tension of his reforms
that my barons restrain themselves in dealing with the sons and to the nation at large.
daughters and wives of their men[2].' The rights of the classes
that had taken the oath of fealty to the Conqueror at Salisbury
are thus guarded, and Henry, whilst attempting, by granting
special boons to each order in the state, to secure the good-will
of all, definitely commits himself to the duties of a national
king. He was the native king, born on English soil, son of the
king, not merely, like Robert and William, of the duke of the
Normans. The return of Anselm, the punishment of Flambard,
and the royal marriage[3] were earnests of what was to result
from the government so claimed and so inaugurated.

[1] Art. 10: 'Forestas communi consensu baronum meorum in manu mea
retinui, sicut pater meus eas habuit.'

[2] Art. 2: 'Similiter et homines baronum meorum justa et legitima rele-
vatione relevabunt terras suas de dominis suis.' Art. 4: 'Et praecipio
quod barones mei similiter se contineant erga filios et filias vel uxores
hominum suorum.' Compare the words of Charles the Bald in the
Capitula at Kiersi, in 877 : 'Volumus atque praecipimus ut tam episcopi
quam abbates et comites seu etiam ceteri fideles nostri hoc erga homines
suos studeant conservare ; ' Pertz, Legg. i. 537.

[3] The historians of the time do not dwell much on the political importance
of the marriage, although it kept England and Scotland in peace for nearly
two centuries; and to a certain extent tended to restore the nationality of
the royal house. That the latter point was not overlooked at the time
seems clear from William of Malmesbury's story that the Norman barons
spoke in derision of the king and queen as Godric and Godgifu ; G. R.
v. § 394.

Struggle
with Duke
Robert.

109. But these measures had scarcely been completed when duke Robert returned from the Holy Land; the echoes of the investiture controversy in the empire were already sounding in the distance, and the great feudatories in Normandy as well as in England were preparing for a trial of strength. The quarrel with Robert broke out early in A.D. 1101. Henry threw himself on the support of the English [1], Robert availed himself of

The struggle
averted.

the discontent of the feudatories and invaded England. But when the armies stood face to face the brothers saw that the fruits of victory must fall to those whose strength would be the destruction of the victor, and that the time was not come for a struggle which would make either of them supreme. The count of Meulan proposed peace, and peace was made. Robert recognised Henry as king and released him from his fealty. Henry undertook to pay Robert a heavy pension, and restored to him the Côtentin, the Norman district which he had purchased of

It is renewed
in 1104.

him in his great necessity. In A.D. 1104 the quarrel was renewed. Robert had again proved himself to be neither wise enough nor strong enough to govern the Normans, and Henry appeared in Normandy as a deliverer. But again the struggle was settled without bloodshed. Robert transferred to his brother the homage of the count of Evreux and Henry was satisfied [2]. The next year, finding his Norman estates imperilled by the irrepressible allies of Robert, he again crossed the sea and added Caen and Bayeux to his possessions [3], leaving Robert on his return destitute alike of funds and supporters. In A.D. 1106

---

[1] 'Licet principibus deficientibus partes ejus solidae manebant, quas Anselmi archiepiscopi cum episcopis suis simul et omnium Anglorum tutabatur favor. Quapropter ipse provincialium fidei gratus et saluti providus, plerumque cuneos circuiens, docebat quomodo militum ferociam eludentes clypeos objectarent et ictus remitterent; quo effecit ut ultroneis votis pugnam deposcerent, in nullo Normannos metuentes;' W. Malmesb. G. R. v. § 395. 'Venerabilis Anselmus archiepiscopus et omnes episcopi et abbates cum sacro clero, et omnes Angli indissolubiliter regi suo adhaerebant, et pro ejus salute regnique statu Regem Sabaoth incessanter orabant. ... Omnes quoque Angli alterius principis jura nescientes in sui regis fidelitate perstiterunt pro qua certamen inire satis optaverunt;' Ord. Vit. x. 18. See too the speech ascribed to Henry in 1106, before the campaign of Tenchebrai, in M. Paris (ed. Luard), ii. 131.

[2] Ord. Vit. xi. 10.

[3] Flor. Wig. A.D. 1105; Ord. Vit. xi. 17.

Robert made an attempt to avert his final fall, and visited Final overthrow of Robert.
England; but it was in vain, Henry followed him home, and
the battle of Tenchebrai in the summer of the same year made
him supreme in Normandy as in England[1]. The point at issue
from the beginning had not been the English crown, but the
power of enforcing obedience on those Norman barons without
whose submission neither country could be at peace. From A.D.
1106 to 1118 the struggle lay between them and Henry. In Claims of William the son of Robert.
the latter year the young heir of Normandy, with the aid of the
king of France and the counts of Flanders and Anjou, made a
bold stroke for his rights, which was defeated by the policy and
good-fortune of his uncle[2]. Again in A.D. 1127 his name was
made the watchword of a renewed struggle[3]; but his early
death set Henry at rest, and for the remainder of his reign he
ruled without fear of a rival. In England his position had
been determined since the year 1103 : but the battle which was
fought out on Norman soil concerned the kingdom scarcely less
closely than the duchy, and every step was marked by an advance in the consolidation of the royal power, by the humiliation
of some great vassal, or the resumption of some great estate.

The process was begun immediately after Robert's departure Humiliation of the baronage.
in A.D. 1101. Robert Malet and Robert de Lacy forfeited their
great estates in Yorkshire and Suffolk[4]. Ivo of Grantmesnil,
who has the evil reputation of being the first to introduce the
horrors of private warfare[5] into England, was suffered to go on
pilgrimage, having divested himself of all his fiefs in favour of
the count of Meulan. Robert of Belesme, earl of Shrewsbury Resistance of Robert of Belesme.
and Arundel and count of Ponthieu and Alençon, was summoned
to answer an indictment of forty-five articles in the king's

[1] Flor. Wig. A.D. 1106.
[2] Hen. Hunt. (ed. Savile), fol. 218 ; Ord. Vit. xii. 1.
[3] Ord. Vit. xii. 45.
[4] Ord. Vit. xi. 1. Ilbert de Lacy, the father of Robert, had 164 manors
in the Domesday Survey; Robert Malet had 221 in Suffolk ; Dugd. Baron.
p. 111.
[5] Ord. Vit. xi. 2. This fact recorded of Ivo is of considerable importance :
'Ivonem quoque, quia guerram in Anglia coeperat et vicinorum rura
suorum incendio combusserat, quod in illa regione crimen est inusitatum,
nec sine gravi ultione sit expiatum.'

Robert of Belesme.

court [1]. He was the son of Roger of Montgomery, the Conqueror's friend, and had been in arms on the side of duke Robert in the last two reigns : he was an utterly selfish tyrant of the worst feudal stamp, cruel, faithless, and oppressive. He determined to resist, fortified his castles of Shrewsbury, Bridgnorth, and Arundel, and was only reduced by the king himself,

His estates confiscated A.D. 1102–3.

who brought the whole force of the nation against him. His life was spared, but his English domains were confiscated [2], and he retired to Normandy, where he lived to do more mischief

Joy of the English.

still. His downfall was regarded by the English with great delight : the cry was, 'Rejoice King Henry and thank the Lord God, for you became a free king on the day when you conquered and banished Robert of Belesme [3].' He had not however yet accomplished his destiny. Having helped to promote the invasion of A.D. 1104, and tried to make a separate peace in A.D. 1105, he escaped capture at Tenchebrai and submitted. But in A.D. 1112 he rebelled, was arrested, and remained captive until

Forfeitures of minor vassals.

his death [4]. Among the forfeitures of A.D. 1102 was also that of William of Warenne, earl of Surrey, who however was afterwards restored [5]; Arnulf of Montgomery, lord of Pembroke, and Roger of Poictou, lord of Lancaster, shared the fate of their brother Robert of Belesme in A.D. 1103 and lost their English fiefs [6]; and thus fell the greatest and most thoroughly representative of the Conquest families.

Humiliation of the feudatories in Normandy.

From A.D. 1103 onwards the battle of English liberty was fought in Normandy. The penalty for rebellion there took the form of confiscation of the English fiefs belonging to the rebels, and each rising left the king richer and stronger, the feudatories more and more depressed. Of the great families which were

[1] Ord. Vit. xi. 3 ; Flor. Wig. A.D. 1101, 1102.

[2] Ord. Vit. xi. 3.

[3] Ord. Vit. xi. 3 : 'Gaude rex Henrice, Dominoque Deo gratias age, quia tu libere coepisti regnare ex quo Rodbertum de Belismo vicisti et de finibus regni tui expulisti.'

[4] Hen. Hunt. fol. 217.   [5] Ord. Vit. x. 18 ; xi. 2.

[6] Ord. Vit. 3. Roger of Poictou had 398 manors in the Domesday Survey. He had great part of Lancashire, and was first of the long line of lords of Lancaster. Both the brothers are called earls by Ordericus, lib. v. c. 14. Arnulf's fief was the castle of Pembroke and its dependencies.

endowed on both sides of the channel, the earls of Chester alone
were unswerving in their faith to the king; some even of the
Beaumonts, after the death of Count Robert of Meulan, fell
away; although the earls of Leicester and Warwick remained
faithful[1]. But Henry's cautious statesmanship led him to make
an important distinction between the Norman and English fiefs.
In the latter case he enforced entire forfeiture, whether the rebellion had taken place on Norman or on English soil. In the
former he contented himself with retaining and garrisoning the
castles of the delinquents, so as, without rendering them desperate, to deprive them of the means of being dangerous. In
accordance with this policy, he abstained from confiscating the
Norman estates of Robert of Belesme, and on the close of the
war in 1119 he allowed his son William Talvas to possess them
as his father's heir, but withheld the castles[2]. An exception to
the rule however was made in the cases in which rebels were
members or connexions of the ducal house; the count of Mortain, the king's cousin, and Eustace of Breteuil, his son-in-law,
forfeited all their estates[3]; but in general Henry seems to have
thought that it was safer to keep a material hold on the
traitors, than by driving them to extremities to throw them
into the hands of the king of France as suzerain, or array them

Difference of Henry's policy in England and Normandy.

Henry's rigour with his own kinsmen.

[1] Earl Robert, who died in 1118, left twin sons, Robert earl of Leicester,
and Waleran count of Meulan. The latter took up arms against Henry in
1123, and was imprisoned. Henry earl of Warwick, brother of Robert I,
died in 1123; his son Roger was now earl.

[2] This, as I have remarked more than once, was one of the great features
of the royal policy in Normandy. Abbot Suger says: 'Fere omnes turres
et quaecunque fortissima castra Normanniae, quae pars est Galliae, aut
eversum iri fecit, aut suos intrudens et de proprio aerario procurans, aut si
dirutae essent propriae voluntati subjugavit;' Vit. Ludovici Grossi, § 15;
Ord. Vit. xii. 15.

[3] Ord. Vit. xi. 21. Eustace of Breteuil received a pension in lieu of his
fief (Ibid. xii. 22), and Breteuil was given to Ralph his cousin, son of Ralph
Guader (see above, p. 316), whose daughter married earl Robert II of
Leicester. This instance shows the extreme reluctance of the king to
extinguish a great fief in Normandy. Breteuil had belonged to William
Fitz-Osbern the justiciar; his two sons divided his inheritance: Roger had
Herefordshire, which he lost in 1075; William had Breteuil, but died
without lawful issue. Henry I adjudged the fief to Eustace, a natural son,
whom he married to his own daughter Juliana. But the Guaders, offspring
of the fatal marriage of 1075, still claimed in the female line, and ultimately obtained Breteuil.

on the side of his brother and nephew. In England, where his title was not really endangered, he could act differently, and employ the great territories which he accumulated in the endowment of a new and more faithful race of vassals. The seizure and retention of the Norman castles is thus the supplement to the measure of reducing the power of the feudatories which in England was carried out by confiscation.

Landmarks of the reign of Henry I.

The critical conjunctures of Henry's reign, after the battle of Tenchebrai, are the rebellion which followed the death of the count of Evreux in A.D. 1118 [1], the loss of the heir in the terrible shipwreck of A.D. 1120, and the revolt of Count Waleran of Meulan in A.D. 1123 [2]. It was not until a few years before his death that he saw himself free from a competitor in the duchy of Normandy, and his last years were embittered by the uncertainty of the succession. By compelling the barons and bishops to swear fealty to Matilda and her infant son [3], and by throwing more and more administrative power into the hands of those servants on whose fidelity he most confidently relied, he probably did all that could be done to avert the evils that he could not fail to foresee. He had however himself set an example which his success had made too tempting for the faith of the generation that followed him.

His precautions for the succession.

Henry gains the support of the English.

110. A double result attended the policy which the love of power, aided by circumstances, thus forced upon Henry. He found himself, as he had from the first day of his reign foreseen, compelled to seek the support of the native English; and the necessities of government called forth in him the exercise of

[1] The leaders in 1118 were Hugh de Gournai, Stephen of Aumâle, Eustace of Breteuil, Richer de l'Aigle, Robert of Neufbourg son of Earl Henry of Warwick, and Henry count of Eu; Ord. Vit. xii. 1. The faithful were Richard earl of Chester, and his cousin and successor Ranulf, Ralph de Conches, William of Warenne, William of Roumare, William of Tankerville, Walter Giffard, and Nigel and William of Albini; Ibid. xii. 14.

[2] The leaders of this revolt were, besides Waleran, who atoned for it by a captivity of five years, William of Roumare, who had claims on the county of Lincoln, Hugh de Montfort, who was imprisoned for the rest of Henry's life, Hugh of Neufchâtel, William Louvel, Baudri de Brai, and Pain of Gisors; Ord. Vit. xii. 34.

[3] See Chap. XI, § 118, below.

great administrative sagacity. Of the former point the contemporary historians, especially Ordericus Vitalis, afford abundant
illustration.   Not only was Henry during the greatest part of
his reign in the closest alliance with the clergy, but the English
people, who saw in the clergy their truest friends and champions,
uniformly supported him.   In the dangers of Robert's invasion Adhesion of
the clergy.
in A.D. 1101, when the count of Meulan, alone among the great
men, kept faith, Anselm with the clergy and people adhered
firmly to the king : 'repudiating the claims of the other prince,
they were constant in their fidelity to their own king, and therefore they were desirous enough to enter the struggle[1].' Their
joy at the conclusion of peace is contrasted with the disgust and
dismay of the feudatories.   In the struggle with Robert of
Belesme, when the barons were anxious to intercede for their
champion[2], the scale was turned in favour of strong measures
by the voice of the native troops ; and the congratulations which
the chronicler puts in the mouth of the people show that in
some quarters at least the real bearing of the contest was duly
appreciated[3]. The nation had accepted Henry as they had
accepted the Conqueror and the great Canute before him.   And Sympathy
of the peo-
ple repaid
by the king.
Henry showed himself to a certain extent grateful.   He restored
the working of the local courts[4], the hundred and the shire, as
they had been in King Edward's time.   He granted to the
towns such privileges as in the awakening of municipal life they
were capable of using[5].   He maintained good peace by severe
and even-handed justice ; and, by strengthening the hands of
Anselm and the reforming prelates who succeeded him, he did,

---

[1] See above, p. 332, note 1.

[2] 'Consules autem et primores regi una convenerunt . . . dicebant enim,
"Si rex magnificum comitem violenter subegerit nimiaque pertinacia, ut
conatur, eum exhereditaverit, omnes nos ut imbelles ancillas amodo con-
culcabit." . . . Pacem igitur inter eos obnixe seramus ut hero comparique
nostro legitime proficiamus, et sic utrumque perturbationes sedando debi-
torem nobis faciamus. . . . Tunc in quodam proximo colle tria millia
pagensium militum stabant et optimatum molimina satis intelligentes ad
regem vociferando clamabant, "Domine rex Henrice noli proditoribus istis
credere;"' Ord. Vit. xi. 3.

[3] See above, p. 334.

[4] Select Charters, p. 99. See below, Chap. XI.

[5] Ibid. pp. 104–108. See below, Chap. XI.

after the arrangement of the question of investiture, win to his side the most stable element of national life.

111. In the second place, his circumstances called forth the display of greater constructive power than had been shown even by his father. Henry was fully awake to the impossibility of governing England with feudal machinery, even clogged and fettered by the checks which the Conqueror had imposed. The faithless and selfish policy of the barons gave him the best excuse for superseding them, gathering the reins of administrative power into his own hands or those of his devoted servants, and forming a strong ministerial body. In this purpose he was seconded by the very admirable instrument that his sagacity selected or his good-fortune threw in his way. Bishop Roger of Salisbury, in the office of Justiciar, acted throughout the reign as the great constructor of judicial and financial organisation. This famous man, whom Henry had first met as a poor priest in Normandy and taken into his service as steward and chaplain, brought to the work of government an amount of laborious and minute attention which to a great extent supplied the want of legal organisation. The regular routine which he instituted was perhaps as great a step towards a safe constitutional system as was possible under so despotic a sovereign : and its elaborate machinery was in itself a check on wanton tyranny. In subordination to Roger, Henry raised up a set of *novi homines*, many of whom were, in nobility of blood, below the ideal standard of the ruling race. Among them Ordericus enumerates the Clintons, the Bassets, and the Trussebuts, who, although not among the tenants-in-chief of Domesday, were of good Norman descent and founders of great English families [1]. They were endowed and elevated in position

[1] Ord. Vit. xi. c. 2 : 'Alios e contra favorabiliter illi obsequentes de ignobili stirpe illustravit, de pulvere, ut ita dicam, extulit, dataque multiplici facultate super consules et illustres oppidanos exaltavit; inde Goisfredus de Clintona, Radulfus Basset et Hugo de Bocalanda, Guillegrip et Rainerius de Bada, Willelmus Trossebot et Haimon de Falesia, Guigan Algazo, et Rodbertus de Bostare.' Of these, Geoffrey de Clinton and Ralph Basset were two of Henry's principal justices ; the latter founded a great legal family: Hugh de Bocland also founded a baronial house. Willegrip had held land in Shropshire and Staffordshire before the Domesday Survey (vol. i. 249, 254); he was no doubt an Englishman, as Hugh

with the distinct purpose of forming a counterpoise to the older
vassals; and they were made useful in the work of administration. This class of men furnished the sheriffs of the counties,
the barons of the Exchequer, and the justices of the Curia regis.
The nobles of the Conquest naturally regarded them as upstarts, who are re-
garded as
and this scornful estimate of them is reflected in the writings upstarts.
of the historians. They were in fact, for the most part, too
poor as yet to make themselves friends among the monks and
clergy, as their rivals did, by founding churches and monasteries; and, being the agents of the strict measures of the king,
they incurred the unpopularity that always awaits economic or
judicial reform. In some cases, it may well be, they showed
too great zeal in carrying out the policy of their master, and in
others they took the opportunity of turning their office to their
own advantage rather than that of the State. But notwithstanding this, they were so far an improvement on the feudal
administrators that they were not too strong to be brought to
justice.

The English, although faithful and submissive to Henry, Causes of
were not disposed to endure his strong government without the misery
prevalent
murmuring. The amount of taxation which he imposed was in the reign
of Henry I.
not so burdensome by its weight as by its regular and inevitable
incidence. The exactions and the misery that they caused are
a frequent subject of lamentation with the native writers. In
A.D. 1103 the Peterborough chronicler explains, 'This was a
year of much distress from the manifold taxes;' in A.D. 1104,
'It is not easy to describe the misery of the land which it
suffered at this time from manifold oppressions and taxations;'
in A.D. 1105, 'The manifold taxes never ceased;' in A.D. 1110,
'This was a year of much distress from the taxes which the
king raised for his daughter's dowry;' in A.D. 1118, 'England

of Bocland was probably. The author of the Gesta Stephani describes their
attitude in the next reign, pp. 14, 15 : ' Exceptis quibusdam regis Henrici
primis et conjunctioribus amicis, quos ex plebeio genere, inter aulanos
juvenculos ad ministrandum assuetos, in tantum postea singulari sibi
dilectione astrinxit, ut eos honoribus ditatos largissimis, praediisque
honoratos amplissimis, et omnium palatinorum archiministros efficeret,
et omnium curialium causarum susceptores praescriberet.' He mentions
as instances only Miles of Hereford and Pain Fitz-John.

paid dearly for the Norman war by the manifold taxes;' in
A.D. 1124, 'He who had any property was bereaved of it by
heavy taxes and assessments, and he who had none starved with
hunger[1].' Allowing for the generally querulous tone of the
writer, it must be granted that there was much truth in the
representation: an extraordinary series of bad harvests and
stormy seasons and the general depreciation of the coinage,
caused by the dishonesty of the moneyers[2], increased no doubt
the distress. But it must not be forgotten that it was by these
exactions that England was saved from the ravages of war,
and that the money so raised was devoted to the humiliation of
the common enemies of king and people. The hateful Danegeld, it was believed, Henry was inclined to remit; partly under
the advice of his physician Grimbald and partly under the impression made by a strange dream, he vowed, it was said, in
1132 to forego the tax for seven years[3]. The amount of taxation, where exact details are recorded, was not greater than
could have been easily borne in a period of prosperity, after
good harvests and in time of peace. The chronicler is obliged
to say of the king, that 'he was a good man and great was the
awe of him; no man durst ill treat another in his time; he
made peace for men and deer[4].' Much the same impression is

---

[1] Chron. Sax. under the several years mentioned. In 1125, which Henry
of Huntingdon describes as the dearest he could remember, the horse-load
of wheat cost six shillings (fol. 219). The Chronicle says that between
Christmas and Candlemas one acre's seed of wheat or barley sold for six
shillings, and one of oats for four. In 1131 there was a cattle plague.

[2] Chron. Sax. A.D. 1124. Hence the very severe measures taken against
the coiners in 1125.

[3] The story of Henry's dream and vow is best known from the so-called
Chronicle of Brompton, but there is contemporary evidence of the popular
belief in it in the continuation of Florence of Worcester; and Gervase,
the Canterbury historian who lived in the same century, knew it. It
was in 1130 that Henry, being in Normandy, saw three visions: ' Primo
vidit in somniis rusticorum multitudinem cum instrumentis in ipsum insilire
et debitum expetere; secundo vidit armatorum copiam omnimodis telis in
ipsum saevire velle; tertio vidit praelatorum catervam cum baculis pas-
toralibus minas fortiter intentare.' The king was so alarmed that he leaped
out of bed and drew his sword. Grimbald, his physician, was present and
told the story. In 1132, in alarm during a storm at sea, he remembered
the vision and made the vow. See Brompton, ap. Twysden, cc. 1018, 1019;
Gervas. Cant. Opp. vol. ii. p. 71; Hardy, Catal. Mat. Hist. ii. 214, 215.

[4] Chron. Sax. A.D. 1135.

made by the more favourable account of Ordericus: 'He Estimate of Henry's policy made by Ordericus Vitalis: governed with a strong hand the duchy of Normandy and the kingdom of England, and to the end of his life always studied peace: enjoying constant good-fortune, he never fell away from his first strength and sternness of justice. The foremost counts and lords of towns and audacious tyrants he craftily over-powered; the peaceful, the religious, the mean people he at all times kindly cherished and protected. From the eighth year of his reign, in which he acquired firm hold on power on both sides of the sea, he always sought peace for the nations under him, and rigidly punished with austere measures the trans-gressors of his laws.' His personal vices were not directly injurious to the welfare of his people. 'Strong in energetic industry, he increased in a manifold degree his temporal gains, and heaped up for himself vast treasures of things which men covet.' 'After a careful examination of the histories of the ancients, I boldly assert that none of the kings in the English realm was, as touching the grandeur of this world, richer or more powerful than Henry[1].' He was the 'Lion of Righteous- and other historians. ness' of Merlin's prophecies[2]. 'Inflexible in the rigour of justice,' says William of Malmesbury, 'he kept his native people in quiet, and his barons according to their deserts[3].' Men thought diversely about him, Henry of Huntingdon tells us, and after he was dead said what they thought. Some spoke of splendour, wisdom, prudence, eloquence, wealth, victories; some of cruelty, avarice, and lust; but, in the evil times that came after, the very acts of tyranny or of royal wilfulness seemed, in comparison with the much worse state of things present, most excellent[4]. He was, it is evident, a strong General estimate of Henry. ruler, with a clear view of his own interests, methodical, saga-cious, and far-sighted: his selfish aims dictated the policy that gave peace and order to his people: destroying his enemies, he destroyed theirs; and by enforcing order he paved the way for

[1] Ord. Vit. xi. 23.
[2] Ibid. xii. 47; Suger, V. Ludovici Gr., § 15; Joh. Salisb. Polycr. vi. 18.
[3] W. Malmesb. G. R. v. § 411.
[4] H. Hunt. ed. Savile, fol. 221.

law.   Such a king neither expects nor deserves love; but he is
regarded with a mixed feeling of confidence and awe, and the
result of his rule is better than that of many who are called
benefactors.

Ecclesias-
tical policy
of Henry I.

112. The ecclesiastical policy of Henry was the same as that
of his father; but the circumstances of the times were different,
and the relations of the king with both the English Church and
the Pope were more complicated [1].   The policy of Anselm was
in contrast with that of Lanfranc, and the tendency of ecclesiastical progress had become too strong to be directed by
political management.   The points at issue between the king
and the Church had become part of the great European quarrel.
The exact importance of those points cannot be discussed here,
and the constitutional results of the dispute on investitures
have their proper place in the history of the national council.
The political consequences of the struggle however were to
draw the clergy and people more closely together, and to force
on the king the conviction that, absolute as he would be, there
were regions of life and thought in which he must allow the

His dispute
with Anselm.

existence of liberty.   In no respect does Henry's ability show
itself more strongly than in this.   At the beginning of his
reign, although the support of the prelates was absolutely necessary to him, and he was willing to win it by renouncing the
evil customs of his brother, he refused to surrender one of the
rights that his father had exercised, or that were in question
among his fellow-rulers on the continent.   Anselm again left
England, but no interruption took place in the ecclesiastical
working: the clergy stood by the king in his struggle with the
feudatories and rejoiced in his victories.   When the early
troubles were over, and Henry was able to apply himself to the
independent treatment of the question, his thoughtful mind at
once struck out the fit line of compromise, and anticipated by
fourteen years the principle on which the Concordat of Worms
was framed between pope and emperor.   His love of order led
him to admit the canonical rights of the chapters of the churches,

---

[1] The unfavourable picture drawn in the Gesta Stephani, pp. 16, 17,
should be compared with that of Eadmer, who is more just to the King.

the synodical powers of the clergy, and even the occasional exercise by the popes of a supreme appellate and legatine jurisdiction. He saw, however, distinctly the point at which his own authority must limit this liberty. The bishops might be elected canonically, but the election must be held in his court; the clergy might be trusted without compulsion to choose his candidates. The councils might be held when the archbishop choose, but the king's consent must be obtained before the assembly could meet or exercise any legislative power. Papal jurisdiction was not excluded, but no legate might visit England without royal licence. In the exercise of this control he showed no self-willed caprice, as William Rufus had done : the licence was never withheld simply to show that it was in his power to withhold it, but only when he was engaged in foreign war which might be complicated by ecclesiastical interference, or when the exertion of sovereign authority was needed to reconcile conflicting interests at home. Henry knew how to yield, with a fairly good grace, or for an adequate purpose. He allowed Ranulf Flambard to make his peace, and found him a useful tool. He allowed himself to be overreached by Archbishop Thurstan and Pope Calixtus II ; but he saw the merits of the archbishop through the disingenuous policy which he had persuaded himself to employ, and after a while placed him in possession of the rights of his see. That in some such cases his favour was purchased by a direct payment is scarcely to be wondered at. The practices that were regarded as simoniacal in the Church, the sale of offices and legal sentences, were not yet regarded as immoral in the secular service of the state. Under an absolute king, whose will is law, that which he chooses to sell passes for justice. Beneath a thin veil of names and fictions, the great ministerial offices and the royal interference by writ in private quarrels were alike matters of purchase. In the Church as well as in the State, if simony, as defined by the canon law, could be avoided, money might pass for money's worth. But setting this aside, Henry felt his own strength to be sufficiently great to spare him the pangs of jealousy. Once firmly seated on his

throne, he indulged in no severities greater than his own security demanded, and, savage as he was by nature, put so far
forth a curb on his own instincts. In the same way he showed

Henry's treatment of the church illustrates his treatment of the people.

no jealousy of the clergy. Certain of his mastery, he found his
interest in using them rather than tormenting them. And this
sheds some light on his treatment of the people : he cared too
little for them to pretend to love them ; he feared them too
little to take pains to propitiate them ; but he saw that for
himself it was best that they should be orderly governed, and
with a strong hand he maintained the order that he may almost
be said to have created [1]. How slender the basis must be on
which the absolute monarch rears his selfish designs ; how little
the strongest will can direct the future course of events ; how
intrinsically treacherous is the most perfect system and order
that results from external will rather than from permanent
organisation under an internal law, may be learned definitely
from the history of the next reign.

Accession of Stephen.

113. The example which Henry had set in his seizure and
retention of the crown was followed in every point by his successor. Stephen of Blois, the son of the Countess Adela and
grandson of the Conqueror, had obtained the county of Mortain
by the gift of his uncle [2], and that of Boulogne by marriage.
His wife, the niece of Godfrey of Bouillon, was a grand-daughter
of Malcolm and Margaret, and descended from the line of Cerdic
in exactly the same degree as the Empress Matilda. His
position as count of Mortain gave him, although he was not the

---

[1] Abbot Suger (V. Ludovici Gr., § 15), commenting on the prophecy of
Merlin : ' Aurum ex lilio et urtica extorquebitur, et argentum ex ungulis
mugientium manabit.'—' In diebus ejus aurum ex lilio, quod est ex reli-
giosis boni odoris, et ex urtica, quod est ex saecularibus pungentibus,
ab eo extorquebatur ; hoc intendens ut, sicut omnibus proficiebat, ab
omnibus ei serviretur. Tutius est enim unum ut omnes defendat ab
omnibus habere, quam non habendo per unum omnes deperire. Argentum ex ungulis mugientium manabat, cum ruris securitas horreorum
plenitudinem, horreorum plenitudo argenti copiam plenis scriniis ministra-
bat.' The last sentence contains the key to much of Henry's administrative policy.

[2] On the forfeiture of Robert of Belesme, Henry I gave Alençon to
Theobald of Blois, who gave it to Stephen in exchange for his French
heritage ; Ord. Vit. xii. 4. Stephen received Mortain instead, when William
Talvas recovered his father's estates in A.D. 1119.

eldest member of his family, the first place among the barons of Normandy, and in this capacity he had thrice pledged his oath to secure the succession of Matilda and her infant heir [1].

The death of Henry I, like that of William Rufus, took both Normandy and England by surprise; and, if on neither side of the channel any respect was paid to the engagements made for the succession, it must be remembered that these engagements had been to all intents and purposes forced upon the barons. The very fact of their repetition had betrayed that they were not on either side regarded as trustworthy. As soon as the king was dead the Norman barons treated the succession as an open question; and Stephen took the decision as respected England into his own hands. Henry died in the night following December 1, A.D. 1135: Stephen immediately on receiving the news crossed over to England. Dover and Canterbury were shut against him [2]. He hastened to London, and was there hailed by the citizens as a deliverer from the danger of a foreign yoke: Geoffrey of Anjou and his wife were disliked, the former as a stranger, and the latter as an imperious self-willed woman [3]; the citizens of the first city in the realm might claim to exercise a prerogative voice in the election of the king, and they, after making a compact, formal or informal, for mutual support, chose Stephen [4]. Encouraged by this success, he passed on to Winchester, where also he was welcomed by the citizens; here he obtained with little delay the royal treasure, having, by the aid of his brother the bishop, overcome the scruples of the justiciar, Bishop Roger of Salisbury [5]. Thus strengthened, he returned to London for formal election and coronation [6]. It was not without deep misgivings that the archbishop, William of Corbeuil,

The succession treated as an open question.

Stephen obtains London and Winchester.

---

[1] Below, Chap. XI.

[2] Gervase, i. 94: 'A Cantuarinis exclusus.'

[3] Cont. Flor. Wig.: 'Volente igitur Gaufrido comite cum uxore sua quae heres erat in regnum succedere, primores terrae juramenti sui male recordantes regem eum suscipere noluerunt, dicentes "Alienigena non regnabit super nos."'

[4] 'Id quoque sui esse juris suique specialiter privilegii, ut si rex ipsorum quoquo modo obiret, alius suo provisu in regno substituendus e vestigio succederet;' 'firmata prius utrinque pactione;' Gesta Stephani, pp. 3, 4.

[5] W. Malmesb. Hist. Nov. i. § 460.

[6] Gervase, i. 94.

Election and
coronation
of Stephen.

disregarded his oath; but the exigency was urgent. The suspension of law and peace owing to the interregnum was becoming dangerous; the news from Normandy brought no prospect of a speedy solution of the difficulty from that quarter. Hugh Bigod, Henry's steward, was ready to swear that the king had released the vassals from their oath and disinherited Matilda [1]. All men were acting as if she had no claim to be considered. Stephen pressed his advantage: the archbishop, with the bishops of Winchester and Salisbury, undertook to act on behalf of the Church, and the citizens of London filled up the gaps in the ranks of the nobles [2]: he was crowned on the 22nd of December. The hurry of the ceremony gave no time to impose new constitutional conditions, nor were the members of the national council who were present likely to demand more than Henry

His first
charter.

had seen good to grant them. A brief charter was issued, by which the new king confirmed the laws and liberties that his uncle had given and the good customs of King Edward's time, and enjoined the observance of them on all, a command which meant little under the weak hand that signed it [3].

He is accepted in
Normandy.

The news of Stephen's boldness and success determined for the time the minds of the Normans who had been talking of electing his elder brother Theobald as their duke [4]: Geoffrey and Matilda were occupied by a revolt in Anjou, and even Earl Robert of Gloucester, the natural son of Henry I, seems to have concluded that it was the moment for politic submission [5]. Only

[1] Gervase, i. 94: 'Quidam ex potentissimis Angliae, jurans et dicens se praesentem affuisse ubi rex Henricus idem juramentum in bona fide sponte relaxasset.' Ralph de Diceto, i. 248: 'Hugo Bigod senescallus regis coram archiepiscopo Cantuariensi sacramento probavit, quod dum rex Henricus ageret in extremis, ortis quibusdam inimicitiis inter ipsum et imperatricem, ipsam exheredavit, et Stephanum Boloniae comitem heredem instituit.' Hist. Pontif. (Pertz, vol. xx.) p. 543.

[2] 'Tribus episcopis praesentibus, archiepiscopo, Wintoniensi, Salesbiriensi, nullis abbatibus, paucissimis optimatibus;' Will. Malmesb. Hist. Nov. i. § 12. Gervase, i. 94, says, 'A cunctis fere in regem electus est.'

[3] 'Sciatis me concessisse et praesenti carta mea confirmasse omnibus baronibus et hominibus meis de Anglia omnes libertates et bonas leges quas Henricus rex Anglorum avunculus meus eis dedit et concessit, et omnes bonas leges et bonas consuetudines eis concedo quas habuerunt tempore regis Edwardi;' Statutes of the Realm, i. 4; Select Charters, p. 113. [4] Ord. Vit. xiii. 20.

[5] 'Post Pascha Robertus comes Gloecestrae ... venit in Angliam ...

the old king of Scots took up arms on behalf of his niece; and
he was pacified by the surrender of Carlisle, although he declined
to do homage, in consideration of his oath to the empress [1]. It
would seem that the necessity of binding Stephen by further
conditions had occurred to the barons who had assembled at the
funeral of the late king. This ceremony had been delayed until
nearly a fortnight after the coronation, and it is probable that it
furnished an opportunity of obtaining some vague promises from
Stephen. He undertook, we are told, to allow the canonical
election of bishops and not to prolong vacancies; to give up the
abuses of the forest jurisdiction which Henry had aggravated,
and to abolish the Danegeld [2]. Whether these promises were
embodied in a charter is uncertain: if they were, the charter is
lost; it is however more probable that the story is a popular
interpretation of the document which was actually issued by
the king, at Oxford, soon after Easter when he had received
the papal recognition [3] and had been joined by the earl of
Gloucester and other chief members of Henry's household.
This charter, which is the second of our great charters of
liberties, is attested by a large number of witnesses [4]; eleven

Stephen's
promises
of good
government.

Burial of
Henry I,
Jan. 4, 1136.

Stephen's
second
charter.

homagium regi fecit sub conditione quadam scilicet quamdiu ille dignitatem suam integre custodiret et sibi pacta servaret;' Will. Malmesb.
Hist. Nov. i. § 463. Robert had been urged to take the crown himself,
but he refused 'dicens aequius esse filio sororis suae, cui justius competebat,
regnum cedere, quam praesumptive sibi usurpare;' p. 8. Notwithstanding
he did homage to Stephen.   [1] Hen. Hunt. fol. 221, 222.

[2] Hen. Hunt. ed. Savile, fol. 221: 'Primo vovit quod defunctis episcopis nunquam retineret ecclesias in manu sua sed statim electioni ca-
nonicae consentiens episcopis eas investiret. Secundo vovit quod nullius
clerici vel laici sylvas in manu sua retineret, sicut rex Henricus fecerat,
qui singulis annis implacitaverat eos, si vel venationem cepissent in silvis
propriis vel si eas ad necessitates suas exstirparent vel diminuerent . . .
Tertio vovit quod Danegeldum, id est, duos solidos ad hidam quos antecessores sui accipere solebant singulis annis in aeternum condonaret.'
These promises were made at Oxford, during the Christmas season, before
the news of the Scottish invasion. The charter, mentioned immediately,
was also issued at Oxford; but, as it is attested by the earl of Gloucester, who landed soon after Easter, it must be dated some time in
the spring.

[3] On the proceedings at Rome, see the important remarks of Mr. Round,
Geoff. de Mandeville, pp. 250 sq.

[4] Statutes of the Realm, i. 3; Select Charters, pp. 114, 115. The earls
are Gloucester, Surrey, Chester, and Warwick, of whom Gloucester was
uniformly, and Chester generally, on the side of the empress. Her most
faithful adherents, Miles of Gloucester and Brian of Wallingford, were also

English and three Norman bishops; the Chancellor Roger; four
earls; four great constables; four royal stewards; two grand
butlers, and seven other vassals, two of whom were of the rank
of count. The privileges conceded by it are chiefly ecclesiastical.
Simony is forbidden; the property, dignities, and customs of the
churches are confirmed as they were in the days of the Conqueror,
and the jurisdiction over ecclesiastics is left in the hands of the
bishops: all interference in the testamentary dispositions of the
clergy and in the administration of vacant churches is disclaimed.
The forests made in the last reign are surrendered[1]. The promise
of peace and justice made at the coronation is renewed, and
amplified by an undertaking to extirpate all exactions, injustice
and chicanery, whether introduced by the sheriffs or by others;
and to maintain good laws and ancient and righteous customs in
reference to judicial procedure generally[2]. As in the charter of
Henry I, each of the three estates has its own clause of conciliation; the forest usurpations being surrendered probably to gain
the support of the lay nobles. But Stephen kept none of these
promises.

Want of
confidence
in Stephen.

He was a brave man, merciful and generous, and had had
considerable military experience; but he was gifted with neither
a strong will nor a clear head, and from the beginning of his
reign neither felt nor inspired confidence. The conditional
adhesion of Robert of Gloucester, who carefully defined the
fealty that he promised as dependent on the king's treatment of
him[3], was not a circumstance likely to reassure Stephen. Much
however might have been done by an honest perseverance in the
Early revolt
against him.
promises of the charter. Unfortunately for the king, a false
report of his death early in the summer produced a general

among the witnesses: probably the retreat of the king of Scots had made
her cause for the time hopeless.

[1] 'Forestas quas Willelmus avus meus et Willelmus avunculus meus instituerunt et habuerunt, mihi reservo. Ceteras omnes, quas rex Henricus
superaddidit, ecclesiis et regno quietas reddo et concedo.'

[2] 'Omnes exactiones et injustitias et mescheningas, sive per vicecomites
vel per alios quoslibet male inductas, funditus exstirpo.' The miskenning,
variatio loquelae, is explained of the arbitrary fines exacted for altering
the terms of indictment, or shifting the ground of an action after it was
brought into court.

[3] Above, p. 346, note 5.

rising.   Hugh Bigod, who had so lately acted as his tool, seized
the castle of Norwich, and Baldwin of Redvers fortified Exeter.
Stephen, with great promptness, marched against the two strong- Stephen's early suc-
holds in succession and took them.   Hugh Bigod and his party cess,
were pardoned, but Baldwin was deprived of his estates in the
Isle of Wight and banished.   The success of the king led him
to forget his engagements, and by holding a forest assize at
Brampton he showed how little weight he allowed to the
promise which in popular estimation was of the most importance [1].   The next year, 1137, was marked by victories in Normandy, and was the crowning period of his prosperity [2].   In
A.D. 1138 all the elements of danger broke out at once into a
blaze.

114. The feudal instinct, notwithstanding the repressive policy Gathering clouds.
of Henry I, was as strong as ever in the great vassals.   Un-
warned by the fate that had overtaken their fellows, and un-
instructed by the good peace that Henry had made, they watched
with eager eyes for the moment when the disputed title to the
throne should give them an opportunity of striking a blow for
themselves.   Matilda's party were gathering resolution and
collecting resources, whilst Stephen was spending his treasures
and wasting his opportunities.   Matters would have been bad Stephen's imprudence.
enough if his policy had been a negative one; but the very
measures which he took for strengthening himself were so ill
chosen as to be fatal.   Notwithstanding the fact that it was by
an outcry against the foreigners that he had been able to exclude
Matilda from the succession, and although he must have known
the intolerant dislike felt both by the Norman barons and by
the English for foreigners, whether as favourites or as merce- His mer-cenaries.
naries, he surrounded himself with an army of hired Flemings [3].
In order, next, to secure more firmly the faith of such barons as

---

[1] Hen. Hunt. fol. 222 ; Gesta Stephani, pp. 20–30.
[2] Hen. Hunt. fol. 222 : 'Hi ergo duo anni Stephano regi prosperrimi
fuerunt: tertius vero, de quo dicemus, mediocris et intercisus ; duo vero
ultimi exitiales et praerupti.'
[3] W. Malmesb. Hist. Nov. ii. § 483; Gervase, i. 105 ; Ord. Vit. xiii. 30 :
'In illis praecipue fisus est.   Unde proceres Normannorum nimis indignati
sunt, suumque regi famulatum callide subtraxerunt.'

Building of
castles.

His creation
of earls.

War of
A. D. 1138.

Attitude of
the bishops.

had adhered to him, he allowed them to fortify their houses and
build castles, where they exercised without limitation all the
tyrannical privileges which the feudal example of France suggested[1]. He went further still. Not satisfied with putting this
weapon into the hand of his enemies, he provoked their pride
and jealousy by conferring the title of earl upon some of those
whom he trusted most implicitly, irrespective of the means
which they might have of supporting the new dignity. On
others of his ministers or supporters he bestowed lavish grants
of lands and castles from the royal estates[2]. Accordingly when,
early in A. D. 1138, the king of Scots again invaded the north,
the party which Robert of Gloucester had been organising in
the south and west of England threw off the mask and broke
into rebellion[3]. Stephen, leaving Yorkshire to be defended by
the barons and commons, who under the exhortations of Archbishop Thurstan mustered as in the days of old and successfully
repelled the invasion, himself led his forces against the rebels
in Somersetshire, where although he was unable to take Bristol,
the stronghold of earl Robert, he achieved some considerable
success[4]. His fortunes might yet have triumphed, but for his
own incredible imprudence.

Up to this time Stephen had contrived to keep on his side
the clergy and the great officers of state. The bishops were
greatly influenced by Henry of Winchester, who early in A. D.
1139 obtained the commission of legate from Rome[5], an office

---

[1] W. Malmesb. Hist. Nov. i. § 467.

[2] Ibid. § 483: 'Denique multos etiam comites qui ante non fuerant
instituit, applicitis possessionibus et redditibus quae proprio jure regi
competebant.' Mr. Round (Geoffrey de Mandeville, pp. 267–278) has
examined most carefully the circumstances of these promotions, and corrected some serious misunderstandings about them.

[3] Henry of Huntingdon, fol. 222, gives a list of the insurgents and their
castles. Talbot fortified Hereford; Robert of Gloucester, Bristol and Sled
(Leeds); William Lovel, Castle Cary; Paganellus, Ludlow; William de
Mohun, Dunster; Robert of Lincoln, Wareham; Eustace Fitz-John,
Malton; William Fitz-Alan, Shrewsbury. Ordericus Vitalis (xiii. 37)
adds Walkelin Maminot, who commanded at Dover; William Peverell,
who had four castles, Burne, Ellesmere, Whittington, and Overton; and
William Fitz-John who fortified Harptree. The Beauchamps at Bedford
had been brought to surrender early in 1138. See also Gesta Stephani,
pp. 30–43 sq.; Ric. Hexham, ed. Raine, p. 84.

[4] Gesta Stephani, p. 41 sq.

[5] The date of Henry's legatine commission, which is often mis-stated, is

which made him more than a match for the newly-elected archbishop, Theobald of Canterbury. Henry of Winchester was a
thorough churchman, and, in spite of his close relationship to
Stephen, never condescended to act as his tool. The adminis- Roger of
Salisbury
trative machinery of the kingdom was still under the control of and his
nephews.
Roger bishop of Salisbury: he yet bore the title of justiciar[1];
his son, also named Roger, was chancellor of the king; one
nephew, Nigel bishop of Ely, was treasurer[2]; another nephew,
Alexander, was bishop of Lincoln. As the whole of the judicial
and financial business of the kingdom depended on the Exchequer,
which had been for thirty years in the hands of this able family,
it was little less than infatuation to break with them. Bishop
Roger had been mainly instrumental in placing Stephen on the
throne. He had, perhaps for the sake of retaining power, done
outrage to the sense of obligation under which gratitude to the
late king should have laid him; probably also he was influenced
not a little by the common idea of statesmen that their first duty
is to see that the government be carried on; without him, he
knew and the event proved, the whole mechanism of the State
would come to a standstill. But he did not shut his eyes to the Their
castles.
uncertainty of his position; he saw the vassals on every side
building castles and collecting trains of followers; and, either
with the thought of defending himself in the struggle which he
foresaw, or perhaps with the intention of holding the balance of
the State firm until the contest was decided, he and his nephews
built and fortified several strong castles in their dioceses[3].
Having great revenues at their disposal, they expended them

given by William of Malmesbury; Hist. Nov. ii. § 471. It was March 1,
1139. Theobald had been consecrated on the 8th of January.

[1] 'Justiciarius fuit totius Angliae et secundus a rege;' Hen. Hunt. fol.
218. 'Cui totius Albionis tutela jamdudum ab avunculo suo, et postmodum ab ipso, commissa fuerat;' Ord. Vit. xiii. 24.

[2] Nigel had been the means of revealing to the king the existence of
a formidable conspiracy, as late as 1137; Ord. Vit. xiii. 32. One of his
clerks, named Ranulf, had contrived a plot for murdering all the Normans;
R. Diceto, i. 253.

[3] Newark and Sleaford were fortified by Alexander; Salisbury, Devizes,
Sherborne, and Malmesbury by Roger. Devizes, according to Henry of
Huntingdon, was as splendid as the most splendid castle in Europe;
fol. 223.

freely; their newly-built fortresses were the noblest works of
the kind north of the Alps; and the train with which they
appeared at court was numerous and magnificent. It is not
clear whether Stephen's course was prompted by a doubt of
Roger's fidelity, or suggested by the petty jealousy of his partisans among the barons, who no doubt resented the maintenance
of Henry's policy[1], or by personal dislike of a too powerful

subject. In June however, at Oxford, he arrested the bishops
of Salisbury and Lincoln, and the chancellor with them, and
compelled them to surrender their castles. The shortsighted-
ness of this policy was immediately apparent; the whole body of
the clergy took umbrage at the injury done to the bishops. A

council was called at Winchester, in which the strongest remonstrance was made, and Stephen was entreated not to render the
breach incurable between the clergy and the royal party. The
king as usual made promises which he either could not or would

not keep[2]. Immediately afterwards the empress landed; and
war broke out again. At the end of the year the bishop of
Salisbury died; the bishop of Ely was banished; and the bishop
of Winchester, as soon as Stephen fell into difficulties, declared
himself on the side of the empress, and procured her election to
the throne[3]. The arrest of Bishop Roger was perhaps the most

---

[1] William of Malmesbury (Hist. Nov. ii. § 468) mentions the jealousy of
the barons; Ordericus (xiii. 40) the suspicions of the bishop's fidelity.
The count of Meulan is described in the Gesta Stephani, p. 47, and by
Orderic, as the chief accuser; he had been sometime a captive under
Henry I, and was a strong supporter of Stephen, in whose interest he had
overrun Normandy in 1138.

[2] William of Malmesbury (Hist. Nov. ii. § 477) says, 'Malorum praeventus consilio, nullam bonarum promissionum exhibuit efficaciam.' Henry
of Huntingdon, 'Rex consilio pravorum tot et tantorum tam verendam
prosternationem despiciens, nihil eos impetrare permisit;' fol. 223. The
Gesta Stephani, p. 51, record a penance done by the king for his attack
on the bishops.

[3] The arrest of the bishops took place June 24, 1139; the council at
Winchester, Aug. 29 to Sept. 1. Earl Robert landed Sept. 30; and the
empress with him. Stephen sent the bishop of Winchester and Count
Waleran of Meulan to escort her. Bishop Roger died Dec. 11. The
bishop of Ely was displaced from his see at the beginning of 1140, as
soon probably as the king knew of bishop Roger's death; Hen. Hunt. fol.
223. The bishop of Winchester, after in vain attempting to mediate,
took the empress's side as soon as Stephen had fallen into her hands, after
the battle of Lincoln in 1141; Ord. Vit. xiii. 43. He is represented in

important constitutional event that had taken place since the Conquest; the whole administration of the country ceased to work, and the whole power of the clergy was arrayed in opposition to the king. It was also the signal for the civil war, which lasted with more or less activity for fourteen years. Civil war.

115. During this time the king was alternately a prisoner and a conqueror, but was never able to restore the administrative machinery; the empress had her turns of good and evil fortune, but was never able to make good her title to the crown. The barons were in earnest only for their own interests; most of them caring little for either candidate; fighting on each side and purchasing new titles or privileges from both by momentary support; supplies were raised from the unfortunate people and clergy. The bishops protested and mediated, but found themselves powerless from the fact that there was no collective interest upon which they could work. The result was that feudal anarchy which had sometimes prevailed abroad, but never before in England. Stephen held his court at London at Whitsuntide, A.D. 1140, but only one prelate, the foreign bishop of Seez, attended[1]. Henceforth, not even the appearance of ancient state was maintained; the solemn courts and coronation days were given up; the treasure was all spent; the king debased the coinage[2]; there was no peace in the realm. 'It is written,' says William of Newburgh[3], 'of one period in the history of the ancient people, "In those days there was no king in Israel, but every one did that which was right in his own eyes." But it was worse in England in King Stephen's days. For because then the King was powerless, and the law weak by reason of the king's powerlessness, some indeed did what was right in their Feudal anarchy during the struggle. Miseries of the country.

the Gesta Stephani, p. 57, as conniving at the empress's designs from the moment of her landing. The election of the empress as 'domina Angliae' took place, April 8, 1141.

[1] Will. Malmesb. Hist. Nov. ii. § 486. The royal pomp had already come to an end: 'Ubi autem ad Natale, vel ad Pascha fuerit, dicere non attinet;' Hen. Hunt. fol. 223. Cf. Joh. Salisb. Polycr. vi. 18.

[2] Will. Malmesb. Hist. Nov. ii. § 34: 'Pro falsitate difficultas monetae tanta erat ut interdum ex decem et eo amplius solidis vix duodecim denarii reciperentur. Ferebatur ipse rex pondus denariorum, quod fuerat tempore Henrici regis, alleviari jussisse.'

[3] Will. Newb. i. 22.

Anarchy of
the period.

own eyes, but many did what by natural reason they knew to
be wrong, all the more readily, now that the fear of the law and
of the king was taken away. At first it seemed that the realm
was rent in two, some inclining to the king, some to the empress.
Not that either king or empress exercised any real control over
their party, but that every one for the time devoted himself to
the pursuit of war. Neither of them could exert command
or enforce discipline; both of them allowed to their supporters
every sort of licence for fear of losing them. The parties fought
for a long time with alternate fortune. As time went on,
wearied of the uncertainty of their luck, they somewhat relaxed
in energy; but even this made it worse for England; for when
the two competitors were tired of strife and willing to rest, the
provincial quarrels of the nobles continued to rage. In every
province, under the impulse of the party struggle, numbers of

Feudal
usurpations.

castles had sprung up. There were in England as many kings,
tyrants rather, as there were lords of castles; each had the
power of striking his own coin[1], and of exercising like a king
sovereign jurisdiction over his dependents. And as every one
sought for himself such pre-eminence, that some would endure
no superior, some not even an equal, they fought amongst themselves with deadly hatred, they spoiled the fairest regions with
fire and rapine, and in the country which had been once most
fertile they destroyed almost all the provision of bread.' The
lamentations of the Peterborough chronicler are as loud and as

The new
castles.

distinct: 'All became forsworn and broke their allegiance; for
every rich man built his castles and defended them against the
king, and they filled the land with castles. They greatly oppressed the wretched people by making them work at these
castles, and when the castles were finished they filled them with
devils and evil men. Then they took those whom they suspected
to have any goods, by night and by day, seizing both men and
women, and they put them in prison for their gold and silver,

---

[1] There are a few relics of the 'adulterine' coinage still in existence;
see Hawkins, English Silver Coinage, ed. Kenyon, pp. 189 sq. Coins are
assigned to Henry of Winchester, Robert of Gloucester, Eustace and William the King's sons, and to Roger Earl of Warwick, besides the Empress
herself.

and tortured them with pains unspeakable. . . . Many thousands
they exhausted with hunger. . . . And this state of things lasted
the nineteen years that Stephen was king, and ever grew worse
and worse. They were continually levying an exaction from The unlaw-
the towns, which they called *tenserie*, and, when the miserable ful taxes.
inhabitants had no more to give, then plundered they and
burned all the towns, so that thou mightest well walk a whole
day's journey nor ever shouldest thou find a man seated in a
town or its lands tilled [1].' John of Salisbury compares England
during this reign to Jerusalem when besieged by Titus [2].

The struggle, unlike most of those civil wars which have Selfish policy
devastated England, is redeemed by scarcely any examples of nobles.
loyalty or personal heroism. Even the fidelity of Robert of
Gloucester to the interests of his sister was an afterthought,
and resulted in no small degree from his distrust of Stephen.
The patriotic resistance offered by the men of Yorkshire to the
Scottish invasion was an act of self-defence against hereditary
enemies, rather than a hearty fulfilment of a national duty.
Among the great earls there is not one whose course can be
certainly affirmed to have been thoroughly consistent. The earl
of Chester, although, whenever he prevailed on himself to act,
he took part against Stephen, fought rather on his own account
than on Matilda's; Geoffrey de Mandeville accepted the title of
earl of Essex from both parties and pillaged both sides; the earl
of Leicester, a mighty man in Normandy as in England, made
his alliances and asserted his neutrality as he pleased. His
brother, the count of Meulan, whose advice had led Stephen to
attack the bishops, condescended to avail himself of the same
policy [3]. The action of the clergy is scarcely more justifiable.
Aiming at the position of an arbitrator, Henry of Winchester The clergy
found himself arguing on each side alternately instead of judging: tration.
and his position was such as to prevent Archbishop Theobald,
who seems to have held consistently, though not energetically,
to the empress, from exercising any authority over his brethren.

---

[1] Chron. Sax. A.D. 1137 (ed. Giles).
[2] Joh. Salisb. Polycr. vi. 18. Cf. Ord. Vit. xiii. 32, 41; Hen. Hunt. fol.
223; Gilbert Foliot, ep. 79, S. T. C. v. 94.
[3] Ord. Vit. xii. 44.

The decided success of one or other of the competitors for the crown might have justified the clergy in either adhesion or resistance; but this was wanting[1]; no one cared enough for either Stephen or Matilda to declare the indefeasible right of either crowned king or legitimate succession. The citizens of London, although from inclination they probably would have supported Stephen, were obliged to receive the empress and offer for a short time a politic submission[2].

The difficulties of the case seemed to admit of no decision save that of military success; and this neither party was strong enough to achieve. Stephen, by destroying the government machinery, had deprived himself of the power of raising a national force; and the mercenaries whom his heroic wife collected on the continent alienated the people whom it was his policy to conciliate. The party of the empress, on the other hand, was mainly supported by the counties in which the personal influence of her brother was strong, and by the adventurers whom she could win to her side by promises. In vain did she go through the process of election as lady of England, hold her courts, and issue her charters in royal form: she had not learned wisdom or conciliation, and threw away her opportunities as lavishly as did her rival.

The course of events was rapid enough at first. The year 1140 was taken up with futile negotiation, local tumult, and general preparation for civil war. In February, 1141, Stephen, while besieging the earls of Chester and Gloucester at Lincoln, was defeated and taken prisoner. This mishap was interpreted as the judgment of God against him: his brother as legate held a great council at Winchester in April, and in it the empress was solemnly chosen as lady of England. Scarcely had she taken the reins of power than she offended her most powerful friends. The Londoners she alienated by her haughtiness; bishop Henry she drove from court by her injustice to the wife and children of Stephen. The brave and politic queen did not despair of her

Attitude of London.

Weakness of both competitors.

Battle of Lincoln.

Matilda elected sovereign, April 8, 1141.

---

[1] Gesta Stephani, pp. 98, 99.
[2] W. Malmesb. Hist. Nov. iii. § 477; Gesta Stephani, pp. 76, 77; Hen. Hunt. fol. 225.

husband's fortunes. In September the empress was a fugitive The king freed.
and Earl Robert a prisoner. On All Saints' Day the two chiefs
of the struggle were exchanged, and then in the exhaustion of
both parties the nation had six months of rest. The empress
had been tried and found wanting.

The year 1142 saw Stephen again in the ascendant: Earl Success of Stephen in 1142.
Robert was attempting to recover Normandy and to interest
Geoffrey of Anjou in his wife's success. The king, taking advantage of his absence, seized his stronghold at Wareham and
besieged the empress in Oxford, whence she had to escape
secretly in December. The dynastic struggle then degenerated
into an anarchic strife. In 1143 and 1144 Geoffrey de Mandeville, whom both Stephen and Matilda had made earl of Essex,
tasked the energies of the king, whilst the earl of Chester at
Lincoln sustained the hopes of the Angevin party. Southern Division of the king-dom.
England seemed to split into two realms; Stephen was acknow-
ledged in the Eastern, Matilda in the Western counties. The
count of Meulan and the earl of Leicester held the balance in
the Midland shires. In 1146 Stephen's fortunes again improved;
the earl of Chester was captured, and the king at Lincoln ventured to wear his crown. In 1147 Earl Robert, who must have
long been weary of his ungrateful task, died; some of his most
powerful friends had already passed from the scene; and the
same year the empress left England, devolving on her son, who
was now approaching manhood, the task of making good his
claim to the succession.

This wearisome story of tergiversation and selfish intrigues, Incidental importance of the period.
although it scarcely concerns constitutional history directly, has
a most important bearing indirectly upon it, as showing the
evils from which the nation escaped. It was the period at
which for once the feudal principle got its own way in England;
it proved the wisdom of the Conqueror and his sons in re-
pressing that principle, and it forced on the nation and its
rulers those reforms by which in the succeeding reign the
recurrence of such a result was made impossible.

The storm of party warfare, as William of Newburgh stated, The storm subsides.
subsided gradually. The changes in the popedom put an end

to the legation of Bishop Henry[1]; the death of Earl Robert removed the main stay of the strength of the empress[2], and the second generation of combatants came into the first ranks with somewhat freer hands. The exhaustion of both sides gave a breathing time, although it was incompetent to restore the national strength or unity. The clergy recovered their influence first, and compelled the king to guarantee as far as he could their personal safety: a series of ecclesiastical disputes followed, which diverted the attention of the bishops from general politics, and threw the king and his brother again more heartily together[3]. In A.D. 1147 the preaching of the Crusade drew from England many of the adventurous spirits who had been disciplined for rapine by the late events[4]. In A.D. 1149 Henry of Anjou, the son of the empress, to whom in his grandfather's time the oath of fealty had been taken in England and in Normandy, was knighted by the king of Scots[5], and a gathering of the barons of Western England, in which the supporters of the empress were chiefly found, threatened a renewal of hostilities. But several years elapsed before Henry saw his opportunity. Having by his father's death gained a firm standing-ground in France, he added, by his politic marriage, the county of Poictou and the duchy of Guienne to Anjou and Normandy[6]. An attempt made by Stephen, with the aid of Lewis VII, to seize the latter terri-

Close of the struggle.

Rise of Henry II.

---

[1] The legation of Henry of Winchester was granted by Innocent II, who died in 1143. Celestine II, who succeeded him, was hostile to Stephen, and Lucius II, who followed in 1144, although friendly to the bishop, did not renew his commission. Eugenius III, who acted under the advice of S. Bernard, and was generally opposed to Stephen, gave the legation to Archbishop Theobald in or before the year 1150.

[2] The Annals of Tewkesbury place the death of Earl Robert in 1147; Gervase in November 1146 (vol. i. p. 131); the Annals of Margam, an abbey founded by the earl, on Oct. 31, 1147. Miles of Hereford died at Christmas, 1143; J. Hexham: Geoffrey de Mandeville, in 1144: H. Hunt. fol. 224.

[3] Hen. Hunt. fol. 225.

[4] See R. de Monte (Bouquet, xiii. 291); Osbern, De expugnatione Lyxbonensi, in the Memorials of Richard I, vol. i. pp. cxliv. sq.

[5] Hen. Hunt. fol. 226; J. Hexham (ed. Raine), p. 159.

[6] Geoffrey of Anjou gave up Normandy to Henry, and Lewis received his homage for it in the summer of 1151; Geoffrey died soon after. The divorce of Lewis and Eleanor took place in March 1152, and the marriage of Henry in May following; R. de Monte (Bouquet, xiii. 292).

tory, was the first note of the renewed struggle. In A.D. 1152 [1] The bishops refuse to accept Eustace as king. Stephen proposed to the assembled bishops that his son Eustace should be associated with him in the kingdom. The prelates, under the influence of Theobald, refused, and suffered forfeiture, which however, with his usual irresolution, Stephen soon after recalled. Early in the following year Henry came to England Henry takes the command against him. and raised a native army [2]. The horrors of active warfare were repeated, not however on so large a scale as before, for Stephen was conscious of his weakness, and Henry was now, as ever, economical of human life. A decisive battle accordingly was avoided; and, when on one occasion the two rivals stood face to face, the great nobles intervened and compelled them to make a truce. Henry of Huntingdon, in describing the attitude of the baronage on this occasion, shows how clearly he understood the real objects of that body. 'Then arose the barons, or rather Mediation of the barons. the betrayers, of England, treating of concord, although they loved nothing better than discord: but they would not join battle, for they desired to exalt neither of the two, lest if the one were overcome, the other should be free to govern them: they knew that so long as one was in awe of the other he could exercise no royal authority upon them [3].' The death however of Eustace, which occurred in August, reduced Stephen's stake in the struggle [4]. The archbishop and bishop Henry, moved at last by the distress of the country, and strengthened by the support of the pope, made a resolute effort for conciliation, and after some preliminary meetings a peace was concluded. Nego- Peace of Wallingford and Westminster. tiations begun at Wallingford before the death of Eustace were completed at Westminster in the following November [5]. In the treaty which was then made the national claims for good

---

[1] Apr. 8, 1152; Chr. S. Aug. ed. Liebermann, p. 82; Hen. Hunt. fol. 226; Gervase, i. 150.

[2] He crossed over to England within the octave of the Epiphany, 1153; R. de Monte. 'Nec tamen hoc [his success against Stephen at Crowmarsh] alienigenae ascribant viribus suis, nostro praecipue milite nitebatur;' Joh. Salisb. Polycr. vi. 18.

[3] H. Hunt. fol. 227; Gervase, i. 154.

[4] Gervase, i. 155; R. de Monte.

[5] Hen. Hunt. fol. 227, 228; Gervase, i. 154, 156. R. de Monte gives Nov. 6 as the date of the final agreement.

Constitutional History.

peace.

government were strongly insisted upon, and an elaborate plan
of reform was drawn up. The result was stated in the form
of a treaty to settle the succession. Each of the parties had
something to surrender and each something to secure. Henry
gave up the present possession of the throne in consideration of
the right of succession; Stephen, who had other children besides
Eustace, gave up their title to the crown to secure to them the
continental estates which he had possessed before his unlucky

Succession
secured to
Henry.

promotion. He adopted Henry as his heir of the kingdom of
England, and Henry did homage and swore fealty: and the
nobles on both sides followed, doing homage and swearing
fealty to both princes. The rights of Stephen's son William
were guaranteed, and a large augmentation of property promised
him: all the kinsmen of the royal family and the clergy were
also bound to the agreement. Two significant clauses complete
the act. 'In the business of the kingdom,' the king says, 'I
will work by the counsel of the duke; but in the whole realm
of England, as well in the duke's part as my own, I will exercise
royal justice [1].'

The scheme
of reform.

116. The scheme of reform, which was drawn up at Wallingford [2], has not been preserved in the form of a document, but
may be extracted from the somewhat rhetorical accounts of the
contemporary historians. The statement made by Roger Hoveden [3], that Henry, in order to enforce the necessary measures,
undertook the office of justiciar, is perhaps an exaggeration,
although he distinctly claimed that they should be carried out
as a part of the pacification [4]: and, when he himself became

[1] Foedera, i. 18: from the Red Book of the Exchequer. See also Will.
Newb. lib. i. cap. 30.
[2] Matt. Paris, ii. 191, 192.
[3] 'Rex vero constituit ducem justitiarium Angliae sub ipso et omnia
regni negotia per eum terminabantur;' Hoveden, i. 212. This is one of
the additions made by Hoveden to the earlier materials which he was
using; it has no contemporaneous authority, and is extremely unlikely to
be true. Even if it were true, Henry stayed in England too short a time
after the pacification to exercise any direct authority. John of Hexham
however says that it was one part of the agreement 'quod Henricus dux
negotia regni disponeret;' ed. Raine, p. 170.
[4] Hen. Hunt. fol. 228. This was at Dunstable early in 1154: 'Displicebat
enim duci, quod castella post mortem Henrici regis in pessimos usus circumquaque constructa non diruerentur, sicut confirmatum et sancitum fuerat

king, he seems to have looked on them as furnishing him with
a programme of the restoration of order. They are stated as
follows. (1) The royal rights, which had everywhere been
usurped by the barons, are to be resumed by the king. (2)
The estates which had been seized by intruders are to return to
the lawful owners who had enjoyed them in King Henry's days.
(3) The adulterine or unlicenced castles[1], by whomsoever
erected during the present reign, to the number of eleven hundred and fifteen, are to be destroyed. (4) The king is to re-
stock the desolate country, employ the husbandmen, and as far
as possible restore agriculture and replace the flocks and herds
in the impoverished pastures. (5) The clergy are to have their
peace, and not to be unduly taxed. (6) The jurisdiction of the
sheriffs is to be revived, and men are to be placed in the office
who will not make it a means of gratifying private friendship
or hatred, but will exercise due severity and will give every
man his own: thieves and robbers are to be hanged. (7) The
armed forces are to be disbanded and provided for: 'the
knights are to turn their swords into ploughshares and their
spears into pruning-hooks;' the Flemings are to be relegated
to their workshops, there to labour for their lords, instead of
exacting labour as lords from the English. The general security is to be maintained, commerce to be encouraged, and
a uniform coinage to be struck[2]. This very comprehensive

The scheme of reform arranged between Stephen and Henry.

---

inter eos in concordiae firmissimo foedere. . . . Quibusdam tamen suorum
castellis regis clementia vel versutia parcens, pacti communionem debilitare
videbatur. Dux igitur super hoc regem angarians, repulsam quidem passus
est;' ibid.

[1] 'Castella adulterina.' The term is not peculiar to England; see
Guibert of Nogent, Opp. ed. D'Achery, p. 517. Robert de Monte gives
375 as the number; Bouquet, xiii. 296. On this point John of Hexham
furnishes further contemporary evidence: 'Continuo exiit edictum ab eis
per omnes provincias violentias comprimi, direptiones interdici, milites con-
ductitios et sagittarios exterarum nationum a regno ejici, munitionesque
quas quisque in sua possessione post mortem Henrici regis construxerat
dirui. Justitia ergo et pax ubique in regno revocata est;' ed. Raine,
p. 171.

[2] The following is the statement of Ralph de Diceto, i. 296, 297: 'Ducem
siquidem Normannorum rex in filium arrogavit; ei et in eum jus suum
transtulit et potestatem, sibi quoad vixerit regiae dignitatis solam imaginem
reservavit. Et si propheticum illud attenderis, jam se induit genitore, jam
ducem arrogavit in filium. In participem regni, et postmodum successorem,

project throws great light on the past as well as on the future, and it is extremely unfortunate that the exact means by which it was to be carried into execution are not recorded. The formal act of adoption was performed at Winchester in November. The treaty of Westminster was published at London before Christmas, and on the 13th of January, 1154, Henry at Oxford received the fealty of the barons. But the task of executing the other clauses seems to have been too much for Stephen, whose spirit was now broken; and Henry, in a meeting at Dunstable before he left England, had to urge the king strongly to do his duty, and especially to enforce the demolition of the castles. The last year of the reign was accordingly devoted to the undoing of the work that seventeen years of war and anarchy had done. Henry, alarmed by the news that there was a plot against his life, left England in the following Lent. Stephen had very incompletely performed his laborious task

Stephen begins the reforms.

universi ducem recipient. In rege ducem, in duce regem singuli venera-buntur. Et ut regem Stephanum nunc regem intelligas, antiqua regni privilegia restaurare proponit. Regalia passim a proceribus usurpata recipiet, munitiones suis fundatae temporibus diruentur, quarum numerus usque ad undecies centum quindecim excrevit. Ut autem ad minora recurras, praediis assignabit colonos, insularios aedificiis, nemoribus saltuarios, feris ditabit indagines, ovibus decorabit montana, pascua re-plebit armentis. Clerus nunc demum dominabitur, pacis tranquillitatem indicet, muneribus sordidis non gravabitur, ab extraordinariis vacationem habebit. Defensivae locorum, seu vicecomites, locis statuentur statutis; non in votum exercendae cupiditatis abibunt, non quenquam ex odio persequentur. Non gratificabuntur amicis, non indulgentiis crimina sub-levabunt, suum cuique reservabunt ex integro. Metu poenarum nonnullos afficient, praemiorum exhortatione plurimos excitabunt: fures terrebuntur in furca; praedones sententia capitali plectentur; milites caligati gladios suos in usum vomeris ligonisque convertent. A castris ad aratra, a tentoriis ad ergasteria Flandrensium plurimi revocabuntur, et quas nostratibus operas indixerunt, dominis suis ex necessitate persolvent. Quid multis? Ab excubiis fatigati a communi laetitia respirabunt: in-nocens et quieta rusticitas otio relevabitur; negotiatores commerciorum vicissitudo locupletabit. Forma publica percussa eadem in regno celebris erit ubique moneta.' The prophecy of Merlin referred to is, 'Nocebit possidenti ex impiis pietas, donec sese genitore induerit;' Geoff. Mon. vii. 3. The terms of the agreement are thus given by Robert de Monte: 'Quod dux post mortem regis, si eum superviveret, pacifice et absque con-tradictione regnum haberet; juratum est etiam quod possessiones quae direptae erant ab invasoribus ad antiquos et legitimos possessores revo-carentur, quorum fuerant tempore Henrici optimi regis. De castellis etiam quae post mortem praedicti regis facta fuerant, ut everterentur, quorum multitudo ad CCCLXXV. summam excreverat;' Bouquet, xiii. 296.

when he died in October, 1154, leaving the throne, for the first He dies. time since the Conquest without a competitor, to the great sovereign who succeeded him.

The reign of Stephen is one of the most important in our whole history, as exemplifying the working of causes and principles which had no other opportunity of exhibiting their real tendencies. It was a period of unprecedented general misery, and a most potent lesson for later times and foreign countries. The moral and social results of it are indeed more distinctly traceable under Henry II, but there can be little doubt that even before the king's death it had had the effect of creating a feeling of national unity among Normans and English, as well as an intense longing for peace. The comparative rarity of notices touching the social life of the period, in the historical memorials of the reign, render it difficult to form any minute conclusions on the material growth of the nation. But that it was a period of great social change there can be no question, when we compare the reign that followed it with the three reigns that preceded it. Some part of the result is of course owing to the equal government and lasting peace of the reign of Henry I : but it would be to disregard the consistent lessons of all history, if we were to suppose that the terrible discipline of anarchy, prolonged for nearly twenty years, during which, the pressure of the legal government being removed, opportunity was given for every sort of development and combination, had no effect in opening the eyes of men in general to the sources of their strength and the causes of their weakness. Although the annalists tell mainly of the feudal usurpations and oppressions, there are not wanting indications that in the town populations, where feudal rule was exercised under more restriction and with less impunity, an important advance towards liberty resulted from the abeyance of government ; or at least that the municipal unity was able so far to hold its own as to prevent disintegration in one of the rising elements of society. But this is an inference from later events rather than a distinctly recorded fact of the reign.

The Norman period closes with the accession of Henry II,

Constitutional importance of Stephen's reign.

whose statesmanlike activity, whose power of combining and adapting that which was useful in the old systems of government with that which was desirable and necessary under the new, gives to the policy which he initiated in England almost the character of a new creation.

CHAPTER XI.

ADMINISTRATION UNDER NORMAN RULE.

117. THE reigns of the Conqueror and his three successors, besides the political interest which they possess as the period of the trial and failure of feudality, have another distinct mark in English history, partly it is true resulting from the former. The Norman period, as we may call it, was the epoch of the growth of a new administrative system, having the source of its strength in the royal power. The constitution of this system distinguishes it from that of earlier and later times. In the earlier history, constitutional life seems to show itself first in the lower ranges of society, and to rise by slow degrees and unequal impulses towards the higher; in the later history, the equilibrium of the governmental system is maintained by regulating the balance between popular liberty and administrative pressure. The foundation of the administrative system marks the period that intervenes: and this foundation was the work of these four reigns. In attempting a sketch of the machinery which was created or developed for making good the hold of the king upon the nation, we must adopt a different arrangement

New character of the constitution in Norman times.

from that under which the Anglo-Saxon polity was examined in a former chapter ; and, beginning with the person and office of the king, descend gradually to the consideration of the powers of the individual subject and the lowest form of collective organisation. For, under the new system, it is from the person, the household, the court, and the council of the king that all constitutional power radiates; and in very many respects both the machinery and the terminology of government bear, down to the present day, marks of their origin in the domestic service of the palace.

118. The Norman idea of royalty was very comprehensive ; it practically combined all the powers of the national sovereignty, as they had been exercised by Edgar and Canute, with those of the feudal theory of monarchy, which was exemplified at the time in France and the Empire ; and it discarded the limitations which had been placed on either system, in England by the constitutional action of the witan, and on the Continent by the usurpations or extorted immunities of the feudatories. The king is accordingly both the chosen head of the nation and the lord paramount of the whole of the land : he is the source of justice and the ultimate resource in appeal for such equity as he is pleased to dispense; the supreme judge of his own necessities and of the method to be taken to supply them. He is in fact despotic, for there is no force that can constitutionally control him, or force him to observe the conditions to which, for his own security or for the regular dispatch of business, he may have been pleased to pledge himself. If the descendants of the Conqueror had succeeded one another by the ordinary rule of inheritance, there can be no doubt but that the forms as well as the reality of ancient liberty would have perished. Owing however to the necessity under which each of them lay, of making for himself a title in default of hereditary right, the ancient framework was not set aside ; and, perfunctory as to a great extent the forms of election and coronation were, they did not lose such real importance as they had possessed earlier, but furnished an important acknowledgment of the rights of the nation, as well as a recognition of the duties of the king.

The crown then continues to be elective: the form of coronation is duly performed: the oath of good government is taken,
and the promises of the oath are exemplified in the form of
charters. Of these charters only those of Henry I and Stephen
are preserved; the document called the charter of William the
Conqueror being a fabrication of the thirteenth or fourteenth
century, composed of several fragments of his legislation thrown
together in the traditional form. The recognition of the king
by the people was effected by the formal acceptance at the
coronation of the person whom the national council had elected,
by the acts of homage and fealty performed by the tenants-in-
chief, and by the general oath of allegiance imposed upon the
whole people, and taken by every freeman once at least in his
life. The theory that by a reversal of these processes, that by
renunciation of homage, by absolution from the oath of allegiance, and by a declaration that the rights conferred by consecration had been forfeited, the person so chosen could be set
aside, was, owing to the existence of competition for the throne,
kept prominently before the eyes of the people; and in the
speech of Henry of Winchester, proposing the election of the
Empress Matilda, it is explicitly stated[1]. The captivity of
Stephen is alleged as a sentence of the judgment of God, not
less convincing than the legal result of a trial by battle: on
this, as the summary decision of the Almighty, the vacancy of
the throne is made to depend, but the neglect of the solemn
promises of good government is forcibly dwelt upon as the
justification of that decision. The oath of allegiance taken to
Stephen is not mentioned, because the previous oath taken to
Matilda in her father's reign is specially insisted on. This declaration, although like the charters themselves it was meant to
serve a temporary purpose, stands on record as an important
statement of principle: it was met by Stephen's friends not by
counter allegations, but by intercessions: neither his misconduct nor the legality of his punishment is formally denied. Yet
against this significant circumstance must be set the fact that
no attempt was made to crown the empress; the legate himself

[1] Will. Malmesb. Hist. Nov. iii. § 493.

simply proposes that she should be elected lady of England and Normandy. It is just possible that the consecration which she had once received as empress [1] might be regarded as superseding the necessity of a new ceremony of the kind; but it is far more likely that, so long as Stephen was alive and not formally degraded, the right conferred on him by coronation was regarded as so far indefeasible that no one else could be allowed to share it.

Right of inheritance.

But whilst the elective principle was maintained in its fulness where it was necessary or possible to maintain it, it is quite certain that the right of inheritance, and inheritance by primogeniture, was recognised as co-ordinate. The dying orders of the Conqueror were so worded as neither to deny the elective right of the English nation, nor to annul the inchoate claims of his eldest son, even when he intended to evade both. 'I make no one of them heir of the realm of England; that I leave to the eternal Creator whose I am and in whose hands are all things; for I got not that so great glory by hereditary right [2].' The arrangement made by William Rufus and Duke Robert at Caen in A.D. 1091, that each should be heir to the other in case of his dying childless [3], proves that something more was involved than the ancient principle of the eligibility of all the members of the royal house; that a power of disposing of the crown was supposed to reside in its wearer, and that the inheritance of England was not materially distinguished from that of Normandy. True, the recognition of the duke of Normandy by his barons was in a manner analogous to that of the king of England by his witan; but in Normandy the right of hereditary succession was established by the precedents of many generations. 'It is for me to appoint my successor, for you to keep faith with him,' were the dying words of Rollo, according to the tradition of his descendants [4]. The measures taken by Henry I for secu-

Set aside by the Conqueror.

---

[1] Flor. Wig. A.D. 1114.

[2] 'Neminem Anglici regni constituo heredem, sed aeterno Conditori Cujus sum et in Cujus manu sunt omnia illud commendo : non enim tantum decus hereditario jure possedi ;' Ord. Vit. vii. 15.

[3] Flor. Wig. A.D. 1091.

[4] 'Meum est mihi illum subrogare, vestrum est illi fidem servare.'

ing the crown to his own children, whilst they prove the accept- Measures taken by Henry I to regulate the succession.
ance of the hereditary principle, prove also the importance of
strengthening it by the recognition of the elective theory. He
did not go so far as his contemporaries in France and the
Empire, and actually obtain the formal election and coronation
of his heir; but in A.D. 1116, in a great council at Salisbury,
homage was done and oaths of fealty taken to his son William[1];
in A.D. 1127, at London, the whole council of the kingdom swore Oaths three times taken to the empress.
that if the king should die without a male heir the empress
should be maintained in possession of the realm of England[2]; a
similar oath, in A.D. 1131, was taken at Northampton[3]; and
after the birth of Henry II, which occurred in A.D. 1133, we are
expressly told by Roger of Hoveden that the prelates, earls, and
barons of the whole of the king's dominions swore fealty to the
empress and her little son whom he appointed to be king after
him[4]. In like manner, in A.D. 1152, Stephen demanded the
recognition of Eustace as his heir, and even went so far, no
doubt under pressure applied by Lewis VII, as to insist that he
should be anointed and crowned[5]. He was indeed defeated, as Stephen fails to secure the crown for Eustace.
we have seen, by the resolution of the bishops, but Constance,
the wife of Eustace, is said in after days to have borne the title
of queen[6]; and the importance which was attached to the adoption of Henry II by Stephen, under the treaty of Wallingford,
shows that the rule commonly adopted in the descent of fiefs
was becoming the accepted theory of succession in the case of
the crown also.

William of Jumiéges particularly mentions the process by which the
Norman dukes before their death procured the acceptance of their successors; lib. ii. c. 22; iv. 20.
[1] Flor. Wig. A.D. 1116.
[2] Cont. Flor. Wig. A.D. 1126; Will. Malmesb. Hist. Nov. i. § 2.
[3] Will. Malmesb. Hist. Nov. i. § 455 : 'Priscam fidem apud eos qui
dederant novavit, ab his qui non dederant accepit.'
[4] Hoveden, i. 187 : 'Fecit archiepiscopos et comites et barones totius
suae dominationis jurare fidelitates Matildi imperatrici filiae suae, et
Henrico filio ejus adhuc minimo, et constituit eum regem post se.'
[5] Hen. Hunt. fol. 227; Gerv. i. 150. See above, p. 359.
[6] Art de Vérifier les Dates, ix. 385. The only evidence that I can find
for the statement is contained in two letters, one of the viscount of
Beziers, the other of the common council of Toulouse, in which she is so
spoken of; Bouquet, xvi. 69, 71.

The queen.

The importance attaching to the position of the queen is not a novelty of the Norman period; the history of Eadburga, the treacherous wife of Brihtric[1], had given it a peculiar interest some centuries earlier: and Judith the wife of Ethelwulf had received a very solemn consecration from the archbishop of Rheims. The queens of William the Conqueror, Henry I, and Stephen play a considerable part in the history of their husbands' reigns. The wives of these kings received special coronation apart from their husbands[2]; they held considerable estates which they administered through their own officers, and which were frequently composed of escheated honours; they had their own chancellors[3]; they acted occasionally as regents or guardians of the kingdom in the absence of the king, and with authority which, if it did not supersede that of the justiciar, had at least an honorary precedence[4]. The payment of queen's gold, that is of a mark of gold to the queen out of every hundred marks of silver paid, in the way of fine or other feudal incident, to the

Coronation of queens.
Their property, court, and authority.

---

[1] According to Asser, who cites Alfred as his authority, the West-Saxons, after the misconduct of Eadburga, refused to allow to the king's wife the name or position of queen: and Ethelwulf's second marriage, together with the coronation and queenly title of his wife Judith, was one ground of his being set aside by Ethelbald in 856; Asser, M. H. B. 471. However this may have been in Wessex, Ethelswitha the wife of Burhred was crowned queen of Mercia (C. D. ccxcix). Eadgifu the wife of Edward the Elder subscribes charters only as *mater regis*. Elfthrytha the wicked wife of Edgar subscribes charters as queen. Emma the wife of Ethelred was also queen, and the rite of crowning the queen appears in the ritua's from this time. Possibly some tradition of the old prejudice may have led Lewis VII to insist so strongly on the coronation of his daughter when married to the heir of the English crown. See Robertson, Essays, pp. 166–171; Freeman, Norm. Conq. i. 565; iii. 48; iv. 179.

[2] The wife of the Conqueror was crowned by the archbishop of York at Whitsuntide 1068; Flor. Wig. The coronation of Matilda the wife of Henry I, by Anselm, Nov. 11, 1100, and that of Adeliza his second wife, Jan. 29, 1121, by Archbishop Ralph, are also specially noticed. Matilda, Stephen's queen, was crowned at Westminster, March 22, 1136, and also at Canterbury with her husband; Gerv. i. 96, 527.

[3] Bernard bishop of S. David's was chancellor to Matilda the first wife of Henry I, and Godfrey of Bath to his second; Flor. Wig. A.D. 1115; Cont. Flor. Wig. A.D. 1123.

[4] Matilda the wife of Henry I, acting with the 'common counsel' of the nobles in the king's absence, sent Archbishop Ralph to Rome in 1116; Eadmer, p. 118; Flor. Wig. A.D. 1116. Charters issued by her are in Elmham, p. 354; Mon. Angl. i. 242; and Hist. Abend. ii. 98; cf. p. 104. Stephen's queen negotiated and commanded during his captivity, and so far maintained the party of her husband that it fell to pieces on her death.

king, even if it is not recognisable in Domesday, is probably as old as the reign of Henry I [1]. The acknowledged importance of her position, the real power and influence with which she was trusted, is in somewhat marked contrast with the treatment of the king's heir. Whether it was to avoid the jealousy of the barons, or to limit the ambition of the presumptive successor, neither William the Conqueror nor Henry I seems to have given to his son a separate establishment by way of appanage [2]. The daughters also were as a rule dowered with treasure, not with land. The illegitimate sons of Henry I were however largely endowed, one of them receiving an extensive and important earldom [3] : and the kinsmen of the king in the second degree were favoured in the same way [4]. But the rebellion of Robert against the Conqueror, and the youth of the etheling William, may perhaps explain more naturally the apparent over-caution of the father in each case.

Position of the heir.

The king's sons.

119. The great officers of the household form the first circle round the throne, and furnish the king with the first elements of a ministry of state. There is from the very first some difficulty in drawing the line that separates their duties as servants of the court from their functions as administrators; a difficulty which is not to be ascribed merely to the deficiency of early records, but appears partly to be the result of a growing policy. It may also have arisen partly from the combination of two or more distinct systems.

Great officers of the household.

The four chief and indispensable servants of the primitive household are named in the ancient Frankish law, as the *major,*

The four necessary servants.

---

[1] Dial. de Scaccario, lib. ii. c. 26 ; Madox, Exchequer, p. 240; Eyton's Shropshire, xii. 156. It is probably the Gersumma reginae of Domesday, i. 154, 238. See Ellis, Intr. i. 172–175.

[2] William the son of Henry I did however issue writs, apparently as his father's representative: two of which are given by Palgrave, Commonwealth, p. clxxix; others are in Madox, Hist. Exch. p. 76, and in Elmham's Chronicle, pp. 353, 354.

[3] Robert earl of Gloucester had the earldom conferred by his father, but the lordship of Gloucester, on which the title was based, was the inheritance of his wife, the daughter of Robert Fitz-Hamon. Reginald earl of Cornwall got his earldom in the struggles of Stephen's reign ; according to the Gesta Stephani, by marriage (pp. 65, 66) ; according to William of Malmesbury, by the gift of his brother the earl of Gloucester ; Hist. Nov. ii. § 34.

[4] Of this Stephen is himself the most important instance.

Officers of the Frank household.

infertor, scantio, and *mariscalcus*[1]. The first of these answers to the praefectus or heah-gerefa of the Anglo-Saxons, the second to the dapifer or discthegn; the scantio to the pincerna or cup-bearer; the mariscalcus to the horsthegn or staller[2]. In this early arrangement may be traced the germ of later differences, for the praefectus and the strator, the master of the household and the master of the horse, must have forced their way into public duties much earlier than the caterer and the butler. The

Officers of the Karolingian court.

Karolingian court had a slightly different rule: the four chief officers are the marshal, the steward, the butler, and the chamberlain[3]; the *major* of the old law disappearing, and his functions devolving, as we know from later history, partly on the dapifer, seneschal or steward, and partly on the chamberlain or account-

In the Empire.

ant. The latter distribution of dignity was permanent, and was observed, with some modifications, down to the latest days of the Empire, in the electoral body, where the Count Palatine was high steward, the duke of Saxony marshal, the king of Bohemia

In Normandy.

cup-bearer, and the margrave of Brandenburg chamberlain. A similar system had been borrowed by the Norman dukes from their titular masters: Normandy had its steward or seneschal,—for whom even the name of comes palatinus[4] is claimed,—its

---

[1] Lex Salica (Herold's Text), xi. 6; Merkel, p. 66; Herold, Origines, p. 9; Waitz, D.V.G. ii. 401. The *Capitula Remedii* mention the camerarius, buticularius, seneschalus, judex publicus, and conestabulus; Pertz, Legg. v. 182. The Alemannic law enumerates, 'seniscalcus, mariscalcus, cocus, and pistor;' Pertz, Legg. iii. 73. The 'seniscalcus' is said to mean the senior servant; Waitz, D. V. G. ii. 401; iii. 420.

[2] The praefectus or praepositus of the king's household, his steward or gerefa, occurs occasionally in Bede: Redfrith is *praefectus* to Egbert king of Kent (H. E. iv. 1); he is apparently the cyninges-gerefa of the laws; Schmid, Gesetze, p. 599. The discthegn or dapifer is mentioned in the Cod. Dipl. dccxv, dcccviii, &c. Oslac the *pincerna* of Ethelwulf was also his father-in-law; and several others who bore the same title are mentioned. The strator or staller was a more important person: Alfred the *strator* of Edward the Confessor is mentioned by Flor. Wig. A.D. 1052; and Osgod Clapa the *staller*, ibid. A.D. 1047; Kemble, Saxons, ii. 108-111.

[3] G. L. von Maurer, Hofverfassung, i. 189. The *dispensator* of Harold is mentioned by Flor. Wig. A.D. 1040; Kemble identifies him with the camerarius or cubicularius, who occasionally appears in the charters; Saxons, ii. 107. Robert the *dispensator* of the Conqueror is mentioned by Ord. Vit. viii. 8, and in Domesday; Ellis, Intr. i. 478.

[4] Stapleton (Rotuli Scaccarii Normanniae, vol. i. p. xvii.) gives an extract from a cartulary of Trinity, Rouen, of A.D. 1068, which speaks of William Fitz-Osbern, 'dapiferi, qui comes erat palatii.'

cup-bearer, its constable, and its chamberlain; and these had become, it would be difficult to say how early, hereditary grand serjeanties. At the time of the Conquest William Fitz-Osbern was, as his father had been, *dapifer* and *comes palatii*. The chamberlainship was hereditary in the house of Tankerville; the lords of Hommet were hereditary constables. The royal household in England reproduced the ducal household of Normandy, and under the same conditions; for although the exact dates for the foundation of the offices cannot be given, nor even a satisfactory list of their early holders, it would seem certain that, before the end of the reign of Henry II, the high stewardship had become hereditary in the house of Leicester, the office of constable in the descendants of Miles of Hereford, that of chamberlain in the family of Vere, and the butlership in that of Albini[1]. But whilst these offices were becoming hereditary, the duties which had originally belonged to them were falling into the hands of another class of ministers, whose titles cause a sort of duplication of official nomenclature which is somewhat puzzling, and which even to the present day occasionally causes confusion[2].

In the court of the Norman kings

The place of hereditary officers supplied by new officials.

---

[1] It is however to be noticed that each of these names appears to have been given to several persons at once; there are certainly several dapiferi and pincernae at the same time. These were honorary distinctions probably, although they may in some instances have been grand serjeanties. The dignity that emerges ultimately may be the chief of each order; the *high* steward, the *great* butler, the lord *high* chamberlain. In later times, when these offices had long become hereditary, and substitutes for their holders were required, they were instituted with special reference to the household; the lord steward of the household and the lord chamberlain are still court officials. Something of the same kind may have taken place in the reign of Henry I, when the ministerial offices were founded.

[2] The Liber Niger Scaccarii contains a document of the age of Henry II, called 'Constitutio domus regis de procurationibus,' which gives the daily allowances of the several inmates of the palace: it is difficult to understand, and domestic servants and great officers of state are mingled in amusing disorder. The following are perhaps the most important particulars for our present purpose: (1) the chancellor has associated with him a Magister Scriptorii; (2) the dapifer, who has the same allowance as the chancellor, is mentioned in connexion with a *magister dispensator panis*, a *clericus expensae panis*, and a company of bakers; (3) the larder has its staff of officials, cooks and kitchen-servants; (4) the buttery, under the *magister pincerna*, whose allowance is the same as that of the steward and chancellor, has under him a *magister dispensator buteleriae*, with several subordinates, and four 'escantiones;' (5) the master chamberlain, the treasurer, the constable, and the master marshal have the same allowances as the steward and chancellor; (6) under the master marshal John (the

The justiciar, the treasurer, and the marshal take their places besides the high steward, the chamberlain, and the constable. Not that the history of these offices is in exact conformity : the constable, as long as he exists at all, retains no small share of his ancient powers ; the high steward, on the other hand, sees every one of his really important functions transferred to the justiciar ; the office of marshal becomes hereditary, those of justiciar and treasurer continue to be filled by nomination or even by purchase ; and only those offices which escape the dangers of hereditary transmission continue to have a real constitutional importance.

The offices have different histories.

120. The chief minister of the Norman kings is the person to whom the historians and later constitutional writers give the name of *justiciarius*, with or without the prefix *summus* or *capitalis*[1]. The growth of his functions was gradual, and even the history of the title is obscure ; for it is often bestowed on officers who, although they discharged the functions which at a later period were attached to it, are not so styled by contemporaries or in formal documents. The office appears first as the lieutenancy of the kingdom or vice-royalty exercised during the king's absence from England. In this capacity William Fitz-Osbern, the steward of Normandy, and Odo of Bayeux, acted during the Conqueror's visit to the Continent in 1067 ; they were left, according to William of Poictiers, the former to govern the north of England, and the latter to hold rule in Kent, in the king's stead, 'vice sua ;' Florence of Worcester describes them as ' custodes Angliae,' and Ordericus Vitalis gives to their office the name of ' praefectura[2].' It would seem most probable that

Growth of the justiciarship.

Holders of the office.

ancestor of the earls marshal of later times) are four marshals, who again have servants of their own. This will account for the number of officers who bear the same names. It exhibits further the retention of the primitive names in the now overgrown establishment of the palace. Probably all the heads of departments were important men. Roger the Larderer was made a bishop by Henry I, a fact which does not show that the king bestowed a bishopric on a mere servant, but that a person who was qualified to be a bishop did not scruple to undertake the office of larderer.

[1] It is observable that in the ordinance referred to in the last note there is no provision for the justiciar. He was not in that capacity a member of the household, although the chancellor was.

[2] Will. Pict. ed. Maseres, p. 151 ; Ord. Vit. iv. 1 ; Flor. Wig. A.D. 1067.

William Fitz-Osbern, at least, was left in his character of steward, and that the Norman seneschalship was thus the origin of the English justiciarship. After the death of William Fitz-Osbern, Odo acted alone ; William of Malmesbury describes him as ' totius Angliae vicedominus sub rege [1].' In 1074, when the king was again in Normandy, William of Warenne and Richard of Bienfaite were left in charge of England ; to these Ordericus [2], who lived a generation later, gives the title ' praecipui Angliae justiciarii ; ' but there is no reason to suppose that the name as yet was definitely attached to a particular post. On another occasion the office seems to have been committed to Lanfranc [3], Gosfrid of Coutances, and Robert of Mortain. In all these cases, although the function discharged was one which belonged to the later justiciar, and they are accordingly stages in the development of that office, it would seem safer to give to the persons employed the more general name of lieutenant or vicegerent. There is no evidence to show that they held any such position during the king's presence in England, or that they exercised even in his absence supreme judicial functions to the exclusion of other great officers of the court. In the placitum held at Pennenden in 1075 Gosfrid acted as president of the court, and in similar trials touching the rights of Ely and Rochester Odo of Bayeux appeared in the same position [4].

Question as to the title borne.

Under William Rufus the functions of the confidential minister were largely extended ; the office became a permanent one, and included the direction of the whole judicial and financial arrangements of the kingdom. It is probable that the king,

Holders of the office under William Rufus.

---

[1] W. Malmesb. G. R. lib. iii. § 277.

[2] Ord. Vit. iv. 14.

[3] Dugdale, Orig. Jurid. 20, quoted in Foss's Judges, i. 11 ; Liber Eliensis, ed. Stewart, i. pp. 256-260. The author of the life of Lanfranc, Milo Crispin, a contemporary of Anselm, seems to imply the same thing : ' Quando gloriosus rex Willelmus morabatur in Normannia, Lanfrancus erat princeps et custos Angliae, subjectis sibi omnibus principibus, et juvantibus in his quae ad defensionem et dispositionem vel pacem pertinebant regni, secundum leges patriae ; ' cap. 15.

[4] At Pennenden, in 1075 (above, p. 301), Gosfrid of Coutances must have been acting as justiciar ; he is described in the Textus Roffensis as ' qui in loco regis fuit et justitiam illam tenuit ; ' Ang. Sac. i. 335. For the Rochester and Ely cases see Ang. Sac. i. 339 ; Liber Eliensis (ed. Stewart), i. 252.

who had no great aptitude for any other business than that of
war, was inclined at first to throw the cares of government on
his uncle Odo and the bishop of Durham, William of S. Carileph; to these prelates later writers give the title of justiciar[1].
But their treason opened the king's eyes to the imprudence of
trusting so great authority to such powerful and ambitious
personages. Ranulf Flambard, who succeeded to the place of
chief adviser[2], seems to have earned his master's confidence by
his ingenious and unscrupulous devices for increasing the royal
revenue, and he may be looked on as the first consolidator of
the functions of the office. It is impossible not to suspect that
he had a share in the work of the Domesday Survey[3]. He was
a native of the diocese of Bayeux, in which Caen, the seat of
the Norman treasury, was situated, and had been brought up
among the inferior officials of the ducal court[4]. He had held,
in the days of Edward the Confessor, a small estate in Hampshire[5], possibly acquired in the service of the Norman bishop
William of London. He was afterwards attached to the household of Bishop Maurice, whom he left to become chaplain to the
king, an office which he had held for some years before he came
into prominent importance[6]. As the annals of the Conqueror's
reign furnish the names of no great lawyers or financiers, as
Ranulf was employed at court during the later years of it, and
as his subsequent career proves him to have possessed great
ability, if not a systematic policy of administration, it is not
unnatural to suppose that he rendered himself useful in the
compilation of the great rate-book of the kingdom. And such
a supposition almost answers the objection taken to the statement of Ordericus, that he made a new survey in the reign of

---

[1] 'Odo episcopus Bajocensis, justitiarius et princeps totius Angliae;'
Hen. Hunt. fol. 212. 'Willelmo Dunelmensi episcopo commendata erat
rerum publicarum administratio;' W. Malmesb. G. R. iv. § 306.

[2] 'Summus regiarum procurator opum et justitiarius factus est;' Ord.
Vit. x. 18. 'Regiae voluntatis maximus exsecutor;' Eadmer, i. p. 20.

[3] Above, p. 324.

[4] Ord. Vit. viii. 8: he had been under Robert the *dispensator* (above,
p. 372), who had given him the name of Flambard.

[5] Domesday, i. 51; Ellis, Intr. i. 420.

[6] Mon. Dunelm., Ang. Sac. i. 706. He is spoken of as a clerk in the
Domesday Book, i. 154, 157; Ellis, Intr. i. 420.

William Rufus, of which there is no other evidence. The
chronicler may have heard that he was employed in the regis-
tration of the revenue, and may have attributed it to him as a
measure adopted during his term of high office.

However this may have been, and by whatever name the post Titles given
him.
was distinguished, it became in Flambard's hands all important.
He is called by Florence of Worcester 'negotiorum totius regni
exactor,' and 'placitator et totius regni exactor[1]:' expressions
which recall the ancient identity of the *gerefa* with the *exactor*[2],
and suggest that one part of the royal policy was to entrust the
functions which had belonged to the praefectus or high steward
to a clerk or creature of the court. Robert Bloett, bishop of
Lincoln, is called by Henry of Huntingdon 'justitiarius totius
Angliae[3]:' he may have succeeded Ranulf, but of his adminis-
tration nothing is known. The next holder of the office is Career of
Bishop
Roger of
Salisbury.
Bishop Roger of Salisbury. He had a history somewhat like
that of Ranulf Flambard. He also was a poor priest of the
neighbourhood of Caen. He had attracted Henry's notice, long
before he came to the throne, by his expeditious way of celebrating divine service, had been enlisted by him as a sort of chaplain steward, and by his economy and honesty had justified the
confidence reposed in him[4]. After Henry's accession he was at
first employed as chancellor, and after the reconciliation of the
king with Anselm was consecrated to the see of Salisbury,
being the first prelate canonically elected since the dispute
about investiture had arisen. He seems to have risen at the
same time to the place of justiciar[5]. Under his guidance,

---

[1] Flor. Wig. A.D. 1099, 1100.   [2] Above, p. 88.
[3] Henry had been brought up in the bishop's court, and can scarcely
have been mistaken as to his right to bear the title. He calls him distinctly 'Justitiarius totius Angliae;' Anglia Sacra, ii. 695.
[4] Will. Newb. i. 6; W. Malmesb. G. R. v. § 408.
[5] 'Rogerius vir magnus in saecularibus, nunc vero regis justitiarius;'
Hen. Hunt. de Cont. Mundi; Ang. Sac. ii. 700. 'Rogerus autem justitiarius fuit totius Angliae et secundus a rege;' Hen. Hunt. Hist. lib. vii.
fol. 219. He is called justiciar also by William of Malmesbury, G. R. v.
§ 408. 'Secundus post regem in omnibus negotiis habebatur . . . curae
palatinae regnique negotiis cunctis specialius est praepositus;' Gesta
Stephani, p. 46. 'Secundus enim a rege in regno praeeminebat universis
judicibus et principibus;' John of Hexham, p. 125. See also Ordericus
Vitalis, xiii. 40.

His adminis-
trative skill.

whether as chancellor or as justiciar, the whole administrative system was remodelled; the jurisdiction of the Curia Regis and Exchequer was carefully organised, and the peace of the country maintained in that theoretical perfection which earned for him the title of the Sword of Righteousness [1]. He is the first justiciar who is called 'secundus a rege.' He retained the title of justiciar until his arrest by Stephen. His personal

Uncertainty
of the appli-
cation of the
title of justi-
ciar.

history need not be further pursued. Roger of Salisbury certainly bore the title of justiciar [2]; whether he acted as the king's lieutenant during his absence is uncertain, and even yet it must be questioned whether the name possessed a precise official significance [3]. Several other ministers receive the same name even during the time at which he was certainly in office: even the title of *capitalis justitiarius* is given to officers of the Curia Regis who were acting in subordination to him [4]. We have, however, been tracing the development of the office rather than the history of the title. The latter, not improbably, gained definiteness of application as the functions of the office developed. The 'magister justitiarius' of the Norman kingdom of Sicily, who possibly took his name from the Norman chief minister of England, appears soon after the middle of the twelfth century [5]. The title of *justiza* of Aragon, a minister

---

[1] In his epitaph, Archaeologia, ii. 190.

[2] Henry uses the term *capitalis justitiarius* in a charter, Foed. i. 12: 'Nisi coram me vel capitali justitiario meo;' but this may not refer to Roger.

[3] In a letter of Henry to Anselm, dated at Rouen, he tells him that he has given notice to the justiciars to act by the Archbishop's advice. Whether these were the regents or the judges, or both, may be questioned. We find the queen and the heir-apparent acting with considerable power in the king's absence; above, pp. 370, 371.

[4] See below, § 127.

[5] Giannone, lib. xi. c. 4, mentions a charter of 1141 as attested by 'Henricus Ollia Dei gratia regalis justitiarius.' The marriage settlement of Queen Johanna in 1177 is signed by a 'magister justitiarius,' a 'regiae curiae magister justitiarius,' a 'regiae curiae justitiarius,' and a 'sacri regii palatii logotheta' as well. Although the Sicilian kings copied Byzantine as well as Western forms, it must not be forgotten that several of their ministers and bishops were Englishmen. Robert of Salisbury, chancellor of Sicily in 1147 (Joh. Salisb. Polycr. vii. 19; John of Hexham, pp. 151, 152), Herbert of Middlesex, bishop of Compsa (R. Diceto, ii. 37), Richard Palmer, archbishop of Messina in 1183, and two contemporaneous archbishops of Palermo, Walter and Bartholomew, were Englishmen. See Hoveden, vol. ii. pref. p. xcii.

not unlike the later chief justices of England, is first found in
the twelfth century[1]. The seneschal of Normandy receives the
name of *justitiar* under Henry II. It is only in the same reign
that the office in England acquires the exclusive right to the
definite name of *summus* or *capitalis justitiarius*, or *justitiarius
totius Angliae*, a title occasionally paraphrased or interpreted as
'*praefectus Angliae*[2].'

For the office, the development of which is thus only obscurely traceable, it is easier to find analogies in foreign systems
than to produce a consecutive history to connect it with known
antecedents. A general view of the Norman policy suggests
that the form taken by the institution on English ground arose
partly from the king's desire to prevent the administration
falling into the hands of a hereditary noble. In a small territory like Normandy, where the duke was always at home, and
where very much of the judicial business was devolved on the
courts of the feudatories, an officer like the seneschal might
suffice for all necessary business of state. But in England,
where the king could not be always resident, where the amount
of public business was increasing rapidly in consequence of the
political changes, and where it was of the utmost importance to
avoid the creation of hereditary jurisdictions, it was absolutely
necessary that a new system should be devised. The same need
was felt in France; and the same tide of events which threw
the administration here into the hands of Bishop Roger, brought
the management of affairs there into the hands of the Abbot
Suger[3]. In each case we see an ecclesiastical mayor of the

Possible reasons for this development.

Necessity for some such officer in England.

---

[1] On the Judex medius of Soprarbe and the Justitia of Aragon, see
Du Cange, sub voc.; Dunham, Hist. of Spain, iv. 178–182; Hallam, M. A.
ii. 49 sq.

[2] This is the title generally given by Gervase to the justiciar; see his
Chronicle, i. 293, 523, &c.

[3] Suger's position at the French court is spoken of in very nearly the
same terms as Roger's : 'praeerat palatio ;' 'nec illum a claustri cura pro-
hiberet curia, nec a consiliis principum hunc excusaret monasterium ;'
'cumque ab eo jura dictarentur nullo unquam pretio declinavit a recto ;'
'praecipua regni incumberent negotia ;' 'ex eo siquidem tempore, quo
primum regiis est adhibitus consiliis, usque ad vitae illius terminum, con-
stat regnum semper floruisse et in melius atque amplius, dilatatis terminis
et hostibus subjugatis, fuisse provectum. Quo sublato de medio statim
sceptrum regni gravem ex illius absentia sensit jacturam ;' Vita Sugeri,

Convenience
of having an
ecclesiastic
in the office.

palace; a representative of the king in all capacities, lieutenant in his absence, chief agent in his presence; prime minister in legal, financial, and even military affairs; but prevented by his spiritual profession from founding a family of nobles or withdrawing from the crown the powers which he had been commissioned to sustain. The expedient was a transitional one; the clerical justiciars were superseded by baronial ones when Henry II felt himself strong enough to stand the risk, and occur again only under his sons, whose exigencies and whose policy compelled them to employ such ministers as they found trained to their hands, and as were otherwise qualified to act as mediators between themselves and their people.

The chancellor.

121. The chancellor, who at a later period entered into many of the rights and dignities of the justiciar, appears in history very much earlier. The name, derived probably from the *cancelli*, or skreen behind which the secretarial work of the royal household was carried on, claims a considerable antiquity; and the offices which it denotes are various in proportion. The chancellor of the Karolingian sovereigns, succeeding to the place of the more ancient *referendarius* [1], is simply the royal

lib. i. ' Rege . . . peregre jam profecto, cum vir egregius rerum dominio potiretur ; ' ibid. lib. ii.

[1] Waitz, D. V. G. ii. 409, traces the history of the Merovingian *referendarius* as a lay officer: the scriptores, notarii, and cancellarii seem to have been part of his staff. In the Ripuarian law, however, he appears with the optimates; and in the Karolingian period, the archi-cancellarius or cancellarius, who keeps the seal, becomes an important officer; ibid. iii. 426. From the time of Lewis the Pious the chancellor was generally in holy orders. The same writer maintains that the arch-chancellor had originally nothing to do with the royal chapel, except so far as it was the storehouse of official documents, and that the union of the office of arch-chancellor and arch-chaplain dates from the reigns of the sons of Lewis. Of course the two functions had been long united before the age of Edward the Confessor, when the title of chancellor was introduced into England. The office held by Dunstan under Edred must have been very much like that of the later chancellors. Reginbaldus, who attests Edward's charter to Waltham (C. D. dcccxiii), is the only person who appears as cancellarius in genuine charters. Leofric bishop of Crediton is called chancellor by Florence of Worcester, A.D. 1045. Helinandus, afterwards bishop of Laon, 1052–1098, seems, from the description given by Guibert of Nogent, to have filled the same office under Edward the Confessor, although he is only called *capellanus* ; Opp. ed. D'Achery, p. 496. It may be remarked that the office of chancellor of a cathedral was unknown in England until some time after the Conquest; the officer who fulfilled the duties later given to the chancellor bearing the title of scholasticus.

notary: the archi-cancellarius is the chief of a large body of such officers associated under the name of the chancery, and is the official keeper of the royal seal. It is from this minister that the English chancellor derives his name and function. Edward the Confessor, the first of our sovereigns who had a seal, is also the first who had a chancellor: from the reign of the Conqueror the office has descended in regular succession. It seems to have been to a comparatively late period, generally if not always, at least in England, held by an ecclesiastic, who was a member of the royal household, and on a footing with the great dignitaries[1]. The chancellor was the most dignified of the royal chaplains, if not the actual head of that body; and he had the especial duty of securing and administering the royal revenue which accrued from vacant benefices. The whole of the secretarial work of the household and court fell on the chancellor and chaplains; the keeping of the royal accounts under the treasurer and justiciar, the drawing up and sealing of the royal writs, and the conducting of the king's correspondence. The chancellor was, in a manner, the secretary of state for all departments[2]. He was generally rewarded for his service with a bishopric, and it was not regarded as fitting that the office should be retained by him after his consecration. Of the early chancellors none are of particular eminence, or perhaps they are overshadowed by the greatness of the justiciar. The office was however held by William Giffard, whose services were influential in procuring the election of Henry I; by Roger of Salisbury himself, before his promotion to episcopal rank and to the justiciarship; and by his son, also named Roger, who was one of the victims of Stephen[3].

A clerical office.

Early chancellors.

[1] Above, p. 373, note 2.
[2] The words of John of Salisbury, 'Hic est qui regni leges cancellat iniquas, et mandata pii principis aequa facit,' are a curious anticipation of the history of the chancellor's equitable jurisdiction as developed at a later period. The play on the word is only a jesting one. The reference to equity is explained when it is remembered that the Curia Regis was by its very nature a court of remedial and equitable jurisdiction in the wider sense of the word equitable. See below, § 127.
[3] It is impossible to construct a trustworthy list of the chancellors of the Conqueror: the title is however given to the following persons, whose dates may be adjusted on the hypothesis that they did not retain office

The trea-
surer.

122. The treasurer during the Norman period was the keeper
of the royal treasure, which was preserved at Winchester : he
was also an important member of the household, and sat in the
Exchequer at Westminster, where he received the accounts of
the sheriffs. William of Pont de l'Arche, who had been
treasurer to Henry I, is mentioned in connexion with the
seizure of the Winchester treasure by Stephen[1]; and the office
was so important that Bishop Roger obtained it for his nephew
the Bishop of Ely[2]. But, like the chancellorship, it falls far

The cham-
berlain.

below the first rank of ministerial dignities. The chamberlain
was another financial officer[3] : his work was rather that of
auditor or accountant than that of treasurer : he held a more
definite position in the household than the officers already enumerated, and in the judicial work of the country he was only
less important than the justiciar.

The offices of steward, butler, constable, and marshal complete

after they became bishops : (1) Herfast, made bishop of Elmham in 1070;
(2) Osbern, made bishop of Exeter in 1072 ; (3) Osmund, made bishop of
Salisbury in 1078 ; (4) Maurice, made bishop of London in 1086; (5)
William, a chancellor known only by the attestation of charters; he has
been identified, but with no certainty, with William of Beaufeu, made
bishop of Thetford in 1086 (R. de Monte), and with William Giffard who
follows. Under William Rufus we find two chancellors, Robert Bloett,
who became bishop of Lincoln in 1094, and William Giffard, who was
chancellor until the accession of Henry I, who appointed him bishop of
Winchester in 1100. The chancellors under Henry I were (1) Roger the
Poor, appointed bishop of Salisbury in 1102 ; (2) Waldric, who was made
bishop of Laon in 1106; (3) Ranulf, 1107-1123; (4) Geoffrey Rufus,
1124-1133, made bishop of Durham in the latter year ; (5) Roger the Poor,
son of the justiciar. It is not improbable that Ranulf the chancellor,
1107-1123, was brother or brother-in-law of Roger of Salisbury. Guibert
of Nogent states that he had two sons in the school of Anselm of Laon,
under the care of William of Corbeuil, afterwards archbishop of Canterbury
(Opp. p. 536) ; and in another place mentions Nigel and Alexander, bishop
Roger's nephews, as scholars of the same teacher (ibid. p. 539); possibly
these may be identified. The seal was kept during Henry I's reign by
the magister scriptorii, as appears from the Constitutio Domus Regis (Lib.
Nig. i. 341 ; p. 373 above); he was probably a subordinate of the chancellor in the position held in Henry II's reign by the vicechancellors.
Richard, 'qui regii sigilli sub cancellario custos erat,' became a bishop in
1121 ; Cont. Flor. Wig.

[1] Gesta Stephani, p. 5. He is called by William of Malmesbury, in
conjunction with Bishop Roger, *custos thesaurorum regalium* ; Hist. Nov.
i. § 11.

[2] Dialogus de Scaccario, i. 8.

[3] See Madox, Hist. Exch. pp. 38 sq.

the machinery of the household. The first of these, as we have
already seen, was eclipsed in his most important functions by
the justiciar, and makes in his official capacity no great figure
in English history. The constable, who exercised the office of
quartermaster-general of the court and army, and succeeded to
the duties of the Anglo-Saxon staller [1]; and the marshal, whose
functions are scarcely distinguishable from those of the constable, reached at a comparatively early date the position of
hereditary dignities. Their military functions however preserved
them from falling into the class of mere grand serjeanties, and at a
later period they had very great importance in the management
of the army [2]. During the Norman reigns neither of them
comes into much prominence. Miles, the constable of Gloucester,
who was made earl of Hereford by the empress, and whose
dignity descended to the Bohuns, is the first of the number who

---

[1] See Coke, 4th Inst. p. 123; Prynne, 4th Inst. pp. 59 sq., 337 sq. Of
the early functions, as well as of the rest of the history, of the constables
we have not much information. The name is derived from the *comes
stabuli* of the Byzantine court, and appears in the West as early as the
days of Gregory of Tours. The duties of the constables of France are
given by Du Cange, s. v.; and those of the constables of Naples by Giannone, xi. 1. But these officers are not exactly parallel with the constables
of England. In Naples the constable kept the king's sword, commanded
the army, appointed the quarters, disciplined the troops, and distributed
the sentinels; the marshals and all other officers being his subordinates.
The French office was nearly the same. In England however the marshal
was not subordinate to the constable. Probably the English marshals
fulfilled the duties which had been in Normandy discharged by the constables. The marshal is more distinctly an officer of the court, the constable one of the castle or army. But the obscurity of the distinction is
accounted for by the hypothesis of the text.

[2] In the reign of Edward I the Earls Bohun and Bigod, the constable
and marshal, refused to exercise their functions except in the king's presence, and helped to bring on the crisis that led to the confirmation of the
charters. Carte, Hist. Engl. ii. 269, gives, from Anstis, an account of
their duties at that time : 'to examine, judge, and determine whether
those who owed services by their tenures answered those services by the
qualities and numbers of the persons required; then to muster those whom
they thought proper to admit, and to assign them quarters ; and, if it was
an expedition to foreign parts, to billet them into ships for their transport-
ation, and to govern them while they were upon the sea; and upon their
landing to direct into what battalions and companies they should be
formed; and during the actual wars to hold court for the determinations of
all offences committed against the laws of war, and for the decision of all
civil causes arising in the army concerning the rights of prisoners and
booties taken, and such like.'

takes the position ordinarily associated with the title of high constable. Both the constable and the marshal had places and definite functions in the Exchequer. Somewhat of the same developing and defining process which we have traced in the justiciarship seems to have taken place in these offices. Not only was there a double set of officials, arising partly perhaps from the consolidation of the Anglo-Saxon and the Norman courts, but each of the offices seems to have been held by several co-ordinate functionaries—there are several dapiferi and camerarii[1]; and as every castle had its own constable, there were many barons who had a right to call themselves the king's constables. The attainment by some one of these of the right to call himself high steward, or high constable, was doubtless a gradual proceeding; and it may conjecturally be referred to the age of Stephen, when both the contending parties sought to retain their fickle partisans by the gift of honours and titles. Probably each one of these offices has a history of its own, for which only scanty materials now exist.

Consolidation of the great offices of the court.

The separation of the great functionaries of the household from those of the State is ultimately marked by the fact of the former becoming hereditary, while the latter continue to be ministerial. And this is further distinguished: the ministerial offices are saleable. The treasurer, the chancellor, even the justiciar, pays a sum of money for his office, or even renders an annual rent or ferm for it[2]. This practice runs on to the thirteenth century, when, so many of the dignities having become hereditary, and the feeling of the nation being strongly expressed in favour of reform, the king was compelled to choose his subordinate ministers with some reference to their capacity for business. Such a history may account for much of the indefinite and complicated character of the offices of State.

Court offices become hereditary:

State offices saleable.

The powers of these officers were very considerable, and were extended by continual encroachments. Each dignitary of the household was a member of the Curia Regis and Exchequer, and in that capacity exercised from time to time judicial functions.

Powers of these officers.

---

[1] See Madox, Exchequer, chap. ii.; and p. 373 above.

[2] See below, § 126.

Each too had under him a staff of servants over whom he exercised judicature and discipline; and this was extended to the cognisance of all offences committed or disputes arising in the department which was nominally under his management. Hence the origin of the courts of the high steward, the constable, and the marshal, which are subjects of complaint down to a late period. These courts were naturally regarded as exceptions to the common law of the land which was administered by the justiciar or under his superintendence.

Judicial powers over their own departments.

123. The witenagemot of the kingdom, now subsisting under the title of the great court or council, forms a second circle round the sovereign [1]. Under the Conqueror this assembly retained very much of its earlier character: the bishops and abbots still attended in virtue of their official wisdom, and with them the great officers of State and the chief of the Norman baronage. It was however rather a court than an organised council. It cannot be certainly affirmed that the tenure of a particular estate of land, held by homage and fealty, either was an indispensable qualification or bestowed the privilege of membership: and before the reign of Henry II it would be rash to maintain that every tenant-in-chief of the crown was a member of the assembly, although every member of the assembly was, after the settlement of the question of investiture, obliged to hold his barony by homage and fealty. It is of course only to the bishops and abbots that that measure directly applies, but its operation in their case necessarily involves the observance

The great council of the kingdom.

Feudal qualification of its members.

Assembly of tenants-in-chief.

---

[1] Gneist, Verwalt. i. 238 sq., argues strongly against the continuance of the witenagemot in the form of a feudal council, and maintains the practically absolute character of the government in the Norman times. It would not now be contended that the assemblies brought together by the Conqueror or Henry I had the definite organisation of the parliaments of Edward I, or even of the councils of Henry II. But that there were such gatherings of magnates, and that those gatherings, when they emerge from obscurity in the reign of Henry II, were assemblies of tenants-in-chief, is clear on the face of the history. The period was one of transition and growth in every way. No legislative act turned the witenagemot into a feudal council, and no legislative act turned the feudal council into a parliament. On the other hand, Gneist's position, that the Norman assemblies were not independent legislative or governing assemblies, needs no proof. The kings were practically absolute, but they retained the theory and the form of a national council.

of the rule in all others. It is sufficiently obvious from the
Domesday record that the tenants-in-chief had long had their
position and character defined. That the forcing of homage
and fealty, with the baronial tenure, upon the bishops had the
effect of annihilating their earlier title to appear in the witenagemot as *sapientes* can scarcely be maintained[1]. It completed
however the symmetry of the baronage, and gave a basis of
uniformity to the court in which they were assembled. The
kings no doubt exercised the right of associating in their deliberations such counsellors as it might seem convenient to admit,
as, for instance, a Roman legate, a Norman prelate who would
be unlikely to have lands in England, or even lawyers, monks,
or clergymen of special skill or sanctity; but it does not follow
that such strangers would be allowed to vote in case of any
difference of opinion. Except in the anomalous period of
Stephen's reign, there are no records of any such discussions as
might lead to divisions. In private perhaps the sovereign
listened to advice, but, so far as history goes, the counsellors
who took part in formal deliberations must have been unanimous or subservient. An assembly of courtiers holding their
lands of the king, and brought together rather for pompous display than for political business, may seem scarcely entitled to
the name of a national council[2]. Such as it was, however, this

*Other coun-
sellors.*

*General un-
animity in
recorded
councils.*

---

[1] Matthew Paris places the commutation of title in A.D. 1070: 'Episcopatus quoque, et abbatias omnes quae baronias tenebant et eatenus ab
omni servitute saeculari libertatem habuerant, sub servitute statuit militari, inrotulans singulos episcopatus et abbatias pro voluntate sua, quot
milites sibi et successoribus suis hostilitatis tempore voluit a singulis exhi-
beri' (ed. Luard, ii. 6). Even if this refers to any real act of William,
and is not a mistaken account of the effect of the Domesday Survey, the
change is not completed until the prelates do homage and fealty for their
temporalities. The exact form and nature of episcopal homage is a matter
of discussion, on which see Taylor, Glory of Regality, pp. 357 sq., and the
third volume of this work, ch. xix. Glanvill (ix. 1) says, 'episcopi vero
consecrati homagium facere non solent domino regi etiam de baroniis suis,
sed fidelitatem cum juramentis interpositis ipsi praestare solent. Electi
vero in episcopos ante consecrationem suam homagia sua facere solent.' As no
bishop could say to the king ' devenio homo vester,' the form was probably
of the nature of fealty rather than homage. Hence the bishops were summoned to parliament 'in fide et dilectione quibus nobis tenemini,' lay lords
' in fide et homagio.' Yet in common language the bishops held their
baronies by homage and fealty.

[2] Gneist (Verw. i. 223) remarks that in the solemn courts held at the

court of bishops, abbots, earls, barons, and knights was the
council by whose advice and consent the kings condescended to
act, or to declare that they acted[1].

A council based on the principle that its members are qualified by feudal tenure of land ought not to confine itself to an
assembly of magnates : it should include all freeholders of town
or country who are not under any mesne lord, and would thus
be in theory a much larger and more liberal representation of
the nation than anything that had existed since the days of the
Heptarchy.   On some occasions, especially at the great councils
of Salisbury in 1086 and 1116, it is probable that a general
muster of the landowners of the kingdom was held, at which all
were expected either to be present or to send their excuses by
the sheriffs, who on the former occasion are especially said to
have been summoned[2].   But the number of persons who were
really consulted on business, or to whom the show of such
attention was paid, must have been always very limited.   As
both earlier and later was the case, only the highest class was
called on to treat of the highest matters; the people, if they
were called at all, would hear and obey.   And thus the constituent parts of the assembly are reduced to the archbishops,
bishops, abbots, earls, barons and knights.   The sheriffs, who
would come invariably under one of these heads, may be left out
of consideration in this relation.   The enumeration is however
in no way based on a logical division; all the members were

The Norman council generally an assembly of magnates :

but sometimes a general meeting of landowners.

Ordinary members of these councils.

festivals the oppressed English might recognise the ancient witenagemot,
and the proud Norman the baronial court; whilst the Conqueror took good
care that they should be neither the one nor the other.   The view which I
have maintained in these chapters is different : I believe that the Conqueror
wished to make these councils both witenagemots and baronial courts, so
maintaining form and reality that the one principle should be a check
upon the other.   But it is a mistake to adopt too strict definitions in such
matter.   The evidence of the Chronicle is sufficient to prove the form and
reality of deliberation.   In 1085, 'At mid-winter the king was at Gloucester
with his witan, and he held his court (hired) there five days: and afterwards the archbishop and clergy held a synod there for three days. . . . .
After this the king held a great consultation (mycel getheaht) ; ' Chron.
Sax. A.D. 1085.

[1] 'Arcebiscopas and leodbiscopas, abbodas and eorlas, thegnas and
cnihtas;' Chron. Sax. A.D. 1086.

[2] 'Archiepiscopi, episcopi, abbates, comites, barones, vicecomites, cum
suis militibus;' Flor. Wig. A.D. 1086.

barons by tenure, greater or less, and all the earls and barons strictly so called were probably knights.

Bishops.

On the ecclesiastical members of the council it is unnecessary to dwell: their character is, except as affected by the acceptance

The archbishop of Canterbury is the first adviser of the crown.

of feudal baronies, exactly the same as it was before[1]. The archbishop of Canterbury is still recognised as the first constitutional adviser of the crown[2]: William Rufus acknowledges the right of Lanfranc as distinctly as Henry I does that of Anselm[3]. And the importance of this position probably lay at the root of the claim made by the kings to decide which of two rival popes should be recognised in the country: the theory that it was by the acceptance of the pall from Rome that the metropolitical status was completed, might have exposed the king to the necessity of receiving his chief counsellor from a hostile power, unless limited by such a condition[4]: and as the papal theory of appeals and legations was not yet applied to England, the power of the archbishop to further or retard the promotion of bishops was practically unlimited, except by means which it would have been highly dangerous for the king to adopt. Even at the best the relations of the archbishops to the Norman kings were hazardous, and depended far more on personal than

His important and independent position.

on legal considerations. The fact that even William Rufus was obliged to except the primatial see of Canterbury from his un-

[1] This is the old question of the title of the bishops to sit in parliament. It is scarcely necessary to say more than that they had sat before the Conquest as witan, and continued to do so without break afterwards. See Selden, Titles of Honour, pp. 695, 696; Hody, Convocation, pp. 128, 129. The bishop of Rochester always sat in parliament, even when he received his temporalities from the archbishop of Canterbury and not from the king; and accordingly the bishops of the sees founded at the Reformation, who never held baronies at all, sit exactly as the other bishops. The qualification is however strictly *official* wisdom, for suffragans, although spiritually equal to diocesan bishops, have never sat. Hody explains this by saying that the bishops sit as governors of the Church; and the same may be said of abbots and priors, although, as their appearance in the national council is for the most part subsequent to the Conquest, and as only the abbots and priors who held baronies were summoned, the question with regard to them is more complicated than that of the bishops.

[2] This fact appears clearly in Lanfranc's letters; e. g. ' hoc est consilium regis et meum;' Ep. 32; cf. Ep. 58. Anselm tried to obtain a promise from William Rufus, that he would act on his advice in the same way; Eadmer, i. p. 20.   [3] Above, p. 330.

[4] Above, p. 309.

scrupulous misuse of patronage, is another proof of the strong constitutional hold of the archbishops ; a hold which their consistent exertions for the protection of the people and the purification of the Church most amply justified. The whole of the episcopal body was until the middle of Henry I's reign sworn to obedience to Canterbury; and the archbishop of York, even after he had obtained recognition of his independence, had so small a body of suffragans as to make his position in fact subordinate. He was very powerful in Yorkshire, but of secondary importance at court.

The archbishop of York.

124. The earls of the Norman period are not numerous, nor are the peculiar characteristics of the rank well ascertained. The tendency towards feudalisation of the governmental machinery, which had been growing since the days of Canute, might have made the assimilation of the English ealdorman to the Norman count easy and obvious; but that tendency was counteracted by the policy of William in more ways than one; and consequently it is difficult to reduce the expedients which he adopted in the several cases to a uniform rule. In the early days of his reign the earls whom he appointed seem to be merely successors to the English magistrates of the same name. William Fitz–Osbern, for instance, succeeds to the earldom of Herefordshire which had been held by the Confessor's nephew Ralph ; Ralph Guader has the earldom of East-Anglia ; and Edwin and Waltheof retain until their fall some portion of the territory which they had inherited with the same title. The three great earldoms of Chester, Shropshire, and Northumberland were created by the Conqueror out of the forfeited inheritances of Edwin, Morcar, and Waltheof, and may likewise be regarded as continuing the line of the ancient magistracies. Hugh of Avranches earl of Chester, Roger of Montgomery earl of Shropshire, and Alberic earl of Northumberland are the only persons who in Domesday hold the title of *comes* by virtue of English earldoms [1]; all the

The earls.

The Conqueror's earls were chiefly holders of old English earldoms.

---

[1] To these may be added the Countess Judith, the widow of Waltheof, who had the counties of Huntingdon and Northampton as earldoms, which descended to her daughter Maud, and through her to the family of Senlis and the kings of Scots.

rest—William of Evreux, Robert of Eu, Robert of Mortain, Eustace of Boulogne, Alan of Brittany, and Robert of Meulan —were counts simply, the first three of Norman, the latter three of French counties[1]. In some other cases the jurisdiction of the ealdorman was held by a bishop, who may have borne the title of earl, although the evidence on this point is not convincing: such was the position of Odo of Bayeux in Kent, of Walcher of Durham, and perhaps of Gosfrid of Coutances, the founder of the fortunes of the Mowbrays, in Northumberland. The third penny of the county, which had been a part of the profits of the English earls, is occasionally referred to in Domesday[2], but generally in connexion with the earldoms of king Edward's time. The title thus sparingly bestowed by the Conqueror was conferred little more lavishly by his sons: Henry of Beaumont, brother of the count of Meulan, was made earl of Warwick[3], Robert Mowbray earl of Northumberland, and William of Warenne earl of Surrey[4], by William Rufus; the count of Meulan himself received the earldom of Leicester from Henry I; the earldom of Gloucester was conferred by the same king on his illegitimate son. In all these cases it is probable that some portion of the traditional authority of the ealdormanship was conferred with the title. The next reign saw a great increase in the number and a change in the character of these officers[5]. Stephen, almost before the struggle for the crown had

Bishops acting as earls.

Earls created by William Rufus and Henry I.

[1] Ordericus Vitalis has unfortunately created a good deal of confusion on this point: he says (lib. iv. c. 7) that the Conqueror gave the county of Buckingham to Walter Giffard, that of Surrey to William of Warenne, and that of Holderness to Odo of Champagne; in each case the comitatus here given was given as a lordship, not an earldom, and accordingly none of the three appear as *comites* in Domesday. The lordship of Holderness was held with the county of Aumâle. The earldom of Surrey was created by William Rufus: that of Buckingham is obscure in its origin, but is probably to be referred to William Rufus. That of Devon is said to have been created for Richard of Redvers by Henry I. The most famous however of the disputed earldoms is that of Richmond, the lordship given by the Conqueror to Alan count of Brittany. On this see the third report of the Lords' Committee on the Dignity of a Peer, pp. 96 sq.; Courthope's Historic Peerage, p. 395.   [2] See above, p. 126.

[3] The count of Meulan had considerable rights in Warwickshire, recorded in Domesday, but the earldom was created for Henry his brother; and he himself obtained the earldom of Leicester in 1103.

[4] In 1089; Ord. Vit. viii. c. 9. See also Ellis, Introd. i. 507.

[5] The *comites* mentioned in the Pipe Roll of 31 Henry I are the counts of

begun, attempted to strengthen his party by a creation of new The earls made by Stephen and Matilda. earls [1]. To these the third penny of the county was given, and their connexion with the district from which the title was taken was generally confined to this comparatively small endowment, the rest of their provision being furnished possibly by new gifts. A similar expedient was adopted by the empress; and, as most of the earls so created contrived to retain their titles, it is possible that the frequent tergiversations which mark the struggle may have been caused by the desire of obtaining confirmation of the rank from both the competitors for the crown. Stephen made Hugh Bigod earl of Norfolk, Geoffrey de Mandeville earl of Essex, Richard de Clare earl of Hertford, William of Aumâle earl of Yorkshire, Gilbert de Clare earl of Pembroke, Robert de Ferrers earl of Derby, and Hugh de Beaumont earl of Bedford [2]. The empress created the earldoms of Salisbury, Hereford, Somerset, Cambridge, and Essex, if not

---

Eu, Beaumont, Brittany, Perche, Flanders, Guisnes, Meulan, Mortain, and Provins; and the earls of Chester, Gloucester, Leicester, Warenne (Surrey), and Warwick.

[1] Whether Stephen granted the third penny of the county to his earls as earls, and whether he or the empress was the first to make such grant, is discussed by Mr. Round, Geoffrey de Mandeville, Appendix H, pp. 287 sq.

[2] As Stephen's earldoms are a matter of great constitutional importance, it is as well to give the dates from Mr. Round's careful lists:—

  Derby, Robert de Ferrers, 1138; John of Hexham, p. 120; Ord. Vit. xiii. 37.
  Yorkshire, William of Aumâle, 1138; ibid.
  Pembroke, Gilbert de Clare, 1138; ibid.
  Lincoln, William de Roumare (? 1139–1140).
  Norfolk, Hugh Bigod (before Feb. 1141).
  Arundel, William de Albini (before Christmas, 1141).
  Hertford, Gilbert de Clare (before Christmas, 1141).
  Essex, Geoffrey de Mandeville, 1140.
  Bedford, Hugh de Beaumont, 1138 (?).
  William of Ypres, called without authority earl of Kent, is thrown out of the list.

The dates and authorities for the empress's earldoms are as follows:—

  William de Mohun, Somerset; Mon. Angl. vi. 335; before June, 1141.
  Patrick of Salisbury, Salisbury; before 1149; Foedera, i. 16.
  Miles of Gloucester, Hereford; July, 1141; Foedera, i. 14; Selden, Titles of Honour, p. 648.
  Aubrey de Vere, Oxford; 1142; Dugdale, Baronage, p. 190; Selden, Titles, p. 650.
  Reginald, Cornwall; appointed by Robert of Gloucester in 1140; W. Malmesb. Hist. Nov. ii. § 34; 1141 (?); Round, p. 271.
  Devon, Baldwin de Redvers; before June, 1141.

more. Two or three earldoms of uncertain creation, such as those of Buckingham and Lincoln [1], which were possibly connected with hereditary sheriffdoms, appear about the same period.

Investiture of earls.

The dignity of an earl was conferred by a special investiture, the girding on of the sword of the county by the king himself, and may be regarded as a personal rather than a territorial office, like knighthood itself. But the idea of official position is not lost sight of, although the third penny of the pleas and the sword of the shire alone attest its original character. The relief of the earl, like the heriot of his predecessor, is much higher than that of the simple baron ; and, although we have no warrant for supposing that a fixed number of knights' fees was necessarily attached to the title, the possessions of the earl were as a rule very much larger than those of the baron.

Jurisdiction of the earl.

The question of the jurisdiction of the earl in his shire is somewhat complicated. In some cases the title was joined to the lordship of all or nearly all the land in the shire; in some it conveyed apparently the hereditary sheriffship [2]; and

Palatine earldoms.

in a few cases the regalia or royal rights of jurisdiction. The earldom of Chester [3] is the most important instance of the latter class. The earl, as we have seen already, was said to hold his earldom as freely by his sword as the king held England by the crown ; he was lord of all the land in his shire that was not in the hands of the bishop; he had his court of barons of the palatinate, the writs ran in his name, and he was in fact a feudal sovereign in Cheshire as the king was in Normandy [4].

[1] On the history of the earldom of Lincoln, see Courthope, Hist. Peerage, p. 287 ; Round, Geoff. de Mandeville, p.

[2] See the grant to Geoffrey Mandeville, Selden, p. 647. The earls of Salisbury were sheriffs of Wilts from the reign of Henry II to the 16th of Henry III : their earldom being in fact based on a hereditary sheriffdom of earlier date. The Beauchamp earldom of Warwick was in the same way founded on a hereditary sheriffdom held almost from the Conquest.

[3] On the palatine earldom in general, see Selden, Titles of Honour, pp. 640 sq. ; above, p. 294. The first creation of a palatine earldom under that name is that of Lancaster in 1351.

[4] The palatine earldom of Chester had its own courts, judges, and staff of officers, constable, steward and the rest : it had its parliament, consisting of the barons of the county, and was not until 1541 represented in the parliament of the kingdom. The eight baronies of the earldom were Halton, Montalt or Mould, Nantwich, Malpas, Shilbroke, Dunham-Mascy, Stockport, and Kinderton : the last was held by the family of Venables,

The bishop of Durham occupied exactly the same position in Palatine earls. Durham, a position of earlier date than the Conquest, founded on the immunities granted by the Northumbrian kings, and confirmed by the Conqueror, in the idea, probably, of placing a strong and inviolable jurisdiction as an obstacle to Scottish invasion[1]. The earldom of Kent is said by Ordericus Vitalis to have been conferred as a palatine earldom on Odo of Bayeux; but, although at the time of the Domesday Survey he is still found in possession of an enormous number of lordships in the county, the day of his greatness was over, and we are left in uncertainty whether he ever really possessed the regalia. Another case is the earldom of Shrewsbury[2]: Roger Montgomery held as lord all the land in Shropshire, save such as belonged to the church and five comparatively insignificant tenants-in-chief: in a charter preserved by Ordericus Vitalis he speaks of the sheriff of the county as 'my sheriff[3]' in a way that leads to the conclusion that he also may have possessed palatine rights; but this earldom was forfeited before the time at which documentary evidence would be found to illustrate it more fully. The other earldoms Possible palatine jurisdictions in other cases. based on the Anglo-Saxon jurisdictions are liable to similar question; William Fitz-Osbern is said to have legislated for Herefordshire[4]; Walcher bishop of Durham ruled the county

which bore the title of baron of Kinderton long before the head of it was called to the House of Lords. The history of this imperium in imperio is curious, and is given in detail in Ormerod's Cheshire, vol. i. The barons spiritual are said to be eight as well as the temporal ones; namely, two bishops, Chester or Lichfield, and Bangor; six abbots, S. Werburgh's, Combermere, Stanlaw, Norton, Birkenhead, and Vale-Royal; ibid. pp. 149, 150. The exact accuracy of the details is questionable.

[1] The organisation of Durham was not quite so complete as the alleged palatine system of Chester: ten baronies are mentioned in the Pipe Roll of 1197, besides the barons of the Wapentake of Sadberge: see Boldon Buke, ed. Greenwell, pp. xi, xii; Hardy, Registrum Palatinum, iii. pr. p. xlvi; Surtees, Durham, ii. 36. The barony of Hilton is the only one of any note among the tenancies-in-chief. But the palatinate had its whole array of officers, courts of justice and record, which were kept in the name of the bishop until 1836: see above, p. 294, note 1. On the origin of this jurisdiction, see Sir T. D. Hardy's prefaces to vols. i. iii. of the Registrum Palatinum.	[2] See above, p. 294.	[3] Ord. Vit. v. 13.

[4] 'Manet ad hunc diem in comitatu ejus, apud Herefordiam, legum quas statuit inconcussa firmitas, ut nullus miles pro qualicumque commisso plus septem solidis solvat; cum in aliis provinciis ob parvam occasiunculam in transgressione praecepti herilis viginti vel viginti quinque pendantur;' W. Malmesb. G R. iii. § 256.

of Northumberland with all the powers of a viceroy[1] : and it is possible that, if we possessed more abundant materials, it would be found that the reduction of great territorial jurisdictions to merely titular dignities was gradually worked out by the Norman kings, instead of being, as is generally presumed, a principle of policy fully developed by the Conqueror himself.

Succession to earldoms. The dignity of earl was, it is scarcely necessary to say, hereditary ; but the heir did not acquire the formal rank until he was invested, although he might obtain possession of his lands, and even his share of the profits of the shire-moots, before he received the sword[2]. There are instances moreover of a division of the inheritance of the great earls : Roger of Montgomery, who held the counties of Shropshire and Sussex, left his Norman fiefs to his elder son, and the English to the second[3]. The first earl of Leicester, who was also count of Meulan, divided his estates between his twin sons, who founded the houses of Meulan and Leicester respectively[4]; and the earldom of Lincoln perhaps owes its origin to a similar partition[5].

The baron. The title of baron, unlike that of earl, is a creation of the Conquest. The word, in its origin equivalent to *homo*[6], receives under feudal institutions, like *homo* itself, the meaning of vassal. Homage (hominium) is the ceremony by which the vassal becomes the man of his lord; and the homines of the king are barons. Possibly the king's thegn of Anglo-Saxon times may answer to the Norman baron; both terms have somewhat the same indefiniteness, being applied sometimes to a personal

[1] Sim. Dun. Hist. Dunelm. ed. Bedford, p. 208 ; W. Malmesb. G. P. lib. iii. ed. Hamilton, p. 271.

[2] See Hoveden's account of the investiture of William Marshall and Geoffrey Fitz-Peter at John's coronation, vol. iv. p. 90.

[3] Ord. Vit. v. 14. [4] Ibid. xii. 33. [5] See above, p. 391, n. 2.

[6] It is explained as connected with the word *wer* (used in *wer*gild), a man. It occurs as early as A.D. 744 in the form of *paro*, meaning a freeman, and is used in the Leges Alamannorum as opposed to a slave : more commonly however for *man* generally; Waitz, D. V. G. ii. 183, iv. 281. It does not occur in the writings of Englishmen before the Conquest ; but appears in Domesday and in the charter of Henry I in its recognised meaning of a tenant-in-chief of the king; see Ellis, Introd. i. 44, 45. Such however is not its exclusive meaning; the barons of Wallingford (Rot. Pip. Hen. II, pp. 5, 20, 23, &c.) are simply the homagers or freeholders of the honour; in the expressions ' barons of the cinque ports,' ' court baron of a manor,' &c., the word has no reference to tenure in chief.

relation, sometimes to a territorial one. In one aspect, any of
the king's dependents are *barones ;* in another, the barony signifies a definite number of knights' fees[1]. But as it has been
found impossible to reduce the territorial baronies to any fixed
area of extension, it is probable that the title or dignity of baron,
or king's baron, involves, from its first entrance into English
history, nothing more than the idea of royal vassal or tenant-in-
chief[2]. Of these there were many grades, besides the great
distinction of majores and minores which appears in Magna
Carta[3]; they varied according to personal qualifications, official
duties, and extent of property ; some received special invitation
to the host, to court and council, were summoned 'propriis
nominibus ;' others not. The baron, as possessor of one manor
or many, had a territorial jurisdiction of a limited sort ; and,
when he possessed by royal grant the profits of the hundred in
which his castle was situated, he acquired an hereditary magistracy somewhat analogous to that of the earl ; but no such
power was attached to the barony by itself. As lord of his
manors, he had his court of tenants in each : he might be great

Different grades in the baronage.

Nature of the courts of the barons.

[1] In the *Modus tenendi Parliamentum* a barony is said to contain
thirteen knights' fees and a third : the relation between knight, baron, and
earl being the same as that of the shilling, mark, and pound ; which is the
proportion of their respective reliefs in some copies of Magna Carta ;
Select Charters, p. 193; Blackstone's Charters, p. 38. But this rule is
quite arbitrary ; there was no such proportion. On the Scottish and Irish
measurements which are called baronies, see Robertson, Essays, pp. 133 sq.,
142 sq.

[2] On the history of the disputed question of barony, see Hallam, Middle
Ages, iii. 6 sq. Selden maintained that all tenants-in-chief by knight-
service were barons; Madox that there was an original but undetermined
difference between tenure by barony and tenure by knight-service. See also
Gneist, Verwalt. i. 270.

[3] The distinction of majores and minores barones, although it appears
perhaps in legal phraseology first in the Dialogus de Scaccario and Magna
Carta, is in usage and language much earlier. Gneist points out that in
the army the difference between the single knight and the leader of 50 or
25; in the Exchequer the difference of relief between a hundred shillings
for the knight and a hundred marks for the baron ; in the court and in the
shire-moot, the interval between the two classes must have made itself
apparent; Dialogus de Scacc. ii. 10. It may indeed be fairly conjectured
that the landowners in Domesday who paid their relief to the sheriff, those
who held six manors or less, and those who paid their relief to the king,
stood in the same relation to one another. See Spence, Equitable Jurisdiction of Chancery, i. p. 40 ; and above, p. 174, note 3 ; and on the special
summons, § 159 below.

enough to have a body of personal counsellors, stewards, chamberlains and constables. In a very few cases he possessed a hereditary sheriffdom, but this was probably never directly attached to a territorial barony, although, as both were hereditary, they might descend for many generations together.

The knights.   The lowest class of tenants-in-chief who are likely to have presented themselves in the national council are the knights[1], who are included in general under the class of barons, but

The knight is the successor of the thegn.   demand some further notice. In tracing the history of the thegn in an earlier chapter[2], the knight has been described as succeeding after the Conquest to his position. He occupies nearly the same extent of land, and in several respects has an analogous history. But the knight proper, at least of the twelfth century, is not merely the possessor of a certain number of hides of land, which he holds by the tenure of chivalry, 'per loricam,' or as a 'fief de hauberc;' he has undergone an honourable initiation in the use of arms, which distinguishes

Institution of knighthood.   him from the unwarlike tenant in socage. The practice of 'dubbing to knighthood' may have had a corresponding usage in Anglo-Saxon times[3]; it certainly is nowhere mentioned as a Norman innovation, and it is unlikely that Ethelred, Canute, or Edward the Confessor, who had great acquaintance with foreign usages, should not have introduced into England the institution

[1] *Cniht* is commonly used in the meaning of *servus*, although it appears occasionally before the Conquest with a somewhat different application, possibly equivalent to *miles*. In the guilds, in the monuments of which it occurs, it is explained as 'young men,' but this is questionable. It had acquired its recognised sense by the middle of the twelfth century. See Chron. Sax. A.D. 1086.

[2] Above, p. 172.

[3] The story of Athelstan's investiture by his grandfather Alfred is told by William of Malmesbury, G. R. ii. § 133 : 'Quem etiam praemature militem fecerat donatum chlamyde coccinea, gemmato balteo, ense Saxonico cum vagina aurea.' The practice is no doubt derived from primitive, almost universal custom, although only occasionally traceable in particular countries. The knighthood of Charles the Bald by his father in 838 (V. Ludovici, c. 59 ; Waitz, D. V. G. iv. 573) may have served as a precedent for Alfred ; and indeed he had as a child received some sort of investiture at Rome ; see Will. Malmesb. ii. pref. p. xlii. Palgrave regards Athelstan's knighthood as the precedent for that of Richard Sans Peur, but, as it seems to me, with very little authority. William the Conqueror was knighted (militiae insignia recipiens) by the king of France ; W. Malmesb. G. R. iii. § 230.

of chivalry, which was then springing up in every country in Europe. But the first mention of it in our annals is in reference to the knighting of the Conqueror and his sons, when it appears to have had somewhat of the character of a religious as well as of a legal rite [1]. Henry I was knighted by his father [2]; William Rufus is said to have received his knighthood from Lanfranc [3]; Henry II was dubbed on his visit to England by his great-uncle King David [4]. But these instances seem to be examples only of a practice usual in much lower ranks of society; and, although the young aspirant might seek lustre for his inauguration by receiving his spurs from a distinguished warrior, it is not necessary to suppose that the right of conferring it was restricted to a smaller body than the knightly class itself. And thus the history of the institution may be referred to the primitive custom of investing the youth in the full assembly of the tribe, by the hand of his king, princeps, or father. Although in general no man would be regarded as entitled to the privileges of knighthood or allowed to call himself a knight who had not been thus initiated, the whole class of landowners who held by knight-service would be for constitutional purposes comprised under the name of knights. The dignity of knighthood was often bestowed on the skilful warrior who had no qualification in land, and it was of course possessed by the initiated members of the great military orders. Here however we have only to notice those members of the great fraternity of chivalry who as vassals of the king were entitled to take their place in his solemn council.

Institution of knighthood.

---

[1] John of Salisbury describes the ceremony as used in the middle of the twelfth century: 'Inolevit consuetudo solemnis, ut, ea die qua quisque militari cingulo decoratur, ecclesiam solemniter adeat, gladioque super altare posito et oblato, quasi celebri professione facta, seipsum obsequio altaris devoveat et gladii, id est, officii sui jugem Deo spondeat famulatum;' Polycraticus, vi. 10.

[2] He is said by Ordericus Vitalis (viii. 1) to have received his arms from Lanfranc. This may have been so, but the Conqueror himself 'dubbade his sunu Henric to ridere;' Chron. Sax. A.D. 1086.

[3] W. Malmesb. G. R. iv. § 305. Abbots were forbidden to make knights, in the council of London in 1102 (Eadmer, p. 68). Thomas Becket knighted the count of Guisnes (Du Cange, s. v. Miles), and William bishop of Ely knighted Ralph Beauchamp as late as 1191; R. Diceto, ii. 99.

[4] Hen. Hunt. fol. 226.

Burghers
and citizens
occasionally
in the coun-
cil.

There were, in some of the towns of the early Norman period, elements of another class of vassals who may occasionally have been brought up to attend the national gatherings ; the great men of London and York for instance. It is certain that on several occasions the citizens of the capital took part in deliberation. In the assembly at which the election of the Empress Matilda took place, the 'Communio' of the city of London was heard pleading for Stephen's liberation ; but we have no evidence for determining in what character they attended [1]. The great citizens of London would most of them be of knightly rank, possessing qualifications in land, and taking rank as barons. The corporate character of the city constitu-

No trace of
representa-
tive mem-
bers of the
Norman
councils.

tion was very grudgingly admitted, and, although it is just possible that some representative functions may have been discharged by its principal members who sat in their own personal right, it is probable that the 'communio' itself could only be heard by petition. The idea of representation which was familiar enough in the local courts might be expected, in a constitution so entirely based on land tenure, to appear in the central council as well. But it is not to be traced in existing records, and, when it does appear later, it is in that intermittent, growing, and struggling form which shows it to be a novelty. Of any representation of the freeholders in general there is not even a suspicion. The sheriffs would, as being barons themselves, have their places in the council, and might report the needs and wishes of their neighbours, but, as royal nominees and farmers of the revenue, they could not be expected to sympathise deeply with the population which they had to assess and to oppress.

General as-
semblies of
the tenants-
in-chief not
frequent.

It is not to be supposed that the assemblies at which all, or even a large proportion, of the tenants-in-chief presented themselves were very frequent. The councils of Salisbury already referred to [2] are perhaps the only occasion on which anything like a general assembly was brought together. These were for the special purpose of taking the oaths of fealty, and comprised other elements besides the tenants-in-chief. The ordinary

[1] See above, p. 356.   [2] See above, p. 387.

courts or councils were of a much more limited character,
seldom containing more than the bishops and 'proceres,' a term
that would include only the earls and greater barons. These
courts were held on the great Church festivals, Christmas,
Easter, and Whitsuntide: generally at the great cities of
southern England, London, Winchester, and Gloucester [1]. The
king appeared wearing his crown; a special peace was maintained, necessarily no doubt in consequence of the multitude of
armed retainers who attended the barons [2]; and magnificent
hospitality was accorded to all comers. 'Thrice a year,' says
the Chronicle, 'King William wore his crown every year that
he was in England; at Easter he wore it at Winchester, at
Pentecost at Westminster, and at Christmas at Gloucester.
And at these times all the men of England were with him,
archbishops, bishops and abbots, earls, thegns and knights [3].' A
similar usage was observed by his sons, although neither he nor
they regularly followed the rotation thus described [4]; they
called together their barons whenever and wherever they
pleased; and many of their courts were held at their forest
palaces in Wiltshire and Berkshire. Under Henry I the number of places of council was largely increased, and the enlarged
accommodation afforded by the growing monasteries was utilised.
Councils were held at Windsor, Rockingham, Woodstock,
among the forest palaces; at Oxford, Northampton, and other
midland towns [5]. The cessation of the solemn courts under

The great annual courts.

Places of council.

[1] See above, p. 291.
[2] See above, p. 200. The crown was placed on the king's head by the
archbishop, on these occasions in his own chamber, before he walked in
procession. See Eadmer, lib. vi. p. 137; Hoveden, iii. 59; Gervase, i. 526.
[3] Chron. Sax. A.D. 1087; W. Malmesb. Vit. S. Wulfst. lib. ii. c. 12:
'Rex Willelmus consuetudinem induxerat, quam successores aliquamdiu
tritam postmodum consenescere permisere. Ea erat ut ter in anno cuncti
optimates ad curiam convenirent de necessariis regni tractaturi, simulque
visuri regis insigne quomodo iret gemmato fastigiatus diademate.' The
custom was restored by Henry II, but disused after the year 1158. Gneist,
who will not allow the continuance of the witenagemot in any shape, or
the existence of a regular feudal court under the Norman kings, sees in
these assemblies only pageants whose splendour would indemnify the
magnates for the absence of all real power; Verwaltungsrecht, i. 224.
[4] 'Quem morem convivandi primus successor obstinate tenuit, secundus
omisit;' W. Malmesb. G. R. iii. § 279.
[5] See Hen. Hunt. fol. 220 sq.

Stephen was regarded by Henry of Huntingdon as a fatal mark of national decline [1].

Theory of the counsel and consent of the baronage.

125. These assemblies must be regarded as legally possessed of the full powers of the old witenagemot : but the exercise of their powers depended on the will of the king, and under the Conqueror and his sons there are scarcely any traces of independent action in them. Their legislative authority is admitted : it is with their counsel and consent [2] that William the Conqueror amends the laws of the Confessor, and divides the ecclesiastical from the secular courts. Henry I mentions in the preamble to the charter [3] that he had received the crown by the counsel of the barons ; with their consent he had retained the forests ; and it was with the counsel of his barons that his father had amended the laws of S. Edward [4];

In legislation.

Stephen, in the corresponding document, asserts his election by the clergy and the people; but neither of them distinctly declares the share of the council in the acts thus prefaced. The writs by which Henry I revived the action of the county courts and declared the penalties for false coining, are drawn in the form of edicts or charters, and contain no mention of counsel or consent. As, however, the historian Eadmer distinctly describes the latter piece of legislation as one of a series of edicts of reform issued by the advice of Anselm and the 'proceres,' the omission of the formal words is not conclusive [5].

In taxation.

The right of the council to join in taxation is nowhere distinctly stated : yet Henry I describes an aid as 'auxilium quod barones mihi dederunt [6] ;' and it must be supposed that the king would lay before his barons any plan for increasing the existing burdens, and that such announcement would be regarded as necessary for the validity of the exaction; the silence

---

[1] See Hen. Hunt. fol. 223.
[2] Above, p. 300, note 1.   [3] Ancient Laws, p. 215.
[4] Statutes of the Realm, i. 4.
[5] See Foedera, i. p. 12 ; Eadmer, Hist. Nov. lib. iv. p. 94.
[6] Chron. Abingd. ii. 113. The article of Henry's charter which relieves the demesne lands of the military tenants, 'ab omnibus gildis et omni opere,' seems also to imply that their consent was required for any taxation, although it does not involve an assembly called to grant it. See First Report on the dignity of a Peer, pp. 38, 39 ; and compare § 128 below.

of the counsellors or their ready assent would be a matter of form.

The judicial proceedings which took place in the king's pre- In judica-
ture. sence are frequently mentioned, but even here a question may be raised as to the freedom of debate. It was by a judicial sentence that Earls Waltheof and Roger were condemned[1]; in a great session of the king's court the bishop of Durham was tried in 1088[2]; in a council at Salisbury in A.D. 1096 William of Eu had his trial by battle and his cruel punishment[3]; in the same council the king sentenced William of Alderi to be hanged, and the other conspirators to be imprisoned; in A.D. 1102 Henry I summoned Robert of Belesme before his court, and alleged forty-five articles of treason against him[4]; in A.D. 1130 Geoffrey de Clinton was accused of treason in the Easter court at Woodstock[5]. In all these, and numerous other cases which might be adduced, it is clearly the full national assembly, and not the mere justices, before whom the trial is conducted. The barons act as judges, the king apparently gives the sentence, although in this respect also he is open to advice. It was by the counsel of Hugh of Chester that William of Eu suffered mutilation[6]; King David of Scotland, as earl of Huntingdon, took an active part in the trial of Geoffrey de Clinton[7]. The mode of trial was probably the same as in the lower courts, Process of
trial in the
council. the accusation by sworn witnesses, compurgation, ordeal and trial by battle[8]. On one occasion, we are informed, the barons

[1] 'Judiciali sententia damnatos;' Flor. Wig. A.D. 1074. 'Censoribus inter se sentientibus, per plures inducias usque in annum [judicium] prote-latum est. . . . Post multos tractatus reum esse mortis definitum est;' Ord. Vit. iv. 15. The trial was at the Christmas court at Westminster; Chron. Sax. A.D. 1075. See Freeman, Norm. Conq. iv. 589.

[2] See below, § 134.

[3] 'Octavis Epiphaniae apud Saresbiriam celebrato *concilio*;' Flor. Wig. A.D. 1096.

[4] Ord. Vit. xi. 3.   [5] Hen. Hunt. fol. 220.

[6] Ord. Vit. viii. 23.

[7] 'Dum David Rex in curia Henrici regis caute judicium indagaret,' &c.; Ord. Vit. viii. 22.

[8] Ordericus tells us that Roger of Hereford was tried by the Norman laws and sentenced to the forfeiture of lands and perpetual imprisonment. By English law the crime was capital; Pollock and Maitland, Hist. Eng. Law, i. 69. If the words refer to the method of procedure it is difficult to see what difference there could have been between the Norman and the

interfered so far as to recommend William Rufus to show mercy; it was by the advice of his wise men that he spared the minor criminals in A.D. 1096 [1].

Jurisdiction of the national councils in questions of right.

Matters of civil jurisdiction were also brought before these assemblies, although the determination in such cases would fall to the lot of the more experienced lawyers of the Curia Regis or Exchequer. A great council at Pedreda in the Conqueror's reign determined the suit between the churches of York and Worcester [2], and a similar quarrel between the bishops of Llandaff and S. David's came before the court more than once in the latter years of Henry I [3]. In A.D. 1126 the king, by the advice of his barons, granted the custody of Rochester Castle to the archbishop of Canterbury [4]. The proceedings of Stephen against the bishops, impolitic as they were, were conducted with a shadow of legality in a similar assembly [5].

General discussions.

Most, however, of the proceedings of the national council at this period, of which any record is preserved, come under the head of general business. The nominations of bishops were always made on these occasions until the right of canonical election was admitted by Henry I [6]: and even then the election took place in the king's court, often at the great festivals when the majority of the barons were present, and when the consecra-

Elections of bishops in the national councils.

English law, except in the use of trial by battle, which does not appear to have been employed in the case; Ord. Vit. iv. 15.

[1] Ord. Vit. viii. 23; 'Consultu sapientum hujusmodi viris pepercit.'

[2] Flor. Wig. A.D. 1070: 'In consilio in loco qui vocatur Pedreda celebrato, coram rege ac Doruberniae archiepiscopo Lanfranco, et episcopis, abbatibus, comitibus et primatibus, totius Angliae.' The dispute between York and Canterbury was heard in an Easter court; 'Uterque igitur in Paschali solemnitate ad regem venit ibique prolatis in medium partium rationibus sententiam de negotio regalis curia dedit;' V. Lanfr. c. 11

[3] Hen. Hunt. fol. 220: 'Post Pascha (A.D. 1132) fuit magnum placitum apud Londoniam, ubi de pluribus quidem et maxime de discordia episcopi Sancti Davidis et episcopi Clamorgensis de finibus parochiarum suarum tractatum est.' The discussion was continued in a conventus at London, and another at Winchester. This suit is described in the Cont. Flor. Wig. (A.D. 1128) as discussed 'in generali concilio' some years before.

[4] Cont. Flor. Wig. A.D. 1126: 'Consilio baronum suorum.'

[5] W. Malmesb. Hist. Nov. ii. § 469: Gesta Stephani, p. 49.

[6] Instances of this proceeding are very numerous: e.g. 'in Nativitate Domini curiam suam Glawornae tenuit, ubi tribus suis capellanis ... dedit praesulatum;' Flor. Wig. A.D. 1085.

tion and the investiture could be celebrated with equal pomp[1]. The ceremony of conferring earldoms and knighthood was a public business of the court[2], as well as the witnessing of the homages paid to the king or his presumptive successor[3]. The foreign and ecclesiastical policy of the king was here canvassed without much jealousy or intimidation[4]; war and peace, royal marriages, and the like. Henry I took the advice of his council on his negotiations with the see of Rome; and even on the choice of a second wife[5]. The see of Ely was founded by the same king with the advice of the archbishop and other magnates[6]. Of the share taken by the baronage in the election of the king enough has been said already: it was a right which each sovereign in turn was politic enough to acknowledge, and of the reality of which he was so far conscious that he took every means of escaping it. The election of Henry I and Stephen, the claim put forward to elect the empress, the acceptance of the heir of King Henry and the rejection of the heir of Stephen, place this prerogative of the nation, however indifferently the council which exercised it represented the nation, upon an incontestable basis.

Election of the king.

[1] Two instances will suffice here. Under Henry I, after the settlement with Anselm,—'Willelmus ... ad archiepiscopatum Cantuariensem Glawornae, ubi in Purificatione Sanctae Mariae rex tenuit curiam suam, eligitur;' Cont. Flor. Wig. A.D. 1123. Under Stephen, after the grant of free election to the clergy,—'Sciatis me dedisse et concessisse Rodberto episcopo Bathoniae episcopatum Bathoniae ... canonica prius electione praecedente et communi vestro (sc. archiepiscoporum, episcoporum, abbatum, comitum, vicecomitum, baronum et omnium fidelium) consilio, voto et favore prosequente ... apud Westmonasterium in generalis concilii celebratione et Paschalis festi solemnitate;' Foedera, i. 16.

[2] See above, pp. 392, 397.

[3] Flor. Wig. A.D. 1086, 1116, 1126.

[4] Henry I writes to Anselm, Eadmer, lib. iv. p. 86: 'in die Ascensionis Domini habebo omnes barones meos mecum congregatos, et per consilium eorum ita convenienter tibi respondebo, quod, cum tecum loquar, non credo te me inde blasphematurum.' And again (Epp. Ans. iii. 94), 'volo legatos meos Romam mittere et consilio Dei et baronum meorum domino papae inde respondere;' see also lib. iv. epp. 4, 6.

[5] Eadmer, lib. vi. p. 136: 'Rex ... consilio Radulfi Cantuariorum pontificis et principum regni quos omnes ... congregavit, decrevit sibi in uxorem Atheleidem ...' See also Hen. Hunt. fol. 220.

[6] The see of Ely was founded by the king with the counsel of the kingdom, 'regi et archiepiscopo ceterisque principibus visum;' Eadmer, p. 9.

Ecclesiastical business in the great councils.

The power of the clergy was so strong during these reigns that we must not expect to find ecclesiastical questions treated in the secular councils except under the greatest reserve. It must however have been a very large gathering that accepted the conditions made by Henry I and Anselm in 1107 [1]: in the following year we find the canons of a Church council at London passed in the presence of the king, with the assent of all his barons [2]; in A.D. 1127, after a similar council, Henry granted his assent to the statutes passed in it, and confirmed them ' by his royal power and authority [3],' on the principle of his father's policy. On this and some other occasions we find distinct traces of a usage which forms a peculiar mark of our ecclesiastical history; the king holds his court at Westminster, whilst the archbishop celebrates his council in the same city; the two assemblies together form a precedent for the coincident summoning of parliament and convocation in later days [4]. The special significance however of the king's ratification of the canons of 1127 lies in the fact that the archbishop had just returned from Rome, invested with that legatine character which was so often a stumbling-block both in civil and ecclesiastical

Coincidence of baronial and episcopal councils.

[1] ' In kalendis Augusti conventus omnium episcoporum, abbatum et procerum regni Lundoniae in palatio regis factus est;' Flor. Wig. A.D. 1107; Eadmer, p. 91.

[2] 'Episcopi statuerunt in praesentia ejusdem gloriosi regis Henrici, assensu omnium baronum suorum;' Flor. Wig. A.D. 1108; Eadmer, p. 95.

[3] See the formal act of confirmation in the Foedera, i. 8. ' Auditis concilii gestis assensum praebuit, auctoritate regia et potestate concessit et confirmavit statuta concilii;' Cont. Flor. Wig. A.D. 1127.

[4] In 1102, ' Celebratum est concilium in ecclesia beati Petri in occidentali parte juxta Lundoniam sita, communi consensu episcoporum, et abbatum et principum, totius regni : in quo praesedit Anselmus. . . . Huic conventui affuerunt, Anselmo archiepiscopo petente a rege, primates regni, quatenus quicquid ejusdem concilii auctoritate decerneretur utriusque ordinis concordi cura et sollicitudine ratum servaretur;' Eadmer, p. 67. Florence's account is based on this; but he adds, 'In festivitate S. Michaelis rex fuit Lundoniae apud Westmonasterium et cum eo omnes principes regni sui, ecclesiastici et saecularis ordinis, ubi duos de clericis duobus episcopatibus investivit . . . , ubi etiam Anselmus tenuit magnum concilium de his quae ad Christianitatem pertinent.' The case of 1127 is even more distinct : ' Rex anxiatus concilium tenuit ad Rogationes apud Londoniam, et Willelmus archiepiscopus Cantuariensis similiter in eadem villa apud Westminster.' The king's assembly was in the palace, the archbishop's in the church : the date of the latter is given by the Continuator of Florence, May 13–16, the Friday, Saturday, Sunday, and Monday after the Rogation days.

affairs. The king had succeeded in obtaining the office for the The canons
of A.D. 1127.
first time for the primate, with whom he was acting in concert;
the canons of the council had thus the threefold sanction of the
national Church, the King, and the Holy See, without any concession being made by either as to the necessity of confirmation
by the other two. These proceedings completed the harmony of
Church and State, which was one of the great objects of Henry's
policy, and which was rudely broken by the quarrels of
Stephen.

In the last reign of the period the ecclesiastical councils claim Ecclesiasti-
cal councils
of Stephen's
reign act in
secular busi-
ness.
and exert more real power than could be decently claimed for
such assemblies of the barons as either party could bring together. The assembly at Winchester in which Matilda was
elected was a synod of the clergy, who were present in three
bodies, bishops, abbots, and archdeacons, and were separately
consulted[1]; but it was largely attended by the barons of the
party. The council of A.D. 1151, in which Stephen, Eustace,
and the barons appeared, and in which both parties appealed
to the pope for the settlement of their claims, was primarily an
ecclesiastical council summoned by archbishop Theobald in his
capacity as legate[2]. It is in fact difficult to discover after the
fourth year of Stephen any assembly to which the name of
national council can be given, although, in the confused accounts
of the final pacification, we may detect evidence that proves
such assemblies to have been held. The abeyance however of
all the constitutional machinery at this period, and the almost
irreconcileable chronological difficulties which meet us in the
annals, may well excuse some hesitation in forcing a general
conclusion from these precedents.

126. The exact relation of the administrative system to the Relation of
the great

[1] William of Malmesbury was present, and describes the council accurately:
'Post recitata scripta excusatoria quibus absentiam suam quidam tutati sunt,
sevocavit in partem legatus episcopos, habuitque cum eis arcanum consilii
sui; post mox abbates, postremo archidiaconi convocati. . . .' Hist. Nov.
iii. § 43.

[2] 'Anno xvi° Teobaldus Cantuariensis archiepiscopus et apostolicae sedis
legatus tenuit concilium generale apud Londoniam in media Quadragesima,
ubi rex Stephanus et filius suus Eustachius et Angliae proceres interfuerunt,
totumque illud concilium novis appellationibus infrenduit;' Hen. Hunt.
fol. 226.

national council is not very easy to define; for the lawyers and historians gave no glimpse of a theory of government, and the documentary evidences of the Norman period are by no means abundant. It would be rash to affirm that the supreme courts of judicature and finance were committees of the national council, although the title of Curia belongs to both, and it is difficult to see where the functions of the one end and those of the other begin. And it would be scarcely less rash to regard the two great tribunals, the Curia Regis and Exchequer, as mere sessions of the king's household ministers, undertaking the administration of national business without reference to the action of the greater council of the kingdom. The historical development of the system is obscure in the extreme. The Conqueror, as Duke of Normandy, had no doubt a high court of judicature and a general assembly of his barons; Edward the Confessor had his national witenagemot, which likewise exercised the functions of judicature; he also, as we must infer from Domesday, had a centralised system of finance, a treasury with its staff of keepers and assessors. How much of the new administrative machinery was imported directly from Normandy, how much was English, how much derived its existence from the juxtaposition of the two, we have to decide on conjecture rather than on evidence; and the materials for answering the question, which concerns

Central sys-
tem of ad-
ministration
from the
reign of
Henry I.

still wider generalisations, will be given further on. It may be enough here to note, that whereas under William the Conqueror and William Rufus the term *Curia* generally, if not invariably, refers to the solemn courts held thrice a year or on particular summons, at which all tenants-in-chief were supposed to attend[1],

---

[1] This of course is not in exact agreement with Gneist's view. He holds that only the great magnates ever attended. It is clear however that on some occasions a large proportion of the landowners were present even in the Norman reigns, and under Henry II these assemblies are distinctly courts of feudal tenants-in-chief, from the very first years of the reign. It seems far more probable that the earlier assemblies were constituted on the same principle, than that that king should begin his reign by a violent innovation. Of course, as a rule, only the great barons would take the trouble or be at the cost of attending. It is of the greatest importance in all our early history to remember that attendance at courts and councils was not regarded as a privilege, but as a burden; *suit* and *service* were alike onerous.

from the reign of Henry I we have distinct traces of a judicial
system, a supreme court of justice, called the Curia Regis, presided over by the king or justiciar, and containing other judges
also called justiciars, the chief being occasionally distinguished by
the title of 'summus,' 'magnus,' or 'capitalis.' The same body also
managed the assessment and collection of the revenue, and for this
purpose had a separate and very elaborate organisation, through
the history of which the character of their judicial work is chiefly
made intelligible : and this may accordingly be stated first.

The Exchequer[1] of the Norman kings was the court in which   The Ex-
the whole financial business of the country was transacted, and   chequer.
as the whole administration of justice, and even the military
organisation, was dependent upon the fiscal officers, the whole
framework of society may be said to have passed annually under
its review.   It derived its name from the chequered cloth which
covered the table at which the accounts were taken[2], a name
which suggested to the spectator the idea of a game at chess
between the receiver and the payer, the treasurer and the sheriff.
As this name never occurs before the reign of Henry I[3], and as   Its name.
the tradition of the court preserved the remembrance of a time
when the business which took place in it was transacted ' ad
taleas,' ' at the tallies,' it seems certain that the date of complete
organisation should be referred to this period[4].   Under the
Anglo-Saxon kings we may presume that the treasure or *hord*

---

[1] The contemporaneous authorities on the Exchequer are the Pipe Rolls,
and the Dialogus de Scaccario, a work on the subject written by Richard
bishop of London the Treasurer, who was son of Bishop Nigel the Treasurer,
and great-nephew of the justiciar Roger of Salisbury.   The great work of
Madox, the *History of the Exchequer*, furnishes an enormous amount of
illustrative matter; and a great deal may be learned from Mr. Hubert
Hall's History of Taxation.

[2] Dialogus de Scaccario, i. 1 : ' Pannus . . . niger virgis distinctus dis-
tantibus a se virgis vel palmae extentae spatio.'

[3] The arguments for a Norman *Exchequer* (eo nomine) existing earlier
than the English are of no account.   There is no genuine mention of it
before the reign of Henry II.   The supposed mention of the Exchequer of
Normandy in a record of 1061 (Gneist, Verwalt. i. 194) is a mistake.   But
the subject will be noticed further on.

[4] As the roll of 31 Henry I is still in existence, it seems quite justifiable
to regard the Exchequer as a fully developed part of the Norman regime,
although a great deal of its political and constitutional importance belongs
to the period of revival under Henry II.

was under the management of a *gerefa* or *hordere*[1], but, although the mention of such an officer is not uncommon, there are no

distinct traces of courts of account : the taxes were collected by the sheriffs and other reeves, and the treasure was preserved in

---

[1] The word occurs in the laws of Athelstan, 'Cyninges hordera oththe ure gerefena;' not however as the name of a great official. The author of the Dialogus says that there were in his time some who referred the institution of the Exchequer back to the English kings; he does not agree with this, because there is no mention in Domesday-book of the 'blanch-ferm.' Mr. Stapleton however in the preface to the Rolls of the Norman Exchequer points out that the 'blanch-ferm' has its origin in a state of things that did not exist in Normandy, and was 'consequent upon the monetary system of the Anglo-Saxons.' The argument is very technical, but quite conclusive. The 'ferm' or pecuniary payment made by the sheriffs was said to be 'blanched,' 'dealbatum,' when it had been tested by fire, weighed, and by additional payment brought to the standard of the royal mint at Winchester. There was no such fixed standard in Normandy, and as the blanch-ferm was an integral part of the English system, it is clear that it could not have been derived from the Norman. Although the blanch-ferm is not mentioned in Domesday, the ferm is in many places described as settled in King Edward's time. This seems to prove the existence of a central department of finance before the Conquest from which the peculiarities of the English Exchequer were derived. It does not of course follow that it bore the name, or that great improvements in it were not effected by the Norman lawyers. But it satisfactorily disposes of the statements of Gneist (Verwalt. i. 194) and Brunner (Schwurgericht, p. 150) that the court of Exchequer was bodily imported from Normandy. Another argument for the Norman origin of the Exchequer is drawn from the notion that there was an Exchequer of Sicily under the Norman kings; Gneist, Verwalt. i. 202; Madox, p. 124. But I can find no evidence that the name 'scaccarium' or 'Exchequer' was ever given to the Sicilian fiscus; and any points of similarity between the procedure of the two courts may be accounted for on the supposition that the Sicilian system was created or elaborated by the great king Roger with the assistance of his English ministers, rather than by supposing them to have been derived from a common Norman fiscal system of the existence of which there is no proof until long after the house of Hauteville had left Normandy. Robert of Salisbury the chancellor of King Roger may have been a pupil of bishop Roger of Salisbury, the organizer of the English Exchequer; and Master Thomas Brown, another minister of the same king, who after his return to his native England was employed by Henry II in the same court, may have introduced some English usages into Sicily. Against the latter hypothesis M. Amari, in a paper read before the 'Reale Accademia dei Lincei' at Rome, in 1878, has urged that the procedure of the Sicilian 'Dohana,' so far from being derived from England, is drawn from the earlier Saracenic institutions ; and that Brown could have had little or nothing to do with it; but the position of Brown at Roger's court is amply vindicated by Dr. Pauli in the Göttingen Gelehrte Anzeige for 1878. If the derivation of the Sicilian system from Oriental sources be admitted, all argument based on the supposition that it is Norman falls to the ground. Brown may even have introduced some points of Sicilian usage into the English court, but such an inference does not affect the main argument. See Dialogus de Scaccario, i. c. 6, and below § 134.

the palace : some machinery for account and guardianship must
be inferred. Under the Conqueror and William Rufus the
word 'fiscus' or 'thesaurus' is commonly used : the word
'scaccarium' comes into use only under Henry I.

The officers of the Exchequer are the great officers of the
household ; the justiciar who is the president, the chancellor,
the constable, two chamberlains, the marshal, and the treasurer,
with such other great and experienced counsellors as the king
directs to attend for the public service, and who share with the
others the title of Barons of the Exchequer. Amongst these,
if not identical with them, are the justices or ordinary judges
of the Curia Regis, who appear to be called indiscriminately
'justitiarii' and 'barones scaccarii.'

Twice a year, at Easter and at Michaelmas, full sessions were
held in the palace at Westminster, attended by all the barons,
with their clerks, writers, and other servants, each of whom had
his assigned place and regular duties. Two chambers were used
for the transaction of business : the upper one, or exchequer of
account, was that in which the reports were received, and all
the legal negotiations carried on and recorded ; and the lower
one, or exchequer of receipt, in which the money was paid down,
weighed, and otherwise tested[1]. The record of the business
was preserved in three great rolls ; one kept by the treasurer,
another by the chancellor, and a third by an officer nominated
by the king, who registered the matters of legal and special
importance[2]. The rolls of the treasurer and chancellor were
duplicates ; that of the former was called from its shape the
great roll of the Pipe, and that of the latter the roll of the
Chancery. These documents are mostly still in existence. The
Pipe Rolls are complete from the second year of Henry II, and
the Chancellor's rolls nearly so. Of the preceding period only
one roll, that of the thirty-first year of Henry I, is preserved,
and this with Domesday-book is the most valuable store of information which exists for the administrative history of the age.

The financial reports were made to the barons by the sheriffs
of the counties. At Easter and Michaelmas[3] each of these

Officers of the Exchequer.

Sessions of the Exchequer.

The rolls of the Exchequer.

System of account.

---

[1] Dialogus, i. 2.   [2] Ibid. i. 5, 6.   [3] Ibid. ii. 2.

Sheriffs'
accounts.

magistrates produced his own accounts, and paid into the Exchequer such an instalment or *proffer* as he could afford, retaining in hand sufficient money for current expenses. In token of receipt a tally was made; a long piece of wood in which a number of notches were cut, marking the pounds, shillings and pence received; this stick was then split down the middle, each half contained exactly the same number of notches, and no alteration could of course be made without certain detection[1]. At the Michaelmas audit these tallies were produced, and the remainder of the accounts made up. If the sheriff were able to acquit himself entirely, he began the new year without arrears; if not, a running account was kept by the same primitive method.

Particulars
of account:
(1) The ferm
of the
county.

The particulars accounted for by the sheriffs afford us a complete view of the financial condition of the country. The first item is the 'firma' or ferm of the shire[2]. This is a sort of composition for all the profits arising to the king from his ancient claims on the land and from the judicial proceedings of the shire-moot: the rent of detached pieces of demesne land, the remnants of the ancient folkland; the payments due from corporate bodies and individuals for the primitive gifts, the offerings made in kind, or the hospitality,—the *feorm-fultum*,— which the kings had a right to exact from their subjects, and which were before the time of Domesday generally commuted for money; the fines or a portion of the fines paid in the ordinary process of the county courts, and other small miscellaneous incidents. These had been, soon after the composition of Domesday, estimated at a fixed sum, which was regarded as a sort of rent or composition at which the county was let to the sheriff, and recorded in the *Rotulus Exactorius;* for this, under

[1] Madox, Hist. Exch. p. 708. The fire which destroyed the old Houses of Parliament is said to have originated in the burning of the old Exchequer tallies.

[2] The farm, ferm, or firma, the rent or composition for the ancient feorm-fultum, or provision payable in kind to the Anglo-Saxon kings. The history of the word in its French form would be interesting. The use of the word for a pecuniary payment is traced long before the Norman Conquest; Stapleton, i. p. xiv. On the Rotulus Exactorius, see Dialogus, i. c. 18.

the name of ferm, he answered annually; if his receipts were in excess, he retained the balance as his lawful profit, the wages of his service; if the proceeds fell below the ferm, he had to pay the difference from his own purse. If land chargeable with these sums fell out of cultivation, he was excused a proportionate amount under the head of waste; if new land was brought under tillage, he had to account for the profit under the title of increment[1]. Before rendering this account, the sheriff discharged the king's debts in the shire, paid the royal benefactions to religious houses, provided for the maintenance of stock on the crown lands, the expenses of public business, the cost of provisions supplied to the court, and the travelling expenses of the king and his visitors incurred within his district[2]. The payments had been long made in kind, and even in the reign of Henry II old men remembered how corn and cattle had been once brought up to the court as the tribute of various shires[3]; horses, hounds, and hawks were still received at a settled valuation, in payment of debt or fine[4].

Sources and burdens of the ferm.

The next item in point of importance is the Danegeld, a tax which had assumed in Norman times the character of ordinary revenue[5], and which, like the ferm, was compounded for by the sheriff at a fixed sum. This tax had been increased heavily by William the Conqueror: in A.D. 1084 it had been trebled[6]; six shillings were exacted from each hide of geldable land, instead of two, the usual sum raised under the Anglo-Saxon king, and the accounts of the sum received from the Western

(2) The Danegeld.

---

[1] Madox, pp. 225, 226.   [2] Dialogus, ii. 6.   [3] Ibid. i. 7.

[4] E. g. Ivo de Heriz pays five dextrarii, destriers or war-horses, that he may have certain lands at fee-farm; Pipe Roll 31 Henry I, p. 7 : Reginald de Muscans pays one *fugator*, or coursing-dog, for the like privilege; ibid. 35 : William de Merlai, a palfrey; p. 36 : Outi de Lincoln, a hundred 'Norrisc' hawks and a hundred gerfalcons; p. 111. The fugator seems to have been worth twenty shillings, p. 35; a hawk, 40s. p. 47; a destrier from 40s. to £20, pp. 11, 85. In Domesday, the count of Meulan (Mellent) receives a large payment in honey as one of the dues of the county. Abundant illustrations of this may be found both in Domesday and in the Pipe Rolls.

[5] 'Hoc autem malum usque in hodiernum diem duravit, et diu, nisi Dei pietas subveniat, durabit. Regibus namque nostris modo persolvimus ex consuetudine quod Dacis persolvebatur ex ineffabili terrore;' H. Hunt. lib. v. fo. 205.

[6] Chron. Sax. A.D. 1083.

counties on this occasion are preserved in the record known as
the Domesday of Exeter. It may be reasonably inferred that
the fixing of the sum of the Danegeld for each county was one
of the results of the Domesday Survey; and it must not be
understood that the sums accounted for under this head afford

Exemptions
and composi-
tions.
any clue to the extent of land in cultivation. Monasteries possessed in many cases immunity from Danegeld; in other cases
they had special commutations; a large extent of land frequently 'defendit se,' that is, was held responsible, or rated, as
one hide; and all persons employed in the king's service were
excepted from the impost. The Danegeld was a very unpopular
tax, probably because it was the plea on which the sheriffs made
their greatest profit; it was believed that Henry I had made a
vow to abolish it; and the abolition was accordingly made a
point among the concessions won from Stephen at the beginning
of his reign. It was really got rid of by Henry II, who however taxed the land in much the same way under other names;
and it was in very nearly the same form reproduced under the

The
*auxilium
burgorum.*
title of carucage by the ministers of Richard I. With the
Danegeld may be noticed another impost which fell in the time
of Henry I on the towns chiefly, and which, although it bore
the feudal name of auxilium [1] or aid, and answers to the later
tallage, was probably the tax which represented in the case of
the towns the same demand as in the country was met by the
Danegeld. It seems, like the Danegeld, to have been a fixed
sum payable annually.

A third head of ordinary or ancient national revenue com-

---

[1] In the Pipe Roll of 31 Henry I, the auxilium burgi or civitatis is in
every case a round sum, varying from £3, the auxilium of Winchcombe,
to £120, the auxilium of London. Besides these *auxilia burgorum* there
are some small payments in Wilts and Berks called *auxilium comitatus,*
and in Surrey, Essex, and Devon, *auxilium militum.* If these are not
arrears from a previous year, in which there may have been some general
impost of the sort, they must be regarded as special payments belonging to
those counties. An *auxilium de militibus* is mentioned in the Liber Niger,
i. 56, where it is said that when the king takes an auxilium of 20s., the
knights of William of Avranches, in Kent, pay only 12s.; if he takes a
mark, they pay 8s.: this seems however to be a scutage. The *auxilium
vicecomitis* was a different payment, made to the sheriff for his services.
These auxilia must be distinguished from the three feudal aids.

prised the proceeds of the pleas of the crown ; the fines and other profits arising from the trial of offences which had been severed from the ordinary operation of the shire and hundred, and which, although tried before the sheriff in his character as justice, were, so far as the fines were concerned, made to contribute directly to the income of the king [1]. Of these the most important is the *murdrum*, the fine payable, as has been already stated, by the hundred in which a murder has taken place in case of its failing to prove the slain man to be an Englishman. The commixture of the populations had so far proceeded in the time of Henry II that it was impossible to decide the question of nationality, and all murders were punished alike [2]. With these may be mentioned a wide class of amercements, some of which have their origin in Anglo-Saxon and some in feudal customs; of the former are fines for non-appearance in the hundred and shire courts, and of the latter penalties for breach of forest law.

(3) Proceeds of the pleas of the crown.

Under the head of feudal income [3] come all the items arising from the transfer of lands, reliefs, guardianship, marriage, escheat, and other incidents ; the sale of public offices included. This was of course a large and comparatively permanent source of revenue. The arbitrary sums exacted under the name of reliefs by William Rufus were one of the grievances which Henry I in his coronation charter undertook to redress. We are not able to discover how this promise was fulfilled, for although in the reign of Henry II a regular arrangement appears to be in force by which the relief of the knight's fee was five pounds, and that of the barony one hundred, the corresponding payments in his grandfather's reign are not to be brought under so simple a principle [4]. It is however probable

(4) Feudal income.

Reliefs.

---

[1] Above, p. 205.

[2] Dialogus, i. 10 ; Select Charters, p. 201. The payments on this head are very various, even in the same hundred; see the Roll of 31 Henry I, pp. 8, 9, &c.

[3] The five marks of feudal tenure, (1) hereditary succession, (2) reliefs, (3) wardship and marriage, (4) aids, and (5) escheats, all receive abundant illustration from the Roll of 31 Henry I.

[4] Madox, Hist. Exch. p. 216 sq.; e. g. under Henry II Hugh de Chaucumb pays £30 for a relief for six knights' fees. But the sums continue to

that a record of the number of knights' fees in England had been made before the death of Henry I, and that it was the basis of the computation adopted by his grandson. Before this was done, the valuation, where the payment was not altogether arbitrary, must have been made according to the record of the hidage preserved in Domesday. And it may be observed, that whilst Henry I took, as an aid for the marriage of his daughter, three shillings on each hide [1], Henry II, on a like occasion, took one mark on the knight's fee [2]. Whatever was the basis of rating, all the feudal incidents would be accounted for in the same way. Henry I may have taken an aid on the occasion of his son's knighthood, as he did on his daughter's marriage, but of this there is no record. The Pipe Roll of the thirty-first year of his reign contains several notices of sums paid for permission to determine suits connected with land, by covenant or by trial by battle; for leave to marry, to avoid answering the claim of another claimant, for cancelling agreements of exchange, and for other liberties which betray the existence of a good deal of legal oppression.

Aids.

The forest law, which, heavy as it was under William the Conqueror, seems to have reached the extreme of severity and cruelty under Henry I, was also made a source of revenue. The fines exacted by the justices under this system form a considerable item in the accounts.

Exactions under the forest law.

Among the great offices of the household which appear from the Pipe Roll to have been saleable are those of dapifer, marshal, and chancellor. The last-mentioned officer in A.D. 1130 owes £3006 13s. 4d. for the great seal [3]; the office of treasurer was bought by Bishop Nigel for his son for £400 [4]. Inferior places in the legal staff are also sold. In Norfolk, Benjamin pays £4 5s. to be allowed to keep the pleas of the crown [5]; in

Sale of offices.

vary occasionally until settled by Magna Carta, which refers to the system mentioned above, as the *antiquum relevium*: and the Dialogus describes the relief of a baron as matter of special arrangement with the king: lib. ii. c. 10.

[1] Hen. Hunt. fol. 217.
[3] Roll 31 Henry I, p. 140.
[5] Roll 31 Henry I, p. 91.
[2] Madox, Hist. Exch. p. 398.
[4] Hist. Eliens., Ang. Sac. i. 627.

Northumberland, Uhtred son of Waltheof makes a payment for
the grant of sac and soc, and a similar transaction is recorded
in Suffolk[1]; John the Marshal pays forty marks for a master-
ship in king's court, Humfrey Bohun four hundred marks to be
dapifer regis[2]; Richard Fitz-Alured pays fifteen marks that
he may sit with Ralph Basset on the king's pleas in Buckinghamshire[3]. At the same time the officers of the ancient courts
are found purchasing relief from their responsibilities; the
judices and *juratores* of Yorkshire pay £100 that they may be
judges and jurors no longer, anxious no doubt to avoid the
heavy fines exacted from them either for non-attendance or for
other neglect of duty[4].

The sum accounted for in the single Pipe Roll of the reign *Gross
amount of
the revenue.*
of Henry I, including all the debts and other gross receipts, is
not less than £66,000 for the year. The exhaustive and
orderly character of the roll is in marked contrast with the
very scanty details of the similar accounts at the beginning of
Henry II's reign, when the whole sum accounted for is not
more than £22,000 : and this fully confirms the statements of
the historians and of the writer of the Dialogus de Scaccario,
as to the ruinous state into which the machinery of government
had fallen under Stephen.

But it is not only in the department of finance that this *System of
assessment.*
most important record illustrates constitutional history, and we
must refer to it again in examining the framework of the
Norman judicature. Before doing this it will be necessary to
recur to the Domesday Survey, which was not only the general
record of the royal revenue, but the rate-book of valuation of
all the land in the kingdom. The formation of this record
afforded a precedent for a rating system which was of no small
importance in its bearing on later history : and it is not a little
singular that a measure taken by the Conqueror, in order to fix
and make available to the utmost his hold upon the country,
should be the first step in a continuous process by which the

---

[1] Roll 31 Henry I, pp. 36, 98.
[2] Ibid. p. 18. Adam de Port pays £9 to be dapifer. Ibid.
[3] Ibid. p. 101.   [4] Ibid. p. 34.

nation arrived ultimately at the power of taxing itself, and thus controlling the whole framework of the constitution and the whole policy of government.

The Domesday Survey was ordered by William in a great council held at Christmas 1085 at Gloucester, when a Danish invasion was supposed to be imminent. It was carried into execution during the following year by officers appointed by the king, who visited the several counties, and called before them all those persons of whom in ordinary times the county court was composed. Tradition recorded that, when the Conqueror wished to confirm the national laws, in order to obtain a true report of those laws he summoned to his court twelve elected representatives of each shire to declare upon oath the ancient lawful customs [1]. A similar plan was now adopted. The king's barons exacted an oath from the sheriff and all the barons and Norman landholders of the shire; every hundred appeared also by sworn representatives, and from each township

the priest, the reeve, and six villeins or ceorls [2]. On the deposition or verdict of these jurors was drawn up the report of the name of each manor or township, and its present and late holder: its extent in hides, the number of ploughs for which it furnished work; the number of homagers, ceorls or villeins,

---

[1] 'Willelmus rex, quarto anno regni sui, consilio baronum suorum fecit summoneri per universos consulatus Angliae Anglos nobiles et sapientes et sua lege eruditos, ut eorum et jura et consuetudines ab ipsis audiret. Electi igitur de singulis totius patriae comitatibus viri duodecim jurejurando confirmaverunt primo ut quoad possent recto tramite . . . legum suarum consuetudinem et sancita patefacerent;' Hoveden, ii. 218; Select Charters, p. 81.

[2] 'Hic subscribitur inquisitio terrarum, quo modo barones regis inquirunt, videlicet per sacramentum vicecomitis scirae et omnium baronum et eorum Francigenarum, et totius centuriatus, presbyteri, praepositi, vi. villanorum uniuscujusque villae. Deinde quomodo vocatur mansio; quis tenuit eam tempore regis Eadwardi, quis modo tenet, quot hidae, quot carrucatae in dominio, quot hominum; quot villani, quot cotarii, quot servi; quot liberi homines, quot sochemanni; quantum silvae, quantum prati, quot pascuorum, quot molendina, quot piscinae; quantum est additum vel ablatum; quantum valebat totum simul, et quantum modo; quantum ibi quisque liber homo vel sochemannus habuit vel habet. Hoc totum tripliciter, scilicet tempore regis Aedwardi et quando rex Willelmus dedit, et quomodo sit modo; et si potest plus haberi quam habeatur;' Ely Domesday, Dom. iii. 497. Henry of Huntingdon gives the commissioners the title of justitiarii; fol. 212.

cotters, and serfs ; how many freemen, how many sokemen ; the extent of wood, meadow, and pasture ; the number of mills and fisheries ; the increase and decrease since King Edward's time ; the several and collective values of every holding. By this report an exhaustive register of the land and its capabilities was formed, which was never entirely superseded ; for although the feudal taxation was, within a century after, based on the knight's fee instead of the hide, much of the general taxation continued to be assessed on the hide, and, the number of hides which the knight's fee contained being known, the number of knights' fees in any particular holding could be easily discovered. Ranulf Flambard, as Ordericus Vitalis informs us, attempted to reduce the number of acres contained in the hide from the English to the Norman computation, and if he had succeeded the measure would have compelled a new assessment[1] ; but, as Domesday continued to be the ultimate authority for the rating of the country, the attempt, if it were ever made, must be understood to have failed. But the changes in the ownership of land, the formation of new forests, and the bringing of old wastes into cultivation, must have made it difficult to secure a fair apportionment of taxation ; and this compelled on the part of the exchequer proceedings which we find in close connexion with the provincial administration of justice. It is unnecessary here to anticipate in detail what

A permanent assessment.

Circuits of the barons of the Exchequer to adjust the rating.

[1] See above, pp. 327, 376. Ord. Vit. viii. 8 : ' Hic juvenem fraudulentis stimulationibus inquietavit regem, incitans ut totius Angliae revisereet descriptionem, Anglicaeque telluris comprobans iteraret partitionem, subditisque recideret tam advenis quam indigenis quicquid inveniretur ultra certam dimensionem. Annuente rege omnes carrucatas, quas Angli hidas vocant, funiculo mensus est et descripsit : postpositisque mensuris quas liberales Angli jussu Edwardi regis largiter distribuerant, imminuit, et regales fiscos accumulans colonis arva retruncavit. Ruris itaque olim diutius nacti diminutione et insoliti vectigalis gravi exaggeratione, supplices regiae fidelitati plebes indecenter oppressit, ablatis rebus attenuavit, et in nimiam egestatem de ingenti copia redegit.' Palgrave, Normandy and England, gives an elaborate amplification of this story, explaining that whereas the productive value of the land was the basis of the earlier system of rating, Ranulf introduced a simple computation of acreage. (Vol. iv. pp. 59–63.) The words of Ordericus will scarcely bear this. Possibly he may refer to a substitution of the short hundred for the long in the reckoning of the hide of land : but it is more probable that the whole story is a misapprehension, and is to be referred to the Domesday Survey, in which Ranulf seems most likely to have taken a part.

must be repeated under the head of judicature: it is enough to remark that, as early as the reign of William Rufus, questions of assessment were referred by the crown to the report of the county court, and that in the reign of Henry I the assessment and levying of taxation seems to have formed one portion of the duty of the justices, who, with the functions if not with the name of itinerant judges, transacted the local business of the Exchequer in each shire [1].

Royal justice a profitable source of revenue.

127. So intimate is the connexion of judicature with finance under the Norman kings, that we scarcely need the comments of the historians to guide us to the conclusion, that it was mainly for the sake of the profits that justice was administered at all. Such no doubt was the principle upon which Ranulf Flambard and his master acted. A deeper and more statesmanlike view probably influenced Henry I and his great minister—the belief that a nation in which justice is done is safer and more contented, and presents therefore an easier and richer body to be taxed. But there is no reason to suppose that Henry acted on any higher motive; the value of justice depended in his eyes very much on the amount of treasure with which it supplied him; and accordingly there is not a single fiscal or judicial measure of his reign by which light is not thrown both on the Curia Regis and on the Exchequer.

The Curia Regis in its judicial character.

The Curia Regis, the supreme tribunal of judicature, of which the Exchequer was the financial department or session, was, as has been stated already, the court of the king sitting to administer justice with the advice of his counsellors [2]; those counsellors being, in the widest acceptation, the whole body of tenants-in-chief, but, in the more limited usage, the great officers of the household and specially appointed judges. The great gatherings of the national council may be regarded as full

---

[1] See below, p. 420.

[2] That William the Conqueror heard causes in person we know from Lanfranc's words in a letter (Ep. 19) addressed to Herfast bishop of Elmham: ' Rex . . . praecepit ut querimonia de clericis abbatis Balduini . . . sopita remaneret, quo ad usque ipsemet ipsam causam audiret vel a me . . . audiri praeciperet.' Down to the reign of John the kings occasionally administered justice in person ; Henry II very frequently.

sessions of the Curia Regis or the Curia Regis, as a perpetual The three annual courts.
committee of the national council, but there is no evidence to
prove that the supreme judicature originated in the idea of
such a devolution of authority.   In the more general meetings,
as at the three annual placita, the king wore his crown, and
consulted, or made a show of consulting, his vassals on all
matters of state.   The courts in the king's absence were presided over by the chief or great justiciar, acting 'ex praecepto
regis' or 'vice sua,' 'in meo loco,' as the Conqueror ex-
pressed it[1].   The other persons who bear the title of jus- Justices of the Curia.
ticiar, the ordinary members, as they may be called, of the
court, were the same as those of the Exchequer; the same
persons who acted as barons in the latter acted as justices in
the former; the fines paid or remitted in the Curia were recorded in the Exchequer, and the writ that was issued in the
one chamber was treated by the other as being, what it was
truly, its own act.   The great officers of the household seem to Place of the officers of the house-hold.
have acted in the business of the Curia Regis, simply however
as justices; we have no record that apportions to them the
definite seats or functions which they held in the Exchequer;
accordingly when we find the chancellor or chamberlain sitting
in judgment, we are not to suppose that the cause on which he

---

[1] Gneist's conclusions on the character of the supreme judicature of the
Norman reigns are as follows:—Under the name of the Curia Regis is to
be understood the personal judicature of the king : the Curia Regis does
not consist of the entire community of tenants-in-chief, for as yet they formed
no distinct body or corporation ; nor of a definite number of great vassals,
for there was as yet no legal line drawn between great vassals and small ;
nor of a definite number of great officials, for the great officials were not so
constituted as to form a court of peers : the justice of the Curia, which was
not administered by the king himself, was administered by special commissions, not by a standing body of judges, or by the barons of the Exchequer.   Verwalt. i. 232, 241-243.   This is an extreme view, and in
harmony with the general idea held by this great jurist of the absolute
despotism of the Norman sovereigns.   On the other hand, it cannot be
denied that the general tendency of English writers has been to ascribe to
the legal institutions of the period greater solidity and definiteness than
they can be proved to have possessed.   The view which I have tried to
indicate in the text and in the Select Charters, regarding the period as one
of transition, in which routine was gradually becoming a check on despotic
authority, will probably not commend itself to the maintainers of either
view.

decides is one belonging specially to the chancery or the chamber ; he is simply a member of the king's judicial court.

The number of justices small.

The number of persons who filled the office of justice or baron of the Exchequer during the Norman reigns was not very large, nor are the relations of the members of the court to one another very well defined ; it is even possible that a close examination of existing records would show that all the officers who discharged judicial functions were members, under some other title, of the king's household. Roger of Salisbury bore the name of 'justitiarius' from the year 1107 to his death ; but there are several other justices[1], mentioned both in records and by the historians, whose position seems to be scarcely inferior to

Justices under Henry I.

his[2]. Ralph Basset appears early in the reign of Henry I as a very influential judge[3]; his son Richard is called by Ordericus Vitalis and Henry of Huntingdon 'capitalis justitiarius[4]' even during the life of Bishop Roger ; and Geoffrey de Clinton, who was the king's chamberlain or treasurer, held pleas in A.D. 1130 over all England[5]. The Pipe Roll of that year furnishes us with the names of other justices : pleas were held not only by

---

[1] Besides the question of the chief justiciarship, treated above, the title of justitia, or justitiarius, has obscurities of its own. (1) It is often used in a very general way, in the salutations prefixed to charters, ' comitibus et baronibus et justitiariis et vicecomitibus ;' in which it seems to include, as it did in France, all landowners who possess courts of their own, or are qualified to act as *judices* in the shire-moot. See Henry I's charter to London, and the Leges Henrici I, § 29; Select Charters, pp. 106, 108. (2) It belongs to the sheriffs, who are called by John of Salisbury (Polycr. v. 15, 16) *justitiae errantes,* and to whom the name *justitia* in the so-called laws of Edward the Confessor seems to belong. It is probable that whilst the sheriff, in his character of sheriff, was competent to direct the customary business of the court, it was in that of *justitia* that he transacted special business under the king's writ. See Bracton, lib. iii. c. 35 (ed. 1640, f. 154). (3) It is specially given to officers of the king's court, e.g. to Miles of Gloucester, ' baroni et justitiario meo ' (Charter of Stephen, Madox, Hist. Exch. p. 135); in which sense it seems to prove that his position was one of judicial authority as well as ministerial. (4) To the chief justice. Henry of Huntingdon gives the name to the commissioners of the Domesday Survey, fol. 212, who are called *barones* in the Survey itself; see above, p. 416.

[2] See the remarks on the development of the chief justiciarship, above, p. 374. Henry I tells Anselm that he has ordered the justiciars to act by his advice. (Ans. Epp. lib. iv, ep. 93.)

[3] Ord. Vit. vi. 10, xi. 2 ; Chron. Abingdon, ii. 170.

[4] Ord. Vit. xiii. 26 ; Hen. Hunt. de Cont. Mundi ; Ang. Sac. ii. 701.

[5] See Mon. Angl. vi. 218. Pipe Roll 31 Hen. I.

the two Bassets and Geoffrey de Clinton, but by William of
Albini the Butler, Eustace Fitz-John and Walter Espec, Miles
of Gloucester the Constable, Pain Fitz-John, Robert Arundel,
and Walkelin Visdeloup [1]. Other names may perhaps be found
in the charters of Henry I and Stephen. The *capitalis justitia*
however seems to be the only one of the body to whom, in
formal documents, a determinate position as the king's representative is assigned [2].

The Curia Regis, in this aspect, was the machinery through
which the judicial power of the crown was exercised in that
wide sphere of legal business on which, in its now complicated
relations, it was brought to bear. That business consisted
largely of causes in which the king's interest was concerned, or
which were brought up by way of appeal when the suitors were
sufficiently powerful to obtain such a favour, or when the
powers of the popular courts had been exhausted or had failed
to do justice [3]. In these particulars it succeeded to the royal
jurisdiction of the Anglo-Saxon kings. It was also a tribunal
of primary resort in cases of disputes between the tenants-in-
chief of the crown, a feudal court in which were arranged the
quarrels of the Norman lords, who were too strong to submit
to the simple justice of the shire and hundred [4]. It was

Character of the Curia Regis.

It inherits something from the Anglo-Saxon system, and something from the Norman.

---

[1] Pipe Roll 31 Hen. I.

[2] See the charter of Henry I to the Canons of Trinity, Aldgate: 'Et
prohibeo super forisfacturam meam quod non ponantur in placitum de aliquo tenemento nisi coram me vel capitali justitia meo;' Foed. i. 12.

[3] The Pipe Roll of Henry I does not expressly mention the jurisdiction
of the Curia Regis, but it is probable that most of the entries 'pro recto
terrae suae' and the like refer to suits in which a writ has been obtained
from the court. Cases in the King's court during the reign of Henry I
will be found in the Chronicle of Battle, p. 51; in the Chronicle of Abingdon, ii. 182; in the Cartulary of Gloucester, i. 236; in Elmham, ed. Hardwick, pp. 355, 362, 366, 382. 'Ric. de Rullos debet i. marcam auri ut
juste tractetur in curia domini sui;' Pipe Roll, p. 143. 'Walterus Mal-
travers reddit computum de 20 marcis argenti ut rex juvet eum versus
Paganum Filium Johannis;' Ibid. p. 124. 'Burgenses de Gloecestra debent 30 marcas argenti si possent recuperare pecuniam suam per justitiam
regis, quae ablata fuit eis in Hibernia;' Ibid. p. 77.

[4] 'Et si amodo exsurgat placitum de divisione terrarum, si est inter
barones meos dominicos, tractetur placitum in curia mea: et, si est inter
vavassores duorum dominorum, tractetur in comitatu;' Writ of Henry I;
below, p. 425. Such a trial is described in a charter of Henry I in the
Cartulary of Gloucester, i. 236: and see the trial of the bishop of Durham;
below, § 134.

Its growing importance as a resource for equity. however more than this: the ancient customary process of the local courts, with that strict maintenance of formalities and that incapacity for regarding equitable considerations which seems inseparable from the idea of compurgation and ordeal, was now becoming antiquated. As a special favour, suits were brought up from the view of the provincial courts to be decided by such new methods as the wisdom of the king and his counsellors might invent; and from the Curia Regis issued the writs which directed inquiry and recognition of rights as to land, the obligations of tenure, the legitimacy of heirs, and the enforcement

System of writs. of local justice [1]. These writs, although not absolutely unknown in England before the Conquest, were derived no doubt in their Norman form from the process of the Karolingian lawyers;

Their origin. they were the expedients by which the 'jus honorarium' of the king, as fountain of justice, was enabled to remedy the defects of the 'jus civile' or 'commune,' the customary proceedings of the local moots [2].

Criminal jurisdiction. The Curia Regis had criminal jurisdiction also, as Ralph Basset proved when he hanged forty-four thieves at Hundehoge [3]. It was in fact a supreme court of justice, both of appeal and, where leave was obtained, of primary recourse.

Review of provincial judicature. But it was also a ministry of justice, before which the whole judicial action of the country passed in review. This was done partly by the Court of Exchequer, in which, as we have seen, the sheriffs annually rendered their accounts; but partly also by direct inspection. The provincial judicature was brought into immediate connexion with the central judicature by journeys of the king's judges. We have seen traces of this arrangement as early as the time of Alfred, who may have been acquainted with the system in use under the Frank emperors [4]. Edgar and Canute had themselves made judicial circuits; the Conqueror's choice of the three great cities of the south of England for his

---

[1] Writs of these kinds will be found in great numbers in most monastic cartularies: e.g. Chron. Abingdon, ii. 84, 85, 92, 93.

[2] On the connexion of the Norman and English Brevia with the Frankish Indiculi, see Brunner, Schwurgericht, pp. 76–84; and below, Chap. XII.

[3] Chron. Sax. A.D. 1124.

[4] See above, p. 202.

annual placita brought the sense of royal justice home to the
country at large. But Henry I went a step further. He sent Circuits of
the justices.
the officers of the Exchequer through the country to assess
the revenue [1]; in one great fiscal iter of the reign the ferms of
the counties were fixed; and during his reign the whole kingdom was visited by justices, officers of the Curia Regis, not
perhaps with the systematic regularity enforced by his grandson,
but with sufficient order to prove that he saw and satisfied the
want of such an expedient. In A.D. 1130 Geoffrey de Clinton,
the chamberlain, had lately visited seventeen out of the thirty-
four counties of which the accounts are preserved; Ralph
Basset had visited seven; Richard Basset five; Eustace Fitz-
John and Walter Espec had held pleas in the northern counties; Miles of Gloucester and Pain Fitz-John in the west-
midland and the Welsh March; William of Albini, Robert
Arundel and others, in the forests and in the south-western
counties. It is probable that this was by no means an excep- Action of the
justices in
the country,
in the county
courts.
tional measure: in A.D. 1124 we find Ralph Basset, as has been
frequently mentioned, holding a court in Leicestershire; Ordericus Vitalis gives an account of a trial held before him in the
county court of Huntingdonshire in A.D. 1115 or 1116[2]. A
measure dictated still more distinctly by this policy may be
traced in the list of sheriffs for A.D. 1130. Richard Basset and
Aubrey de Vere, a judge and a royal chamberlain, act as joint
sheriffs in no less than eleven counties: Geoffrey de Clinton,
Miles of Gloucester, William of Pont l'Arche the Treasurer, are
also sheriffs as well as justices of the king's court. That such The sheriff-
doms held
by the
justices.
a system was open to much abuse is self-evident; these officers
sitting as judges and barons in the Exchequer actually audited

---

[1] Dialogus de Scaccario, lib. i. c. 7: 'Rex, diffinito magnorum consilio,
destinavit per regnum quos ad id prudentiores et discretiores cognoverat,
qui, circeuentes et oculata fide fundos singulos perlustrantes, habita aesti-
matione victualium quae de hiis solvebantur, redegerunt in summam
denariorum.'
[2] 'Radulfo autem Basset sedente pro tribunali, congregatis etiam pro-
vincialibus universis apud Huntedoniam, ut mos est in Anglia;' Ord. Vit.
vi. 10. Ralph may have been sheriff of Huntingdonshire at the time, but
he was in attendance on the queen, and seems to have acted on the same
business in London shortly after.

the accounts which they presented as sheriffs; but they were under the strong control of the king and Bishop Roger; and although there were scandals no doubt, such as that for which Geoffrey de Clinton was tried in this very year[1], the important fact remains that by these means the king and the justiciar kept in their hands the reins of the entire judicial administration. The justices whilst employed in provincial work sat in the shire-moot; and this usage of Henry I, with the series of similar measures initiated by Henry II, forms the link between the old and new organisations of the country, by which that concentration of local machinery was produced, out of which the representative system arose. The parliament of the thirteenth century was the concentration of local representation in and

Step toward self-government.

with the national council. It was no small step in that direction when the action of the Curia Regis was brought into direct connexion with that of the shire-moot. The Norman curia met the Anglo-Saxon gemot in the visitations of the itinerant justices.

The county courts.

128. We thus come to the constitution of the shire-moot. In a former chapter the history of this institution has been traced up to and past the date of the Conquest; and it has already been shown how in the inquest which preceded the Domesday Survey, as well as in the production of the record of Edward's laws, the means of gaining information which it afforded were utilised. The existence of the shire-moot through the reigns of the Conqueror[2] and William Rufus is proved by the existence of writs addressed, as in the preceding reigns, to the sheriffs and other leading members[3]. There is in existence a writ directed by William Rufus to the sheriff of Northamptonshire ordering him to call together his shire to examine into the rights of the monks of Ramsey[4]. It appears from the very charter by which

---

[1] See above, p. 401.

[2] 'Requiratur hundredus et comitatus sicut antecessores nostri statuerunt;' Ll. Will. I; Select Charters, p. 84.

[3] 'Willem king gret Willem biscop and Swein scirefen and alle mine thegnes on Estsexen freondlice;' Mon. Angl. i. 301. See a similar writ in favour of Chertsey Abbey, ibid. i. 431.

[4] 'Rex Willelmo de Cahannis, salutem. Praecipio tibi ut facias convenire sciram de Hamtona et judicio ejus cognosce,' &c.; Palgrave, Common-

Henry I orders the restoration of the ancient courts that they Abuses of
these courts.
had been used under his brother for the purposes of extortion [1],
and the same may be inferred from the description of Ranulf
Flambard 'as driving all the gemots' throughout all England.
From the year 1108 onwards these courts, as well as those of
the hundred, were held 'as in king Edward's days and not
otherwise.' The lords of land and their stewards attended, and
from each township the reeve and four men [2], and the parish
priest. The full court met twice a year under the sheriff or The shire-
moot.
his deputy, and was still competent to declare folk-right in every
suit ; the pleas of the crown were recorded in it for the view
of the Curia Regis, whether reported by the sheriff to the Exchequer or examined by the justices in a provincial visit [3]. It
had a criminal as well as a civil jurisdiction as before, although
the management of the pleas of the crown on the one side, and
the interference by royal writ on the other, must have materially

wealth, clxxix ; 29th Report of the Deputy Keeper of the Records, App.
p. 44.

[1] 'Henricus rex Anglorum Samsoni episcopo et Ursoni de Abetot, et
omnibus baronibus suis Francis et Anglis de Wirecestresira, salutem.
Sciatis quod concedo et praecipio ut amodo comitatus mei et hundreda in
illis locis et eisdem terminis sedeant sicut sederunt in tempore regis Eadwardi et non aliter ; ego enim quando voluero faciam ea satis summonere
propter mea dominica necessaria ad voluntatem meam ; et si amodo exsurgat placitum de divisione terrarum, si est inter barones meos dominicos
tractetur placitum in curia mea ; et si est inter vavassores duorum dominorum tractetur in comitatu ; et hoc duello fiat nisi in eis remanserit. Et
volo et praecipio ut omnes de comitatu eant ad comitatus et hundreda sicut
fecerunt in tempore regis Eadwardi, nec remorent propter aliquam causam
pacem meam vel quietudinem, qui non sequuntur placita mea et judicia
mea, sicut tunc temporis fecerunt. Teste R. episcopo Lundoniae et Rogero
episcopo et Ranulfo cancellario et R. comite de Mellent, apud Rading ;'
Foedera, i. 12. Compare Leges Henrici I, c. vii. § 1 : 'Sicut antiqua fuerat
institutione formatum, salutari regis imperio, vera *nuper* est recordatione
formatum, generalia comitatuum placita certis locis et vicibus et diffinito
tempore per singulas Angliae provincias convenire debere, nec ullis ultra
fatigationibus agitari nisi propria regis necessitas vel commune regni com-
modum saepius adjiciat.'

[2] 'Intersint autem episcopi, comites, vicedomini, vicarii, centenarii,
aldermanni, praefecti, praepositi, barones, vavasores, tungrevii, et ceteri
terrarum domini. . . . Si uterque (sc. baro et dapifer) necessario desit,
praepositus et quatuor de melioribus villae assint pro omnibus qui nominatim non erunt ad placitum submoniti ;' Leges Henrici I, c. vii. §§ 2, 6.

[3] 'Agantur itaque primo debita verae Christianitatis jura ; secundo regis
placita ; postremo causae singulorum dignis satisfactionibus expleantur et
quoscunque scyresmot discordantes inveniet, vel amore congreget vel se-
questret judicio ;' Ibid.

affected its independence.   It retained however all its authority
in matters of voluntary jurisdiction, witnessing transfers of land,
and sanctioning by its testimony private charters and documents
of all sorts.   The ancient forms were also in use; witness,
compurgation, and ordeal; and the old theory that in these
popular courts the suitors were the judges.

Antiquity of
its customs.

The new light thrown on the shire-moot, by the increased
number of records, makes it a little difficult to know what particulars of custom, now for the first time discoverable, are new
or old.   The composition of the court and its times of session
are however clearly ancient.   The custom of interference of the
crown by writ, although not unprecedented [1], is, as a custom,
new [2].   The references to trial by battle, which now become
common, show that the Normans had introduced that custom in
its legal completeness.   But the most important novelty is the
inquest by oath, which has been already referred to, and which
forms an important link in the history of the jury.   William
the Conqueror directs the justiciars on one occasion to assemble
the shire-moots which had taken part in a suit touching the
rights of Ely; that being done, there were to be chosen a number
of the English who knew the state of the disputed lands in the
reign of Edward; these were to swear to the truth of their
depositions; and action was to be taken accordingly [3].   A similar
writ of William Rufus to the sheriff of Northamptonshire, already

Trial by
battle and
inquest by
jury.

Inquest by
sworn jurors.

---

[1] See above, p. 206.

[2] For example: 'Henricus rex Anglorum Nigello de Oilli et Willelmo
vicecomiti de Oxeneforde salutem.   Praecipio vobis ut faciatis abbati de
Abbendona plenariam rectitudinem de exclusa sua,' &c.   Chron. Abingd.
ii. 92.   'H. rex Anglorum, W. vicecomiti de Oxeneforde, salutem.   Fac
cito et sine mora plenam justitiam Faritio,' &c.   Ibid.

[3] 'W. rex Anglorum Lanfranco archiepiscopo et Rogero comiti Moritonii
et Gauffrido Constantiensi episcopo salutem.   Mando vobis et praecipio ut
iterum faciatis congregari omnes scyras quae interfuerunt placito habito
de terris ecclesiae de Heli, antequam mea conjunx in Normanniam novissime
veniret; cum quibus etiam sint de baronibus meis qui competenter adesse
poterunt et praedicto placito interfuerunt et qui terras ejusdem ecclesiae
tenent.   Quibus in unum congregatis eligantur plures de illis Anglis qui
sciunt quomodo terrae jacebant praefatae ecclesiae die qua rex Edwardus
obiit, et quod inde dixerint ibidem jurando testentur;' Liber Eliensis, i.
256.   The result of the inquiry is referred to by Henry I as final: 'Sicut
dirationatum fuit in tempore patris mei apud Keneteford, coram baronibus
patris mei . . . et testimonio plurium syrarum'; Mon. Angl. i. 482.

mentioned, directs a like proceeding in the affairs of Ramsey; whilst two writs of William the Etheling to the sheriff of Kent order, and direct action to be taken upon, the verdict or recognition of the good men of that county in reference to the rights of S. Augustine's [1].

The employment of a number of sworn thegns to report on the character of accused persons, which has been traced to the laws of Ethelred, may probably have continued to be usual; and thus the growth of the jury in criminal matters may have kept pace with its development in civil affairs. But of this we have slight evidence, unless the session of Hundehoge, where the thegns of Leicestershire acted with the king's justiciar, may be again appealed to. But however this may be, it is certain that the administration of justice in the shire-moot was now vested in persons who were bound by oath to the fulfilment of their duties and to speak the truth [2]. The Pipe Roll

Question as to a jury of presentment.

---

[1] 'Willelmus filius regis Willelmo vicecomiti de Chent salutem. Praecipio quod praecipias Hamonem filium Vitalis et probis vicinis Santwic quos Hamo nominabit, ut dicant veritatem de nave abbatis de Sancto Augustino, et, si navis illa perrexit per mare die qua rex novissime mare transivit, tunc praecipio ut modo pergat quousque rex in Angliam veniat et iterum resaisiatur inde abbas praedictus. Testibus episcopo Sarisb. et cancellario apud Wodestoc.' 'W. filius regis W. vicecomiti salutem. Praecipio quod resaisias abbatem de Sancto Augustino de nave sua sicut ego praecepi per meum aliud breve et sicut recognitum fuit per probos homines comitatus, quod inde abbas erat saisitus die qua rex mare novissime transivit, et in pace teneat, et hoc sine mora, ne inde clamorem amplius audiam. Teste cancellario apud Windesor;' Palgrave, Commonwealth, clxxix.: Elmham, ed. Hardwick, pp. 353, 354: in the latter place these acts are referred to William Rufus during his father's life; but this is very improbable. The same authority furnishes another writ of the same sort; p. 356: 'Fac recognosci per homines hundredi de Middeltone quas consuetudines Abbas S. Augustini habere debet in villa de Newingtone.' A writ of Stephen ordering restitution to the church of S. Martin, London, in pursuance of a like recognition, 'Sicut recognitum et testificatum fuit coram M. vicecomite in hundredo apud Meldonam,' is printed in Madox, Formulare Angl. p. 40. In 1106 Henry I commissions five barons to ascertain the customs of the church of York by the oath of twelve men; Thoroton, Nottinghamshire, iii. 177.

[2] The promissory oath, such as that taken by the twelve thegns to accuse no one falsely, and by modern jurymen to 'well and truly try and true deliverance make,' as well as that of the modern witness, differs widely from the declaratory oath of the ancient popular courts, which was confined to the affirmation of a single fact, prescribed by the judges as the point to be proved, or to the confirmation by compurgators of the oath of a principal. The observance of the distinction would have served to prevent

of Henry I proves the existence of large bodies of judices and juratores. Whether the terms are equivalent; whether they merely mean the qualified members of the courts who were summoned *nominatim*[1] and from whose body witnesses and compurgators must be chosen; whether the judices were a permanent body of local proprietors[2], and the juratores a selection of freemen sworn to declare the truth in the particular case; whether the judices may not have been the presenters of the criminals, and the juratores the witnesses in the civil suits, it would be dangerous even to guess. They appear however to be distinguished, probably by special summons, from the 'minuti homines,' 'smale-manni' or mean men, who were likewise bound to attend the shire-moot and hundred-moot, either in person or by the reeve, and who probably did not possess so much land as was necessary to qualify a man for acting as judge in a suit in which land was in question. That these persons were very numerous is certain from the very large fines imposed on them for neglect of duty. In Yorkshire the sheriff accounts for thirty-one marks drawn from nine 'judicatores comitatus;' and for 336 marks five shillings and sixpence 'de minutis judicibus et juratoribus comitatus.' It is no wonder that we find almost immediately after that the unfortunate payers have undertaken to compound for their attendance: The judges and jurors of Yorkshire owe a hundred pounds that they may no more be judges or jurors[3].' The

the construction of many improbable theories of the origin of juries. The oath of the jury-inquest was a promise to speak the truth, 'Sacramentum quod verum dicent' (Assize of Clarendon), or 'Quod inde veritatem secundum conscientiam suam manifestabunt' (Const. Clarendon).

[1] See Ll. Henr. cc. vii, xxix. Cf. p. 425, note 2 above.

[2] The judices in the county court are described in the Leges Hen. I, c. xxix.: 'Regis judices sunt barones comitatus, qui liberas in eis terras habent per quos debent causae singulorum alterna prosecutione tractari; villani vero vel cotseti vel ferdingi vel qui sunt viles vel inopes personae non sunt inter legum judices numerandi.'

[3] Pipe Roll Hen. I, pp. 27, 28. The entry 'Judices et juratores Eboraciscire debent £100 ut non amplius sint judices nec juratores,' ibid. p. 34, is sometimes quoted as referring to Walter Espec and Eustace Fitz-John. This is however not the case: it is the first entry among the accounts accruing from the county of York in consequence of their visitation. The exact meaning of the entry is uncertain: Brunner (Schwurgericht, p. 355) adduces it as an illustration of the attempts made from the beginning of

sheriff of Kent accounts for £17 3s. 4d. from the jurors of Kent, and another sum from Sussex; in Essex, £5 6s. 8d. is raised from the 'minuti homines;' in Lincolnshire, seventy four marks and a-half; in Bedfordshire, forty shillings from the 'juratores et minuti homines;' and four judges of the isle of Axholm render account for eight marks due for the pleas of William of Albini[1]. It can scarcely be doubted that all these fines were incurred for non-attendance, and that they prove either the dislike of the free-holders to attend the court of the justice itinerant, or a serious decline in the ancient constitution of the county courts. But this does not affect the main question, which is the continuance of the custom of employing jurors to transact the judicial work.

The use made of the shire-moot for the purpose of raising money may account for the reluctance of the suitors to attend. That this was the practice is clearly shown by Henry's writ for the restoration of the ancient custom : 'I will cause those courts to be summoned when I will for my own proper necessities, at my pleasure[2];' an important engagement intended to deprive the sheriffs of their opportunities of wanton exaction, but to secure to the king the right of asking for or taking money when he should deem it necessary. Unfortunately this is the only evidence that we have of the method of raising money from the shire-moot[3]; but it seems almost

the jury system to escape the responsibility. It appears to me rather to refer to the old system which was gradually being replaced by the jury system, and to be a sort of composition for the fine incurred by non-attendance at the shire-moot and hundred-moot. But the same desire to avoid jury-work appears constantly later on, when fines 'pro defectu recognitionis' are frequent. To the scarcity of qualified jurors the following passage refers : 'Si opus est, licet in placitis judicibus qui aderunt respectare placitum ex abundanti, donec senatores absentes interesse possint, vel ipsi judicium inquisierint ; nec jure cogendi sunt ad jurandum quod nesciant judicium inde;' i. e. in cases in which at the county court there is not a sufficient number of qualified judices informed on the particular case, the trial may be respited until either they have informed themselves, or the absent *witan* can be present. Leges Hen. I, c. 29.

[1] Pipe Roll Hen. I, pp. 65, 69, 118, &c.   [2] Above, p. 425.
[3] The following curious writ of Henry I proves both the formal demand of an aid from the barons of his court and the negotiation of the particulars through the officers of the Exchequer : 'H. rex Anglorum R. episcopo, et Herberto camerario et Hugoni de Bochelanda, salutem. Sciatis quod clamo quietas v. hidas abbatis Faricii de Abendona de eleemosyna de Wrtha,

certain that when the occasion arose, the counties would be
consulted by the barons of the Exchequer and not by the
sheriffs. The same writ directs that suits between the barons
of the king's demesne for the division of land are to be decided
in the Curia Regis; similar suits between vassals, 'vavassores,'
in the county court and by trial by battle.

The hun-
dred-moot.

Nearly all the general statements made about the shire-moot
are true also of the hundred-moot. This also is restored by
Henry I as it was in King Edward's days. The same reluctance to attend is proved by the entry of penalties on the Pipe
Roll; the sheriff of Sussex accounts for 102 marks 'for the
pleas of Richard Basset from the minuti homines for default of
the hundred-moot;' and in Middlesex a small payment of the
same kind is entered[1]. The 'Leges Henrici I,' as they are
called, attest the existence of the two courts of the hundred,
the great one for view of frankpledge, held twice a year under
the sheriff, and afterwards called the great court of the hundred, or Sheriff's tourn and leet[2]; and the lesser court, the
Curia parva Hundredi, held twelve times a year, and presided
over by the bailiff of the hundred[3]: in the latter the chief
business was probably the disputes about small debts, which
long continued to furnish its sole employment[4].

The mano-
rial courts.

129. The manorial constitution, which is the lowest form of
judicial organisation, was by this time largely if not completely
developed. The manor itself was, as Ordericus tells us, nothing
more nor less than the ancient township, now held by a lord who
possessed certain judicial rights varying according to the terms
of the grant by which he was infeoffed. Every manor had a

de omnibus rebus, et nominatim de isto auxilio quod barones mihi dederunt,
et hoc dico, sicut clamavi quietas eas per aliud breve meum in omni tempore. Testibus,' &c.; Chron. Abingd. ii. 113.

[1] Pipe Roll Hen. I, pp. 71, 151; cf. pp. 28, 30, 56, 117, 143.

[2] Ll. Hen. I, c. viii: 'Bis in anno conveniant in hundretum suum quicunque liberi . . . ad dinoscendum inter cetera si decaniae plenae sint.'

[3] Ibid. c. vii: 'Hundreta vel wapentagia duodecies in anno congregari.'
Under Henry II these courts were held every fortnight, 'de quindena in
quindenam.' Henry III fixed them every three weeks; Rol. cl. 18 Hen.
III, m. 10; Ann. Dunst. pp. 139, 140.

[4] See Eyton's Shropshire, xii. 168; Viner's Abridgment, s. v. Court.
Early notices of transactions in the court of the hundred will be found in
Madox, Formulare Anglicanum, p. 40.

court-baron [1] or hall-moot, the ancient gemot of the township [2], Court-baron, court-cus- in which by-laws were made and other local business transacted, tomary, and court-leet. and a court-customary in which the business of the villenage was dispatched.   Those manors whose lords had under the Anglo-Saxon laws possessed sac or soc, or who since the Conquest had had grants in which those terms were used, had also a court-leet, or criminal jurisdiction, cut out as it were from the criminal jurisdiction of the hundred [3], and excusing the suitors who attended it from going to the court-leet of the hundred.   If the lord had a grant of view of frankpledge also, his tenants were released from attendance at the sheriff's tourn. It was only the great baronial jurisdictions, which were almost shires in themselves, that freed their suitors from all attendance at the popular courts.   These greater jurisdictions, liberties, or Liberties and honours. honours [4], the growth of which in Anglo-Saxon times we have

[1] The term ' court-baron ' is commonly understood as if it meant 'curia baronis,' the court of the lord ; but it may be questioned whether it is not really ' curia baronum,' the court of the vassals or homagers who were the judges.   The manorial court of the Archbishop of York at Ripon was called the court military, i. e. the court of the knightly vassals of the church of S. Wilfrid.

[2] The tunscipesmot occurs in a charter granted by Richard I to Wenlock Priory : the king grants that all the prior's men, tithes, and effects shall be quit of all oppressions and exactions, from shire-moot and hundred-moot, from pleas and plaints, from husteng, portmanmot (court of portreeve in boroughs), and tunscipesmot ; Eyton, Shropshire, iii. 237.

[3] On the institution of the court-leet, see Scriven on Copyholds ; Gneist, Self-government, i. 89, 101 sq.   Although the documentary history of these courts belongs to a later age, there can be little risk in tracing their origin back to the sac and soc of the older jurisdictions, and not regarding them as mere creations of Norman feudalism.   If they had been so, there must have been some evidence of their creation after the Conquest ; but, so far from this being the case, the language in which they are mentioned in documents of the Norman period is distinctly borrowed from the Anglo-Saxon.   The history of the leet-jury, which might throw some considerable light on the early development of the jury principle in England, is still a desideratum.   It may be regarded as quite certain that, if the manorial jurisdictions had been created in the feudal period, they would have taken the feudal form ; their courts would have been courts of baronies, not of single manors, and their process would not have been identical with that of the old popular courts, as for the most part it is.

[4] The honour may contain several manors and hold one court-day for all, but the several manors retain their separate organisation under it ; and it has no independent organisation irrespective of them.   ' Although an honour consists of many manors, and there is for all the manors only one court held, yet are they quasi several and distinct courts ;' Scriven, ii. 737 ; quoted by Gneist, Verwalt. i. 164.

already traced, were multiplied under the Norman sovereigns [1]. They presented to the great feudatories the most favourable opportunities for extending the principles of feudal law, and making themselves absolutely supreme among their dependents. It tasked accordingly the energies of the national courts to watch them: they attracted to their own courts the poorer freemen of the neighbourhood, to the diminution of the profits of the hundred and the shire and to the impoverishment of the crown; they served as a basis for the judicial tyranny of the petty castellans, which we have seen break out into anarchy in the wretched times of Stephen; and it was no small triumph when Henry II forced them to admit his itinerant justices to exercise jurisdiction in them [2], although the proceeds of the assizes continued no doubt to increase the income of the lords. The legal records of Henry I's reign furnish us with but little information respecting either the smaller jurisdictions of the manor or the greater ones of the honour or liberty. There is however no doubt that the same principles of legal procedure were used in these as in the popular courts; the juratores and judices were there as well as in the shire and the hundred; compurgation and ordeal; fines for non-attendance; the whole accumulation of ancient custom as well as Norman novelty. They were in fact, as they had been earlier, public jurisdictions vested in private hands [3]; descending hereditarily in connexion

Procedure in the manorial courts.

[1] The jurisdiction of the hundreds fell more especially into the hands of the territorial proprietors; so much so, that before the end of the period, perhaps in a majority of cases, these courts had become part of the fief of the lord whose castle or manor-house was the stronghold of the neighbourhood; e. g. Robert d'Oilli had a grant of the hundred outside the Northgate of Oxford: and, besides these, a great number of hundreds were held by the monasteries; any good county history will furnish illustrations. In these cases the *bailiff* of the hundred was nominated by the lord and presided in the courts, except at the sheriff's tourn. In the case of an honour such as that of Peverell, the sheriff was excluded even from the tourn. Dep. Keeper's Report, xvi. app. 41.

[2] Assize of Clarendon, Select Charters, p. 144.

[3] An example of a transaction in the court of Bath under Bishop John of Tours will be found in Madox, Hist. Exch. p. 76. The Bishop sits with his friends and barons. A letter is produced from the regent William, son of Henry I, directing the delivery of an estate to a person who had inherited it. The bishop reads the letter, and asks the opinion of the court. The prior of Bath states the claim of the convent on the land in question. A

with the hereditary estate, and only recoverable by the crown
either by a forcible resumption of the estate, or by a series of
legal enactments such as reduced the dangers of private authority by increasing the pressure of central administration. The
latter process was one part of the reforms of Henry II, but the
former, owing to the strangely conservative policy of the kings,
was very seldom resorted to. When a great barony fell by
forfeiture or escheat into the hands of the crown, instead of
being incorporated with the general body of the county or
counties in which it lay, it retained a distinct corporate existence and the whole apparatus of jurisdiction which it had possessed before. Under the title of an Honour, it either continued in the possession of the king and was farmed like a
shire[1], or was granted out again as a hereditary fief. Whilst
it remained in the king's hands, the fact that he was the lord
of the honour did not raise the immediate tenants of the barony
to the rank of tenants-in-chief, or entitle the crown to claim
from them the rights that it claimed from such tenants[2]. It
was therefore separable from the estates of the crown at a
moment's notice, and was not used to promote the uniformity or
symmetry of the provincial organisation.

Treatment of escheated honours.

discussion follows, ' variis ab alterutro contradictionibus :' the bishop ad-
journs, that those members of the court who are 'neither advocates nor
favourers of either side' may have time for consideration. Having deliberated, they return into court, and one of them delivers the sentence :—
the claimant must produce his title-deeds or witnesses; if he can do
neither, he must be heard no more. He makes no reply, and the sentence
is approved by the court; two bishops, three archdeacons with many
clerks and chaplains, and five laymen, probably the friends and barons
mentioned before; and the document is attested by twelve witnesses.
A writ from the king confirms the decision of the court, directing that
the prior and convent shall retain the land. This proceeding is certainly
more like that of a witenagemot than that of a court of law, but it is
recognised by the king ' sicut dirationaverunt [monachi] ... per judicium
curiae tuae.'

[1] So the Honour of Wallingford is specially mentioned in the Assize of
Clarendon; and those of Wallingford, Nottingham, Boulogne, and Lancaster in Magna Carta. Some of these were set apart as a provision
for the king's ministers: e. g. the Honour of Berkhampstead was held
by the chancellor in the reign of Henry II. The Honour of Peverell long
retained a separate existence, having been forfeited early in the reign
of Henry II. Its courts were only abolished by statute in the 12 and 13
Victoria.

[2] Dialogus de Scaccario, ii. 24; Magna Carta, art. 43.

Demesne of
the crown.

130. Somewhat analogous to the franchises of the nobles was the jurisdiction of the demesne estates of the crown, the profits of which are recorded in the Pipe Rolls, although they were not in all cases farmed by the sheriffs of the counties in which they lay. The royal estate of Windsor was accounted for in the year 1130 by William de Bocland, who was steward also of several other royal manors. In these estates, which, when they had been held by the crown since the reign of Edward the Confessor, bore the title of manors of ancient demesne [1], very much of the ancient popular process had been preserved without any change; and to the present day some customs are maintained in them which recall the most primitive institutions. In one great division however of the royal lands, the forests, this is not the case, although the forest administration itself was to a certain extent modelled upon the popular system. The forests, we are told by the author of the Dialogus de Scaccario, were peculiarly subject to the absolute will of the king; they were outside the common law or right of the kingdom; they were not liable to be visited by the ordinary judges of the Curia Regis, but by special commission and by special officials; they had laws and customs of their own, and these were drawn up rather to insure the peace of the beasts than that of the king's subjects [2].

The forests.

Abuses of
forest juris-
diction.

The abuses of this close jurisdiction furnish a frequent theme for the declamations of contemporary historians, and form no unimportant element in constitutional history down to the reign of Edward I. The chief grounds of complaint were the constant attempts made by the kings to extend the area of forest

[1] ' A manor of ancient demesne was extra-hundredal; it was as it were a hundred in itself, owing no suit nor having any concern in other hundred courts, but like the latter, controlled by the county court and responsible to the king's justiciars in many matters, but chiefly in those which were connected with the criminal law, and came under the class called Pleas of the Crown;' Eyton, Shropshire, iii. 73, 74.

[2] Dialogus de Scaccario, i. 11: 'Sane forestarum ratio, poena quoque vel absolutio delinquentium in eas, sive pecuniaria fuerit sive corporalis, seorsum ad aliis regni judiciis secernitur et solius regis arbitrio vel cujuslibet familiaris ad hoc specialiter deputati subjicitur. Legibus quidem propriis subsistit, quas non communi regni jure, sed voluntaria principis institutione subnixas dicunt, adeo ut quod per legem ejus factum fuerit, non justum absolute sed justum secundum legem forestae dicatur.'

territory, the severity of the forest law, and the stringency of
its execution. The first of these involved a temptation to the
exercise of arbitrary power which the best of the early kings
were unable to resist, and gave a point of attack of which both   Extension of
barons and people persistently availed themselves. The ground   forest area.
and nature of the claim which the sovereign exercised are
alike uncertain ; whether he regarded himself as the sole proprietor of all beasts of chase, or as having peculiar rights of
chase over all the land in his kingdom, cannot be decided. It
is however evident that no such claim was either formulated,
recognised by the laws or acquiesced in by the owners of land.
Yet for nearly two centuries the process of extension went on   Extension of
in spite of constant protest and as constant promises of redress.   forests.
William I had made the New Forest, as it was believed, with a
wanton sacrifice of popular rights and at such a cost of popular
hardship as brought his posterity under a special curse: and
William Rufus was a no less mighty hunter than his father.
Yet Henry I was able ' by the common consent of his barons to
retain the forests which his father had had[1].' Stephen was
compelled to resign the forests which Henry had made, while
he retained those of the Conqueror and William Rufus, but he
did not keep his engagement[2]. Henry II in his turn re-   Efforts at
tained all that the anarchy of the preceding reign had spared   limitation.
and left his invidious position to Richard and John. John
again in the Great Charter was compelled to renounce the
forests that he himself had afforested[3]; Henry III had to surrender all that had been made since the accession of his uncle
Richard[4], and to submit to a forest survey or perambulation
which was to define the extent of the forests for all time[5]. It

---

[1] ' Forestas *communi consensu baronum meorum* in manu mea retinui,
sicut pater meus eas habuit ; ' Carta Hen. I ; art. 10.
[2] ' Forestas quas Willelmus avus meus et Willelmus avunculus meus
instituerunt et habuerunt, mihi reservo; ceteras omnes, quas rex Henricus
superaddidit, ecclesiis et regno quietas reddo et concedo;' Statutes of the
Realm ; Charters, i. 3.
[3] Art. 47 : ' omnes forestae quae aforestatae sunt tempore nostro statim
deafforestentur.'
[4] Charter of 1216, art. 38 ; Charter of the Forest, art. 1-3.
[5] Charter of the Forest, art. 1.

was an attempt to annul this restriction in 1227 that brought about one great crisis of his reign[1], and his illustrious son seventy years after was engaged in the same struggle. Edward I had in the end to submit to a practical decision of the question by the nation itself, which strained to the utmost the honesty and self-sacrifice of his political character[2].

Cruelty of the forest law. The cruelty of the forest law is constantly ascribed to Henry I, who shared with William Rufus the traits of bloody ferocity from which the Conqueror, Robert and Stephen were comparatively free. The first forest code now extant is of the reign of Henry II: but it records the severities of his grandfather, and the inferences drawn from it are borne out by the words of Ordericus and other contemporaries. Cruel mutilation and capital punishment, not to be redeemed by any forfeiture, are a leading feature of a code so tyrannical that even its authors screened its brutality by a circumlocution[3]. The stringency of the law and the severity of its execution were, not less than its cruelty, a cause of national complaint. Henry II succeeded by the connivance of a papal legate, in subjecting to the operation of the forest law even the clergy whom the common law failed to touch[4]. Richard I compelled the whole population of the counties in which there were any forests to attend the forest courts of the itinerant justices as rigorously as he enforced their attendance on the popular courts of shire and hundred[5]; an

Severity of its execution.

---

[1] See below, vol. ii. c. xiv. § 171.　　　[2] Below, vol. ii. c. xiv. § 181.

[3] The assize of Woodstock; printed in Hoveden, ii. 245; Select Charters, pp. 157–159; Bened. Abb. ii. pf. clxi. The blinding and emasculation are screened by the form 'justitia qualis fuit facta tempore regis Henrici avi sui.' The forest assize of Richard I gives the punishment in full.

[4] See the letter of Henry II to the pope: 'Clericus de cetero non trahatur ante judicem saecularem in persona sua de aliquo criminali, neque de aliquo forisfacto, excepto forisfacto forestae meae, et excepto laico feodo,' &c.; R. de Diceto, i. 410. And in the assize of Woodstock, art. 9 : ' rex defendit quod nullus clericus ei forisfaciat de venatione sua nec de forestis suis.' Many are the complaints of the clerical and monastic annalists, and illustrations are found in the Pipe Rolls. See Bened. i. 105; Hoveden, ii. 86; R. de Diceto, i. 402, 403.

[5] The assize of Woodstock, art. 11, orders them to attend on the summons of the Master forester; that of Richard directs the justices in eyre to enforce the attendance, 'convenirent coram eis ad placita forestae, archiepiscopi, episcopi, comites et barones et omnes libere tenentes ; et de unaquaque villa praepositus et quatuor homines ;' Hoveden, iv. 63.

obligation from which they were only relieved by the legislation of the Great Charter and the Charter of the Forest[1]. John asserted over the fowls of the air the same exclusive right that his ancestors had claimed over the beasts of the chase[2]. But the same progressive legislation, which in the thirteenth century stayed the extension of the forests, amended most of the oppressive regulations of the law by which they were administered.

A system so abhorrent to the nation at large, and working on principles so much opposed to those on which the maintenance of national life depended, involved the existence of a large staff of officers and a fabric of local judicature. The Master-forester of England seems to have been independent even of the great justiciar: the justices in eyre of the forests were analogous to the justices in eyre of the royal courts of law; the four verderers of each forest county, elected by the votes of the full county court[3], the twelve knights appointed to keep vert and venison, the foresters of the king and of the lords who had estates within the limits of the forests[4], answered to the array of sheriffs, coroners, stewards and bailiffs of the common law jurisdiction. The courts of the forest stood in the same way side by side with the courts of law[5]. Every three years the justices in eyre held a court of justice-seat, to determine all suits, claims of right, and presentments; a supreme court of civil and criminal jurisdiction. A triennial regard[6], or visitation of the forests by the officers themselves, was held in preparation for the justice-seat. The inferior courts were the wood-mote, held every forty days, a sort of minor 'regard' in

Courts of forest jurisdiction.

Court of justice-seat.

Regard of the forests.

Woodmote and Swain-mote.

---

[1] M. C. art. 44: 'Homines qui manent extra forestam non veniant de cetero coram justiciariis nostris de foresta per communes summonitiones.' Cf. Carta de Foresta, art. 2.

[2] M. Paris. ii. 524: 'A.D. 1208 Rex Anglorum Johannes ad Natale Domini fuit apud Bristollum, et ibi capturam avium per totam Angliam interdixit.'

[3] Examples of writs for the free election of verderers, analogous to those for the election of coroners, are to be found in abundance in the Foedera; see below, c. xv. § 216.

[4] Assize of Woodstock, art. 7.

[5] See Coke, 4th Institute, pp. 289, sq.; Prynne, 4th Instit. pp. 218, sq.; and Manwood on the Forest Laws.

[6] See the articles of the 'Regard' under Henry II, in Benedict. ii. pf. p. clix.; Hoveden, ii. 243 sq.

which presentments were made, and attachments received by the
verderers and enrolled: and the swain-mote held three times a
year before the verderers as judges, in which all the suitors of
the county court were obliged to attend to serve on juries and
inquests.   These may be regarded as parallel to the courts of
the hundred and the shire : some part of their proceedings were
regulated on the same principles, and, as time went on, they
shared the same reforms.

In this brief survey we have run beyond the limits of the
Norman period; but the whole forest system has its root and
development during that age, and it will not be necessary here-
after to recur to it except where incidentally it falls in with the
current of political history [1].

131. A scarcely less important feature of administrative
history at this period is the growth of the towns [2].   This has
been traced in a former chapter down to the date of the Conquest.   We have seen that they were originally no more than
large townships or collections of townships, whose constitution
cannot be shown to have differed from the general type of the
ancient village, but which had accumulated rights and functions
answering more strictly to those of the hundred.   And at the
time of the Conquest they had gained such importance as to
have in many cases special compositions for taxation, and
tribunals of their own [3].   With the exception however of London,

---

[1] On the number and position of the forests, see Pearson's Historical
Maps, pp. 44–48 ; Ellis's Intr. i. 103–116.   'The royal domains consisted
of 1422 manors, 30 chases, 781 parks, and 67 forests;' Gneist, Verwaltungsrecht, i. 190 (from Cowell?), but this computation does not apply
to the Domesday Survey, or even to the Norman period with any strict-
ness.

[2] The fortified towns mentioned in Domesday are Canterbury, Nottingham, York, Oxford, Hereford, Leicester, Stafford, Chester, Lincoln, and
Colchester.   The customs of forty-one cities or boroughs are either given
in detail or briefly noticed.   Most of these are the county towns of the
present day.   In the laws of Athelstan, ii. § 15, 2, Canterbury, Rochester,
London, Winchester, Lewes, Hastings, Chichester, Southampton, Wareham, Dorchester, Shaftesbury, and Exeter are particularly mentioned as
having moneyers ; very many others are specified in Domesday, and still
more are discoverable from coins.   See Ellis, Intr. i. 174–177.

[3] See above, pp. 99–102.   Oxford paid £20 and six sextaries of honey
in the time of King Edward ; £60 at the Survey.   Stafford paid £9 at the
former period ; Shrewsbury £7 16*s.* 8*d.* ; Norwich £20 to the king, £10 to

no town yet shows itself to have arrived at anything like the later civic constitution; and London under its port-reeve and bishop, the two officers who seem to give it a unity and identity of its own, is only a bundle of communities, townships, parishes, and lordships, of which each has its own constitution.

The charter granted by the Conqueror to the chief city of the kingdom is of a curiously jealous and scanty character: 'William the king greets William the bishop and Gosfrith the port-reeve[1], and all the burghers within London, French and English, friendly: and I do you to wit that I will that ye twain be worthy of all the law that ye were worthy of in King Edward's day. And I will that every child be his father's heir after his father's day; and I will not endure that any man offer any wrong to you. God keep you[2].' Here is no grant of corporate privileges; the son may succeed to his father's franchise, but there is no corporate succession; the state of things that had existed in King Edward's day is guaranteed and no more. The charter of Henry I shows a marked advance[3]. The city is recognised as a distinct unity, although that unity depends on hereditary succession only: it is independent of county organisation, the county in which it lies is itself let at ferm to the citizens; it is placed on a level with the shires, it is to have a sheriff of its own and a justiciar: as a greater privilege still, it is to elect its own sheriff and justiciar, and to be open to no other jurisdiction than that of its own elected officers. The citizens are not to be called before any court outside their own

Charter of the Conqueror to London.

Charter of Henry I to London.

Shire constitution of London recognised.

Other privileges.

---

the earl; at Huntingdon two-thirds of the *firma burgi* were paid to the king, one-third to the earl; Ellis, Intr. i. 190 sq.

[1] The word *port* in *port-reeve* is the Latin 'porta' (not portus), where the markets were held, and, although used for the city generally, seems to refer to it specially in its character of a mart or city of merchants. The port-gerefa at Canterbury had a close connexion with the 'ceapmanne gilde;' and the same was probably the case in London, where there was a cnihten-gilde, the estates of which were formed into the ward of Portsoken. From the position assigned to the port-reeve in this writ, which answers to that given to the sheriff in ordinary writs, it may be inferred that he was a royal officer who stood to the merchants of the city in the relation in which the bishop stood to the clergy: and if he were also the head of the guild his office illustrates very well the combination of voluntary organisation with administrative machinery which marks the English municipal system from its earliest days.

[2] Select Charters, p. 82.   [3] Ibid. pp. 108, 109.

walls, and are freed from Danegeld, from scot and lot, from
responsibility from the murder-fine and obligation to trial by
battle: they are freed from toll and other duties of the kind
throughout all England, at the ports as well as inland. They
are to possess their lands, the common lands of their townships,
and their rights of coursing in Chiltern, Middlesex, and Surrey.
Yet with all this no new incorporation is bestowed: the churches,
the barons, the citizens, retain their ancient customs; the churches
their sokens, the barons their manors, the citizens their township
organisation, and possibly their guilds. The municipal unity
which they possess is of the same sort as that of the county and
hundred. They have their folk-moot, answering to the shire-
moot outside[1]; their hustings-court every Monday, which may
be regarded as a general meeting of the citizens, although later
lawyers regarded this also as a county court. There is no mention
of any merchant-guild, the membership of which is a requisite for
civic magistracy. No guild is mentioned at all, although we
know from the laws of Athelstan that a frith-guild existed in
London in his days, and from another charter of Henry himself
that there was a 'cnihten-gild,' or confraternity of citizens which
had possessed its own lands with sac and soc and other customs
in the days of King Edward. Whatever may have been the
position of the guilds at this time, it would seem certain that
they were not a part of the constitution of the city, which
clearly was organised under a sheriff like any other shire. It is
possible that this charter of Henry I conferred a new constitution, and that the elective sheriff was a substitute for the
ancient port-gerefa; whilst the English cnihten-gild, with which
the port-gerefa and his soken are closely connected, was dissolved,
to reappear perhaps at a later period in the form of the merchant-guild and 'communa'; its property was bestowed on the
church of the Holy Trinity in Aldgate, a community of
Augustinian canons. But, however this may have been, before
the end of the reign the trade-guilds force their way into notice.

Their moots.

London guilds.

[1] On the current mistake about 'wardemota' for 'vadimonia,' see Round,
Geoff. de Mandeville, p. 370, where the whole history of London at this
period is treated.

In A.D. 1130 Robert the son of Lefstan pays for the guild of weavers £16 into the Exchequer. He was probably the alderman of the guild; and his father Lefstan seems to have occupied the same position in the cnihten-gild[1]. But the guild, so far as it is illustrated by documents, comes into prominence almost as early in the provincial towns as it does in London, and requires more special mention in relation to them.

Between the date of Henry's charter and that of the great Pipe Roll some changes in the organisation of the city must have taken place. In A.D. 1130 there were four sheriffs or vice-comites who jointly account for the ferm of London, instead of the one mentioned in the charter; and part of the account is rendered by a chamberlain of the city. The right to appoint sheriffs has been somehow withdrawn, for the citizens pay a hundred marks of silver that they may have a sheriff of their own choice, whilst the four sheriffs in office pay two marks of gold each in order to be quit of it[2]. There is no charge for the Danegeld, but instead there is an 'auxilium civitatis' amounting to £120. These facts may not indeed point to any oppressive or repressive policy on the part of the king, but it may be inferred, from the great dislike of the guild system shown by Henry II and his ministers, that it was no part of the royal policy to encourage municipal independence where it could not be made directly serviceable to the humiliation of the nobles.

It is possible that the disappearance of the port-reeve, the conversion of the cnihten-gild into a religious house, and the later particulars which have been noticed, signify a civic revolution, the history of which is lost, but which might account for the earnest support given by the citizens to Stephen, and the struggle for the establishment of the Communa which marks the reign of Richard I.

[1] Pipe Roll 31 Hen. I, p. 144: 'Robertus filius Levestani reddit compotum de £16 de gilda Telariorum Londoniarum.' In the charter of Henry I, which confirms to the church of the Holy Trinity the rights of the old cnihten-gild, it is said that they are to be held as they were 'tempore patris mei et fratris mei, et meo, et tempore Leostani;' Foedera, i. 11. In the Pipe Roll, Witso the son of Levestan pays half a mark of gold for his father's office. Alestan is 'praepositus Lundon.,' in Domesday, i. 2 b.

[2] Pipe Roll 31 Hen. I, pp. 143, 145, 148, 149.

London
under
Stephen.

Our next glimpse of the state of London is in the reign of Stephen, when, as we have already seen, the chief men of the city were allowed to join the small body of barons and bishops who elected the king. To Stephen the Londoners were for the most part faithful, although Thomas Becket, the son of one of them, was the adviser and executor of the policy which prevented the coronation of Eustace and secured the throne to Henry II [1]. In that council at Winchester by which the empress was elected to be lady of the English, the citizens appeared by messengers acting on behalf of the *communio* [2], a description of municipal unity which suggests that the communal idea was already in existence as a basis of civic organisation. That idea was fully developed in the next reign, but in the case cited the word may possibly mean nothing more than the folkmoot which had been recognised in Henry's charter.

The 'Communio.'

Composite
character of
the constitu-
tion of
London.

During the Norman period, then, London appears to have been a collection of small communities, manors, parishes, churchsokens, and guilds, held and governed in the usual way; the manors descending by inheritance, the church jurisdictions exercised under the bishop, the chapter, and the monasteries; and the guilds administered by their own officers and administering their own property: as holding in chief of the king, the lords of the franchises, the prelates of the churches, and even the aldermen of the guilds, where the guilds possessed estates, might bear the title of barons. It was for the most part an aristocratic constitution, and had its unity, not in the municipal principle, but in the system of the shire.

Provincial
towns.

The growth of the provincial towns is more distinctly traceable. We have in a former chapter seen their origin in the township of Anglo-Saxon times, generally in the dependent township which acquired wealth and solidity under the protection of a great earl or bishop, or of the king himself. In the time of the Confessor, as represented to us in Domesday, the boroughs had obtained a clearly recognised status. Their customs are recorded as fully as they would have been in later times by charter; their constitution is set before us as by its

Boroughs in
Domesday.

[1] Gervase, Chron. i. 150.　　　　[2] W. Malmesb. Hist. Nov. iii. § 495.

judicial character approaching that of the hundred rather than
that of the mere township, although the jurisdiction is manorial
rather than civic : the existence of guilds is likewise recorded ;
the men of Dover have a guild-hall, and there are guilds
possessed of land at Canterbury[1].

Regarded as a subject for historical analysis, the medieval *Analysis of the munici-pal institute.*
municipality may be resolved into three principles ; the primitive
organisation of the hundred or township with its judicial and
police functions : the voluntary association of the guild formed
for the regulation of trade, and authorised to enforce its by-laws :
and the further association of the burghers, whether as townsmen or as guildsmen, for the purpose of obtaining emancipation
from arbitrary imposts and external interference, an association
to which we may assign the name of *communa* or *communio*.
It is not however necessary to look for the development of town
life in any such regular forms, and we may, perhaps more safely,
examine the several points enumerated in that order in which
documentary illustration is most readily available.

The first point to be noticed is, then, that of jurisdiction, *Jurisdiction in the towns.*
which both before and after the Conquest is almost inseparable
from that of tenure. In some of the Domesday towns the sac
and soc belongs, as in Lincoln, to the owners of manorial
estates which are united within the walls[2]. In some it belongs
entirely to the king, or to the earl or bishop[3]; and in some it
is divided between the crown, the bishop, the earl,—each
of whom may be regarded as a public magistrate,—and one or
more private lords. In all these cases, unless expressly excluded *Subject to the sheriff.*
by grant, the sheriff exercised the same superintendence over
the towns as he did over the country : they were exempt from

[1] ' Willelmus filius Goisfridi iii. [mansuras habet] in quibus erat gihalla
burgensium ;' Domesd. i. 1. In Canterbury, ' Ipsi quoque burgenses habe-
bant de rege xxxiii. acras terrae in gilda sua ;' ' habet archiepiscopus xii.
burgenses et xxxii. mansuras quas tenent clerici de villa in gildam suam ;'
ibid. pp. 2, 3.

[2] ' In ipsa civitate erant xii. lagemanni, id est habentes sacam et socam ;'
Lincoln, Domesd. i. 336. Besides these twelve, several other great proprietors had their halls with sac and soc.

[3] Sandwich belongs to the Archbishop of Canterbury ; Domesd. i. 3;
Exeter belongs to the king; ibid. 100; Warwick to the earl ; Madox,
Firma Burgi, p. 16, where many other cases are given.

the hundred court, either as being themselves hundreds, or as being held by lords possessing sac and soc, but they were not exempt from the shire administration. The sheriff collected from them the rents which formed a portion of the ferm, and watched the royal rights in the courts of justice. The Norman Conquest produced no change in the towns, save this, that the tenure became a more prominent feature of dependence than the jurisdiction. They were regarded as held in demesne by the lords who had the jurisdiction, and, where no other lord claimed it, they were held in demesne of the king. The difference between the towns thus held is not perhaps very great until the age of charters begins: then, when a town belongs to the king, it has a royal charter; other towns have charters from their lords which sometimes express the consent of the king to the grant of liberties. Of the boroughs which possess early charters, Northampton is in the king's demesne [1], Beverley in that of the archbishop of York [2]. Leicester early in the twelfth century was divided into four parts, held by the king, the Bishop of Lincoln, Simon of Senlis who represented the old earls of Mercia, and Ivo of Grantmesnil the sheriff and farmer of the king's share [3]. Subsequently Count Robert of Meulan got all four shares into his own hands, and left the town as a borough in demesne to the earls of Leicester his descendants. The city of Winchester, like that of London, scarcely appears in Domesday at all [4]; its citizens had already, it would seem, something of the same status as those of London: their support was given to Stephen at his election in the same way, and they shared with the Londoners, and occasionally disputed with them, the privilege of service in the kitchen and the buttery at the coronations [5]. One result of the doctrine of tenure in the case of the towns was to leave the different classes of men in the

Margin notes: Tenure in towns. Towns in royal demesne. Leicester under several lords. Position of Winchester.

---

[1] Madox, Firma Burgi, p. 7.   [2] Foedera, i. 40.

[3] Ord. Vit. xi. 2. The Leicester charters, a most interesting series, are translated by Thompson in his book on *English Municipal History.*

[4] '[The customs, services, and charges of] London, Winchester, Abingdon, and a few others, were omitted probably on account of charters of immunity previously granted;' Ellis, Intr. i. 190.

[5] Hoveden, iii. 12, 248.

same condition in which they were in the country: the burgage tenure answers to the socage of the rural manors, and the lowest class of townsmen, until admitted into the guild, is on an exact level with the rustici or nativi, the class into which the Normans ultimately threw no small portion of the ceorls and villeins of the Anglo-Saxon days. *The population of towns answers to that of the country.*

The first step towards a separate administration and distinct organisation is, as usual, one connected with fiscal arrangements. *Fiscal changes in the towns.* It was quite natural that the city communities, growing in wealth and strong in social unity, should wish to be divided from the country districts. The sheriff was answerable to the crown for a certain sum, and whatever he could make above that sum was his own profit: nothing was easier than to exact the whole of the legal sum from the rich burghers, and take for himself the profits of the shire; or to demand such sums as he pleased of either, without rendering any account. The burghers made it a point then to have such a valuation of their town as would show what was really due, apart from the profits of the shire; and this done, they would pay to the sheriff no more, except as a free gift or in return for special services. The Domesday Survey accordingly gives the profits of the towns at distinct round sums, which had probably been long before agreed on. The next point gained was to take the collection of this sum out of the hands of the sheriff; which was done by obtaining from the crown a charter letting the town to the burghers at a fee farm rent equal to the sum thus deducted from the ferm of the shire. This was called the *firma burgi*, a rent paid to the crown from the borough, for which the burghers were responsible, and which they collected amongst themselves by strict apportionment[1]. *The Firma Burgi.*

It must have been however a primary question, to whom could such a charter be granted, and what organisation existed *Who bought the Firma Burgi?*

---

[1] See Madox, Firma Burgi, p. 18; Hist. Exch. pp. 226 sq.; Brady on Boroughs, pp. 40 sq.; Gneist, Self-government, i. 104–110, 847–850, Verwalt. i. 134 sq. The arrangement might be either at fee farm or for a term of years. The *firma burgi* (totidem verbis) first appears in Domesday in the case of Huntingdon. The ferms of Northampton £100, Wallingford £53 10s. (£80 in 1156), and Colchester £40, are specified in the Pipe Roll of 31 Henry I, pp. 135, 138, 139.

among the burghers that was capable of entering into such an engagement. Various answers have been given to the question: sometimes the guild, sometimes the leet jury, sometimes the germ of a corporation, the existence of which is somewhat hastily presumed, has been assumed as the recipient of the grant. But it seems most natural to refer it to the only organisation of the existence of which we have certain evidence, the fully qualified members of the township or hundred court of the

The tenants in burgage were the original *communitas civitatis.*

town, as already constituted. These were the owners of land, the owners of houses, shops, or gardens; the burgage-tenants, from whose burgages the rent was originally due, and from which it must, if raised legally, be paid: these men met in the church-yard or town-hall as the men of the township; in a trading town they would be the members of the guild; and, in the judicial work of the town, they were the class who furnished the judices and juratores, the leet jury in fact, when that jury first comes to light[1]. Under the reeve, the praepositus as the Norman lawyers called him, there was already a *communitas civitatis*, although of a very primitive form. The acquisition of the Firma Burgi by the inhabitants, whether in the character of a township or in the character of a guild, invested them with the further character of a 'communio' a partnership or corporate society.

Additional privileges purchased.

The body thus recognised speedily discovered its own strength, and obtained further grants of perpetual liberties, or purchased the occasional enjoyment of privileges: the city of London serving as the standard to which all attempted to rise. In A.D. 1130 the citizens of Lincoln paid 200 marks of silver and four marks of gold that they might hold their city of the king in chief[2]: a charter would probably be the result of this payment, or at all events the bestowal of the privileges enume-rated in the charter of Henry II. That king specifies, as one of

---

[1] See Gneist, as above referred to. He distinctly regards the *communa*, the origin of the corporation, as the result of a combination of the firma burgi with the leet jurisdiction. This I entirely agree with, but the ad-justment of the relation of these two elements with the guild presents some difficulties as to its universal applicability.

[2] Pipe Roll 31 Hen. I, p. 114.

the existing rights of the burghers of Lincoln, that they had a Cases of Lincoln and Beverley.
merchant-guild composed of the men of the city and the
merchants of the county [1]. The charter of Archbishop Thurstan
to Beverley places the 'hans-hus' or guild-hall among the fore-
most of the privileges conferred on his men. 'I will that my Early charters of towns.
men of Beverley shall have their hans-hus [2], that they may there
treat of their by-laws, to the honour of God and S. John and
the canons, and to the improvement of the whole township,
freed according to the same law as that which those of York
have in their hans-hus.' In other towns the guilds were already
making their way: the Pipe Roll records payments by the
weavers of Oxford of two marks of gold that they may have
their guild; the shoemakers pay five that they may recover
theirs; the weavers of Huntingdon pay forty shillings; those
of Lincoln a mark of gold [3]. But the most significant indica- Rise of the guilds.
tion of growth is found in the curious payment of Thomas of
York, the son of Ulviet, who gives the king a coursing dog that
he may be alderman of the merchant-guild of York: the value
of a coursing dog was twenty shillings [4], so that either the
position was an unimportant one, or Thomas's hold upon it so

[1] 'Gildam suam mercatoriam de hominibus civitatis et de aliis mercatoribus comitatus, sicut illam habuerunt tempore Edwardi, Willelmi et
Henrici regum Angliae;' Foed. i. 40; Select Charters, p. 166.
[2] The word *hansa* is used by Ulfilas for a band or company. As a historical word it appears first in England, later in Germany. G. L. von Maurer,
Städteverfassg. ii. 254; Sartorius, Urk. Gesch. d. Deutsch. Hanse, i. 73.
It seems to be indentical with *guild*, and it is also used in the sense of a
tax; Sartorius, i. 75, 76. We have here a hanshus at York and another at
Beverley. The men of York had in the time of John their guild at home
and several *hansas* both in England and in Normandy. The men of Dunwich
have their *hansa et gilda mercatoria* confirmed by the same king; Select
Charters, p. 311. In the second year of Henry III the citizens of Hereford
paid for a charter, and to have for ever a merchant-guild, with a *hansa* and
other liberties; Madox, Hist. Exch. p. 284. There was a *hansa* also at
Montgomery (Eyton, Shropshire, xi. 134); at Liverpool, Wigan, and Preston
(Harland's Mamecestre, i. 182, 198, 204).
[3] Pipe Roll 31 Hen. I, pp. 2, 5, 48, 109.
[4] Ibid. pp. 34, 35. Ulviet, the father of Thomas, was, as we learn from
the inquest into the customs of the church of York (above, p. 427 note 1),
a lageman or magistrate of the city. Perhaps we may infer from this a
gradual change from the lageman to the guild system produced by continuing the substantial power, under different names, but in the hands of
the same families. Compare the relations of Leofstan and his son Robert
with the cnihten-gild and weavers' guild of London, above, p. 441.

strong as to make the king's consent a matter of small value. There is as yet no indication that the guild aspires to modify the constitution of the city.

Ancient origin of guilds.

The origin of guilds, as has been already remarked, runs back to remote antiquity. The simple idea of a confraternity united for the discharge of common or mutual good offices, supported by contributions of money from each member and celebrating its meetings by a periodical festival, may find parallels in any civilised nation at any age of the world. The ancient guild is

Guilds of Anglo-Saxon times.

simply the club of modern manners[1]. In England it appears early, if not first of all, in a religious form, and that form it retained throughout the middle ages, although it does not engross the name. Three of these religious guilds are known to us by their statutes, which date from the early years of the

The Abbotsbury guild.

eleventh century[2]. At Abbotsbury in Dorset, Orcy grants a guild-hall as property to the guild, in honour of God and S. Peter, and lays down rules for the members. The contributions are to be in wax, bread, wheat and wood : the wax is for the maintenance of lights in the minster. Fines are ordered for the neglect of duty, for offensive words, and for bringing more than the due number of guests to the guild-feast. The only specified duty is that of contributing to the comfort of the dying, and attending the burial and praying for the souls of deceased members : a steward and 'feormeras,' or caterers for the feast, are the only officers mentioned, but there are two classes of guild brothers, one distinguished by full membership. The

[1] On the subject of guilds see an essay by Brentano, prefixed to Toulmin Smith's *English Gilds*, which condenses the results of the investigations of Wilda and others. The rules laid down by Hincmar for the geldoniae or confratriae of his time show that they were identical with the religious guilds of the Anglo-Saxons. Gneist, Self-government, i. 110, Verwalt. i. 139, thinks that too much importance has been attached to the guilds by modern writers and that their constitutional importance was much less in England than on the Continent.

[2] The statutes of these guilds are given in English by Kemble, Saxons, i. 511–514. Those of Abbotsbury are in the Cod. Dipl. dccccxlii ; and the other two in Hickes, Dissert. Epist. pp. 20–22. The objects of the guilds are thus stated by Hincmar ; 'In omni obsequio religionis conjungantur, videlicet in oblatione, in luminaribus, in oblationibus mutuis, in exsequiis defunctorum, in eleemosynis et ceteris pietatis officiis ;' especially the offering of candles and maintenance of lights ; Brentano, p. lxxxi.

rules of the Exeter guild direct three annual feasts, with masses The Exeter
guild. and psalm-singing for quick and dead ; the contributions are in malt and honey ; the fines are for neglect of the feast or the contribution, and for offensive words. On the death of a brother an additional subscription of fivepence is called for; at a house-burning one penny ; and there is a provision for funeral services. The second order of membership appears under the name of ' cniht.' In these two cases the duties of the members are purely religious, and nowhere concern questions of law or police. The statutes for the thegns' guild at Cambridge [1] con- The Cam-
bridge guild. tain similar provisions : there are directions for the burial of members, fines for misgreeting and violence, and regulations for mutual help in difficulties. But there is much more : if a brother be robbed, the guild undertakes to exact eight pounds from the thief; if a brother slay a man righteously, the guild helps to pay the wergild; if unrighteously he bears his own penalty ; if one slay another, he must redeem his place as a guild-brother by a fine of eight pounds ; and if any eat and drink with one who has slain a guild-brother, he pays a pound or clears himself by compurgation. It can scarcely be doubted that this form of guild had legal recognition ; the law of Ethelred prescribes a fine for breach of ' peace given in an alehouse,' which apparently refers to something of this kind [2].

The Cambridge statutes thus connect the religious guild with The 'frith-
gild.' the ' frith-gild,' a form of association of which, although it is of a more advanced and complex character, there are even earlier documentary traces. The provision of the laws of Ini and Alfred, that the ' gegildan,' or guild-brethren, of the kinless man should share in the receipt and responsibility of the wergild, may possibly be referred to an institution of the sort existing

---

[1] Kemble, Saxons, i. 513. The thegns' guild naturally calls to mind the *lagemanni* of Cambridge, mentioned in Domesday, and referred to above, p. 100. The heriot of the Cambridge lagemanni was eight pounds, a palfrey, and the arms of a knight. They were certainly thegns, and this guild may be a rudimentary form of a corporation ; for it is observable that the guild brethren make some rules which, without the aid of the magistrates, they would find it very difficult to enforce.

[2] Ethelred, iii. 1. Cf. Ll. Henr. c. lxxxi ; ' de pace regis danda in potatione.'

among the foreign settlers in the seaport towns of Wessex[1]: it is possible that it may denote a wide extension of the guild system amongst the English; but no further light can now be thrown upon it.   Under Athelstan however we have the complete code of a 'frith-gild' of the city of London, in which may be recognised a distinct attempt on the part of the public authorities to supplement the defective execution of the law by measures for mutual defence[2].   It is drawn up by the bishops and reeves belonging to London, and confirmed by the pledges of the 'frith-gegildas'; and, if it be indeed the act of a voluntary association, forms a curious precedent for the action of the Germanic leagues and the Castilian hermandad of later ages. By this statute a monthly meeting is directed, at which there is to be 'bytt-fylling[3]' and a refection, the remains of which are to be bestowed in alms: on the death of a member each brother gives a loaf, and sings, or pays for the singing of, fifty psalms. Thus far the common form of the religious guild is preserved. The other articles refer to the enforcement of mutual defence: each member pays fourpence for common purposes, towards a sort of insurance fund from which the guild makes good the losses of members; and a contribution of a shilling towards the pursuit of the thief.   The members are arranged in bodies of ten, one of whom is the head-man; these again are classed in tens under a common leader, who with the other head-men acts as treasurer and adviser of the hundred members.   The special objects, for which minute directions are given, are the pursuit and conviction of thieves and the exacting of compensation, the

The Judicia civitatis Lundoniae.

Social and police system of the London 'frith-gild.'

Its arrangement in tens.

---

[1] Ini, 16, 21; Alfred, 27, 28; Schmid, Gesetze, 587–589; see above, p. 96.

[2] Athelstan, vi. § 1–12: 'Judicia civitatis Lundoniae.'

[3] The byttfylling is in the Latin version *buccellorum impletio*, the filling of butts or vats: whether the ale brewed at one meeting was drunk at the same, or at the next, or sold for the benefit of the guild, it is hard to say. No contribution of malt is mentioned in these statutes, as was the case in those of Exeter.   The Chronicle of Battle mentions four guilds, adding that the abbot pays to each the regular contribution of a member 'ad cervisiam faciendam,' and has a poor man to represent him and drink his share at each meeting: pp. 20, 21.   Giraldus Cambrensis (Ang. Sac. ii. 397) describes the guildhall of London as 'Aula publica quae a potorum conventu nomen accepit.'   See above, p. 31, note.

carrying out of the law which Athelstan and the witan had
passed at Greatley, Exeter and Thundersfield. It is improbable
that any institution on so large a scale existed in any other town
than London, although the Cambridge statute may have been
drawn up on the same model; and it would be rash to connect
the 'Cnihtengild' of Henry's reign with this guild in particular,
although the existence of the one, taken in connexion with the
'cnihts' of the Exeter guild, irresistibly suggests the mention
of the other.

A charter of the reign of Edgar mentions three 'geferscipas' Guilds at
Canterbury.
or fraternities existing at Canterbury[1]; one of these may be the
priests' guild which is recorded in Domesday as possessing land,
another the 'ceapmanne gild,' the third a cnihtengild[2].

The third form of guild, the merchant-guild, 'ceapmanne The
merchant-
guild:
gilde,' or hansa, must be at least as old as the Conquest. The
charters of the twelfth century refer to the gilda mercatoria as
existing in king Edward's time[3]. The guild-hall of the men of
Dover, 'Gihalla burgensium,' is not likely to have been merely
the meeting-place of a private religious club[4]. The guilds of owning
property:
Canterbury possessed messuages and lands at the time of the
Domesday Survey; and the 'ceapmanne-gild' in the days of
Anselm exchanged eight houses with the monks of Christ
Church, each party conveying the right of sac and soc as they
themselves had held it[5]. In the hans-hus of Beverley and York and making
by-laws:
the burghers met to make their statutes, the by-laws by which
they regulated the trade and other municipal business of the
town which did not fall under the view of the more ancient

---

[1] Somner, Canterbury, part i. p. 178, describes a charter of Edgar dated
A.D. 956, and attested by Hlothwig the port-reeve, and the congregation
at Christ Church, and the congregation at S. Augustine's, and the three
'*geferscipas* innan burhwara utan burhwara miccle gemittan.'

[2] Somner, p. 179; below, note 5. An imperfect Canterbury charter of
the reign of Ethelbert (860-866) is attested by 'ego Æthelstan and
ingan burgware, ego Æthelhelm and cniahta gealdan;' Kemble, C. D. ii.
p. 83. If this is genuine it is the earliest extant instance of such a guild
in England.

[3] Charter of Lincoln, Foedera, i. 40.   [4] Domesday, i. 1.

[5] There is an agreement 'betwux than hirede˙æt Christescircean and
than cnihtan on Cantwareberig of cepmanne gilde;' and it is attested by
Calveal the 'portegerefa and tha yldista men of tham heape;' Somner,
p. 179.

courts; and this right to regulate trade was not the least important privilege granted or recognised by charter. A merchant-guild which possessed land, exercised jurisdiction, and enacted by-laws, must have already assumed the character of an official organisation, supplementary perhaps in the first place to the township administration, but gradually coalescing with it. Possibly the merchant-guild may have sometimes purchased the firma burgi. For in the great mercantile towns all the land and houses would be held by merchants and their dependents: from the merchant who had made three voyages over the sea at his own cost and so thriven to thegn-right, to the mere retailer, every one who was in the position of a free-holder was connected with trade, every one who would have a claim on public office or magistracy would be a member of the guild[1]. Further still, the merchant-guild supplied machinery of enfranchisement; the villein, the nativus of the Norman times, who could obtain admission into the guild and was unclaimed by his lord for a year and a day became a freeman[2]. His membership was allowed to give him that status which otherwise the law refused to landless men.

The merchant-guild contained all the traders, whether or no they possessed an estate of land. The charters of Oxford and other towns direct that no one shall exercise any merchandise in the town who does not belong to the merchant-guild or cannot plead ancient custom[3]. Such a fraternity would of course aim

(marginal notes:) a supplementary organisation: including all traders. Enfranchising power of the merchant-guild. Its monopoly of local trade.

---

[1] The charters of Henry II and Richard I to Winchester are granted to the citizens of the merchant-guild; Select Charters, pp. 165, 265. Whether this means that all the citizens of the town were in the guild, or that there were others dependent on the bishop who were not in the guild, can only be decided by local records. The privileges granted are much the same as those generally bestowed on *burgenses*.

[2] See Glanvill, de Legibus, v. 5; Select Charters, pp. 111, 166; and on the whole subject, Gross, The Gild Merchant (Oxford, 1890).

[3] So also that of Montgomery; Eyton's Shropshire, xi. 134; and that of Chester; Harland's Mamecestre, i. 189. It is probable that this arrangement was of the essence of the guild, and that the power of enforcing the regulation was the great privilege secured by the confirmation of the guilds by charter. The same exclusive right is exercised, occasionally at least, by the craft-guilds: in 1157 the shoemakers of Magdeburg ordained that no shoes should be sold in the city except by members of their guild

at engrossing among its own members the local authority : they
would furnish the great majority, if not the whole of the members of the court-leet ; they would be the electors of the reeve,
the recipients of the charters.   There were craft-guilds besides, Craft-guilds.
those of the weavers and shoemakers for instance, which might
in small manufacturing towns aim at the same position, but
which would as a rule content themselves with making regulations for their own crafts and with possessing property to pay
the expenses of their own festivals.   The fines paid by these
bodies show that the king or the sheriff viewed them with
jealousy ; the confirmation of their position by charter proves
that they were originally voluntary associations and not the
creation of the State.   The right of the merchant-guild to Relation of
the mer-
exclude from the privileges of trading all who were not members chant-guild
to the craft-
of its own body seems to imply necessarily either that these guilds.
craft-guilds originally stood in a filial relation to it, or that the
membership of the narrower involved also the membership of
the wider society.   The struggles between the patrician burghers
of the merchant-guild and the plebeians of the craft-guilds,
which mark the municipal history of Germany, have no exact
parallel in England, although there are traces of disputes between
the mayor and citizens of London and the guild of weavers in
the fourteenth century which show that the relations of the
two bodies were not satisfactorily determined[1].   That these
relations were created by a distinct and deliberate convention,
such as that by which the several guilds at Berwick[2] coalesced
in a single merchant-guild, is scarcely probable.   For the
present period however the existence of the merchant-guild and
its prominence in the charters are nearly all the data that we
possess.   In the reign of Henry II there can be little doubt that Constitutional posi-
the possession of a merchant-guild had become the sign and tion of the
merchant-
token of municipal independence : that it was in fact, if not in guild.
theory, the governing body of the town in which it was allowed

or by their licence ; G. L. von Maurer, Städteverfassg. ii. 397.   Compare
the case of the weavers of York, Rot. Cl. i. 421.

[1] Madox, Firma Burgi, pp. 192 sq.

[2] Houard, Traités, ii. 467 ; Smith, English Gilds, pp. 338 sq.; Acts of
Parliament of Scotland, i. 89.

to exist. It is recognised by Glanvill as identical with the communa of the privileged towns [1], the municipal corporation of the later age.

Relation of the guild to the communa.

Yet the merchant-guild and the governing body of the town are not identical in idea. The business of the guild is the regulation of trade, the business of the governing body is the administration of justice and police; the chief of the guild is the alderman, the chief of the magistracy is the praepositus or reeve. The merchant-guild of York may be recognised, but the communa of London is watched and discouraged; the formation of new guilds without authorisation is punishable; they are adulterine like the adulterine castles of the barons; their object is suspected to be not the maintenance of their craft, or of peace

Illegal guilds.

or religion, but the defeating of the king's rights. In the twenty-sixth year of Henry II, eighteen adulterine guilds in London are fined in various sums; amongst these are the goldsmiths, the butchers, and the pilgrims; each is mentioned as

Illegal communa.

having its own alderman [2]. The offence of Ailwin at Gloucester [3] and of Thomas 'from beyond the Ouse [4]' at York was probably of the same sort, they had set up a 'communa' without authority. There must have been in London, and in a less number in York and Winchester also, some other influential men who were not connected with trade, and whom the aggressive policy of the

Relation of the guild to the land-owning community.

guilds would necessarily exclude from municipal power: these continued probably to hold their own courts as lords of manors or to claim exemption from the jurisdiction of magistrates from whose election they were excluded; but they can never have been strong enough to oppose the popular current: the great men of Lincoln who possessed sac and soc must either have been absorbed in the merchant-guild or have been bought up by it before Henry II recognised it by charter; possibly before Henry I sold to the burghers the status of tenants-in-chief.

---

[1] Glanvill, De Legibus, v. 5.

[2] 'Admerciamenta de gildis adulterinis;' Hist. Exch. pp. 390, 391.

[3] 'Ailwinus Merciarius reddit compotum de £100 pro Communa;' Rot. Pip. 16 Henry II; Hist. Exch. p. 391.

[4] 'Thomas de Ulträusa reddit computum de xx. marcis pro Communa quam volebant facere;' Rot. Pip. 22 Henry II; Firma Burgi, p. 35.

But doubtless every trading town had its own special history, and made its own special sacrifices for unity and freedom. In London the struggle lasted the longest and took the most various forms. The communa there did not obtain legal recognition until 1191; it was not until the reign of Edward II that all the citizens were obliged to be enrolled among the trade-guilds, and in the reign of Edward III the election of the city magistrates was transferred from the representatives of the ward-moots to the trading companies[1].

The growth of the corporation of London.

The history of this feature of our local institutions will always be read with different feelings; whilst municipal independence has in many cases helped the cause of liberty, it has in others encroached largely on wider rights; and so far as it is based on the guild, it must be regarded as a series of infringements on the ancient rights of free inhabitants, as one out of many cases in which an organisation originally created for the protection of the weak has been allowed to monopolise their rights and to usurp the functions of government[2]. The dislike with which the communa was viewed outside the towns is marked by Richard of Devizes, a free-speaking author, who furnishes some important data for the civic history of the reign of Richard I. The communa is 'tumor plebis, timor regni, tepor sacerdotii.'

Political importance of these bodies.

The process then by which the guilds gained their municipal position is obscure; and it was not completed within the Norman period. Its history can scarcely be interpreted without reference to the development of town organisation which was going on abroad. In France the communal constitution was during this period encouraged, although not very heartily, by Lewis VI, who saw in it one means of fettering the action of the barons and bishops and securing to himself the support of a strong portion of his people[3]. In some cases the commune of

Growth of the communes in France.

[1] See Dr. Brentano's Essay in Smith's English Gilds, p. cxi.

[2] That this was the case with the French communes occasionally may be seen by the charter of Philip II, withdrawing the privileges of Étampes in consequence of the oppression of the churches and knights by the commune; Ordonnances des Rois, xi. 277.

[3] Thierry divides the municipalities of France into five zones or regions: (1) the North, the home of the sworn commune, comprising Picardy, Artois, Flanders, the Isle of France, Champagne, and Normandy; (2) the South,

The commune.

France is, like the guild, a voluntary association, but its objects are from the first more distinctly political. In some parts of the kingdom the towns had risen against their lords in the latter half of the eleventh century, and had retained the fruits of their hard-won victories[1]. In others, they possessed, in the remaining fragments of the Karolingian constitution, some organisation

Charters of communes.

that formed a basis for new liberties. The great number of charters granted in the twelfth century[2] shows that the policy of encouraging the third estate was in full sway in the royal councils, and the king by ready recognition of the popular rights gained the affections of the people to an extent which has few

The character of their liberties.

parallels in French history. The French charters are in both style and substance very different from the English. The liberties which are bestowed are for the most part the same[3], exemption from arbitrary taxation[4],—a privilege which closely

the home of the consular forms, dating (by a bare possibility) from Roman times; (3) Central France, where the administration was generally in the hands of a prévôt, and the constitution, something like that of the English unchartered towns, based on the ancient usage in the rural districts; (4) the West, comprising Brittany and the Poictevin provinces; in the former the parish church was the centre of administration, and the system was generally parochial, half ecclesiastical and half civil; in the latter sworn communes were founded on the model of Normandy; (5) the Eastern, which had been part of the medieval German empire and shared the general history of the German municipalities. Tableau de l'Ancienne France Municipale; Hist. du Tiers État, ii. 42 sq.

[1] The commune of Le Mans appears as early as 1072, 'facta igitur conspiratione quam communionem vocabant;' Gesta Pont. Cenomann., Mabillon, Analecta, p. 308; that of Cambray dates from 1076, and that of Beauvais from 1099; Thierry, Tiers État, ii. 62; Waitz, D. V. G. vii. 388 sq.; on those of Laon and Amiens, see Guibert of Nogent, Opp. pp. 503–505, 509, 515.

[2] Many of these may be found in the Ordon. des Rois; in Baluze's Miscellanea, vols. iii. iv., and in the Recueil des Monuments Inédits de l'Hist. du Tiers État, ed. by Aug. Thierry. See also Kemble, Saxons, ii. pp. 512–544; and the Historical Illustrations appended to Guizot's Lectures on Civilisation in France.

[3] Many of the provisions of the communal charters recall the early guild customs; e. g. the direction that the members shall not abuse one another (Stabilimentum Rothomagense, Duchesne, p. 1066); the entrance into the body is effected by a payment to the common fund (charter of Noyon, A.D. 1191; Baluze, iii. 79).

[4] See the charter of Tours, A.D. 1181; Baluze, iii. 80; Chaumont, A.D. 1182; Ordonnances, xi. 225. In the latter case the words are, 'ut omnes qui in eadem permanebunt communitate, ab omni talliata, injusta captione, creditione et universa irrationabili exactione, cujuscunque sint homines, liberi et immunes, jure perpetuo permaneant.' Guibert of Nogent, describ-

corresponds with the acquisition of the Firma Burgi in England
—the right to local jurisdiction [1], the privilege of enfranchising
the villein who has been for a year and a day received within
the walls [2], and the power of electing the officers [3]. But, whilst
all the English charters contain a confirmation of free and good
customs, the French are filled with an enumeration of bad ones [4].
The English recur in thought to a time when, in tradition at
least, they possessed all that is granted, and even more ; the
French regard only the present oppressions from which they
are to be delivered. The English have an ancient local constitution the members of which are the recipients of the new
grant, and guilds of at least sufficient antiquity to render their
confirmation typical of the freedom now guaranteed ; the French
communia is a new body which, by a sum of money has purchased, or by the action of a sworn confederacy, has wrung from

---

ing the Communio of Laon (cir. 1110), makes this the chief point : 'Clerus
cum archidiaconis ac proceres, . . . causas exigendi pecunias a populo aucu-
pantes, dant eis per internuntios optionem, ut si pretia digna impenderent,
communionis faciendæ licentiam haberent. Communio autem, novum ac
pessimum nomen, sic se habet, ut capite censi omnes solitum servitutis
debitum dominis semel in anno solvant, et si quid contra jura deliquerint
pensione legali emendent ; ceterae censuum exactiones, quae servis infligi
solent, omnimodis vacent ;' Opp. p. 503.

[1] Only however where the king's own right of demesne was clear ; the
commune of Beauvais was under the justice of the bishop ; Ordonnances,
xi. 198. The privilege of not being called to plead outside the town is
common ; e. g. charter of Corbie, Ordonn. xi. 216.

[2] 'Si quis moram fecerit per annum et diem in communia Senonensi in
pace et sine juris vetatione, et aliquis postea eum requisierit quod sit
homo suus, non illi de eo respondebunt jurati ;' Charter of Sens, A.D. 1189 ;
Ordonn. xi. 263. The privilege was not peculiar to communes : 'Quicunque vero in villam venientes, per annum et diem ibi in pace manserint,
nec per regem, nec per praepositum, nec per monachum justitiam vetu-
erint, ab omni jugo servitutis deinceps liberi erunt ;' Charter of the vill of
Seaus, A.D. 1153 ; Ordonnances, xi. 199. Cf. the charter of Voisines, A.D.
1187 ; ibid. iv. 456. It was probably an understood right, which required
limitation : the free rustic who wished to join the commune of S. Riquier
had to resign his land to his lord ; Ordonn. xi. 184. Cf. charters of Roye,
ibid. 233 ; and Bray, ibid. 296. The *parish* of Lorris has the enfranchising
clause ; Ordonn. xi. 202.

[3] Charter of Tours ; Baluze, iii. 80 ; Beauvais ; ibid. 81 : Chateauneuf,
A.D. 1181 ; ibid. 221.

[4] See the charter of Bourges, A.D. 1145 ; Ordonnances, i. 9 : that of
Orleans, A.D. 1168 ; ibid. i. 15 : that of Amiens ; ibid. xi. 264 ; Baluze,
iii. 84 : Beauvais, A.D. 1115 ; Ordonnances, xi. 177 : Laon, A.D. 1128 ;
ibid. 187.

The French commune

its oppressors, a deliverance from hereditary bondage[1]. The French charters abound in saving clauses protecting the rights of the feudal lords which the grant infringed, or setting aside those rights in accordance with the principle of alliance between king and commune against their common foes. In the English charters there are no signs of such antagonism as marks the one case, or of such cautious liberality as distinguishes the other.

contrasted with the English guild.

The commune lacks too the ancient element of festive, religious, or mercantile association which is so conspicuous in the history of the guild. The idea of the latter is English, that of the former is French or Gallic. Yet notwithstanding these differences, the substantial identity of the privileges secured by these charters seems to prove the existence of much international sympathy. The ancient liberties of the English were not unintelligible to the townsmen of Normandy; the rising freedom of the German cities roused a like ambition in the towns of Flanders[2]; and the struggles of the Italian municipalities awoke the energies of the cities of Provence. All took different ways to win the same liberties.

Town life of Germany.

The town life of Germany presents in its mercantile development a closer parallel with that of England, but there is not between the two systems the direct historical connexion which, through the long union of the Norman, Angevin, and Poictevin inheritances with the English crown, subsists between the institutions of France and England. The German hansa may have been derived from England; the communa of London was certainly derived from France. Hence for points of common history we must look further back, to the township and the mark: the later growth of German city life, the colonial character of the great Saxon towns with their artificial patriciate and strict caste system, the independent mercantile communities of the Rhine and Franconia, the imperial history of Worms, Cologne,

Varieties of civic constitutions there.

---

[1] ' Universi homines infra murum civitatis et in suburbio commorantes, in cujuscunque terra maneant, communiam jurabunt;' Charter of Beauvais, A.D. 1182; Baluze, Misc. iii. 80: cf. the charter of Compiegne, A.D. 1153; ibid. p. 83: of Soissons, A.D. 1181; ibid. 79.

[2] See the Flemish charters in Kemble, Saxons, ii. 528 sq. In that of S. Omer the guild has an important place.

and Frankfort, the mercantile principalities of Augsburg and
Nüremberg, have, if some slight coincidences in London history
be excepted, no parallels in England. The cities of Spain again,
whilst they unite in one form or other most of the elements existing separately elsewhere,—the colonial character of the Saxon,
the communal spirit of the French, the mercantile association
of the English town system,—are in the details of their historical
growth far removed from the conditions of English society; and
they are, it must be added, too little illustrated by accessible
documentary history to furnish either a parallel or a contrast.
The Italian towns have a distinct development of their own, *Italian
towns.*
rather owing, it is true, to their external relations than to any
peculiar element inherent in their institutions, but sufficiently
marked to make us set them aside in a view so general as that to
which we must limit ourselves. Great in mercantile enterprise,
great in political ambition, centres of life and progress, they
were no integral part of the system in which they were em-
bedded : they were, whether bound to, or in league against,
imperial power, practically independent of any higher authority
than their own ; and by their jealousies, enmities, and ambitions,
they constituted themselves political unities, too weak to stand
alone, too proud to throw themselves into the general interest
of the peoples among which they were placed, destined by their
very temper and circumstances to a short and brilliant career,
but allowed to claim a very slight share in the benefits, for the
winning of which their own history had been both a guiding
and a warning light.

The communa of London, and of those other English towns *Relics of
older sys-
tems survive
in the
modern cor-
porations.*
which in the twelfth century aimed at such a constitution, was
the old English guild in a new French garb : it was the ancient
association, but directed to the attainment of municipal rather
than mercantile privileges : like the French communia, it was
united and sustained by the oaths of its members and of those
whom it could compel to support it. The major and the jurati, *The mayor,
aldermen,
and coun-
cillors.*
the mayor and jurats, were the framework of the communa, as
the alderman and brethren constituted the guild, and the reeve
and good-men the magistracy of the township. And the system

which resulted from the combination of these elements, the history of which lies outside our present period and scope, testifies to their existence in a continued life of their own. London, and the municipal system generally, has in the mayor a relic of the communal idea, in the alderman the representative of the guild, and in the councillors of the wards the successors to the rights of the most ancient township system. The jurati of the commune, the brethren of the guild, the reeve of the ward, have either disappeared altogether, or taken forms in which they can scarcely be identified.

Chartered towns not numerous in the Norman period.

Although the importance of this rising element of English life is sufficiently great to justify the place that we have here given it, it is not to be supposed that during the period before us it was very widely diffused. The English municipalities were neither numerous, nor, with the exception of London, in possession of much political power : their liberties took the form of immunities and exemptions, rather than of substantial influence : they were freed from the exactions of the sheriffs, but not empowered to take a representative share in the administration of the county; they were enabled to try their own prisoners, to oust strange jurisdictions, to raise their taxes in their own way, but not to exercise jurisdiction outside their walls, or to raise their voice in granting or refusing a contribution to the wants of the State. Even their charters were received with misgiving; they were purchased with solid gold, and had as a matter of fact to be redeemed in the form of confirmation from each successive king. Still the history of the twelfth century is one of distinct and uniform progress.

Their growth continuous.

Points of development.

The close of the Norman period saw the English towns thus far advanced, and aiming at further growth. They had secured the firma burgi, and freed themselves from the pecuniary exactions of the sheriffs ; they had obtained a recognition by charter of their free customs, that is of the special rules of local administration which they had immemorially observed, especially the exemption from the Norman innovation of trial by battle ; their constitution was still that of the township and the hundred, but the relief from the financial administration of the sheriff had

suggested the possibility of liberation from his judicial administration also. The guilds were operating so as to produce a
stronger cohesion among the townsmen; they met frequently
in their drinking-halls, and drew up their own regulations for
the management of trade; their leading men possessed the
ancient burgages on which the king's dues were payable, and
this was enough to entitle them to such social power as was left
in local hands; they possessed, if not the sole right to trade,
something very like a monopoly of all mercantile dealings, and
a claim to immunity from tolls throughout the shire or the
realm, and in some cases even in the foreign dominions of the
king. Accordingly the membership of the guild is indispensable
to the full and perfect status of the burgher. Some, if not all,
the towns so privileged, could confer freedom on the villein by
allowing him to stay for a year and a day within their walls, or
enrolling him in their guild. The most offensive of the services
demanded from tenants of demesne land were remitted to them.
They could still be tallaged, taxed at the will of the king, but
so could the rest of the nation. Except through the agency of
their own magistrates they could not be forced by a stranger to
appear in the courts of law. Diversities of custom there doubtless were, but in all this there was a strong tendency towards
liberty. How well the towns repaid the confidence shown by
the kings in the gift of these privileges appears in the history of
Henry II and his sons.

The example set by the sovereign in the cities and boroughs
that were under his direct control was followed by the lords who
held boroughs in demesne. The earl of Leicester chartered his
town [1], and the earl of Chester the boroughs of the palatine

Advantages really se-cured by the towns.

Towns in the hands of mesne lords.

---

[1] Thompson, Municipal Antiquities, pp. 29, 39, 41, 44, &c. The history
of Leicester supplies a story illustrative of the process by which new
liberties were obtained. In order to avoid the necessity of trial by battle,
the men of Leicester, in or about the reign of Henry I, petitioned the earl
that they might have a body of twenty-four men chosen out of their own
number to decide all pleas; and they promised to pay 3*d.* yearly for each
house in the High-street that had a gable: these twenty-four were the
jurors of the portman-mote; a court which appears in some other cor-
porations in the north, and answers to the court-leet, or lagh-moot.
The story is found in an inquest of 39 Hen. III, which, I fear, is not
good authority. Compare, however, the charters printed in Harland's

earldom : Durham received its privileges from the bishop, and
the great prelates whose rights excluded the interference of
sheriff and shire-moot were able to bestow on their towns
privileges scarcely less extensive than those given by the crown.

Unchartered
towns.
But there were other town communities outside all these
classes, depending on mesne lords who were without the power
of granting immunities, or depending on the crown but not rich
enough to purchase charters. These subsisted under the ancient
township or manorial system, and down to a comparatively late
period were distinguished only by external features from the

Market
towns.
rural communities. From this class sprang the largest part of
the market towns of the present day : the privilege of having a
market was not grudged by the rulers whose revenues it helped
to swell ; and once established, the market involved a humble
machinery of police and magistracy, which gave to the place,
otherwise undistinguished from the villages around it, some
semblance of municipal constitution [1].

The villein
class.
132. The history of that extensive portion of the population
which lay outside the classes thus accounted for, is, during the
Norman period, extremely obscure. The man who had no
political rights, and very little power of asserting his social
rights, who held his cottage and garden at the will of a master
who could oppress him if he could not remove him, and could
claim without rewarding his services,—who had no rights
against his master, and who could only assert such rights as he

The rusticus
or nativus.
had against others through the agency of his master,—the
rusticus, the *nativus*, the *servus*,—fell only occasionally within
the view of the writer who chronicled great events, and then
but to add an insignificant feature to his picture. The villein
possessed no title-deeds, by the evidence of which his rights were
attested ; he carried his troubles to no court that was skilled
enough to record its proceedings. It is only by a glimpse here
and there that we are enabled to detect his existence ; and the

Mamecestre, i. 182, 183, 188, 195, 198, 199, where important illustrations
are given from the constitutions of Chester, Preston, Liverpool, Lancaster,
and Salford.

[1] For the continuation of this investigation see below, vol. iii. ch. xxi.
§§ 484-490.

glimpses are too uncertain to furnish a clue by which his history
can be traced. Yet when he reappears, as he does in the
thirteenth and fourteenth centuries, he bears marks of a history
on which some conjectures must be hazarded. Under the Anglo-
Saxon system there is no difficulty in estimating his position :
it is one of depression but not of helplessness : when he comes
before us in the reign of Richard II his condition is one which
suggests that, however much social causes may have served to
ameliorate his actual lot, the legal theory of his status has
become hardened and sharpened so as to warrant almost wanton
oppression.

Depression into servitude.

The Anglo-Saxon laws recognised, as we have seen, a class of
serfs, or theows, who were the mere chattels of their master [1].
The landless man, on the contrary, was free in all personal
relations, although he must have a surety, or a patron, to answer
for his forthcoming, or to assert his rights in all matters of
which the law took cognisance. The landless man might settle
on the land of another, or take service in his household ; he
might act as a hired labourer, or as a small rent-paying tenant ;
he might be attached hereditarily to his master, or to the land
that his master owned. And the lowest class of landowner, that
is, the ceorl who possessed a little alod of his own, had often,
perhaps generally, found it necessary to put himself under the
protection of his powerful neighbour, who would defend his
rights and discharge his public services in consideration of a
rent paid or labour given, or an acknowledgment of dependence.
The barons who took the Domesday Survey recognised the
existence of all these classes, and of distinctions among them
much more minute than can be interpreted at the present day [2].

Anglo-Saxon servitude.

Servitude in Domesday.

[1] The law of the Conqueror, 'Ego prohibeo ut nullus vendat hominem
extra patriam super plenam forisfacturam meam,' would have its primary
application in the case of such slaves. The law is an amplification of one
of Ethelred and Canute which forbids the sale of men to heathen masters.
This slave trade, the chief seat of which was at Bristol, was put down by
the preaching of S. Wulfstan in the age of the Conqueror; see W. Malmesb.
V. S. Wulfstani, Ang. Sac. ii. 258.

[2] Ellis, Intr. ii. 511 sq., gives the following numbers : bordarii, 82,119 ;
cotarii, 5054 ; coscets, 1749 ; servi, 25,156 ; villani, 108,407 ; besides small
numbers of different classes which may be referred to the same heads. The
distinctions among these classes are generally based on the variety of

That record attests the existence of more than 25,000 servi, who must be understood to be, at the highest estimate of their condition, landless labourers; over 82,000 bordarii; nearly 7000 cotarii and cotseti, whose names seem to denote the possession of land or houses held by service of labour or rent paid in produce; and nearly 110,000 villani. Above these were the liberi homines and sokemanni, who seem to represent the medieval and modern freeholder. The villani of Domesday are no doubt the ceorls of the preceding period, the men of the township, the settled cultivators of the land, who in a perfectly free state of society were the owners of the soil they tilled, but under the complicated system of rights and duties which marked the close of the Anglo-Saxon period had become dependent on a lord, and now under the prevalence of the feudal idea were regarded as his customary tenants; irremoveable cultivators, who had no proof of their title but the evidence of their fellow ceorls. For two centuries after the Conquest the villani are to be traced in the possession of rights both social and to a certain extent political: their oaths are taken in the compilation of Domesday, their representatives attend the hundred-moot and shire-moot; they are spoken of by the writers of the time as a distinct order of society, who, although despicable for ignorance and coarseness[1], were in possession of considerable comforts, and whose immunities from the dangers of a warlike life compensated for the somewhat unreasoning contempt with which they were viewed by clerk and knight. During this time the villein could assert his rights against every oppressor but his master; and

Villenage in Domesday.

Advantages of the villein.

services to which they were liable or the extent of the land they were allowed to hold; but local customs differed, and the warning, 'Videat qui scyram tenet, ut semper sciat quae sit antiqua terrarum institutio vel populi consuetudo,' was very necessary; Rectitudines, in the Ancient Laws, ed. Thorpe, p. 186. Most of the terms are explained in the Rectitudines Singularum Personarum; in Greenwell's edition of Boldon Buke, pp. l. sq.; in Robertson's Scotland under her Early Kings, ii. 158 sq.; in Hale's Domesday of S. Paul's, and Register of Worcester; in Pearson's Early and Middle Ages, Thorpe's Lappenberg, and Ellis's Introduction to Domesday.

[1] E. g. 'Servi vero, quos vocamus rusticos, suos ignominiosos et degeneres in artibus eis indebitis enutrire contendunt, non ut exeant a vitiis sed ut abundent divitiis ... Redimunt suos a dominis servi. ...' W. Map, de Nugis Curialium, p. 9.

even against his master the law gave him a standing-ground if he could make his complaint known to those who had the will to maintain it. But there can be little doubt that the Norman Tendency towards depression. knight practically declined to recognise the minute distinctions of Anglo-Saxon dependence, and that the tendency of both law and social habit was to throw into the class of *nativi* or born villeins the whole of the population described in Domesday under the heads of servi, bordarii, and villani [1]. Not but that, if it Legal status of the villein. came to a question of fact, the local witnesses might in each case draw a distinction as to the status of the villein concerned; the testimony of the township or the hundred might prove that this man was descended from a family which had never been free, this from a bought slave, this from a commended ceorl; but the law administered by Norman jurists classed nativi and villani together [2]: the nativus could not be made a knight or a clerk without the leave of his master, or without formal emancipation; the villanus, with his sequela, his service, and his progeny, could be disposed of in the same deed of sale or gift that alienated the land on which he had been settled for ages [3]: the villein could not leave his home except to go on pilgrimage, for so his lord lost his services. It is true that in a state of society in which the land is far too wide for its inhabitants, and in which accordingly the wages of labour may be said to be paid in land, such a state of dependence may be compatible with

---

[1] In one entry on the Pipe Roll of Henry I they seem to be treated as part of the stock upon an estate: 'Restoldus debet £239 15s. 2d. numero, pro defectu comitatus, videlicet in annona, et domibus, et grangiis, et molendinis, et piscariis, et villanis, et bordariis, et buris et bubulcis et foeno;' p. 2.

[2] The fifth book of Glanvill is devoted to the question of villenage, or the status of the *nativus*: ' Omnia catalla cujuslibet nativi ita intelliguntur esse in potestate domini sui quod propriis denariis suis versus dominum suum a villenagio se redimere non poterit; si quis vero extraneus eum ad liberandum emeret suis nummis, posset quidem perpetuo versus dominum suum qui eum vendiderat se in statu libertatis tueri;' ch. 5. 'Ascriptitii qui villani dicuntur, quibus non est liberum obstantibus quidem dominis suis a sui status conditione discedere;' Dialogus de Scaccario, i. 10. The chattels of the ascriptitii might be sold to pay their lord's debts, but not until all his own saleable property had been sold; and in case of a scutage, those of the knights holding under a defaulting lord might be sold as well as those of the villein; Ibid. ii. 14.

[3] See examples in Madox, Formulare Anglicanum, pp. 416 sq. None of them however belong distinctly to the Norman reigns.

much personal comfort and some social ambition; but it is in itself a degraded position, and has a tendency to still further degradation. Incidentally however it is probable that the influx of Norman ideas helped to raise the lowest rank of dependents; for although the free ceorl becomes the villein, the servus or theow disappears altogether. Not to anticipate here the further conclusions which still lie far ahead of us, it may be said that under the Norman kings such slight indications as we possess of the state of the villeins show them to have been in possession of considerable social privileges. They were safe in the possession of their homes; they had a remedy against the violence of their masters [1]; they could, if they chose to renounce their holdings and take refuge in a town, become members of the guild, and there, when unclaimed for a year and a day, obtain the full rights of free men; they could obtain manumission by the intervention of the Church, which always proclaimed the liberation of the villein to be a work of merit on the part of the master. But it by no means followed that manumission was a material benefit, if thereby the newly enfranchised man lost his title to be maintained on his lord's land, and must forthwith look for new service or throw himself on the chances of war or trade. Under a fairly good lord, under a monastery or a college, the villein enjoyed immunities and security that might be envied by his superiors; he had a ready tribunal for his wrongs, a voice in the management of his village; he might with a little contrivance redeem his children and start them in a higher state of life. His lord had a peremptory claim on his earnings, but his lord had a lord whose claims on him were as irresistible if not as legally binding. He was excluded from juries and assizes touching property, but by that exemption he was freed from the risk of engaging in quarrels in which he would be crushed without pity by the more powerful neighbour against whom he might have to testify. If he was without political rights, so were also the great majority of his superiors.

Advantages of the villein in the Norman period.

His disabilities not disadvantageous to him.

---

[1] 'Aluredus de Cheaffeword reddit compotum de 40s. pro rustico verberato;' Pipe Roll 31 Hen. I, p. 55. This must have been his own *rusticus*, for an assault on another man's villein would not have been reported in the royal accounts.

The few laws of the Norman period do not much affect the Legal notices
of the
villein.
villein. The fabricated charter of William the Conqueror [1] con-
tains a form of manumission which seems to be not later in
origin than the reign of Henry I; it is only by a bold inference
that we can argue from the words of the charter of Henry I
that the villeins came within the provision that the barons
should treat their men as the king treated the barons. The
enfranchising power of the borough or the guild may be inferred,
but cannot be proved [2]. The restriction imposed by the Constitutions of Clarendon on the ordination of the rustics seems
to imply that that practice had reached a point at which it was
liable to be abused [3]. The exclusion of the villani, cotseti, and
ferdingi, of mean and poor persons, from the judicial duties of
the shire-moot, was a measure which common prudence and
policy alike must have dictated [4]. It may however be doubted
whether the word *villani* had during the twelfth century fully
acquired the meaning of servitude which was attached to it by
the later lawyers.

[1] Thorpe, Ancient Laws, p. 213: 'Si qui vero velit servum suum liberum
facere, tradat eum vicecomiti per manum dexteram in pleno comitatu,
quietum illum clamare debet a jugo servitutis suae per manumissionem, et
ostendat ei liberas vias et tradat illi libera arma, scilicet lanceam et
gladium, deinde liber homo efficitur.' In the Leges Henrici I the form is
this: 'Qui servum suum liberat in ecclesia, vel mercato, vel comitatu, vel
hundreto, coram testibus et palam faciat, et liberas ei vias et portas con-
scribat apertas, et lanceam et gladium vel quae liberorum arma sunt, in
manibus ei ponat;' Hen. I, § 78. Compare the act of manumission in
Hist. Ramsey, c. 29 (Gale, p. 407), 'ut in quadrivio positi pergerent quo-
cunque voluissent;' and Grimm, R. A. p. 331.

[2] The enfranchising clause in the fabricated charter of William the
Conqueror cannot be safely appealed to as evidence of this privilege:
'Item si servi permanserint sine calumpnia per annum et diem in civitatibus nostris vel in burgis vel muro vallatis, vel in castris nostris, a die illa
liberi efficiantur et liberi a jugo servitutis suae sint in perpetuum.' This
clause does not appear in the Leges Henrici I, drawn up probably before
A.D. 1118; but the privilege was granted by charter during that reign to
particular towns; and in Glanvill's time the principle at least was recognised.

[3] 'Filii rusticorum non debent ordinari absque assensu domini de cujus
terra nati dignoscuntur;' Const. 16; Select Charters, p. 140. This legislation however is by no means peculiar to this age or country; see the law
of Charles the Great in Labbe and Cossart, Conc. vii. 1061; that of Lewis
the Pious, ibid. vii. 1480; and the Lateran Council of 1179, ibid. x. 1730.

[4] See the passage quoted above, p. 428, note 1. In the Pipe Roll of 31
Henry II are several cases of amercements imposed for placing *rustici* on
juries and assizes; Madox, Hist. Exch. p. 379.

133. The military system of the Normans, so far as it is connected with their doctrine of tenure, need not be further discussed here. We have seen that the distribution of the land into knights' fees was a gradual work, which was not completed in the reign of Henry II. When therefore Ordericus Vitalis describes the regular feudal force of the kingdom as consisting of sixty thousand knights, to whom a proper provision in land had been assigned by the Conqueror, it is clear that he is stating an inference drawn from some calculations which we do not possess, unless, as seems probable, it was based on a misunder-

standing of the Domesday Survey [1]. The apparently inexplicable diversities in the computation of the acreage of the hide, the variation of the number of hides contained in the knight's fee, and the fact that the system of assessment by knights' fees furnishes no real clue to the number of warriors actually producible, are sufficient reason for not hazarding a conjectural estimate. The number of knights who could be brought into the field at once was by no means large; the whole number furnished by the tenants-in-chief from the ten counties south of the Thames and Avon was, as we learn from the Liber Niger, only 2047 [2]: and these counties probably contained a fourth part of the

---

[1] Above, p. 287. It is certain that even the officials of the Exchequer had no certain computation of the number of knights' fees. Alexander Swerford, the original compiler of the Liber Ruber Scaccarii, who wrote in 1230, tells us that Longchamp when Chancellor had endeavoured in vain to ascertain it: ' Illud commune verbum in ore singulorum tunc temporis divulgatum fatuum reputans et mirabile, quod in regni conquisitione dux Normannorum Rex Willelmus servitia xxxii. millia militum infeodavit;' Hunter, Three Catalogues, p. 13. Stephen Segrave however, the minister of Henry III, reckoned 32,000 as the number; Ann. Burton. p. 367. The calculation of Higden in the Polychronicon, lib. i. c. 49, makes the whole number 60,015, of which 28,015 are held by the religious; but as he makes the parish churches 45,002 in number, his calculation is only a contrivance to reconcile the 60,000 of Ordericus with the 32,000 of popular opinion. From Higden the statement is taken by the author of the chronicle called Eulogium (vol. ii. p. 154); from these two books it was taken by a host of copyists: Selden in his notes on Fortescue quotes it from the Eulogium.

[2] Pearson, Early and Middle Ages, i. 375; ii. 209, 496, 497. Mr. Pearson's conjecture that the number of 32,000 really applied to the hides, and that the knights' fees, calculated at five hides each, would be 6400, is ingenious; but the statement, wherever it is made, is distinctly referred to the knights' fees only.

population of England.   The official computation, on which the
scutage was levied, reckoned in the middle of the thirteenth
century 32,000 knights' fees, but the amount of money actually
raised by Henry II on this account, in any single year, was very
far from commensurate.   The exact obligation of the knight's
service was to furnish a fully-armed horseman to serve at his
own expense for forty days in the year.   This service was not
in practice limited to the defence of the country in which the
estate lay ; the Norman knights served the Norman king both
in England and abroad, nor did the question of foreign service
arise during this period of our history.   The baron led his own
knights under his own banner, the host was arranged by the
constable or marshal under the supreme command of the king :
the knights who held less than baronial fees under the crown
appeared with the rest of the forces of the shires under the
command of the sheriffs.   The infantry must have been furnished
almost entirely by the more ancient fyrd system, or by mercenaries.   It is however improbable that anything like a regular
force of infantry was maintained by the Norman kings.   It was
enough, after the pacification of the country by the Conqueror,
that a force of knights should be kept together for such hurried
expeditions on the Welsh or Scottish borders as received the
name of wars.   The like body accompanied the king in his visits
to Normandy.   Where more was required, as was the case in
the struggles of the early years of Henry I, recourse was had to
the native population.   Every free man was sworn, under the
injunction of the Conqueror, to join in the defence of the king,
his lands and his honour, within England and without [1] : nor
was any fixed period for such service defined by the law ; although
custom must have restricted the demand for it to cases in which
the kingdom was imperilled by invasion, and must have limited
its duration according to the provision made by the county for
the force it furnished.   The oath thus taken must have legalised

Obligation of military service.

Union of the shire-forces under the sheriff.

Obligation to foreign service.

---

[1] ' Statuimus etiam ut omnis liber homo foedere et sacramento affirmet,
quod infra et extra Angliam Willelmo regi fideles esse volunt, terras et
honorem illius omni fidelitate cum eo servare et ante eum coram inimicos
defendere ; ' Select Charters, p. 83.

the employment of English troops for the war in Maine in 1073[1], and the summons issued by William Rufus to the English, in obedience to which 20,000 foot-soldiers were furnished for war

Provision made by the shire for the fyrd.

in Normandy[2]. Each of these received from the shire a sum of ten shillings, which, compared with the twenty shillings which in the county of Berks were paid towards the expenses of each knight for two months[3], may perhaps imply that two months was the customary period of service. On these terms then it is probable that the English forces which assisted Henry against

Action of the fyrd.

Robert of Belesme were collected; and although the long peace which followed gave but few opportunities for the king to demand the fulfilment of the obligation, the invasion by King David in 1138 found the Yorkshiremen still mindful of their duty and capable of discharging it successfully[4].

Mercenary soldiers.

But there can be little doubt that for the Norman wars of Henry I, and for the partisan warfare which desolated England under Stephen, mercenaries were largely employed. In 1085 the Conqueror's army raised for the defence against Canute of Denmark was composed of 'solidarii[5],' footmen and archers collected from all parts of France and Brittany; and after the first Crusade the hosts of veteran adventurers who survived their pilgrimage were at the disposal of Henry I. The mercenaries drawn by him from Flanders gave Stephen and Matilda a precedent for a practice which to a great extent indeed economised the blood and sinew of the native English, but yet was productive of much misery and great irritation. The rapacity of

Unpopularity of mercenaries in England.

the Flemings created in the people an intense feeling of hatred, and one of the most popular provisions of the reform carried out by Henry II was the expulsion of these plunderers. The fact that each of these three sources of military strength, the feudal array, the national militia, and the mercenary companies, was available on both sides of the channel, placed a very powerful engine of warfare in the king's hands; and we shall see as we proceed that among the very first steps towards a reorganisa-

---

[1] W. Malmesb. G. R. lib. iii. § 258.   [2] Flor. Wig. A.D. 1094.
[3] Above, p. 131, note 3.   [4] Ric. Hexham, ed. Twysden, c. 321.
[5] Flor. Wig. A.D. 1085.

tion of the national unity were measures which forbade the
introduction of mercenaries into England, a growing reluctance,
culminating in a positive refusal, on the part of the feudal
tenants to fight the king's battles abroad, and the actual cessation of any attempt to use the English free population for foreign
warfare.

134. This survey of the history of the Norman sovereigns, How much of this system was Norman?
whilst it furnishes but a broken outline of their administrative
system in general, suggests questions which it is by no means
easy to answer. How far was the machinery, the recorded
facts of which have been here given, the national system of the
Normans in their earlier seats? how far was it a mere translation
of English institutions into Norman forms? how far was it the
result of a combination which forced both elements into new
developments? What was purely Norman, what was purely
English, what was new? The opinions of lawyers and historians
have widely differed on this point; and the differences seem in
many cases traceable rather to the mental constitution than to
the political or national prepossessions of the writers. One Variety of opinions.
authority insists on the immemorial antiquity of every institution the origin of which cannot be fixed by date; another refuses to recognise the possible existence of a custom before it
appears definitely in contemporary records: this writer regards
the common features of the two systems as positive proofs that
the one is derived from the other; that refuses to receive any
amount of analogy as proof of historical connexion. The result
has been on the one hand to treat the Norman system of government as an entire novelty, and on the other to reduce its influences to the merest and most superficial shades of change. The
view that has been taken in the earlier chapters of this book
has recognised to the fullest extent the permanence of the
Anglo-Saxon institutions, and under each head of the present
chapter have been noted the features of the Norman reigns
which appeared really strange to the older rule. In the policy Idea of this work.
of the Conqueror we have traced the existence of an idea of
combination, of dovetailing or welding together the administrative framework of the two races. In taxation the Danegeld is

distinctly English, the feudal aid is distinctly Norman: William maintained both. In legal procedure the hundred-moot and the shire-moot are English, the custom of trial by battle is Norman ; in military organisation the fyrd is Anglo-Saxon, the knight-service is Norman : in each case the Conqueror intro-

Principle of combination.

duced the one without abolishing the other. This principle was dictated in the first instance by the necessity of providing institutions for two distinct nationalities, and was perpetuated as the nationalities coalesced, because it furnished the king with a power of holding the balance of the kingdom with a firm purpose of strong government. Just as the nationalities combined to produce one nation strengthened in character and polity by the union, so the combination of the institutions produced a new growth in which, whilst much that is old can be detected, there is much else that could not have existed but for the combination. The increase of official records in the reigns of Henry II and his sons enables us to trace this influence more accurately as we advance. But there are some points which demand notice at our present stage of inquiry.

We have considered the leading principle of the system of the Conquest to be the combination of the strongest part of the Norman system with the strongest part of the early English system ; the maintenance of the local and provincial machinery of the latter with the central and sovereign authority character-

Origin of the Curia Regis and Exchequer.

istic of the former. The most important parts of the centralising system of the Norman kings are the Curia Regis and Exchequer; and here the most opposite opinions have been

Norman, English, or merely the work of despotism?

put forth for many years with the utmost confidence. The Curia Regis has been regarded as the simple reproduction in conquered England of the Curia Ducis of Normandy [1], which again was a reproduction of the court of the Karoling kings of the West Franks as it existed under Charles the Simple when he bestowed Normandy on Rollo. From another point of view it is represented merely as the English court of Edward the Confessor, the small witenagemot of the Anglo-Saxon kings,

---

[1] Brunner, in his Entstehung der Schwurgericht, and also in Holtzendorf's Encyclopädie.

which has under the influence of feudal ideas sustained a change rather nominal than constitutional, and which gradually tends to devolve upon the king and his more immediate household the central administration of justice in cases calling for such administration. From another point the whole central administration is viewed as the operation of the personal omnipotence of the king as conqueror and supreme administrator[1]. Each of these theories contains a great truth: the Norman kings were despotic in fact; their highest attempts at organised government advance in the direction of law no further than that stage which has been more than once described as the stage of routine. The system of routine by which they worked was primarily the system on which they had governed Normandy; the court of the duke was reproduced in principle, as it was in the persons who constituted it, in the court of the king. The English administrative system was also so far advanced under Edward the Confessor that the transformation of the ancient witenagemot into the great court and council was—after the great change of actors caused by the substitution of Norman for native lords and prelates—possible without any still more violent innovation. But there are other facts to be considered besides theories conceived *à priori*. We possess a large stock of Anglo-Saxon records; laws and charters which shed a great deal of broken light on every department of the life of our forefathers. The constitutional history of Normandy, and the legal history of the whole of that kingdom of which Normandy was a nominal province, is, during the century and a half that intervenes between the extinction of the Karolingian power and the reign of Lewis VI, illustrated only in a very slight degree by fragments of legislation and scattered charters. The most ancient text-books of Norman law are later than the reign of Henry II, both in composition and in materials[2]. No one at

Element of truth in each theory.

Scantiness of Norman records.

---

[1] Gneist, Verwaltungsr. i. 228 sq.

[2] Brunner, in an Excursus contained in his work, Das Anglonormannische Erbfolgesystem, gives a careful account of the existing *origines* of Norman law. These are to be found in two books: (1) Statuta et consuetudines Normanniae, printed in French by Marnier in his Établissements et Coûtumes, Assises et Arrêts de l'Echiquier de Normandie (Paris, 1839);

the present day would contend that the legal reforms of Henry II were drawn from the Grand Coûtumier of Normandy, any more than that they were the result of the lessons of his great-uncle King David of Scotland. Yet it would be almost as rash to maintain that the similarities of Norman and later English law are to be ascribed solely to the fact that both were developed under the force of Henry I and under the genius of Henry II. If, again, we ascribe to Norman sources all that is Karolingian in the measures of the Norman and Angevin kings, we are underrating the probable and almost demonstrable influence which the association of the West-Saxon dynasty with the Karoling, Saxon, and Franconian courts must have produced on native custom. Under the circumstances it might seem almost the safest plan to abstain from attempting a conclusion. But this is scarcely possible.

Difficulty of tracing the connexion of Norman and Karolingian institutions.

The regular action of the central power of the kingdom becomes known to us, as we have seen, first in the proceedings of the Exchequer. The English Exchequer appears first early in the reign of Henry I: the Norman Exchequer appears first under Henry II. There is nothing in the name to determine whether it was originally given to the court in England or in Normandy. The method of accounting in the English Exchequer is based on the English coinage, that of the Norman on the French: both England and Normandy must have had fiscal audits long before the Conquest; the systems of account, almost all the processes of the two courts, are different. Yet the results have necessarily a resemblance; the officers of the one were occasionally trained in the work of the other, and when reforms

Growth of the Exchequer in England and in Normandy.

and in Latin by Warnkönig in the Staats- und Rechts-Geschichte, vol. ii. This compilation, as Brunner shows, contains two works, (*a*) a Tractatus de brevibus et recognitionibus, drawn up soon after 1218; and (*β*) a Très ancienne coûtume de Normandie, which belongs to the justiciarship of William Fitz-Ralph, about 1190-1200. (2) The second book is the Grand Coûtumier of Normandy, the older form of which appears to be the Latin Somma de legibus consuetudinum Normanniae, which is found in J. P. de Ludewig's Reliquiae Manuscriptorum, vol. vii. pp. 149-418. The date of this work, which Brunner shows to be an original composition, and not founded on the preceding, as Warnkönig and Marnier supposed, falls between 1270 and 1275. Brunner's arguments on the Inquest by Jury are taken from charters of much earlier date.

were needed in the one, a change of administrators was easy; the Treasury of Caen could lend an abbot to the Exchequer of Westminster, or the Exchequer of Westminster could lend a baron to revise the accounts of Caen. The same exigencies, so long as the rulers of England and Normandy were the same, would be met by much the same measures. There is no evidence but that of tradition for deriving the English Exchequer from Normandy : there is far more antecedent probability that whatever the Norman Exchequer has in common with the English was derived from the latter. Yet the English Exchequer was organised by Norman ministers: the Domesday Survey was carried out by Normans : Ranulf Flambard and Roger of Salisbury were both natives of the neighbourhood of Caen. If there is no Norman roll of the reign of Henry I, there is but one English roll: in the latter case all but one have perished, so that no one can safely maintain that in the former case none ever existed. Yet at the time at which the English fiscal system was developed, during the reign of William Rufus and in the early years of Henry I, the two countries were not under the same ruler.

The two Exchequers grow side by side.

The conclusion seems to depend on a balance of probabilities : it is most probable that in both countries there was a fiscal court or audit, that the two were developed and more fully organised under the same superintendence, and each may have borrowed from the other: but there is no historical proof, and no historical necessity to assume, that the one was an offshoot of a transplantation of the other. The importance of the name is only secondary ; it matters little whether the chequered cloth were first used at Westminster or at Caen. It appears only in those countries which are connected with Normandy after the Conquest and with the Norman kings of England, so that from this point of view the English origin seems most probable.

Probable conclusion.

Name of Exchequer.

The history of the Curia Regis, in its judicial aspect, is, as we have seen, even more complicated. The Anglo-Saxon kings heard causes in person: the judgment of the king was the last resort of the litigant who had failed to obtain justice in the hundred and the shire. He had also a court in which the disputes

Growth of the idea of the Curia Regis.

of his immediate dependents were settled, the 'theningmanna-
gemot,' the existence of which is proved, but no more than its
existence[1]. The Norman duke had his feudal court of vassals
like every other feudal lord, and a tribunal of supreme judicature which may or may not have been personally identical with
the court of vassals. The royal judicature in England was in
the reigns of the Conqueror and William Rufus exercised either
by the king or justiciar in person on the great festivals, or by
special commission in the shire-moot. The question then is
this, Was the Curia Regis as developed under Henry I the
Curia Ducis of Normandy? or was it the king himself acting as
judge with the council of his witan or a portion of them? or
was it not rather a tribunal in a stage of growth, springing
from a combination of the two older systems, and tending to
become something very different from either?

Trial of the bishop of Durham in the Curia Regis in 1088.

The report of the court held on Bishop William of S. Carileph,
after the rebellion of 1088[2], supplies us with convincing proof
that the last is the true account of the matter. The bishop had
joined in the conspiracy of the earls during Lent 1088; and the
king's officers had on the 12th of March seized his estates; he
demanded restitution; the king insisted that he should purge
himself of his treason. The bishop pleaded his right to be tried
as a bishop, but offered to defend himself from the charge of
having broken his oath of fealty. The parties met on the 2nd of
November at Salisbury, where all the bishops, earls, barons, and
royal officers assembled. Lanfranc refused to listen to the
bishop's plea, and he was appealed of treason by Hugh de
Beaumont on the king's part. After much deliberation, every
stage of which is recorded, the bishop still insisting on his
right[3], Lanfranc declares that he must first answer the king's

[1] Above, p. 205, note 1.
[2] 'De injusta vexatione Willelmi episcopi primi;' printed first by Bedford
in an appendix to his edition of Simeon of Durham, pp. 343–375; and
afterwards in the Monasticon, vol. i. pp. 244–250.
[3] At one point the bishop of Durham is sent out of court whilst the barons
deliberate whether he should be restored to his possessions or acquit himself
to the king first. The archbishop of York states the result of the consultation: 'Domine episcope, dominus noster archiepiscopus et regis Curia
vobis judicat quod rectitudinem regi facere debeatis antequam de vestro
feodo revestiat;' Bedford, p. 359.

demand: 'We are not judging you in the matter of your bishopric but of your fee, and so we judged the bishop of Bayeux before the king's father concerning his fee; nor did the king in that plea call him bishop, but brother and earl[1].' The bishop struggles against this and appeals to Rome. The court then deliberates on the sentence, which is finally pronounced by Hugh de Beaumont, in the name of the king's court and the barons[2]: as the bishop will not answer the charge brought against him, he forfeits his fee. Ultimately he spends three years in exile. The record is drawn up by a friend of the bishop, and is very long; but these details are sufficient to prove that the court in which the trial was held was the witenagemot acting as a feudal court of peers.

The Curia Regis of Henry I was a regulated and modified form of that of William Rufus, as that of Henry II was an organised development of that of Henry I. The trial of Henry of Essex early in the reign of Henry II, and that of Robert of Belesme in the reign of Henry I, are links in a series which proves the fundamental identity of the earliest and latest forms.

Development of the Curia Regis under Henry I.

But although we may assert an English element in the Curia Regis, and confidently deny its exclusively Norman origin, it must be granted that very much of the new forms of process was foreign. Whether Lanfranc brought it from Pavia, or William inherited it from the Norman dukes, we can scarcely on existing evidence decide. Lanfranc had been an eminent lawyer[3] before he became a monk, and his Norman home at

The process of the Curia Regis was foreign: especially the system of writs.

---

[1] 'Nos non de episcopio, sed de tuo te feodo judicamus, et hoc modo judicavimus Bajocensem episcopum ante patrem hujus regis de feodo suo; nec rex vocabat eum episcopum in placito illo, sed fratrem et comitem; p. 361.

[2] 'Domine episcope, regis curia et barones isti vobis pro justo judicant, quando sibi vos respondere non vultis de hiis de quibus vos per me appellavit, sed de placito suo invitatis eum Romam, quod vos feodum vestrum inde forisfacitis.' The bishop demurs: Hugh answers, 'Ego et compares mei parati sumus judicium nostrum in hac curia confirmare;' p. 362.

[3] 'Nam, ut fertur, pater ejus de ordine illorum qui jura et leges civitatis asservabant fuit;' Vita Lanfranci, c. 1. 'Saecularium legum peritiam ad patriae suae morem intentione laica fervidus edidicit. Adolescentulus orator veteranos adversantes in actionibus causarum frequenter praecipitavit, torrente facundia apposite dicendo senes superavit. In ipsa aetate

Caen was the central seat of the ducal administration. However they were introduced, the great development of the system of writs, and especially the custom of inquest by sworn recognitors, are features of Norman jurisprudence which must be traced ultimately to Karolingian usage. The provincial visitations of the royal judges, which under Henry II grow into a regular system of judicial eyres, are less certainly

Itinerant judicature of Frank origin.

Norman. They may as an expedient of government be of Karolingian origin; but the historical connexion between the judges of Henry I and those of Charles the Great may be traced perhaps with as much probability on English as on Norman

Itinerant judicature under Alfred:

ground[1]. If the Capitularies of Charles the Bald include the territory which was afterwards Normandy in the plan for the operation of the imperial *missi*, there is sufficient evidence that a measure of the same sort was taken in England as early as the days of Alfred. But in this point as well as in the others it seems far more natural to suppose that similar circumstances suggested similar institutions, than that the latter were historically connected. The judicial visitations of the judges of Henry I were really rather circuits of the royal officers than

and under the Norman kings.

special commissions. The special commissions of the Norman period, such as was the tribunal at Pennenden, already more than once referred to, were, as we have seen, attempts to combine the inquisitorial process of the Norman Curia with the local machinery of the Anglo-Saxon shire.

Much of the nomenclature of the Norman system is of course

sententias promere statuit quas gratanter jurisperiti, aut judices aut praetores civitatis, acceptabant;' Ord. Vit. iv. c. 6.

[1] Lappenberg, ed. Thorpe, iii. p. 4. The argument of Brunner (Schwurgericht, pp. 152 sq.) for the priority of the itinerant justices of Normandy to those of England will scarcely be regarded as convincing. The reference to the 'Ancient Custom of Normandy,' which belongs to the last decade of the twelfth century, for proof that once or twice a year three or four sworn barons or knights held assizes in each Norman viscounty at a period earlier than the judicial reforms of Henry II, is unsatisfactory in the extreme; and the documentary examples are of still later date. There is the strongest probability that Henry II was as great a legal innovator in Normandy as he was in England. Brunner's use of this argument does not however in the least derogate from the convincing authority of the main argument of his book, which proves the descent of the Norman and English Inquest by Jury from the Karolingian *Inquisitio*.

French; and the influence of the nomenclature in modifying the character of the offices and processes which it denotes must always be allowed for. The terms justiciar, account, feoffment, amercement, forfeiture, tallage, homage, chattels, assize, seisin, summons, and innumerable others are derived from the Norman usage of Latin as the language of records; and the Latin of the Norman charters is not the Latin of the Anglo-Saxon charters[1]. The story that William the Conqueror forbade the use of the native tongue in the courts of law, notwithstanding the high authority of the fourteenth-century schoolman on which it rests, is no doubt a fabrication[2]; the popular courts transacted their business in English, and the kings issued their charters in English as well as Latin. Richard I is the first king of whom no English document is preserved[3], and our first French record belongs to the reign of John. But by far the great majority of the writs and other legal records must have been kept in Latin, as those of the Exchequer certainly were. The question then, so far as it is of significance at all, concerns the thing rather than the name: it will be found on careful examination that very many of the Norman-Latin names are merely translations of the Anglo-Saxon, not into the corresponding dialectic forms, but into the forms which represented the ideas which to the Norman mind they most nearly resembled. The Norman translated the word shire, not by sectio or even provincia, but by comitatus; the word scir-gerefa, not by praepositus provinciae, but by vicecomes; the gemot is far more frequently the curia than the conventus; the misericordia and

[marginal notes] New nomenclature of the Norman period not a conclusive argument of Norman innovation.

The language of legal proceedings.

Norman translation of English terms.

---

[1] Madox, Hist. Exch. p. 127.

[2] 'Narrant historiae quod cum Willelmus dux Normannorum regnum Angliae conquisivisset, deliberavit quomodo linguam Saxonicam posset destruere, et Angliam et Normanniam in idiomate concordare; et ideo ordinavit quod nullus in curia regis placitaret nisi in Gallico, et iterum quod puer quilibet ponendus ad litteras addisceret Gallicam et per Gallicam Latinam, quae duo usque hodie observantur;' Robert Holkot (ob. 1349), in his lectures on the Book of Wisdom, lect. xi.; cited by Selden in his notes on Fortescue. See too Fortescue, de Laudibus, &c., ch. 48. The authority of the pseudo-Ingulf is worthless.

[3] The English grants of Stephen and Henry II to Canterbury, and also to S. Paul's, are still preserved. See Mon. Angl. i. 111 ‡ MS. Lambeth 1212; Hickes, Thesaurus, praef. p. xvi. The first French Record is a charter of 1215 of Stephen Langton, preserved on the Charter Rolls, p. 209.

amercement have their exact correlatives in the Anglo-Saxon laws. The proper feudal terminology stands on a different footing : the oath of fealty in Norman law was different in matter and form from the Anglo-Saxon hyld-ath; the heriot was not the relief; the tallage rested on a different principle from the Danegeld; yet under the combining process that was necessary to the Norman king, the one might be prudently taken to represent the other, the obligation and the burden being much the same under either name. The analogy of the changes introduced by S. Osmund into the liturgy of the Church may suffice to show how greatly, under the circumstances of the Conquest, such innovations are magnified in the popular estimation : the mere revision of the service-books is represented as the introduction of a new rite; the institution of a new cantus provokes a monastic revolution. The fact, however, that the Norman influences introduced at the Conquest are so liable to be exaggerated if they are judged on a superficial view, must not lead us to underrate them. They were strong and penetrating rather than ostentatiously prominent. The careful study of the institutions of this period reveals the fact that not only in England but in Normandy it was a season of growth and transition; and it is far more consonant with historical probability to suppose that the development of two states so closely connected proceeded, if not by the same, still by equal steps, than that the one borrowed its whole polity from the other : for that England in the twelfth century continued to borrow from Normandy the system of the tenth, whilst Normandy remained stationary, neither developing her own nor imitating her neighbour's growth, seems altogether inconceivable. The absence of records throws us back upon hypothesis, but no sound criticism will allow us to see in the Norman Coûtumier of the thirteenth century the model of the legal measures taken in England by the Conqueror and his sons.

The conclusion that is suggested by the survey of the administrative machinery of the period corresponds almost exactly with that which is drawn from the political history. The royal policy is a policy of combination, whereby the strongest and

Marginal notes:

Novelties of feudal terminology.

Analogy of ritual with law.

Transitional character of the period.

Comparison of constitutional with political history.

safest elements in two nations were so united as to support one sovereign and irresponsible lord; the alliance between the king and the English is reflected in the measures taken to strengthen the Curia Regis and to protect the popular courts. It is the first stage in the process of amalgamation; a process which Henry I probably never contemplated as possible, but which Stephen's reign with all its troubles helped to begin, and which that of Henry II made practically safe. The age of routine dependent on the will of a despot passes by almost perceptible stages into the age of law secured by the organisation of a people which has begun at least to realise its unity and identity.

CHAPTER XII.

HENRY II AND HIS SONS.

135. General features of the period.—136. Henry II, his character and training.—137. His accession and first measures.—138. The years 1158–1163.—139. The contest with Becket.—140. Constitutions of Clarendon.—141. The Assize of Clarendon.—142. The year 1170.—143. The years 1171–1173.—144. The rebellion of 1173-4.—145. Reforms after the rebellion.—146. Latter years of Henry II.—147. Summary of the reign.—148. Richard I.—149. William Longchamp.—150. Administration of Walter of Coutances and Hubert Walter.—151. Accession of John.—152. Loss of Normandy.—153. Quarrel with the Church.—154. Quarrel with the barons.—155. The Great Charter.

General features of the reigns of Henry II, Richard, and John.

135. THE sixty years that followed the death of Stephen comprise a period of English history which has a special importance. It is a period of constant growth, although the growth is far from being regular or uniform. The chain of events that connects the peace of Wallingford and the charter of Runnymede is traceable link by link. The nation which at the beginning of the period is scarcely conscious of its unity, is able, at the end of it, to state its claims to civil liberty and self-government as a coherent organised society. Norman and Englishman are now one, with a far more real identity than was produced by joint ownership of the land or joint subjection to one sovereign. England has been enabled, by the fortunate incapacity of John, to cut herself free from Normandy; and the division of interest between the two races has ceased. The royal power has curbed the feudal spirit and reduced the system to its proper insignificance. The royal power, having reached

Growth of the royal power through the people,

its climax, has forced on the people trained under it the knowledge that it in its turn must be curbed, and that they have the strength to curb it. The church, the baronage, and the people have found by different ways their true and common interest. This has not been done without struggles that have seemed at certain times to be internecine. The people, the baronage, and the church have been severally crushed, reformed, revived, and reorganised. More than once the balance of forces has been readjusted. The crown has humbled the baronage with the help of the people, and the church with the help of the baronage. Each in turn has been made to strengthen the royal power, and has been taught in the process to know its own strength. By law the people have been raised from the dust, the baronage forced to obedience, the clergy deprived of the immunities that were destroying their national character and counteracting their spiritual work. The three estates, trained *who thereby learn their own strength.* in and by royal law, have learned how law can be applied to the very power that forced the lesson upon them. What the king has reformed and reorganised in order to gain a firm and real basis for his own power, has discovered its own strength and the strength of law, and has determined to give its service and sacrifices no longer without conditions. The history is to be worked out in some detail.

Henry II is the first of the three great kings who have left on *Individual impression made by Henry II.* the constitution indelible marks of their own individuality. What he reorganised Edward I defined and completed. The Tudor policy, which is impersonated in Henry VIII, tested to the utmost the soundness of the fabric: the constitution stood the shock, and the Stewarts paid the cost of the experiment. Each of the three sovereigns had a strong idiosyncrasy, and in each case the state of things on which he acted was such as to make the impression of personal character distinct and permanent.

136. Henry II at his accession found the kingdom in a state *Henry II at his accession, 1154.* of dissolution: his only advantage was the absolute exhaustion of all the forces which had produced that dissolution. The task before him was one which might have appalled an experienced legislator, and Henry was little more than twenty-one years old.

He did not succeed to the inheritance of a band of veteran
counsellors; the men with whom he had to work were the

survivors of the race that had caused the anarchy. He was a
young man of keen bright intellect, patient, laborious, methodical;
ambitious within certain well-defined limits, tenacious of power,
ingenious even to minuteness in expedients, prompt and ener-

getic in execution; at once unscrupulous and cautious. These
characteristics mark also the later stages of his career, even
when, disappointed of his dearest hopes and mortified in his
tenderest affections, he gave way to violent passion and degrading
licence; for his private vices made no mark on his public career,
and he continued to the last a most industrious, active, and
business-like king. There was nothing in him of the hero, and
of the patriot scarcely more than an almost instinctive knowledge
of the needs of his people, a knowledge which can hardly ever
be said to be the result of sympathy. Thus much all the
historians who have described him join in allowing; although
they form very different estimates of his merit as a ruler, and of

the objects of his policy. These objects seem to have been mainly
the consolidation of his power: in England the strengthening
and equalising of the royal administration; on the Continent
the retention and thorough union of the numerous and variously
constituted provinces which by marriage or inheritance had
come into his hands. The English nation may gratefully
recognise his merit as a ruler in the vastness of the benefits
that resulted from the labours even of a selfish life.

Henry II was born at Le Mans on the 5th of March, 1133 [1],
when his grandfather was despairing of an heir. When quite an
infant, he received the fealty and homage of the barons as their

future king. He was the child of parents singularly ill-matched:
his father was of the weak, unprincipled, and impulsive type into
which the strong and astute nature of the Angevin house sank
in its lowest development; his mother a Norman lady who had
all the strong characteristics of her race, and had too early exchanged the religious training which would have curbed them for

---

[1] Chron. Andegavense, in Labbe's Bibliotheca Manuscriptorum, i. 277;
Ordericus Vitalis, lib. x. c. 1; R. de Monte, A.D. 1133.

the position of the spoiled child-wife of the cold-blooded despotic emperor. As empress she had enjoyed the power and splendour of her position too heartily to endure the rule of a husband so personally insignificant as Geoffrey of Anjou, or to submit to the restraints of a policy which would have been desperate but for the craft and energy of Robert of Gloucester. Yet in spite of her imperious behaviour and her want of self-control, Matilda was a woman of considerable ability; in her old age she was a safe and sagacious counsellor ; and some part at least of her son's education must be put to her credit. Henry was brought to England when he was nine years old to be trained in arms ; four years were spent at Bristol under the instructions of a master named Matthew who is afterwards called his chancellor[1] ; at the age of sixteen he was knighted by his great-uncle David of Scotland; in 1151 he received the duchy of Normandy, and soon after succeeded his father in the county of Anjou ; the next year he married Eleanor, and added Poictou and Guienne to his dominions ; at the age of twenty he undertook the recovery of England, brought Stephen, partly by war and partly by negotiation, to terms which insured his own succession, and in less than a year after the pacification succeeded to the English throne.

The Empress Matilda.

Henry comes to England in 1142 ; becomes duke in 1151, and king in 1154.

An education so disturbed and so curtailed can hardly have contained much legal or constitutional teaching, and Henry's own peculiar genius for such lore could scarcely have been as yet developed ; but by the urgency with which he forced Stephen to take in hand the necessary reforms, he showed at least a consciousness of the importance of the task, even if we may not venture to ascribe to him an actual share in the draught of the scheme of reform. That Henry acquired at the Scottish court any real acquaintance with the principles or forms of legal knowledge, that in his titular office of seneschal of France[2] he really discharged any duties of a judicial character,

He could not have had much legal education before his accession.

---

[1] Gervase, i. 125 ; Epp. G. Foliot, S. T. C. v. 201. He attests, as chancellor, an undated charter of Eleanor to S. Paul's, 'per breve regis de ultra mare.' He was possibly the archdeacon of Gloucester who died in 1177 ; Ann. Wigorn. p. 384; Ann. Theokesb. p. 52. On the dates of this part of Henry's life, see Mr. Howlett's note on the Gesta Stephani, pp. 130, 131.

[2] R. de Monte, A.D. 1177 ; Gir. Camb. de Inst. Pr. lib. iii. c. 28.

or that he acted as justiciar in England during the latter years
of Stephen, are theories alike improbable, and indeed opposed
to historical evidence. The court of King David might have
furnished training for either a warrior or a monk, but not for a
lawyer or a constitutional king; in France Henry had scarcely
spent more time than can be accounted for by the business of
his succession and marriage; and in England he had remained
only a few weeks after the pacification. He had in his wife and
mother two counsellors of ability and experience, but his own
genius for government must have been innate; and next to his
genius the most important element in the creation of his
characteristic policy must be looked for in his choice of advisers.
Of these the first must have been Earl Ranulf of Chester, with
whom as duke of Normandy he had made a close alliance in
1152, but who died before his accession; Archbishop Theobald,
who had been firmly attached to the interests of the empress
throughout the later years of the struggle; Bishop Henry of
Winchester; Nigel of Ely who represented the family and the
official training of Roger of Salisbury the justiciar of Henry I;
the earl of Leicester, Robert de Beaumont; and Richard de
Lucy, who had charge of the castle of Windsor and the Tower
of London at the peace [1], who had possibly acted as justiciar
during the last year of Stephen, and who filled the office for the
first twenty-five years of Henry's reign, during part of the time
in conjunction with the earl of Leicester. In a subordinate
capacity was Thomas Becket of London, the pupil of Theobald
and future archbishop and martyr. None of these, except Nigel
and Thomas, had as yet given great proofs of administrative
skill; the bishop of Winchester, who had had the fairest opportunity, had made the most signal failure. There must have
been in Henry himself some gift that called forth or detected the
ability of his servants.

[1] Foedera, i. 18. The Tower of London and Windsor Castle were
peculiarly in the custody of the justiciar; and he also signed the royal
writs, as we find Richard de Lucy signing the charter of Henry II.
The charter of Stephen however, in which he is addressed as justiciar,
does not necessarily imply that he was chief justiciar; Madox, Formulare
Angl. p. 40.

137. Stephen died on the 25th of October, 1154, and Henry Interregnum after Stephen's death, 1154. landed in England on the 8th of December[1]. Nothing can show more clearly the exhaustion of society than the fact that the interregnum of two months was peaceful. Archbishop Theobald seems to have taken the helm of state, and notwithstanding the presence of Stephen's mercenary troops, which were yet undismissed, no man laid hands on his neighbour[2]. After re- Coronation of Henry; Dec. 19, 1154. ceiving the fealty of the chief barons at Winchester the duke of Normandy hastened to London, where he was elected and[3] crowned on the 19th of December, and issued a charter of liberties as brief and comprehensive as that of Stephen had been. He grants and confirms all the gifts, liberties, and His charter. customs that his grandfather had granted, promises the abolition of all evil customs that he had abolished, and enjoins that the church, his earls, barons, and all his men, shall have and hold, freely and quietly, well, in peace and wholly, of him and his heirs, to them and their heirs, all the liberties and free customs that King Henry I had granted and secured by his charter[4]. The reference to the charter of Henry is as marked as the omission of all mention of Stephen. The charter is attested by Richard de Lucy, who therefore was probably in the office of justiciar. On Christmas Day the king held his court at The mercenaries banished. Bermondsey, and having debated with the barons on the measures necessary to the state of the kingdom, directed the expulsion of the mercenaries and the demolition of the adulterine castles[5]. William of Ypres consequently departed with his Fleming soldiers, and the demolition of the fortified houses was speedily begun. The bishop of Ely was recalled to the Restoration of the Exchequer, 1154–1155. Exchequer[6]; Thomas Becket was made chancellor[7], and the

---

[1] Gervase, i. 159.

[2] Ibid.

[3] 'Ab omnibus electus est;' R. de Monte, A.D. 1154.

[4] Statutes of the realm, Charters, p. 4; Select Charters, p. 135.

[5] 'In nativitate Domini tenuit rex curiam suam apud Beremundeseiam ubi cum principibus suis de statu regni et pace reformanda tractans, proposuit animo alienigenas gentes de regno propellere et munitiunculas pessimas per totam Angliam solotenus dissipare;' Gervase, i. 160; R. de Monte, A.D. 1155.

[6] Dialogus de Scaccario, Prol. i. c. 8.

[7] Gervase, i. 160, states that Thomas was made chancellor at the accession;

official dignity of the court was replaced on its old footing. Whether at this assembly new sheriffs were appointed, or that measure had been already taken before Stephen's death, is uncertain; the persons who are found in the office, so soon as the regular Exchequer accounts furnish us with authentic names, are generally barons of great local importance. In Devonshire and Wiltshire the earls of the county, and in Herefordshire the claimant cf the earldom, appear as sheriffs; Richard de Lucy accounts for Essex and Hertfordshire; but as a rule the sheriffs seem to be persons of local importance only, and chosen from what may be called the second rank of the baronage. The earls must have felt that they were in a critical position; Henry might have been expected to annul the creations of Stephen, and reduce the *pseudo-comites* to the rank from which they had been raised. We have no record of actual displacement; it may however have taken place at the time of the coronation; the earldoms of Bedford, Somerset, York, and perhaps a few others, drop out of the list; those of Essex and Wilts remain. Some of the earls had already made their peace with the king; some, like Aubrey de Vere, obtained a new charter for their dignity: this part of the social reconstruction was dispatched without much complaint or difficulty[2].

The new sheriffs, 1155-1156.

Question of the earls.

see also R. de Diceto, i. 300. Stephen's chancellor, after the dismissal of Roger the Poor in 1139, was Philip of Harcourt, archdeacon of Evreux, who became bishop of Bayeux in 1142; Ord. Vit. xiii. 42; Cont. F. Wig. ii. 124.

[1] 'Rex Henricus coepit revocare in jus proprium urbes, castella, villas quae ad coronam. regni pertinebant, castella noviter facta destruendo, et expellendo de regno maxime Flandrenses, et deponendo quosdam imaginarios et pseudo-comites quibus rex Stephanus omnia pene ad fiscum pertinentia minus caute distribuerat;' R. de Monte, A.D. 1155. The earldom of Kent, assigned on insufficient authority to William of Ypres, came to an end on his departure; and the earldom of York is heard of no more until Richard I bestowed it on his nephew Otto. The earl of Hereford, Roger, died in the first year of Henry, after having obtained a confirmation of his earldom; but his brother Walter did not succeed; it was however given to his great-grandson Henry de Bohun many years after. On the whole question see Round, Geoff. de Mandeville, pp. 267–277. It can hardly be doubted that there was exaggeration and perhaps misapprehension even among contemporary writers.

[2] 'Ubi sunt, ut de domesticis loquar, Gaufridus, Milo, Ranulfus, Alanus, Simon, Gillebertus, non tam comites regni quam hostes publici? Ubi Willelmus Sarisberiensis?' Joh. Salisb. Polycr. viii. 21.

Not so the more substantial part of the work. The great nobles were not unwilling to see the humiliation of their smaller neighbours, but very loath to surrender the royal demesne, and especially the castles that had been placed in their hands by the two contending parties[1]. The command of the king was summary and comprehensive; the royal estates, by whatever charters of the late king they were conferred, must be restored; the royal castles, however obtained, must be surrendered. Charters were produced and services pleaded in vain[2]. A very few only were able to offer any real resistance. This came, as might be expected, from both sides. The count of Aumâle, who had won the battle of the Standard, who was a near kinsman of both kings, who had been generally faithful to Stephen, and was almost sovereign of the north, declined to surrender Scarborough. Roger of Hereford the son of Miles, who had been one of the great supporters of the empress, fortified the castles of Hereford and Gloucester against the king. Hugh Mortimer, who since the fall of the house of Montgomery had been the most powerful man on the Welsh march, prepared for open revolt. The Scots too showed no readiness in restoring Northumberland and Cumberland, which King David had undertaken to hold in trust for Henry.

The king lost no time in negotiation; in January 1155 he went northwards, and compelled the count of Aumâle to surrender Scarborough[3]: on his return he visited Nottingham, where the news of his approach frightened into a monastery the great baron of the Peak, William Peverell, who had been accused of attempting to poison the earl of Chester[4]. Early in March

Resumption of royal demesne; 1155.

Resumption of castles.

Resistance of the great barons.

Henry takes the castles in 1155.

---

[1] The right of the duke of Normandy to garrison the castles of the barons has been mentioned already, and Henry's exercise of the right is an important illustration of his action on this occasion. In 1161 he occupied and garrisoned the castles of the count of Meulan and others; in 1166 those of the count of Ponthieu and Alençon: in 1165 he seized the castles of the Lusignans in Poictou, and in 1171 those of the Leonois in Brittany. He also in 1171 resumed the ducal demesnes which had been alienated since the death of Henry I. See R. de Monte under these dates.

[2] W. Newb. ii. c. 2; R. Dicet. i. 371.

[3] W. Newb. ii. c. 3; Gervase, i. 161.

[4] Gervase, i. 161; R. de Monte, A.D. 1155. William Peverell's crime had been committed and his punishment determined on long before this.

Henry was again in London, where he held a great council, renewed the general peace, and confirmed the old customs [1], but declared his intention of extinguishing every element of dis-

He reduces Roger of Hereford; March, 1155.

order and of bringing the contumacious barons to account. The manifesto was no sooner issued than it was enforced; the terrors of the king's approach wrought wonders; before the middle of the month Roger of Hereford had, under the advice of Gilbert Foliot, made his formal submission [2], and Hugh Mortimer, with his three castles of Wigmore, Cleobury, and

Oaths taken to the heir; April, 1155.

Bridgnorth, alone held out. Before proceeding against him Henry held another great assembly, on April 10, at Walling-ford [3], where he exacted the oaths of the bishops and barons to the succession of his son William, and in case of his death to Henry his second son. The subjugation of the border proved no easy task. Bridgnorth, which had been fortified fifty years before by Robert of Belesme, tasked the skill of the royal forces, and Henry was obliged to call out the whole military power of

Submission of Hugh Mortimer.

England before it was brought to submission [4]. Hugh Mortimer made his peace in July [5]. Before the end of his first year Henry had thus disarmed the feudal party, restored the regular administration of the country, banished the mercenaries, de-stroyed the castles, and showed an intention of ruling through

Proposed conquest of Ireland.

the means, if not under the control, of his national council. In September he held another council at Winchester, in which he discussed the project of conquering Ireland as a provision for his brother William of Anjou [6]; he ordered that the castles of

Henry had promised his fiefs to the earl of Chester, in case of his proved guilt, in 1152, in which year the earl died; Foedera, i. 16.

[1] 'In sequenti Quadragesima congregavit generale concilium apud Lun-doniam et renovavit pacem et leges et consuetudines per Angliam ab antiquis temporibus constitutas;' Chron. de Bello, p. 72. 'Convocatis universis fere regni primoribus coepit rex rationem ponere cum eis qui adhuc tenebant praesidia regii juris; erat enim fixa in animo ipsius sententia omnem re-bellionum materiam exstirpare et suspicionum causas submovere;' Gervase, i. 161.

[2] March 13th; Gervase, i. 162.

[3] 'Factus est conventus generalis praesulum et principum totius Angliae apud Wallingefordiam;' Gervase, i. 162; R. de Monte, A.D. 1155.

[4] Chron. de Bello, p. 75; R. de Monte, A.D. 1155.

[5] 'Mense Julio, nonis ejusdem;' R. de Monte.

[6] The empress objected and the design was given up for the present; R. de Monte.

the bishop of Winchester, who had gone abroad without leave, should be demolished; and he wound up the business of the year by a solemn gathering at Westminster at Christmas [1]. The history of the year furnishes abundant illustration of the energy and capacity of a king of two-and-twenty.

The year 1156 was spent by Henry on the Continent. He was accompanied by his chancellor Becket, who had already become his most intimate friend and most influential adviser [2]. The chief object of the expedition was to secure Normandy and to bring to submission the king's brother Geoffrey, who had under his father's will claims on Anjou which Henry denied. England was left under the management of earl Robert of Leicester and Richard de Lucy, the justiciars; the queen likewise took part in the government during the first half of the year. The year is marked by no event of importance, but it furnishes us with the first of an unbroken series of Exchequer Rolls, from which we learn much as to the reconstruction of the administrative system. The Pipe Roll of the second year of Henry II [3] exhibits the account for the year ending at Michaelmas, 1156: no sheriff appears for the northern counties, which are still in the hands of the Scots; the diminished amount of revenue shows that the treasury was but slowly recovering from the exhaustion of the last reign, not more than £22,000 being raised in the gross from the whole kingdom. A general visitation of the country had not been yet attempted, but the constable, Henry of Essex, had heard pleas in eight of the southern counties; in two of them, Essex and Kent, in company with the chancellor, who for the first time appears in the character of a judge. The general taxation is of much the same sort as in the roll of Henry I, but the term *scutage*, which does not appear in 1130, indicates that the assessment of the knights' fees was now in use; and as it is mainly in reference to the spiritual baronies that the word occurs, it follows that the liability of these estates to the public duties was not confined

Marginal notes:

Expedition to France in 1156.

Revenue of 1156.

Itinerant justices in 1156.

Scutage in 1156.

---

[1] R. de Diceto, i. 301; Chron. de Bello, p. 76.
[2] Gervase, i. 162.
[3] Printed by Hunter with the Rolls of the 3rd and 4th years, in 1844.

to military defence. The practice was, as we learn from John
of Salisbury, opposed by Archbishop Theobald[1], but it was
perhaps advised by the chancellor, who did not until a much
later period betray any sympathy with the cause of clerical
immunities.

Henry's acts in 1157.

138. Henry returned to England soon after the 7th of April,
1157, and immediately found his hands full of work. Some
few of the royal castles had been allowed to remain in the
hands of the barons who were half trusted, in order perhaps to
avoid provoking them to rebel. The son of the late king,
William count of Mortain, Warenne and Surrey, whose rights
had been secured at the peace, now placed in the king's hands
all the castles that he possessed both in England and Normandy, and received in return the patrimony of his father and

Restoration of the northern counties.

mother[2]. Hugh Bigod, the veteran intriguer, who had yet
again to signalise himself as a rebel, surrendered his castles[3];
and king Malcolm of Scotland restored the northern counties.
The king made a pilgrimage to S. Edmund's, where he wore
his crown on Whitsunday and held a great court[4]; and directly
after began to prepare for his first expedition to Wales. In
contemplation of this undertaking he assembled the whole
baronage at Northampton on the 17th of July[5]; and having
received the ambassadors of Frederick Barbarossa, and done

Expedition to Wales in 1157.

some legal business, he proceeded into the west. The force
necessary for the expedition was raised by an arrangement new
at least in England—every two knights joined to furnish a
third; so that a third of the whole body took part in the expedition[6]. The war was short, and not brilliant. The constable,

---

[1] John of Salisbury (ep. 128) mentions this scutage as levied to enable
Henry to make war on his brother: ' Verum interim scutagium remittere
non potest, et a quibusdam exactionibus abstinere, quoniam fratris gratia
male sarta nequidquam coiit.'

[2] R. de Monte, A.D. 1157.　　　　　　　　　　　　　　　[3] Ibid.

[4] Chron. de Bello, pp. 84, 85; Pipe Roll, p. 107.

[5] ' Convocati sunt ad eum praesules et principes regni, abbates nonnulli,
aliique inferioris ordinis personae;' Gervase, i. 163, 165; Radewic, ap.
Urstis. p. 325.

[6] ' Circa festivitatem S. Johannis Baptistae rex Henricus praeparavit
maximam expeditionem ita ut duo milites de tota Anglia tertium pararent
ad opprimendum Gualenses terra et mari;' R. de Monte, A.D. 1157.

Henry of Essex, was charged with cowardice in letting fall the royal standard ; and the king returned, scarcely claiming the fame of victory. The negotiations with Malcolm went on through the summer; part of the time the two kings were hunting in the Peak [1]. The king of Scots did homage at Chester. Then or soon after the final surrender of Northumberland and Cumberland was made, and Malcolm received, as the inheritance of his grandmother, the daughter of Waltheof, the county of Huntingdon. Henry wore his crown that Christmas at Lincoln, not however venturing into the cathedral, for this was forbidden by a superstition already of old standing, but attending mass in the church of S. Mary Wigford [2]. The year is not marked as one of great judicial activity.

Coronation at Lincoln in 1157.

Six months of 1158 were spent in England; at Easter the king wore his crown at Worcester [3]. In the summer he went into Cumberland, where he knighted William of Warenne on Midsummer Day [4]; and in August he went to France, where he secured the inheritance of his brother Geoffrey who was just dead, and negotiated the marriage of his eldest son with a daughter of Lewis VII. Early in the next year he betrothed his second son Richard to a daughter of the count of Barcelona, and formed a plan for enforcing the claim of his wife on the county of Toulouse [5].

The year 1158.

Expedition to France in 1158.

Henry's foreign wars affect our subject only as being the causes which prompted some of those financial measures which illustrate his genius for organisation. And amongst them the war of Toulouse is perhaps the most important : for it is the epoch at which the institution of scutage, as a pecuniary commutation for personal service in the host, is fixed by the common consent of lawyers and historians. The king's position was a somewhat difficult one. It was scarcely fair to call on the military tenants of England and Normandy to fight as a

The war of Toulouse, in 1159.

---

[1] Pipe Roll, pp. 90, 152 ; R. de Monte, A.D. 1157.
[2] Pipe Roll, p. 136; W. Newb. ii. c. 9 ; Hoveden, i. 216.
[3] Hoveden, i. 216 ; Pipe Roll, p. 175.
[4] 'In festivitate S. Johannis Baptistae ;' R. de Monte ; Hoveden, i. 216 ; Chron. Mailros. p. 168 ; Pipe Roll, pp. 119, 175.
[5] R. de Monte, A.D. 1158, 1159.

matter of duty for the aggrandisement of the estates of the duke
of Aquitaine.   The English baronage might indeed rejoice in
the opportunity of signalising themselves before so splendid a
king and in a new land; but not so the bulk of the knightly force.
Still less could the national force of the country be armed in
such a cause.   Henry was willing to fight with mercenaries, if
England and Normandy would provide him with the funds:
such a force would be far more manageable during the campaign, and less dangerous when it was over.   A precedent was
found in the ancient fyrdwite, the fine paid by the Anglo-Saxon
warrior who failed to follow his king to the field[1].   But instead of being a punishment, it was now regarded as a privilege; those tenants of the crown who did not choose to go to

war, paid a tax of two marks on the knight's fee[2].   With this,
and a very large accumulation of treasure from other sources,
amounting, according to the contemporary writers, to £180,000,
Henry undertook the subjugation of Toulouse.   The whole
court accompanied him : the king of Scots, the first of the
tenants-in-chief, William of Boulogne, son of the late king,
and the chancellor Becket, are especially mentioned.   The expedition lasted for three months, and, although marked by some
brilliant exploits, was unsuccessful.   Henry did not take Toulouse, although he reduced most of the territory to submission.
He would not bear arms against Lewis VII[3], who was his

[1] Above, p. 209.

[2] A scutage of two marks on the knight's fee is accounted for in the
Rolls of the fifth year.   According to Alexander Swerford, the author of
the Liber Ruber, it was for an expedition to Wales ; Madox, Hist. Exch.
p. 436 : but no such expedition was made.   Gervase, i. 167, says that the
king exacted £180,000 by way of scutage from England this year.   The
sum is impossible, and is probably made by multiplying the supposed
number of knights' fees (60,000) by the sum of sixty shillings, which was
the amount levied on the knight's fee in Normandy; R. de Monte, A.D.
1159.   But the shillings are Angevin, i.e. worth one-fourth of the English;
and the knights' fees were very far from being 60,000.   See above, p. 468.
Becket's enemies alleged that he advised the impost, and his friends regarded his subsequent troubles as a judgment on that account.   See Gilbert
Foliot, ep. 194; Joh. Salisb. ep. 145.   There is no doubt about the character of this scutage.   John of Salisbury says : 'Tolosam bello aggressurus,
omnibus contra antiquum morem et debitam libertatem indixit ecclesiis, ut
pro arbitrio ejus satraparum suorum conferrent in censum ;' ep. 145 : he
regards the chancellor as accountable for it.

[3] Robert de Monte simply says, 'urbem tamen Tolosam noluit obsidere,

feudal lord, and with whom he was at peace, although Lewis
was actively supporting the count of Toulouse against him, and
the Norman lords were fighting on their own border. This
war was however followed by a quarrel between the two kings,
which detained Henry at a distance from England until the
month of January, 1163.

Long absence of Henry from England.

During this long period the country was administered by
the justices, the queen or the young Henry occasionally presiding in the court or at the councils : the rolls of account show
that the business of justice and taxation went on without difficulties, and the historians detail little more than the successions
of bishops and abbots.   The most important of these was the
election of the chancellor to the see of Canterbury, which took
place in the presence of the justiciar, in May, 1162 ; the electors
on this occasion being the bishops of the province.   This event
closes the ministerial career of Becket, and forms an epoch in
the reign of Henry, which serves to mark off one period of his
political activity.

Quiet administration during the years 1158–1163.

Up to this time his labours had been confined mainly to the
work of restoration.   The scheme adopted at Wallingford had
deferens honorem Ludovico.'   The Draco Normannicus gives more details,
which are worthy of note :—

> 'Rex velut orator legiones convocat, adsunt
>   Et regni proceres, militiaeque duces.
>   *   *   *   *
> Orditur, narrat, confirmat, sicque refutat,
>   Claudit, et ex istis quatuor illa regit ;
> An dominum regem clausum subvertat et urbem,
>   An vivum capiat consul et ipsa ruat ;
> Urgeat an clausos muris ad deditionem,
>   Exspectet potius hanc sine rege capi ?
>   *   *   *   *
> Consulit inde duces, quaerit, deliberat, ex his
>   Quatuor utilius quid sibi quidve suis.
> Quidlibet ex primis tribus his vis militis audax
>   Expetit, hortatur, id feritate cupit.
> Ingenium procerum simul experientia rerum
>   Ut quartum teneat consulit illud agat ;
> Regibus Anglorum facinus miserabile regem
>   Frangere Francorum, deditione premi.
> Clausis parcendum, pietatem solvere victis,
>   Urbem ne repleat planctibus, igne, nece.
> Consilio procerum rex regi parcit et urbi,
>   Pars patriae fuerat jamque subacta sibi.'
>   Lib. i. c. 12.

Completion
of the
scheme of
reform.
been carried out strictly: the castles had been demolished or
taken into the royal hands, and the mercenaries with their
foreign leaders dismissed; the royal estates had been as far as
was possible restored to cultivation, farmhouses and palaces had
alike been rebuilt[1]; the courts of justice had been in full
activity, and severe sentences had everywhere been executed
upon the malefactors who had enjoyed impunity for many
years: in particular the coiners of false or debased money had
been rigidly punished. The successive scutages had shown
that the king needed an increased revenue, and that he knew
how to raise it; and the measures taken for levying a force
against the Welsh in 1157, and for the war of Toulouse, showed
that, young as Henry was, he had a plan and policy of his own.

Disarming
of the feudal
party.
Nothing in fact could have been wiser than to disarm that
feudal party from which he had most to fear, by accepting their
money instead of leaning on their armed support. It is not to
be supposed that during these years Henry showed no signs of
that ingenuity in the development of legal institutions which
especially marks the next period of the reign. William of
Newburgh mentions, among his very first acts, the careful provision made for provincial as well as for central judicature[2].

Improve-
ments in
judicial pro-
cedure.
We learn from the lives of S. Thomas that the chancellor himself was constantly employed in hearing causes[3], and so great
was the interest which Henry took in such matters that, on one
occasion during the constant litigation in which the abbey of
Battle was involved, the ordinary form of charter being insufficient for the emergency, the king himself drew up the
document required[4]. It is almost certain then that some part

---

[1] R. de Monte marks the year 1161 as a period of building. Among
other erections, ' domum leprosorum juxta Cadomum mirabilem aedificavit:
aulam et cameras ante turrim Rothomagi nihilominus renovavit, et non
solum in Normannia sed etiam in regno Angliae, ducatu Aquitaniae,
comitatu Andegaviae, Cenomanniae, Turonensi, castella, mansiones regias,
vel nova aedificavit, vel vetera emendavit.'

[2] ' Ordinatisque in cunctis regni finibus juris et legum ministris qui vel
improborum audaciam coercerent, vel interpellantibus secundum causarum
merita justitiam exhiberent. . . . Quoties autem, judicibus mollius agentibus,
provincialium querimoniis pulsabatur, provisionis regiae remedium adhibe-
bat;' W. Newb. ii. c. i.

[3] Roger of Pontigny, Vita S. Thom. (ed. Giles), i. 102.

[4] Chron. de Bello, p. 165.

of the legal reforms of the reign had been set on foot already, although the text of no formal document of the kind is now extant.   The references made in the Constitutions of Clarendon to the system of recognitions and juries of presentment, seem to justify us in inferring that, whether or no these customs are rightly described as belonging to the reign of Henry I, there is the utmost probability that they had been recognised as part of the ordinary course of law since the beginning of the reign of Henry II, although not in the complete form which was given them in his later acts.   In Normandy he had been active in the same way.   In the beginning of the year 1160, having held his Christmas court at Falaise, he had ordained that no dean should accuse any man without the evidence of neighbours who bore a good character; and that in the treatment of all causes, the magistrates of the several districts at their monthly courts should determine nothing without the witness of the neighbours, 'should do injustice to no man, inflict nothing to the prejudice of any, should maintain the peace, and punish all robbers summarily; and that the churches should enjoy their own in peace[1].'   It is improbable that England should not have felt the same innovating policy; but in the absence of distinct record it cannot be proved.   And accordingly it is impossible to say with certainty that any of the known reforms of the reign were the work of the chancellor, whose influence during these early years was supreme with the king.

Similar reform in Normandy.

Law reforms, 1155-1162.

139. As soon however as Henry returned to England after five years' absence, in January, 1163, he began to apply to public business even more zealously than before.   Early in March he is found in council, hearing the wearisome cause of Richard de Anesty, at London[2]; at the end of the month, at

The year 1163.

---

[1] R. de Monte, A.D. 1160; Bouquet, xiii. 304 : 'Rex Anglorum Henricus ad Natale Domini fuit apud Falesiam et leges instituit ut nullus decanus aliquam personam accusaret sine testimonio vicinorum circum manentium qui bonae vitae fama laudabiles haberentur.   De causis similiter quorumlibet ventilandis instituit ut, cum judices singularum provinciarum singulis mensibus ad minus simul convenirent, sine testimonio vicinorum nihil judicarent, injuriam nemini facerent, praejudicium non irrogarent, pacem tenerent, latrones cunctos statim punirent, quaeque quiete tenerent ecclesiae sua jura possiderent.'   [2] Palgrave, Commonwealth, p. xxii.

Windsor, he presided at the trial in which Henry of Essex the Constable was appealed for treason by Robert de Montfort, and having been defeated in trial by battle, forfeited his great inheritance [1]. After a hurried expedition into Wales, he was on the 1st of July at Woodstock, where the king of Scots and the princes and lords of Wales did homage to the heir, and where the king's first great trouble, the quarrel with Becket, began [2].

History of Becket.

This famous person, who had been selected by Archbishop Theobald as the fittest adviser of the young king, was endowed with many brilliant and serviceable gifts. He was an able man of business, versatile, politic; liberal even to magnificence; well skilled in the laws of England, and not deficient in the accomplishments of either clerk or knight. His singular career illustrates at once the state of the clergy at the time and his own power of adapting himself, apparently with a good conscience, to each of the three great schools of public life in turn. The clergy of the Norman reigns may be arranged under three classes: there is the man of the thoroughly secular type, like Roger of Salisbury, a minister of state and a statesman, who has received high preferment in the Church as a reward for official service; there is the professional ecclesiastic, like Henry of Winchester, who looks to the interests of the Church primarily, whose public course is dictated by regard for clerical objects, who aims at a mediatorial position in the conflicts of the State, and who has close relations with the great ecclesiastical centre at Rome; and there is, thirdly, the man who, not less patriotic than the first and not less ecclesiastical than the second, acts on and lives up to higher principles of action, and seeks first and last what seems to him to be the glory of God. This last class is represented to some extent by Anselm; it is not numerous and in an age of monastic sanctity and pretension is especially exposed to the intrusion of false brethren, such as the fanatic who is ambitious of martyrdom, or the

Becket a representative man of three schools.

---

[1] Palgrave, Commonwealth, p. xxii; R. de Monte, A.D. 1163. See also the Chronicle of Jocelin of Brakelond (ed. Camden Soc. pp. 50–52).

[2] R. Diceto, i. 311.

hypocrite who will endure the risks of persecution provided he obtains the honour of popularity. Thomas Becket lived through all three phases, and friends and enemies to the present day debate to which of the two divisions of the last class his life and death assign him. His promotion to Canterbury put an end to the first act of his career. Until then he had been the chancellor, the lawyer, judge, financier, captain, and secretary of state. Now he became the primate, the champion of the clergy, the agent or patron of the Pope, whom he probably had persuaded Henry to recognise; the assertor of the rights of his Church and of his own constitutional position as first independent adviser of the Crown. The date at which he resigned the chancellorship is uncertain, but it seems clear that, before Henry's return from France, he had made himself enemies among his former associates by demanding from them restitution of estates belonging to the see of Canterbury which, as he maintained, they held unjustly, and by otherwise asserting the temporal claims of his see [1]. Henry was no doubt hurt by the resignation of the chancellor, but was scarcely prepared to find his late minister placing himself in an attitude of opposition which had no precedent in the history of the last hundred years. Anselm's quarrels arose from spiritual questions. Those of Thomas began on a purely secular point.

His alienation from the king.

Henry's resentment.

The account given by the contemporary writers of this first dispute is very obscure: it concerned however some question of taxation in which the king was anxious to make a change beneficial to the royal revenue. Every hide of land, we are told [2], paid to the sheriff two shillings annually, in consideration of his services in the administration and defence of the shire. This sum the king wished to have enrolled as part of the royal revenue, intending probably to reduce, as he afterwards did, the power of the sheriffs, or to remunerate them from some other fund. A tax so described bears a strong resemblance to the Danegeld, which was an impost of

Dispute at Woodstock on the revenue of 1163.

---

[1] Gervase, i. 174.
[2] Grim, V. S. Th. i. 21; ed. Robertson, ii. 375; R. Pont., S. T. C. i. 113; Garnier, p. 65; Will. Cant. ed. Robertson, i. 12; S. T. C. ii. 5. Round, Feudal England, p. 498, rejects the idea of connecting it with the Danegeld.

two shillings on the hide, and was collected by the sheriffs, being possibly compounded for at a certain rate, and paid by them into the Exchequer. As the Danegeld from this very year 1163 ceases to appear as a distinct item of account in the Pipe Rolls, it is impossible to avoid connecting the two ideas, even if we may not identify them. Whether the king's object in making this proposition was to collect the Danegeld in its full amount, putting an end to the nominal assessment which had been long in use, and so depriving the sheriffs of such profit as they made from it, or whether he had some other end in view, it is impossible now to determine; and consequently it is difficult to understand the position taken by the archbishop.

Becket's opposition to the king on a matter of taxation, July 1, 1163.

'We will not,' he is recorded to have said, 'my lord king, saving your good pleasure, give this money as revenue; but if the sheriffs and servants and ministers of the shires will perform their duties as they should, and maintain and defend our dependents, we will not be behindhand in contributing to their aid.' The king in anger answered, 'By the eyes of God, it shall be given as revenue, and it shall be entered in the king's accounts; and you have no right to contradict; no man wishes to oppress your men against your will.' Becket replied, 'My lord king, by the reverence of the eyes by which you have sworn, it shall not be given from my land, and from the rights of the Church not a penny[1].' We are not told further of the immediate result: but the king and his minister never met again as friends. This is, however the details may be understood, the first case of any opposition to the king's will in the matter of taxation which is recorded in our national history; and it would seem to have been, formally at least, successful.

Council of Westminster, Oct. 1163.

Three months after, in October, in the council of Westminster, a fresh constitutional quarrel broke out. Ever since the Conqueror had divided the temporal and spiritual courts of justice, the treatment of criminal clerks had been a matter of difficulty; the lay tribunals were prevented by the ecclesiastical ones from enforcing justice, and the ecclesiastical ones were able only to inflict spiritual penalties. The reasonable compromise which

---

[1] Grim, S. T. C. i. 22; ed. Robertson, pp. 376 sq.

had been propounded by the Conqueror himself, in the injunction that the lay officials should enforce the judgments of the bishops [1], had been rendered inefficacious by the jealousies of the two estates; and the result was that in many cases grossly criminal acts of clerks escaped unpunished, and gross criminals eluded the penalty of their crimes by declaring themselves clerks. The fact that the king took up the question at this moment seems to show that he was already undertaking the reform of the criminal law which he carried into effect three years after. He proposed that the anomalous state of things should cease; that clerical criminals should be brought before the temporal court and accused there; if they pleaded not guilty they were to be tried in the ecclesiastical court; if found guilty, to be degraded there and brought back to the temporal court for punishment as laymen [2]. Becket resisted; it was sufficient that the criminal should be degraded; if he offended again, he offended as a layman, and the king might take him; but the first punishment was sufficient for the first offence. The king on the same occasion complained heavily of the exactions of the ecclesiastical courts, and proposed to the assembled bishops that they should promise to abide by the customs which regulated those courts and the rights of the clergy generally, as they had been allowed in the days of his grandfather. The archbishop saw that to concede this unreservedly would be to place the whole of the clergy at the king's mercy: he prevailed on the bishops to assent 'saving their order,' and the king, irritated by the opposition, left the assembly in anger. Immediately after he ordered the archbishop to resign the honours of Eye and Berkhampsted which had been committed to him as chancellor [3].

After two or three unsatisfactory interviews with Becket, the

Marginal notes: Dispute about the criminous clerks. Disputes in 1163. Henry complains of the extortion of the ecclesiastical courts. Open quarrel.

---

[1] See above, p. 307. If the excommunicated person was obdurate for forty days, the king issued a writ to the sheriff to seize him and compel him to satisfy the church; Rot. Cl. ii. 166.

[2] I have adopted the conclusion of Pollock and Maitland, Eng. Law, i. 431: but the matter is far from clear, and was not clear at the time. See Hoveden, i. 219; Gervase, i. 174; Grim, S. T. C. i. 22; ed. Robertson, ii. 376; R. Pontigny, S. T. C. i. 115 sq.; Anon. Lambeth, S. T. C. ii. 88.

[3] Herbert of Bosham, S. T. C. iii. 111; ed. Robertson, iii. 275. He had held them since 1156, and probably from his first appointment as chancellor; Pipe Roll, 2 Hen. II.

king called together at Clarendon, in January 1164, the whole
body of the bishops and barons[1]. Again the archbishop was
bidden to accept the customs in use under Henry I; and again
he declined doing anything unconditionally. Then the king
ordered that they should be reduced to writing, having been
first ascertained by recognition. The recognitors, according to
the formal record, were the archbishops, bishops, earls, barons,
and most noble and ancient men of the kingdom; according to
the archbishop, Richard de Lucy the justiciar and Jocelin de
Bailleul[2], a French lawyer of whom little else is known, were
the real authors of the document, which was presented as the
result of the inquiry, and which has become famous under the
name of the 'Constitutions of Clarendon.'

140. The Constitutions of Clarendon are sixteen in number,
and purport to be, as the history of their production shows
them to have been, a report of the usages of Henry I on the
disputed points. They concern questions of advowson and
presentation, churches in the king's gift, the trial of clerks, the
security to be taken of the excommunicated, the trial of laymen
for spiritual offences, the excommunication of tenants-in-chief,
the licence of the clergy to go abroad, ecclesiastical appeals,
which are not to go further than the archbishop without the
consent of the king; questions of the title to ecclesiastical
estates, the baronial duties of the prelates, the election to
bishoprics and abbacies, the right of the king to the goods of
felons deposited under the protection of the Church, and the
ordination of villeins[3]. Such of these as are of importance to
our subject may be noticed elsewhere: it is enough at present
to remark that, while some of the Constitutions only state in
legal form the customs which had been adopted by the Conqueror
and his sons, others of them seem to be developments or expansions of such customs in forms and with applications that belong
to a much more advanced state of the law. The baronial status

---

[1] ' Ex mandato regis, concurrentibus episcopis et proceribus ;' R. Diceto,
i. 312. Cf. Gervase, i. 176; 'generale concilium;' W. Fitz-Stephen (S. T. C.
i. 215; Robertson, iii. 46). [2] Robertson, Becket, p. 97.
[3] Gervase, i. 178–180; Select Charters (ed. 3), pp. 137–140. With the
Constitutions generally compare the *Stabilimentum* of Philip II; Ordonn.
des Rois, i. 39, sq.

of the bishops is unreservedly asserted, the existence of the Their importance as Curia Regis as a tribunal of regular resort, the right of the illustrating bishops to sit with the other barons in the Curia until a question the progress of Henry's of blood occurs, the use of juries of twelve men of the vicinity schemes for the reform for criminal causes and for recognition of claims to land, all of law. these are stated in such a way as to show that the jurisprudence of which they were a part was known to the country at large. Accordingly, the institution of the Great Assize—the edict by which the king empowered the litigant who wished to avoid the trial by battle to obtain a recognition of his right by inquest of jury—must be supposed to have been issued at an earlier period of the reign: and the use of the jury of accusation, which is mentioned in the Laws of Ethelred but only indistinctly traceable later, must have been revived before the year 1164. And if this be so, the Constitutions of Clarendon assume a character which the party statements of Becket's biographers have not allowed them. They are no mere engine of tyranny, or secular The Constitutions of spite against a churchman: they are really a part of a great Clarendon part of the scheme of administrative reform, by which the debateable general scheme of ground between the spiritual and temporal powers can be legal reform. brought within the reach of common justice, and the lawlessness arising from professional jealousies abolished. That they were really this, and not an occasional weapon of controversy, may be further inferred from the rapidity with which they were drawn up, the completeness of their form, and the fact that, notwithstanding the storm that followed, they formed the groundwork of the later customary practice in all such matters.

To Becket however and his followers they presented them- Becket's reception of selves in no such light. The archbishop had come the year them, 1164. before from the council of Tours[1] in an excited state of mind, of which the council of Woodstock saw the first evidence. He best of all men must have known the beneficial effects which the kingdom at large had experienced from the king's legal measures. Yet he declared them to be incompatible with the freedom of the clergy. At last, moved by the entreaties of his brethren, whom the king's threats had frightened, he declared his

[1] May 19, 1163; Gervase, i. 173.

acceptance of the Constitutions : but with so much reluctance and with so many circumstances on which no consistent testimony is attainable, that the impression given at the time was that he was temporising, if not dealing deceitfully. He sent immediately to ask the forgiveness of the pope, as having betrayed the interests of the Church [1].

Fatal quarrel.

From this moment the intrigues of the archbishop's enemies, intrigues for which his own conduct had given the opportunity, although it afforded no justification, left him no rest. In vain he appealed to the king: Henry was too deeply wounded to forgive, and was too much determined on his own policy of reform to think of yielding; and the courtiers were resolved *Council of Northamp-ton, October, 1164.* that no reconciliation should take place. In the following October a council was called at Northampton [2], to which the archbishop was summoned, not, as was the custom, by the first summons issued specially to him as the first counsellor of the crown, but by a common summons addressed to the sheriff of Kent and ordering him to cite the archbishop to answer the claims of John the Marshal [3]. At that council his ruin was completed: he was overwhelmed by the king's demand that he should produce the accounts of the chancery, and by the charges *Becket goes into exile.* of his enemies. In despair of justice, in fear of his life, or in the new ambition of finishing the third phase of his career by exile or martyrdom, he fled from Northampton and soon after took refuge in France, where, partly by threats of spiritual punishment, partly by intrigues, and partly by invoking the legal interference of a pope who had little sympathy with his sufferings, he conducted a struggle which fills the chronicles of the next six years.

---

[1] Robertson, Becket, pp. 101–103.

[2] 'Convenerunt illuc episcopi, comites, barones totius regni, mandato regis urgente;' R. Diceto, i. 313. 'Solemne statuens celebrare concilium, omnes qui de rege tenerent in capite mandari fecit; citatus est et archi-episcopus;' Grim, S. T. C. i. 39; ed. Robertson, ii. 390. 'Generale con-cilium;' W. Fitz-Steph. S. T. C. i. 218; ed. Robertson, iii. 49. 'Episcopos et abbates, comites etiam et proceres, et omnes officiales suos, omnesque omnino qui alicujus essent auctoritatis vel nominis;' Roger of Pontigny, S. T. C. i. 132.

[3] W. Fitz-Stephen, S. T. C. i. 220; ed. Robertson, iii. 51.

During the greatest part of this time Henry also was absent Henry's movements, 1164–1166.
from England. He paid a hurried visit to Normandy in 1165,
and on his return made his third expedition to Wales. Early
in 1166 he held a council of the clergy at Oxford [1], and a great
assembly of the bishops and baronage at Clarendon [2]. He had Affairs of 1166.
just negotiated a marriage for his eldest daughter with Henry
the Lion Duke of Saxony, who was now in close alliance with
Frederick Barbarossa, and was supposed to be intending to join
the party of the anti-pope. Harassed by the attacks of Becket,
in want of money for the dowry of his daughter, invited by the
emperor to join the schismatic party, committed to it by his
own envoys, and drawn back from such a gross mistake by
Earl Robert of Leicester the justiciar, who refused the kiss of
peace to the archbishop of Cologne when acting as the imperial
ambassador [3], Henry showed himself still the master of the
situation. It is to this period that we owe the Assize of The Assize of Clarendon, 1166.
Clarendon, which remodelled the provincial administration of
justice, and the valuable series of documents which are contained
in the Black Book of the Exchequer. Immediately after the
council of Clarendon the king went to France, where he was
employed in the acquisition of Brittany and in counteracting
the intrigues of Becket until March, 1170. In these years he
lost some of his oldest counsellors; the empress in 1167,
Geoffrey de Mandeville in 1166, Earl Robert of Leicester in
1168, and Bishop Nigel of Ely in 1169. He had however now
gained sufficient experience in affairs to be independent of his
ministers—he never again submitted to the advice of a friend

---

[1] R. Diceto, i. 318; Ann. Theokesb. (ed. Luard), p. 49; W. Newb. ii. c.
13. This council is sometimes misdated, as if it belonged to 1160 or 1161.
But the king was abroad in those years, and the direct evidence of Ralph
de Diceto is amply sufficient to fix the year.

[2] This assembly is mentioned by Grim, and Roger of Pontigny, as one
in which an oath was exacted from the bishops that they would not appeal
to the pope; S. T. C. i. 55, 156; ed. Robertson, ii. 405. The Pipe Rolls
for the year mention the king's residence at Clarendon, and give several
payments made for wine, carriage, fish, etc.; as well as for wax to seal the
summonses, for the conduct of approvers, and for the wages of the summoners. See Bened. Pet. ii. pref. lxi; Eyton, Court, Household and Itinerary of Hen. II, pp. 89, 90.

[3] R. Diceto, i. 318.

such as Becket had been; and in the family of the old ministers of the Exchequer he found a number of trained clerks who, without aspiring to influential places in the government, were skilful and experienced in every department of ministerial work. Bishop Nigel had left a son for whom he had purchased in 1159[1] the office of treasurer, Richard Fitz-Neal, the author of the Dialogus de Scaccario, afterwards bishop of London. Another of his clerks, probably a kinsman, earned an unhappy notoriety during the Becket quarrel as Richard of Ilchester[2]; he was a man of consummate skill in diplomacy as well as finance, acted as justiciar of Normandy, and was constantly employed as a justice and baron of the Exchequer at home. The office of chancellor was not filled up during Becket's life, some distinguished chaplain of the king usually acting as protonotary, vice-chancellor or keeper of the seal[3]. The office of justiciar was retained by Richard de Lucy, whose fidelity to the king, notwithstanding his devotion to the memory of Becket[4], and his frank determination, where he could, to assert the rights of the nation, earned him the honourable title of Richard de Lucy the Loyal[5].

141. The credit of having drawn up the Assize of Clarendon[6]

---

[1] Hist. Eliens. Ang. Sac. i. 627.

[2] Richard of Ilchester was a writer or clerk in the Curia and Exchequer from the beginning of the reign of Henry II; Pipe Roll, pp. 30, 31, 98. He became archdeacon of Poictiers before 1164, and was made bishop of Winchester in 1174. His illegitimate son, Herbert bishop of Salisbury, was called *Pauper* or *le Poor*, a name which belonged peculiarly to the family of Roger of Salisbury the justiciar. So that it is most probable that Richard was a kinsman of Nigel, whose son, the bishop of London, speaks of him with great respect in the Dialogus de Scaccario. He was a kinsman also of Gilbert Foliot; S. T. C. v. 291.

[3] Matthew, the king's chancellor, who is mentioned in a letter of Foliot to the pope (S. T. C. v. 201), is probably the king's old tutor. See above, p. 485. A clerk named Walter kept the seal in 1166; S. T. C. iv. 185. Geoffrey Ridel also appears as keeper. But the most important functions seem to have been discharged by John of Oxford and Richard of Ilchester. See Eyton, Court, &c. of Hen. II, pp. 100, 174.

[4] He founded the Augustinian abbey of Lesnes in Kent in honour of the martyr, and became a canon there after his resignation; Ben. Pet. i. 238; Mon. Angl. vi. 456.

[5] Jordan Fantosme (ed. Michel), p. 70.

[6] The Assize of Clarendon was long known only through the Assize of Northampton, published ten years later: it was first printed by Sir F. Palgrave, Commonwealth, pp. clxvi–clxxi. It will be found, edited from a

must be divided between the king and his advisers. Whether
or no it owes some part of its importance to the loss of the legal
enactments that had preceded it, it is the most important document of the nature of law, or edict, that has appeared since the
Conquest; and, whether it be regarded in its bearing on legal
history, or in its ultimate constitutional results, it has the
greatest interest. The council in which it was passed is described as consisting of the archbishops, bishops, abbots, earls,
and barons of all England; Becket however was not present,
and the assembly probably, amongst its minor acts, issued some
sentence against him and his relations. The Assize contains no
mention of him. It is arranged in twenty-two articles, which
were furnished to the judges about to make a general provincial
visitation[1]. Of these the first six describe the manner in which
the presentment of criminals to the courts of the justices or the
sheriff is henceforth to be made. Inquest is to be held, and
juries of twelve men of the hundred, and four men of the township, are to present all persons accused of felony by public
report; these are to go to the ordeal, and to fare as that test
may determine. By the other articles all men are directed to
attend the county courts, and to join, if required, in these presentments[2]; no franchise is to exclude the justices, and no one
may entertain a stranger for whom he will not be responsible
before them; an acknowledgment made before the hundred
court cannot be withdrawn before the justices[3]; even the result
of the ordeal is not to save from banishment the man of bad

better MS., in Select Charters (ed. 3), pp. 143–146; also in my edition of
Benedict of Peterborough, vol. ii. app. pp. cxlix–cliv; Hoveden, ii. cii–cv,
248–252. It has not unnaturally been confused with the Constitutions of
Clarendon; and even Gervase, who was a contemporary, describes the
Assize of Northampton as a re-enactment of the act of Clarendon: 'Pro
cujus exsecrandis institutis beatus martyr Thomas Cantuariensis usque in
septennium exulavit;' i. 258. The Assize and the Constitutions have
nothing in common.

[1] This Assize seems to be referred to in the Dialogus de Scaccario, ii. c.
10: as 'arctior assisa quam rex propter sceleratos constituit;' and 'Regia
constitutio quae est pro bono pacis;' ibid.

[2] 'Homines de Tichesoura debent v. marcas quia noluerunt jurare assisam
regis;' Pipe Roll of 1166.

[3] Compare this with Glanvill, lib. viii. c. 9. It seems to be the first
mention of the distinction of a court of record from one not of record; but
see Ll. Will. c. 24.

character who has been presented by the inquest; one sheriff is to assist another in the pursuit and capture of fugitives. The sessions of the justices are to be held in full county court. Two curious articles touching the ecclesiastical relations of the State follow; no convent or college is to receive any of the mean people into their body without good testimony as to character, and the heretics condemned at the recent council of Oxford are to be treated as outlaws. The Assize is to hold good so long as the king shall please.

Its import-
ance as a
legal monu-
ment.

In this document we may observe several marks of the permanence of the old common law of the country. Not only is the agency of the shire-moot and hundred-moot—the four best men of the township, and the lord with his steward— applied to the execution of the edict, but the very language of the ancient laws touching strangers and fugitive felons is repeated [1]. The inquest itself may be native or Norman, but there is no doubt as to the character of the machinery by which it is to be transacted. In the article which directs the admission of the justices into every franchise may be detected one sign of the anti-feudal policy which the king had all his life to maintain.

It is enforced
by a judicial
eyre.

The visitation took place in the spring and summer of 1166; two justices, the earl of Essex and Richard de Lucy, travelled over the whole country [2], and the proceeds of their investiga-tions swell the accounts of the Pipe Roll of the year to an

Strict en-
forcement.

unusual size. The enormous receipts under the heads of placita [3], the chattels of those who failed in the ordeal [4], fines exacted from the men who refused to swear under the king's assize [5], the goods of those hanged under the Assize of Claren-don [6], the expenses of the gaols which the Assize ordered to be

---

[1] Compare with the clause about strangers, the Laws of Edward the Confessor, c. 23; Canute, sec. 28; William I, i. 48; Henry I, 8, § 5.

[2] In eighteen counties assizes were held by Richard de Lucy, who was accompanied by the earl of Essex in seventeen out of the number.

[3] Some extracts will be found in Madox, Hist. Exch. pp. 235, 236.

[4] 'De catallis fugitivorum et eorum qui perierunt in judicio aquae;' Roll of 1166: this entry occurs in a large number of counties.

[5] See above, p. 507: cf. pp. 428, 429, above.

[6] 'De catallis fugitivorum et suspensorum per assisam de Clarendon;' Roll of 1169.

built or to be put in good repair[1], mark the accounts of this and several succeeding years. These entries, which have nothing corresponding with them in the rolls of the earlier years, seem to suggest the conclusion that the act from which they resulted was really a great measure of innovation; an attempt to invigorate the local administration of justice, and the initiative measure of a newly-developed principle of judicial process; a distinct step forwards in the policy of bringing the royal jurisdiction into close connexion with the popular courts, and thus training the nation to the concentration of the powers of the people in the representative parliaments of later ages.

The immediate results of the Assize were by no means transient; the visitation of 1166 was followed by an itinerant survey of the forests in 1167, and in 1168 by a thorough circuit of the shires[2], held by the barons of the Exchequer mainly for the purpose of collecting the aid which Henry demanded for the marriage of his eldest daughter. It is not improbable that the discussion of this aid took place in the council of Clarendon in 1166[3], for Henry was not in England between that date and the time when the money was collected; but it is possible that it was taken as a matter of course under the recognised feudal principles in such cases. The assessment was one mark on the knight's fee[4]; and the number of knights' fees on which it was assessed was certified by the landowners themselves. The collection of the money occupied the barons for two years[5], and, as appears from the action of the next

Subsequent measures of provincial jurisdiction.

The aid of 1168.

---

[1] The expenses of gaols at Canterbury, Rochester, Huntingdon, Cambridge, Sarum, Malmesbury, Aylesbury, and Oxford are accounted for in the Roll of 1166.

[2] Alan de Nevill held the forest courts in 1167; in 1168 the barons who took the aid were Richard of Ilchester, Reginald of Warenne, William Basset, and Guy the Dean of Waltham; besides these, Richard de Lucy acted in Yorkshire and Cumberland, Henry Fitz-Gerold in Kent, and William Fitz-John in Dorset and Somerset; Roll of 1168.

[3] The purchase of a hutch, 'Una huchia ad custodiendas cartas baronum de militibus' (Roll of 1166), would seem to fix the date of the documents preserved in the Liber Niger; Madox, Hist. Exch. p. 400. See also Eyton, Court, &c. of Henry II, pp. 89–91. On the importance of this measure, see Round, Feudal England, pp. 236–246.

[4] Madox, Hist. Exch. p. 398.

[5] The same officers acted as in 1168, with the addition of John Cumin, afterwards archbishop of Dublin, and Gervase of Cornhell.

year, did not satisfy the king, whilst it called forth great complaints on the part of the people. The visitation of the barons
was used for judicial as well as financial purposes, the sheriffs
had great opportunities of enforcing justice as well as of making perquisites, and the exaction, following so close on the
severe assize of 1166, led men not unreasonably to regard the
mechanism employed for the repression of crime as one of a
series of expedients for increasing the receipts of the Exchequer. The murmurs of the people reached the king in
Normandy; and he had by this time other reasons for paying
a visit to England.

142. He was now thoroughly weary of the Becket controversy, and the pertinacious underhand hostility of Lewis VII.
He had succeeded in compelling the Bretons to submit to
Geoffrey his third son, whom he had married to the heiress of
Count Conan; and he was anxious to obtain for his son Henry
the right to govern England as viceroy or sharer in the rights
of the crown, which could be conferred only by the rite of
coronation. With this object in view he returned in March,
1170, and held a great court at Easter at Windsor, and another
immediately after at London. In the second assembly, which
coincided probably with the Easter session of the Exchequer,
he, by an extraordinary act of authority, removed all the
sheriffs of the kingdom from their offices, and issued a commission of inquiry into their receipts, which was to report to
him on the 14th of June, the day fixed for the coronation of
the younger Henry[1]. The commission of inquiry, the text of
which is extant, contains thirteen articles, which specify both
the matters to be investigated and the particular method by
which the information is to be obtained. The barons to whom
it is intrusted are to take the oaths of all the barons, knights,
and freeholders of each county, and to receive their evidence
as to the receipts of the sheriffs and the whole staff of their
servants, of the bishops and the whole host of their temporal
officers, of all the special administrators of the royal demesne,
of the itinerant officers of the Exchequer, and of all others who

[1] Bened. Pet. i. 5.

have had the opportunity of touching the public money: in Articles of inquest of Sheriffs, 1170.
particular, inquiry is to be made into the execution of the
Assize of Clarendon, whether it has been justly enforced, and
whether the officers employed in it have taken bribes or hush-
money; into the collection of the aid pur fille marier, and into
the profits of the forests: a supplementary article directs inquiry into the cases in which homage due to the king and his
son has not been paid[1]. The great amount of business which
thus accrued could not be dispatched in so short a time by the
same staff of officers; the inquest was taken by twelve 'Barons
errant,' clerk and lay, in the counties nearest London, and by
similar large commissions in the more distant shires; they
were probably composed mainly of the baronage of the district,
who would naturally scrutinise with some jealousy the pro-
ceedings of both the sheriffs and the judges[2]. The result was Removal of the sheriffs.
apparently the acquittal of the officials: whether or no this
was obtained by purchase[3], no further proceedings were taken
against them, but the sheriffs were not restored to their sheriffdoms, and had no further opportunity given them of making
their office a stepping-stone to greater wealth and position[4].
Henry placed in the vacant magistracies the officers of the Ex- New sheriffs.
chequer whom he knew and trusted; adopting in this respect

[1] Gervase, i. 217–219; Bened. Pet. ii. clvi. sq.; Select Charters (ed. 3),
pp. 148 sq. On the points of likeness between this document and the
Instructions given to the Karolingian Missi, see below, chap. xiii. § 164.

[2] Gervase gives the names of the Commissioners for the counties of Kent,
Surrey, Middlesex, Berkshire, Oxford, Buckingham, and Bedford:—the
abbots of S. Augustine's and Chertsey; the earl of Clare, William of
Avranches, Manasser of Dammartin, Gerold Fitz-Ralph, Gilbert de Pinkeni,
William Fitz-Helton, William Fitz-Neal, William Fitz-Martin, Ralph of
the Hospital, and Ralph de Dene. In Warwickshire and Leicestershire
Walter de Insula and Eustace Fitz-Stephen acted 'de Inquisitione Vice-
comitum Angliae;' Madox, Hist. Exch. p. 97.

[3] William Basset, who had been sheriff of Leicestershire, owed in the
19th year of Henry II 100 marks 'pro fine quem fecit cum rege de
jurata facta super eum de Inquisitione Vicecomitum Angliae;' Madox,
Hist. Exch. p. 97.

[4] The Chronicle of Benedict, i. 5, says that some of the sheriffs were
shortly after replaced; but an examination of the list of the sheriffs, given
in the thirty-first Report of the Deputy-Keeper, shows that it was done in
very few cases, and that none of the sheriffs now removed were employed
again, except those who were members of the Curia Regis, as Ranulf
Glanvill and William Basset.

the plan of his grandfather, who had used his judges for sheriffs, although he avoided throwing too many of the counties into any single hand : the Curia Regis and the shire thus are brought together closer than ever, whilst a blow is struck at the local influence of the feudal lords.

Coronation of the young king, 1170.

The Whitsuntide of 1170 was however marked by a more critical event than the inquest of sheriffs. The heir was crowned as Henry III; the ceremony was performed not by Thomas of Canterbury, but by Roger of York, and the wife of the young king was not crowned with him. This act, which was intended by Henry as a sign and seal of power, was a most unfortunate mistake. He had, not unnaturally, supposed that it would strengthen the supreme authority to have in each division of his dominions a sufficient representative of royal majesty [1] : he found that he had placed a dangerous weapon in the hands of an undutiful son. The minor irregularities of the

It produces a crisis in the Becket quarrel.

coronation-day roused his enemies to frenzy; Thomas Becket asserted that the rights of Canterbury, of the English Church, of Christianity itself, were outraged by Archbishop Roger's intrusion ; and Lewis VII, hurt at the neglect of his daughter, and backed by the support of the family of Champagne, who combined careful orthodoxy with intense hatred of the house of Anjou, urged the pope to put the kingdom under interdict. Before these invitations took effect, Henry, alarmed as he might well be, hastened into France, reconciled his long quarrel with

Murder of the arch-bishop, Dec. 29, 1170.

the archbishop, and authorised his return. Becket returned in December, excommunicated the opposing bishops, provoked the king to utter his angry and hasty wish to be rid of him, and expiated his imprudent and unchristian violence by a cruel death, on the 29th of December, 1170.

He is hailed as a martyr.

He was at once hailed as a martyr by Lewis VII and the house of Champagne; the monks of Canterbury were ready to accept him as their patron saint after death, although they

---

[1] Benedict, i. 132 : 'Addens etiam in illo mandato quod quando ipse solus erat in regimine regni, nihil de jure suo amittebat, et modo dedecus esset cum sint plures in regenda terra, aliquid inde perdere.' These words, written in 1177, seem to furnish one clue to Henry's policy.

had cared little about him during his life: the tide of miracle began to flow immediately, and with it the tide of treason and disaffection around the person of the king.

143. Henry's anger and horror at the murder of the arch- Henry applies for absolution. bishop—an act which showed in its perpetrators not only great brutality, but a profound disregard for the king's reputation and for the public safety—urged him to apply at once in self-defence to Rome. That done, he must keep out of the way of the hostile legation which had been dispatched to Normandy. He collected his forces in the duchy, crossed to England in He visits Ireland, 1171. August, 1171, and thence to Ireland, where he remained, receiving the homages of the bishops and princes of that divided country, until he heard that the legates who were sent to absolve him had arrived in Normandy. This was in March, 1172. His absolution, May 21, 1172. On receiving the news he returned as rapidly as he had come, made his submission to the papal representatives, clearing himself by oath of all complicity in the death of Becket, renouncing the Constitutions of Clarendon, and swearing adhesion to Alexander III against the antipope. The submission was completed Repeated Sep. 27, 1172. at Avranches in September [1]. As one portion of the pacifica- Second coronation of the heir, Aug. 27, 1172. tion, the younger Henry was crowned a second time, on this occasion in company with his wife, at Winchester instead of Westminster, and by the archbishop of Rouen instead of the archbishop of York [2]. The long storm seemed to have ended in a profound calm. The king found time to demand a scutage from those barons who had not joined him in his Irish expedition [3], and set to work with characteristic elasticity on a scheme for a marriage of his youngest son John with the heiress of Maurienne.

144. But the momentary quiet was preparatory to the real burst of the storm, which had been long gathering in regions far more dangerous to Henry's power than the council-chamber of the pope. The long strain of the Becket quarrel had worn

---

[1] See Benedict, i. 31, 32; Hoveden, ii. 35–39.

[2] Bened. i. 31. The queen was anointed as well as crowned: the young king was crowned only.

[3] Madox, Hist. Exch. p. 438: 'De scutagio militum qui non abierunt in Hiberniam nec denarios nec milites pro se miserunt.'

out his patience, and the humiliation which attended the visit of the legates placed him before his barons in a position which no English sovereign had yet filled. He had become irritable and exacting, had alienated his wife, and failed to secure the love of his children. His very measures of reform had arrayed against him the many whose interests were affected by his reforms. A conspiracy against his life, contrived by Adam de Port, was discovered[1]. The feudal spirit was ready for its opportunity, which Lewis VII was eager to make. The old men who remembered Stephen's time were passing away, and the young ones were looking forward to the rule of a new generation. The Maurienne negotiation was the spark that set

the mass of disaffection in flame. The king's proposition, that a proper provision should be made for John, was opposed by his eldest son : he demanded a substantive share in the administration of the government; he would have England or Normandy to himself, or at least some territory of his own where he and his wife might be a real king and queen[2]. That he was prompted by Lewis VII and encouraged by promises of the lords of Normandy, England, and Anjou, the historian of the time distinctly asserts[3]; and the result gives some probability to the statement, although it is not probable that in England an actual conspiracy of any wide extent was on foot. At Midlent, 1173, the young Henry fled from his father, and went at

once to Lewis. The king immediately suspected treason, and set the castles of Normandy in a condition of defence. No time was lost on either side. Lewis called a council at Paris, in which he proposed to assist the young king to dethrone his father, and found a ready assent from the counts of Flanders, Boulogne, and Blois : the king of Scots, his brother David, and Hugh Bigod the earl of Norfolk, also undertook to support him, and received the promise of extensive honours to be bestowed if the rebellion were successful[4]. Each of the allies had

---

[1] Adam would not stand his trial, and was outlawed, but restored a few years after; Bened. i. 35. He joined the rebels in 1173 ; J. Fantosme, p. 62.
[2] Bened. i. 41. [3] Ibid. p. 42.
[4] Bened. i. 44, 45 ; Jordan Fantosme (Surtees Society), pp. 2–6, 15. The latter writer, who was a contemporary, describes a debate held by the

a different ground of offence : the count of Boulogne had a Henry's enemies in France. claim on Mortain—he had married the daughter of Stephen, and Henry had tried to purchase his rights over the Norman county; the counts of Blois and Flanders, besides their ancestral hatred to Normandy and their pious indignation on behalf of the martyr, had each his own private grudge; Henry had spared no man's interest in his determination to round off his territorial boundaries.

The war broke out in June; and the news of the invasion Outbreak of war in June, 1173. of Normandy provoked an immediate rebellion in England. The English earls had watched with disgust Henry's progressive measures for the extinction of feudal power. Their castles had been taken from them, their franchises invaded, their military service exacted or money taken in commutation: every advantage that the feudal obligation gave to the king he had used, but he had allowed them no liberty of tyranny in return. The most influential amongst them had still very Henry's enemies in England. great interests in Normandy: the earl of Leicester had the great fief of Breteuil; the earl of Chester was hereditary viscount of Avranches and Bayeux; William of Aumâle, the son of that Stephen who had been set up as a competitor against William Rufus, had both his lordship of Holderness and his great Norman county. Others had the fancied wrongs of a century to avenge; the Bigods and the Mowbrays, who had risen on the ruins of earlier feudatories, longed to realise their strength and consolidate their local power; the king of Scots, William the Lion, and his brother David, united the grudges of jealous neighbourhood with those of national dislike and feudal The English war was a rebellion of the Normans. discontent. The English rebellion comprised nearly all that portion of the baronage which inherited the traditions of the Conquest and the ancient Norman spirit. It was a Norman rebellion on English soil. They hated Henry as Count of Anjou not less heartily than they feared him as king of England.

The war of 1173 began in France. The count of Flanders War in France, 1173. invaded Normandy from the north, and took Aumâle and its

king of Scots before waging war in 'sun plenier parlement,' an early use of the word; p. 14.

count, too easily for the credit of the latter; Lewis invaded it
from the south-east, and besieged Verneuil; the earl of Chester

Henry's
victories.

at the same time raised Brittany in revolt. Henry, who had
an army of 10,000 Brabançon mercenaries in his pay[1], marched
to the relief of Verneuil, and drove Lewis out of the country:
he then moved with the utmost rapidity on Brittany, and took
the earl of Chester, with a host of Breton nobles, prisoners at
Dol. This energetic defence induced Lewis and the disobedient
sons to propose peace; but in the intervals of negotiation
Henry made the best use of his time; he brought Vendôme to
submission, and had completely humbled his enemies before
Christmas.

War in
England.

In England the struggle began later, and was practically
decided without the king's personal intervention. The govern-

The faithful
earls.

ment was still in the hands of Richard de Lucy: of the great
earls, William de Mandeville of Essex was faithful; so also
were William of Arundel the husband of Queen Adeliza,
Reginald of Cornwall the king's uncle, and Hamelin of Warenne
the king's brother; so too were Strongbow the conqueror of
Ireland, and the earls of Salisbury, Warwick, and Northampton,
but these earls were by no means a match in power or position for those of Chester, Leicester, and Derby[2]. The earl of
Gloucester, the king's cousin, tried to avoid taking part in the
struggle. All the bishops on both sides the water were
faithful, except Arnulf of Lisieux and Hugh of Durham, who

Proceedings
of the justi-
ciar in 1173.

tried to temporise[3]. Two of the faithful earls, those of
Essex and Arundel, were with the king in France; and the
defence of the country fell chiefly on the justiciar, who, on
hearing that the war had broken out in Normandy, determined
to strike the first blow. In July, accompanied by the earl of
Cornwall, he besieged Leicester, where the officers of the earl
had set up the standard of revolt: he burned the town, but
failed to take the castle. Leaving a force to continue the

---

[1] Benedict, i. 51.
[2] The list of the king's supporters is given in one of the MSS. of Benedict (vol. i. p. 51).
[3] Jord. Fantosme, pp. 26, 73.

siege, the justiciar, this time in company with Humfrey Bohun War in the
the constable, advanced on Berwick, where they were detained north in 1173.
until September, when the earl of Leicester with his wife and a
large force of Flemings landed in Norfolk, and was welcomed by
Hugh Bigod. On this news the justiciar hastened southwards Capture of
and, having been joined by the earls of Cornwall and Arundel, the earl of Leicester.
defeated and took prisoner the earl and countess at Fornham,
where more than 10,000 of the Flemish mercenaries were slain.
The prisoners were sent to the king, who now had in his own
hands the two of his enemies who were most dangerous to
him [1].

The contest however was not over. Early in 1174 the king Invasion of
of Scots invaded Northumberland, sent his brother David to the north in 1174.
the relief of Leicester, and reduced the border fortresses one by
one to surrender. Roger Mowbray who held the castles of
Thirsk, Malessart, and Axholm, and the earl of Ferrers who
had fortified Tutbury and Duffield, co-operated with the earl of
Leicester's knights and with Hugh Bigod, who was ravaging Conduct of
his own county with another Flemish army. Norwich and Hugh Bigod.
Nottingham were burned by the rebels, and Northampton, in
spite of the gallant defence of the townsmen, was plundered [2].
The justiciar was detained in middle England, apparently uncertain against which of the enemies he should march first [3],
and employed himself in besieging Huntingdon : he could not
leave the country unsettled behind him ; the king of Scots Threatened
might be in Northumberland, but the younger Henry and invasion from
Philip of Flanders with a great fleet were waiting for a fair Flanders.
wind at Gravelines ; the king had his hands full in Poictou ;
the count of Bar had landed with mercenaries at Hartlepool,
and it was uncertain which side the great Hugh de Puiset,
bishop of Durham, and the most magnificent lord of the whole
north country, was about to take [4].

In this great emergency the victory of the royal party was Fidelity of
secured by the fidelity of the people. The barons of Yorkshire the York-shiremen, 1174.

---

[1] Benedict, i. 58–62 ; Jordan Fantosme, pp. 45–50.
[2] J. Fantosme, pp. 53 sq.   [3] Ibid. pp. 38, 40.
[4] Benedict, i. 64, 65.

and the whole force of the county rallied round the sheriff, Robert Stuteville; Archbishop Roger sent his vassals under his constable, Robert de Thilli; Ranulf Glanvill, William de Vescy, and Bernard of Balliol brought up their knights; and the assembled army overtook King William at Alnwick, took him by surprise, and captured him with the leading men of his court. In Lincolnshire, Geoffrey, the king's natural son, the bishop-elect of Lincoln, collected the army of the shire and took Axholm; he then marched into Yorkshire, where, his force increasing as he proceeded, he captured the other castles of the Mowbrays[1]. In the meantime the king himself had arrived. Immediately on landing he went on pilgrimage to Canterbury, where he completed his penance on the day that the king of Scots was captured: at the head of his Brabançons he hastened to London, and thence to Huntingdon, which surrendered immediately. From Huntingdon he moved against Hugh Bigod, in whom now the rebellion centred. The veteran conspirator saw that the contest was hopeless; without a battle he made his submission to the king at Seleham, and surrendered his castles: a week after the bishop of Durham arrived, and by a like submission and surrender obtained permission for his nephew, the count of Bar, to leave the kingdom with his forces: the same day the constables of the earl of Leicester, Roger Mowbray and the earl Ferrers, surrendered their fortresses, and the struggle was over in England. The king returned hastily to relieve Rouen which his son was besieging, but his short stay had been enough to prove that the opportunity of his enemies was over. Peace was made in September[2] at Mont Louis with the rebellious sons, and in December at Falaise with the king of Scots.

The importance of this struggle, the last which the feudal baronage undertook in arms against the royal power, may excuse some amount of detail[3]. The result in France may testify to

Marginal notes:

Capture of the king of Scots, July 13. Prowess of the bishop-elect of Lincoln.

Arrival of the king, July 8, 1174.

Submission of the rebels, July 25–31.

Peace, Sept. 30.

---

[1] Benedict, i. 65–69.   [2] Ibid. 72–79.
[3] 'Seignurs, en la meie fei, merveille est mult grant
Pur quei li suen demeine le vunt si demenant,

the skill and energy of Henry: the result in England testifies chiefly to the constitutional hold which he had obtained on the body of the nation, on the Church, and on the newer, less thoroughly Norman, portion of the baronage. The great earls had indeed conducted their revolt as if they had never intended to be successful. They had had no settled plan, no watchword, no cry by which they could attract the people. They trod in the very footsteps of the rebel earls under William Rufus and Henry I, and they shared in their evil fortune, more happy than they in that they had to deal with a more politic and more merciful conqueror. The bishops had stood firmly on the king's side, with the exception of Hugh de Puiset, whose temporising policy had redounded to his own confusion. The free men of town and country had been faithful at a great cost. Norwich, Nottingham, and Northampton had paid dearly for their fidelity, for the earls, where they had the power, burned and ravaged the towns with twofold satisfaction. The shires had contributed their force willingly, and had done good work. The baronage which had sprung up since the beginning of the century from the families promoted and enriched by Henry I which in many cases were free from the influence of Norman connexion,—possessing no Norman lands, and unaffected by Norman prepossessions,—which was learning the benefit of law and social security, and being amalgamated day by day in sympathy and hopes with the bulk of the English people,—the baronage too had shown both faith and gratitude. The administration itself, the justiciar and his subordinates, had proved equal to the strain : there was no treason among the ministers ; and, if they had shown some symptoms of weakness, it was owing to the sudden and bewildering character of the revolt.

Henry's victory was so complete that he could afford to be

Le plus honurable e le plus conquerant
Que fust en nule terre puis le tens Moysant,
Fors sulement li reis Charle, ki poesté fud grant
Par les dudze cumpaignuns Olivier e Rodlant.'
                                Jordan Fantosme, p. 6.

generous[1]; he saw that his true policy was not to revenge himself by executions and confiscations, but, whilst he turned his enemies into friends by his mercy, to disarm them effectually. He kept a tight hand on their castles, many of which he dismantled[2]; he is said, somewhat doubtfully, to have exacted no ransoms; he shed no blood and seized no inheritances.

145. He took further advantage of his practical supremacy in the country to go on with the work of organisation which he had begun; and one result of the rebellion was his more continuous residence in England. After his return from France in 1175 he stayed two whole years in the country; holding constant councils and enforcing fresh measures of consolidation. He had now filled up the episcopal sees that had been vacant since the Becket quarrel; Richard of Ilchester and John of Oxford had become bishops of Winchester and Norwich: the chancellorship, which had long been in abeyance or in commission, was given to Ralph de Warneville, treasurer of York, who lived in Normandy and discharged his duties by means of a vice-chancellor, Walter of Coutances[3]. The reality of the king's reconciliation with the Church was exhibited by his attendance with his son at an ecclesiastical council held by the new archbishop, Richard of Dover, at Westminster, the week after his arrival, in May 1175. That Whitsuntide he held his royal court at Reading[4], where he compelled the earl of Gloucester to

Henry's clemency in 1174.

Henry stays in England during 1175 and 1176.

Councils of 1175.

---

[1] Dialogus de Scaccario, ii. c. 2 : ' Contra numerosam hostium multitudinem solius Divinae gratiae magnitudo subvenit, et quasi pugnante pro se Domino, sic in brevi pene rebelles omnes obtinuit ut longe fortius quam prius, eo quo infirmari debuit, confirmaretur in regno. . . . . . Tam enormis sceleris incentoribus inaudita pepercit misericordia, ut eorum pauci rerum suarum, nulli vero status sui vel corporum dispendia sustinerent.'

[2] R. Diceto, i. 395 ; Will. Newb. ii. c. 83. The series of measures touching the castles runs over several years. Orders were given for dismantling them immediately after the war; R. Diceto, i. 398. These were executed in 1176; Bened. i. 121, 124, 126 (see below, p. 522). On the restoration of the earls in 1177 their castles were still retained in the king's hands (Bened. i. 134, 135). The same year all the royal castles in the north changed their officers (Bened. i. 160), and shortly after (ibid. i. 178) the council advised the king to keep in hand those of the bishop of Durham.

[3] R. Dic. i. 367. He held it till 1181, when the king gave it to his son Geoffrey.

[4] 'Curiam et festum regium ; ' Bened. i. 91, 92.

surrender the castle of Bristol, and showed his consciousness of his own strength by severely enforcing the forest-law against the barons. After a conference with the Welsh princes at Gloucester [1], in which he forced them and the border barons to swear peace, he held a great council at Woodstock [2], where he filled up the vacant abbacies, and issued an edict by which the persons who had been lately in arms against him were forbidden to come to court without a summons; no one was to remain at the court between sunset and sunrise without permission; and no one on this side the Severn was to wear arms as a part of his ordinary habit; men had gone about with bows and arrows and sharp knives too long [3]. Thence he went to Lichfield, where he hanged four knights for the murder of a forester : thence to Nottingham, where he held a great visitation of the forests, and, notwithstanding the expostulation of the justiciar, exacted large sums as fines for the waste of the vert and venison, which he had himself during the war authorised his supporters to destroy [4]. This conduct, which was in itself unjustifiable, was probably provoked by the extravagance with which the permission had been used. He next went to York, to receive the submission of the Scots and the homage promised by the king at the peace of Falaise. In October he held a great council at Windsor [5], and concluded a treaty with the king of Connaught. Immediately after Christmas he called a great council at Northampton, in which he renewed and amplified the Assize of Clarendon [6].

Henry at Woodstock,

at Lichfield,

at Nottingham,

at York,

at Windsor.

The state of the kingdom since the death of Becket had been so unsettled, that the measures which the inquest into the conduct of the sheriffs was intended to promote must necessarily

Internal administration.

---

[1] 'Magnum tenuerunt concilium apud Gloucestriam;' Bened. i. 92.

[2] 'Magnum coram praedictis regibus celebraverunt [episcopi] concilium;' Bened. i. 93.

[3] Ibid. : 'In ipso autem concilio praecepit rex publico edicto,' &c.

[4] Ibid. p. 94.

[5] Ibid. p. 101 : 'Congregatis apud Windeshovers . . . archiepiscopo Cantuariensi et episcopis Angliae et comitibus et baronibus terrae suae.'

[6] 'Magnum concilium de statutis regni;' Bened. i. 107. 'Coram episcopis, comitibus, baronibus, militibus et aliis hominibus suis;' R. Diceto, i. 404.

have been suspended : but the administration had not for one
moment been disturbed in its ordinary course. The king had exacted the scutage for the Irish expedition in 1172, and in 1173 six
detachments of Exchequer officers had taken a tallage throughout the country, and held courts of justice at the same time [1].
The next year, a year of war, left no time for judicial business,
but in 1175 the shires were visited by justices again. Each
year's account presents a different arrangement of circuits, or a
different staff of judges. The Assize of Northampton placed
this jurisdiction on a more permanent footing.

The Assize of Northampton was issued in January, 1176 [2],
and formed, like that of Clarendon, a body of instructions for
the itinerant justices. It contains thirteen articles, many of
them marked by a severity which contrasts unfavourably with
the character of the earlier document, but which was no doubt
called for by the condition in which the country had been left by
the late war. The punishment of felons is made more cruel than
before ; stringent measures are directed against fugitives and
outlaws, and the manner of presenting the report of the inquest
is defined in nearly the same language. But the influence of
the commission of 1170 is traceable ; the sheriffs are not now
associated with the justices as the persons to whom the report
is to be made, and a particular inquiry is ordered into the
receipts of the king's bailiffs. Other articles have special reference to the recent rebellion ; every man, be he earl, baron, knight,
freeholder, or villein, is to take the oath of fealty, or to be
arrested as the king's enemy ; the castles, the destruction of
which had been ordered, are to be really destroyed ; and report
is to be made to the king as to the performance of the duty of
castle-guard by those who are liable to it. Nor was the visitation confined to criminal jurisdiction ; the judges were to take
recognitions of novel disseisin, and to hear every sort of plea that
was cognisable under royal writ touching fiefs of half a knight's
fee or less. In their fiscal capacity they were to examine into
the escheats, wardships, crown lands and churches. The fourth

Marginal notes:

Taxes of 1172 and 1173.

Visitation of 1175.

Assize of North-ampton, Jan. 1176.

New in-structions of the itinerant justices.

Political articles.

Civil and fiscal work.

---

[1] Pipe Rolls of the several years ; Madox, Hist. Exch. pp. 84 sq.
[2] Bened. i. 107 sq. ; Hoveden, ii. 89 sq. ; Select Charters (ed. 3), p. 150.

article directs that, in the case of the death of a freeholder, the rights of his family, his will and his debts, are to be provided for before the relief is paid to his lord: and that questions arising as to the nature of his tenure are to be decided by a recognition of twelve men. This clause is probably the text of the law on which the assize of *Mort d'ancester* as a part of the regular process was founded. The execution of the Assize of Northampton was committed to six detachments, each consist- ing of three judges[1]; to each detachment a cluster of counties or circuit was assigned: of the eighteen judges, eight were barons acting as sheriffs at the time, and in most cases one of the three was sheriff of one of the counties in his circuit. The lists of the sheriffs show a considerable change of officials in the year following the assize, with the marked result of throwing the sheriffdoms more entirely into the hands of the court.

Division of the country into six circuits.

The years 1176 and 1177 were occupied with constant councils, in which all sorts of business were transacted: the disputes between the two archbishops furnished occupation for more than one[2]; the marriage of the king's daughter with the king of Sicily was considered in another[3]; in a great council at Winchester, on Michaelmas-day, 1176, the king took all the castles of the kingdom into his hands, not even sparing those of the faithful Richard de Lucy[4]; and in a court held at Westminster, November 12[5], he received the ambassadors of both emperors and several minor princes. In 1177, as in 1176, Northampton was the place chosen for the January council[6]; in a court held in February at Winchester, the king

Councils of 1176 and 1177.

Inquest into receipts.

---

[1] The names of the judges are given in the Chronicle of Benedict, i. 107, 108.

[2] There was a council of clergy, March 14, 1176, at Westminster to meet the Roman legate; there the two archbishops quarrelled; on the 15th of August a council of bishops, earls, and barons met to settle the strife; Bened. i. 112, 118.

[3] On the arrival of the Sicilian ambassadors Henry called together the archbishops, bishops, earls, and *sapientiores* of the kingdom on the 25th of May, 1176; the subject was discussed and 'habito tractatu communi' the proposal was accepted; R. Diceto, i. 408; Bened. i. 116.

[4] Bened. i. 124; R. Diceto, i. 414.

[5] R. Diceto, i. 416.

[6] 'Magnum celebravit concilium cum episcopis, comitibus et baronibus suis;' Bened. i. 132.

directed a new inquest into the conduct of the royal bailiffs, and issued summonses for a general feudal levy[1]; at the beginning of Lent a great assembly was held in London, in which Henry arbitrated between the kings of Castille and Navarre with the advice of his court[2]; in May the king held a council at Geddington to treat 'of the peace and stability of the realm,' and another at Oxford to witness the nomination of John as king of Ireland, and the partition of that country among the barons who had joined in the adventure of the conquest[3]. The next month at Winchester all the tenants-in-chief were called together to hear the king's purpose of going to Normandy, and to prepare to accompany him[4]. A great expedition was contemplated, but the necessity for war was averted for the time, and the forces returned home, spared from the danger of affording a precedent for foreign service in time to come. But although the army was not needed in Normandy the king's presence was indispensable, and in August he left England for a year; during which the country enjoyed profound quiet.

He returned in the following July, and, as usual, signalised his presence by some energetic reforms. This time his zeal took the shape of an attack on the Curia Regis. He had heard that the measures of the justices had been oppressive, that their

Spanish award in 1177.

Feudal levy for an expedition to France.

Henry leaves, August, 1177.

He returns in July, 1178.

---

[1] The sheriffs were to report at the Easter Exchequer: 'Praeterea ibidem per consilia familiarium suorum mandavit omnibus comitibus et baronibus et militibus regni qui de eo in capite tenebant, quod omni occasione remota essent bene parati equis et armis apud Londonias in octavis clausi Paschae secuturi eum inde in Normanniam et moraturi secum per unum annum in partibus transmarinis ad custamentum eorum;' Bened. i. 138.

[2] 'Mandavit archiepiscopis, episcopis, comitibus et baronibus totius Angliae quod essent ad eum apud Lundonias Dominica proxima post caput jejunii; habiturus enim erat illorum consilia de quodam judicio faciendo inter duos reges Hispaniae;' Bened. i. 139. 'Venerunt tot abbates, tot decani, tot archidiaconi quot sub numero non cadebant. Venerunt etiam illuc comites et barones regni quorum non est numerus;' ibid. 145. 'Archiepiscopus Cantuariensis et episcopi Angliae qui aderant et comites et barones regni . . . adjudicaverunt;' ibid. 151.

[3] Bened. i. 160, 162.

[4] 'Venerunt etiam illuc ad eum comites et barones et milites regni sui per summonitionem suam. . . . Congregatis itaque omnibus in urbe Wintoniae rex per consilium eorum transfretationem suam distulit;' Bened. i. 178. The king himself sailed August 17; Bened. i. 190; and returned July 15, 1178; ibid. 207.

number was far too great: eighteen judges are said by the chronicler to have been acting at once; possibly the eighteen who had gone on circuit in 1176. Without actually dismissing these, the king by the advice of his council chose five of his own immediate servants, two clerks and three laymen, before whom he ordered all the complaints of his people to be brought, reserving the harder cases for his own hearing as before, to be decided with the council of the wise[1]. In this measure is traced the foundation of the Court of King's Bench as a separate committee of the Curia Regis; whilst the power of hearing appeals, as now reserved to the king, marks an important step in the development of the judicial system out of which the equitable and appellate jurisdictions sprang. The immediate effect of this measure is uncertain, for the two following years produced great changes, both personal and official.

His changes in the Curia Regis.

The germ of the King's Bench, and jurisdiction of the Council.

Soon after Easter, 1179, Richard de Lucy, who had been chief justiciar for twenty-five years, and who had been faithful to the king and just to the people during the whole time, resigned his office, and retired to the monastery of Lesnes, which he had founded[2]. Henry took advantage of the event to re-model the provincial administration: in a great council held at Windsor, setting aside the arrangement of six circuits so lately devised, he divided England into four districts, East, West, Midland, and North. To each of these five judges were assigned, one bishop, one or two chaplains or clerks, and three or four laymen. The northern circuit had no bishop, but six judges, one of whom was Ranulf Glanvill. Of the whole body only eight had been before employed in a judicial capacity, and most of the new justices are traceable as succeeding in process of time to sheriffdoms and other high offices[3]. The report of the commission was made to the king in August, but the accounts appear in the roll of 1180. Ralph de Diceto explains the measure as an attempt on the king's part to use the bishops of

Richard de Lucy resigns in 1179.

New division and distribution of judicial work, 1179.

Three bishops among the judges.

---

[1] Bened. i. 207. See below, § 163.

[2] Bened. i. 238. 'Tunc rex congregatis episcopis et comitibus et proceribus regni . . . communi eorum consilio, coram rege filio suo divisit in quatuor partes Angliam;' ibid.

[3] Bened. i. 238, 239.

Winchester, Norwich, and Ely as checks on the lay officials, or
at least so to blend lay and clerical influences in the arrangement as to secure equitable treatment for the litigants [1]. The
expedient seems scarcely to have been successful: it was not
repeated; Ranulf Glanvill, the great lawyer, was almost immediately after appointed to the place which Richard de Lucy had
held [2], and under his administration the king's long and varied
experiments came to an end. It is probable that, in faithful
discharge of duty, and an inventive or adaptative genius for
legal proceedings, he came up to his master's ideal of a good
judge.

*Ranulf
Glanvill
justiciar,
1180.*

146. The remaining years of Henry furnish little that is of
constitutional importance. He paid during the time four long
visits [3] to England, and on each occasion left the impress of his
presence. In 1180 he ordered a new coinage, the second coinage
of the reign; for the promise made at the treaty of Wallingford
had been redeemed in 1158 [4]. In 1181 he issued the Assize of

*Latter
years of
Henry II.*

*New coin-
age in 1180.*

[1] R. Diceto, i. 434–437.
[2] Hoveden, ii. 215.
[3] The dates are as follows:—In April, 1180, the king went to Normandy; he returned July 27, 1181. He left again March 3, 1182; returning
June 10, 1184. He left again April 16, 1185, and returned April 27,
1186. Leaving next February 17, 1187, he returned January 30, 1188.
His final departure from England took place July 10, 1188, and he died
July 6, 1189.
[4] See above, p. 361. The offences of the coiners had called forth some
very severe measures on the part of Henry I, who by his charter had
promised to secure the purity of the coinage. William of Malmesbury
(Hist. Nov. ii. § 34) mentions the depreciation of the coin as an act of
Stephen, and the private coinage of the barons was one of the points noted
by William of Newburgh at the same period (above, p. 354). Henry had
very early taken measures to restore the coin to its due weight, and had
ordered a common coinage for the whole country to be struck, which alone
was to be taken at the Exchequer; Dialogus i. c. 3. In the Pipe Roll of
the second year of the reign are some notices of the punishment of fraudu-
lent moneyers; but the first mention of the 'commutatio monetae' is in
1158. The new coinage of 1180 was received by the people with suspicion
(W. Newb. iii. c. 5); but the severe measures against the moneyers were
again necessary. An assize was issued by which the payment of the old
coin was declared unlawful after Martinmas, and the new coinage, struck
under the management of Philip Aymar, a native of Touraine, was thus
forced into circulation. Unluckily Philip was found conniving at the
frauds of the moneyers; the minor offenders were punished, but he was
pardoned, and escaped to France. Ralph Niger lays the blame on the king
and the archbishop of Canterbury: 'Being himself corrupted by Archbishop

Arms, by which he directed the whole of the freemen of the country to provide themselves with armour according to their means, and the inquiry by oath of legal juries to determine the liability of each[1]. The same year he made his son Geoffrey chancellor. In 1184 he promulgated the Assize of Woodstock, a code of forest ordinances, which were very stringent, but somewhat less inhuman than the customs of his grandfather[2]. In 1186 he filled up the vacant churches, objecting in a significant way to the election of the officers of his court to the bishoprics, and thus delaying the promotion of Richard the Treasurer, Godfrey de Lucy, Herbert the Poor, and other rising men[3]. The same year he assembled an army for an expedition to Galloway, but at Carlisle he received the homage of the rebellious lords, and returned home taking a scutage of his barons[4]. In 1188, after the shock of the capture of Jerusalem, he obtained from a great national council at Geddington[5] a

Richard, he suffered the coin to be corrupted, and nevertheless hanged the corrupters of it;' Ralph Niger (ed. Anstruther), p. 168. Cf. R. Diceto, ii. 7; Gervase, i. 294; Madox, Hist. Exch. 189 sq.; Benedict, ii. pref. pp. ci–civ.

[1] Benedict, i. 278 sq.; Hoveden, ii. 261; Select Charters (3rd edit.), p. 153.

[2] Benedict, i. 323, 324; Hoveden, ii. 243; Select Charters (3rd edit.), p. 156.

[3] Benedict, i. 346: 'Rex ... electioni de illis factae consentire noluit, respondens illos satis divites esse, et se de cetero nunquam daturum episcopatum alicui pro amore, vel consanguinitate, vel consilio, vel prece, vel pretio, sed illis quos elegerit sibi Dominus.'

[4] Benedict, i. 348; Madox, Hist. Exch. p. 441.

[5] 'Convocatis archiepiscopo et episcopis et comitibus et baronibus regni;' Benedict, ii. 33. The ordinance is in Benedict, ii. 30; Hoveden, ii. 335; Select Charters (ed. 3), p. 159. The councils of the later years which have not been mentioned in the above notes were as follows :—

In 1184 Ranulf Glanvill held a council to deliberate on the pope's demand of an aid from the clergy; Bened. i. 311. The king returned to England on the 10th of June, and held a council with the bishops and monks, at Reading, Aug. 5; at Windsor, Oct. 23; and at London, Dec. 2; R. Diceto, ii. 22.

In 1185 the king held a council of bishops, abbots, earls, and barons on the 17th of March, at Clerkenwell, to discuss a crusade; Bened. i. 336; R. Diceto, ii. 33. At the Easter court he knighted John, and gave the county of Huntingdon to the king of Scots. On April 16 he went abroad.

In 1186, having returned April 27, he met the bishops and clergy at Eynsham, May 25; the council, which was held for the election of bishops, sat for eight days; R. Diceto, ii. 41, 42: and a similar assembly was held at Marlborough, Sept. 14. At Christmas, at Guildford, a very solemn court

promise of a tithe to be contributed towards the Crusade, for
the assessment and collection of which his favourite plan of
inquest by jury was again employed.   But although these acts
have an importance of their own, the real interest of this period
of Henry's life lies outside of England, in his contest with his
disobedient sons and King Philip of France.   During these
struggles the English baronage, as a rule, was faithful: but,
had the great earls even wished to renew their pretensions, they
were too tightly bound by the royal policy of precaution or by
personal gratitude.   Hugh Bigod had closed his uneasy career in
1177: the earl of Chester had been restored to the royal favour
and made useful in Ireland the same year; he died in 1181: the
earl of Leicester had recovered his estates, with the exception of
the castles, in 1177, and continued faithful; although, when the
young king rebelled in 1183, it was thought necessary to imprison
him as well as his wife[1], to keep them out of mischief: and
the same precaution was taken with respect to the earl of Gloucester and others: Roger Mowbray went on a crusade in 1186.

There is no trace of any sympathy felt in England for the
revolt of the king's sons in 1183; and, if there had been any
such feeling, the short duration of the struggle, which closed at
the death of the young king in June, would have prevented its
manifestation: but the war was really confined to the Poictevin
provinces.   The rebellious son, on whom much empty sentiment
has been wasted, was a showy and ambitious man, possessed of
popular accomplishments, and professing sympathy with the
baronial party which his father was constantly employed in re-
pressing[2].   He had some gifts that his father wanted, or did

---

was held, and the grand-serjeanties usual at the coronations were performed;
Bened. ii. 3.

In 1187, on Feb. 17, the king went abroad; he returned Jan. 30, 1188.

In 1188, on Feb. 11, he held the council at Geddington; on the 10th of
July he went abroad, and never returned.

[1] Bened. i. 294.   The importance of the countess, who is almost always
mentioned as present where her husband was, is worth notice.   She was
Petronilla, the heiress of the family of Grantmesnil.   The earl's mother,
Amicia, was daughter of Ralph II, son of Ralph Guader by the daughter of
William Fitz-Osbern: he and his wife thus represented three families which
attributed their downfall to the policy of the Conqueror and his sons.

[2] This appears especially in Aquitaine, where he was regarded as a

not take the pains to exhibit; and either by these, or as a result Character of the younger Henry. of his father's unpopularity, won from the annalists of the time the character of a popular favourite. His conduct however was that of an unprincipled, ungrateful son, a faithless brother, and a contemptible politician; he was in fact a puppet in the hands of his father-in-law, of his mother, or of the feudal party in England, Normandy, and Aquitaine.

The contest with Richard, which occupied the last year of Quietness of England during the king's last troubles. the king's life, was watched by the English with even less anxiety; for they had little fear of the issue, and knew very little about Richard. The sudden, profound, and fatal discomfiture of the king took the nation, as it took the whole western world, by surprise[1].

The internal administration of these years was regular and Judicial and financial progress. peaceful. Year after year the judicial and financial officers make their circuits and produce their accounts: both judicial and financial receipts accumulate; and the gross income of the last year of the reign reached the sum of £48,000[2]. Ranulf Glanvill also during this time drew up or superintended the composition of the *Liber de Legibus Angliae*, on which our knowledge of the Curia Regis in its earliest form depends: to a somewhat earlier period belongs the *Dialogus de Scaccario* of Richard Fitz-Neal[3], and the recension of the English laws which may have been revised by Glanvill[4]. It is possible that all three works[5] were drawn up at the king's command, to put on record the methods of proceeding which had depended too much hitherto on oral and hereditary tradition.

Henry died on the 6th of July, 1189, having to the last week Henry's death, July, 1189. of his life refused to allow to Richard the recognition of the

---

martyr, and where it was said that miracles were wrought at his tomb. See the extracts from the sermon of Thomas Agnellus, in Hoveden, ii. pref. p. lvii.

[1] Hoveden, ii. pref. pp. lix–lxxii.

[2] Pipe Roll of the 1st of Richard I, i.e. the year ending at Michaelmas, 1189; a month after Richard's coronation.

[3] It was begun in 1176, but contains notices of events as late as 1178.

[4] Hoveden, ii. 218 sq.

[5] The Dialogus is dedicated to the king: 'Rex illustris, mundanorum principum maxime;' Præf.: Select Charters (ed. 3), p. 169.

barons as his successor, and possibly, in his irritable and exhausted condition, nursing some idea of disposing of his kingdom, as the Conqueror had done, in favour of his younger son [1]. The discovery of John's treachery rendered this of course impossible, and that discovery broke his heart.

147. The examination of the administrative measures of Henry in the order of their adoption is necessary to enable us to realise at once the development of his policy, and the condition of affairs which compelled it. Nor, although in the investigation much detail is needed which at first sight seems irrelevant to the later or to the more essential history of the Constitution, is the minute inquiry to be set aside as superfluous. Henry II was, it is true, far more than an inventor of legal forms or of the machinery of taxation. He was one of the greatest politicians of his time; a man of such wide influence, great estates, and numerous connexions, that the whole of the foreign relations of England during the middle ages may be traced directly and distinctly to the results of his alliances and his enmities. He was regarded by the Emperor Frederick, by the kings of Spain and Sicily, by the rising republics of Lombardy, by the half-savage dynasts of Norway, and by the fainting realm of Palestine, as a friend and a patron to be secured at any cost. He refused the crowns of Jerusalem and Sicily; he refused to recognise the antipope at a moment when the whole influence of the papacy was being employed to embarrass and distress him. His career is full of romantic episodes, and of really great physical exploits.

His greatness on the Continent.

He is chiefly distinguished as a legislator and administrator.
Yet the consent of the historians of the time makes him, first and foremost, a legislator and administrator. Ralph Niger, his enemy [2], tells how year after year he wore out men's patience

---

[1] The story of Giraldus (De Inst. Pr. lib. iii. c. 2), that he intended to annul his marriage with Eleanor and exclude all her children from the succession, is no doubt a fabrication: the same writer attributes to Archbishop Geoffrey the thought of surviving his brothers, and putting in a claim to the throne notwithstanding his illegitimacy. (V. Galfridi, Ang. Sac. ii. 383; Gir. Camb. Opp. ed. Brewer, iv. 374.) Henry had meditated a divorce in 1175, and discussed the matter with the legate; Gervase, i. 256, 257.

[2] 'Nactus autem regnum Anglorum servos, spurios, caligatos, cubili,

with his annual assizes ; how he set up an upstart nobility; how His politic he abolished the ancient laws, set aside charters, overthrew ment. municipalities, thirsted for gold, overwhelmed all society with his scutages, his recognitions, and such like. Ralph de Diceto explains how necessary a constant adaptation and readjustment of means was to secure in any degree the pure administration of justice, and lauds the promptness with which he discarded unsatisfactory measures to make way for new experiments[1]. William of Newburgh[2] and Peter of Blois[3] praise him for the

mensae, regno praefecit et ex iis quaestores, praetores, proconsules, tribunos, municipes, forestarios, super provincias constituit : illustres ignominiis oneratos, sed ceteris rebus vacuos, patrimoniis omnino privavit vel sub- dole portionibus detractis decrustando sensim adnihilavit. Ex cubiculariis et aulae nugatoribus episcopos, abbates, factos auctoritate propria ad officium apparitorum revocavit, et quem praesulem crearat a praeside, in praesidatum recreavit ex praesule. . . . Nulli infra metas forestae habitanti in lucis propriis aut virgas colligendi, aut sylvestria et invia in agriculturam agendi, potestatem concessit sine forestariis. Legem quoque de forestis inauditam dedit, qua delicti alieni immunes perpetuo mulctabuntur. . . . Illustribus uxores ducere, filias nuptui dare, praeter regis conscientiam in- hibuit et transgressores tanquam reos laesae majestatis punivit. Heredes omnium quos avus suus extulerat et qui ei in subigenda Anglia constanter adsistebant, cognatos quoque suos quasi aspides exosos habuit. . . . Nullo quaestu satiatus, abolitis legibus antiquis, singulis annis novas leges quas assisas vocavit edidit. Danegeldum avitum innovavit. . . . Corruptus a Ricardo archiepiscopo monetam corrumpi permisit, corruptores tandem suspendio decedere compellens. Avibus caeli, piscibus fluminum, bestiis terrae immunitatem dedit et sata pauperum loca pascuae fecit. Causam fidei laesae et advocationis ecclesiarum in curia decidi constituit. Tribu- tarius exteris, in domesticos praedo, scutagiis, recognitionibus et variis angariarum alluvionibus fere omnes depressit. Omne jus poli jure fori demu- tavit. Scripta authentica omnium enervavit, libertatibus omnium insidians, quasi e specula, solotenus egit innoxiorum municipia. Filias miserae con- ditionis, corruptas et oppressas, copulans clarissimis, heredes omnes mechanicos creavit. . . . Hereditates retinuit aut vendidit. . . . In causis differendis cavillantissimus ut saepe jus venderet ; ' R. Niger (ed. An- struther), pp. 167-169.

[1] ' Rex pater Anglorum his plurimum quaerens prodesse qui minimum possunt . . . de communi salute magis et magis sollicitus . . . intentissimus ad justitiam singulis exhibendum . . . animum a proposito non immutans circa personas mutabiles immutabilem semper saepe mutavit sententiam ; ' R. Dic. i. 434, 435.

[2] ' Fuit enim in illo regni fastigio tuendae et fovendae pacis publicae studiosissimus, in portando gladium ad vindictam malefactorum. . . . Nullum grave regno Anglorum vel terris suis transmarinis onus unquam imposuit . . . tributum more aliorum principum . . . ecclesiis . . . nunquam indixit ; ' W. Newb. lib. iii. c. 26. See too John of Salisbury, Polycrat. lib. vi. c. 18.

[3] ' Non enim sicut alii reges in palatio suo jacet, sed per provincias currens explorat facta omnium, illos potissimum judicans quos constituit judices aliorum. Nemo est argutior in consiliis, in eloquio torrentior. . . .

Different
opinions
about him.

very measures that Ralph Niger condemns; his exactions were
far less than those of his successors; he was most careful of the
public peace; he bore the sword for the punishment of evildoers, but to the peace of the good; he conserved the rights
and liberties of the churches; he never imposed any heavy tax
on either England or his continental estates, or grieved the
Church with undue exactions: his legal activity was especially
meritorious after the storm of anarchy which preceded. In
every description of his character the same features recur,
whether as matters of laudation or of abuse.

How far
was he an
original
legislator?

The question already asked recurs, How many of the innovating expedients of his policy were his own? Some parts of
it bear a startling resemblance to the legislation of the Frank
emperors, his institution of scutage, his assize of arms, his
inquest of sheriffs, the whole machinery of the jury which he
developed and adapted to so many different sorts of business,—
almost all that is distinctive of his genius is formed upon Karolingian models, the very existence of which within the circle
of his studies or of his experience we are at a loss to account

General
revival of
legal study.

for. It is probable that international studies in the universities
had attained already an important place; that the revived study
of the Roman law [1] had invited men to the more comprehensive

Quoties enim potest a curis et sollicitudinibus respirare, secreta se occupat
lectione aut in cuneo clericorum aliquem modum quaestionis laborat evol-
vere. . . . Apud dominum regem Anglorum quotidiana ejus schola est,
litteratissimorum conversatio jugis et discussio quaestionum. . . . Rex noster
pacificus, victoriosus in bellis gloriosus in pace, super omnia hujus mundi
desiderabilia zelatur et procurat pacem populi sui. . . . Nullus mansuetior
est afflictis, nullus affabilior pauperibus, nullus importabilior est superbis;
quadam enim divinitatis imagine semper studuit opprimere fastuosos, op-
pressos erigere et adversus superbiae tumorem continuas persecutiones et
exitiales molestias suscitare. . . .' Pet. Bles. Epp. (ed. Busaeus), ep. 66.
Giraldus Cambrensis, like Ralph Niger, takes the opposite view : 'Fuerat
enim et ab initio et usque ad finem nobilitatis oppressor, jus et injuriam,
fasque nefasque pro commodo pensans' (De Inst. Pr. ii. c. 3); 'acer in in-
domitos, clemens in subactos, durus in domesticos, effusus in extraneos;
largus in publico, parcus in privato. . . . Auctor pacis diligentissimus et
observator . . . humilitatis amator et superbiae calcator . . . zelo justitiae
sed non ex scientia, regni sacerdotiique jura conjungens vel confundens
potius. . . .' (Ibid. c. 29.)

[1] Magister Vacarius gente Longobardus, vir honestus et juris peritus,
cum leges Romanas anno ab Incarnatione Domini 1149 in Anglia discipulos
doceret, et multi tam divites quam pauperes ad eum causa discendi con-

examination of neighbouring jurisprudence. But whilst the Roman
law dis-
Roman law met with a cold reception in England, and whilst the couraged in
minutiae of feudal legislation as it was then growing up gained England.
admission only at a later period, and were under Henry repressed
rather than encouraged, we here and there come across glimpses
of the imperial system which had died out on the soil from which
it sprang. The illustration of this phenomenon will come in its
own place.

148. Richard had no opposition to fear in any of his father's Accession
dominions, and he was already in possession of his mother's of Richard,
July, 1189.
inheritance; but he had to make terms with Philip his late
ally, who from the moment of his succession saw in him only
his father's son and his own hereditary enemy. In England the
public peace was maintained by the queen, who, acting in conjunction with the justiciar, put forth a proclamation in her own
name directing the release of prisoners and claiming the allegiance
of the whole nation for her son[1]. The archbishop, who had been
in France at the time of Henry's death, was sent home to
prepare for the coronation. As soon as Richard had concluded He is in-
his treaty with Philip, and received investiture as duke of vested as
duke, and
Normandy, he crossed over to England. From his first arrival comes to
England.
it was clear that his mind was set upon the Crusade, and his

---

fluerent, suggestione pauperum de Codice et Digesta excerptos novem
libros composuit qui sufficiunt ad omnes legum lites quae in scholis frequen-
tari solent decidendas, si quis eos perfecte noverit;' R. de Monte, A.D.
1149. 'Tunc leges et causidici in Angliam primo vocati sunt quorum
primus erat magister Vacarius. Hic in Oxenfordia legem docuit;' Gervase,
ed. Twysden, c. 1665. He was silenced by Stephen : 'Rex quidam Angliae
Stephanus allatis legibus Italiae in Angliam publico edicto prohibuit;'
Roger Bacon, Opus Minus (cited by Selden in his notes on Fortescue,
p. 39). 'Tempore regis Stephani a regno jussae sunt leges Romanae quas in
Britanniam domus venerabilis patris Theobaldi Britanniarum primatis
asciverat; ne quis etiam libros retineret edicto regio prohibitum est et
Vacario nostro indictum silentium;' John Salisb. Polycr. viii. c. 22.
Glanvill's preface to his book on the laws is adapted from the Institutes of
Justinian; many extracts from the civil and canon law are found in the
so-called Leges Henrici Primi, written probably before the year 1118; and
before the end of the reign of Henry II the procedure of the Roman civil
law had become well known to the English canonists, although its influence
was not allowed much to affect the common law of the kingdom. See the
case of the monks of Canterbury, drawn up by a civilian, in Epistolae
Cantuarienses, pp. 520 sq.

[1] Bened. ii. 74, 75.

whole policy directed to providing funds and making the necessary arrangements for the kingdom during his own absence. He began by seizing his father's treasures, which amounted to a fabulous sum [1]; he called Ranulf Glanvill to a strict account, and imprisoned him until he had paid a heavy ransom [2] and resigned the justiciarship; he disposed in marriage of most of the royal wards, and in a magnificent progress through the west of England wiled away the three weeks which intervened between his landing and the coronation. The latter event took place on the 3rd of September, in such splendour and minute formality as to form a precedent for all subsequent ceremonies of the sort. But although every detail of the ancient rite was preserved and amplified,—the crowning and anointing, the solemn oath of the king and the consequent homage and fealty of bishops and barons,—whilst the form of election, although not specially mentioned by the historians, was no doubt performed; no charter of liberties was issued, as had been done at the last three coronations. Richard was frankly accepted by the people as well as by the barons as his father's heir; nor was there during the whole of his reign any attempt made by any one in the kingdom, except John, to overthrow, either in name or in substance, his royal authority. After the coronation he continued his royal progress, visiting the most famous English sanctuaries. On the 16th of September he brought together a great council at Pipewell in Northamptonshire [3], where he gave away the vacant bishoprics, appointed a new ministry, and raised a large sum of money by the sale of charters of confirmation. Shortly after he changed the sheriffs in almost every county [4]. The acquisition of treasure seems to have been the chief object of these measures; for, although the offices were transferred to different holders, the same persons

Marginal notes:

Glanvill displaced.

Richard makes a progress and is crowned, Sept. 3, 1189.

Council of Pipewell.

Ways of raising money.

---

[1] More than nine hundred thousand pounds, Bened. ii. 77; more than one hundred thousand marks, Hoveden, iii. 8 : the former estimate seems much too high and the latter too low.

[2] R. Devizes, p. 7. According to this writer, Glanvill paid a ransom of £15,000.

[3] Bened. ii. 85.

[4] R. Devizes, p. 8; Bened. ii. 90. The latter historian places the resignation of Glanvill at this point.

remained in authority. Richard had no desire to disgrace his father's friends, and had very few of his own to supply their places. He stayed two months longer in the country, and, after selling to the Scots their freedom from the obligation which his father had extorted, left for Palestine on the 11th of December. *Release of Scotland.*

Richard was not at this period of his life an accomplished politician. He had two distinct objects to provide for before he went—the maintenance of the administration of the kingdom in faithful hands, and the securing of his brother John in his reluctant allegiance. The means he took for these ends were inadequate. John was indulged with a considerable gift of revenue and authority : besides the great Gloucester inheritance which he received with his wife, he was put in possession of so many counties and royal honours as seriously to impoverish the crown[1], while the only restraint imposed on him was the retention of some of his castles in the hands of the government, and an oath by which he undertook to absent himself for three years from England. From this oath John was released before Richard left France ; but his ambition was further tantalised by the recognition of Arthur of Brittany as heir to Richard. The king seems to have trusted mainly to his mother's influence to keep his brother out of mischief. The other object, the maintenance of sound government, was to be provided for by the choice of ministers. A chancellor the king had already found in William Longchamp, a clerk of Norman extraction, who had been in the service of his half-brother Geoffrey, and whom at Pipewell he promoted to the see of Ely. The justiciarship was bestowed on William Mandeville, earl of Essex and count of Aumâle, who had been unswervingly faithful to Henry ; a share of the power, probably the administration of the northern counties, being reserved for Hugh de Puiset, the aged bishop *Richard's policy.* *His provision for John, 1189.* *The new ministry.* *William Mandeville.*

[1] He had the county of Mortain in Normandy, the honour of the earldom of Gloucester, the castles and honours of Marlborough, Lancaster, Ludgershall, the Peak, and Bolsover ; the town and honour of Nottingham, and the honours of Wallingford and Tickhill without the castles ; the counties of Derby, Devon, Dorset, Somerset, and Cornwall. See Hoveden, iii. pref. p. xxv.

of Durham. The arrangement however was broken up by the death of the earl soon after his appointment, and England was

Hugh de Puiset.

left nominally in charge of Bishop Hugh [1], although the chancellor and several of the justices were associated with him as colleagues. The bishop of Durham had paid heavily for his honours; he had bought the justiciarship and the earldom of Northumberland [2]; the chancellor too had paid for the chancery £3,000 [3], although he was the king's most trusted friend.

Struggle between the Bishops of Durham and Ely, 1190.

Scarcely however had Richard left England when the two bishops quarrelled at the Exchequer. Both had recourse to the king in Normandy, and in March, 1190, a new appointment was made; William Longchamp became chief justiciar, and to Bishop Hugh the jurisdiction of the north was again entrusted [4]. But on the return of the latter to England he was arrested by his colleague, no doubt under the king's orders, and kept in forced retirement as long as the power of the chancellor was maintained [5].

Career of Longchamp.

149. Longchamp was now both justiciar and chancellor: in the June following he was made papal legate [6], and, as the archbishop of Canterbury had gone on crusade, whilst Geoffrey of York, the king's half-brother, was unconsecrated and in disgrace, he was supreme in both Church and State. He took full advantage of his opportunities, lived in pomp and luxury, obtained great wardships and rich marriages for his relations, sold judicial sentences, exacted money by every possible title from every possible payer, and offended both the baronage and his own colleagues in the government. But he was faithful to his

[1] Bened. ii. 101.

[2] He gave 2,000 marks for the county; and for the justiciarship a large sum which is described in Benedict (ii. 91) as 1,000 marks; but Richard of Devizes fixes the whole sum wrung from him at £10,000; p. 8.

[3] Reginald the Lombard, bishop of Bath, had bidden £4,000; R. Devizes, p. 9.

[4] Bened. ii. 106.

[5] Bened. ii. 109, 110. The king gave him full powers by letter dated at Bayonne, June 6: ' Mandamus vobis et praecipimus quid sicut de nobis consulitis et sicut vos ipsos et omnia vestra diligitis, sitis omnino intendentes dilecto et fideli cancellario nostro Elyensi episcopo super omnibus quae ad nos spectant, et pro ipso faciatis sicut pro nobismet ipsis faceretis, de omnibus quae vobis ex parte nostra dixerit;' R. Diceto, ii. 83.

[6] R. Diceto, ii. 83.

master ; and his public policy, as distinct from his personal behaviour, was intelligent and energetic. His rule kept the kingdom in peace so long as Eleanor, whether in France or in England, was able to keep John in order. On her departure to Italy, whither she had to convey Richard's betrothed wife, John took the opportunity of overthrowing his brother's minister and securing to himself a prospect of constitutional succession to the defeat of the pretensions of Arthur.

He maintains peace until Eleanor's departure to Sicily.

In the spring of 1191 Longchamp was attempting to get into the king's hands some of the castles[1] whose owners or governors he suspected of treason : one of these, Gerard Camville, the sheriff of Lincolnshire, was a friend of John, who took up arms in his favour. Twice during the summer war seemed imminent ; but, as Richard had already been informed of the unpopularity of his representative, and as the barons and prelates cared little for either John or Longchamp, the actual use of force was avoided, and means were taken, by arbitration, of preserving the balance of power between the two[2]. Before the second occasion however presented itself, the king's envoy, Walter of Coutances, archbishop of Rouen, had arrived from Messina with mysterious instructions, to act on the king's part as circumstances should dictate. He took a share in the second truce which was concluded at Winchester in July, and which placed the principal royal castles in the hands of safe men, bishops and barons, who were all inclined to support Richard's authority, although they differed as to the policy of securing John's succession. In September however a new difficulty arose : the archbishop of York returned from Tours, where he had been consecrated, alleging that he as well as John had been released from his oath to stay away from England. Immediately on landing he was arrested by Longchamp's order, and treated with unnecessary ignominy. He at once appealed to John, who on this occasion

Quarrel about Gerard Camville.

Civil war imminent.

Truce, April 1191.

Truce at Winchester, July 1191.

Arrest of Archbishop Geoffrey, September 1191.

---

[1] Gloucester (R. Devizes, p. 13), Wigmore (ibid. p. 30).
[2] On the sequence of these events see Hoveden, iii. pref. pp. lviii. sq. The first truce was arranged April 25, 1191, at Winchester, before the archbishop of Rouen arrived ; the second, in which he took part, on the 28th of July.

found the sympathy of the barons and bishops on his side. The chancellor, speedily discovering his error, disavowed the action of his servants and released Geoffrey; but he had given his

Council of the barons, Oct. 1191.

enemies their opportunity. A council of the barons[1] was called at London, and John laid the case before them: a conference was proposed near Windsor, but the chancellor failed to present himself. Excommunicated by the bishops and deserted by his colleagues, he hastened to London and

Longchamp accused, Oct. 8.

shut himself up in the Tower. John, who was now triumphant, brought together a great council at S. Paul's[2], and there, before the barons, bishops, and citizens of London, accused Longchamp.

The Archbishop of Rouen claims the justiciarship.

Then the archbishop of Rouen produced a commission signed by Richard at Messina in the preceding February, appointing him supreme justiciar, with William Marshall, Geoffrey Fitz-Peter, Hugh Bardulf, and William Briwere as coadjutors[3]. The nomination was welcomed with delight; the archbishop had been vice-chancellor to Henry II, and was known to be an honest man of business, with no ambition to be a statesman. John was hailed as *summus rector totius regni*, but he saw himself deprived of the fruit of his victory over the chancellor, and

Flight of Longchamp.

acquiesced for a time with a good grace. Longchamp, after a protest somewhat more dignified than was to be expected, surrendered his castles, and was allowed to escape to the Continent, where he excommunicated his enemies and intrigued for his return. He contrived to purchase the consent of John and Eleanor, but was repelled by the firm attitude of the baronage[4], who were disinclined alike to submit to his dictation and to

Return of Eleanor, Feb. 1192.

afford John a new opportunity. Eleanor soon after returned to England, and, although constantly harassed by the underhand conduct of Philip and by the treachery of John, she contrived to maintain the peace of the kingdom until the news of Richard's capture reached her in February 1193.

[1] Bened. ii. 212.
[2] 'Fere omnes episcopi et comites et barones Angliae, et cives Lundoniae cum illis;' Bened. ii. 213.
[3] Bened. ii. 213; Hoveden, iii. pref. p. lxi. p. 96; R. Diceto, ii. 98–101; Gir. Camb. V. Galfr. Ang. Sac. ii. 396; Opp. ed. Brewer, iv. 400, 401.
[4] Bened. ii. 239, 257; R. Devizes, p. 57.

The deposition of Longchamp, although it scarcely merits the Constitu- constitutional importance which is sometimes given to it, has a tional im- certain significance. It shows the hold which legal system had the crisis. on the barons; irregular as was the proceeding of John, and in- explicable as was the policy of the archbishop of Rouen, the assembly at S. Paul's acted as a council of the kingdom, heard the charges brought against the minister, and defined the terms of his submission; debated on and determined in favour of the nomination of the archbishop. Their action was, strictly speaking, unconstitutional; there was as yet neither law nor custom that gave them a voice in the appointment or deposition of the justiciar, nor could they even assemble constitutionally without a summons, which the existing justiciar would never have issued. Yet they acted on that critical principle which more than once in our later history has been called into play, where constitutional safeguards have proved insufficient to secure the national welfare; and the result justified their boldness: they acted as if in substance, though not in strict form, they repre- sented the nation itself.

150. The government of Walter of Coutances subsisted, The Arch- although with some difficulty, during the rebellion of John bishop of Rouen in 1193 and the rigorous measures taken for the raising the justiciar, 1191-93. king's ransom,—being sustained by the presence of Eleanor, the adhesion of the barons, and the general good-will of the nation. The ransom, as one of the three ordinary feudal aids, Ransom of the king. scarcely required from the national council more than a formal recognition of liability; but the amount was too great to be raised by a mere scutage on knights' fees. A meeting of the magnates was summoned at Oxford on the 28th of February, 1193. Messengers were sent in April from the king to all arch- bishops, bishops, abbots, earls, barons, clerks, and freeholders, asking for an aid, but not specifying the amount required. The same month the king wrote to his mother and the justices, saying that the sum required was 70,000 marks; thereupon the queen and justices, by a public edict, ordered the collection of money for the purpose, according to a scheme which would enable every class of subjects to aid in the release of the

sovereign. The sum ultimately fixed was 150,000 marks,

Means taken
for raising
Richard's
ransom,
1193.

or £100,000; double the whole revenue of the crown [1]. The national assent was taken for granted; and the justiciars propounded a somewhat complicated scheme : an aid was taken on the principle of scutage, twenty shillings on the knight's fee ; it was supplemented by a tallage, hidage, and carucage, which brought under contribution the rest of the land of the country : the wool of the Gilbertines and Cistercians was also demanded, and the treasures of the churches, their plate and jewels: but the heaviest impost was the exaction of one-fourth of revenue or goods from every person in the realm, a most important and dangerous precedent, although justified on this occasion by the greatness of the necessity. The result proved inadequate, although sufficient money was raised to secure the release of the

Hubert
Walter
justiciar.

king. But before this was done the archbishop of Rouen resigned the justiciarship, being succeeded by Hubert Walter, archbishop of Canterbury, at Christmas 1193 [2].

Previous
career of
Hubert.

Hubert Walter was an old servant of the court, the nephew and pupil of Ranulf Glanvill, and a constant attendant on Henry II. Richard had at the beginning of his reign given him the bishopric of Salisbury, and had taken him with him to Palestine, where he exhibited the due admixture of religious zeal, charity, and prowess that befitted the prelate on pilgrimage. He had acted as chaplain, as captain, as treasurer, and as ambassador. On the failure of the crusade Hubert had led back the English army, had visited his master in captivity, and had been sent home by him to raise the ransom, and to be made

His victory
over John,
Feb. 1194.

archbishop. He had proved his right to Richard's confidence by the energy he had shown in the cause; and his appointment as justiciar was almost immediately followed by a complete victory over John, whose rebellion on the news of Richard's release he

---

[1] Hoveden, iii. 208–217; R. Coggeshale, ed. Stevenson, p. 60. See Hoveden, iv. pref. pp. lxxxii–lxxxv ; W. Newb. iv. c. 38. Ralph de Diceto says that the arrangement for raising the money 'statutum est communi assensu ;' ii. 110; but this does not necessarily imply any deliberation in the national council, nor is there any distinct proof that such an assembly was held. But the chronicles are not very full on the subject.

[2] R. Diceto, ii. 112.

quelled by the prompt use of spiritual as well as temporal arms:
in one week he obtained from the clergy a sentence of excommunication and from the assembled barons a declaration of outlawry against him, and he was engaged in the reduction of the
castles when Richard landed.

Richard's second visit bore a strong resemblance to his first. Richard's
second visit
to England
in 1194.
It was occupied mainly with attempts to raise still more money;
an object easily made consistent with a show of judicial severity
and a politic caution against the treachery of John. After the Great coun-
cil of Not-
tingham.
surrender of the last of John's castles, a great court and
council was held at Nottingham, attended by the queen-mother,
both the archbishops, and several bishops and earls[1]. The
business lasted four days, from the 30th of March to the 2nd
of April. On the first day Richard removed the sheriffs of Sale of
offices
Lincolnshire and Yorkshire, and put up the offices for sale.
Yorkshire fell to Archbishop Geoffrey, whose bid of an immediate payment of 3,000 marks and 100 marks of increment was
accepted in preference to the lower offer of the chancellor, who
proposed 1,500 marks for Yorkshire, Lincolnshire, and Northamptonshire, with an annual increment of 100 marks from
each. On the second day the king demanded from his court a John and
his friends
sentenced.
sentence of outlawry against his brother John, and Hugh of
Nunant bishop of Coventry, who had been his chief adviser.
The court determined that they should be summoned; and, in
case of their non-appearance within forty days, John was to be
banished, and Hugh to be tried as a bishop by the bishops, and
as a sheriff by the lay judges. The third day, the 1st of April, Financial
measures.
was devoted to finance: Richard asked for a carucage,—two
shillings on each carucate of land,—a third part of the service
of the knights, and the wool of the Cistercians. For the latter
item he accepted a pecuniary fine. On the last day of the Accusation
of Arch-
bishop
Geoffrey
and Gerard
Camville,
April 1194.
council he devoted himself to hearing the complaints made
against his brother Geoffrey the archbishop of York, and to
the trial of Gerard Camville. The archbishop refused to answer,
and Gerard, after summarily denying the charges laid against

---

[1] Hoveden, iii. 240 sq.; Select Charters (ed. 3), pp. 253, 254.

him, gave security for a trial by battle. The king before the assembly broke up announced his intention of being crowned at Winchester on the Sunday after Easter. The political meaning of the several measures taken on this occasion is probably this: Richard recognised distinctly the fidelity of the chancellor, and thought it necessary to displace all the officers who had shown any sympathy with John. But he was not prepared to continue to Longchamp the confidence which he by his imprudence had so dangerously abused. The sheriffs, as we learn from the Rolls [1], were nearly all displaced; and in particular William Briwere, Hugh Bardulf, Geoffrey Fitz-Peter, William Marshall, Gilbert Pipard, and others who had taken a prominent part in the removal of Longchamp, were transferred to other counties, as if the king, although he could not dispense with their services, wished to show his disapproval of their conduct in the matter. Richard however was never vindictive, and would condone any injury for a substantial fine.

Removal of the sheriffs.

His second coronation was understood to have an important significance. He had by his captivity in Germany, if not, as was alleged, by a formal surrender of the kingdom of England to the emperor to be received again as a fief, impaired or compromised his dignity as a crowned king [2]. The Winchester coronation was not intended to be a reconsecration, but a solemn assertion that the royal dignity had undergone no diminution. The ceremony of anointing was not repeated, nor was the imposition of the crown a part of the public rite. Richard went in procession from his chamber to the cathedral, and there received the archbishop's blessing [3]. The occasion resembles the crown-wearing festivals of the Norman kings, and was a revival of the custom which had not been observed since Henry II wore his crown at Worcester in 1158. The few remaining days of the king's stay in England were occupied in arranging the quarrel of the chancellor with Archbishop Geof-

Richard's second coronation, April 17, 1194.

Negotiations with the King of Scots.

---

[1] Thirty-first Report of the Deputy-Keeper of the Records.

[2] See the next chapter of this work, § 158.

[3] See R. Coggeshale, ed. Stevenson, p. 64; Gervase, i. 524–526; Hoveden, iii. 247.

frey, and in negotiation with the king of Scots. Hugh de
Puiset surrendered the county of Northumberland, and William
the Lion offered the king 15,000 marks for the succession.
Richard would have accepted the bid, but would not surrender
the castles, and this disgraceful negotiation fell to the ground[1].
On the 12th of May the king sailed for Normandy, where he
was almost immediately reconciled with John, and soon after
restored to him the county of Mortain, the earldom of Gloucester, and the honour of Eye, giving him a pension of eight
thousand pounds Angevin in lieu of his other estates and dignities[2]. No more is heard from this time of Arthur's rights as
heir to the crown; the immediate danger of Richard's death
was over, and it was by no means unlikely that he might have
children. For the remainder of the reign, those persons whose
rivalry constitutes the interest of the early years fall into insignificance; Richard himself and his chancellor leave the kingdom to return no more; Hugh de Puiset dies shortly after;
the archbishop of Rouen returns to his province; John intrigues
in secret; and Archbishop Geoffrey, whose calamities fill the
annals of the time, scarcely comes as yet within the ken of
constitutional history.

The kingdom was practically for the remainder of the reign
under the rule of Hubert Walter, who became papal legate in
1195, and acted as justiciar until 1198. The period, as might
be expected from the character and training of the minister,
was devoted mainly to the expansion and modification of the
plans by which Henry II had extended at once the profits and
the operations of justice. The constant appeals of Richard for
money gave the archbishop constant opportunities of developing the machinery by which money could be procured, with as
little oppression and as much benefit to the State as were
compatible with the incessant demand[3]. Immediately after
the king's departure a visitation by the justices was held in

*Richard leaves Eng-
land, and is
reconciled
with John.*

*Temporary
peace.*

*Adminis-
tration of
Hubert
Walter.*

*The Iter
of 1194.*

---

[1] Hoveden, iii. 249.   [2] Ibid. 286.
[3] Ralph of Coggeshale says of him: 'Crudelia edicta in quantum potuit
repressit et delenivit, afflictorum miseratus calamitatem et exactoriam de-
testans servitutem;' pp. 92, 93.

September 1194, under a commission of the most extensive

Articles of
the Iter of
1194.
character. By the articles of this 'iter' [1] the constitution of the grand jury of the county is defined; four knights are to be chosen in the county court, these are to select on oath two knights from each hundred, and these two, also on oath, are to add by co-optation ten more for the jury of the hundred; a long list of pleas of the Crown and other agenda of the judges is furnished, which is comprehensive enough to cover all occasions of quarrel and complaint since the beginning of the reign. The sheriffs are forbidden to act as justices in their own shires. The election of officers to keep the pleas of the Crown, which is ordered by another article, is the origin of the office of coroner, another limitation of the importance of the sheriffs. The justices are empowered to hear recognitions by great assize, where lands are concerned up to the amount of five pounds of annual value: the Jews and their persecutors, the dead crusaders, the friends, debts and malversations of John, are to be

Feudal and
other articles
of inquiry.
brought into account. Inquiry is to be made into the king's feudal claims, wards, escheats, ferms, and churches: and the financial work of the judges is to be completed by the exaction of a tallage from all cities, boroughs, and demesnes of the king. It was further intended that a general inquest into the conduct and receipts of the sheriffs, such as had taken place in 1170, should form part of the business, but the archbishop, thinking the work of the judges sufficient already, cancelled for the time

Importance
of the Iter
of 1194.
that article of the commission. This visitation, which comprehends almost all the points of administrative importance which mark the preceding reign, constitutes a stage in the development of the principles of election and representation. The choice of the coroner, and the form prescribed for the election of the grand jury, whether this act originated them or merely marked their growth, are phenomena of no small significance.

Whilst this measure was in contemplation Richard was busily

---

[1] Hoveden, iii. 262–267; Select Charters (ed. 3), pp. 258–263; Gervase, i. 528, 530, 531. Gervase gives an account of the session of these *justitiarii errantes* at Canterbury: they were Oger Fitz-Oger, Geoffrey of Sundridge, and Hugh of Dudington; Henry of Cornhell was the sheriff. They tried pleas under the Assize of Clarendon.

employed in his French provinces in forcing his bailiffs and other Oppressive
acts of
Richard. officers to account for their receipts and to redeem their offices. Amongst other oppressive acts he is said to have taken the seal from his unscrupulous but faithful chancellor, and, having ordered His new
seal. a new one to be made, proclaimed the nullity of all charters which had been sealed with the old one [1]. He also issued licences Licences
for tourna-
ments. for the holding of tournaments, which were expected to bring in a considerable revenue. One act of justice was however done; the chalices of the churches which had surrendered their plate for the royal ransom were replaced by the king's special command [2].

The following year was one of peace and consequent activity. Proceedings
of the year
1195. The tallage of 1194 was followed by a scutage in 1195, levied on those tenants-in-chief who had not accompanied the king to Normandy. This is the second scutage of the reign; the first was taken in the king's first year on the pretence of an expedition to Wales [3]. The justiciar immediately on the reception Hubert at
York as
justiciar
and legate,
June 12–15,
1195. of his legatine commission, in June 1195, proceeded to York, where he held a great court of the most ample description for four days. On the first he directed his servants to hear pleas of the Crown and assizes, whilst he himself and his officials held a spiritual court and heard pleas of Christianity; on the second he acted as legate and visited S. Mary's abbey; on the third and fourth he held a provincial council, which passed fifteen important ecclesiastical canons [4]. One document of interest

---

[1] Hoveden, iii. 267; R. Coggeshale, p. 93. Mr. Round (Feudal England, p. 541) shows that this measure was taken in 1198 rather than in 1194. Richard's first seal was lost when the vice-chancellor was drowned between Rhodes and Cyprus in 1191; but it was recovered with his dead body. The seal that was now superseded may have been the one which the chancellor had used during the king's absence. Richard, however, when he was at Messina, had allowed his seal to be set to various grants for which he took money, but which he never intended to confirm. Therefore probably he found it convenient now to have a new seal in lieu of both the former ones, although he threw the blame of the transactions annulled upon the chancellor. The importance of the seal is already very great. Archbishop Geoffrey was credibly accused of sealing writs with the seal of Henry II after the king's death.   [2] Hoveden, iii. 290.

[3] Madox, Hist. Exch. p. 444. The tax raised on the knight's fee for the king's ransom was called an aid, and not a scutage : a proof that the latter term was now becoming restricted to the payment made in commutation of service.

[4] Hoveden, iii. 293–298; Gervase, i. 529; W. Newb. lib. v. c. 12.

The oath of the peace.

was issued the same year; a proclamation of an oath of the peace, which was to be taken by all persons above the age of fifteen. They swore, according to the old law of Canute, not to be thieves or robbers, or receivers of such, and to fulfil their duty of pursuing the thief when the hue and cry is raised[1]. The enforcement of the edict was committed to knights assigned for the purpose; this is probably the origin of the office of conservator of the peace, out of which, in the reign of Edward III, the existing functions of the justices of the peace were developed; and the record thus forms an interesting link of connexion between the Anglo-Saxon jurisprudence and modern usage.

Effect of pecuniary exactions.

The steady judicial and financial pressure had its usual effect. The archbishop was unable to satisfy the king, and he offended the people. He had constant difficulties with his subordinates, and the Church, which should have been his especial care, was disturbed by quarrels which he had not time to attend to.

Intended inquiry into the Exchequer frustrated.

Early in 1196, Richard, impatient at the delay of the inquiry which he had directed in 1194 to be made into the receipts of the royal officers, sent over two of his confidential servants, Philip of Poictiers the bishop-elect of Durham, and the abbot of Caen, to conduct the investigation[2]. The purpose was defeated by the death of the abbot, but the archbishop seems to

Hubert offers to resign.

have regarded the mission as a sign of the king's distrust. He offered to resign the justiciarship, and with some difficulty prevailed on the king to accept the offer: but before the resignation was completed he saw reason to withdraw it, and, having represented to the king the enormous sums which had been raised during his administration, continued two years longer in office[3]. Almost at the same moment the discontent felt by the poorer citizens of London at the way in which the taxes were collected broke into open revolt. William Fitz-Osbert, who was an old crusader and apparently a hot-headed politician,

[1] See the Laws of Canute, ii. 21; Hoveden, iii. 299; Select Charters (ed. 3), pp. 263, 264; and p. 226, above.
[2] Hoveden, iv. 5; W. Newb. lib. v. c. 19.
[3] Hoveden, iv. 12, 13.

took the lead in the rising. The poorer citizens complained Riot of William Fitz-Osbert, 1196. that the whole burden fell upon them: the tallages were collected by poll, 'per capita;' William insisted that they should be assessed in proportion to the property of the payers. Unfortunately for the citizens, their leader by his violence brought down upon him the vengeance of the archbishop, and, having fallen a victim in the strife, was regarded by the one party as a felon and by the other as a martyr[1]. We do not learn that the Londoners received any benefit from the outbreak. The monks of Canterbury however, who hated the archbishop, took advantage of the fact that the blood of the rioter had been shed at the command of the justiciar in their peculiar church of S. Mary le Bow, and added a fresh accusation to the list of charges on account of which Innocent III ultimately ordered Hubert to resign his secular office. A third scutage was levied in this Scutage of 1196. Assize of Measures. year. In 1197 the justiciar issued an assize intended to secure the uniformity of weights and measures in all parts of the kingdom. This proposition was unable to make way against the usages of the nation: the amount of traffic was not yet so great or so generally diffused as to make it indispensable, and the severity of some of the penalties induced the judges to set it aside early in the reign of John. But it had considerable importance in itself, and formed the basis of one of the articles of the Great Charter[2].

The history of the next year, 1198, furnishes two events of In 1198 the king's demand for money is refused. great importance. In a council of the barons held at Oxford, the archbishop laid before them a demand made by the king that they should provide him a force for his war in Normandy; three hundred knights were to be furnished, each to receive three English shillings every day and to serve for a year.

---

[1] Hoveden, iv. 5; R. Diceto, i. 533; W. Newb. lib. v. c. 20; Gervase, ii. 143. Hoveden, unless he is speaking ironically, applauds the conduct of William Fitz-Osbert: Ralph de Diceto, the dean of S. Paul's, who was an eye-witness, speaks of him as a mere demagogue. William of Newburgh gives a long account of the events, and treats him judicially. He was a disreputable man who, having failed to obtain the king's consent to a piece of private spite, made political capital out of a real grievance of the people. The whole story is worked out by Palgrave in the preface to the Rotuli Curiae Regis.

[2] Hoveden, iv. 33, 34, 172.

There can be no doubt that the demand was unprecedented, whether we consider the greatness of the amount, £16,425, or the definiteness of the proposition. But neither point caused

Opposition of S. Hugh of Lincoln,

the actual objection. The bishop of Lincoln, Hugh of Avalon, the Carthusian friend of Henry II, declared that he would not assent to the grant. In vain the archbishop, and the treasurer the bishop of London, pleaded the royal necessities; the independent prelate declared that the lands of his church were bound to render military service within England and there only: he had, he said, fought the battle of his church for thirteen years; this impost he would not pay; rather than do

and Herbert of Salisbury.

so, he would go back to his home in Burgundy. To the archbishop's further discomfiture, the example of Hugh was followed by Bishop Herbert of Salisbury, who had had the regular ministerial training and was closely connected with the ruling

Resignation of the justiciar.

officers of the Exchequer. The opposition was so far successful that the archbishop withdrew the proposal, and shortly after resigned [1]. This event is a landmark of constitutional history: for the second time a constitutional opposition to a royal demand for money is made, and made successfully. It would perhaps be too great an anticipation of modern usages to suppose that the resignation of the minister was caused by his defeat.

The scheme for collecting the carucage of 1198.

The other remarkable matter of the year is the imposition of a carucage—a tax of five shillings on each carucate or hundred acres of land. This was the Danegeld revived in a new and much more stringent form; and, in order to carry out the plan, a new survey on the principle of Domesday was requisite. Even from this the justiciar did not shrink. A knight and a clerk were sent out into each county, to report on the 31st of May on the extent, liability, and tenure of the land to be taxed: these officers were, in conjunction with the sheriff in each county, to call before them the members of the county court, the stewards of barons, lords and bailiffs, the reeve and four men of each township, whether free or villein, and two knights

[1] Hoveden, iv. 40; Vita S. Hugonis, p. 248; Select Charters, pp. 255, 256. See also Round, Feudal England, pp. 528 sq.

for every hundred : an oath was to be taken from all parties,
that they would speak the truth, and declare how many carucates, or what wainage for ploughs, there were in each township.
Even the words of the Domesday commission were repeated.
The account was registered in four rolls; three kept by the
knight, the clerk, and the sheriff, and one divided among the
stewards of the barons whose interests it concerned. The money
was collected by two knights and the bailiff of each hundred,
who accounted for it to the sheriff; and the sheriff accounted
for it at the Exchequer[1]. The inquiry, which so forcibly recalls
that of 1086, has a significance which does not belong to the
great precedent, unless we regard the machinery of the oath
taken by the representatives of the townships and hundreds in
the two commissions in contrary lights. It may be questioned
whether the jurors of 1086 or those of 1198 had greater freedom
and responsibility: but we look on the former as part of an institution then for the first time adapted to the administration
of the English government ; whilst the latter appear as part of
a system the disciplinary force of which had nearly completed
its work : the plan adopted in the Assize of Arms and in the
ordinance of the Saladin Tithe is now applied to the assessment
of real property ; the principle of representation is gradually
enlarging its sphere of work, and the process now used for the
calculation will before long be applied to the granting of the
tax, and ultimately to the determination of its expenditure.

   This demand of carucage is by no means the last constitutional act of the reign. It is not known whether the survey
was really carried into execution. The resignation of the archbishop took place a few weeks after the date fixed for the
report[2] : and the tax was not collected without difficulty. The
religious houses having demurred to the payment, the king
directed a proclamation to be made by which the clergy were
practically outlawed : if any man injured a clerk or regular he
was not to be forced to compensate him ; but if the clerk or
regular were the aggressor, he must be brought to justice. The

*A new
Domesday
Inquest.*

*Importance
of the caru-
cage of 1198.*

*The religious
are com-
pelled to pay
the tax.*

<hr>

[1] Hoveden, iv. 46 sq.   [2] Ibid. iv. 47, 48.

threat was sufficient to bring the monks to submission, and they purchased a reconciliation[1].

Geoffrey Fitz-Peter justiciar.

Geoffrey Fitz-Peter, the successor of Hubert, who came into office on the 11th of July, 1198, began his career as minister by a severe forest visitation, in the conducting of which he reissued

Iter of 1198.

and enlarged the Assize of Woodstock[2]. He also directed a new 'iter' of the justices on nearly as large a scale as that of 1194[3]. The agenda of this 'iter' contain a direction for the elections of the nominators of the Great Assize to be made before the justices: a proof that these functionaries were not now appointed by the sheriffs, but elected by the suitors of the county court. The Forest Assize also directs that the whole body of the suitors of that assembly shall attend at the sessions

Severity of the government.

of the forest justices[4]. These two measures, together with the severe treatment of the clergy just mentioned, seem to mark the character of the new justiciar as austere and even oppressive. Richard no doubt found in him a servant whose conscience was less strict than Hubert's, and whose position as a layman and an earl was less assailable than that of the archbishop. His real importance as a public man belongs to the next reign.

Richard dies, April 6, 1199.

The laborious and quarrelsome career of Richard came to an end in April, 1199. His subjects, fortunately for themselves, saw very little of him during the ten years of his reign. They heard much of his exploits, and reconciled themselves in the best way they could to his continual exactions. Under his ministers they had good peace, although they paid for it heavily: but the very means that were taken to tax them trained them and set them thinking. The ministers themselves recognised the rising tendency to self-government in such measures as those we have described. To Richard the tendency would be

His character.

probably unintelligible. He was a bad king: his great exploits, his military skill, his splendour and extravagance, his poetical tastes, his adventurous spirit, do not serve to cloak his entire want of sympathy, or even consideration, for his people. He was no Englishman, but it does not follow that he gave to

[1] Hoveden, iv. 66.
[2] Ibid. 63.
[3] Ibid. 61.
[4] Ibid. 63.

Normandy, Anjou, or Aquitaine the love or care that he
denied to his kingdom. His ambition was that of a mere
warrior : he would fight for anything whatever, but he would
sell everything that was worth fighting for. The glory that he
sought was that of victory rather than conquest. Some part of His reputa-
his reputation rests on the possession of qualities which the   tion.
English had no opportunity of testing : they were proud of a
king whose exploits awakened the wonder of Christendom,
they murmured against ministers whose mediation broke the
force of an oppression which would otherwise have crushed
them. Otherwise the latter years of the reign were years of
progress in wealth and in the comfort which arises from security :
a little respite before the tyranny that was coming. The reign Comparative
of Richard is marked by no outbreak of feudal insubordination : peace of
had there been any such, the strength of the administration   England.
would have been sufficient to crush it. But the great nobles Quietness
were, like the king himself, partly engaged abroad ; those of of the
                                                               barons.
them who were left at home had learned the lesson of submission ; they saw themselves surrounded by a new body of equals,
sprung from and working with the ministerial families, and
they were assimilating themselves to this new nobility in forming hopes and ambitions more truly national. The feeling
towards union that was working in society generally was
affecting the barons not less than the people whom they were
to lead on to liberty.

151. The death of Richard was so sudden, and the order of Interreg-
the kingdom so complete at the time, that John, who had re- num after
                                                             the death
ceived the fealty of the barons by his brother's order [1], might of Richard,
have secured the throne without difficulty before the country 1199.
generally knew that it was vacant. Instead of doing this he
allowed an interregnum of six weeks. Secure, as it would
seem, of England, he spent the time in taking possession of the
treasures of Richard, and attempting to obtain the continental

---

[1] Hoveden, iv. 83 : 'Cum autem rex de vita desperaret, divisit Johanni
fratri suo regnum Angliae, et fecit fieri praedicto Johanni fidelitates ab
illis qui aderant.' John was not present ; R. Coggeshale, p. 99. There is
surely in this anxiety of the dying king to provide for his brother and for
the succession at least one redeeming trait : Richard knew how to forgive.

provinces on which Arthur, as the son of his elder brother, had

Archbishop Hubert and William Marshall enforce order.

a half-acknowledged claim. Whilst he was receiving the surrender of the castles of Anjou and Maine and the investiture of the duchy of Normandy, Archbishop Hubert and William Marshall were doing their best to strengthen his position in England[1]. John's six weeks' delay in France gave to the discontented barons an opportunity of reviewing their grievances. The traditional principle, that when the king dies the peace dies with him, was now in full force: seventy years were to elapse before it was superseded by the doctrine of the immediate succession of the heir, expressed later in the maxim that the king never dies: now it had time to work. All who had castles in their hands fortified and garrisoned them; and not a few broke out into open rapine immediately on hearing of the fate of Richard[2]. The archbishop found it no easy task to enforce order, when once the spell was broken. His first measure was to direct that the oath of fealty and peace should be everywhere taken: the sheriffs brought together the force of the shires for the purpose, and all attempts at resistance were put down, the spoil restored, and the offenders brought to

Apprehensions of the great earls.

justice[3]. It was more difficult to allay the apprehensions and secure the adhesion of the earls and other great vassals, who, although they had acquiesced in Richard's oppressions, were by no means inclined to accept the same treatment from John. He had made himself personal enemies during his short tenure of power; some feared and some despised him. The feudal spirit was not extinct, and every one who had anything to gain thought this a fair time for the attempt. The king of Scots might press his claim on the northern counties, the earl of Chester might even support the cause of his stepson Arthur; Roger de Lacy had hanged two knights for betraying his castles to John; the earl of Hertford had claims on the earldom of Gloucester, which John held in right of his wife; the earl Ferrers held his earldom with no very sure hand. The arch-

---

[1] Hoveden, iv. 86.
[2] R. Coggeshale, pp. 98, 99.
[3] Hoveden, iv. 88; R. Coggeshale, p. 99.

bishop, acting in conjunction with the justiciar and William *The arch-bishop pro-cures their adhesion to John.* Marshall, called together at Northampton all those of whom any apprehension was entertained, and made them the most ample promises on behalf of John: not a grievance, public or private, was to remain without redress. Even the Scottish claims should receive due attention; and, wherever a right was in danger, the king, as soon as there should be a king, would confirm and enforce it[1]. The promises of the three ministers were accepted as sufficient security, and all the barons, including Earl David of Huntingdon, the brother of the king of Scots, took the required oaths. In the meanwhile John, having *Arrival of John.* made good his hold on Normandy, crossed over to England for his coronation, which took place on the feast of the Ascension, May 27, 1199.

The ceremony was performed with the same pomp as had *His corona-tion, May 27, 1199.* been used for Richard: the form of election and the solemn promises of good government were repeated. But a speech is preserved by Matthew Paris, which, whether or no the words are genuine, seems to show that there was something exceptional *Speech of Hubert Walter.* in the proceedings; some attempt on the archbishop's part to give to the formality of the election a real validity, which perhaps might be useful if the claims of Arthur should ever be revived. Hubert declared, the historian tells us, that the right to reign *Principle of election enunciated.* is conferred by the election which the nation makes after invoking the grace of the Holy Ghost: Saul and David were made kings, not because they were of royal race, but the one because of his strength and fitness, the other because of his sanctity and humility. Still, if in the royal stock there were one of distinct pre-eminence, the choice should fall more readily on him. Richard had died without an heir; the grace of the Holy Ghost had been asked for: in John were united royal blood, and the good qualities of prudence and energy: all together then elected John. The cry 'Vivat rex' was the answer of the assembled crowd. The archbishop moreover, *Oath of good govern-ment.* when he received the coronation oath, adjured him on God's

[1] Hoveden, iv. 88.

behalf that he would not take the honour to himself without a
full purpose to keep his oath, and John replied that by God's
help in good faith he would keep all that he had sworn[1]. Later
events gave to both these declarations a character which, in the

John's coro-
nation,
May 27,
1199.

case of ordinary kings, they might not have had. Matthew
Paris supposes that the archbishop, warned of John's utter
faithlessness and foreseeing the troubles of his reign, wished to
impress upon him and upon the people that as an elected king
he must do his duty under pain of forfeiture. But the speech
of Hubert was probably in itself nothing more than a declaration of John's fitness to be elected, the recollection of which
would naturally recur to those who heard it when they found
out how unfit he was to reign. The enunciation however of
the elective character of the royal dignity is of very great importance. The circumstances too of John's accession recall
forcibly those which attended that of William Rufus, when
Lanfranc strove in vain to bind the conscience of the prince in
whose exaltation he had so large a share. In more than one
respect Hubert Walter played the part of Lanfranc to John.

Investiture
of earls.

The business of the coronation was followed by the investiture of William Marshall and Geoffrey Fitz-Peter as earls[2]; a

Hubert
chancellor.

ceremony which had been long delayed. The chancellorship
was undertaken by the archbishop, notwithstanding the warning of Hugh Bardulf, who told him plainly that he was de-
rogating from his dignity and making a dangerous precedent.

Faithful-
ness of
Hubert.

Hubert probably saw that John would need both advice and
restraint, which no one of inferior position or weaker character
would be able to enforce. The justiciar continued in office; but
most of the sheriffs were either removed to other counties or
dismissed altogether. No charter of liberties is known to have
been issued; if any such had existed it could scarcely have
failed to be brought forward in the struggle that followed.

John had no time to lose in England: he hurried to Notting-

---

[1] Matthew Paris, ii. 454, 455. In the declaration made by Lewis, on
his invasion of England in 1216, long before Matthew Paris wrote,
this speech of Hubert is distinctly referred to as affecting the claim of
inheritance. See Foedera, i. 140.

[2] Hoveden, iv. 90.

ham to meet the king of Scots, who did not come; and then, on John goes to Normandy, but makes peace and returns early in 1200. the 20th of June, left England, taking with him a large number of the barons to prosecute the war in Normandy [1]. Immediately on his arrival he made a truce with Philip, who for the moment was supporting the claims of Arthur in Anjou and Maine: after Christmas a treaty was concluded between the two kings, and John returned to England to raise money for the purchase of peace, a sum of 30,000 marks. He stayed in the kingdom from New taxes. the 27th of February to the 28th of April, 1200, and took a carucage of three shillings on the hide; a scutage of two marks had just been taken on account of the expedition to Normandy. Both these exactions were in excess of the usual rate [2], and the chroniclers furnish us with no further evidence of the way in which they were imposed and levied, than that the king demanded the aid, and an edict went forth from the justices that it should be paid; a grant of a fortieth of moveables for the Crusade was obtained in the following year by letters addressed by the king to the barons and by the justiciar to the sheriffs [3]. After a second John returns to France in April 1200, and marries a new wife. vain attempt to secure the homage of the king of Scots, John again sailed for France, where he remained until September; employed, after the conclusion of the peace in May, chiefly in divorcing his wife, Hawisia of Gloucester, and marrying Isabella of Angoulême,—acts which caused in England the alienation of the whole of the Gloucester influence from the king, and in France the active and malicious hostility of the house of Lusignan, to whose head Isabella had been betrothed. The month after his On his return he is crowned, Oct. 8, 1200; receives the Scottish homage, Nov. 22; and is crowned a third time, Mar. 25, 1201. return John and his wife were crowned at Westminster [4]; the fealty of the king of Scots was finally received in a great council of bishops and barons of the two kingdoms, and the court made a progress through the north [5]. At Easter, 1201, the coronation ceremonial was again performed at Canterbury [6]; and the state

---

[1] Hoveden, iv. 92, 93.   [2] Ibid. 107; R. Coggeshale, p. 101.
[3] Ibid. 188, 189.
[4] Ibid. 139. R. Coggeshale says more particularly that the king wore his crown, but the queen was consecrated; p. 103. R. Diceto says, ' ipse rex eadem die pariter coronatus est;' ii. 170.
[5] Hoveden, iv. 140 sq.
[6] Ibid. 160. R. Diceto, ii. 172: ' instinctu archiepiscopi.'

of peace and order which had lasted for two years began almost immediately afterwards to break up. The remainder of the history of the reign may be briefly examined under the three heads of foreign affairs, the great ecclesiastical quarrel, and the struggle which led to the granting of Magna Carta.

Foreign politics of John's early years.

152. John possessed in his mother, Queen Eleanor, who was now nearly eighty, a counsellor of much experience in continental politics, of great energy and devoted faithfulness. As long as she lived his fortunes in France were not hopeless; she had herself headed an army against Arthur, and her last public act was to fetch her granddaughter, Blanche of Castille, from Spain, in order to strengthen the new alliance between Philip

Peace in 1200 with France.

John goes to Normandy in 1201.

Philip in 1202 declares that he has forfeited his fiefs.

and John by a royal marriage. Unfortunately the peace so made was very shortlived; quarrels on the Norman frontier called John from England in June, 1201, and he did not return until the inheritance of his fathers had passed away from him. Early in 1202 Philip, having obtained a respite from his matrimonial troubles, and found time to listen to the complaints of Hugh of Lusignan, summoned John to trial after Easter at Paris for oppressing the barons of Poictou[1]. John refused to attend, and was declared to have forfeited his fiefs as a contu-

Arthur captured.

macious vassal[2]. Arthur, taking advantage of the confusion, raised a force and besieged his grandmother in the castle of Mirabel, where he was captured by John; and, after some mysterious transactions, he disappeared finally on the 3rd of

John a second time condemned to forfeiture.

April, 1203. Philip, who believed with the rest of the world that John had murdered him, summoned him again to be tried on the accusation made by the barons of Brittany[3]. Again John was contumacious, and this time Philip himself undertook to

Loss of Normandy.

enforce the sentence of the court. City after city, castle after castle, fell before him. The Norman barons were unwilling to

---

[1] Rigord (Bouquet, xvii. 54); R. Coggeshale, p. 135; R. Wendover, iii. 167; Alberic of Trois Fontaines, p. 423; Will. Armoric. (Bouquet, xvii. 75).
[2] M. Paris, ii. 480, states that John visited England and was again crowned at Canterbury, April 14, 1202. But we know, from his Itinerary, that he was on that day at Orival near Rouen.
[3] See Le Baud, Hist. Bret. p. 210; Morice, Hist. Bret. i. 132; Foedera, i. 140; R. Wendover, iii. 273; M. Paris, ii. 657; Chron. Lanercost, p. 2; Ann. Margam, p. 27; Walter of Coventry, ii. pref. xxxii, xxxiii.

fight the battles of a king who wasted his opportunities and would scarcely strike a blow for himself. In November, 1203, John returned to England and left Normandy to its fate[1]; he distrusted the barons, and they distrusted him. In the following spring both Normandy and Anjou were lost; John pretending to raise an army in England, and selling to the barons his licence to absent themselves, or exacting scutages on the pretence that they had deserted him. Eleanor died on the 1st of April, 1204[2]; and the month of July saw Philip supreme in the whole of Normandy, Maine, Anjou, and Touraine. John never again set foot in Normandy: in 1205 he raised an army, but dismissed it. In 1206[3] he made an attempt to recover Poictou, where he still had some ground, but was obliged to purchase a truce of two years by surrendering his last hold on the Norman and Angevin inheritance. In 1214 again, after his quarrel with the Church was settled, he made an expensive and fruitless expedition to Guienne, which likewise ended in a truce.

John returns to England in 1203.

Death of Eleanor, 1204.

John's faint attempts to recover his states.

Normandy was at last separated from England; the prophecy of Merlin was fulfilled, the sword of the duchy was separated from the sceptre of the kingdom[4]. The Norman barons had had no choice but between John and Philip. For the first time since the Conquest there was no competitor for their allegiance, no son, brother, or more distant kinsman. John could neither rule nor defend them. Bishops and barons alike welcomed or speedily accepted their new lord. The families that had estates on both sides of the Channel divided into two branches, each of which made terms for itself; or, having balanced their interests in the two kingdoms, threw in their lot with one or other, and renounced what they could not save. Almost immediately Normandy settles down into a quiet province of France; a province which Philip was willing to govern by Norman law,

Separation of Normandy from England.

Importance of the separation.

---

[1] M. Paris, ii. 483. [2] Ann. Waverley, A.D. 1204.
[3] M. Paris, ii. 494; Foedera, i. 95.
[4] 'Gladius a sceptro separatus est;' R. Coggeshale, p. 146. An illustration of the process of separation may be found as early as 1199, when the earls of Pembroke and Clare divided the Giffard estates, the former taking the 'esnecia et caput' in Normandy, the latter in England.

and to indulge in such free customs as the Normans could challenge as their own. For England the result of the separation was more important still. Even within the reign of John it became clear that the release of the barons from their connexion with the Continent was all that was wanted to make them Englishmen. With the last vestiges of the Norman inheritance vanished the last idea of making England a feudal kingdom. The Great Charter was won by men who were maintaining, not the cause of a class, as had been the case in every civil war since 1070, but the cause of a nation. From the year 1203 the king stood before the English people face to face; over them alone he could tyrannise, none but they were amenable to his exactions: and he stood alone against them, no longer the lord of half of France, or of a host of strong knights who would share with him the spoils of England. The royal power and the royal dignity that had towered so haughtily over the land in the last two reigns was subjected to a searching examination: the quarrels of the next few years revealed all the weakness of the cause which had lately been so strong, and the strength of the nation which had so lately been well contented to sustain the strength of its oppressor.

153. As the death of Eleanor marks the collapse of John's continental power and the end of the dynastic system of the Conqueror, that of Hubert Walter marks the termination of the alliance between the king and the clergy which had been cemented by Lanfranc and had not been completely broken by the quarrel of Anselm, or even by that of Becket. The archbishop died in July, 1205; John lost his wisest adviser by an event which itself launched him in circumstances requiring the most prudent counsel. Engaged in a quarrel from which a little circumspection would have saved him, he chose to enter the lists against Innocent III; matching his own low cunning at once against the consummate diplomacy of the Curia and the aspiring statesmanship of the greatest of all the popes. Foiled in his attempt to place a creature of his own on the throne of Canterbury, and unwilling to agree in a compromise which he had himself made imperative, he refused

Margin notes:

Consolidation of the English nationality.

The king face to face with his people.

The death of Hubert Walter produces the quarrel between John and the clergy in 1205.

John with a fair cause puts himself in the wrong.

to receive the newly-consecrated archbishop, and exposed the country to the shame and horrors of an interdict.

Not to dwell in this place on the important question of the bearing of this quarrel on the history of the Church, it may be sufficient to mark the epochs of the struggle, during the whole of which John continued in the British islands. Hubert Walter died on the 12th of July, 1205; the appeals of the monks of Canterbury and of the suffragan bishops, with an application from John for the confirmation of his nominee, were carried to Rome before Christmas. The pope decided against all the claims in December, 1206, and, taking advantage of the presence of the monks with letters of authorisation from John, prevailed on them to elect Stephen Langton. John refused the royal assent, and Innocent chose to regard it as dispensable. In June, 1207, he consecrated the new archbishop. John persevered in his refusal to receive Langton; the kingdom was placed under interdict on the 23rd of March, 1208; and in 1209 the king was declared excommunicate. Year after year the pope attempted to renew negotiations, but each year the attempt failed. The king seized the estates of the clergy, and many of the bishops fled from the kingdom[1]. The large revenues thus made available were used by John in making enormous military preparations : he made expeditions to Wales and Ireland, and grew richer and stronger as he grew more contumacious. In 1211 the pope, by the mouth of his envoys Pandulf and Durand, declared that unless the king would submit he would issue a bull absolving his subjects from their allegiance, would depose him from his throne, and commit the execution of the mandate to Philip of France. The news of this determination brought into action a widely-spread feeling of disaffection which, if it existed before, had not yet found vent. The barons had sat still whilst the bishops were plundered. Some of the ministers, if not all, sympathised with John, and made their profit out of the spoil. But the great majority of the people, noble as well as simple, watched in anxious suspense for the event of the struggle.

Chronology of the struggle.

The Interdict, 1208.

John's use of it to exact money.

Threat of deposition, 1211.

Neutrality of the barons.

---

[1] Walter of Coventry, ii. pref. pp. liv–lix.

John however had made private enemies as well as public ones; he trusted no man, and no man trusted him. The threat of deposition aroused all his fears, and he betrayed his apprehensions in the way usual with tyrants. The princes of Wales had just concluded a peace with him; they were the first to take advantage of the papal threat, and renewed the war. John hanged their hostages and summoned an army for a fresh invasion of their country; the army assembled, but John, warned of the existence of a conspiracy, did not venture to lead it into Wales. In panic fear he dismissed his host, and shut himself up in Nottingham Castle. Gathering courage after a fortnight's seclusion he arrested some of the barons, whom he suspected not so much of conspiring as of having power to injure him, and seized their castles [1]. This proceeding alarmed the few nobles who had really entertained designs against him. Eustace de Vesci and Robert Fitz-Walter, the chiefs of the party, fled to France. The king next tried to propitiate the people: he remitted the fines which had been exacted during a recent visitation of the forests; he abolished some vexatious customs which prevailed in the ports; and took other measures for the preservation of peace [2]. He then compelled those bishops who still remained in England to acknowledge by letter that the sums of money which he had exacted from them since the beginning of the reign had been paid by them as their own free gift. In the meantime he was negotiating continually with the pope; and Philip of France was collecting his forces for an invasion.

The spring of 1213 saw the close of this part of the struggle: John had every reason to fear the strength of Philip, and no reason whatever to trust in the attachment of his people. In

---

[1] Walt. Cov. ii. 207; M. Paris, ii. 534.

[2] 'Nam cum novis exactionibus forestarii totam fere Angliam plurimum vexassent, rex sortem miseratus afflictorum eas omnino remisit. Insuper et forestariorum capitaneos jurare compulit ut ea tantum exigerent quae in diebus patris sui exigere consueverant. Alios etiam qui obtentu servandorum portuum plurimas tum civibus tum peregrinis et mercatoribus intulerant molestias, et novas adinvenerant exactiones, ab hujusmodi molestatione compescuit, et novas exactiones remisit. Sed et viduis dicitur propitius exstitisse, et pacis provisioni, quantum ad temporalia attinet, satis sedulus exstitisse;' Walt. Cov. ii. 207; M. Paris, ii. 537.

John's misgivings.

Welsh war, 1212.

He seizes the castles of the barons whom he suspects.

He courts the people,

and negotiates with the pope.

In 1213 he prepares to submit.

spite of his own scoffing disregard of religion, he trembled at
the papal excommunication, the dire effects of which he saw in
the downfall of his nephew the Emperor Otto; but above all he
dreaded the fulfilment of the prophecy of Peter of Wakefield,
that on the approaching feast of the Ascension he should be no
longer king[1]. In abject alarm he surrendered every point for *He surrenders his*
which he had been struggling. He made his submission to the *crown to*
pope, accepted Langton as archbishop, undertook to repay the *the pope, May 15, 1213.*
money exacted from the churches, and, as a crowning humilia-
tion, surrendered his kingdom to the see of Rome, receiving it
again as a papal vassal subject to tribute, and swearing fealty
and promising liege homage to the pope. The pacification was
arranged on the 15th of May. For a moment it was accepted
as a solution of all difficulties[2]: no one seemed to see that it
created a new one which was greater than all and comprehended
all that had preceded it: but it was only for a moment; before
the first measures preliminary to the execution of the treaty
were taken, a new and still more formidable question arose,
from the determination of the barons not to obey John's command to serve in France.

154. The attitude of the barons had been more or less *Formidable*
threatening since the beginning of the reign: they had indeed *attitude of the barons.*
acquiesced in the plunder of the churches, partly because they
saw in it one way of diverting the king's oppressive policy from
themselves. The moment the ecclesiastical difficulty was overcome, the question of their rights and of the king's infringement
of them emerged. We have seen that their adhesion to John at *Their grievances.*
his accession had been purchased by a promise that he would
do them justice: they had claimed the fulfilment of the promise
in 1201, when, on their refusal to go to Normandy until they
were satisfied, John seized their castles and demanded their
sons as hostages[3]. Since then their grounds of complaint had
been accumulating. They had been shamelessly taxed: the *Heavy*
carucage had been in John's first year raised from two to three *scutages.*

[1] Walt. Cov. ii. 208; M. Paris, ii. 535, 541, 547.
[2] Walt. Cov. ii. 210, 211; M. Paris, ii. 539 sq.
[3] Hoveden, iv. 161.

shillings on the carucate: the scutage from a pound to two marks on the knight's fee: year after year the scutage had been taken as a matter of course, and when Geoffrey of York had raised his voice against the imposition of the carucage he had been summarily silenced[1]. In 1203 the king had exacted a seventh of the moveable property of his barons[2]; in 1204 he had taken an aid from the knights[3]: in 1207 a thirteenth of moveables from the whole country. In this last case Archbishop Geoffrey of York, following the example of S. Thomas and S. Hugh, resisted the demand when it was laid before the council; the clergy refused to give, but the king exacted the tax notwithstanding, and sent their champion into exile[4]. Again and again he had demanded the military service of the barons, and each time he had shown his distrust and cowardice. In 1201 the forces assembled at Portsmouth were allowed to return home on payment of money to the king[5]; in 1202 and 1203, when they reached Normandy, they found the king unwilling to fight, and having returned home in disgust found themselves obliged to redeem their desertion by enormous fines[6]. In 1205, under alarm of invasion, he collected a great force; insisted on new oaths of fealty being taken by the whole nation, and in preparation for national defence ordered an elaborate new organisation to be created for the levying of the old armed militia. He himself was obliged at Oxford to swear to observe the rights of the kingdom[7]. But notwithstanding this show of earnestness, when he had brought his great host together at Portsmouth, and had even pretended to sail for France, he had gone no farther than Wareham, and on his return had accepted money and dismissed the army[8]. The barons were not without the military pride natural to a warlike race; they despised the king who dared not lead them; they hated him for his mistrust of them; they looked with

Resistance of archbishop Geoffrey in 1207.

Disgust of the barons.

---

[1] Hoveden, iv. 140.
[2] M. Paris, ii. 483.
[3] Ibid. ii. 484.
[4] Ibid. ii. 511; Ann. Waverley, p. 258.
[5] Hoveden, iv. 163.
[6] M. Paris, ii. 483.
[7] Gervase, Gesta Regum, Opp. ii. 97. See below, cap. xiii. § 162.
[8] M. Paris, ii. 490.

disgust on the mean trickery by which he qualified his capricious despotism. But they endured it all.

Geoffrey Fitz-Peter, the earl of Essex, had continued to be John's justiciar ever since his accession. He was a man trained in the school of Henry II under Glanvill and Hubert Walter, and had attained his earldom partly by a fortunate marriage and partly by making the best of his opportunities as one of the king's counsellors[1]. He had shown the qualities necessary to the minister of such a king, had worked out his master's plans, and allowed the unpopularity which they involved to fall upon his own head. It must be said in excuse for him, as for Hubert Walter, that he probably retained his position partly from a feeling that, if he resigned it, it would fall into worse hands. Both ministers were hated by the king, who felt that they restrained him; yet both were indispensable. Hubert had governed both the Church and the nation, Geoffrey governed the nation and allowed the king to ruin the Church. He had won by age and ability a commanding position even amongst those who were at first inclined to regard him as an upstart[2]; and the extent of his influence must be calculated from the permanent breach which followed his death.

Character of Geoffrey Fitz-Peter, justiciar, 1198-1213.

He acted as a restraint on John.

To return however to the events of the year 1213. The submission of the king to the pope had been accomplished; the fatal anniversary had passed over, and John was still a king: Peter of Wakefield was hanged. It was time to reply to the threats of Philip; and this could not be done better than by an expedition to France. John, elated by the naval victory at Damme, proposed it to the barons; they alleged that he was still excommunicate, and refused to follow him[3]. This plea was

John prepares to go to France: reluctance of the barons.

[1] Hoveden, iii. pref. pp. xlviii, xlix; W. Cov. ii. pref. lxi, lxii.

[2] M. Paris, ii. 558: 'Erat autem firmissima regni columna, utpote vir generosus, legum peritus, thesauris, reditibus et omnibus bonis instauratus, omnibus Angliae magnatibus sanguine vel amicitia confoederatus, unde rex ipsum prae omnibus mortalibus sine dilectione formidabat, ipse enim lora regni gubernabat.'

[3] M. Paris, ii. 549. Ralph of Coggeshale and the monk of Barnwell, copied by Walter of Coventry (ii. 212), give other reasons for the refusal of the barons; the literal terms of their tenure, their exhaustion after their long march, and their poverty. 'Barones Northanhumbrenses

His absolution, and new oath.

soon set aside: the archbishop landed on the 16th of July, and absolved the king at Winchester, exacting from him an express renewal of his coronation oath and a promise to abolish all evil customs[1].   Again the king laid his proposals before the barons,

The barons refuse foreign service.

and again he was met by a refusal : this time the northern barons declared that their tenure did not compel them to serve abroad and that they would not follow the king[2].   It was the same ground which had been taken up by S. Hugh in 1198, and, although deficient in historical proof, was in accordance both with equity and with the altered state of things.   It might be fair enough, when John was duke of Normandy, for his English barons to maintain him by arms in his existing rights; but when Normandy was lost, and lost by his fault, it by no means followed that they should engage in war to recover it.   Whether he had a right to take them to Poictou was more than doubtful.

Conduct of the northern barons.

The northern barons who alleged this plea were for the most part members of that second aristocracy which had grown up on the ruins of the Conquest families and had no stake in Normandy. They had been trained under the eye of Glanvill and Richard de Lucy; had been uniformly faithful to the king against the greater feudatories; had manfully discharged their duties in the defence against the Scots ; and had already begun to show that propension towards political liberty and self-government which marks them during later history; for they were the forefathers of that great north country party which fought the battle of the constitution during the fourteenth and fifteenth centuries.   In-

---

invitavit ut secum transfretarent : at illi pari animo eademque sententia contradixerunt asserentes non in hoc ei obnoxios esse secundum munia terrarum suarum, sed et in expeditionibus Anglicanis se nimis exhaustos et vehementer extenuatos ;' R. Coggeshale, p. 167. 'Quippe qui longa expeditione vexati non facile possent tantum opus exhaustis aggredi cistarchiis ;' W. Cov. ii. 212.

[1] M. Paris, ii. 550: 'Juravit rex, tactis sacrosanctis evangeliis, quod sanctam ecclesiam ejusque ordinatos diligeret, defenderet et manuteneret contra omnes adversarios suos pro posse suo, quodque bonas leges antecessorum suorum et praecipue leges Edwardi regis revocaret, et iniquas destrueret, et omnes homines suos secundum justa curiae suae judicia judicaret, quodque singulis redderet jura sua.'

[2] M. Paris, ii. 551, refers to this second application the excuse of poverty alleged by the barons : and no doubt the reasons mentioned by Ralph and Walter belong to this juncture ; see above, p. 563, note 3.

dignant at their attitude of resistance, John prepared to take John goes into the his usual prompt vengeance. He marched rapidly northwards : north, Aug. at Northampton the archbishop overtook him and prevailed on 25 to Sept. 28, 1213. him to promise a legal and judicial investigation before proceeding to extremities[1]. John however went on his way; advanced to Durham by way of a demonstration, but returned without doing anything, in as great haste as he had gone[2]. On the 3rd of October he completed his transactions with the pope He does homage to the legate. by doing homage to the legate Nicolas at London[3].

Whilst John was thus employed, a series of very important Assembly at S. Alban's, meetings had been held by the justiciar and archbishop. In August 4, 1213; order to ascertain the amount due by way of restitution to the plundered bishops, a general assembly was called at S. Alban's on the 4th of August, which was attended not only by the bishops and barons, but by a body of representatives from the townships on the royal demesne, each of which sent its reeve and four legal men. In this council, for such is the name given it by the historians[4], a much wider range of subjects was discussed than the assessment of the losses of the Church. The in which the laws of justiciar laid before the whole body the king's recent promise of Henry I are mentioned. good government, he issued an edict forbidding the illegal exactions, and referred to the laws of Henry I as the standard of the good customs which were to be restored[5]. This is the

---

[1] W. Cov. ii. 212 ; M. Paris, ii. 551. Ralph of Coggeshale, p. 167, says that the king was prevailed on to renew his promises to the northern barons : 'Northanhumbrenses regi concordantur, mediantibus legato, archiepiscopo Cantuariensi et aliis episcopis et baronibus, ea conditione ut liceat eis gaudere atavis libertatibus.' But he places the agreement after the arrival of Cardinal Nicolas.

[2] See Sir T. D. Hardy's Itinerary of John, in the Introduction to the first volume of the Patent Rolls.

[3] W. Cov. ii. 214; M. Paris, ii. 570.

[4] M. Paris, ii. 550 : 'In crastino (sc. May 16) autem misit rex litteras ad omnes vicecomites regni Angliae praecipiens ut de singulis dominicorum suorum villis quatuor legales homines cum praeposito apud Sanctum Albanum pridie nonas Augusti facerent convenire. . . . Interfuerunt huic concilio apud Sanctum Albanum Galfridus filius Petri et episcopus Wintoniensis cum archiepiscopo et episcopis et magnatibus regni.'

[5] Ibid. ii. 551: 'Ubi cunctis pace regis denunciata, ex ejusdem regis parte firmiter praeceptum est quatenus leges Henrici avi sui ab omnibus in regno custodirentur et omnes leges iniquae penitus enervarentur. Denunciatum est praeterea vicecomitibus, forestariis, aliisque ministris regis,

first occasion on which the laws of Henry I are recurred to as a
basis of liberty, and it may be regarded as a mark of the vast
increase in royal power which had accrued since the early years
of Henry II.   Probably few knew what the laws of Henry I
were; but the archbishop took care that they should soon be

Council of
London.
The charter
of Henry I
produced,
Aug. 25, 1213.

informed.   Another council was called at S. Paul's on the 25th
of August, and there Henry's charter was produced [1].   It was
seen at once that it furnished both a safe standing-ground and a
precedent for a deliberate scheme of reform.   The justiciar laid
before the king the claims of the council, and died almost
immediately after, on the 2nd of October [2].

The king's
remark on
the death
of the jus-
ticiar, Oct. 2,
1213.

With him the king lost his hold upon the baronage, but his
first thought was one of relief: 'When he arrives in hell,' he
said, 'he may go and salute Hubert Walter; for, by the feet of
God, now for the first time am I king and lord of England.'
This speech recalls the words addressed by the English to
Henry I when he had humbled Robert of Belesme; but the
circumstances were very different.   The people had then rejoiced in the humiliation of a tyrant who was persecuting the
king and themselves alike; John rejoices in the death of a
faithful servant who had until now stood between him and the
hatred of the people,—between the tyrant and his destined

victims [3].   Geoffrey's successor was a foreigner; the king, to
the great disgust of the barons, confided the justiciarship to
Peter des Roches, the Poictevin bishop of Winchester [4].

The meeting at S. Alban's is the first occasion on which we
find any historical proof that representatives were summoned to
a national council.   The reeve and four men were probably
called upon merely to give evidence as to the value of the royal
lands; but the fact that so much besides was discussed at the
time, and that some important measures touching the people at
large flowed directly from the action of the council, gives to

sicut vitam et membra sua diligunt, ne a quoquam aliquid violenter extor-
queant, vel alicui injuriam irrogare praesumant, aut scotalla alicubi in
regno faciant sicut facere consueverunt.'
[1] M. Paris, ii. 552.
[2] M. Paris, ii. 558; W. Cov. ii. 215; R. Coggeshale, p. 168.
[3] M. Paris, ii. 559; see above, p. 334.   [4] R. Coggeshale, p. 168.

their appearance there a great significance. To the first It is a general meeting of representatives.
representative assembly on record is submitted the first draught
of the reforms afterwards embodied in the Charter: the action
of this council is the first hesitating and tentative step towards
that great act in which Church, baronage, and people made
their constitutional compact with the king, and their first
sensible realisation of their corporate unity and the unity of
their rights and interests. How the justiciar would have
carried on the undertaking we cannot even guess. Unfortu- Obscurity of the historians.
nately, as is so often the case in great crises of history, the
attention of the historians is devoted to points of minor interest;
and, when we should hear of great constitutional debates, we find
only the record of the doings of the legates and the bishops.
The one significant fact is this,—that the king on the 7th of The writ of November 7, 1213.
November summoned a council at Oxford to which, besides the
armed force of the knights, each sheriff is directed to send four
discreet knights from his county to discuss with the king the
business of the country [1]. The four legal men of the demesne
townships are replaced by the four discreet men of the shire:
the very words, 'ad loquendum nobiscum de negotiis regni
nostri,' are an omen of the institution of representative parliaments. Again however the historians forsake us, and we do not
even know that the assembly was ever held.

The eventful year came to a close without overt action. Early In 1214 John goes abroad until Oct. 19.
in 1214 John went abroad and stayed there until October; when
immediately on his return he called the northern barons to
account for not accompanying him. But they had been before-
hand with him. They had met on the pretence of pilgrimage Confederation of the barons at S. Edmund's.
at S. Edmund's, and had there sworn that if the king delayed
any longer to restore the laws and liberties, they would withdraw
their allegiance, and would make war upon him until he should
confirm the concession by a sealed charter. The propositions
were to be laid before him immediately after Christmas; in
the meantime a force was to be raised sufficient to begin if not
to decide the struggle [2]. The king however accelerated the

---

[1] Report on the Dignity of a Peer, App. i. p. 2 ; Select Charters, p. 287.
[2] M. Paris, ii. 582, 583. The northern barons again took the lead.

crisis by demanding a scutage, which the barons refused to grant[1].

John grants freedom of election to the bishops, November, 1214.

John's first thought was to attempt to divide his enemies. The clergy might be detached from the barons by a promise of the freedom of election which had been so long withdrawn from them; and on the 21st of November a charter was issued to that effect[2]. This failed of its purpose; for the bishops, with Langton at their head, had of course not taken part in the oath at S. Edmund's; they were one in counsel with the barons, but had not been compelled to break off relations with the king; nor could they have armed their retainers in the cause without throwing the country at once into civil war. Nothing more was done until after Christmas. On the feast of the Epiphany, John at the Temple received a deputation from the barons and heard their demands: smothering his indignation, he requested a truce until the first Sunday after Easter[3]. This was agreed to; and the king employed the respite in renewed attempts to sow distrust among his enemies. He again, on the 15th of January, issued the charter of freedom to the Church[4], directed the oath of allegiance and fealty to be taken throughout England[5] to him alone, and demanded a renewal of

He receives the barons, Jan. 6, 1215.

His measures of precaution.

' Barones Northanhumbriae in unam coeuntes sententiam ut regem compellerent ad reformandam ecclesiae et regni libertatem et ad abolendas pravas consuetudines, quas ad depressionem ecclesiae et regni tam pater quam frater regis, cum his abusionibus quas idem rex adjecerat, olim suscitaverant, secundum quod rex anno praeterito juraverat, regem super his . . . . orant et adhortantur, insuper et cartam Henrici primi proferunt;' R. Coggeshale, p. 170.

[1] 'Dissensio orta est inter Johannem regem Angliae et quosdam de proceribus pro scutagio quod petebat ab illis qui non ierant nec miserant cum ipso in Pictaviam. Dantibus enim illud plurimis, contradixerunt ex Aquilonaribus nonnulli, illi videlicet qui anno praeterito regem ne in Pictaviam transiret impedierunt, dicentes se propter terras quas in Anglia tenent non debere regem extra regnum sequi nec ipsum euntem scutagio juvare. E contrario rege id tanquam debitum exigente, eo quod in diebus patris sui necnon et fratris sic fieret, res ulterius processisset nisi legati praesentia obstitisset. Prolata est carta quaedam libertatum ab Henrico primo Anglis data, quam quasi in observandam cum sibi confirmari a rege proceres jam dicti postularent, dilata est res in annum alterum;' W. Cov. ii. 217, 218.

[2] Statutes of the Realm, i. 5; Select Charters, pp. 279–281.
[3] M. Paris, ii. 584.   [4] Ibid. 608–610.
[5] M. Paris, ii. 584; W. Cov. ii. 218.

homage from his tenants-in-chief. Not content with this, on the 2nd of February, he took the vow of Crusade [1], involving in the guilt of sacrilege all who should raise their hands against him. But the barons were undismayed; they collected an army at Stamford, and marched as soon as the truce expired to Brackley in Northamptonshire where they encamped on the 27th of April. The king, who was at Oxford, sent the archbishop and William Marshall to demand their conditions; and the messengers brought back a long schedule of demands, which the king at once refused to grant. After an attempt to gain time by proposing, on the 10th of May, that the quarrel should be settled by arbitration by the pope and eight arbitrators, four chosen by each side, John had nothing left but to await the attack of the barons who had already on the 5th of May renounced their allegiance [2]. As soon as they knew that their demands were rejected they proceeded by way of Northampton, Bedford, and Ware to London, where they were received with a hearty welcome on the 24th of May. The adhesion of the Londoners was followed by a great defection from the king's party; nearly all the members of his court and household obeyed the summons addressed to them by the confederacy, and left John without any power of resistance. Under these circumstances he set his seal to the articles proposed by the barons, and issued the Great Charter of liberties on the 15th of June at Runnymede [3].

Progress of the barons.

The barons enter London, May 24, 1215.

John is deserted by his court and grants the Charter.

155. The Great Charter, although drawn up in the form of a royal grant, was really a treaty between the king and his subjects; it was framed upon a series of articles drawn up by them [4], it contained the provision usual in treaties for securing its execution, and, although in express terms it contained only one part of the covenant, it implied in its whole

Summary of the articles of the Charter.

[1] W. Cov. ii. 219.
[2] Lib. de Antt. Legg. p. 201; Ann. Dunst. p. 43. See Blackstone, Charters, p. xiii.
[3] M. Paris, ii. 585–589; W. Coventry, ii. 219–222; R. Coggeshale, pp. 171–173. The best account of the crisis is to be found in the preface prefixed by Blackstone to his edition of Magna Carta.
[4] Foedera, i. 129, 130.

tenour the existence and recognition of the other. The king
granted these privileges on the understanding that he was to

Its treaty
character.

retain the allegiance of the nation. It is the collective people
who really form the other high contracting party in the great
capitulation,—the three estates of the realm, not it is true
arranged in order according to their profession or rank, but
not the less certainly combined in one national purpose, and
securing by one bond the interests and rights of each other
severally and of all together. The Charter contains a clause
similar to that by which Henry I tried to secure the rights of
his subjects as against the mesne lords ; but now the provision
is adopted by the lords themselves for the security of fair and

It includes
the whole
people.

equal justice : ' All the aforesaid customs and liberties that we
have granted to be held in our kingdom, so far as pertains to us,
with reference to our vassals, all men of our kingdom, as well
clerk as lay, shall observe, so far as pertains to them, with
reference to their men [1].' The barons maintain and secure the
right of the whole people as against themselves as well as

It protects
the rights of
the com-
mons.

against their master. Clause by clause the rights of the
commons are provided for as well as the rights of the nobles ;
the interest of the freeholder is everywhere coupled with that
of the barons and knights ; the stock of the merchant and the
wainage of the villein are preserved from undue severity of
amercement as well as the settled estate of the earldom or
barony [2]. The knight is protected against the compulsory
exaction of his services, and the horse and cart of the freeman against the irregular requisition even of the sheriff [3]. In
every case in which the privilege of the simple freeman is not
secured by the provision that primarily affects the knight or
baron, a supplementary clause is added to define and protect his

---

[1] Articles of the Barons, § 48 ; Magna Carta, § 62. See above, p. 331.

[2] Art. Bar. § 8 ; Magna Carta, § 20 : ' Liber homo non amercietur pro
parvo delicto nisi secundum modum delicti, et pro magno delicto amercietur secundum magnitudinem delicti, salvo contenemento suo ; et mer-
cator eodem modo salva mercandisa sua ; et villanus eodem modo amercietur salvo wainnagio suo, si inciderint in misericordiam meam ; et nulla
praedictarum misericordiarum ponatur nisi per sacramentum proborum
hominum de visneto.'

[3] Art. Bar. § 20 ; Magna Carta, § 30.

right; and the whole advantage is obtained for him by the comprehensive article which closes the essential part of the charter.

This proves, if any proof were wanted, that the demands of the barons were no selfish exaction of privilege for themselves; it proves with scarcely less certainty that the people for whom they acted were on their side. The nation in general, the people of the towns and villages, the commons of later days, the Englishmen who had fought the battles of the Norman kings against the feudatories, had now thrown themselves on the side of the barons: John's tyranny had overthrown that balance of the powers of the State which his predecessors had striven with so much earnestness and so much policy to adjust. We do not indeed find, in the list of those who forced the king to yield, any names that prove the commons to have been influential in the drawing up of the articles: the conspicuous names are those of the northern barons, of the men of the great ministerial houses, and of that remnant of the Conqueror's baronage that had cut themselves loose from Normandy and Norman principles and reconciled themselves to the nobler position of leaders of their brother Englishmen. It was probably by the bishops, Langton in particular, and the legal members of the confederacy, that the rights of the freeholder were so carefully fenced round with provisions. These men and their successors led the commons and acted for them until the Reformation, with little discord and still less jealousy of their rising influence; and it was the extinction of the class which furnished their natural leaders that threw the Church and the nation under the tyranny that followed the Wars of the Roses.

The Great Charter is the first great public act of the nation, after it has realised its own identity: the consummation of the work for which unconsciously kings, prelates, and lawyers have been labouring for a century. There is not a word in it that recalls the distinctions of race and blood, or that maintains the differences of English and Norman law. It is in one view the summing up of a period of national life, in another the starting-point of a new period, not less eventful than that which it closes.

The barons did not act selfishly.

The people were on their side.

Debt of the people to the bishops and lawyers.

The barons as leaders of the people.

The Great Charter, a corporate act of the nation.

It is based
on the
Charter of
Henry I.

Magna Carta in its completed form attests the account given by the historians of its origin and growth. It is based on the charter of Henry I; it follows the arrangement of that famous document, and it amplifies and expands it, so as to bring under the principles, which were for the first time laid down in A.D. 1100, all the particular rights, claims, and duties which had come into existence during the developments of the intervening century. As the whole of the constitutional history of England is little more than a commentary on Magna Carta, a brief summary of the articles, regarded as the outgrowth of the previous history, is all that is necessary or possible at this stage of our work.

Motive
clause of
the Charter.

The king declares himself moved to issue the charter, as his great-grandfather had done, by his pious regard for God and his desire for the benefit of his people : the counsellors by whose advice he acts, and whose names he enumerates, are the bishops and barons who had not taken an overt part against him, or who only at the last moment had joined the confederation which compelled him to yield.

Grant of
Church
liberties.

The first clause, again, as in the charter of Henry I, secures the rights of the Church; repeats and confirms the charter, twice issued already, for the free election to bishoprics, and the great principle so often appealed to both earlier and later, ' quod Anglicana Ecclesia libera sit [1].'

Remedy
of feudal
abuses in
the matters
of relief,
wardship,
and mar-
riage.

This is followed by a series of clauses protecting the tenants-in-chief of the Crown from the abuses of feudal right; a fixed sum is determined for the relief, as 'the ancient relief,' the very statement betraying the nature of the grievances [2]; the relief is altogether abolished where the right of wardship is exercised ; the latter right is carefully limited; the disparagement of heirs by unequal marriages is forbidden ; and the widow is secured against spoliation as well as against compulsion to take

---

[1] Magna Carta, § 1. Cf. the Charter of Henry I, § 1 ; Stephen, Charter ii. ; Select Charters, pp. 100, 120.

[2] Magna Carta, §§ 2–4 ; Art. Bar. §§ 1–3. Cf. Charter of Henry I, § 2 ; Assize of Northampton, § 4 ; Dialogus de Scaccario, lib. ii. c. 10 : where the rule that a relief is not to be taken on the coming to age of a royal ward, is laid down as it is in the charter itself.

another husband [1]. The latter concession John had already
declared himself willing to grant in that scheme of abortive
reforms which he propounded, before his submission to the
pope, in A.D. 1212. This portion of the charter closes with three articles in which the king renounces the oppressive means which had been used to secure the payment of debts to the Crown and to the Jews, in whose debts the Crown had an ulterior and contingent interest. These clauses show that the king's servants had departed from the rules which had prevailed in the Exchequer under Henry II, and which had been carefully drawn up so as to secure the rights of the Crown with the greatest regard to the safety of the debtor [2].

Remedy of the tyrannical exaction of debts.

The twelfth and three following articles are those to which the greatest constitutional interest belongs; for they admit the right of the nation to ordain taxation, and they define the way in which the consent of the nation is to be given.

The constitutional articles.

No scutage or aid, other than the three regular feudal aids, is henceforth to be imposed but by the common counsel of the nation, and the common counsel of the nation is to be taken in an assembly duly summoned; the archbishops, bishops, abbots, earls, and greater barons are to be called up by royal writ directed to each severally; and all who hold of the king in chief, below the rank of the greater barons, are to be summoned by a general writ addressed to the sheriff of their shire; the summons is to express the cause for which the assembly is called together; forty days' notice is to be given; and when the day has arrived the action of those members who obey the summons is to be taken to represent the action of the whole [3]. This most important provision may be

Limitation of aids and scutages.

Method of summons to the national council.

---

[1] Art. Bar. §§ 4, 17; Magna Carta, §§ 6–8. Cf. Charter of Henry I, §§ 3, 4. Walter of Coventry says, 'sed et viduis dicitur propitius exstitisse,' of the reforms proposed in 1212; ii. 207; see above, p. 560.

[2] Magna Carta, §§ 9–11; Art. Bar. §§ 5, 15, 16, 34, 35. Cf. Charter of Henry I, §§ 6–8; Dialogus de Scaccario, ii. 12–17; Assize of Northampton, § 4.

[3] Magna Carta, §§ 12, 14; Art. Bar. § 32: 'Nullum scutagium vel auxilium ponatur in regno nostro, nisi per commune consilium regni nostri, nisi ad corpus nostrum redimendum, et primogenitum filium nostrum militem faciendum, et ad filiam nostram primogenitam semel maritandam,

regarded as a summing-up of the history of parliament so far
as it can be said yet to exist. It probably contains nothing
which had not been for a long time in theory a part of the
constitution: the kings had long consulted their council on
taxation; that council consisted of the elements that are here
specified, and had been summoned in a way analogous to if not
identical with that here defined. But the right had never yet
been stated in so clear a form, and the statement thus made
seems to have startled even the barons; they had not ventured
to claim it, and when they had the reins of power in their own
hands they seem in the subsequent editions of the charter to
have shrunk from repeating the clauses which contained it [1]. It
was for the attainment of this right that the struggles of the
reign of Henry III were carried on; and the realisation of the
claim was deferred until the reign of his successor. In these
clauses however the nation had now obtained a clear, or comparatively clear, definition of the right on which their future
political power was to be based.

The limitation of royal exaction is supplemented by a corresponding limitation of the power of the mesne lords; the king
is not to empower them to take aids except for the three
recognised purposes, and then only such sums as are reasonable:
nor is any one to be distrained to perform more than the proper
service of his tenure [2].

The next series of clauses concern judicial proceedings: the

---

et ad haec non fiat nisi rationabile auxilium : simili modo fiat de auxiliis
de civitate Londoniarum . . . . Et ad habendum commune consilium regni, de
auxilio assidendo aliter quam in tribus casibus praedictis, vel de scutagio
assidendo, summoneri faciemus archiepiscopos, episcopos, abbates, comites,
et majores barones, sigillatim per litteras nostras ; et praeterea faciemus
summoneri in generali, per vicecomites et ballivos nostros, omnes illos
qui de nobis tenent in capite ; ad certum diem, scilicet ad terminum
quadraginta dierum ad minus, et ad certum locum ; et in omnibus litteris
illius summonitionis causam summonitionis exprimemus ; et sic facta sum-
monitione negotium ad diem assignatum procedat secundum consilium
illorum qui praesentes fuerint, quamvis non omnes summoniti venerint.'
The provision for the summoning of the council is not among the barons'
articles, and probably expresses the earlier practice ; see above, pp. 395, 504.

[1] The clause is not found in any of the numerous confirmations of the
Great Charter.

[2] Magna Carta, §§ 15, 16; Art. Bar. §§ 6, 7.

suitors who are involved in Common Pleas are no longer to be common pleas,
compelled to follow the Curia Regis[1] : the trials are to be heard
in some fixed place. The recognitions of novel disseisin, mort assizes, amerce-
d'ancester, and darrein presentment are henceforth to be taken ments,
in the county courts, before two justices who will visit each
shire every quarter, and four knights chosen by the county
court for the purpose[2]. The freeman is not to be amerced in a
way that will ruin him, the penalty is to be fixed by a jury of
his neighbourhood ; earls and barons are to be amerced by their
peers, and clerks only in proportion to their non-ecclesiastical
property[3]. Such a clause proves that the careful provisions of
the Exchequer on this point had been transgressed by the king
who had, as we learn from the historians, imposed amercements of
scandalous amount and with wanton tyranny, just as he com-
pounded by fines for imaginary offences. The sheriffs, constables, limitation of the power of
coroners, and bailiffs of the king are forbidden to hold pleas of the sheriff.
the Crown[4] ; a further limitation on the power of the local
magistrates, which had been already curtailed by the direction
issued in Richard's reign that no sheriff should be justice in his
own county. Such a provision shows some mistrust of the
sheriffs on the part of both king and barons ; but it was probably disregarded in practice. This is the first of a series of Remedy of Exchequer
articles by which the abuse of the sheriff's authority is re- abuses, and petty exac-
strained[5] ; the ferms of the counties and other jurisdictions are tions.
not to be increased ; the debts due to the Crown which are

---

[1] Magna Carta, § 17; Art. Bar. § 8.

[2] Magna Carta, §§ 18, 19; Art. Bar. 8. See the Assize of Northampton, § 5.

[3] Magna Carta, §§ 20-23; Art. Bar. §§ 9-11; p. 570, above. Cf. Dialogus de Scaccario, lib. ii. c. 14, where the order to be observed by the sheriffs in sales is prescribed : ' Mobilia cujusque primo vendantur, bobus autem arantibus, per quos agricultura solet exerceri, quantum pote-rint parcant, ne ipsa deficiente debitor amplius in futurum egere cogatur.' This is a piece of Henry's special legislation ; Select Charters, p. 237.

[4] Magna Carta, § 24; Art. Bar. § 14. The barons had asked that the sheriffs should not interfere in pleas of the Crown *sine coronatoribus* : the charter forbids both sheriffs and coroners (vel coronatores) to hold such pleas ; a fact which seems to suggest that there was some jealousy of the elective officer. Cf. Assize of Richard I, A.D. 1194, art. 21 ; Glanvill, lib. i. c. 1 ; and see above, p. 544.

[5] Magna Carta, §§ 25-33; Art. Bar. §§ 14-16, 18-23.

collected by the sheriff are to be collected under the view of the
lawful men of the neighbourhood ; the goods of intestates are
to go to their natural heirs ; the royal officers are to pay for all
the provisions which they take by requisition ; they are not to
take money in lieu of service from those who are willing to
perform the service in person; they are not to seize the horses
and carts of the freeman to do royal work, nor his wood without
his consent ; the lands of convicted felons are to be held by the
Crown for a year and a day, and then to revert to the lords[1];
and the weirs in the Thames, the Medway, and the other rivers
in England are to be removed.

The remaining articles of general application are of a miscellaneous character; some laying down great principles, and
others defining points of minute and occasional import. The
use of the writ of Praecipe is limited so as not to defeat the
judicial rights of the lords[2]: the uniformity of weights and
measures is directed in the words of Richard's assize[3]; the writ
of inquest in cases where life and limb are concerned is to be
granted freely[4]: the king will not claim the sole wardship of
the minor who has other lords, except where he is the king's
tenant by knight service[5]: no bailiff is to force a man to compurgation or ordeal without witnesses[6]. Merchants may go out
and come in without paying exorbitant customs; and all lawful
men may leave the kingdom and return except in time of war,
or when the traveller belongs to a nation at war with the king[7].

Miscel-
laneous
articles.
Writ of
Praecipe :
measures :
inquests.
Privileges of
merchants.

[1] See Dialogus de Scaccario, lib. ii. c. 10 ; Assize of Clarendon, § 5.

[2] Art. Bar. § 24 ; Magna Carta, § 34 ; Glanvill, lib. i. c. 6. See Blackstone, Comm. iii. 274; Brunner, Schwurgericht, pp. 405–407. The writ of
Praecipe is a peremptory writ enjoining the sheriff to command the person
in question to do some act, or show why he should not be compelled. It
was in fact an evocation of the particular cause to the king's court.

[3] Art. Bar. § 12 ; Magna Carta, § 35 ; Hoveden, iv. 33.

[4] Art. Bar. § 26 ; M. C. § 36.

[5] Art. Bar. § 27 ; M C. § 37.

[6] Art. Bar. § 28 ; Magna Carta, § 38.

[7] Art. Bar §§ 31, 32 ; Magna Carta, §§ 41, 42 : 'Omnes mercatores
habeant salvum et securum exire de Anglia, et venire in Angliam, et
morari et ire per Angliam, tam per terram quam per aquam, ad emendum
et vendendum, sine omnibus malis toltis, per antiquas et rectas consuetudines, praeterquam in tempore gwerrae, et si sint de terra contra nos
gwerrina ; et si tales inveniantur in terra nostra in principio gwerrae,

The vassals of an escheated honour are not to be treated by the king as tenants-in-chief of the Crown, but only to pay such reliefs and aids as they would owe to the mesne lord if there were one[1]. The forest courts are not to compel the attendance of any man who is not directly concerned in the forest jurisdiction: this clause relieves the people of the shires in which the forests lie from the compulsory attendance directed by the Assize of Woodstock[2]. It is followed by a still greater concession; all the forests made in the present reign are disforested, and all rivers placed in fence are thrown open; a thorough investigation of all the forest usages is to be made by an inquest of twelve sworn knights, and all the bad customs are to be abolished forthwith[3]. By these clauses, which form the only forest charter issued by John[4], a great yet reluctant concession is made to a demand which had been increasing in intensity and listened to with stubborn disregard for a century and a half.

Remedy of the forest abuses.

Other clauses are of a more general character. The thirty-ninth and fortieth are famous and precious enunciations of principles. 'No free man shall be taken, or imprisoned, or disseized, or outlawed, or exiled, or any wise destroyed; nor will we go upon him, nor send upon him, but by the lawful judgment of his peers or by the law of the land. To none will we sell, to none will we deny or delay, right or justice[5].' The judicium parium was indeed no novelty; it lay at the

Enunciation of general principles of justice.

The judicium parium.

attachientur sine dampno corporum et rerum, donec sciatur a nobis ve capitali justiciario nostro quomodo mercatores terrae nostrae tractentur, qui tunc invenientur in terra contra nos gwerrina; et si nostri salvi sint ibi, alii salvi sint in terra nostra.' A similar privilege had been granted by charter as early as April 5, 1200. See Charter Rolls, p. 60.

[1] Art. Bar. § 36; Magna Carta, § 46.

[2] Art. Bar. § 39; Magna Carta, § 44. See the Assize of Woodstock, § 11; Select Charters, pp. 159, 258.

[3] Art. Bar. § 47; Magna Carta, § 47. Cf. Charter of Henry I, § 10; and Stephen's second Charter.

[4] The Forest Charter ascribed to him by Matthew Paris belongs to Henry III.

[5] Art. Bar. §§ 29, 30; Magna Carta, §§ 39, 40: 'Nullus liber homo capiatur, vel imprisonetur, aut dissaisiatur, aut utlagetur, aut exuletur, aut aliquo modo destruatur, nec super eum ibimus, nec super eum mittemus, nisi per legale judicium parium suorum vel per legem terrae. . . . Nulli vendemus, nulli negabimus, aut differemus, rectum aut justiciam.'

foundation of all German law; and the very formula here used is probably adopted from the laws of the Franconian and Saxon Caesars; but it was no small gain to obtain the declaration in such terms from a king who by giving the promise made a confession of past misgovernment [1].

Judges to be skilled in the law.

Another significant article pledges the king to confer the sheriffdoms and other judicial offices of the local courts only on men skilled in the law [2]. Another secures to the founders of religious houses their rights of custody during vacancy [3]; and another forbids that any one should be taken or imprisoned on the appeal of a woman, except for the death of her husband [4].

Rights of patrons.

General application.

Such, with the provision for the application of the rules thus enunciated to the whole nation, are what may be called the general articles of the Charter. The remainder is composed of clauses of special and transient interest: the king undertakes to surrender all charters and hostages placed in his hands as securities, and to dismiss the detested group of foreign servants whom he had gathered round him either as leaders of mercenaries or as ministers of small tyrannies. As soon as the pacification is completed he will dismiss all his mercenaries, forgive and recall all whom he has disseized or exiled; he will then reform, on the principles already adopted, the forests made by his father and brother, and do justice in other ways, for many of the promises made in the earlier part of the Charter had no retrospective validity. The rights of the Welsh who have

Temporary provisions.

Dismissal of mercenaries.

The Scots and Welsh.

[1] Compare the following passages from the Libri Feudorum : Conrad the Salic (A.D. 1024–1036) says, 'Praecipimus . . . ut nullus miles . . . tam de nostris majoribus valvassoribus quam eorum militibus sine certa et convicta culpa suum beneficium perdat nisi secundum consuetudinem antecessorum nostrorum et judicium parium suorum. . . . Si contentio fuerit de beneficio inter capitaneos, coram imperatore definiri debet ; si vero fuerit contentio inter minores valvassores et majores de beneficio, in judicio parium suorum definiatur per judicem curtis ;' Lib. Feud. I. xviii. Lothar II says, 'Sancimus ut nemo miles adimatur de possessione sui beneficii nisi convicta culpa quae sit laudanda per judicium parium suorum sicut supra dictum est ;' ibid. c. xxii ; Pertz, Legg. ii. 39 ; app. p. 185. In the laws of Henry I (so called) the same principle is laid down : ' Unusquisque per pares suos judicandus est.'

[2] Art. Bar. § 42 ; Magna Carta, § 45. On this principle the steward of a court-leet must be a learned steward.

[3] Art. Bar. § 43 ; Magna Carta, § 46.

[4] Magna Carta, § 54.

been oppressed are at the same future period to be determined and recognised; the Welsh princes and the king of Scots are to have justice done; and a general amnesty for all political offences arising out of the present quarrel is to be given [1].

The enforcement of the Charter is committed to twenty-five barons, to be chosen by the whole baronage. These are empowered to levy war against the king himself, if he refuse to do justice on any claim laid before him by four of their number; and in conjunction with the communa—the community of the whole realm—to distrain him, saving his royal person and queen and children [2].

Means of execution.

The twenty-five executors.

The last clause contains the enacting words, 'We will and firmly enjoin,' and the oath to be taken on the part of the king and on the part of the barons, that all these articles shall be observed in good faith and without evasion of their plain construction [3].

Enacting words and oath.

In this mere abstract of the Great Charter we have the summing up of the rights and duties that have been growing into recognition whilst the nation was growing into consciousness. The *Communa totius terrae*, which is to join with the twenty-five barons in the execution of the Charter, has at last entered upon its career of constitutional life.

Recognition of the national unity.

So great a boon as Magna Carta might almost excuse the men by whose agency it was won from a trial at the bar of history. But so much of the earlier fortunes of the constitution turns upon personal history, on the local, official, and family connexions of the great men, that we cannot dismiss the subject without the inquiry, Who were the men, and what was their training? Who were the barons that now impose limits on royal tyranny, and place themselves in the vanguard of liberty? How have they come to sit in the seats and wield the swords of those whom so lately we saw arrayed in feudal might against king and people?

Inquiry as to the persons who won the Charter.

The barons who took part in the transactions out of which

---

[1] Magna Carta, §§ 49–59, 62; Art. Bar. §§ 44–46.
[2] Magna Carta, § 61; Art. Bar. § 49.
[3] Magna Carta, § 63.

Fourfold
classification
of the
baronage.
Magna Carta emerges—and the whole baronage was in one way or another directly concerned in it—fall into four classes: those who began the quarrel in A.D. 1213 by refusing to follow the king to France; those who joined them after the councils held at S. Alban's and in S. Paul's; those who left the king in the spring of A.D. 1215 after the adhesion of the Londoners; and those who continued with him to the last. Each of these divisions contained men who acted on the ground of public right, and others who were mainly influenced by private friendship and gratitude, or by the desire of avenging private wrongs.

The first
class; the
northern
lords.
The first class was chiefly composed of the north country barons, the Northumbrani, Norenses, Aquilonares of the chroniclers. No list of them is given, but they can easily be distinguished in the roll of chiefs enumerated by Matthew Paris in connexion with the assembly at Stamford: they are Eustace de Vesci, Richard de Perci, Robert de Ros, Peter de Bruis, Nicolas de Stuteville, William de Mowbray, Simon de Kyme, Gilbert de la Val, Oliver de Vaux, John de Lacy the constable of Chester, and Thomas of Multon. All these are well-known names in the north; many of them appear in Domesday; but, with the exception of Mowbray and Lacy, not among the greater tenants-in-chief at the time of the Survey. They had sprung into the foremost rank after the fall of the elder house of Mowbray, and had many of them done service under Richard de Lucy and Ranulf Glanvill in the defence of the north. Eustace de Vesci, however, was closely connected by marriage with the king of Scots, and is said to have had, like Robert Fitz-Walter and William of Salisbury, cruel wrongs to avenge upon the king.

The second
class; the
feudal and
ministerial
lords.
The second division, containing the rest of the confederates who met at Stamford, embraced the remnant of the Conquest baronage, and the representatives of the families which had earned lands and dignities under Henry I and Henry II.
The Stamford confederates.
Amongst these the most prominent is Robert Fitz-Walter, a grandson of Richard de Lucy and a descendant in the male line from the Norman house of Brionne. With him are Saer de Quenci earl of Winchester, the possessor of half the inheritance of the great house of Leicester; Henry Bohun earl of

Hereford, and Roger Bigod earl of Norfolk, who appear side by side as their descendants did when they defied Edward I; Richard of Clare earl of Hertford, the brother-in-law, and Geoffrey de Mandeville earl of Essex, the husband, of the king's divorced wife; William Marshall the younger, the son of the great earl whose adhesion was the main support of John; Roger de Creissi, William Malduit, William de Lanvalei, and others, whose names recall the justices of Henry II's Curia; and with them Robert de Vere, Fulk Fitz-Warin, William Mallet, William de Beauchamp, two of the house of Fitz-Alan, and two of the house of Gant[1]. Many of these have names the glories of which belong to later history: such of them as are of earlier importance may be referred to the two sources already indicated; the great baronial families that had been wise enough to cast away the feudal aspirations of their forefathers, and the rising houses which had sprung from the ministerial nobility.

The third class, which clung to John as long as he seemed to have any hope in resistance, was headed by those earls who were closely connected by blood or by marriage with the royal house[2]: Earl William of Salisbury, the king's natural brother; William of Warenne, the son of Earl Hamelin and cousin of John, and Henry earl of Cornwall, grandson of Henry I. With them were William de Forz, titular count of Aumâle and lord of Holderness, a feudal adventurer of the worst stamp, whose father had been one of the captains of Richard's crusading fleet; Ranulf earl of Chester, and William Marshall earl of Pembroke, two men of long and varied experience as well as great social importance, who seem up to the last moment to have hoped that their own influence with the king might make it unnecessary for them to go into open opposition. In the second rank come Geoffrey de Lucy, Geoffrey de Furnival, Thomas Basset, Henry de Cornhell, Hugh de Neville, and William Briwere, the men who were at present in power in the Curia Regis and Exchequer; who were bound in honour to adhere to their master or to resign their dignities and who had

The third class, who joined the barons after their entry into London.

The present ministry.

[1] M. Paris, ii. 585.   [2] Ibid. 587.

in many cases been too willing ministers of the iniquities that provoked the struggle.

The fourth class; John's personal adherents. The few who adhered to John to the last were chiefly those who had everything to fear and nothing to hope from the victory of the confederates ; Richard de Marisco, the chancellor, Peter de Mauley, Falkes de Breauté, Philip son of Mark, Gerard de Atie, Engelard de Cygonies, Robert de Gaugi, and others whose names testify to their foreign extraction, and some of whom were expressly excluded by the Great Charter from ever holding office in England[1].

The king's party among the bishops. Of the bishops, Peter des Roches the justiciar was probably the only one who heartily supported John : he was a foreign favourite and an unpopular man. Pandulf the papal envoy was also on the king's side ; and some of the bishops who had been lately consecrated, such as Walter Gray of Worcester, who had been chancellor for some years, and Benedict of Rochester, probably avoided taking up any decided position. Even archbishop Langton himself, although he sympathised with, and partly inspired and advised the confederates, remained in attendance on the king.

Classification of the twenty-five executors. It is worth while to compare with these lists the names of those counsellors by whose advice John declares that he issues the charter, as well as those of the twenty-five barons to whom the execution was committed. The former body is composed of the bishops, with Stephen Langton and Pandulf at their head, and those earls and barons who only left John after the adhesion of the Londoners : it contains none of the northern barons, none of the second list of confederates ; and the selection was perhaps made in the hope of binding the persons whom it includes to the continued support of the hard-won liberties. The twenty-five executors are selected from the two latter classes ; they are as follows : of the north country lords, Eustace de Vesci, William de Mowbray, Robert de Ros, John de Lacy, Richard de Perci ; of the Stamford confederates, the earls of Hertford, Gloucester, Winchester, Hereford, Norfolk, and Oxford ; Robert Fitz-Walter, William Marshall the younger, Gil-

[1] Art. 50.

bert de Clare, Hugh Bigod, William Mallet, John Fitz-Robert, Roger de Mumbezon, Richard de Muntfitchet, William de Huntingfield. Two of the third list, William of Aumâle and William of Albini, represent a body less hostile to John. Geoffrey de Say, who is found shortly after in arms against John, and the mayor of London, complete the number [1].

In a further stage of our inquiry we shall be able to trace the subsequent divisions of party and policy that sprang out of these several combinations, in that altered state of affairs which followed the French invasion, and through the difficulties which beset the minority of Henry III. The analysis of the lists confirms the evidence of the historians, and proves that the first cry for freedom came from the North, that it was taken up and maintained by the strength of the baronial party, which had learned the benefit of law, peace, and good government, and that the demands of the confederates took a definite and defensible form under the hand of the archbishop, and on the model of Henry I's charter: that this basis of agreement was accepted by the people at large, and especially by the Londoners, who to some extent represent the town population of the kingdom; and was finally adhered to by the most important members of the government, with William Marshall at their head. John remained contumacious till all but his foreign creatures had forsaken him, and, when he yielded, he yielded with a full intention of eluding by papal connivance all his promises. The Great Charter is then the act of the united nation, the church, the barons, and the commons, for the first time thoroughly at one. It is in form only the act of the king: in substance and in historical position it is the first effort of a corporate life that has reached full consciousness, resolved to act for itself and able to carry out the resolution.

(margin note: Importance of these lists.)

[1] M. Paris, ii. 604, 605; Select Charters, p. 298. Matthew Paris, ii. 605, gives a further list of thirty-eight barons who swore to obey the orders of the twenty-five: this list includes the Earls Marshal, Arundel and Warenne, Hubert de Burgh, Warin Fitz-Gerold, Philip of Albini, and William Percy.

CHAPTER XIII.

GROWTH OF ADMINISTRATIVE AND REPRESENTATIVE
INSTITUTIONS.

Distinctive character of the consti- tution.

156. The great characteristic of the English constitutional system, in that view of it which is offered in these pages,—the principle of its growth, the secret of its construction,—is the continuous development of representative institutions from the first elementary stage, in which they are employed for local purposes and in the simplest form, to that in which the national parliament appears as the concentration of all local and provincial machinery, the depository of the collective powers of the three estates of the realm. We have traced in the Anglo-Saxon history the origin and growth of the local institutions, and in the history of the Norman reigns the creation of a strong administrative system. Not that the Anglo-Saxon rule had no administrative mechanism, or that the Norman polity was wanting in its local and provincial organism, but that the strength of the former was in the lower, and that of the latter in the upper ranges of the social system, and that the stronger parts of each were permanent. In the reigns of the three kings, whose history was sketched in the last chapter, we trace a most important step in advance, the interpenetration, the growing

Anglo-Saxon local institu- tions.

Norman central in- stitutions.

together, of the local machinery and the administrative organ-
isation. We have already examined the great crisis by which Period of
interpene-
tration.
they were brought together; now we begin to trace the process
by which the administrative order is worked into the common
law of the people, and the common institutions of the people
are admitted to a share in the administration of the state; the
beginning of the process which is completed in national self-
government.

The period is one of amalgamation, of consolidation, of continuous growing together and new development, which distinguishes the process of organic life from that of mere mechanic
contrivance, internal law from external order.

The nation becomes one and realises its oneness; this real- Realisation
isation is necessary before the growth can begin. It is com- of national
pleted under Henry II and his sons. It finds its first distinct unity.
expression in Magna Carta. It is a result, not perhaps of the
design and purpose of the great king, but of the converging
lines of the policy by which he tried to raise the people at large,
and to weaken the feudatories and the principle of feudalism in
them. Henry is scarcely an English king, but he is still less a
French feudatory. In his own eyes he is the creator of an The result
empire. He rules England by Englishmen and for English policy.
purposes, Normandy by Normans and for Norman purposes;
the end of all his policy being the strengthening of his own
power. He recognises the true way of strengthening his power,
by strengthening the basis on which it rests, the soundness,
the security, the sense of a common interest in the maintenance
of peace and order.

The national unity is completed in two ways. The English Union of
have united; the English and the Norman have united also. blood.
The threefold division of the districts, the Dane law, the West- Extinction
Saxon and the Mercian law, which subsisted so long, disappears tinctions.
after the reign of Stephen. The terms are become archaisms
which occur in the pages of the historians in a way that proves
them to have become obsolete [1]; the writers themselves are

---

[1] Simeon of Durham, ed. Hinde, i. 220-222.

uncertain which shires fall into the several divisions. Traces of slight differences of custom may be discovered in the varying rules of the county courts, which, as Glanvill tells us, are so numerous that it is impossible to put them on record[1]; but they are now mere local by-laws, no real evidence of permanent divisions of nationality. In the same way Norman and Eng-

Inter-
marriages.

lishmen are one. Frequent intermarriages have so united them, that without a careful investigation of pedigree it cannot be ascertained,—so at least the author of the Dialogus de Scaccario affirms,—who is English and who Norman[2]. If this be considered a loose statement, for scarcely two generations have passed away since the Norman blood was first introduced, it is conclusive evidence as to the common consciousness of union. The earls, the greater barons, the courtiers, might be of pure Norman blood, but they were few in number : the royal race

Uncertain
infusion of
Norman
blood.

was as much English as it was Norman. The numbers of Norman settlers in England are easily exaggerated ; it is not probable that except in the baronial and knightly ranks the infusion was very great, and it is very probable indeed that, where there was such infusion, it gained ground by peaceable settlement and

Value of
Norman
name and
lineage.

marriage. It is true that Norman lineage was vulgarly regarded as the more honourable, but the very fact that it was vulgarly so regarded would lead to its being claimed far more widely than facts would warrant : the bestowal of Norman baptismal names would thus supplant, and did supplant, the old English ones, and the Norman Christian name would then be alleged as proof of Norman descent. But it is far from improbable, though it may not have been actually proved, that the vast majority of surnames derived from English places are evidence of pure English descent, whilst only those which are derived from Norman places afford even a presumptive evidence of Norman descent. The subject of surnames scarcely rises into prominence before

---

[1] Glanvill, De Legibus Angliae, lib. xii. c. 6.

[2] 'Jam cohabitantibus Anglicis et Normannis et alterutrum uxores ducentibus vel nubentibus, sic permixtae sunt nationes ut vix discerni possit hodie, de liberis loquor, quis Anglicus quis Normannus sit genere ; exceptis dumtaxat ascriptitiis qui villani dicuntur ;' Dialogus, i. c. 10; Select Charters, p. 201.

the fourteenth century; but an examination of the indices to Increase of English surnames.
the Rolls of the Exchequer and Curia Regis shows a continuous
increase in number and importance of persons bearing English
names: as early as the reign of Henry I we find among the English names.
barons Hugh of Bochland, Rainer of Bath, and Alfred of Lincoln, with many other names which show either that Englishmen had taken Norman names in baptism, or that Normans
were willing to sink their local surnames in the mass of the
national nomenclature.

157. The union of blood would be naturally expressed in Unity and growth of language.
unity of language, a point which is capable of being more
strictly tested. Although French is for a long period the language of the palace, there is no break in the continuity of the
English as a literary language. It was the tongue, not only of
the people of the towns and villages, but of a large proportion
of those who could read and could enjoy the pursuit of know-
ledge. The growth of the vernacular literature was perhaps Modifica-tions of vernacular literature.
retarded by the influx of Norman lords and clerks, and its
character was no doubt modified by foreign influences under
Henry II and his sons, as it was in a far greater degree affected
by the infusion of French under Henry III and Edward I: but
it was never stopped. It was at its period of slowest growth
as rapid in its development as were most of the other literatures
of Europe. Latin was still the language of learning, of law,
and of ritual. English had to struggle with French as well
as with Latin for its hold on the sermon and the popular poem:
when it had forced its way to light, the books in which it was
used had their own perils to undergo from the contempt of the
learned and the profane familiarity of the ignorant. But the Continuity, survival, and victory of English.
fact that it survived, and at last prevailed, is sufficient to prove
its strength. The last memoranda of the Peterborough
Chronicle belong to the year 1154: the last extant English
charter can scarcely be earlier than 1155. There are English
sermons of the same century, and early in the next we reach
the date of Layamon's Brute and the Ormulum. These are Fragment-ary charac-ter ac-counted for.
fragments of the literature of a language which is passing
through rapid stages of growth, and which has not attained a

classical standard. Only fragments are left, for the successive stages pass so quickly that the monuments of one generation are only half intelligible to the next. The growth of the language and that of the literature proceed in an inverse ratio. If we were to argue from these fragments, we should infer, that whilst in the department of law the use of the native tongue was necessarily continuous, it had to rise through the stages of the song and the sermon to that point of development at which those who required history and deeper poetry demanded them in their own language. Such a sequence may imply the increase of education in the English, but it more probably implies the disuse of French in the classes that had a taste for learning : and it is still more probable that the two literatures advanced by equal steps until the crisis came which banished French from popular conversation. There are traces that seem to show that English was becoming the familiar conversational language of the higher classes. The story of Helewisia de Morville, preserved by William of Canterbury in his life of Becket, exhibits the wife or mother of one of the murderers as using English. 'Huwe of Morvill, war, war, Liulf haveth his sword ydrawen,' was her cry when she invoked the aid of her husband to punish the stubborn virtue of her English favourite [1]. Giraldus Cambrensis, a man of high Norman descent, could not only read but criticise the language of the Chronicles and of Alfred, and compare the dialects of northern and southern England [2]. Hugh of Nunant, a Norman of the Normans, mentions it as a strange thing that William Longchamp the chancellor was ignorant of the language of the people, and regards it in special connexion with his hatred and contempt of the English [3]. Latin was the ordinary language of the monks of Durham, yet they conversed in English with S. Godric, who spoke French only by miracle [4]. The hymn which the Blessed Virgin taught

Relation of language and literature in the process of development.

Scraps of English in conversation.

---

[1] Will. Cant., ed. Robertson, i. 128.

[2] Gir. Cam. Opp. vi. 177, 178.

[3] Ben. Pet. ii. 219 : ' Ille non respondebat quia linguam Anglicanam prorsus ignorabat.' See also Gir. Camb. V. Galfridi, in Anglia Sacra, ii. 406, 407 ; Opp. iv. 424.

[4] V. S. Godric, pp. 203, 206.

the same saint was in English [1] and in English it is recorded
for the reading of bishop Hugh de Puiset. At Canterbury, in
the miraculous history of Dunstan, written by Eadmer, it is
the devil that speaks French [2] and corrects the indifferent idiom
of an English monk. S. Hugh of Lincoln, who was a Bur- *English
commonly
spoken.*
gundian by birth, did not understand the dialects of Kent and
Huntingdonshire, but he was addressed by the natives as if it
were naturally to be expected that he would comprehend what
they said [3]. Little can be safely inferred from such scattered
notices, but that it was not uncommon for educated people to
speak both languages. Of any commixture of French and *No commixture of
French with
English.*
English at this period there is no trace: the language of
Chaucer owes its French elements to a later infusion: the
structure of our language is affected by the foreign influence as
yet in a way which may be called mechanical rather than
chemical: it loses its inflexions, but it does not readily accept
new grammatical forms, nor does it adopt, to any great extent,
a new vocabulary.

The uniformity of legal system in its application to Norman *Consolidation of the
legal system.*
and Englishman alike, would of necessity follow from a state of
society in which Norman was undistinguishable from Englishman: but, except in one or two points of transient interest, it
is not likely that any great distinctions of legal procedure had
ever separated the two races. The Norman character of the
Curia Regis and the English character of the shiremoot stand in
contrast not so much because the former was Norman and the
latter English, as because of the different social principles
from which they spring. The Englishman where he is a tenant-
in-chief has his claims decided in the Curia Regis; the Norman
vavassor and the English ceorl alike are treated in the shiremoot [4].
The trial by battle and the inquest by jury in its several forms
are, after the first pressure of the Conquest is over, dealt with
by both alike. The last vestige of difference, the presentment
of Englishry, loses what significance it ever had. The tenures

[1] V. S. Godric, p. 208.
[2] Eadmer, V. S. Dunstani, p. 236.
[3] Magna Vita S. Hugonis, pp. 157, 268.
[4] Writ of Henry I, quoted above, p. 425.

are the same for all; the Englishman is not disqualified from being a tenant-in-chief: the Norman may hold land in villenage: the free and common socage of the new system is really the free possession of the old, and the man who holds his acres by suit and service at the county court[1] is as free as if he continued to call his land *ethel* or *bocland*, over which none but the king had soken. The one class which is an exception to all these generalisations, that of the *rustici* or *nativi*, is, it would appear, exclusively English: but even these, where they have recognised claims to justice, claim it according to its fullest and newest improvements. The system of recognition is as applicable to the proof or disproof of villein extraction as to the assize of mort d'ancester or novel disseisin: nor does the disqualification under which the rustic lies, for ordination or for the judicial work of the jury and assize, arise from his nationality, but from his status. The claims of his lord forbid him to seek emancipation by tonsure; the precarious nature of his tenure forbids him to testify in matters touching the freer and fuller tenure of other men's property.

The villein class.

Englishmen rarely promoted.

Still great promotion in Church and State does not yet commonly fall to the lot of the simple Englishman. Wulfstan of Worcester, the last of the Anglo-Saxon bishops, dies in 1095; Robert, the scholar of Melun, the first English bishop of any note after the Conquest, belongs to the reign of Henry II[2]. The Scot, the Welshman, and the Breton reach episcopal thrones before the Englishman. Archbishop Baldwin, who was promoted to Canterbury by Henry II, seems to have been an Englishman of humble birth; Stephen Langton also was an Englishman, but by this time the term includes men of either descent, and henceforth the prelates of foreign extraction form the exceptions rather than the rule. In the service of the State however it is, as we have seen already, by no means improbable that English sheriffs and judges were employed by Henry I:

---

[1] 'Per sectam comitatus et de hendemot, unde scutagium dari non debet;' Rot. Pip. 3 Joh.; Madox, Hist. Exch. p. 467.

[2] Robert is distinctly described by Robert de Monte, as *genere Anglicus* (ed. Pertz, vi. 513); John of Pagham, who was made bishop of Worcester in 1151, may also have been English.

and English scholars and lawyers were rising into distinction in
Sicily and even in France.

The union of the races resembles not merely the mechanical
union of two bodies bound together by force, or even by mutual
attraction, in which, however tight the connexion, each retains
its individual mass and consistency : it is more like a chemical
commixture in which, although skilled analysis may distinguish
the ingredients, they are so united both in bulk and in qualities,
that the result of the commixture is something altogether distinct from the elements of which it is composed.   The infusion
of a little that is Norman affects the whole system of the
English, and the mass which results is something different from
either the one or the other.   True the great proportion of the
bulk must be English, but for all that it is not, and nothing
will ever make it, as if that foreign element had never been
there.

Character of the union of races.

Result of the commixture.

The commixture of institutions is somewhat similar : the new
machinery which owes its existence to the new conception of
royal power, the Curia Regis and Exchequer, does not remain
side by side and unconnected with the shiremoot and the kindred
institutions ; it becomes just as much a part of the common law
as the other : the ancient system of the shire rises to the highest
functions of government ; the authority of royal justice permeates
the lowest regions of the popular organisation.   The new consolidating process is one of organism, not of mere mechanism :
the child's puzzle, the perfect chronometer, the living creature,
symbolise three kinds or stages of creative skill, order, organisation, law ; the point that our history reaches at the date of
Magna Carta may be fixed as the transition from the second to
the third stage.

Commixture of institu- tions.

Growth of the common law.

In tracing the minute steps of the process by which the commixture of race and institutions was so completed as to produce
an organisation which grew into conscious life, we may follow a
principle of arrangement different from that used in the eleventh
and earlier chapters ; and after examining the position of the
king, divide the discussion under the four heads of legislation,
taxation, the military system, and judicature ; closing the history

Plan of the following Chapter.

of the period with an attempt to trace the origin and development of that representative principle, which we shall find running through all the changes of administrative policy, and forming as it were the blending influence which enables the other elements to assimilate, or perhaps the breath of life which turns mere organism into living and conscious personality.

The King.

Growth of the idea of kingship.

158. The very idea of kingship had developed since the age of the Conqueror. This had been one result of the struggle with the Church. The divine origin of royalty had been insisted on as an argument to force on the kings the sense of responsibility. This lesson had been familiar to the ancient English rulers, and its application had been summarily brought home. Edwy, like Rehoboam, had spurned the counsels of the fathers, and the men of the north had left him, and taken Edgar to be king. But the truth was less familiar, and the application less impressive to the Norman. The Conqueror had won England by the sword; and, though he tried to rule it as a national king, it was not as one who would be brought to account: William Rufus had defied God and man: Henry I had compelled Anselm to give him a most forcible reminder of the source from which both king and prelate derived their power: Stephen had sinned against God and the people, and the hand of supreme power was traced in his humiliation. The events that were taking place on the Continent conveyed further lessons. In the old struggles between pope and emperor the zeal of

Moral and religious position of the king.

righteousness was on the side of the latter: since the reign of Henry IV the balance of moral influence was with the popes; and the importance of that balance had been exemplified both

Scholastic view of kingship.

in Germany and in France. The power of the pen was in the hands of the clergy: Hugh of Fleury had elaborately explained to Henry I the duties and rights which his position owed to its being ordained of God[1]. John of Salisbury, following Plutarch and setting up Trajan as the model of princes, had urged the contrast between the tyrant and the king such as he hoped to find in Henry II[2]. Yet these influences were thwarted by another

[1] See his work in Baluze's *Miscellanea*, ii. 184 sq.
[2] In the *Polycraticus*, throughout.

set of ideas, not indeed running counter to them, but directed
to a different aim. The clergy had exalted royalty in order to Legal theory of absolute sovereignty.
enforce its responsibilities on the conscience of the king; the
lawyers exalted it in order to strengthen its authority as the
source of law and justice; making the law honourable by mag-
nifying the attributes of the lawgiver. And, as the lawyers Influence of the imperial idea.
grew more powerful as a class, the theory of royalty approached
more closely to absolutism: their language has a tone, a force,
and a consistent logic that is wanting to the exhortations of the
churchmen. Yet even to the lawyer this ideal king was not the
man who sat on the throne, but the power that would enforce
the law. Glanvill cites and applies to Henry II the maxim of
the Institutes, 'quod principi placuit, legis habet vigorem,'—a
principle which, as Fortescue points out, is absolutely foreign to
the ideas of English law [1]; and the author of the Dialogus de
Scaccario, who, although himself an ecclesiastic, represented
both in life and in doctrine the ministerial lawyer, lays down
that the deeds of kings are not to be discussed or condemned by
inferior men, their hearts are in the hands of God, and it is by
divine not by human judgment that their cause must stand or
fall [2]. Happily a theory of absolutism is compatible with very Practical limitations.
strong and strict limitations in practice: yet it was probably
under the idea that the king is the sovereign lord of his people
that Richard I and John forsook the time-honoured practice of
issuing a charter of liberties at the coronation. John's idea of John's idea of his own position.
his own position was definitely that of an absolute prince: when
he heard the demands of the barons he inquired why they had
not asked for the kingdom also, and swore that he would never
grant them such liberties as would make himself a slave [3]: yet
the liberties they asked were those which his forefathers had
been glad to offer to their people. Curiously enough it is in
John that the territorial idea of royalty reaches its typical
enunciation: all the kings before him had called themselves on
their great seals kings of the English: John is the first whose

[1] De laudibus Legum Angliae, ch. 9.
[2] Dialogus, praef.; Select Charters, p. 169.
[3] M. Paris, ii. 586.

title appears on that solemn and sovereign emblem as *Rex Angliae*.

Growth of real power.

The growth of real power in the king's hands had advanced in proportion to the theory. Every measure of internal policy by which the great vassals had been repressed, or the people strengthened to keep them in check, had increased the direct influence of the crown ; and the whole tendency of the ministerial system had been in the same direction. Hence it was that John was able so long to play the part of a tyrant, and that the barons had to enforce the Charter by measures which for the time were an exercise on their part of sovereign power.

Claim of the king to the rule of the British islands.

Somewhat of the greatness of the royal position was owing to the claim, which at this period was successfully urged, to the supreme rule of the British islands ; a claim which had been made under the descendants of Alfred, and was traditionally regarded as really established by Edgar. The princes of Wales had acknowledged the suzerainty of the Conqueror, and had been from time to time forced into formal submission by William Rufus and Henry I : but Stephen had been able to do little on that side of the island. The three Welsh wars of Henry II were

Homage of Wales.

not amongst his most successful expeditions, yet by arms or by negotiations he managed to secure the homage of the princes [1], on one of whom he bestowed his own sister in marriage [2]. On Richard's accession the homage was again demanded, and a scutage was raised on the pretext of an expedition to enforce it. Yet when Rhys ap Griffith, the king of South Wales, came to Oxford for the purpose of negotiation, Richard refused to meet him [3], and it does not appear that he ever renewed his homage. On the death of Rhys, the disputed succession to his principality was settled by archbishop Hubert as justiciar [4], and Griffith his

---

[1] Henry's three Welsh wars were in 1157, 1163, and 1165. Homage was performed by the princes at Woodstock July 1, 1163 : and they attended his court at Gloucester in 1175. In 1177 they swore fealty at Oxford in May. In 1184 they provoked the king to prepare for another expedition ; but when he had reached Worcester, Rhys ap Griffith met him and did homage. The South Welsh were again in arms in 1186. The princes of North Wales, after the marriage of David with the king's sister, were faithful, and adhered to Henry in the rebellion of 1173.

[2] Bened. i. 162.   [3] Bened. ii. 97.   [4] Hoveden, iv. 21.

successor appeared as a vassal of the English king at the court
of John [1]. There seems to have been no reluctance to accept the
nominal superiority of England, so long as it was compatible
with practical independence. But the fact that their bishops *Ecclesiasti-*
received their consecration at Canterbury, and were, from the *cal depend-*
reign of Henry I, elected and admitted under the authority of the *Wales.*
kings of England, is sufficient to prove that anything like real
sovereignty was lost to the so-called kings of Wales. They were *Policy of*
divided amongst themselves, and the highest object of their *the Welsh*
political aims was from time to time to throw their weight on *princes.*
the side of the disaffected barons who were their neighbours:
creating difficulties in the way of the king of England, which
prevented him from meddling with them. But his formal
suzerainty was admitted. 'What Christian,' says Matthew
Paris, 'knows not that the prince of Wales is a petty vassal
(vassalulus) of the king of England [2]?'

It was very different with Scotland, although Malcolm *Question of*
Canmore had under the spell of the Conqueror's power done *the Scottish*
formal homage to him [3], and each of the sons of Margaret *homage.*
had in turn sought support against his competitors at the
court of Henry I. The complicated question of the Scottish
homage, an obligation based, it is said, on the commendation of
the Scots to Edward the Elder, on the grant of Cumberland by
Edmund to Malcolm, and on the grant of Lothian by Edgar or·
Canute to the king of Scots, was one of those diplomatic knots
which are kept unsolved by mutual reservations until the time
comes when they must be cut by the sword. And to these *Its compli-*
obscure points a new complication was added when David of *cations.*
Scotland, who had obtained the English earldom of Huntingdon,
succeeded to his brother's throne. Henry the son of David
received the earldom of Northumberland from Stephen, and his
father kept during the whole of Stephen's reign a hold on that
county as well as Cumberland and Westmoreland, partly in the
alleged interest of his niece the empress, partly perhaps with the

---

[1] Hoveden, iv. 142.   [2] M. Paris, iv. 324.
[3] Guibert of Nogent, Opp. p. 384, speaks of William the Conqueror,
'Qui Anglorum Scotorumque sibi regna subegit;' also p. 469.

intention of claiming those territories as rightfully belonging to his Cumbrian principality. Henry II not only obtained the restoration of the northern counties from Malcolm IV, but compelled him to do homage [1]: William the Lion, who succeeded Malcolm, acted throughout his whole reign as a vassal of England, attending the royal courts and acquiescing for the most part in a superiority which it would have been folly to

Scottish homage from 1174 to 1189.

dispute [2]. After the unsuccessful attempt in 1174 to assist the rebellious earls, in which he was defeated and captured, Henry II imposed on him the most abject terms of submission : compelling him to surrender the castles of Lothian, and to enforce on his bishops and barons a direct oath of fealty to the English crown. From that obligation Richard released him for the sum of ten thousand marks; but neither Henry's exaction of the homage, nor Richard's renunciation of it, affected the pre-existent claims. With William the Lion it was a far more important object to recover Northumberland, Cumberland, and Westmoreland, than to vindicate his formal independence. The states he ruled or claimed to rule were as yet unconsolidated : he had little authority in the real Scotland that lay beyond the Forth, and from which his royal title was derived. The English-speaking provinces, which he held as lord of Lothian and of Strath Clyde, were as yet no more Scottish than the

[1] Malcolm IV did homage to Henry II at Chester in 1157 ; he attended him at the siege of Toulouse, and was knighted by him at Tours in 1159. He did homage to the younger Henry at Woodstock in 1163. These homages were apparently due for the county of Huntingdon.

[2] William succeeded his brother in 1165 ; in 1166 he followed Henry II to Normandy, according to the Chronicle of Melrose, as a vassal, but returned shortly after. In 1170 he and his brother David did homage to the younger Henry, according to Lord Hailes for Huntingdon, according to Lord Lyttelton for Lothian : there is no decisive evidence on the point. After his release from imprisonment he frequently attended the English court ; especially at Northampton in 1176, at Winchester in 1177, at Nottingham in 1179, in Normandy in 1181, at Nottingham in the same year, at London in 1185, at Marlborough in 1186. He attended on Richard at Canterbury in 1189, and was there relieved from the bondage imposed by Henry II ; and was again at court in 1194 at Nottingham. In 1200 he did homage to John at Lincoln, 'salvo jure suo.' At this time the county of Huntingdon was in the hands of his brother David ; it is therefore difficult to see for what the homage could have been due, unless it were for the traditional claim. Possibly William yielded it in the hope of recovering the northern counties, in which he did not succeed.

counties which he wished to add to them. Yet both he and his people aimed at an independence very different from that of Wales. The Scottish bishops, who from the beginning of the twelfth century had struggled against the attempt to reduce them to dependence on York or Canterbury, refused to submit themselves to the English Church, even when they swore fealty to the English king; and actually obtained from Pope Clement III a declaration that they were subject immediately and solely to the apostolic see itself. The Scottish barons, even before they had been released by Richard, refused to be bound by the English undertaking to pay the Saladin tithe [1]. When it is remembered that a large portion of these barons were adventurers of Norman descent, who had obtained estates in the Lowlands, too far from the English court to fear royal interference, it is not difficult to see how the feudal principle gained its footing in Scotland in such strength as to colour all its later history. The Scottish constitution, as it appears under king David, was a copy of the English system as it existed under Henry I, but without the safeguards which the royal strength should have imposed on the great vassals. Hence the internal weakness which so long counteracted the determined efforts of the people for national independence.

The anomalous condition of the principality of Galloway, which, as an outlying portion of the Strath Clyde kingdom, clung to English protection to evade incorporation with Scotland, and was from the beginning of the twelfth century subject ecclesiastically to York, gave the English kings another standing-point beyond the border [2]. But although

The Scottish Church made immediately dependent on Rome.

Refusal to pay the Saladin tithe.

English influence in Scotland.

Relation of Galloway to England and Scotland.

---

[1] Bened. ii. 44.

[2] Galloway was under the rule of Fergus, an almost independent prince (princeps), who was connected by marriage with Henry I, until the year 1160, when the country was subdued by Malcolm. Fergus then became a canon and died the next year. On the outbreak of war in 1173, the sons of Fergus expelled the Scottish officers from their country, and in 1174 Henry sent envoys to invite them to become his vassals. They however quarreled among themselves, and Henry, finding that they intended to make a tool of him, abstained from further negotiations; and William the Lion did homage for Galloway as well as Scotland. In 1176 the king of Scots compelled Gilbert of Galloway, who had murdered his own brother Uhtred, to do homage to Henry, as a Scottish baron, under the terms of the treaty of Falaise.

Henry II raised an army for the reduction of Galloway in 1186, and even marched as far northwards as Carlisle, his successors did not regard the question as worthy of a struggle.

Galloway dependent ecclesiastically on York.

Alan of Galloway appears amongst the barons by whose counsel John issued the charter, and the bishops of Whithern received consecration and mission at York, down to the middle of the fourteenth century ; but the territory was gradually and completely incorporated with Scotland, as Scotland gradually and completely realised her own national identity : Dervorguilla, the heiress of the princes of Galloway, was the mother of John Balliol, king of Scots.

Claims of the kings on Ireland.

Over Ireland as a whole the claims of the Anglo-Saxon kings were only titular. Edgar however, who had obtained the submission of the Northumbrian Danes, had apparently acted as patron also of the Ostmen in Ireland[1]. Canute may not improbably have done the same ; and, when those settlers sought and obtained an ecclesiastical organisation in the reign of the Conqueror, they received their bishops from Canterbury. But nothing more had been done ; and it is uncertain whether in the most extensive claims of the Anglo-Saxon kings to the ' imperium' of all the British isles[2], Ireland was even in thought included. Henry II however, very early in his reign, conceived

The bull *Laudabiliter.*

the notion of conquering the sister island. In his first year he obtained from the English Pope, Adrian IV, the bull *Laudabiliter*, in which, by virtue of a forced construction of the

---

In 1184 Gilbert rebelled against William the Lion, and died before the war was over, in 1185, leaving his heir in Henry's hands. The territory was seized by his nephew, Ronald, against whom Henry marched in 1186. Ronald however met him at Carlisle and did homage : he retained the principality until he died in 1200 at the English court. Alan, his son and successor, married a daughter of David of Huntingdon, and was the father of Dervorguilla Balliol. Galloway furnished a portion of Henry II's mercenary troops.

[1] Coins of Ethelred and Canute, if not also of Edgar, were struck at Dublin ; Robertson, Essays, p. 198 ; Ruding, Annals of the Coinage, i. 262-276 ; and Nicolas of Worcester in a letter to Eadmer counts the king of Dublin among Edgar's vassals ; Memorials of Dunstan, p. 423. Cf. Kemble, Cod. Dipl. ii. 404.

[2] ' Ego Aethelred gentis gubernator Angligenae totiusque insulae coregulus Britannicae et ceterarum insularum in circuitu adjacentium ; ' Kemble, Cod. Dipl. iii. 323 ; cf. 348, iv. 23.

forged donation of Constantine, the pontiff, as lord of all islands, bestowed Ireland on the English king[1]. In a council at Winchester, held the same year, Henry proposed an expedition to conquer the country as a kingdom for his brother William, but was dissuaded by the empress[2]; and the gift remained a dead letter until 1167, when the quarrels of the native princes opened the way for the piratical attempts of Richard of Clare. In 1171 Henry himself, determined to avoid the Roman legation, went, as we have already seen, to Ireland and received the formal obedience of both kings and prelates; the king of Connaught, who alone resisted, making his submission by treaty in 1175[3]. In 1177 John was made lord of Ireland, and received the homage of some of the barons, amongst whom his father portioned out the country, which was as yet unconquered[4]. In 1185 he was sent over to exercise authority in person, but he signally failed to show any capacity for government, and was recalled in disgrace. Henry seems to have thought that a formal coronation might secure for his son the obedience of the Irish, and obtained from Urban III licence to make him king, the licence being accompanied by a crown of gold and peacock's feathers[5]. But, although a special legate was sent for the purpose in 1187, John was never crowned, and the kings of England remained lords only of Ireland until Henry VIII took the title of king without coronation. John, during the years of the Interdict, made an expedition to Ireland, in which he had some success, bringing the English settlers, who already aimed at independence, into something like order. But the lordship of Ireland was little more than honorary; the native population were driven into semi-barbarism, and the intruding race were scarcely subject even in name to the English crown. The resignation of the kingdom of England to the pope in 1213 was, however, accompanied by the surrender and restoration of Ireland also; and of the annual tribute of a thousand

Marginal notes:
Henry proposes a conquest of Ireland.

The submission of the Irish princes; and the feudal division of Ireland.

John and his successors lords of Ireland.

---

[1] Giraldus Cambrensis, Opp. v. 316. Cf. Joh. Salisb. Metalogicus, iv. c. 42. John of Salisbury brought an emerald ring from the pope to Henry II by way of investiture.

[2] Robert de Monte, A.D. 1155.

[3] Benedict, i. 101–103.   [4] Ib. i. 161, 165.   [5] Hoveden, ii. 307.

marks, three tenths were assigned to Ireland, whilst seven
tenths were to be paid for England. The fact that Ireland
had in 1151 received a new ecclesiastical constitution from
Pope Eugenius probably saved it from annexation to the province of Canterbury, or to the jurisdiction of the primate of
England.

New ecclesiastical constitution of Ireland.

Whilst the king of England was thus asserting and partially
realising imperial claims over his neighbours in the British
islands, he was in his continental relations involved in a net of
homages and other kindred obligations, which might seem to
derogate from the idea of royalty as much as the former
magnified it. As duke of Normandy he was a vassal of the
king of France; and as dukes of Aquitaine, counts of Poictou,
and counts of Anjou, Henry II and his sons stood in still more
complicated feudal connexion. The Norman kings had avoided
as much as possible even the semblance of dependence. The
Conqueror was not called on after the Conquest to do homage
to his suzerain, and William Rufus never was duke of Normandy. Henry I claimed the duchy during the life of Robert,
but he avoided the necessity of the ceremony by making his son
receive the formal investiture [1]; and Stephen followed the same
plan, to secure Normandy for Eustace [2]. In these cases the
royal dignity was saved by throwing the duty of homage upon
the heir; David king of Scots had allowed his son Henry to
take the oath to Stephen, and thus avoided a ceremony which,
although it might not have humiliated, would certainly have
compromised him [3]. Henry II had performed all the feudal
ceremonies due to Lewis VII before he obtained the English
crown [4]; and on the succession of Philip would willingly have
devolved the renewal of homage on the sons amongst whom his

Homages paid by the kings for foreign fiefs.

Homage for Normandy.

Homage of Henry II for Normandy, Anjou, and Aquitaine.

---

[1] William the Etheling did homage for Normandy in 1119; Cont. F.
Wig.; W. Malmesb. G. R. lib. v. § 419.

[2] In 1137; Hen. Hunt. fol. 222; Hoveden, i. 192.

[3] Hen. Hunt. fol. 221, 222; Hoveden, i. 190, 191.

[4] He did homage for Normandy in 1151 to Lewis VII; R. de Monte
(Bouquet, xiii. 292). John of Salisbury (ep. 285) says that Henry, notwithstanding his oath that he would never return to homage to Lewis,
did unreservedly renew his homage in the conference at Montmirail in
1169. Cf. R. de Monte, A.D. 1169.

great foreign dominion was to be divided[1]. When however, after the death of his eldest son, he found himself in 1183 obliged to make a fresh settlement of his estates, with that politic craft which he embodied in his saying that it was easier to repent of words than of deeds, he sacrificed his pride to his security, and did formal homage to his young rival[2]. Richard had done the same before his accession, and was not called on to repeat it[3]. John, after in vain attempting to avoid it, and after seeing Arthur invested with Normandy and the other paternal fiefs, yielded, as his father had done, to expediency, and performed in A.D. 1200 the homage which was a few years later made one of the pleas for his forfeiture[4]. His mother was still alive, and from her he chose to hold Aquitaine, she in her turn doing the homage to the suzerain[5].

Homage of John.

If the royal consecration was supposed to confer such dignity that it was a point of honour to avoid, if possible, the simple ceremonies of homage and fealty for fiefs for which it was justly due, it was only in the greatest emergency and under the most humiliating circumstances that the wearer of the crown could divest himself of his right and receive it again as the gift of his temporary master. Yet this, if we are to believe the historians, happened twice in the short period before us. Richard was compelled to resign the crown of England to Henry VI during his captivity; and John surrendered his kingdom to Innocent III: in both cases it was restored as a fief, subject to tribute: and in the former case the bargain was annulled by the emperor before his death, although Richard was regarded by the electors who chose Otto IV as one of the principal members of the

Disparagement of the Crown by surrender.

Cases of Richard and John.

[1] The younger Henry acted as seneschal of France at the coronation of Philip II; Bened. i. 242. He had received the office in 1169; R. de Monte, A.D. 1169.   [2] Hoveden, ii. 284; Bened. i. 306.

[3] At least no mention is made of the repetition of the ceremony in the account of his interview with Philip immediately after his father's death; Bened. ii. 74.

[4] 'Recepit homagium regis Angliae de omnibus terris et feodis et tenementis quae unquam rex Ricardus aut Henricus pater ejus tenuit de eo vel de praedecessoribus suis;' R. Coggeshale, p. 101. Cf. Hoveden, iv. 115.

[5] Rot. Chart. p. 130; Rigord (Bouquet, xvii. 50); W. Covent. ii. pref. xxxiv.

empire[1]. It has been stated that Henry II made a similar surrender, or took a similar oath to the pope on the occasion

No such act done by Henry II.

of his absolution at Avranches : this however was not the case; the fealty which he swore was merely promised to Alexander III as the Catholic pope, not as his feudal lord, and the oath simply bound him not to recognise the antipope[2]. John during his brother's life was said to have undertaken to hold the kingdom as a fief under Philip II if he would help him to win it; but

View of the pope and emperor.

this may have been a mere rumour[3]. It can scarcely be thought probable that either Henry VI or Innocent III, although both entertained an idea of universal empire, deliberately contrived the reduction of England to feudal dependence ; both took advantage of the opportunity which deprived their victims for the

Humiliating character of the act.

moment of the power of resistance. Richard made his surrender with the advice of his mother, his most experienced counsellor; and John accepted his humiliation with the counsel and consent of all parties, bitterly as they felt it, and strongly as they resented the conduct by which he had made it necessary[4]. In neither case would much heroism have been shown by resistance

[1] Hoveden, iii. 202, 203; iv. 37, 38.

[2] It is not clear however that the pope did not intend Henry to bind himself to homage and fealty, and so to hold the kingdom of the papacy. The curious expression found in a letter addressed in Henry's name to Alexander III, among the letters of Peter of Blois, has been understood to imply that the king on the occasion of his absolution placed the kingdom in that feudal relation which was afterwards created by John's submission : ' Vestrae jurisdictionis est regnum Angliae et quantum ad feudatarii juris obligationem vobis duntaxat obnoxius teneor et astringor;' Opp. ed. Busæus, p. 245. It is possible that the papal legates were instructed to obtain such a concession from Henry, as, in the Life of Alexander III, the king is said to swear ' quod a domino Alexandro papa et ejus catholicis successoribus recipiemus et tenebimus regnum Angliae.' But no such concession is mentioned in any contemporary account of the purgation, nor could it have been unknown to English historians if it had really taken place. The letter of Peter has of course no claim to be authoritative, and may be only a scholastic exercise. The matter is however confessedly obscure. See Robertson, Life of Becket, p. 303, and the authorities there quoted.

[3] Hoveden, iii. 204.

[4] Matthew Paris says that the surrender was made by the unanimous consent of all parties (ii. 541). The Barnwell canon, copied by Walter of Coventry, allows that the act was politic, although it appeared to many an ' ignominious and enormous yoke of slavery ' (ii. 210). In the document itself John states that he acts ' communi consilio baronum suorum.'

to the demand : Richard's misfortune and John's misgovernment had left them practically without alternative.

The ceremonial attributes and pomp of royalty changed but
little under these sovereigns. The form and matter of the
coronation service remained, so far as we have documentary
evidence, unaltered : Henry II during his first three years wore
his crown in solemn state on the great festivals, though he so
far varied the ancient rule as sometimes to hold his court on
those days at S. Edmund's, Lincoln, and Worcester : but after
A.D. 1158 he gave up the custom altogether. Richard only once,
after his consecration, wore his crown in state ; and John went
through the ceremony thrice at least, once on the occasion of his
wife's coronation [1]. The venerable practice was distasteful to
Henry II, who disliked public ceremonial and grudged needless
expense. Richard's constant absence from England, and John's
unfriendly relations with Archbishop Langton and the barons,
prevented its revival. The improvement in the legal machinery
of the kingdom had deprived it of its former usefulness, and the
performance of the grand serjeanties which were due at the
coronations might by agreement take place on other occasions,
as at the great court held at Guildford in 1186 [2]. In other
points both Richard and John showed themselves inclined to
advance rather than abate the pomp of their position. Richard
is the first king who regularly uses the plural 'we' in the granting
of charters ; John, as we have seen, is the first who formally calls
himself the king of the land instead of the king of the people.

The long absences of the kings threw additional power, or a
firmer tenure of power, into the hands of the justiciars. Yet it
may be questioned whether Henry II did not contemplate the
institution of a practice according to which either himself or
his eldest son should be constantly present in England. The
younger Henry is found, both before and after his coronation, acting in his father's place : not only as the centre of
courtly pomp, but transacting business, issuing writs, presiding
in the Curia, and discharging other functions which seem to

Disuse of the coronation-days.

The custom obsolete.

Pomp of Richard and John.

John is Rex Angliae.

Regency in the king's absence.

The younger Henry.

---

[1] Hoveden, iv. 169, 182 ; above, pp. 554, 555.
[2] Benedict, ii. 3 ; above, p. 527, n. 5.

Queen
Eleanor.

belong to regency[1]. During the interregnum which followed Henry's death, his widow acted in her son's name, proclaiming his peace and directing the oaths of fealty to be taken to him; and during his captivity she is found at the head of the administration both in England and Normandy, acting with

John.

rather than through the justiciar. John, after the fall of Longchamp in 1191, was recognised by the barons as ruler of the

The justiciar.

kingdom[2] in his brother's stead. These facts seem to indicate that the viceregal character, which the justiciar certainly possessed, was not without its limits: whilst from the fact that earl Robert of Leicester is found acting together with the justiciar Richard de Lucy[3] during the absence of Henry and his sons, it may be argued that the king avoided trusting even that most loyal servant with a monopoly of ministerial power. But we have not sufficient evidence to define the exact position of either the members of the royal family or the justiciar; and it is very probable that it was not settled even at this time by any other rule than that of temporary convenience.

The national
council in
two aspects;
as a feudal
court and
as a stage
towards the
representation of
estates.

159. The national council under Henry II and his sons seems in one aspect to be a realisation of the principle which was introduced at the Conquest, and had been developed and grown into consistency under the Norman kings, that of a complete council of feudal tenants-in-chief. In another aspect it appears to be in a stage of transition towards that combined representation of the three estates and of the several provincial communities which especially marks our constitution, and which perhaps was the ideal imperfectly grasped and more imperfectly realised, at which the statesmen of the middle ages almost unconsciously aimed. The constituent members of this assembly are the same

[1] He was present at Becket's election to the primacy in 1162; R. de Diceto, i. 306: also when Becket received the quittance, in the Exchequer, of his accounts as chancellor; Grim, S. T. C., p. 15; ed. Robertson, ii. 367; Roger of Pontigny, S. T. C. pp. 107, 108. He must have been quite an infant at the time. After his coronation he had a chancellor and a sealbearer or vice-chancellor, and that at a time when his father had dispensed with a chancellor.

[2] 'Summus rector totius regni;' R. Devizes, p, 38; above, p. 538.

[3] As for example in 1165, when he refused the kiss of peace to the archbishop of Cologne as a schismatic; R. Diceto, i. 318.

as under the Norman kings, but greater prominence and a more Gradual de-
finition of
definite position are assigned to the minor tenants-in-chief; the position
there is a growing recognition of their real constitutional im- of the feudal
portance, a gradual definition of their title to be represented
and of the manner of representation, and a growing tendency to
admit not only them, but the whole body of smaller landowners,
of whom the minor tenants-in-chief are but an insignificant
portion, to the same rights. This latter tendency may be
described as directed towards the concentration of the representation of the counties in the national parliament,—the
combination of the shiremoots with the witenagemot of the
kingdom.

The royal council, as distinct from the mere assembly and Possible ar-
court of the household, might consist of either the magnates, of the
the greater barons, the 'proceres' of the Conqueror's reign; council.
or of the whole body of tenants-in-chief, as was the accepted
usage under Henry II; or of the whole body of landowners,
whoever their feudal lords might be, which was the case in the
great councils of 1086 and 1116, and which, when the representative principle was fully recognised, became the theory of
the medieval constitution. These three bodies were divided by
certain lines, although those lines were not very definite. The The greater
greater barons held a much greater extent of land than the barons.
minor tenants-in-chief: they made a separate agreement with the
Crown for their reliefs, and probably for their other payments
in aid [1]: they had, as we learn from Magna Carta, their several
summonses to the great councils, and they led their vassals to the
host under their own banners. The entire body of tenants-in- The entire
chief included besides these the minor barons, the knightly body, tenants-in-
and the socage tenants of the crown, who paid their reliefs to the chief.
sheriff, were summoned to court or council through his writ, and
appeared under his banner in the military levy of the county.
The general body of freeholders comprised, besides these two The general
bodies, all the feudal tenants of the barons and the freemen of freeholders.
the towns and villages, who had a right or duty of appearing in
the county court, who were armed in the fyrd or under the

[1] Dialogus de Scaccario, ii. cc. 10, 24.

assize of arms, who were bound to the Crown simply by the oath of allegiance taken in the shiremoot, and were qualified to determine by their sworn evidence the rights of their neighbours, the assessment of their goods, and the report of their neighbourhood as to criminals.

Ordinary, extraordinary, and theoretical forms.

These three possible assemblies may be regarded again as the assembly in its ordinary, extraordinary, and theoretical form : the national council usually contained only the magnates ; on great occasions it contained the whole body of the tenants-in-chief ; in idea it was the representation of the nation ; and on one or two very rare occasions that idea was partially realised. But there were departments of national action in which the uncertainty and indefiniteness of such a theory were inadmissible. For the payment of taxes all men must be brought under contribution ; for the efficiency of the national host all men must be brought together in arms. For the first of these purposes they might be visited in detail, for the second they must be

Military levies a general assembly of the nation.

assembled in person. Accordingly we find that the military levies in which Henry II brought together the whole kingdom in arms, as for the siege of Bridgnorth in 1155 or for the expedition to Normandy in 1177, may have really been steps towards the assembling of the nation for other purposes ; and when, as in the latter case, we find the king acting by the counsel of the assembled host [1], we recur in thought to that ancient time when the only general assembly was that of the

National concentration in arms.

nation in arms. But the nation in arms was merely the meeting of the shires in arms : the men who in council or in judgment made up the county court, in arms composed the 'exercitus scirae :' on occasion of taxation or local consultation they were the wise men, the legales homines of the shiremoot. The king's general council is then one day to comprise the collective wisdom of the shires, as his army comprises their collective

---

[1] Bened. i. 178 : ' Venerunt etiam illuc ad eum comites et barones et milites regni per summonitionem suam, parati equis et armis secum transfretare in Normanniam. . . . Congregatis itaque omnibus in urbe Wintoniae, rex *per consilium eorum* transfretationem suam distulit.' Immediately after, the 'consiliarii' of the king are mentioned as advising him about the garrisons of the castles.

strength. But it is very rarely as yet that the principle of national concentration, which has been applied to the host, is applied to the council.

The point at which the growth of this principle had arrived during the period before us is marked by the fourteenth article of the Great Charter: 'To have the common council of the kingdom' for the assessment of extraordinary aids and scutages, 'we will cause to be summoned the archbishops, bishops, abbots, earls, and greater barons singly by our letters; and besides we will cause to be summoned in general by our sheriffs and bailiffs all those who hold of us in chief; to a certain day, that is to say, at a term of forty days at least; and to a certain place; and in all the letters of such summons we will express the cause of the summons; and the summons having been so made, the business shall on the day assigned proceed according to the counsel of those who shall be present, although not all who have been summoned shall have come.' The council is thus no longer limited to the magnates: but it is not extended so as to include the whole nation, it halts at the tenants-in-chief: nor are its functions of advising on all matters recognised, it is simply to be assembled for the imposing of taxation. The provision, that the determination of the members present shall be regarded as the proceeding of the whole body summoned, enunciates in words the principle which had long been acted upon, that absence, like silence, on such occasion implies consent.

The use of a written summons to call together the council must have been very ancient, but we have no evidence of the date at which it became the rule. The great courts held on the festivals of the Church might not indeed require such a summons, but every special assembly of the sort—and very many such occur from the earliest days of the Norman reigns—must have been convoked by a distinct writ. Such writs were of two kinds: there was first a special summons declaring the cause of meeting, addressed to every man whose presence was absolutely requisite; thus for the sessions of the Exchequer each of the king's debtors was summoned by a writ declaring the sum for

Marginal notes:

Constitution of the national council as stated in the Great Charter.

A stage of transition.

Writs of summons.

Two sorts of writs of summons: the special,

and the general.

which he was called upon to account[1] : and secondly there was a general summons such as those addressed to the several counties through their sheriffs to bring together the shiremoot to meet the justices or the officers of the forest[2]. The former was delivered directly to the person to whom it was addressed; the latter was proclaimed by the servants of the sheriff in the villages and market towns, and obeyed by those who were generally described in the writ itself, as their business, inclination, or fear of the penalty for non-attendance, might dispose

Summons of the greater barons.

them. On this analogy the writs of summons to the national council were probably of two sorts : those barons who in their military, fiscal, and legal transactions dealt directly with the

Summons of the minor tenants.

king were summoned by special writ : those tenants-in-chief who transacted their business with the sheriff were convened, not by a writ in which they were severally named, but by a general

Importance of summons.

summons. Of the greater barons the first person summoned was the archbishop of Canterbury, and it is from the mention by the historians of the offence offered to Becket by neglecting this customary respect that we learn the existence of the double system of summons in the early years of Henry II[3]. There is still earlier evidence of the special summons : Gilbert Foliot, in reference to the homage and oaths taken to the empress, describes the greater magnates as those who were accustomed to be summoned to council in their own proper names; evidently as distinguished from those who were cited by a collective summons[4]. The Pipe Rolls contain very frequent mention of payments made to the summoners, and that in direct connexion with meetings of the council[5]. In 1175 Henry went so far as to forbid those who had been lately in arms against him to appear

First extant writ, of 1205.

at his court at all without summons[6]. It is a strange thing that so very few of these early writs are now in existence : the most

[1] See the chapters on Summons in the Dialogus de Scaccario, i. cc. 1, 2.
[2] Such are the 'communes summonitiones' mentioned in Art. 44 of the Great Charter.
[3] See above, p. 504.
[4] 'Eorum namque qui statuto consilio propriis, ut dicitur, consueverant appellari nominibus, nemo plane relictus est qui non ei consilium de obtinendo et tuendo post regis obitum regno . . . promitteret;' S. T. C. v. 98.
[5] See above, p. 505, note 2. [6] See above, p. 521.

ancient that we have is one addressed to the bishop of Salisbury
in 1205, ten years before the granting of the charter. This
document fixes the date of the assembly, which is to be held at
London on the Sunday before Ascension Day, and the cause of
the meeting, which is to discuss the message brought by the
envoys from Philip of France; and it also contains a clause of
general summons, directing the bishop to warn the abbots and
priors of his diocese to be present on the occasion [1]. Of the
general forms of summons addressed to the sheriffs, we have no
specimens earlier than the date at which representative institutions had been to a great extent adopted: but, if we may judge
of their tenour from the like writs issued for military and
fiscal purposes, they must have enumerated the classes of
persons summoned in much the same way as they were enumerated in the writs ordering the assembly of the county court [2].
Of this however it is impossible to be quite certain. That the
county court had a special form of summons for the purpose of
taxation we learn from a writ of Henry I, which has been
already quoted [3]. It is probable that the fourteenth clause of
Magna Carta represents no more than the recognised theory of
the system of summons; a system which was already passing
away; for, besides that council at S. Alban's in 1213, in which
the several townships of royal demesne were represented as in
the county court by the reeve and four best men, a council was
called at Oxford in the same year, in which each county was
represented by four discreet men, who were to attend on the king
'to talk with him on the business of the kingdom.' In the writ
by which this council is summoned, and which is dated on the
7th of November at Witney, we have the first extant evidence
of the representation of the counties in the council [4]; they were
already accustomed to elect small numbers of knights for legal
and fiscal purposes, and the practice of making such elections to
expedite the proceeding of the itinerant justices is confirmed by

Summons of the county court.

Summons of four discreet knights in 1213.

[1] Select Charters, p. 282.
[2] Examples, of the reign of Henry III, are in the Select Charters (ed. 3),
pp. 343, 358, 374, &c.
[3] Above, p. 425.
[4] Select Charters, p. 287; above, p. 567.

the Great Charter itself. It is then just possible that the 14th clause may have been intended to cover the practice of county representation which had been used two years before. The further development of the system belongs to a later stage of our inquiries.

Members of the Council.The character of the persons summoned requires no comment: the archbishops and bishops were the same in number as before, but the abbots and priors were a rapidly increasing body. The number of earls increased very slowly: it may be questioned whether Henry II founded any new earldoms, or whether the two or three ascribed to him were not merely those which, having been created by his mother or Stephen, he vouch-

Earldoms and great baronies.safed to confirm[1]. None were created by Richard; and by John only the earldom of Winchester, which was founded in favour of one of the coheirs of the earldom of Leicester, the latter title being taken by the other coheir. The number of great baronies however was probably on the increase, although we have not sufficient data, either as to the possessors or as to the exact character of such baronies, to warrant a very positive

Minor tenants and clergy.statement. The number of minor tenants-in-chief who attended cannot even be conjectured: but, as the clergy of inferior dignity formed an appreciable part of the council, it is probable that the knights who, without yet possessing a representative character, came up from the shires in consequence of the general summons, were a considerable body: and sometimes they were very numerous. The presence of a large number of deans and archdeacons is mentioned on some special occasions[2], which seem to indicate a plan of assembling the three estates in something like completeness: but we have no reason to suppose that

---

[1] William of Albini of Arundel was made earl of the county of Sussex by charter in 1155; and Aubrey de Vere, earl of Oxford, about the same time. Henry confirmed the earldoms of Norfolk and Hereford, and the grant to Aubrey de Vere was no doubt a confirmation also. Richard gave charters to William of Arundel and Roger Bigod: John restored the earldom of Hereford in favour of Henry de Bohun, and created that of Winchester for Saer de Quincy. See the Fifth Report on the Dignity of a Peer, App. pp. 1–5.

[2] For example on the occasion of the Spanish award in 1177, Bened. i. 145; and at S. Paul's in 1213, M. Paris, ii. 552.

they were ever summoned as a matter of right or as tenants-in-chief.

The times of assembly were very irregular. In many cases, Times of
holding
councils. especially in the early years of Henry II, they coincided with the great festivals, or with the terminal days which were already beginning to be observed by the lawyers. But so great a number of occasional councils were called by Henry, and so few by his sons, that obviously no settled rule can have been observed. And the same remark is true as regards the place of meeting. The festival courts were still frequently kept at Winchester and Westminster ; but for the great national gatherings for homage, for proclamation of Crusade, or the like, some central position, such as Northampton or its neighbourhood, was often preferred. Yet some of Henry II's most important acts were done in councils held in the forest palaces, such as Clarendon and Woodstock. Richard's two councils were held in middle England, one at Pipewell in Northamptonshire, the other at Nottingham ; both places in which the weariness of state business might be lightened by the royal amusement of the chase.

The name given to these sessions of council was often ex- Name of
parliament. pressed by the Latin *colloquium*[1] : and it is by no means unlikely that the name of parliament, which is used as early as 1175 by Jordan Fantosme[2], may have been in common use. But of this we have no distinct instance in the Latin Chroniclers for some years further, although when the term comes into use it is applied retrospectively ; and in a record of the twenty-eighth year of Henry III the assembly in which the Great Charter was granted is mentioned as the ' Parliamentum Runimedæ.'

The subjects on which the kings asked the advice of the body Subjects of
deliberation. thus constituted were very numerous : it might almost seem

---

[1] E. g. M. Paris, ii. 552.
[2] Jordan Fantosme, p. 14. It is used also by Wace. It is applied by Otto Morena to the diet or parliament of Roncaglia held by Frederick I in 1154 ; Leibnitz, Scr. Rer. Brunswic. i. 809. It is first used in England by a contemporary writer in 1246, namely by M. Paris, iii. 518. See Hody, History of Convocation, p. 326.

General de-
liberations.

that Henry II consulted his court and council on every matter
of importance that arose during his reign; all the business that
Richard personally transacted was done in his great councils;
and even John, who acted far more in the manner and spirit of a
despot than did his father or brother, did little in the first half
of his reign without a formal show of respect towards his constitutional advisers. Nor is there any reason to suppose that
such a proceeding was, in the great proportion of instances,
merely a matter of form: a sovereign who is practically absolute asks counsel whenever he wants it; and such a sovereign,
if he is a man of good sense, with reason for self-confidence, is
not trammeled by the jealousies or by the need of self-assertion
which are inseparable from the position of a monarch whose

Miscella-
neous mat-
ters.

prerogatives are constitutionally limited. Hence it was perhaps that these kings, besides constantly laying before their
barons all questions touching the state of the kingdom [1],—
matters of public policy such as the destruction of the illegal
castles and the maintenance of the royal hold on the fortresses,
matters relating to legislation, to the administration of justice,
to taxation, and to military organisation,—also took their
opinion on peace and war, alliances, royal marriages, and even
in questions of arbitration between foreign powers which had
been specially referred to the king for decision [2]. Of such deliberations abundant instances have been given in the last
chapter. It is very rarely that any record is preserved of

Opposition
to the royal
will.

opposition to or even remonstrance against the royal will. In
1175 Richard de Lucy ventured to remind Henry II, when he
was enforcing the law against the destroyers of the forests, that
the waste of vert and venison had been authorised by his own

---

[1] Such was the assembly at Bermondsey in 1154 'de statu regni;'
Gervase, i. 160: that 'de statutis regni' at London in 1170, and that at
Northampton in 1176; Bened. i. 4, 107.

[2] In 1176 Henry II consulted his council before assenting to the marriage of his daughter Johanna; in 1177 he consulted the great assembly of
feudal tenants held at Winchester, on the expediency of proceeding with
the war. In 1184 on the question of an aid demanded by the pope;
Bened. i. 311. In 1155 he had consulted them on an expedition to Ireland.
In 1177 he took their advice on the Spanish arbitration; Benedict, i. 116,
142, 178; R. de Monte, A.D. 1155.

writ; but his mediation was summarily set aside[1]: the remon-
strances likewise of the one or two counsellors, who during the
Becket quarrel interposed on behalf of the archbishop, were
either tacitly disregarded or resented as an advocacy of the
king's enemy. Still less are we to look for any power of in-
itiating measures of either public policy or particular reform in
any hands but those of the king. Yet the assize of measures in
1197 was made not only with the advice but by the *petition* of
the magnates[2]. The justiciar however probably advised the
king on all these matters, and perhaps suggested the administrative changes which he had to work out in their details; in
this respect acting as the spokesman of the barons, as the archbishop acted as the spokesman of the Church, and exercising
over the king a less overt but more effectual influence than
could have been asserted by the barons except at the risk of
rebellion. John certainly chafed under the advice of the justiciar, without venturing to dismiss him. In all these matters
the regard, even if merely formal, shown by the king to the
advice and consent of his barons has a constitutional value, as
affording a precedent and suggesting a method for securing
the exercise of the right of advising and consenting when the
balance of power was changed, and advice and consent meant
more than mere helpless acquiescence. The part taken by the
national council in legislation, taxation, and judicature may be
noticed as we proceed with the examination of those departments of public work.

Position of the justiciar as spokesman of the council.

The ecclesiastical councils of the period did their work with
very little interference from the secular power, and with very
little variation from the earlier model. Their privilege of
legislating with the royal acquiescence was not disputed, and
their right to a voice in the bestowal of their contributions
towards the wants of the state came into gradual recognition in
the reign of John: but although his expedients for the raising
of money may now and then have served as precedents upon
which the claim to give or refuse might be raised on behalf of
the several orders in Church and State, no complete system of

Position of the Church councils.

[1] Bened. i. 94.　　　　　[2] See p. 616.

separate action by the clergy on secular matters was as yet devised, nor was their position as a portion of the common council of the realm defined by the Great Charter apart from that of the other tenants-in-chief. The theory of the Three Estates had yet to be worked into practice ; although there were signs of its growing importance.

Legislation.

160. Great as was the legal reputation of Henry II, and greatly as the legal system of England advanced under him and his sons, the documentary remains of the legislation of the period are very scanty. The work of Glanvill is not a book of statutes, but a manual of practice ; and, although it incorporates no doubt the words of ordinances which had the force of laws,

Form of legislation : the Assize.

it nowhere gives the literal text of such enactments. The formal edicts known under the name of Assizes, the Assizes of Clarendon and Northampton, the Assize of Arms, the Assize of the Forest, and the Assizes of Measures, are the only relics of the legislative work of the period. These edicts are chiefly composed of new regulations for the enforcement of royal justice. They are not direct re-enactments or amendments of the ancient customary law, and are not drawn up in the form of perpetual statutes : but they rather enunciate and declare new methods of judicial procedure, which would either work into or supersede the procedure of the common law, whether practised in the popular or in the feudal courts. In this respect they strongly resemble the Capitularies of the Frank kings, or, to go farther back, the edicts of the Roman praetors : they might indeed, as to both form and matter, be called Capitu-

Origin of the Assize.

laries. The term Assize, which comes into use in this meaning about the middle of the twelfth century, both on the Continent and in England, appears to be the proper Norman name for such edicts[1]; but it is uncertain whether it received this par-

---

[1] Looking at the word *assisa* simply we might incline to regard it as the *lex assisa* or *sententia assisa*, the settled edict of the king, just as the *redditus assisus* was the fixed or assessed rent of an estate. It is however used so early in the sense of a *session* that the former cannot be regarded as the sole explanation. In the Assize of Jerusalem it simply means a law : and the same in Henry's legislation. Secondarily, it means a form of trial established by the particular law, as the Great Assize, the Assize

ticular application from the mere fact that it was a settlement
like the Anglo-Saxon *asetniss* or the French *établissement*, or
from a verbal connexion with the session of the court in which
it was passed, or from the fact that it furnished a plan on which
sessions of the courts reformed by it should be held. The assize
thus differs widely from the charter of liberties, the form which
the legislation of Henry I and Stephen had taken, and is
peculiar in English history to the period before us, as the form
of Provisions marks the legislative period of Henry III, and that
of Statute and Ordinance belongs to that of Edward I and his
successors. The special sanctity of the term *law*, as used in
Holy Scripture and in the Roman jurisprudence, may perhaps
account for the variety of expressions, such as those quoted
above, by means of which men avoided giving the title of law
to their occasional enactments. The Assizes of England, Jerusalem, Antioch, Sicily, and Romania, the Establishments of
S. Lewis, the Recesses of the German diets, and many other like
expressions, illustrate this reluctance.

The Assize possesses moreover the characteristic of tentative Its character
or temporary enactment, rather than the universal and per- decree.
petual character which a law, however superficially, seems to
claim : its duration is specified in the form ; it is to be in force
so long as the king pleases ; it may have a retrospective effi-
cacy, to be applied to the determination of suits which have
arisen since the king's accession, or since his last visit to Eng-

of Mort d'Ancester; and thirdly, the court held to hold such trials; in
which sense it is commonly used at the present day. Yet it occurs in the
Norman law-books in the twelfth century, and apparently in the Pipe Roll
of 2 Henry II, in the sense of a session, and that is taken by many antiquaries as the primary meaning. The formation of assisus from a barbarous
use of assido or assideo (instead of assessus) might be paralleled with the
derivation of tolta in *malatolta* from tollo in the sense of taking toll ; but
the word accido, to tax, may, so far as the *assisus redditus* is concerned,
be the true origin of this form, as it is of the modern *excise*. On the
other hand, it is impossible not to associate the *assize* of Henry II with
the *asetniss* of Ina and Edmund. Possibly the use of the word in so many
senses may point to a confusion of three different origins. Cf. the derivation of *taxo*, to tax, from τάσσω, to ordain, or regulate : and the use of
the word *tallare*=*accidere*, *taxare*. The form *assisia* suggests further
difficulties, but there is no reason to look for an Arabic derivation, as is
done in the editions of Du Cange.

land [1]; it is liable to be set aside by the judges where they find it impossible to administer it fairly. But, on the other hand, it is to the assize that the most important legal changes of the period owe their origin: the institution of jury and the whole procedure of the Curia Regis can have come into existence in no other way.

Assizes issued with the counsel and consent of the council.

In the drawing up of the assize, the king acted by the advice and consent of his national council. This is distinctly stated in the preamble or title of the Assizes of Clarendon and Woodstock: the former is made 'de assensu archiepiscoporum, episcoporum, abbatum, comitum, baronum, totius Angliae [2];' the latter 'per consilium et assensum archiepiscoporum, episcoporum et baronum, comitum et nobilium Angliae [3].' The Assize of Northampton was the work, we are told, of the king, made by the counsel of King Henry his son and by the counsel of his earls, barons, knights, and vassals (homines) in a great council, consisting of bishops, earls, barons, and the rest, held 'de statutis regni [4].' The ordinance by which trial by the Great Assize was instituted was, according to Glanvill, an act of royal beneficence, bestowed on the nation by the clemency of the

Instances of Assizes.

prince according to the counsel of the magnates [5]. The Assize of Measures was issued in the name of Richard I by the justiciar in 1197, as made by the lord Richard king of England at Westminster, although the king was at the time in France, by the petition and advice of his bishops and all his barons [6]. In this act of legislation the justiciar represented the king. The instructions

[1] The Assize of Clarendon is to be held good as long as it pleases the king. That of Northampton directs inquiry into disseisins made since the king's last coming to England; and the view of this Assize is to extend from the date of the Assize of Clarendon to the time of its own publication; 'atenebit a tempore quo assisa facta fuit apud Clarendonam continue usque ad hoc tempus.' Richard's Assize of Measures was set aside by the justices because the merchants declared it to be impracticable. See Select Charters, pp. 146, 151; Hoveden, iv. 172. John's Assize of Wines was set aside in the same way; ibid. p. 100.

[2] Select Charters, p. 143.

[3] Select Charters, p. 157.

[4] Bened. i. 107.

[5] 'Est autem magna assisa regale quoddam beneficium, clementia principis de consilio procerum populis indultum;' Glanvill, ii. c. 7.

[6] Hoveden, iv. 33.

given to the itinerant justices had likewise the force of laws, and might with justice be termed Assizes. They too were issued by the justiciar in the king's absence, and contained old as well as new regulations for the courts. The Assize of Arms issued in 1181 is not distinctly said to be framed under the advice of the council, and it may possibly have been regarded by the barons with some jealousy as putting arms into the hands of the people ; but, when John in 1205 summoned the nation to arms in conformity with the principle embodied in his father's assize, he declares that it is so provided with the assent of the 'archbishops, bishops, earls, barons, and all our faithful of England [1].' These instances are sufficient to prove the share taken by the national council in legislation. The duty of proclaiming the law in the country fell upon the sheriffs and the itinerant justices, whose credentials contained perhaps the first general promulgation. The Great Charter was read, by the king's order, publicly in every county, no doubt in the shiremoot and hundred court [2]; duplicates of it were deposited in the cathedral churches.

Proclamation of the new laws in the country.

In all this there was nothing new : it was simply the maintenance of ancient forms, which prove their strength by retaining their vitality under the strongest of our kings. The advice and consent of the council may have been, no doubt in many cases was, a mere formality : the enacting power was regarded as belonging to the king, who could put in respite or dispense with the very measures that he had ordained. Yet in this an advantage may be incidentally traced. If the barons under Henry II had possessed greater legislative power, they might have kept it to themselves, as they did to a certain extent keep to themselves the judicial power of the later parliament; but, as it was, legislation was one of the nominal rights that belonged to the whole council as the representative of the nation, and the real exercise of which was not attained until the barons had made common cause with the people, and incorporated

Importance of constitutional forms.

Legislative power not really acquired by Parliament until it has become representative.

[1] Select Charters, p. 281.
[2] Select Charters, p. 306 : 'quam etiam legi publice praecipimus per totam bailliam vestram.' See above, p. 130.

their representatives in their own assembly. The period of national as distinct from royal legislation begins when the council has reached its constitutional development as the national parliament. The legislation of the Great Charter was to a certain extent an anticipation, a type, a precedent, and a firm step in advance towards that consummation.

Taxation; three points.

161. The subject of taxation may be arranged under three heads,—the authority by which the impost is legalised, the description of persons and property on which it is levied, and the determination of the amount for which the individual is liable; in other words, the grant, the incidence, and the assessment.

Norman taxation.

The reticence of historians during the reigns of the Norman kings leaves us in doubt whether the imposts which they levied were or were not exacted simply by their own sovereign will. Two records have been mentioned, however, of the reign of Henry I, in one of which the king describes a particular tax as

Form of imposing a tax, by signifying the king's necessities.

'the aid which my barons gave me,' whilst in another he speaks of the summoning of the county courts in cases in which his own royal necessities require it[1]. From the two passages it may be inferred that some form was observed, by which the king signified, both to his assembled vassals and to the country at large through the sheriffs, the sums which he wanted, and the plea on which he demanded them. The same method was observed by Henry II and Richard I; and it is only towards the end of the reign of Richard that we can trace anything like a formal grant or discussion of a grant in the national council[2]. It was commonly said that the king took a scutage, an aid, or a

[1] Above, pp. 400, 425.

[2] In 1159 Henry 'scutagium accepit;' Gerv. i. 167; in 1194 Richard 'constituit sibi dari' a carucage; Hoveden, iii. 242: in 1198 'cepit . . . quinque solidos de auxilio;' ib. iv. 46. In 1200 we find the word ' expostulans' used of the king's proposition of a tax for the collection of which 'exiit edictum a justitiariis;' R. Coggeshale, p. 101. In 1203 John 'cepit ab eis septimam partem omnium mobilium suorum;' M. Paris, ii. p. 483. In 1204 'concessa sunt auxilia militaria;' ibid. ii. 484. In 1207 'convenit episcopos et abbates ut permitterent personas dare regi certam summam;' Ann. Waverl. p. 258. A gradual change in the tone of demand may be traceable in this, yet John was really becoming more despotic all the time.

carucage ; and, where the barons are said to have given it, the
expression may be interpreted of the mere payment of the money.
Of any debate or discussion on such exactions in the national   Cases of
council we have rare evidence : the opposition of S. Thomas to   debate on
taxation.
the king's manipulation of the Danegeld, and the refusal by S.
Hugh of Lincoln to furnish money for Richard's war in France,
are however sufficient to prove that the taxation was a subject
of deliberation, although not sufficient to prove that the result
of such discussion would be the authoritative imposition of the
tax [1]. For the shadow of the feudal fiction, that the tax-payer   Want of a
system of
made a voluntary offering to relieve the wants of his ruler, seems   representa-
to have subsisted throughout the period : and the theory that   tion.
the promise of the tax bound only the individual who made it,
helped to increase the financial complications of the reign of
John. Archbishop Theobald had denounced the scutage of 1156,   Opposition
to taxation,
and it is doubtful whether it was raised on his lands. S. Thomas   personal
had declared at Woodstock that the lands of his church should   not representative.
not pay a penny to the Danegeld ; the opposition of S. Hugh
was based not on his right as a member of the national council,
but on the immunities of his church ; and, when Archbishop
Geoffrey in 1201 and 1207 forbade the royal officers to collect
the carucage on his estates, it was on the ground that he himself had not promised the payment. The pressing necessity of
raising the ransom of Richard probably marks an epoch in this
as in some other points of financial interest. The gentle terms
donum or *auxilium* had signified under his father's strong hand
as much as Danegeld or tallage ; but now not only was the
king absent and the kingdom in a critical condition, but the
legal reforms in the matter of assessment had raised up in the
minds of the people at large a growing sense of their rights.
The taxes raised for the ransom were imposed by the justiciar,   Taxes for
Richard's
probably but not certainly, with the advice of the barons [2], and   ransom.
were no doubt collected without any general resistance ; but
both the amount and the incidence were carefully criticised,
and in some cases payment was absolutely refused. The clergy

[1] See above, pp. 500, 548.   [2] Above, p. 540.

of York, when the king's necessities were laid before them by
the archbishop in their chapter, declared that he was infringing
their liberties, and closed their church as in the time of
interdict[1].

Growth of
the idea of
connecting
taxation
with repre-
sentation.

This idea, which is indeed the rudimentary form of the
principle that representation should accompany taxation, gained
ground after the practice arose of bringing personal property
and income under contribution. It was the demand of a quarter
of their revenues, not a direct tax upon their land, that provoked
the opposition of the canons of York; and although Archbishop
Geoffrey is found more than once in trouble for forbidding the

Protest of
the Church
against taxa-
tion in 1207.

collection of a carucage, the next great case in which resistance
was offered to the demands of the Crown occurred in reference
to the exaction of a thirteenth of moveable property in 1207.
On this occasion it was not an isolated chapter, but a whole
estate of the realm that protested. The king in a great council
held on January 8 at London proposed to the bishops and
abbots that they should permit the parsons and beneficed clerks
to give him a certain portion of their revenues. The prelates
refused to do so. The matter was debated in an adjourned
council at Oxford on February 9, and there the bishops repeated

Imposition
of the
thirteenth.

their refusal in still stronger terms. The king therefore gave
up that particular mode of procedure, and obtained from the
national council a grant of an aid of a thirteenth of all chattels
from the laity. That done, having on the 26th of May forbidden
the clergy to hold a council at S. Alban's, he issued, the same
day, a writ to the archdeacons and the rest of the clergy, inform-
ing them of the grant of aid, and bidding them follow the good

Exile of
Geoffrey.

example[2]. Archbishop Geoffrey, who acted as the spokesman of

---

[1] Hoveden, iii. 222 : ' Vocavit, monuit et rogavit ut quartam partem
reddituum suorum ad praefati regis liberationem conferrent ; . . . qui
renuentes et concanonicos suos in partes suas trahentes, asserebant eum
. . . libertates ecclesiae suae velle subvertere.'

[2] Ann. Waverley, p. 258 ; M. Paris, ii. 511. The writ addressed to the
archdeacons, after rehearsing the grant made by the archbishops, bishops,
priors, and magnates, proceeds : ' Verum quia de vobis confidimus quod
nos et honorem nostrum diligitis et defensionem regni nostri et recupera-
tionem terrarum nostrarum affectatis, vos rogamus attentius, quatenus
tale auxilium nobis ex parte vestra faciatis ut inde vobis gratias dare
debeamus ; et quod alii rectores ecclesiarum vicini vestri ad auxilium

the clergy, now gave up the struggle and went into exile; other circumstances were leading to a crisis: the thirteenth was no doubt generally collected; but early in the following year the interdict was imposed and constitutional law was in abeyance during the remainder of the reign. The twelfth article of the charter, in which the king promises that no scutage or aid, save the three regular aids, should henceforth be imposed without the advice and consent of the national council, does not explicitly mention the imposition of a tax on moveables, nor does it provide for the representation in the council of the great majority of those from whom such a tax would be raised. But in this, as in other points, the progress of events was outstripping and superseding the exact legal definitions of right. The fourteenth article does not provide for the representation of the shires, or for the participation of the clergy as an estate of the realm, distinct from their character as feudal freeholders, yet in both respects the succeeding history shows that the right was becoming practically established. So neither is the principle as yet formally laid down that a vote of the supreme council is to bind all the subjects of the realm in matter of taxation without a further consent of the individual. The prevalence of the idea that such consent was necessary brings the subject of the grant into close connexion with that of the assessment. But before approaching that point, the question of incidence requires consideration.

Growth of the taxative principle in advance of the Great Charter.

The principle of taxation by the nation itself not yet enunciated.

The indirect taxation of this period is obscure and of no great importance. The prisage of wine, the fines payable by the merchants for leave to import particular sorts of goods, the especial temptation which the stores of wool held out to the king's servants, the whole machinery of the customs, although referred to in the Great Charter as 'antiquae et rectae consuetudines [1],' were, so far as touches constitutional history, still in embryo. The existing practice rested on the ancient right of toll, and not on any historical legislative enactment. Although,

Indirect taxation of the period.

nobis faciendum exemplo vestro facilius invitentur;' May 26, 1207; Patent Roll, 8 John; ed. Hardy, i. 72.

[1] Article 31.

then, these sources furnished an appreciable revenue to Richard I
and John[1], the general taxation of the country may for our
present purpose be regarded as direct taxation only.

Incidence of taxation.

The taxable property may be divided into land and moveables,
and again, according to the character of their owners, into lay
and clerical; these may be subdivided in the former case according as the layman is a tenant-in-chief, a knight, a freeholder, a
burgher, or a villein, in the latter according as the possessor is

Realty and personalty, lay and clerical.

a prelate, a beneficed clerk, a chapter, or a religious house. Each
division of property was brought under contribution at a different period, and for each there was a distinct name and method
of taxation.

All early taxation borne by the land.

All the imposts of the Anglo-Saxon and Norman reigns were,
so far as we know, raised on the land, and according to computation by the hide: the exceptions to the rule would be only
in the cases of those churches which claimed entire immunity,
and those boroughs which paid a composition for their taxes in
a settled sum, as they paid the composition for the ferm in the
shape of an annual rent. This generalisation covers both the
national taxes like the Danegeld, and the feudal exactions by
way of aid; both were levied on the hide. Henry I had exempted from such payments the lands held in demesne by his
knights and barons, in consideration of the expenses of their
equipments[2]; but this clause of his charter can have been only
partially observed. Henry II, from the very beginning of his
reign, seems to have determined on attempting important

Of Church lands.

changes. He brought at once under contribution the lands held
by the churches, which had often claimed but had never perhaps
secured immunity.

Taxation of goods intro- duced.

In the Assize of Arms in 1181 he took a long step towards
taxing rent and chattels, obliging the owner of such property
to equip himself with arms according to the amount which he
possessed[3]. In the ordinance of the Saladin Tithe personal
property is rendered liable to pay its tenth[4]. Under Richard I

[1] Madox, Hist. Exch. pp. 529 sq.
[2] Above, p. 331.   [3] Ib. p. 527.
[4] Ib. p. 528. An act, which preceded the Saladin tithe and is dated in

the rule is extended: for the king's ransom every man pays a fourth part of his moveables[1]: in 1204 John exacted a seventh of the same from the barons[2], and in 1207 a thirteenth from the whole of the laity[3]. This change in the character of taxation serves to illustrate the great development of material wealth in the country which followed the reforms of Henry II. The burdens would not have been transferred from the land to the chattels if the latter had not been found much more productive of revenue than the former.

Sevenths and thirteenths.

But this was not the only change. Henry II adopted the knight's fee instead of the hide as the basis of rating for the knights and barons: and on this basis established a somewhat minute system of distinctions. As early as his second year we find him collecting a scutage, at twenty shillings on the 'scutum' or knight's fee, from the knights who held land under the churches[4]. In 1159, for the war of Toulouse, he raised a much larger sum under the same name, from the tenants by knight service; as a commutation for personal service he accepted two marks from each, and with the proceeds paid an army of mercenaries[5]. The word scutage, from its use on this occasion, acquired the additional sense of a payment in commutation of personal service, in which it is most frequently used. In 1163, as has been already mentioned[6], the ancient Danegeld disappears from the Rolls; but it is succeeded by a tax which, under the name of donum or auxilium, and probably levied on a new computation of hidage, must have

New system of rating land.

The scutage.

Disappearance of Danegeld.

1184, directing a contribution for the Holy Land, is given in the Liber Custumarum, p. 653; Spelman, Conc. ii. 115; Labbe, Conc. x. 1739; Bessin, Conc. Normanniæ, p. 90; Wilkins, Conc. i. 490. It purports to be an ordinance made by Henry and Philip for their respective dominions in consequence of the legation of Albert de Suma (1179), but possibly may belong to the year 1185; Hoveden, ii. 304. According to this ordinance, every person possessing more than 100s. in moveables was to pay 'in Anglia unus sterlingus' on each pound for three years; and higher in proportion. But the authority and authenticity of the document are not sufficiently great to allow us to regard it as a piece of real legislation. It is stated to be issued by the two kings, 'communi consilio episcoporum et comitum et baronum terrarum suarum.'

[1] Above, p. 540.   [2] Ib. p. 562; M. Paris, ii. 484.   [3] Above, p. 562.
[4] Ib. p. 492. For earlier use of the term scutage, see Round, Feudal England, pp. 268–270.   [5] Above, p. 494.   [6] Ib. p. 500.

been a reproduction of the old usage. Such a change must indeed have been necessary, the Danegeld having become in the long lapse of years a mere composition paid by the sheriff to the Exchequer, while the balance of the whole sums exacted on that account went to swell his own income. Under Richard the same tax appears under the name of carucage: the normal tax being laid on the carucate instead of the hide, and each carucate containing a fixed extent of one hundred acres[1].

Its reappearance as carucage.

Class taxation.

Each of these names represents the taxation of a particular class: the scutage affects the tenants in chivalry; the donum, hidage or carucage, affects all holders of land; the tenth, seventh, and thirteenth, all people in the realm. Each has its customary amount; the scutage of 1156 was twenty shillings on the fee[2]; those of 1159 and 1161 were two marks; the scutage of Ireland in 1171 was twenty shillings, and that of Galloway in 1186 at the same rate. The scutages of Richard's reign,—one for Wales in the first year and two for Normandy in the sixth and eighth,—were, in the first case ten, in the other cases twenty shillings. John in his first year raised a scutage of two marks; on nine other occasions he demanded the same sum, besides the enormous fines which he extorted from his barons on similar pretexts. Other aids to which the name is not commonly given were raised in the same way and at similar rates. Such were especially the aid pur fille marier, collected by Henry in 1168 at twenty shillings on the fee, and that for the ransom of Richard I at the same amount.

Customary amount of scutage and aid.

Rate of carucage.

The carucage of Richard was probably intended, as the Danegeld had been, to be fixed at two shillings on the carucate. In 1198 however it was raised to five, and John in the first year of his reign fixed it at three shillings[3].

The tallages.

Under the general head of donum, auxilium, and the like, come a long series of imposts, which were theoretically gifts of the nation to the king, and the amount of which was determined

---

[1] Hoveden, iv. 47.

[2] The following particulars are from the Pipe Rolls and Red Book of the Exchequer, as cited by Madox; the Rolls, down to the 12th year of Henry II, are printed by the Pipe Roll Society.

[3] Above, p. 555.

subject of taxation illustrates the gradual way in
and people were realising the idea of self-govern-
e application of a representative scheme to the
essment, and the recognition that the liability of the
ased on his own express consent, either to the grant
the amount of his own contribution, mark a state of
which the concentration of local interests in one
council was all that was needed to secure the tax-payer
arbitrary treatment on the part of either the sovereign
s ministers. This becomes still more evident as we approach
wider but equally important sphere of judicial action, in
which not only the principle, but the actual details of the
representative system seem progressively to assert themselves.
Before entering upon this, however, some notice must be taken
of the military system of Henry II and his sons, which, as exemplified both in the scutage and in the Assize of Arms, may be
regarded in close connexion with his expedients of taxation.

162. Henry found on his accession the three kinds of military
force, which we have described in a former chapter[1], in full
existence, but very incompletely organised, and, in consequence
of the recent troubles, either burdensome to the nation or
thoroughly ineffective. The standing army of mercenaries he
was bound by the treaty, which secured him the succession, to
disband and banish ; the general body of tenants in chivalry
was broken up among the feudatories who had been fighting
each for himself; and the national force of the fyrd, which by
its very nature was capable of only slight discipline and occasional usefulness, had shared in the general disorder of the
country consequent on the paralysis of government. Henry
from the very first years of his reign saw that peace was his
true interest, but that with so wide an extent of territory to
defend, and so many jealous enemies to keep in check, he could
have no peace unless he were strong enough to prevent war.
Each then of these three expedients he saw would have its uses,
while each had its defects. The mercenary force was hateful to
the nation ; the feudal levy was divided according to the interests

[1] Above, pp. 468 sq.

of its leaders, was not trustworthy in emergency, ﾠ
the strict rules as to the nature and duration of serv
capable of being freely handled : the national militia
useless for foreign warfare, or could be made usef
being treated as a mercenary force, an expedient wh
at once the blood and the treasure of the kingdom. Tʜ
policy was to use mercenaries for foreign warfare, and ﾠ
the national militia for defence and for the maintenance ﾠ
The feudal levy, like the rest of the machinery of feudﾠ
which could not be got rid of, might be made occasionally uﾠ
in both ways, but would be more useful still, if it could be maﾠ
to contribute to the support of the crown in ways which would
leave the king unembarrassed by the minutiae of feudal
custom.

The mercenaries, employed by Henry, Richard, and John.

This policy Henry maintained more or less continuously. He
fought his wars on the Continent by means of mercenaries [1] :
he had a standing force of 10,000 Brabançons, and a large
number of Welsh and Galwegian soldiers. Richard followed
the example, and in addition to these embodied a force of
Basques and Navarrese, two races whose military malpractices
had been condemned by the Lateran Council of 1179, and who
with the Brabançons and Catalans enjoy the evil reputation of
being the forerunners of the free companies of the next age.
Many of these were probably Crusaders who had returned penniless from the East, or mere bandits and brigands who by taking
foreign service had escaped the justice of their native lords.
John, like his father and brother, maintained a great host of
these adventurers, and with them fought the battles and conducted the cruel ravages which mark the close of his reign. The
mercenary force only comes within our view in two points : it
was a breach of the compact of Wallingford, in spirit at least,
that such a host ever set foot on English soil; and it was only
from the revenue of his kingdom that Henry could draw funds

---

[1] 'Mavult enim princeps stipendiarios quam domesticos bellicis apponere
casibus ; ' Dialogus, i. c. 9. ' Nolens vexare agrarios milites nec burgensem
nec rusticorum multitudinem ... duxit, solidarios vero milites innumeros ; '
R. de Monte, A.D. 1159.

to pay its expenses. The king faithfully observed the condition : on one occasion only were his mercenaries brought to England, and then it was to repel invasion, for the purpose of which a force of Flemish soldiers had already landed. They stayed in England for a month, and left with the king on his return to France [1]. Richard had no inclination, as he had indeed no temptation, to break the rule: and John's mercenary army, raised to repel the French invasion of 1213, in itself perhaps justified by the emergency, became one of the great occasions of his downfall. The direct question of the payment of the mercenaries only once arises, that is in 1198, when the justiciar proposed that it should be met by a grant for the express purpose of maintaining a body of knights, and was defeated by the resolution of S. Hugh [2]. But in this case the force required was asked rather as a substitute for personal service than as an engine of national defence, and on that ground it was refused.

Mercenaries brought to England only in exceptional cases.

Payment of mercenaries refused.

Henry's manipulation of the feudal host is a more complex matter, for there can be little doubt that he desired to weaken the great feudatories by disarming their vassals, as well as to obtain a more complete command of the resources that lay within his reach. The first expedient to which he had recourse was to break through the net of feudal custom by demanding that every three knights should, instead of serving in person, equip one of their number, probably for a threefold term of service. This was done in the Welsh war of 1157, and furnished the king with a body of knights, one-third of the whole knightly force of the kingdom, for a space of four months instead of the usual forty days [3]. A similar, if not the same, plan was adopted by Richard, who in the council of Nottingham in 1194 demanded a third part of the knight-service of the kingdom for his war in Normandy [4]: and John in 1205, by the advice of the council, directed that every nine knights should join to equip a tenth with wages of two shillings a day for the defence of the country [5]. The principle involved in this arrangement

Henry's management of the feudal force.

Joint equipment.

Combination for purpose of equipment.

---

[1] Bened. i. 74.	[2] Above, p. 548.
[3] R. de Monte, A.D. 1157.	[4] Hoveden, iii. 242.
[5] Patent Rolls, i. 55 ; Select Charters, pp. 281, 282.

is exactly analogous to that adopted by Charles the Great in the capitulary of A.D. 807, in which he directs that, when there is war in Spain or with the Avars, every five Saxon warriors are to join to equip a sixth; when the war is in Bohemia, every two are to equip a third; for the direct defence of the country each

Coincidence of the Frank laws. is to present himself in person[1]. The rule is in direct agreement with the Frank system of armament by which the poorer landowners combined to equip a fully-armed warrior, as was the Berkshire custom recorded in Domesday[2]. The coincidence may be accidental, but it forms one of a great number of small points in which Henry's administrative expedients seem to be borrowed from the Karolingian laws.

Scutage as commutation of service. A second and more comprehensive measure is found in the institution of scutage, which we have already examined under the head of taxation. The transition by which the fyrdwite or penalty for neglecting the summons to arms—a fine which was provided for also in the most ancient laws of the Germanic races[3]—was so modified as to become an honourable commutation for personal service, was not so great as might appear at first sight. Richard Fitz-Neal distinctly ascribes it to Henry's wish to spare the blood of his subjects[4]; it had however the further merit of providing the king with money to pay an army which he could handle as he pleased; it helped to disarm a dangerous element in the country; and it solved, or rather waived for the time, the already threatening question of the liability to foreign service. That it was used by John, like everything else, as an engine for extortion, or that in later reigns it was made an excuse for unrighteous exaction, is no argument against its original usefulness. The land-tax of the present day is the link which binds us, directly in this point, with the custom of our forefathers.

The Assize of Arms in 1181 was intended to reform and

[1] Pertz, Legg. i. 149.

[2] Pertz, Legg. i. 149; Baluze, i. 317, 318; above, p. 131; Waitz, D. V. G. iv. 471 sq.

[3] See Waitz, D. V. G. iv. 470; Pertz, Legg. i. 134; Baluze, i. 299, 300. The heribannum of the Franks, in the sense of a fine for not going to war, corresponds with the Anglo-Saxon fyrdwite.

[4] Above, p. 630, note 1.

Assize of
Arms, a re-
constitution
of the fyrd.

re-arm the national force of the fyrd.   It directed that the
whole free population, the *communa liberorum hominum*, should
furnish themselves with arms.   The owner of a knight's fee
must possess a coat of mail, a helmet, a shield, and a lance;
the freeman possessing sixteen mark___ ___nt or chattels must
have the same;   the owner o___ ___t possess a hauberk,
a head-piece of iron, an___ ___ll burghers and freemen a wambais, hea___ ___.   Here again we find a
strict analogy wi___ ___system, which no doubt had
had in this ___ ___existence on the Continent;
a similar ___ ___nilip of Flanders and Philip of
France ___ ___ Every man who possessed twelve
mansi ___ ___ry of A.D. 805, obliged to possess a
brunia c___ ___ by one of A.D. 779 it is forbidden that
any sho___ ___ll such arms to a stranger [4]: by that of
A.D. 812 ___ ___ssesses more than the necessary equipment
must employ ___, or alienate it, in the royal service [5]: all these
are minor points in which the language of the Assize almost
exactly coincides.   It stands however in still closer relation to
the system of the Lombard kings.

The Assize of Arms embodied a principle of perpetual utility,
and one the history of which is easily traceable, from the first
germ of the obligation in the trinoda necessitas, down to the
militia armament of the present times : the several questions, all

[1] Bened. i. 278.   [2] Ib. i. 269, 270.
[3] Pertz, Legg. i. 133; Baluze, i. 297, 301, &c.   The capitulary 'de expeditione Romana,' which directs that each man shall have a brunia for
every ten mansi, is a fabrication; Pertz, Legg. ii. App. p. 3; but the edict
of the Lombard king Haistulf (A.D. 750) furnishes a very important parallel:
'Stetit ut ille homo qui habet septem casas massarias habeat loricam suam
cum reliqua conciatura sua, debeat habere et cavallos; et si super habu-
erit per isto numero debeat habere caballos et reliqua armatura: item
placuit ut illi homines qui non habent casas massarias et habent 40 jugis
terrae habeant cavallum et scutum et lanceam; item de minoribus hominibus principi placuit ut, si possunt habere scutum, habeant coccora cum
sagittas et arcum; item de illis hominibus qui negotiantes sunt et pecunias
non habent, qui sunt majores et potentes habeant loricam et cavallos,
scutum et lanceam; qui sunt sequentes habeant caballos, scutum et lanceam;
et qui minores habeant coccoras cum sagittas et arcum;' Edictus, &c.
Longobardorum, ed. Bluhme, Hanover, 1869; Pertz, Legg. iv. 196.
[4] Pertz, Legg. i. 38, 133; Baluze, i. 277, 297, 301.
[5] Pertz, Legg. i. 173; Baluze, i. 340.

Provision
of ships.

depended for existence on the three principles by which the army was sustained, but in different proportions and combinations. The usage of the reign of Ethelred, according to which each shire furnished its quota of ships [1], had disappeared before the Domesday Survey, although England had continued to be a naval power throughout the reign of the Confessor. Possibly the fleet had become less important as the danger of Danish invasion was less constantly imminent. The great vassals of the Conquest had, it is said, merited their great rewards by their contributions to the Norman fleet [2], but none of them received or held

Ships of
Dover.

their English lands on the condition of service by sea. The inland counties in some cases reported in Domesday book special services due when the king went to sea; and Dover held its liberties in return for a provision of twenty ships to be kept for fifteen days annually in the king's service [3]. The fleet however is not a prominent object in the Survey.

The fleets
arranged
according
to the ports
from which
they came.

Yet the kings, possessing so extensive a sea-board in both England and France, were never at a loss for ships; and the ships when assembled were, like the fyrd, ranged according to the counties from which they came. The crusading expedition of A.D. 1147, by which Lisbon was taken, was to a certain extent a volunteer expedition, and may not be a fair instance of the usual practice: in it however the ships of Norfolk and Suffolk sailed under Hervey Glanvill, a local magnate; those of Kent under Simon of Dover; those of London, Hastings, Southampton, and Bristol under their own captains [4]. The London crusaders of 1188 and 1190 seem to have had an organisation of their own, although in the latter case they formed part of a fleet commanded by royal officers who bore the names of justiciars

Richard
made laws
for the fleet.

and constables [5]. Richard made laws for this fleet, with the counsel of his 'probi homines,' and enjoined the observance of them on his own subjects in the strictest terms, compelling

---

[1] Above, p. 131. [2] Ib. p. 279.

[3] Domesd. i. 1. Sandwich owed the same service; and Romney with other ports owed sea-service.

[4] Expugnatio Lyxbonensis, Chron. Rich. I, i. p. cxliv.

[5] Hoveden, iii. 46 sq.; Benedict, ii. 120 sq. The commanders are called constables by Hoveden, iii. 36, justiciars by Bened. ii. 110.

them to swear obedience, and commanding them as they cared for their fortunes at home to act in proper submission to their justiciars.

Even of the fleet of 1190 a large proportion was in no respect national property: the vessels of transport which composed no small part of it were no doubt hired by the king, or possibly impressed for the occasion. Dover and Hastings held their liberties by furnishing twenty ships each for the king's service, and the rest of the Cinque Ports doubtless contributed in proportion. The vessels of war however, the galleys, must have been the property of the king, and it is probably to this crusade that we owe the germ of a permanent navy. Such a navy must have been from remote antiquity an institution among the Mediterranean powers; at this moment the Pisans, the Genoese, and the Venetians possessed large fleets of armed transports, which were hired by the French and German Crusaders: the king of Sicily had his 'stolium fortunatum,' for whose commander he borrowed the Arabic title of Emir or Admiral[1]. The Danes and the Flemings likewise possessed naval forces, but those probably belonged to individual adventurers, amongst whom the king or the count might be the first. In England itself Hugh de Puiset, the bishop of Durham, had his own great ship, which became royal property at his death[2]. Except for the distant expeditions to Palestine, the king needed only such a squadron as would carry him and his court from time to time across the Channel[3]: the defence of the coast must have been maintained as of old by local resources. The permanent fleet then was from its very origin a fleet of mercenaries, and was maintained from the royal revenue just as a band of Brabançons might have been, although, as the English merchant service was the readiest resource for recruits, the royal fleet was chiefly manned by Englishmen. John's naval armament was organised

The beginning of a permanent navy.

Growth of navies.

The permanent fleet a fleet of mercenaries.

---

[1] Bened. i. 171; ii. 128.   [2] Madox, Hist. Exch. p. 493.
[3] Henry II had one ship of his own until Becket ordered three very good ones to be built and equipped; these he presented to his master; W. Fitz-Stephen, S. T. C. i. 193; ed. Robertson, iii. 26. The full number furnished by the Cinque Ports under Edward III was fifty-seven, twenty-one each by Dover and Hastings, five each by Romney, Hythe, and Sandwich.

on this plan; but it is not until after the date of the Charter, which limits our present inquiries, that its importance comes into historical prominence. The legislation of the Admiralty, which is referred to the present period by writers of the fifteenth century, is either antedated, or so modified by translation and adaptation that it is not to be recognised as twelfth-century work.

The king was the paymaster.

It is clear from what has been said that the mercenary force of army and navy was, so far as its maintenance is concerned, dependent on no authority but that of the king, who paid its expenses, as he did all other national and personal expenses, out of the general fund accruing to the Exchequer, over which the national council neither possessed nor as yet claimed control.

Judicature.

163. The judicial measures of Henry II constitute a very im-

Recapitulation of the judicial policy of Henry II.

portant part of his general policy. They have been noticed in their personal and political bearing in the last chapter. We have there seen how the original impulse was given to his reforms by the terms on which the Crown was secured to him, how those reforms were moulded by his peculiar genius or by the influence of well-chosen advisers, the tradition of the Exchequer forming an important element; how the several steps in advance were partly guided by a desire to limit the judicial power of the great feudal vassals, and to protect the people against the misuse by the local magnates of that influence in the county courts which had fallen into their hands. We have accordingly noted the chief occasions on which the sheriffs, and even the royal judges, were brought to special account, and displaced to make way, either for men who had received a better legal training, or for such as were less closely connected with the ruling families of the district, or for those who would bring the shire adminis-tration into more thorough concert with the supreme administra-

Policy of Richard s ministers.

tion, if not completely under its control. We have traced, under the history of Hubert Walter and Geoffrey Fitz-Peter, a growing spirit of legal reform, a rapid invention of new machinery or adaptation of the old machinery to new ends, not indeed free from the imputation that it was chiefly stimulated by financial considerations, but still in its ultimate results con-

ducive to the growth and conscious realisation of the idea of
self-government. And we have further inferred that the attitude
taken by the clergy, the barons, and the commons at the date of
the Great Charter was produced by the altered circumstances in
which the kingdom was placed by these changes: that whilst
on the one hand they had given to the king an overwhelming
power, they had on the other revealed to the Three Estates the
unity of their interests, and the possibility of erecting a well-
compacted fabric of liberty. We have now to trace the mechanical workings involved in this history.

Henry at his accession found the administrative system in the
most attenuated state. Twenty years of misrule had seen the
polity of his grandfather broken up rather than suspended, and
very few of the old servants of the State survived. Such
judicial machinery as existed seems to have been sustained by
Richard de Lucy, but the year which had elapsed since the
pacification had only given time to attempt the uprooting of the
evils of misrule, not to lay the foundations or to rebuild the
fabric of a sound government. Hence Henry's reforms, although, so far as he was able to get aid from his grandfather's
ministers, they were based upon the older system, owe very much
to the king himself, and, from the outset of the reign, exhibit
marks of decided growth and difference from the former state
of things. The Exchequer was restored under Bishop Nigel as
it had existed under Bishop Roger, but the Curia Regis from
the first presents a much more definite appearance than before.
Still one with the Exchequer in its personal staff, it has much
more independent action and a wider sphere; it developes a
new and elaborate system of rules and customs. The king's
personal tribunal continues to be a supreme and ultimate resort,
but the royal judicature from time to time throws off offshoots,
which before the end of the period constitute a system of courts
and jurisdictions that with some developments and modifications have subsisted to our own day.

The judicature may be divided into three branches, the central
and supreme court or courts, the provincial, popular, or common
law tribunals, and the visitatorial jurisdiction by which the first

Condition of things in 1155.

Reforms of Henry II, his own work.

Division of the subject of judicature.

interfered with, regulated, and remodelled the second: and these may be noticed in the order of their authority; first, the king's courts; secondly, the itinerant justices; thirdly, the local tribunals.

The Exchequer and the Curia Regis continue throughout this period to exist in that close union which proves their original identity; but whereas under Henry I the financial character of the board is the most prominent, under Henry II more importance attaches to its judicial aspect. In the former reign the Curia Regis, except when the king takes a personal share in the business, seems to be a judicial session of the Exchequer, an adaptation of Exchequer machinery to judicial purposes; under the latter the Exchequer seems to be rather a financial session of the Curia Regis. The king is ostensibly the head of the one[1], the justiciar the principal actor in the other; but still the fabric is the same: the judges are the same; the transactions of the Curia frequently take place in the chamber of the Exchequer, and are recorded in its Rolls; and, through all the changes by which the Curia is modelled and divided, the Exchequer forms a rallying-point, or common ground, on which all the members of the supreme judicature seem to meet, as in the more modern Court of Exchequer Chamber in modern days.

The financial system of the Exchequer, as it existed under Henry I, has been already described, and illustrated from the single Pipe Roll of the reign as well as from the Dialogus de Scaccario[2]. The latter work describes the practice of the year 1178, in language which shows a substantial agreement with the system presented in the Roll of 1130. This organisation therefore it is unnecessary to recapitulate here. The points in which change and development are traceable are either minute matters of procedure, which scarcely come within the view of constitutional history, or matters of legal interest which belong more strictly to the history of the Curia Regis and itinerant jurisdictions. The

The Exchequer and Curia Regis.

Close union of the two.

Continuity of Exchequer usages.

---

[1] 'Regis Curia, in qua ipse in propria persona jura decernit; ... ex officio principaliter residet [in scaccario] immo et praesidet primum in regno capitalis scilicet justitia;' Dialogus, i. c. 4.

[2] Above, pp. 407 sq.

Court of Exchequer, taking special cognisance of suits touching the revenue, possessing a different body of judges and a distinct code of customs, has not yet a separate existence; but it may be justly presumed that, where such suits were entertained, the judges before whom they were tried would be those who were most familiar with the financial work. The fines levied for legal purposes, which were originally the determinate agreements between litigants drawn up and recorded in the king's court, and were a source of constant income to the Crown, were regularly concluded 'ad scaccarium[1];' but the judges who witnessed the transaction were not a permanent committee of officers; they were apparently a selection for each occasion from the whole body of the Curia, all of whom were, it is probable, equally eligible and of equal authority. The records of the Exchequer grow during the period in bulk and in number: the Pipe Rolls of Henry II[2] are supplemented under John by Oblate, Liberate, and Mise Rolls[3], in which the particular outgoings on the heads of royal allowances, benefactions, and other payments are circumstantially recorded. The Great Rolls of the Pipe however continue to contain the summaries and authoritative details of the national account.

The Curia Regis of Henry II attained its ultimate constitu- tion by a long series of somewhat rapid changes. In the early years of the reign it appears to be, as it had been under Henry I, a tribunal of exceptional resort to which appeals, although increasing in number, were still comparatively rare, and the action of which is scarcely distinguishable from that of the national council. The king himself took a leading part in the business,

[1] See illustrations of business done 'ad scaccarium' in the reign of Henry II in Madox, Hist. Exch. pp. 144, 145.

[2] The Pipe Rolls down to the eleventh year of Henry II are in print, also one of Richard, and one of the reign of John. They are the only complete series of records for the period, and throw a great deal of light on every department of history, although commonly known only through the medium of Madox's work.

[3] The Fines of the reigns of Richard and John were edited by Hunter among the publications of the Record Commission, in 1835 and 1844; the Rotuli de oblatis of John and the Rotuli 'de Liberate ac de Misis et Praestitis' in 1844 by Sir T. Duffus Hardy; the Rotuli Curiae Regis of Richard and John by Sir F. Palgrave in 1835; and the Close and Patent Rolls of John between 1833 and 1844 by Sir T. D. Hardy.

much of which was done in his presence ; and even in his absence
the action of the justiciar seems to depend on the royal pleasure
as indicated by special writs.   Such at least is the impression
made by the long details of litigation contained in the Chronicle
of Battle, and in the account of Richard de Anesty, who has
preserved the record of his delays and expenses in a suit which
lasted from 1158 to 1163[1].   Yet side by side with this there
appears a show of judicial activity among the subordinate members of the household, the court, and the Exchequer.   The
Chancellor, as we learn from the Lives of S. Thomas, was constantly employed in judicial work, whether in attendance on the
king, or, as the Pipe Rolls also testify, in provincial visitations.
As early as the second year of the reign, Henry of Essex the
Constable, Thomas the Chancellor, and the earl of Leicester the
co-justiciar, are found hearing pleas in different counties[2].   The
Chancellor, if we may believe the consistent evidence of his
biographers, habitually relieved the king of the irksome part of
his judicial duties[3].   From the Constitutions of Clarendon
again we learn that the Curia Regis possessed the organisation
of an established tribunal, the action of which in ecclesiastical
cases must be held to prove a still wider action in secular causes.
In 1165, the year after the enactment of the Constitutions, we
have an agreement between the abbots of Westminster and
S. Alban's attested by several of the ministers of the Exchequer
under the title of justices[4], and in 1166 we come to the Assize
of Clarendon, which marks an epoch in the administration of,
at least, the criminal law.   During these years—for such is the
reasonable inference—the judicial work of the Curia Regis had
been growing until it was more than the king and his regular

*Personal
sessions of
the king.*

*The Chan-
cellor.*

*Trials in the
country.*

*The Curia in
1164.*

In 1166.

---

[1] This important record is only to be found in Sir F. Palgrave's Rise
and Progress of the English Commonwealth (vol. ii), where it is illustrated
by most interesting notes : it is well illustrated by Mr Hubert Hall, in his
'Court Life under the Plantagenets,' London, 1890.

[2] Pipe Rolls of Henry II, pp. 17, 26, 65.   An assize of the Chancellor
and Henry of Essex is mentioned in Essex, pleas of the Chancellor and the
earl of Leicester in Lincolnshire, in the second year.   In the fourth year
are entered pleas of the Chancellor in Middlesex.

[3] Roger of Pontigny (V. S. Thom. ed. Giles), i. 102 ; W. Fitz-Stephen,
ibid. i. 171, 186 ; ed. Robertson, iii. 1, 18.

[4] Madox, Hist. Exch. p. 30 ; Formulare Angl. p. xix.

ministers of state could dispatch, and was thus falling, even more completely than it had done under Henry I, into the hands of the officers of the Exchequer. The system of recog- Increase of
business. nitions was, as the Constitutions of Clarendon prove, in full play, and the superior chances of justice which that system afforded were drawing larger business to the court, and at the same time involved a vast 'officina brevium,' with a body of trained clerks [1] and a regular code of practical jurisprudence. Unfortunately we are unable to discover the date at which the Great Assize was issued; if this were known, it would probably be found to coincide with one of the periods at which great changes were made in the judicial staff.

The first however of these epochs is the year 1166. The Judicial changes in the Curia Regis at this date were so great as to call 1166. for especial notice from John of Salisbury, even in the height of the Becket controversy [2]; and the Assize of Clarendon, which belongs to the same year, denotes the character of the changes. Yet the Assize of Clarendon was directed to the improvement of provincial justice; and it was carried out, not by a new body of judges, but by two of the king's ministers, the justiciar and the earl of Essex, with the assistance of the sheriffs, who, acting under royal writ as administrators of the new law, still engrossed the title of 'justitiae errantes [3].' The development of the central jurisdiction is traceable by inference from that of the provincial judicature. The four Exchequer officers [4] who assessed the aid In 1168. *pur fille marier* in 1168 are found hearing placita and attesting concords shortly after; it follows that they acted not only as taxers but as judges. The six circuits of the tallagers of 1173 were no doubt suggestive of the two circuits of the justices in 1175 and the six circuits of the judges in 1176 [5]. It is then to In 1176.

[1] Under Becket as Chancellor were fifty-two clerks; some of them however belonged to his private retinue; W. Fitz-Stephen, S. T. C. i. 196; ed. Robertson, iii. 29.

[2] 'Quae autem circa Anglorum curiam innovantur, ubi rerum crebrae mutationes sunt, vobis notiora esse arbitror quam nobis.' John of Salisbury writes thus to Bartholomew bishop of Exeter; Ep. 145.

[3] Above, p. 420, note 1.

[4] Richard of Ilchester, Wido dean of Waltham, Reginald of Warenne, and William Basset, were the four. See Madox, Hist. Exch. pp. 102, 145.

[5] See the lists for 1176, in Bened. i. 107; Madox, Hist. Exch. p. 86;

these years, from 1166 to 1176, that we must refer the creation or development of the large staff of judges in the Curia Regis which we find acting in 1178. All the eighteen justices of 1176 were officers of the Exchequer; some of them are found in 1175 holding 'placita Curiae Regis' in bodies of three or four judges[1], and not in the same combinations in which they took their judicial journeys. We can scarcely help the conclusion that the new jurisprudence was being administered by committees of the general body of justices, who were equally qualified to sit in the Curia and Exchequer and to undertake the fiscal and judicial work of the eyre.

Growth of the staff of judges.

The year 1178 furnishes another epoch. Henry finding that the eighteen judges of the Curia were too many, that they caused entanglements in the business of the court, and expense and distress to the suitors, reduced them at once to five[2]. Some were dismissed perhaps for misconduct; but very many of the existing judges reappear again in functions scarcely distinguishable from those which they had discharged before. Yet the statement of the diminution of their number, which is made by a historian singularly well informed as to the affairs of the court, has considerable significance. From this date we may fix the existence of the sittings of the Curia Regis 'in Banco.' Their proceedings are still nominally transacted 'coram rege,'

Henry reduces the number in 1178.

The Curia Regis 'in Banco.'

and those for 1173 are in the Pipe Rolls only. In 1175, Ranulph Glanvill and Hugh de Cressi visited the eastern and midland counties, William de Lanvalei and Thomas Basset the south and west; ibid. p. 85.

[1] For instance, in 1177 William Fitz-Ralph, Bertram de Verdun, and William Basset hear pleas in Curia Regis touching Buckinghamshire and Bedfordshire: yet, on the eyre, these two counties are visited by three other judges; moreover Bertram de Verdun visited Worcestershire, and the other two with Hugh de Gundeville visited seven midland counties. The first placita Curiae Regis mentioned by Madox are in 1175; Hist. Exch. pp. 64, 65.

[2] Benedict, i. 207: 'Itaque dominus rex moram faciens in Anglia quaesivit de justitiis quos in Anglia constituerat, si bene et modeste tractaverunt homines regni; et cum didicisset quod terra et homines terrae nimis gravati essent ex tanta justitiarum multitudine, quia octodecim erant numero; per consilium sapientium regni sui quinque tantum elegit, duos scilicet clericos et tres laicos: et erant omnes de privata familia sua. Et statuit quod illi quinque audirent omnes clamores regni, et rectum facerent, et quod a Curia Regis non recederent, sed ibi ad audiendum clamores hominum remanerent, ita ut, si aliqua quaestio inter eos veniret quae per eos ad finem duci non posset, auditui regio praesentaretur et sicut ei et sapientioribus regni placeret terminaretur.'

but nominally only. 'The five are to hear all the complaints of the kingdom and to do right, and not to depart from the Curia Regis.' Questions which are too hard for them are to be referred to the king in person, who will decide them with the advice of the wise men of the kingdom.

The year 1179 witnessed another change, possibly however *Changes in* of persons rather than of system. The great justiciar had re- *1179.* signed, and Henry had put the office as it were into commission, employing the bishops of Norwich, Ely, and Winchester as heads of three bodies of itinerant judges, each containing two clerks and three knights. A fourth body, to which the northern *The Curia* counties were assigned, contained Ranulf Glanvill, who was to *in 1179.* succeed, the next year, to the justiciarship, with five other judges. This fourth committee, according to the chronicler, entered into the place assigned in 1178 to the five judges retained in the Curia; 'these six are the justices constituted in the Curia Regis to hear the complaints of the people [1] :' why the circuit most remote from the capital was assigned to them we are not told, but as the whole business of the eyre was concluded between April 1 and August 27, there could have been no insuperable difficulty.

This is the last notice of the constitution of the Curia Regis which the historians of Henry's reign have preserved to us : and the modifications which are traceable in records from this point to the date of Magna Carta are of personal rather than legal importance. The work of Glanvill furnishes us with the rules of procedure; the Rotuli Curiae Regis which begin in 1194 afford a record of the actual business done, and the names of the judges employed are discoverable from these and other records.

So far then as concerns the framework of the supreme judi- *General con-* cature, our conclusion for the present is this : from the year *clusion as to* *the growth* 1179 the sessions of 'justitiarii in Banco [2]' are regularly held in *of the Curia.*

---

[1] Bened. i. 238; R. de Diceto, ii. 435.

[2] Glanvill, lib. ii. c. 6; viii. c. 1; xi. c. 1 : 'coram Justitiis Domini Regis in banco residentibus.' Coke's notion that by this session of the judges the Common Bench or Court of Common Pleas is meant, is mentioned by Madox only to refute it; Hist. Exch. p. 546. Foss also argues conclusively

the Curia Regis, nominally but not actually 'coram rege.' These justices are a selection from a much larger staff, before whom Exchequer business is done, and who undertake the work of the circuits: and it would appear probable that the selection was altered from time to time, possibly from year to year. Their work was to hear all suits that were brought before the king, not only criminal but civil, cases in which the revenue or rights of the king were touched, and cases of private litigation with which the king, except as supreme judge, had no concern: all the business in fact which came at a later period before the courts of King's Bench, Exchequer, and Common Pleas. Although their deliberations were not held in the king's presence, they followed his person, or the justiciar in the king's absence; a rule which must have been most burdensome to ordinary suitors, and which accordingly, so far as touches private civil suits or 'communia placita,' was abolished by Magna Carta.

The later divisions of the courts. The fixing of the Common Pleas at Westminster broke up the unity of the Curia [1]; but it was not until the end of the reign of Henry III that the general staff was divided into three distinct and permanent bodies of judges, each under its own chief.

The court of royal audience. But the court or courts thus organised must no longer be regarded as the last resource of suitors. The reservation of knotty cases to be decided by the king with the council of his wise men [2], cases which, as we learn from the Dialogus de Scaccario, included questions of revenue as well as of law in general [3], continues the ancient personal jurisdiction of the sovereign.

against it; Judges of England, ii. 161. See also Hardy's Introduction to the Close Rolls, vol. i. pp. xxv. sq. Instances of Final Concords made before the justices of the Curia, answering to those described by Glanvill as made before the justices in Banco, will be found in Madox, Formulare Anglicanum, pp. 217 sq., and in the Fines published by the Record Commission; above, p. 641, note 3.

[1] By the seventeenth article of Magna Carta. The Provisions of the Exchequer, 12 Edw. I, and the Articuli super Cartas, 28 Edw. I, c. 4, forbid Common Pleas to be holden henceforth in the Exchequer.

[2] Above, p. 645. The same principle is stated in the Articles of the Assize of Northampton: ' Nisi tam grandis sit querela quod non possit deduci sine domino rege, vel talis quam justitiae ei reportent pro dubitatione sua.'

[3] Dialogus, i. c. 8: 'Si . . . fieri contigerit, ut inter ipsos majores dissensionis oriatur occasio . . . horum omnium cognitio ipsi principi reservabitur.'

The very act that seems to give stability and consistency to the ordinary jurisdiction of the Curia, reduces it to a lower rank. The judicial supremacy of the king is not limited or fettered by the new rule; it has thrown off an offshoot, or, as the astronomical theorists would say, a nebulous envelope, which has rolled up into a compact body, but the old nucleus of light remains unimpaired. The royal justice, diffused through the close personal council[1], or tempered and adapted by royal grace and equity under the pen of the chancellor[2], or exercised in the national assembly as in the ancient witenagemot, or concentrated in the hands of an irresponsible executive in the Star Chamber, has for many generations and in many various forms to assert its vitality, unimpaired by its successive emanations.

The judicial supremacy of the king.

Its continuity.

In tracing the history of the central judicature we have had to anticipate the leading points of interest in the development of the visitatorial jurisdiction. The whole may be briefly summed up. The circuits of the royal officers for fiscal and judicial

The growth of the itinerant judicature.

---

[1] See Sir Francis Palgrave's Essay on the Jurisdiction of the King's Council, and Dicey's Essay on the Privy Council.

[2] The growth of the Chancellor's jurisdiction does not fall within the present period; but the increased importance of his position is remarkable, and the germ of his future functions was in being already. William Fitz-Stephen, who was one of Becket's clerks, writes thus: 'Cancellarii Angliae est ut secundus a rege in regno habeatur, ut altera parte sigilli regii, quod et ad ejus pertinet custodiam, propria signet mandata; ut capella regis in ipsius sit dispositione et cura, ut vacantes archiepiscopatus, episcopatus, abbatias et baronias cadentes in manu regis ipse suscipiat et conservet; ut omnibus regis adsit consiliis, et etiam non vocatus accedat; ut omnia sigilliferi regii clerici sui manu signentur, omnia cancellarii consilio disponantur; item ut, suffragantibus ei per Dei gratiam vitae meritis, non moriatur nisi archiepiscopus aut episcopus, si voluerit. Inde est quod cancellaria emenda non est:' V. S. Thom. i. 186; ed. Robertson, iii. 18. The Dialogus de Scaccario represents the justiciar as 'primus post regem;' the term 'secundus a rege' probably means next after the justiciar; the form is frequently used by Becket's friends. The Dialogus (lib. i. c. 5) confirms most of the statements of the biographer just cited; nothing is done without the chancellor's consent and advice either in the Curia or in the Exchequer; he has charge of the royal seal, sealing it up into its loculus or purse, which is kept by the treasurer.

The fact that the chancellor was always in attendance on the king led to the petitions for royal grace and favour being entrusted to him, first for custody, and afterwards for hearing. Hence arose the equitable jurisdiction by which he remedied the 'summum jus' of the common law or promised remedies in cases which were not provided for by the common lawyers. The statement that the chancery is not purchaseable is disproved by some important exceptions. See above, pp. 414, 541.

purposes, which we have traced in the reign of Henry I, continue
to have the same character under Henry II, the judicial forms
following rather than preceding the fiscal. In 1166 the itinerant
court receives new and full instructions from the Assize of
Clarendon, but it is still the Curia Regis in progress, a great

Formation
and changes
of circuits.

part of the work being done by the sheriffs[1]. In 1176 six
circuits are formed, eighteen judges are specially told off in six
detachments, as had been done in the fiscal iter of 1173: in
1178, 1179, and 1180 there seem to be four circuits, and the
arrangements in the later years vary between two and six.
Under Richard we have still further modifications, and the
same in the early years of John, none of them however involving
a new principle of construction, but all perhaps implying a restriction of the local jurisdictions of the sheriff and the shire-

Itinerant
justices.

moot[2]. At last, in the eighteenth clause of Magna Carta, the
king undertakes to send two justices four times a year to take
the Assizes of Mort d'ancester, Novel disseisin, and Darrein
presentment. This arrangement proved no doubt far too burdensome to be continued, but the changes indicated in the re-issues
of the Charter and carried into effect in periodical iters of the
judges lie beyond our present inquiry. The justices of the
year 1176 are the first to whom the name *Justitiarii Itinerantes*
is given in the Pipe Rolls: the commissioners of 1170 are called
Barones errantes : ' perlustrantes judices ' is the term used by
the author of Dialogus; the sheriffs were the ' errantes justitiae'
known to John of Salisbury in 1159. The various applications
of the terms may mark the growth and consolidation of a system
by which the sheriffs were deprived of the most important of
their functions.

The courts
of these
justices are
full county
courts.

The visits of the itinerant justices form the link between the
Curia Regis and the Shire-moot, between royal and popular
justice, between the old system and the new. The courts in
which they preside are the ancient county courts, under
new conditions, but substantially identical with those of the

---

[1] The action of a justice itinerant at Bedford in 1163 was one of the
grounds of the quarrel between the king and Becket; the judge was Simon
Fitz-Peter, who had ceased to be sheriff of Bedfordshire two years before;
Rog. Pont. S. T. C. i. 114.　　　　　　　　　　　[2] Above, pp. 544 sq.

Anglo-Saxon times. The full shire-moot consists, as before, of all the lords of land and their stewards, and the representatives of the townships, the parish priest, the reeve and four men from each; but the times of meeting, the sphere of business, and the nature of procedure during the period before us have undergone great and significant changes, some of which can be minutely traced, whilst others can be accounted for only by conjecture.

The Anglo-Saxon shire-moot was held twice a year: the county court of Henry I was held as it had been in King Edward's days, that is, according to the 'Leges Henrici I,' twice a year still. Yet in the confirmation of the Great Charter, issued by Henry III in 1217, it is ordered that the county court shall meet not more than once a month, or less frequently where such has been the custom; the sheriff is to hold his tourn twice a year in the hundreds. An edict issued in 1234 further provides that the hundred courts, which under Henry II had been held fortnightly, should be held from three weeks to three weeks, but not under general summons[1]. It is not easy to determine the date or the causes of so great a multiplication of sessions of the shire-moot, unless, as it would be rash to argue, we suppose the sessions of the hundred court to be included in the term *comitatus*. Possibly the sheriffs had abused their power of summoning special meetings and of fining absentees; a custom which comes into prominence in the reign of Henry III, and which shows that it was the direct interest of the sheriffs to multiply the occasions of summons. Possibly it may have arisen from the increase of business under the new system of writs and assizes, which involved the frequent adjournment of the court for short terms: possibly from an earlier usage by which the practice of the county court was assimilated to that of the hundred with the special object of determining suits between litigants from different hundreds or liberties. Or it may have been caused by the gradual withdrawal of the more important suits from the shire-moot, the natural result of which would be the increase of the number of less important meetings for the convenience of petty suitors.

Times of holding the county court.

Increase of small suits in the county courts.

[1] Ann. Dunst. pp. 140, 141. See above, p. 430.

comitatus' which elects, according to Magna Carta, the knights who are to take the assizes, and the twelve knights who are to inquire into the abuses which Magna Carta was designed to reform.

Institution of juries, a step in the growth of a representative system.

164. It is in the new system of recognition, assizes, and presentments by jury that we find the most distinct traces of the growth of the principle of representation; and this in three ways. In the first place, the institution of the jury was itself based on a representative idea: the jurors, to whatever fact or in whatever capacity they swore, declared the report of the community as to the fact in question. In the second place, the method of inquest was in England brought into close connexion with the procedure of the shire-moot, and thus the inquisitorial process, whether its object was the recognition of a right or the presentment of a criminal, was from the moment of its introduction carried on in association with the previously existing representative institutions, such as were the reeve and four best men, the twelve senior thegns, and the later developments of the same practice which have been just enumerated in our account of the formation of the county court and the usage of legal assessment. In the third place, the particular expedients adopted for the regulation of the inquests paved the way in a remarkable manner for the system of county representation in the parliament as we saw it exemplified on the first occasion of its appearance in the reign of John. The use of election and representation in the courts of law furnished a precedent for the representation of the county by two sworn knights in the national council. On each of these heads some detail is necessary which may throw light incidentally on some kindred points of interest.

Trial by jury variously treated.

The history of the Jury has been treated by various writers from every possible point of view[1]: its natural origin, its historical development, the moral ideas on which it is founded, and

[1] See Palgrave, Rise and Progress of the English Commonwealth; Forsyth, History of Trial by Jury; Biener, das Englische Geschwornengericht; Gneist, Self-Government, i. 74 sq.; K. Maurer in the Kritische Ueberschau, v. pp. 180 sq., 332 sq.; and Brunner, Entstehung der Schwurgerichte.

the rational analysis of its legal force, have all been discussed
many times over with all the apparatus of learning and the
acute penetration of philosophical research. Some of these
aspects are foreign to our present inquiry. Yet the institution
is of so great interest both in itself and in its relations that
some notice of it is indispensable.

We have sketched, in an earlier stage of this work, the formation of the primitive German courts : they were tribunals of
fully qualified members of the community, a selection it might
be from a body of equally competent companions, able to declare the law or custom of the country, and to decide what,
according to that custom, should be done in the particular case
brought before them. They were not set to decide what was
the truth of facts, but to determine what action was to be taken
upon proof given. The proof was itself furnished by three
means, the oaths of the parties to the suit and their compurgators, the production of witnesses, and the use of the ordeal : the
practice of trial by battle being a sort of ultimate expedient to
obtain a practical decision, an expedient partly akin to the
ordeal as a judgment of God, and partly based on the idea that
where legal measures had failed recourse must be had to the
primitive law of force,—the feud or right of private war,—only
regulated as far as possible by law and regard for the saving of
life. For each of these methods of proof there were minute
rules and formalities, the infringement or neglect of which put
the offender out of court. The complainant addressed his charge
to the defendant in solemn traditional form; the defendant
replied to the complainant by an equally solemn verbal and
logical contradiction. The compurgators swore, with joined
hands and in one voice, to the purity and honesty of the oath of
their principal [1]. Where the oath was inconclusive, the parties
brought their witnesses to declare such knowledge as their
position as neighbours had given them; the court determined
the point to which the witnesses must swear, and they swore to

*Modes of
trial among
the German
races.*

*Oaths,
evidence,
ordeal.*

*Formalism
of the sys-
tem.*

---

[1] The Anglo-Saxon forms of oath may be found in the Ancient Laws, ed.
Thorpe, pp. 76, 77. The oath of the compurgator runs thus : ' On thone
Drihten se ath is clæne and unmæne the N. swor.'

that particular fact[1]. They were not examined or made to testify all they knew; but swore to the fact on which the judges determined that evidence should be taken. If the witnesses also failed, the ordeal was used. And where the defeated party ventured to impugn the sentence thus obtained, he might challenge the determination of the court by appealing the members of it to trial by combat; or as was the later practice, by applying to the king for a definitive sentence. Trial by combat, however common among some branches of the German stock, was by no means universal, and, as has been pointed out, was not practised among the native English.

The germ of the jury not contained in this.

In these most primitive proceedings are found circumstances, which on a superficial view seem analogous to later trial by jury: but on a closer inspection they warrant no distinct impression of the kind. The ancient judges who declare the law and give the sentence—the rachinburgii, or the scabini—are not in any respect the jurors of the modern system, who ascertain the fact by hearing and balancing evidence, leaving the law and sentence to the presiding magistrate; nor are the ancient witnesses, who depose to the precise point in dispute, more nearly akin to the jurors who have to inquire the truth and declare the result of the inquiry, than to the modern witnesses who swear to speak not only the truth and nothing but the truth, but the whole truth. The compurgators again swear to confirm the oath of their principal, and have nothing in common with the jury but the fact

Yet the oath and evidence are of a representative character.

that they swear[2]. Yet although this is distinctly the case, the precedure in question is a step in the history of the jury: the first form in which the jury appears is that of witness, and the principle that gives force to that witness is the idea that it is the testimony of the community: even the idea of the compurgatory oath is not without the same element; the compurgators must be possessed of qualities and legal qualifications which shall secure their credibility.

[1] The number of witnesses required varied in the different nations : the Saxon and Lombard laws required two at least ; the Bavarian, three or more ; the Frank laws, seven or twelve, according to the importance of the matter in question ; Brunner, Schwurgericht, p. 51.

[2] Forsyth, Hist. of Jury, p. 83 ; see also Sohm, i. 130.

Beyond this stage, modified it is true here as elsewhere by Anglo-Saxon system. different circumstances and local usages, the Anglo-Saxon system did not proceed. The compurgation, the sworn witness, and the ordeal, supplied the proof; and the sheriff with his fellows, the bishop, the shire-thegns, the judices and juratores, the suitors of the court, declared the law. Only in the law of The twelve thegns in the shire-moot. Ethelred, by which the twelve senior thegns in each wapentake are sworn not to accuse any falsely[1], do we find the germ of a more advanced system, in which the community seems to undertake the duty of prosecution : but the interpretation of the passage is disputed, and its bearing contested, although it seems to imply no more than that the English were not far in arrear of the Frank jurisprudence.

The whole system of recognition by sworn inquest, with the Recognitions introduced into England by the Normans. single exception, if it be an exception, which has just been mentioned, was introduced into England by the Normans : the laws of Edward, the Domesday Survey, the fiscal recognitions of the reigns of William Rufus and Henry I[2], are distinctly a novelty, a part of the procedure of the newly-developed system of government. Various theories have been invented for their origin. Many writers of authority have maintained that the entire jury system is indigenous in England, some deriving it from Celtic tradition based on the principles of Roman law and adopted by the Anglo-Saxons and Normans from the people they had conquered[3]. Others have regarded it as a product of

---

[1] Above, pp. 129, 427.   [2] Above, pp. 416, 426, 427.

[3] According to Brunner, pp. 11-19, the origin of the jury among the Welsh, from whom it was borrowed by the Anglo-Saxons, is maintained by Phillips (On Juries) and Probert (On the Ancient Laws of Cambria) ; Selden, Spelman, Coke, Turner, Phillips, and G. L. von Maurer regard it as a product of Anglo-Saxon genius. Of the authors who hold that it was imported from primitive Germany, Brunner mentions Bacon, Montesquieu, Blackstone, Savigny, and Nicholson in the preface to Wilkins' Anglo-Saxon Laws ; Wormius and Worsaae held that it was derived from the Norsemen through the Danes ; Hickes, Reeves, and others, that it was derived from the Norsemen through the Normans of the Conquest ; and Konrad Maurer, who has investigated the analogous system in use among the Norsemen, argues for a common *North* German origin, from which the principle of jury has been developed in different ways by the several races in which it is found. Of those writers who allow that it is of Norman introduction, Daniels maintained that the Normans found it existing in France ; Möhl derived it from the usages of the canon law ; Meyer supposed

Various opinions on the national origin of jury.

that legal genius of the Anglo-Saxons of which Alfred is the mythic impersonation; or as derived by that nation from the customs of primitive Germany or from their intercourse with the Danes. Nor, even when it is admitted that the system of recognition was introduced from Normandy, have legal writers agreed as to the source from which the Normans themselves derived it. One scholar maintains that it was brought by the Norsemen from Scandinavia; another that it was derived from the processes of the canon law; another that it was developed on Gallic soil from Roman principles; another that it came from Asia through the Crusades, a theory which has little more to recommend it than the still wilder supposition that it is of Slavonic origin, and borrowed by the Angles and Saxons from their neighbours in Northern Europe. But all these theories on examination show that their inventors have either been misled by superficial coincidences, or argue on hypothesis only. The only principle which the systems on which the theories are built have in common is the use of the oath as an instrument of judicial procedure, and this use is universal.

The Inquests of the Frank kings.

The truth seems to be that the inquest by sworn recognitors is directly derived from the Frank Capitularies, into which it may be adopted from the fiscal regulations of the Theodosian Code[1], and thus own some distant relationship with the Roman jurisprudence. The Karolingian kings issued instructions to their Missi very much as Henry II issued instructions to his itinerant justices, and they gave special commissions of inquiry into fiscal and judicial matters to be answered by the

that it came from Asia by way of the Crusades; Maciejowski claimed it for the Slavonic neighbours of the Angles and Saxons. The theory given in the text is mainly that of Palgrave, but corrected and adjusted by the recent writings of Dr. Brunner.

[1] Palgrave, English Commonwealth, p. 271; Brunner, p. 87. The following passages from the Theodosian Code are cited by Brunner: 'Super vacantibus ac caducis ... certi etiam dirigantur qui cuncta solerter inquirant et cujus fuerint facultates, et si nemo eas sibi jure nititur retentare. Ac si locum fisco factum esse claruerit occupatis prius bonis et rerum omnium descriptione perfecta ...;' Cod. Theod. x. 10. l. 11. 'Ex privatorum ... sollicitudine contractuum ... illis ... personis a quibus publici muneris injuncta curantur, nullum fomitem calumniae patimur litis accendi. Cur enim continentiam venditionis alienae inquisitio palatina rimetur?' ibid. l. 29.

oath of sworn witnesses in the district court[1]. These answers
then embodied the belief or knowledge of the local court as
representing the community, every qualified member of the
community being a member also of the court. The persistence
of the inquisitorial system is proved not only by Norman
charters and customs, but by the existence of the kindred
principle, undeveloped indeed and early forgotten, in the jurisprudence of the rest of France[2]. The order to hold such inquest was a royal, or in Normandy a ducal privilege, although
it was executed by the ordinary local officers; primarily it was
employed to ascertain the rights and interests of the Crown;
by special favour permission was obtained to use it in the

The Inquest perpetuated in Normandy from the Karolingian times.

---

[1] The following instances show that this usage was applied primarily to
cases in which the royal interests were concerned, and that the witnesses
supplied the evidence of the neighbourhood : ' Item volumus ut omnis inquisitio quae de rebus ad jus fisci nostri pertinentibus facienda est, non
per testes qui producti fuerint sed per illos qui in eo comitatu meliores et
veraciores esse cognoscuntur, per illorum testimonium inquisitio fiat, et
juxta quod illi inde testificati fuerint vel contineantur vel reddantur ; '
Capit. 829. § 2; Pertz, Legg. i. 354. ' Ut pagenses per sacramentum
aliorum hominum causas non inquirantur nisi tantum dominicas ; ' Capit.
819. § 1; Brunner, p. 88 ; Baluze, i. p. 409; Pertz, Legg. i. 227. ' Ut in
omni comitatu hi qui meliores et veraciores inveniri possunt eligantur a
missis nostris ad inquisitiones faciendas et rei veritatem dicendam et ut
adjutores comitum sint ad justitias faciendas ; ' Cap. 829 ; Pertz, Legg. i.
351; Baluze, i. 449. The best instances for comparison are the Assizes
of Clarendon and Northampton, the Inquest of Sheriffs, and the Capitula
of 1194; they may be compared with the capitula data missis in 802,
e.g. ' de fidelitate jusjurandum ut omnes repromittant ; ' Pertz, Legg. i. 97 ;
Baluze, i. 267. ' Inquiratur qui sunt qui debent domino regi homagium
et non fecerunt ; ' Inquest of Sheriffs, art. xi. ' Item justitiae capiant
domini regis fidelitates ; ' Ass. Northampt. art. 5. Or again on the subject
of criminals, fugitives, strangers, forgers, the effects of war, abundant coincidences of the most striking character will be found in the capitularies of
802, 806, 819, 829, 854, 860, 865. The following extract from a capitulary
of 868 is in close parallel with the instructions for the Domesday Inquest :
' Inquirant quoque quot (canonici, etc.) tempore avi nostri Karoli et domini
genitoris nostri Hludovici unoquoque in loco fuerint et quot modo sint ; et
ubi loca a Nortmannis sive a quibuslibet aliis destructa et penitus adnullata,
quot ibi nunc propter paucitatem rerum et devastationem eorundem constitui vel ordinari possint ; ' Baluze, ii. 139.

[2] The continuance of the system in France from the Karolingian times
and through the Norman period is proved by Dr. Brunner in his work so
frequently referred to above. The most curious phenomenon in connexion
with it is the fact that it was only on English soil that it gained much
development, the Norman lawyers seeing themselves rapidly outstripped
by those of England, and the institution withering away in the rest of
France until it became extinct.

concerns of the churches and of private individuals [1]. Even
under this system the sworn recognitors were rather witnesses
than judges ; they swore to facts within their own knowledge ;
the magistrate to whom the inquiry was entrusted was the
inquirer, and he inquired through the oath of men sworn to
speak the truth and selected in consequence of their character
and local knowledge.

This was the source of trial by jury.

Such was the instrument which, introduced in its rough simplicity at the Conquest, was developed by the lawyers of the
Plantagenet period into the modern trial by jury. Henry II
expanded and consolidated the system so much that he was not
unnaturally regarded as the founder of it in its English character.
From being an exceptional favour, it became under his hand a
part of the settled law of the land, a resource which was open

Recognition by jury said to be an invention of Henry II.

to every suitor. The recognitions are mentioned by Ralph
Niger [2] as one of his expedients of tyranny ; by Ranulf Glanvill
as a boon conferred by royal benevolence on the people, and
with the counsel and consent of the nobles. John, in a charter
granted to the church of Beverley, forbids that the rights of that
church should be damaged by assizes or recognitions, and adds
that the pleas shall be held in the court of the provost as they
were in the reign of Henry I, before recognitions or assizes had
been ordained in the kingdom [3]. So early had Henry II

[1] The coincidences between the practice described by Glanvill and the
usages of the Great Coûtumier of Normandy have of course led to two
opposite theories ; one that the Norman usage was a faulty imitation of
the English ; the other that the system was transplanted full-grown from
Normandy to England. Neither is true ; the system of recognition existed
in Normandy before it was brought to England, but it was developed in
England, and that development probably had a reflex influence on Normandy. It would be wrong to suppose that the Great Coûtumier affords
an exact picture of the Normandy even of Henry II's reign, much
more that the English system developed from a germ which is represented
by the Great Coûtumier. There are however, in the minute legal peculiarities of the Norman recognitions as described in that work, signs of a
primitive character, a simplicity and general applicability which seem to
show that it had been naturalised there in a much earlier form than it was
in England, and this confirms the historical and documentary evidence.
The whole subject is interesting, but it involves a great quantity of
minute legal details which have very slight connexion with our present
inquiries.

[2] Above, p. 531, note 1.

[3] ‘Ubi placita inde fuerunt et esse consueverunt tempore regis Henrici

acquired the fame of having instituted the system, which he had indeed remodelled and made a part of the common right of his subjects, but which had certainly existed under his four predecessors.

The application of the principle to legal matters—for we have already noticed its fiscal use—may be placed under two heads: the inquest in civil matters exemplified in the Great Assize and in the Assizes of Novel disseisin, Mort d'ancester, Darrein presentment, and others; and the inquest of presentment in criminal matters, which appears in the Assizes of Clarendon and Northampton. The Great Assize is, according to Glanvill, a royal boon by which wholesome provision is made for the lives of men and the integrity of the State, so that in maintaining their right to the possession of their freeholds the suitors may not be exposed to the doubtful issue of trial by battle. This institution proceeds from the highest equity, for the right, which after much and long delay can scarcely be said to be proved by battle, is by the beneficial use of this constitution more rapidly and more conveniently demonstrated[1]. It is in fact the most distinct mark of the original equity with which the royal jurisdiction, as civilisation and legal knowledge advanced, was applied to remedy the evils inherent in the rough and indiscriminating formality of the popular tribunals: such the inquest had been under the Karolings, such was the recognition or assize under the Plantagenets. The trial by battle was in England an innovation; it was one from which the English recoiled as an instrument associated with tyranny, if not devised for the purposes of tyrants; and the charters of the boroughs frequently contain a provision, dearly bought no doubt but greatly valued, that the burghers shall not be liable to its use[2]. In the place of this barbarous foreign custom, the following machinery is applied; the possessor of the freehold in dispute

His use of it in the assizes.

The Great Assize.

An equitable institution.

Trial by battle disliked.

patris nostri vel tempore Henrici regis avi patris nostri, antequam recognitiones vel assisae in regno nostro essent constitutae ... d .. 8⁰ Oct. anno regni nostri quarto;' Houard, Anciennes Loix, ii. 288.
[1] Glanvill, de Legibus, ii. 7; above, p. 616, note 5.
[2] See the Charter of London, Select Charters, p. 108; Winchester, ib. p. 266; Lincoln, ib. p. 267; above, p. 461, note 1.

applies to the Curia Regis to stop all proceedings in the local courts until a recognition has taken place as to the right of the claimant[1]: and thereupon a writ is issued to the sheriff to that

Process of the Great Assize.

effect. The party in possession is thus said to have placed himself on the assize; and the next step is taken by the claimant, who demands a writ by which four lawful knights of the county or neighbourhood shall be empowered to choose twelve lawful knights of the same neighbourhood, who shall declare on oath which of the two litigants has the greater right to the land in question[2]. The writ accordingly is issued, addressed to the sheriff, directing him to summon four knights to appear at Westminster to choose the twelve. They appear in due course, and under oath nominate the twelve recognitors, who are then summoned to appear before the king or his justices prepared to make their declaration[3]. On the day fixed they present themselves, and the suit proceeds; if the twelve are acquainted with the circumstances in dispute and are unanimous, the

Oath of the recognitors.

transaction is complete; they are sworn 'that they will not speak falsehood nor conceal truth' according to knowledge gained by eye-witness or 'by the words of their fathers and by such words as they are bound to have such confidence in as if they were their own[4].' The declaration made, the sentence is issued. If however the twelve knights or any of them are ignorant, or if they disagree, others are to be called in who have the requisite information; and, when the complete number of twelve unanimous witnesses will depose to the fact, their verdict

Other assizes.

is of the same account. The proceedings in the other assizes are of the same kind, save that the twelve recognitors are nominated by the sheriff himself without the intervention of the four knights electors[5].

Recognitions before the itinerant justices.

The date of the original enactment of the Great Assize is unknown; but the use of recognition by twelve sworn witnesses is prescribed in the Constitutions of Clarendon for cases of dispute as to lay or clerical tenure[6]. It there appears as a part

[1] Glanvill, ii. 7. [2] Ibid. c. 10. [3] Ibid. c. 12.
[4] Ibid. c. 17. [5] Ibid. xiii. cc. 1, 2 sq.
[6] 'Recognitione duodecim legalium hominum;' Art. 9; Select Charters, p. 139.

of the work of the 'capitalis justitia.' From Glanvill it is clear
that such litigation might be transacted before the itinerant
justices; and the Assize of Northampton of 1176 places among
the agenda of the eyre recognitions of the seisin of heirs, and of
'disseisin upon the assize,' under which descriptions we may
detect the cases of Mort d'ancester and Novel disseisin[1]. In
1194 the grand jury of the hundred are empowered to act on
all the business of the session, in which are included all recognitions and assizes ordered by the king's writ, and even recognitions under the Great Assize where the property in dispute
is worth five pounds a year or less[2]. In 1198 the sum is raised
to ten pounds, and the elections under the Great Assize are to be
made before the itinerant justices. The great charter of John
likewise retains the three recognitions of Novel disseisin, Mort
d'ancester, and Darrein presentment, to be heard in the quarterly
county courts by the justices and four chosen knights[3]: and the
charter of 1217 orders the same rule to be observed once a year[4],
except in cases of Darrein presentment, which are reserved for
the justices of the bench. The recognitions have become a permanent and regular part of the county business.

The development of the jury of presentment is, after its The jury of
reconstitution or creation by Henry II, marked by correspond- presentment
ing stages of progress. But its origin is less clear. By some of criminals.
jurists it is brought into close connexion with the system of
compurgation, the jurors who present the list of criminals
representing the compurgators of the accuser[5], and the jury
which at a later period was impanelled to traverse the presentment representing the compurgators of the accused. Others
again connect it with the supposed institution of the collective
frankpledge, the corporate responsibility of the tithing, the
hundred, and the shire for the production of offenders, which has
played so large a part in constitutional theories, but which rests

---

[1] Art. 5; Select Charters, p. 155.
[2] Articles 2 and 18; Select Charters, pp. 259, 260.
[3] Art. 18.   [4] Articles 13 and 15; Select Charters, p. 345.
[5] This is the theory of Rogge, as stated by Brunner, pp. 25, 26. Hickes
long ago stated the fact that there is no real connexion between jury and
compurgation. The common use of the number twelve is misleading.

on very slight foundation of fact[1]. The *frithborh* was neither a
body of compurgators nor a jury of presentment. As a matter
of history it seems lawful to regard the presentment as a part of
the duty of the local courts for which an immemorial antiquity
may be claimed with at least a strong probability. The leet juries
of the small local courts do not draw their origin from any legal
enactment, and bear every mark of the utmost antiquity. By
them amercements are still made and presentments offered under
oath, although their action is restricted and superseded by newer
expedients. But their procedure affords some warrant for be-
lieving that the twelve senior thegns, who swore in the county
court to accuse none falsely, were a jury of presentment. The
juratores synodi, in the ecclesiastical courts of the ninth century,
might furnish a precedent or parallel[2]. If so, the mention of the
juratores of the shire and hundred which occurs in the Pipe
Roll of Henry I is accounted for, and with it the mention of a
criminal jury in the Constitutions of Clarendon[3]. The obscurity
of this side of the subject may be regarded as parallel with the
scantiness of evidence which we have already noticed as to the
recognition. From the year 1166 however the history of the

Assize of
Clarendon.

criminal jury is clear. By the Assize of Clarendon inquest is to
be made through each county and through each hundred, by
twelve lawful men of the hundred and by four lawful men of
each township, 'by their oath that they will speak the truth.'

Procedure
on present-
ment.

By these all persons of evil fame are to be presented to the
justices, and then to proceed to the ordeal : if they fail in the
ordeal they undergo the legal punishment ; if they sustain the ordeal, yet, as the presentment against them is based on the evidence
of the neighbourhood on the score of bad character, they are to

Assize of
Northamp-
ton, and
eyre of 1194.

abjure the kingdom[4]. The jury of presentment is reduced to a still
more definite form, and receives a more distinct representative
character, in the Assize of Northampton[5], and in the Articles of

---

[1] The theory of G. L. von Maurer ; Brunner, p. 26.

[2] See especially Regino of Prüm, de causis synodalibus, lib. ii. cap. 2.
But there the jurors of the synod do not present, only reply to the inquiry
of the visiting bishop.

[3] Const. Clar. art. 6.

[4] Assize of Clarendon, art. 1 ; Select Charters, p. 143.

[5] Assize of Northampton, art. 1 ; Select Charters, p. 152.

Visitation in 1194: in the latter capitulary the plan used for
nominating the recognitors of the Great Assize is applied to the
Grand Jury, for so the body now constituted may be termed:—
'In the first place, four knights are to be chosen from the
whole county, who by their oath shall choose two lawful knights
of each hundred or wapentake, and those two shall choose upon
oath ten knights of each hundred or wapentake, or, if knights be
wanting, legal and free men, so that these twelve may answer
under all heads concerning their whole hundred or wapentake[1].'
The heads on which they answer include not only the assizes
which have been already referred to in connexion with the jury,
but all the pleas of the Crown, the trial of malefactors and their
receivers as well as a vast amount of fiscal business. The later *Later de-*
development of these juries does not fall under our present *velopment of the jury.*
inquiry, but it may be generally stated thus: at an early period,
even before the abolition of ordeal by the Lateran Council of
1215, a petty jury was allowed to disprove the truth of the
presentment, and after the abolition of ordeal that expedient
came into general use[2]. The further change in the character *Later cha-*
of the jurors, by which they became judges of fact instead of *racter of jury.*
witnesses, is common to the civil and criminal jury alike. As it
became difficult to find juries personally well informed as to the
point at issue, the jurors summoned were allowed first to add to
their number persons who possessed the requisite knowledge,
under the title of afforcement. After this proceeding had been
some time in use, the afforcing jurors were separated from the
uninformed jurors and relieved them altogether from their
character of witnesses. The verdict of the jury no longer
represented their previous knowledge of the case, but the result
of the evidence afforded by the witnesses of the fact; and they
become accordingly judges of the fact, the law being declared by
the presiding officer acting in the king's name.

In all these points we see distinctly the growth of a principle *Judicium*
of representation, expecially applied to the work of the county *parium.*

---

[1] Hoveden, iii. 262 ; Select Charters, p. 259.
[2] On the subsequent history of criminal jury, see Forsyth, Trial by
Jury, pp. 199 sq., where the legal growth of the institution is traced with
admirable clearness.

courts or growing up in them. The 'judicium parium' however, which is mentioned in Magna Carta, has a wider application than this. It covers all cases of amercement in the county, the hundred, and the manorial courts, and exhibits a principle which, rooted in primitive antiquity, is capable of infinite development and beneficial application ; and this we have seen exemplified in the assessment processes described above.

Connexion of jury with the representative system.

It remains then briefly to point out the direct connexion between the jury system and county representation. In the earliest existing records of recognitions, the way in which the jurors are to be selected is not clearly laid down[1]. The recognitions of the Norman reigns are regarded as acts of the county court, and the possibility of election by the suitors is not excluded : it is however more probable that the recognitors were selected by the sheriff, possibly by rotation from a general list, possibly according to their nearness to the spot or acquaintance with the business in hand. On the institution of the assizes of Novel disseisin, Mort d'ancester, and Darrein presentment, the sheriff summoned the requisite number of jurors at his discretion, and the plea was held at a place named in the writ of summons in such a way as to imply that it was to be heard not in the regular county court, but in a special session[2]. The

The Recognitions held in the county court.

Great Assize was differently constituted : there the sheriff nominated four electors to choose the twelve recognitors, and the trial took place before the justices itinerant in the county, or before the court at Westminster[3]. The articles of 1194 place the election of the recognitors, with all the other business of the eyre, in the hands of the grand jury[4]; those of 1198 direct that it shall take place before the justices in the full county

---

[1] In the early instances given by Palgrave, pp. clxxviii sq., we have (1) 'quibus (sc. scyris) congregatis, *eligantur* plures de illis Anglis qui sciunt quomodo terrae jacebant,' &c. ; (2) 'Praecipio quod praecipias Hamonem filium Vitalis et probis vicinis de Santwic, *quos Hamo nominabit*, ut dicant veritatem.' See above, p. 427.

[2] Glanvill, xiii. 3 : 'Ab initio eligendi sunt duodecim liberi et legales homines de vicineto secundum formam in brevi expressam.' The writ merely orders the sheriff to summon and 'imbreviate' twelve recognitors. Even here however there was room for a real election.

[3] Glanvill, ii. 10–12.

[4] Art. 2 : 'Item de omnibus recognitionibus,' &c. ; above, p. 661.

court[1]; Magna Carta completes the process, enacting that the assizes shall be taken quarterly in the county court before two justices sent by the king, and four knights of the county, chosen by the county[2]. The constitution of the grand jury of inquest is similarly developed. The twelve legal knights of the shire, the twelve lawful men of the hundred, and the four men of the township mentioned in the Assize of Clarendon, may have appeared in rotation, or may have been selected by the sheriff or the hundredman or the reeve: but in 1194 they are nominated, through a process of co-optation, by four elected knights[3]. These elected knights may still have been nominated by the sheriff, but it is more probable that they were chosen by the suitors, first because the appointment of coroners, which is directed in the same document, was made by election of the freeholders, and intended as a check on the power of the sheriff[4]; and, secondly, because the term 'eligendi' may be reasonably interpreted by the clause of Magna Carta just referred to[5]. The mode of nominating the grand jury was modified in later practice, and the element of popular election was altogether eliminated; in the period before us, however, it furnishes an important illustration of the usage of election which was so soon to be applied to parliamentary representation. In both the systems of judicial jury we have thus the same result, a body of four knights representing the county court for this special purpose, in one case certainly, and in the other probably, chosen by the county court itself. In the fiscal business we have another analogy; the carucage of 1198 is assessed before a knight and a clerk of the Exchequer acting on behalf of the Crown, and the sheriff and

Method of electing the Grand Jury.

Probably a free election by the suitors.

Elective principle.

Illustration from fiscal usages.

[1] 'Et capientur coram eis electiones magnae assisae per mandatum domini regis vel ejus capitalis justitiae;' Hoveden, iv. 61.

[2] Art. 18.

[3] 'In primis eligendi sunt quatuor milites de toto comitatu, qui per sacramentum suum eligant duos legales milites de quolibet hundredo vel wapentacco, et illi duo eligant super sacramentum suum x. milites de singulis hundredis vel wapentaccis; vel, si milites defuerint, legales et liberos homines, ita quod illi xii. in simul respondeant de omnibus capitulis de toto hundredo vel wapentacco;' Hoveden, iii. 262.

[4] Art. 20. Hoveden, iii. 263.

[5] 'Cum quatuor militibus cujuslibet comitatus electis per comitatum;' Art. 18.

Magna Carta
executed on
inquest by
twelve
chosen
knights of
each shire.

Council at
Oxford in
1213.

The ele-
ments of a
representa-
tive system
at work
before the
Great
Charter.

lawful knights 'electi ad hoc' acting on behalf of the shire: it
was collected by two knights of the hundred, who paid it to the
sheriff, and he accounted for it at the Exchequer[1]. We are
thus prepared for the great executory measure of 1215, under
which the articles of the charter were to be carried out by an
inquest of twelve sworn knights in each county, chosen in the
county court and of the county itself[2]: and we understand the
summons to the council at Oxford of 1213, in which the sheriff
of each county is ordered to send four discreet men of his county
to speak with the king on the business of the realm[3]. In the
four discreet men of the shire we detect the old representative
idea of the four good men of the township, who appeared in the
shire-moot: now they are summoned to a national assembly
which is itself a concentration of the county courts. It is not
however yet certain whether the four discreet men, the predecessors of the two discreet knights of later times, were on this
occasion elected by the shire. On the analogy of the other
elections it might be presumed that they were; but the fact
that only a week's notice was given to the sheriffs seems to preclude the possibility of a general election. Nor is it necessary
to antedate the growth of an institution, when the later steps of
its development are distinctly traceable. Whether or no the
fourteenth article of the Great Charter intended to provide for
a representation of the minor tenants-in-chief by a body of
knights elected in the county court, we see now the three principles involved in such representation already in full working,
although not as yet distinctly combined for this purpose. We
have a system of representation, we have the practice of election,
and we have a concentration of the shires in the great council.
The struggle of eighty years which followed the act of Runnymede not only had to vindicate the substantial liberties involved

---

[1] Hoveden, iv. 46 sq.; Select Charters, p. 257; above, p. 549.
[2] Art. 48: 'Statim inquirantur per duodecim milites juratos de eodem
comitatu, qui debent eligi per probos homines ejusdem comitatus.' See
also Patent Rolls, i. 180; Select Charters, p. 307.
[3] 'Et quatuor discretos homines de comitatu tuo illuc venire facias ad
nos ad eundem terminum ad loquendum nobiscum de negotiis regni nostri;'
Report on the Dignity of a Peer, App. i. p. 2; Select Charters, p. 287.

in that act, but to sharpen and perfect and bring into effective and combined working every weapon which, forged at different times and for different purposes, could be made useful for the maintenance of self-government. The humble processes by which men had made their by-laws in the manorial courts and amerced the offenders; by which they had assessed the estates or presented the report of their neighbours; by which they had learned to work with the judges of the king's court for the determination of questions of custom, right, justice, and equity, were the training for the higher functions, in which they were to work out the right of taxation, legislation, and political determination on national action.

The process of training.

165. The history of the towns presents some points of marked contrast with that of the shires; and these shed light on the later separation of interest between the two classes of communities. The whole period was one of great development in this respect; Henry II and the ministers of his sons encouraged the growth of the mercantile spirit, and reaped the benefit of it in a very great increase of revenue. The privileges of self-government and self-assessment, exemption from the interference of the sheriffs and their arbitrary exactions, the confirmation of guilds, the securing of corporate property, the free election of magistrates, and the maintenance of ancient customs, in many cases to the exclusion of the general reforms, are all of them matters of grant liberally bestowed or sold without reservation. The charters of Richard and John are very numerous; those of Henry II are fewer in number, and do not furnish us with a clue to any progressive policy on the king's part, such as might have been inferred from his general practice in other matters. In those few to which an approximate date can be assigned, the privileges granted are not much greater than was the case in the reign of Henry I: but the Pipe Rolls contain great numbers of instances in which the purchase of additional favours is recorded. In some of these, perhaps, the favour is obtained merely for the single occasion, and in such cases no charter need have been drawn up. In others, where a permanent privilege was bought, the charter in which it was contained must have been

Growth of towns.

Purchase of privileges.

Charters of towns.

Privileges of towns obtained by fine and charter.

lost or destroyed when its importance had been diminished by
a new grant of still greater favours. The charters of Richard
belong chiefly to his early years, especially to the first year,
Charters of when he was anxiously raising money for the Crusade. Those
John,
of John, however, extend throughout the reign, and, being enrolled among the royal records[1], have survived in great measure
Growth of a the dangers in which the earlier grants perished. They exhibit
burgher
spirit. the town constitution in almost every stage of development, and
in every part of the kingdom. Helston and Hartlepool are alike
striving for municipal organisation[2] : one town is rich enough
to purchase a constitution like that of Oxford or Winchester,
another is too poor or too humble to ask for more than the
merchant guild, or the *firma burgi*, or the condition of a free
borough[3]. Amongst the more privileged communities great
varieties of custom prevail, and provincial laws of considerable
antiquity probably underlie the customs of the larger towns.
London, Winchester, Oxford, Norwich, and others, appear as
typical constitutions on the model of which privileges are granted
to the more humble aspirants[4] ; and to their practice the newly-
enfranchised boroughs are referred, in case of a dispute as to the
interpretation of the charter. Thus, beside the common instinct
which would lead the mercantile communities to act together in
cases in which there was no ground for rivalry, and beside the
common privilege which exempted them from the jurisdictions
to which their country neighbours were amenable, they possessed
in common a quantity of peculiar customs, which kept the *burgenses* of the kingdom as a class by themselves, although they

[1] Rotuli Chartarum, edited by Sir T. Duffus Hardy in 1837.
[2] Rot. Chart. pp. 86, 93 ; Select Charters, pp. 313, 314.
[3] The Hartlepool charter confirms to the *homines* of Hartlepool that
they be free burghers ; that of Helston begins with a grant that it be a
free borough, and have a merchant guild : a second charter to Helston
contains the settlement of the ferm. The charter of Kingston lets the
ferm to the *homines* ; Rot. Chart. p. 52.
[4] Hartlepool is to have the same rights as Newcastle ; Beverley as York ;
Norwich, Lincoln, and Northampton as London ; Winchester is the model
town for Wallingford, Andover, Salisbury, Ilchester ; Oxford for Yarmouth
and Lynn ; Winchester or Oxford for Portsmouth and Marlborough ;
Winchester or London for Wilton ; Launceston for Helston ; York for
Scarborough ; Bristol for Dublin ; Northampton for Grimsby ; Hastings
for Romney.

never, as was the case in Scotland and in Germany, adopted a confederate bond of union or organised themselves in leagues.

The boroughs under Henry I had probably, when they obtained any privilege at all, obtained the confirmation of the merchant guild, and by the agreement for the *firma burgi* had limited the exactions of the sheriff, so far as regarded the ferm, although the taxes properly so called, especially the tallage, were still collected by him. They had also in some cases obtained a right to have all causes in which they were engaged tried within their own boundaries. If then the sheriff still retained judicial authority over them he must come and hold his court among them. But such a practice, whilst in one respect it saved them from the risks of the county court, in another exposed them to the exactions of the sheriff, who might come and hold 'scotale' at his convenience, and so wring money from his entertainers. It was therefore a great point to exclude the sheriff altogether; and in order to do this, an independent magistracy must be founded, the right of election obtained, and a power to treat directly with the royal officers on the questions of taxation. These then are the points most commonly secured by a fine or charter.

The boroughs obtain the right of paying their own ferm and excluding the intermeddling of the sheriff.

The right of excluding the sheriff and having their own pleas decided on their own ground[1] involved their exemption from the ordinary sessions of the county court; and, as their customs were confirmed by the same act that served to exempt them, they lost the benefit, or escaped the burden, of innovation. The exemption of the citizens of London, Winchester, and other towns from the duellum[2], after it had been introduced into the shire-moot, no doubt arose in some degree from this: when the

They are exempted from the shire-moot and hundred.

---

[1] E.g. in the thirty-first year of Henry II the men of Cambridge pay 300 marks of silver and a mark of gold to have their town at ferm and 'ne vicecomes se inde intromittat;' here *inde* may refer only to the ferm. John's charter (Rot. Chart. p. 83) grants to them 'quod nullus eorum placitet extra muros burgi de Cantebruge de ullo placito praeter placita de tenuris exterioribus, exceptis monetariis et ministris nostris.' The charter to Dunwich grants that the burghers 'nullam sectam faciant comitatus vel hundredorum nisi coram justitiis nostris;' ib. p. 51.

[2] 'Quod nullus eorum faciat duellum, et quod de placitis ad coronam pertinentibus se possint disrationare secundum consuetudinem civium civitatis Londoniarum;' Charter of Northampton, Rot. Chart. p. 45.

Assize of Clarendon, by introducing the inquest by presentment into the county court, abolished there the practice of compurgation, sending the accused persons directly to the ordeal, the burghers lost the benefit of the change, and long retained compurgation as the customary mode of defence guaranteed to them by their charters [1]. From the visitations of the itinerant justices however they were not exempted; but in their courts they obtained special privileges. The burghers of Dunwich and other towns were represented by twelve lawful men just as if they were independent hundreds; and they were amerced by a mixed jury, six men of their own body and six strangers [2].

They are represented in the courts held by the itinerant justices.

These privileges involved almost of necessity a remodelling of the local magistracy: the right of electing their own reeve or *praepositus* was not the least important of the royal gifts. This does not appear in the charters of Henry II; it is found occasionally in those of Richard [3], and very commonly in those of John. It does not however seem certain that this difference implies an advance towards freedom in the matter; and it is not improbable that, whilst the boroughs continued under the management of the sheriff, an office of so little practical importance as that of the reeve may have been filled up by election. When however the reeve and the probi homines became the governing body, it may well be supposed that the appointment would be a matter of serious question. The citizens of Lincoln are empowered by Richard to make their own reeve, who is however to be a person qualified to serve both them and the king; by John they are directed to choose two, who will be received as their representatives at the Exchequer. The burghers of Nottingham, according to John's Charter, may appoint their reeve annually, but the king reserves the power of removing an unfit person: those of Shrewsbury choose two, of whom the

They obtain a right of electing their magistrates.

Election of the praepositus or reeve.

[1] See Palgrave, English Commonwealth, pp. 217, 259.

[2] 'Et cum summoniti fuerint esse coram justitiis, mittant pro se xii legales homines de burgo suo qui sint pro eis omnibus; et si forte amerciari debuerint, per sex probos homines de burgo suo et per sex probos homines extra burgum amercientur;' Rot. Chart. p. 51. See above, p. 651.

[3] 'Et cives Lincolniae faciant praepositum quem voluerint de se per annum, qui sit idoneus nobis et eis;' Foedera, i. 52.

sheriff presents one at the Exchequer: those of Northampton, by the common counsel of the town, are to choose two fit persons and present them to the sheriff, who will present one of them at the Exchequer to pay their own ferm[1]. Both Lincoln and Northampton are to choose four coroners, to keep the pleas of the Crown and be a check on the reeves. Under these magistrates the old local courts retained their organisation, or modified it only by the mixture of the guild customs, which were also of great antiquity[2]. The new borough courts were the old courts[3] of the township, the hundred and the shire, under new names[4].

The financial arrangements of the towns have been already mentioned under the head of taxation. From the Pipe Rolls and the Dialogus de Scaccario we learn that they made their separate terms with the justices of the Exchequer. Besides the common payment however, the richer burghers were often prevailed on, by force or persuasion, to promise additional sums to relieve the king's necessities[5]: as demesne of the Crown, for such most of them continued to be even by the terms of their enfranchisement, they were subject to tallage which, although it might be occasionally mentioned in the national council, was levied by the feudal right of the king as lord. Next to this the

(margin: Election of borough coroners.)

(margin: Negotiations of the boroughs with the Exchequer.)

(margin: Taxation of the boroughs.)

---

[1] The Charters will be found in the Rot. Chartarum; that of Shrewsbury, p. 46; Northampton, p. 45; Nottingham, p. 39; Lincoln, p. 56; Gloucester, p. 57; Ipswich, p. 65.

[2] See above, pp. 448 sq. The passages in charters which refer to the men of the merchant guild as distinct from the body of burghers, as at Winchester and Gloucester, probably indicate that in those towns the private jurisdictions of the bishop or other lord remained apart from the general borough organisation, or were not consolidated with the guild.

[3] John grants to the burghers of Leicester that all sales of land of the town that take place in the *portmanmote* shall be valid; Rot. Chart. p. 32. The courts-leet of the Lancashire boroughs are often called *lagh-moots*: and there are many other forms. See above, p. 461.

[4] I have not thought it necessary to recapitulate what was said above, pp. 452, 457, about the clause of enfranchisement: which became probably a part of the common law before the reign of John.

[5] Like the benevolences or the compulsory loans of later times: e.g. in the 19th of Henry II, after the citizens of London had paid £666 13s. 4d. *de novo dono*, Reiner son of Berengar pays 100 marks *de promissione sua*. These promises are however more frequent in the cases of ecclesiastical persons, in which it might be more important to recognise the voluntary character of the payment. See Madox, Hist. Exch. pp. 404, 405.

The scotale. 'scotale' seems to have been the most burdensome local custom. The nature of this exaction is very obscure. It was however levied by the sheriff for his own emolument, probably as a reward for his services in maintaining the peace; and was raised by a process similar to that by which the guilds raised their common funds. Whether the sheriff could compel the burghers to make offerings of malt from which a 'scotale' was brewed, the proceeds of which went into his purse; or the name simply means a gathering of the burghers at which they were compelled to promise contributions to the same end, or at which heavy fines for non-attendance were inflicted, it is difficult to say [1]. Whatever it was, however, it was a burden from which the towns were anxious to be relieved, and the relief was either a step towards, or a result of, the exemption from the authority

Summary of town privileges.

of the sheriffs [2]. Free election of magistrates, independent exercise of jurisdiction in their own courts and by their own customs, and the direct negotiation of their taxation with the

---

[1] 'Scotales were abuses put upon the king's people by his officers, who invited them to drink ale, and then made a collection to the intent that they should not vex nor inform against them for the crimes they had committed or should commit;' Brady, Boroughs, App. p. 13. The derivation of the word is questionable: Spelman thought that it might be derived from *Scot* and *tallia*, in the sense of a payment: it is possible that the latter syllable may be connected with *hall* (as in Gildhalla); but the connexion with the drinking customs is quite clear, so that the probability is in favour of the more obvious derivation from scot (payment) and ale. The Constitutions of 1236 forbid *scotallae* along with *aliae potationes*; Wilkins, i. 636. The later *church-ale* was a custom of collecting contributions of malt from the parishioners, with which a quantity of ale was brewed, and sold for the payment of church expenses. The custom of fining absentees and drinking the fines may also be connected with it.

[2] E.g. see Richard's charter to Winchester, Select Charters, p. 266. Other officers however could make scotale besides the sheriff, and the prohibition is generally extended to the reeve and other royal officers. Sad to say, even the archbishop of Canterbury occasionally did it, as is shown by the following passage from Somner on Gavelkind, which further illustrates the nature of the burden: 'Item si dominus archiepiscopus fecerit scotallam infra boscum, quilibet terram tenens dabit ibi pro se et uxore sua 52 ob. et vidua vel kotarius 1 ob.;' 'memorandum quod predicti tenentes debent de consuetudine inter eos facere scotalium de 16 den. et ob. ita quod de singulis 6 denariis detur unus denarius et obolus ad potandum bedello domini archiepiscopi supra dictum feodum.' Walter abbot of Malmesbury (1205–1222) released the townsmen from compulsory attendance at three scotales, at Christmas, Passion-tide and Michaelmas, for a fine of 13s. 4d. and annual payment of 30s.; Reg. Malmesb. ed. Brewer, i. 446.

officers of the Exchequer, were no unimportant steps in the
attainment of municipal independence. Nor was any such step
retraced ; every new charter confirmed, and many of them rehearsed in detail, the customs allowed by the earlier grants
which they superseded.

The city of London still furnishes the type of the most ad- Changes in
vanced privilege, and the greatest amount of illustrative detail. the consti-
Yet even the history of London is obscure. We can trace changes London.
in the constitution of the sheriffdom, we have the date of the
foundation of the *communa* and the mayoralty; we come upon
occasional marks of royal jealousy, and exaggerations of civic independence ; we can see two parties at work, the one moved by
the court, the other by the municipal instinct ; we can discern
the points at issue between the rich and the poor. Still these
features scarcely blend into a distinct picture, or furnish a consecutive story.

London was represented at the Exchequer, during the first The sheriffs
fifteen years of Henry II, by two sheriffs, instead of the four of London.
who appeared in 1130, and who reappear in the sixteenth year.
In 1174 the smaller number recurs : from 1182 to 1189 only
one sheriff acts[1]. At the coronation of Richard I the two
sheriffs are Richard Fitz-Reiner and Henry of Cornhell, the
latter of whom was Master of the Mint and sheriff of Kent[2] ;
the former was the head of a great civic family; his father
Reiner had been sheriff from 1155 to 1170, and Berengar his
grandfather may not improbably have served before him. In Two parties
the struggle between John and Longchamp in 1191 these two among the
magnates are found on different sides : Richard Fitz-Reiner is citizens.
the host and supporter of John, Henry, as his duty to the court
compelled him, takes the part of the chancellor. When accordingly in the midst of the struggle John took the oath to the
communa of London and was followed by the whole body of
barons who adhered to him, it is probable that he acted at the
suggestion of Richard Fitz-Reiner, and gave completeness to a

[1] See the thirty-first Report of the Deputy Keeper of the Records, pp.
307, 308; Madox, Firma Burgi, pp. 164, 165.
[2] Madox, Hist. Exch. p. 631 ; Hoveden, iii. pref. pp. lxxvii, lxxviii.

municipal constitution which had long been struggling for

Establishment of the communa under a mayor.

recognition [1]. Immediately after this confirmation of the communa we find Henry the son of Alwyn mayor of London [2]: the sheriffs cease to be the ruling officers, and become merely the financial representatives of the citizens, who are themselves properly the 'fermers' or sheriffs of London and Middlesex [3]. It is a saying among the citizens, that 'come what may, the

The mayor annually elected.

Londoners should have no king but their mayor.' Henry Fitz-Alwyn is mayor for life; two years after his death, when John, a month before the Great Charter was extorted from him, was buying help on every side, he granted to the 'barones' of the city of London the right of annually electing the mayor [4]. The privilege was ineffectual so far as it was intended to win the support of the Londoners, for a fortnight after it was granted they received the barons with open arms [5]. The duty of sustaining their privileges fell accordingly on the barons: their customs were guaranteed by the thirteenth article of the Charter, and a clause was added preserving like rights to all the cities, boroughs, towns, and seaports of the realm. Lastly, as one of the twenty-five barons chosen to execute the Charter, appears the Mayor of London.

Supremacy of the mercantile element.

The establishment of the corporate character of the city under a mayor marks the victory of the communal principle over the more ancient shire organisation which seems to have displaced early in the century the complicated system of guild and franchise. It also marks the triumph of the mercantile over the aristocratic element. Henry Fitz-Alwyn may have been an hereditary baron of London [6], but his successors, Serlo le Mercer, Ralph Eswy the goldsmith, and others, were clearly

[1] Gir. Camb. Ang. Sac. ii. 397; Opp. iv. 404. Cf. R. Devizes, p. 38; R. Diceto, ii. 99.

[2] Liber de Antiquis Legibus, p. 1. He was one of the treasurers of the sum raised for the king's ransom; Hoveden, iii. 212.

[3] Madox, Firma Burgi, p. 165.

[4] It is dated May 9, 1215; Rot. Chart. p. 207; Select Charters, p. 314.

[5] On the 24th of May; M. Paris, ii. 587.

[6] He was most probably descended from Ailwin Cild who founded Bermondsey priory in 1082; and he was himself a benefactor of Bermondsey; Stapleton, Lib. de Antt. Legg. vi.

tradesmen [1]. It would, doubtless, be unsafe to argue that mercantile pursuits were at this time regarded with anything like
contempt in England. The feeling is one of the results of the
growth of fictitious and superficial chivalry in the fourteenth
century. The men of London had made their pilgrimages to
Palestine, and fought their sea-fights on the way, in company or
in emulation with the noblest of the Norman lords. The story
of Gilbert Becket may be fabulous, but Andrew of London and
his fellow-citizens in 1147 had done good work for Christendom
at the capture of Lisbon, the only real success of the second
Crusade [2]; and in 1190 William Fitz-Osbert and Geoffrey the
goldsmith of London were among the chief men of the fleet
which saved the infant kingdom of Portugal from Moorish
conquest [3]. The struggle, so far as we can trace it, was not
between nobility and trade, but between the territorial franchise
and the mercantile guild. Nor was the victory of the communa
to any appreciable degree a victory of the Englishman over the
foreigner. The population of London was less English probably
than that of the other great towns such as Winchester and York.
The names of the leading citizens who are mentioned throughout the twelfth century are with few exceptions, such as Henry
Fitz-Alwyn, of alien derivation. Richard the son of Reiner the
son of Berengar was very probably a Lombard by descent: the
influential family of Bucquinte, Bucca-uncta, which took the
lead on many occasions, can hardly have been other than
Italian [4]; Gilbert Becket was a Norman. The form of the communa in which the corporate life asserted its independence was
itself foreign. From the beginning of its political importance
London acts constantly as the purse, sometimes as the brain,
never perhaps in its whole history as the heart, of England.

Expedition of the citizens.

Foreign element in the city.

[1] Liber de Antiquis Legibus, pp. 2, 3, sq.
[2] Expugnatio Lyxbonensis, p. cxliv. Henry of Huntingdon specially
remarks that this great victory was won not by the nobles, but by men of
middle rank.
[3] Hoveden, iii. 42; Bened. ii. 116.
[4] Andrew of London, the leader of the Londoners at Lisbon in 1147, is
not improbably the Andrew Bucquinte whose son Richard was the leader
of the riotous young nobles of the city who in 1177 furnished a precedent
for the Mohawks of the eighteenth century; Benedict, i. 155. Cf. Pipe
Roll 31 Henry I, pp. 145, 147.

A mercantile oligarchy.

The victory of the communa is no guarantee of freedom or fair treatment to the poorer citizens; we no sooner find it in supreme authority than the riot of William Fitz-Osbert occurs to prove that an oligarchy of the purse has as little of tender mercy as an oligarchy of the sword. The real importance of London in this region of history is rather that it affords an example of local independence and close organisation which serves as a model and standard for other towns, than that it leads the way to the attainment of general liberties or peculiarly English objects. Still its position and the action of its citizens give it no small political power, and no insignificant place in history.

Importance of the clergy.

166. The action of the clergy in the great struggles of the period has been already noted, in its proper proportion to the general detail. They by their vindication of their own liberties showed the nation that other liberties might be vindicated as well, and that there are bounds to the power and violence of princes. They had fought the battle of the people in fighting their own. From them too, as subjects and not merely as churchmen, the first movements towards national action had

Their independence.

come. They had bound up the wounds of the perishing State at the accession of Henry II; they had furnished the first if not the only champions of freedom in the royal councils, where S. Thomas, S. Hugh, and Archbishop Geoffrey had had courage to speak where the barons were silent. They had, on the other side, not, it may be fairly allowed, without neglecting their spiritual work, laboured hard to reduce the business of government to something like the order which the great ecclesiastical organisation of the West impressed on every branch of its administration. What the Church had borrowed from the Empire in this respect it repaid with tenfold interest to the rising

Their sense of unity.

State system of Europe. And this was especially the case in England. We have seen that the Anglo-Saxon Church made possible and opened the way to national unity: it was the common Church which combined Norman and Englishman in one service, when law and language, land tenure and political influence, would have made them two races of lords and slaves. It was the action of Lanfranc and Anselm that formed the

strongest link between the witenagemot of the Confessor and the
court and council of the Conqueror and his sons. It was the
hard and systematic work of Roger of Salisbury that gave order
to the Exchequer and the Curia. The work of Becket as
Chancellor is thrown into the shade by his later history, but
he certainly was Henry's right hand in the initial reforms of
the reign, and the men who carried on those reforms, in a
direction contrary to the policy which Becket as archbishop
adopted, were men who trod in the footsteps of his earlier life.
Hubert Walter, the administrator of Henry's system, who under
Richard and John completed the fabric of strong government
by means of law, and Stephen Langton, who deserves more than
any other person the credit of undoing the mischiefs that arose
from that system, maintaining the law by making the national
will the basis of the strength of government, were both representative men of the English Church. No doubt there were
evils in the secular employments of these great prelates : but if
for a time the spiritual work of the Church was neglected, and
unspiritual aims fostered within her pale, the State gained
immensely by being administered by statesmen whose first ideas
of order were based on conscience and law rather than on brute
force. Nor was the spiritual part of the work unprovided for.
Three archbishops of Canterbury, Anselm, Ralph, and William,
all of them belonging to the religious rather than the secular
type, had sanctioned the employment of Bishop Roger as
justiciar ; and without the consent of the Pope, it is said, he
refused to bear the title [1]. Innocent III, when he insisted that
Hubert Walter should resign the like office, showed that the
growing sense of the age forbade what so great a saint as
Anselm had connived at; but that growing sense had been
educated in great measure by the system which it was soon to
discard.

It is however in the details of mechanical work that these
remarks help to illustrate the subject of this chapter. The
systematic order of the growing polity was not a little indebted
to the fact that there existed in the Church system a set of

[1] W. Malmesb. G. R. v. § 408; R. Diceto, i. 435, ii. 77.

models of work. The Church had its ranks and degrees, codes
of laws and rules of process, its councils and courts, its central
and provincial jurisdictions, its peculiar forms of trial and arbitration, its system of writ and record. In a crisis in which
representation and election were growing into importance, and
in which all forms were manipulated by clerical administrators,
the newer forms must needs be moulded in some degree on the
on legisla-tion; older. The legislation of the period, the assizes and constitutions, bear, in common with the Karolingian capitularies, a
strong resemblance to ecclesiastical canons, a form which was
local organi-sation; universal and vigorous when the capitulary was forgotten. The
local and territorial divisions of the dioceses made indelible the
civil boundaries which feudal aggression would have gladly
obliterated. The archdeaconries, deaneries, and parishes preserved the local unities in which they had themselves originated;
and the exempt jurisdictions of the convents were in their
nature an exact parallel with the franchises of the feudal lords,
and, in the case of great ecclesiastical establishments, possessed
legal prac-tice. both characters. The assemblies of the clergy kept up forms
that were easily transferred to the local moots: the bishop's
visitation was a parallel to that of the sheriff; the metropolitical
visitation to that of the Curia or Exchequer; spiritual excommunication was parallel with civil outlawry; clerical procurations
with royal purveyance and the payments to the sheriff for his aid;
the share of the clergy in determining their assessments suggested the like action on the part of the lay communities, or at
least familiarised men with a system of the kind.

Clerical in-fluence on representa-tion. In no particular is this more apparent than in the very important question of election and representation. In the latter
point we shall be able to trace, as we proceed, very close
analogies: the fact that the early representative members in
the national council were frequently, if not always, invested with
the character of procurators or proxies, bearing letters of
credence or ratification that empowered them to act on behalf of
their constituents, suggests at once that the custom was borrowed
from the ecclesiastical practice, of which such procuratorial
representation was a familiar part, in negotiation with the Holy

See, and in the formation of Church councils at home. The appearance of the proctors of the cathedral and diocesan clergy in the central assemblies of Church and State precedes by a few years the regular incorporation of the knights of the shire in parliament; and Convocation as well as the House of Commons owes its representative character to the great period of definition, the reign of Edward I. In the case of election the connexion is perhaps less close : but there can be little doubt that the struggles for ecclesiastical freedom of election kept in use forms which made the extension of elective liberty possible in other quarters. The Church recognised three modes of elec- Modes of tion : the 'via compromissi,' by which the electors deputed to a clerical election. small committee of their body—an uneven number, three or five—the function of choosing the bishop or abbot; the 'via scrutinii,' in which the several votes were taken in order and the choice determined by the majority; and the 'via inspirationis Spiritus Sancti,' in which at one moment, and in one breath, the whole body uttered the name of the same person, just as in the court of justice the compurgators took their oath. The last-mentioned method in its exact form was of course in- Analogy of applicable to the cases of popular election ; but the acclamations of lay elections. the crowd of suitors at the county court represents a similar idea ; the show of hands corresponds with the 'via scrutinii ;' and the 'via compromissi' has its parallel doubtless in the gradual reservation of the choice of members, both in town and shire, to a small deputed body [1], who in the former case finally engrossed the right of election.

The common arrangement of the early medieval courts, by System of which the king's chapel was made the repository of writs and record. records, and his clerks or chaplains the framers and writers of such documents, illustrates another side of the same general truth. The ecclesiastical system of writ, summons, and record was probably, in England, derived from the extensive docu-

---

[1] It is not perhaps too much to say that the election of the sworn knights to nominate the recognitors of the Great Assize was a distinct parallel with elections made 'via compromissi.' The deputies of the convent at Canterbury who carried full powers to the Curia Regis or to Rome were compromissarii, proctors in fact of that church.

Records and
Registers. mentary machinery of the Church of Rome, which in its turn
was derived from the similar practice of the later Empire[1].
The writs of the Norman Curia may not improbably have been
drawn by continuous practice from the formulae of the imperial
system of the Franks, great stores of which are to be found in
the collections of Marculf and other jurists[2]. The growth of
the system is accordingly complex, the written forms of procedure, both lay and clerical, being developed side by side, or in
constant entanglement with one another, as might well be the
case when they were drawn up by the same writer. It is however
interesting to observe that the custom of registering the acts of
court, and retaining copies of all letters issued by the king,
seems to have been introduced either late in the reign of
Henry II or under Richard and John, under whom, as has been
already mentioned, the great series of national records begin.
William Longchamp, the chancellor and justiciar of Richard,
who with all his great faults must have also had a great
capacity for business, and who, as we learn from the Red Book
of the Exchequer[3], took pains to make himself familiar with its
details, must have authorised, perhaps suggested, the enrolment
of the acts of the Curia: it was carried out under his vice-
chancellor and successor Bishop Eustace. The enrolment of
charters and of letters patent and close begins in the chancellorship of Hubert Walter, and is continued by Walter de Grey,
afterwards archbishop of York, who has left in the register of
his archiepiscopal acts one of the earliest existing records of the
kind. The Lincoln registers begin with the acts of Bishop
Hugh of Wells, who had been a deputy of the chancellor from
1200 to 1209[4]. If the episcopal registers were drawn up in

**Increase
after the
accession of
John.**

**Episcopal
registers.**

**Papal
Registers.**

---

[1] On the registration of papal letters see the preface to Jaffé's Regesta
Pontificum, and also to his Monumenta Gregoriana. Gregory VII, in a
letter to Hubert of Terouanne, mentions his own register. The practice
existed at Rome from the days of Gregory I or earlier; the most ancient
remains however are those of the registers of Gregory I, John VIII, and
Gregory VII. The series from Innocent III to Pius V is complete.

[2] Illustrations of this will be found in Brunner, as quoted above, p. 422.

[3] Quoted above, p. 468, note 1.

[4] Of course there may have been episcopal registers, as there may have
been royal records, earlier, but there is no evidence that such existed.

imitation of the royal rolls, the latter owed both idea and form to the papal registry, the influence of which was under Innocent III supreme in Europe, and which could trace its method, through the 'regesta' of Gregory VII and the earlier popes, to the practice of the ancient republic. In such matters it would not be fair to say that Church and State borrowed from each other; each had a vitality and a development of its own, but each gained strength, versatility and definiteness from their close union; and that close union was made closer still whilst the business of the two was conducted by the same administrators.

167. We have now, however imperfectly, traced the process of events by which the English nation had reached that point of conscious unity and identity which made it necessary for it to act as a self-governing and political body, a self-reliant and self-sustained nation,—a power in Europe, basing its claims for respect not on the accidental position or foreign acquisitions of its kings, but on its own internal strength and cohesion, its growth in good government, and its capacity for a share in the common polity of Christendom. We have also tried to trace the process by which its internal organisation has been so framed, modified, and strengthened, that when the occasion came it was able to answer to the strain : by which, when the need of representative institutions made itself felt, the mere concentration and adaptation of existing machinery supplied all that was required. The century that follows Magna Carta was an age of growth, of luxuriant, even premature, development, the end of which was to strengthen and likewise to define the several constituent parts of the organic whole. The three estates made their way, through this time of training, to a realisation of

Summary of the steps of national growth and organisation.

The York and Lincoln registers are the most ancient; those of Canterbury begin in 1278; Winchester in 1282; Exeter in 1257; Hereford in 1275; Worcester in 1268; Salisbury in 1297; Lichfield in 1296; Norwich in 1299; Carlisle in 1292; the other sees have records beginning early in the next century. The collection of letters, such as those of Lanfranc, Anselm and Becket, seems to have been a literary work and not a regis-tration, although in many points it answers the same purpose.

their distinct identity, and gained such a consciousness of their
distinct spheres of work as enabled them to act without
entanglement of machinery or waste of power. The constitution
which reached its formal and definite maturity under Edward I
had to learn easy and economic working under his successors.
In that lesson it had also severe experiences of struggle, defect,
and failure : its representative men lose the grace and simplicity
of the earlier times; personal and territorial aims waste the
energies of the better and wiser, and divide into permanent
factions the ignorant and more selfish. Yet the continuity of
life, and the continuity of national purpose, never fails : even
the great struggle of all, the long labour that extends from the
Reformation to the Revolution, leaves the organisation, the
origin of which we have been tracing, unbroken in its conscious
identity, stronger in the strength in which it has preserved, and
grown mightier through trial. The further investigation of this
history, in its political as well as in its mechanical aspect, must
begin from Magna Carta as a new starting-point.

INDEX.

END OF VOL. I.

OXFORD: HORACE HART, PRINTER TO THE UNIVERSITY

CLARENDON PRESS, OXFORD.
SELECT LIST OF STANDARD WORKS.

1. DICTIONARIES.
A NEW ENGLISH DICTIONARY
ON HISTORICAL PRINCIPLES,
Founded mainly on the materials collected by the Philological Society.
Imperial 4to.

EDITED BY DR. MURRAY.

PRESENT STATE OF THE WORK.

				£	s.	d.
Vol. I. A, B By Dr. MURRAY	Half-morocco	2	12	6
Vol. II. C By Dr. MURRAY	Half-morocco	2	12	6
Vol. III. D, E By Dr. MURRAY and Dr. BRADLEY	Half-morocco	2	12	6
Vol. IV. F, G By Dr. BRADLEY	Half-morocco	2	12	6
Vol. V. H—K By Dr. MURRAY	Half-morocco	2	12	6

	£	s.	d.
Vol. VI. L—N By Dr. BRADLEY			
L–Lap	0	2	6
Lap–Leisurely . . .	0	5	0
Leisureness–Lief . .	0	2	6
Lief–Lock	0	5	0
Lock–Lyyn	0	5	0
M–Mandragon . . .	0	5	0
Mandragora–Matter .	0	5	0
Matter–Mesnalty . .	0	5	0
Vol. VII. O, P By Dr. MURRAY			
O–Onomastic . . .	0	5	0
Onomastical–Outing .	0	5	0
Outjet–Ozyat . . .	0	2	6
P–Pargeted	0	5	0
Pargeter–Pennached.	0	5	0
Pennage–Pfennig .	0	5	0
Ph–Piper	0	5	0
Vol. VIII. Q—S By Mr. CRAIGIE			
Q	0	2	6
R–Reactive	0	5	0
Reactively–Ree . .	0	5	0
Ree–Reign	0	2	6
Reign–Reserve . . .	0	5	0

The remainder of the work is in active preparation.

Vols. IX, X will contain S–Z with some supplemental matter.

Orders can be given through any bookseller for the delivery of the remainder of the work in complete *Volumes* or in *Half-volumes* or in *Sections* or in *Parts.*

HALF-VOLUMES. The price of half-volumes, bound, with straight-grained persian leather back, cloth sides, gilt top, is £1 7s. 6d. each, or £16 10s. for the twelve now ready, namely, A, B, C–Comm., Comm.–Czech, D, E, F, G, H, I–K, L–Matter, O–Pf.

SECTIONS. A single Section of 64 pages at 2s. 6d. or a double Section of 128 pages at 5s. is issued quarterly.

PARTS. A Part (which is generally the equivalent of five single Sections and is priced at 12s. 6d.) is issued whenever ready; M–Meet is now ready.

Nearly all the Parts and Sections in which Volumes I–V were first issued are still obtainable in the original covers.

FORTHCOMING ISSUE, July 2, 1906. Ph–Piper, by Dr. MURRAY.

Oxford: Clarendon Press. London: HENRY FROWDE, Amen Corner, E.C.

K. 3000

A Hebrew and English Lexicon of the Old Testament, with an Appendix containing the Biblical Aramaic, based on the Thesaurus and Lexicon of Gesenius, by F. Brown, S. R. Driver, and C. A. Briggs Parts I–XI.   Small 4to, 2s. 6d. each.

Thesaurus Syriacus : collegerunt Quatremère, Bernstein, Lorsbach, Arnoldi, Agrell, Field, Roediger: edidit R. Payne Smith, S.T.P.   Vol. I (Fasc. I–V), sm. fol., 5l. 5s.   Vol. II, completion (Fasc. VI–X), 8l. 8s.

A Compendious Syriac Dictionary, founded upon the above. Edited by Mrs. Margoliouth. Small 4to, complete, 63s. *net.* Part IV, 15s. *net.*   *Parts I–III can no longer be supplied.*

A Dictionary of the Dialects of Vernacular Syriac as spoken by the Eastern Syrians of Kurdistan, North-West Persia, and the Plain of Moṣul. By A. J. Maclean. Small 4to, 15s.

An English-Swahili Dictionary. By A. C. Madan. *Second Edition,* Revised.   Extra fcap. 8vo, 7s. 6d. *net.*

Swahili-English Dictionary. By A. C. Madan.   Extra fcap. 8vo, 7s. 6d. *net.*

A Sanskrit-English Dictionary. Etymologically and Philologically arranged, with special reference to cognate Indo-European Languages. By Sir M. Monier-Williams. *New Edition.*   Cloth, bevelled edges, 3l. 13s. 6d. ; half-morocco, 4l. 4s.

A Greek-English Lexicon. By H. G. Liddell and Robert Scott. *Eighth Edition, Revised.* 4to. 1l. 16s.

An Etymological Dictionary of the English Language, arranged on an Historical Basis. By W. W. Skeat. *Third Edition.* 4to. 2l. 4s.

A Middle-English Dictionary. By F. H. Stratmann. A new edition, by H. Bradley. 4to, half-morocco. 1l. 11s. 6d.

The Student's Dictionary of Anglo-Saxon. By H. Sweet. Small 4to. 8s. 6d. *net.*

An Anglo-Saxon Dictionary, based on the MS. collections of the late J. Bosworth. Edited and enlarged by T. N. Toller. Parts I–III. A–SÁR. 4to, stiff covers, 15s. each. Part IV, § 1. SÁR–SWÍÐRIAN. Stiff covers, 8s. 6d.   Part IV, § 2, SWÍÞ-SNEL–ÝTMEST, 18s. 6d.

An Icelandic-English Dictionary, based on the MS. collections of the late R. Cleasby. Enlarged and completed by G. Vigfússon. 4to. 3l. 7s.

2. LAW.

Anson. *Principles of the English Law of Contract, and of Agency in its Relation to Contract.* By Sir W. R. Anson. *Tenth Edition.* 8vo. 10s. 6d.

Anson. *Law and Custom of the Constitution.* 2 vols. 8vo.
Part I. Parliament. *Third Edition.* 12s. 6d.
Part II. The Crown. *Second Ed.* 14s.

Bryce. *Studies in History and Jurisprudence.* 2 Vols. 8vo. By the Right Hon. J. Bryce, M.P. 25s. *net.*

Digby. *An Introduction to the History of the Law of Real Property.* By Sir Kenelm E. Digby. *Fifth Edition.* 8vo. 12s. 6d.

Grueber. *Lex Aquilia.* By Erwin Grueber. 8vo. 10s. 6d.

Goudy. *Von Jhering's Law in Daily Life.* Translated by H. Goudy. Crown 8vo. 3s. 6d. net.

Hall. *International Law.* By W. E. Hall. *Fifth Edition.* Revised by J. B. Atlay. 8vo. 21s. net.

—— *A Treatise on the Foreign Powers and Jurisdiction of the British Crown.* 8vo. 10s. 6d.

Holland. *Elements of Jurisprudence.* By T. E. Holland. *Tenth Edition* (1906). 8vo. 10s. 6d.

—— *Studies in International Law.* 8vo. 10s. 6d.

—— *Gentilis, Alberici, De Iure Belli Libri Tres.* Small 4to, leather back. 21s.

—— *The Institutes of Justinian.* *Second Edition.* Extra fcap. 8vo. 5s.

—— *The European Concert in the Eastern Question,* a collection of treaties and other public acts. 8vo. 12s. 6d.

Holland and Shadwell. *Select Titles from the Digest of Justinian.* By T. E. Holland and C. L. Shadwell. 8vo. 14s. Also in Parts, paper covers — I. Introductory Titles. 2s. 6d. II. Family Law. 1s. III. Property Law. 2s. 6d. IV. Law of Obligations (No. 1), 3s. 6d. (No. 2), 4s. 6d.

Ilbert. *The Government of India.* Being a Digest of the Statute Law relating thereto. By Sir C. Ilbert. 8vo, leather back. 21s.

—— *Legislative Forms and Methods.* 8vo, leather back. 16s.

Jenks. *Modern Land Law.* By Edward Jenks. 8vo. 15s.

Jenkyns. *British Rule and Jurisdiction beyond the Seas.* By the late Sir H. Jenkyns. 8vo, leather back. 16s. net.

Markby. *Elements of Law* considered with reference to Principles of General Jurisprudence. By Sir W. Markby. *Sixth Edition, Revised,* 8vo. 12s. 6d.

Moyle. *Imperatoris Iustiniani Institutionum Libri Quattuor,* with Introductions, Commentary, Excursus and Translation. By J. B. Moyle. *Fourth Edition.* 2 vols. 8vo. Vol. I. 16s. Vol. II. 6s.

—— *Contract of Sale in the Civil Law.* 8vo. 10s. 6d.

Pollock and Wright. *An Essay on Possession in the Common Law.* By Sir F. Pollock and Sir R. S. Wright. 8vo. 8s. 6d.

Poste. *Gaii Institutionum Juris Civilis Commentarii Quattuor;* or, Elements of Roman Law by Gaius. With a Translation and Commentary by E. Poste. *Fourth Edition,* revised and enlarged. 8vo. 16s. net.

Radcliffe and Miles. *Cases Illustrating the Principles of the Law of Torts.* By F. R. Y. Radcliffe and J. C. Miles. 8vo. 12s. 6d. net.

Sohm. *The Institutes.* A Text-book of the History and System of Roman Private Law. By R. Sohm. Translated by J. C. Ledlie. *Second Edition.* 8vo. 18s.

Stokes. *The Anglo-Indian Codes.* By Whitley Stokes.
Vol. I. Substantive Law. 8vo. 30s.
Vol. II. Adjective Law. 8vo. 35s.
First and Second Supplements to the above, 1887–1891. 8vo. 6s. 6d.
Separately, No. 1, 2s. 6d.; No. 2, 4s. 6d.

Young. *Corps de Droit Ottoman* Recueil des Codes, Lois, Règlements, Ordonnances et Actes les plus importants du Droit intérieur, et D'Études sur le Droit coutumier de l'Empire Ottoman. Par George Young. Part I (Vols. I–III), cloth, 2l. 17s. 6d. net; paper covers, 2l. 12s. 6d. net. Part II (Vols. IV–VII), cloth, 1l. 17s. net; paper covers, 1l. 11s. 6d. The complete Parts I and II separately, will cost 2l. 12s. 6d. net in paper covers, or 2l. 17s. 6d. net in cloth each.

3. HISTORY, BIOGRAPHY, ETC.

Asser. *Life of King Alfred,* together with the Annals of St. Neots, erroneously ascribed to Asser. Edited with Introduction and Commentary by W. H. Stevenson. 2 vols. Crown 8vo. 12s. net.

Aubrey. '*Brief Lives,' chiefly* of Contemporaries, set down by John Aubrey, between the Years 1669 and 1696. Edited from the Author's MSS., by A. Clark. With Facsimiles. 2 vols. 8vo. 25s.

Ballard. *The Domesday Bor*-oughs. By Adolphus Ballard. 8vo. With four Plans. 6s. 6d. net.

Barnard. *Companion to Eng*-lish History (Middle Ages). With 97 Illustrations. By F. P. Barnard. Crown 8vo. 8s. 6d. net.

Boswell's *Life of Samuel* Johnson. Edited by G. Birkbeck Hill. In six volumes, medium 8vo. With Portraits and Facsimiles. Leather back. 3l. 3s.

Bright. *Chapters of Early* English Church History. By W. Bright. Third Edition. Revised and Enlarged. With a Map. 8vo. 12s.

Bryce. *Studies in History* and Jurisprudence. By J. Bryce. 2 vols. 8vo. 25s. net.

Butler. *The Arab Conquest* of Egypt and the last thirty years of the Roman Dominion. By A. J. Butler. With Maps and Plans. 8vo. 16s. net.

Chambers. *The Mediaeval* Stage. By E. K. Chambers. With two illustrations. 2 vols. 8vo. 25s. net.

Clarendon's *History of the* Rebellion and Civil Wars in England. Re-edited by W. D. Macray. 6 vols. Crown 8vo. 2l. 5s.

Fisher. *Studies in Napole*-onic Statesmanship.— Germany. By H. A. L. Fisher. With four Maps. 8vo. 12s. 6d. net.

Freeman. *The History of* Sicily from the Earliest Times.
   Vols. I and II. 8vo, cloth. 2l. 2s
   Vol. III. The Athenian and Carthaginian Invasions. 24s.
   Vol. IV. From the Tyranny of Dionysios to the Death of Agathoklês. Edited by A. J. Evans. 21s.

Freeman. *The Reign of* William Rufus and the Accession of Henry the First. By E. A. Freeman. 2 vols. 8vo. 1l. 16s.

Gardiner. *The Constitutional* Documents of the Puritan Revolution, 1628–1660. By S. R. Gardiner. Second Edition. Crown 8vo. 10s. 6d.

Gross. *The Gild Merchant* a Contribution to British Municipal History. By C. Gross. 2 vols. 8vo, leather back. 24s.

Hill. *Sources for Greek* History between the Persian and Peloponnesian Wars. Collected and arranged by G. F. Hill. 8vo. 10s. 6d.

Hodgkin. *Italy and her In*-vaders. With Plates & Maps. 8 vols 8vo. By T. Hodgkin.
   Vols. I–II. 42s. Vols. III–IV 36s. Vols. V–VI. 36s. Vols VII–VIII. 24s.

Hollis. *The Masai; their Lan*-guage and Folklore. By A. C. Hollis With Introduction by Sir Charles Eliot. 8vo, with 27 full-page Plates of Illustrations, and a Map. 14s. net

Johnson. *Letters of Samuel* Johnson, LL.D. Collected and Edited by G. Birkbeck Hill. 2 vols. 8vo leather back, 24s. net; cloth, 21s. net

—— *Johnsonian Miscellanies* 2 vols. 8vo, leather back, 24s. net cloth, 21s. net.

—— *Lives of the Poets.* With a Memoir of Dr. Birkbeck Hill, by his nephew, H. S. Scott, and a full Index. 3 vols. 8vo, leather back 42s. net; cloth, 36s. net.